H

D0091832

CANADIAN ROCKIES

ANDREW HEMPSTEAD

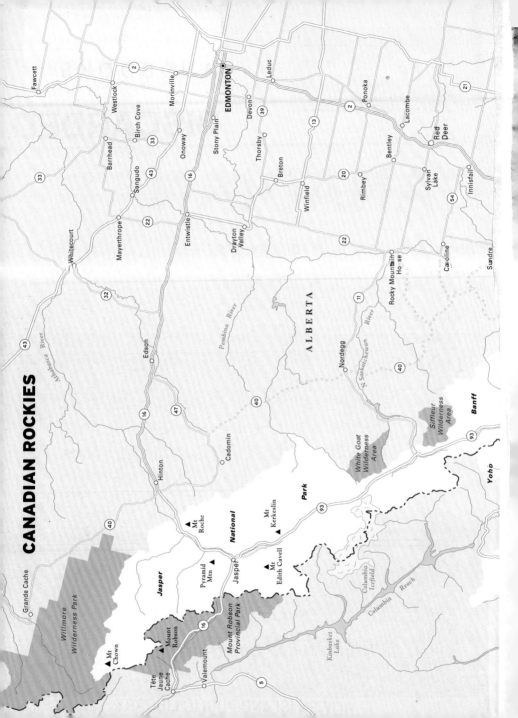

CANADIAN ROCKIES

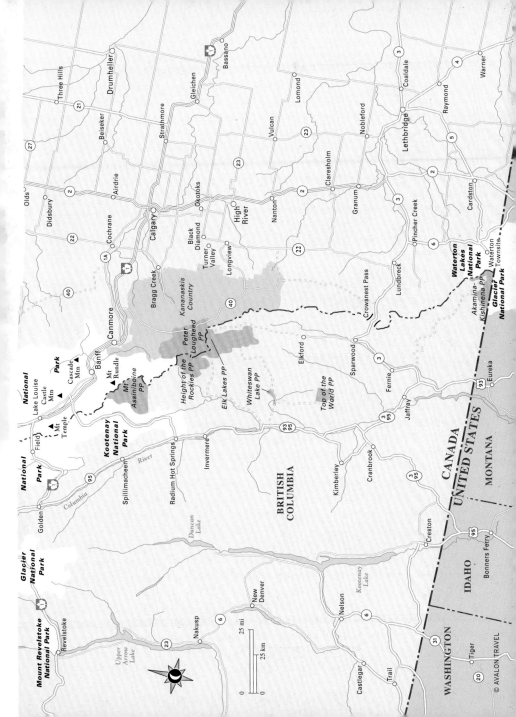

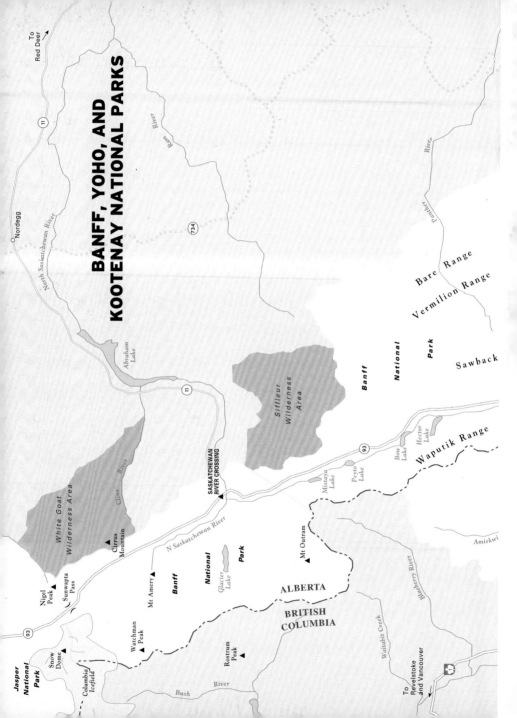

BANFF, YOHO, AND KOOTENAY NATIONAL PARKS

To Red Deer

Nordegg

11

734

11

93

North Saskatchewan River

Ram River

River

Puniller River

Abraham Lake

Cline River

Sifleur Wilderness Area

White Goat Wilderness Area

SASKATCHEWAN RIVER CROSSING

Bare Range

Vermilion Range

Sawback

Banff National Park

Waputik Range

Hector Lake

Bow Lake

Peyto Lake

Mistaya Lake

Amiskwi

Citrus Mountain

N Saskatchewan River

Glacier Lake

Mt Outram

Mt Amery

Banff National Park

ALBERTA

BRITISH COLUMBIA

Nigel Peak

Sunwapta Pass

Watchman Peak

Rostrum Peak

Blaeberry River

Waitabit Creek

To Revelstoke and Vancouver

93

Jasper National Park

Snow Dome

Columbia Icefield

Bush River

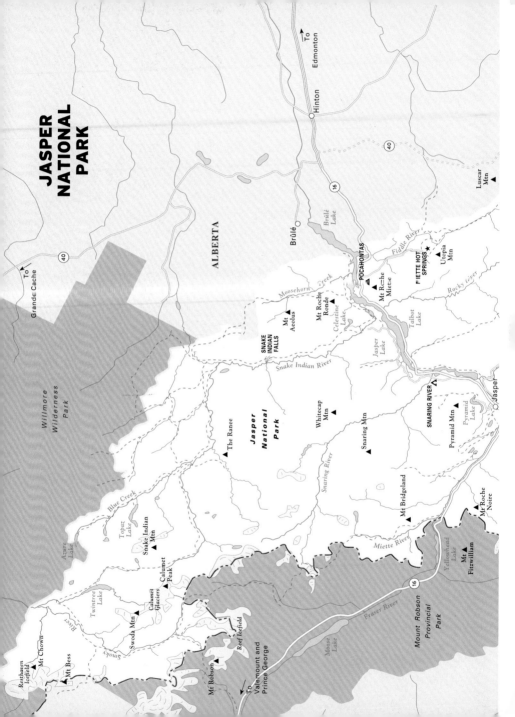

Contents

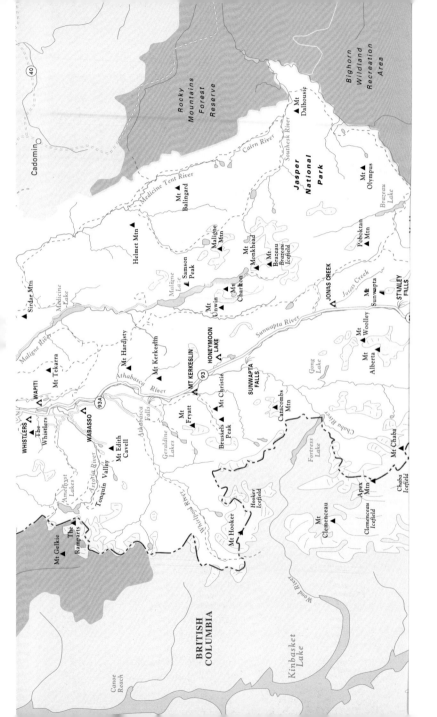

Discover the Canadian Rockies

Snowcapped peaks, glaciers and ice fields, multihued lakes, rushing rivers, alpine meadows, and abundant wildlife make the Canadian Rockies a travel destination that is rivaled by few places in the world. Although Mother Nature dealt a winning hand to the Canadian Rockies, early governments had the foresight to protect most of the land for all time in a string of contiguous parks—each with its own character but combining to create one massive swath of wilderness blessed with dramatic beauty.

It is the outstanding recreational opportunities that make the Canadian Rockies unique. Hiking tops the list in popularity. Over 3,000 kilometers (1,860 miles) of hiking trails lace the mountains, ranging from wheelchair-accessible boardwalks to backcountry treks. Biking, canoeing, kayaking, white-water rafting, golfing, and fishing are also high in the summertime popularity stakes, while in winter visitors don skis, snowboards, and snowshoes. An abundance of wildlife can be found in the most unexpected places—an elk grazing on a golf course, a bear feasting on dandelions as you ride overhead on a gondola.

The Canadian Rockies' parks are filled with tourism infrastructure. For many visitors, the opportunity to vacation in a wilderness setting without sacrificing the amenities of a resort destination is unequaled.

Nowhere is this more apparent than in the town of Banff. Its main street is lined with boutiques and restaurants, and hotel rooms serve every budget. To the north, the town of Jasper offers a toned-down version of similar services. Outside of the parks, the city of Calgary is known around the world for the Calgary Stampede, while smaller towns such as Canmore, Radium Hot Springs, and Invermere thrive. Throughout the region, campgrounds cater to those who like to sleep under the stars—even if it is in an RV with all the trimmings.

While natural beauty is the main selling point, the growth of towns as tourist resorts makes the Canadian Rockies an ideal destination for all interests and budgets. One visitor may spend the day golfing one of the world's most scenic courses, taking a gondola to a mountain peak, soaking in a European-style spa, and then dining in a fine French restaurant before retiring to a luxurious suite. Another visitor may strike out early on foot for a remote alpine lake, go white-water rafting in the afternoon, and then return to pitch a tent and grill dinner over a campfire. Two very different experiences of a most singular destination.

Planning Your Trip

▶ WHERE TO GO

Banff National Park

Banff is the crown jewel in Canada's national park system and home to the world's most photographed lakes. Lake Louise, Moraine Lake, and the Icefields Parkway are just some of the park's awe-inspiring highlights. Biking along the shoreline of Lake Minnewanka, exploring Larch Valley when fall colors are at their height, canoeing across Bow Lake, and

hiking in to backcountry Mount Assiniboine Provincial Park may not be as well known, but each activity allows a glimpse of the park you won't see in the tourist brochures.

Canmore

Canmore is the largest population center in the Canadian Rockies, but don't let that put you off including it in your itinerary. In a little

IF YOU HAVE . . .

Emerald Lake, Yoho National Park

· **ONE WEEKEND:** Spend your time in the towns of Banff and Lake Louise.

· **ONE WEEK:** Add Yoho and Jasper National Parks.

· **TWO WEEKS:** Add Canmore, Kananaskis Country, Kootenay National Park, and Calgary.

over three decades, it has transformed itself from a coal-mining town without a coal mine to a hotbed of recreational pursuits. The surrounding mountains are legendary among the climbing fraternity. Hiking trails lead to crystal-clear lakes and mountain peaks. But Canmore should also factor into your vacation plans for more practical purposes, such as the range of excellent restaurants and a choice of well-priced family-friendly accommodations.

Kananaskis Country

Pronounced exactly as it reads, this recreational playground lies adjacent to Banff National Park and is handy for Calgarians who flock west to revel in a diverse range of activities or simply to do nothing at all. Along with scenery that rivals the national parks, the facilities are top-notch—wonderful golfing, 1,300 kilometers (800 miles) of hiking trails, 30 lakes stocked for fishing, accommodations ranging from tepees to upscale hotels, and over 2,000 campsites in 31 campgrounds. The catch? There's not one—even entry is free.

Kootenay National Park and Vicinity

Kootenay may not have the famous resort towns of Banff and Jasper, but what it has it does well: vast areas of wilderness, abundant wildlife, and a network of hiking trails that are suited to all levels of fitness. Highway 93 provides access to natural attractions like

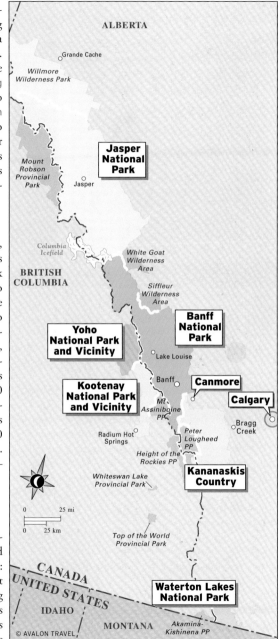

Lake Minnewanka, Banff National Park

Wedge Pond, Kananaskis Country

Marble Canyon and the Paint Pots, as well as phenomena such as Radium Hot Springs, which have been tweaked for human enjoyment. Visitors looking for creature comforts can travel beyond the park to the towns of Radium Hot Springs and Invermere.

Yoho National Park and Vicinity

Thousands of people pass through Yoho, one of the jewels of Canada's national park system, daily, most traveling along the TransCanada Highway on their way to somewhere else. If only they knew what they were missing. Instead of rushing through, detour to Emerald Lake or up the Yoho Valley. Lake O'Hara is not accessible by public road, but this is a good thing. It makes one of the most scenic regions in all of the Canadian Rockies even more special.

Jasper National Park

Beyond a simple sign at Sunwapta Pass is a natural attraction that will leave you breathless—the Columbia Icefield, the largest and most accessible glacier field in the Canadian Rockies. Continuing north, the Icefields Parkway eventually reaches the town of Jasper, a smaller, quieter version of Banff. Take a walk down Maligne Canyon or a boat tour on Maligne Lake, hike the trails below Mount Edith Cavell, and head west to Mount Robson Provincial Park, and you'll be following in the footsteps of millions before you.

Waterton Lakes National Park

The old cliché that good things come in small packages couldn't be a truer description of Waterton Lakes National Park, separated only by an international border from Glacier National Park in Montana. The scenery is dramatic, ranging from prairie to glaciated peaks and from bird-rich wetlands to high alpine lakes. If you're looking for wildlife, Waterton Lakes will exceed your expectations. Mule deer and bighorn sheep are common within the town site, and both black and grizzly bears are often sighted along park highways.

Calgary

Yahoo! Welcome to Cowtown, gateway to the Canadian Rockies, where in 1875 a North West Mounted Police detachment set up camp and today you'll find a world center for the oil-and-gas industry, with ultra-modern skyscrapers going up faster than any town planner ever imagined. While oil drives the economy, you'll experience a different type of energy during the second week of July, when the Calgary Stampede transforms the city into party central, Western-style.

▶ WHEN TO GO

While the Canadian Rockies and Calgary can be visited year-round, there are two influxes of visitors—one in the warmer months and the other in winter. Summer (late June–mid-Sept.) is definitely high season, especially the school holiday period of July through August and, in Calgary, the second week of July (Calgary Stampede). Simply said, the weather is unbeatable. The season is dominated by long, warm—and sometimes hot—days, everything is open, and there's plenty to do and see. Crowded parks, high prices, and difficulty securing reservations are the downside of summer travel.

Late spring and early fall are excellent times to visit the Canadian Rockies for two reasons: You'll avoid the crowds, and you'll save money. Spring (mid-Apr.–late June) is notable for long days of sunlight (in late June it stays light until after 10pm) and a sense of optimism for the upcoming warm months. Fall (mid-Sept.-Nov.) can be delightful, especially September, with lingering warm temperatures and a noticeable decrease in crowds immediately after the long weekend (at the beginning of the month). While fall colors in general lack the intensity of those in the

skating on Lake Louise

eastern provinces and New England, larch turn a brilliant yellow throughout high alpine areas in late September.

Local ski resorts begin opening for the winter season (Dec.-mid-Apr.) in late November.

The best snow conditions are January-February, although for enthusiasts looking for a combination of good snow and warmer weather, March is an excellent time of year to visit.

▶ BEFORE YOU GO

Passports and Visas

To enter Canada, a passport is required by citizens and permanent residents of the United States. At press time, the U.S. government was developing alternatives to the traditional passport. For further information, see the website http://travel.state.gov. For current entry requirements to Canada, check the Citizenship and Immigration Canada website (www.cic.gc.ca).

All other foreign visitors must have a valid passport and may need a visa or visitors permit depending on their country of residence and the vagaries of international politics. At present, visas are not required for citizens of the United States, British Commonwealth, or Western Europe. The standard entry permit is for six months, and you may be asked to show

onward tickets or proof of sufficient funds to last you through your intended stay.

No vaccinations are necessary for visiting Canada.

Transportation

Visitors to the Canadian Rockies have the option of arriving by road, rail, or air. The main gateway city for flights from North America and Europe is Calgary, while Vancouver is also a popular starting point. From these two cities, as well as points across Canada, scheduled train and bus services pass through the region year-round.

Driving, whether it be your own vehicle or a rental car, is by far the best way to get around the Canadian Rockies, although most towns are served by bus.

Moose are not particularly common in the Rockies, but you may be lucky enough to spot one.

Explore the Canadian Rockies

▶ BEST OF THE CANADIAN ROCKIES

This itinerary combines the best of the best—the best—known natural highlights, the hikes you won't want to miss, and the most scenic drives. Understand that you will not see all of the Canadian Rockies in one week, but you won't miss anything major either.

Day 1

Fly into Calgary, pick up a rental car, and head for the mountains. After settling in to your Banff accommodation, spend the afternoon exploring the town, including a stop at the information center and a walk along the Bow River to the Fairmont Banff Springs.

Day 2

Head to Lake Minnewanka for the morning's first tour boat departure. After a picnic lunch at Two Jack Lake (the prime picnic table is on a chunk of forested rock attached to the mainland by a rock causeway), take the Bow Valley Parkway to the village of Lake Louise. This is your overnight destination, but it's worth driving up to the lake itself to watch the sunset.

Day 3

Rise early to visit Lake Louise, one of the world's most photographed lakes, before the crowds arrive. Nearby Moraine Lake is surrounded by mountains and glaciers, but it gets crowded, so hike into Larch Valley. Head to

Peyto Lake, Banff National Park

TOP 12 DAY HIKES

Iceline Trail, Yoho National Park

The Canadian Rockies is renowned for hiking—in fact, many visitors plan their entire vacation around hiking. Here is a list of 12 personal favorites, each of which can easily be completed in a day by anyone with a reasonable level of fitness.

- **Sunshine Meadows,** Banff National Park (p. 51)
- **Bourgeau Lake,** Banff National Park (p. 53)
- **Lake Agnes,** Banff National Park (p. 87)
- **Larch Valley,** Banff National Park (p. 89)
- **Ha Ling Peak,** Canmore (p. 117)
- **Rawson Lake,** Kananaskis Country (p. 148)
- **Floe Lake,** Kootonay National Park (p. 173)
- **Iceline Trail,** Yoho National Park (p. 195)
- **Wilcox Pass,** Jasper National Park (p. 218)
- **Bald Hills,** Jasper National Park (p. 232)
- **Cavell Meadows,** Jasper National Park (p. 232)
- **Crypt Lake,** Waterton Lakes National Park (p. 271)

Yoho National Park and spend the afternoon driving through the steep-sided Yoho Valley and visiting turquoise-colored Emerald Lake.

Day 4

Go white-water rafting down the Kicking Horse River. Head north along the Icefields Parkway, stopping at the Crowfoot Glacier overlook, beautifully blue Bow Lake, and the high lookout platform above Peyto Lake. As dusk falls, keep your eyes out for wildlife such as bears, elk, and moose. Bunk down for the night en route to Jasper.

Day 5

Continue to Jasper and take a boat tour on Maligne Lake to photogenic Spirit Island. As

a general rule, the lake is less windy in the morning and there are fewer crowds. After lunch, head west to Mount Robson Provincial Park and view the park's namesake peak as the sun sets. Return to Jasper for the night.

Day 6

The Icefields Parkway is dotted with scenic pullouts and day-use areas. You will have stopped at many of them on the way north, but the Columbia Icefield was left for this return trip. Here, choose between an Ice Explorer tour onto the glacier and the hike to Wilcox Pass, for a sweeping view of the glacier-filled valley. Continue south to Canmore to take in Oh Canada Eh! dinner theater.

Mistaya Canyon, along the Icefields Parkway

Day 7

Allow time to visit Calgary's Canada Olympic Park before heading out to the airport for your flight home.

▶ TWO-WEEK ROAD TRIP

One option for a two-week tour of the Canadian Rockies is simply to pad the preceding itinerary with more hikes and activities. Although that's what many travelers do, two weeks gives you the opportunity to explore beyond the core national parks and also include major Calgary attractions, as laid out in this itinerary.

Day 1

Arrive in Banff for a two-night stay. Explore the town and start your mountain journey with an easy walk—maybe along the Bow River or to Vermilion Lakes, where birdlife such as Canada geese is prevalent.

Day 2

Expand your exploration of the town to include Lake Minnewanka and the Bow Valley Parkway, which passes through a corridor filled with wildlife. Depending on your interests, take an afternoon gondola ride up Sulphur Mountain or book a tee time at the hallowed Banff Springs Golf Course.

Day 3

Spend the day exploring Kananaskis Country. At Canoe Meadows, just off Highway 40, kayakers often put on quite a show in the rapids of the Kananaskis River.

Day 4

If you leave Kananaskis Village early, you should arrive in Waterton Lakes National Park for a late lunch, even with a one-hour stop at Highwood Pass. Choose between a

WINTER ADVENTURES

Downtown Banff becomes a winter wonderland.

If you enjoy winter sports, you'll love traveling to the Canadian Rockies between December and April. Winter travel and the focus of your vacation will be very different than a summer trip. Instead of hiking and canoeing and barbecuing, you'll be skiing and snowshoeing in a magical mountain setting purified by snow, then retreating to relax around a roaring fire each evening.

Banff National Park holds three major ski resorts–**Lake Louise, Sunshine Village,** and **Ski Norquay.** Kananaskis Country's **Nakiska** was developed for the downhill events of the 1988 Winter Olympic Games. Today, it serves mainly a regional market, offering runs for all skill levels. Meanwhile, to the north in **Jasper National Park, Marmot Basin** is renowned for its uncrowded slopes and sweeping views, and to the east at Calgary's **Canada Olympic Park,** you can ski the slopes used during the 1988 Winter Olympic Games.

Summer hiking trails are perfect for **cross-country skiing** in winter; many of those around the towns of Banff and Jasper are groomed. The **Canmore Nordic Centre** is laced with cross-country trails–and hosts world-class competitions through the winter months.

Snowshoeing is a traditional form of northern transportation but is still a popular recreation. Many sports stores have rentals and will lead you in the right direction. If you would like to try **dogsledding,** head to Canmore or Lake Louise, where commercial operators offer trips.

One of the most unusual winter activities in the Canadian Rockies are **ice walks** to frozen waterfalls. Guided tours operate in **Johnston Canyon (Banff)** and **Maligne Canyon (Jasper).**

Finally, after a long day of winter sports, there's no better way to soothe sore muscles than soaking in one of the region's many **hot springs.**

hike to Bertha Lake, a strenuous outing to a scenic alpine body of water, or afternoon tea at the Prince of Wales Hotel.

Day 5

Take a border-crossing tour boat to Goat Haunt, Montana, which is at the far south end of Upper Waterton Lake and surrounded in steep mountains that drop precipitously into the water. Keen hikers will want to give the boat trip a miss and instead visit Crypt Lake, which is reached along a strenuous trail that includes a rope ladder and natural tunnel. Spend another night in Waterton. You may see deer, elk, and bears on an evening drive to Cameron Lake.

Day 6

This is the longest day on the road, around six hours of driving to the lakeside town of Invermere, where the best beach is within walking distance of downtown. The trip can be broken up with a chairlift ride at Fernie Alpine Resort and a detour to Whiteswan Lake Provincial Park, where hot springs have been left in their natural state.

Day 7

Drive north to Radium Hot Springs and Kootenay National Park. Pick a local hike that suits your level of fitness, then rest your weary bones in the hot springs.

Day 8

It's a two-hour drive between Radium Hot Springs and Golden, but there's no hurry as the Kicking Horse Mountain Resort gondola doesn't begin running until 11am. Arrive at your Yoho National Park accommodation in the early afternoon and take an easy hike around Emerald Lake, where the water is an impossibly rich turquoise color.

Day 9

If you've done your planning thoroughly, you'll be booked on the shuttle bus to Lake O'Hara in the morning. This is the premier hiking region in all of the Canadian Rockies, and it's possible to hit the highlights (Lake Oesa, Opabin Plateau, and Lake McArthur) in a single day. Spend the night along the Bow Valley Parkway.

Emerald Lake, Yoho National Park

FAMILY FUN

Children love the Columbia Icefield in Jasper National Park.

The focus of your vacation in the Canadian Rockies should be the outdoors, even with children. Mix up the places you think the children should see with places you know they will enjoy. If you're traveling to the Canadian Rockies as a family, renting a vehicle will make your holiday more enjoyable—upgrade to a minivan for everyone's sanity. With those tips in mind, here are some favorite family-friendly places and activities:

- **Louise Lakeshore Trail (Banff National Park):** A walking path for all ages along one of the world's most beautiful lakes.

- **Banff Park Museum (Banff National Park):** Learn about local wildlife at this downtown museum.

- **Lake Agnes Teahouse (Banff National Park):** Families with older children that reach this historic teahouse can reward themselves with sweet treats.

- *Oh Canada Eh!* **(Canmore):** All ages will enjoy a rollicking good time at this nationalistic dinner theater.

- **Mount Lorette Ponds (Kananaskis Country):** Try fishing at these shallow ponds, which are stocked with rainbow trout.

- **Radium Hot Springs (Kootenay National Park):** Take a soak in these outdoor mineral pools.

- **Kicking Horse Mountain Resort (Golden):** Ride this gondola for sweeping views only mountaineers usually enjoy.

- **Columbia Icefield (Jasper National Park):** Just riding in an oversized Ice Explorer will excite most children, but the real fun is bumping along over a glacier.

- **Maligne Lake (Jasper National Park):** A safe, enjoyable way to enjoy this beautiful lake is to jump aboard a tour boat.

- **Telus Spark (Calgary):** It's easy to spend a full day in this modern science center.

Columbia Icefield

Day 10

Rise early for the short drive to Moraine Lake; climb onto the rock pile beyond the parking lot for the most magnificent lake-and-mountain view you could possibly imagine. The rest of the day is yours to spend in the village of Lake Louise.

Day 11

The earlier you hit the road for Jasper, the better your chances of spotting wildlife along the Icefields Parkway. Stop at Bow Lake and Peyto Lake to take a selection of classic Canadian Rockies photographs, and then allow three hours at the Columbia Icefield to take in the displays and ride a bus out onto the glacier.

Day 12

Hike through steep-sided Maligne Canyon and drive out to Maligne Lake for more magical mountain views (maybe hike into the Bald Hills if time allows). Make either Mount Robson Provincial Park or Mount Edith Cavell Road your main detour on the leisurely southbound journey back through Banff National Park to Canmore.

Day 13

In Canmore, do some shopping, play a round of golf, take a helicopter ride, or mountain bike on the trails of the Canmore Nordic Centre.

Day 14

Leaving the mountains behind and heading back to Calgary, make time to take in the Olympic legacy that is Canada Olympic Park before heading out to the airport. If your flight doesn't leave until later in the day, also plan stops at Calgary Tower and the Glenbow Museum.

▶ A WEEK UNDER THE STARS

Camping out is a great way to experience the Canadian Rockies, and you'll save some money to boot. This itinerary works for both tent campers and those who have their own or a rented RV (recreation vehicle). It's important to remember that not all campgrounds have powered sites or accept reservations.

Day 1

Turn down Highway 40 as you travel west from Calgary to Kananaskis Country. Spend the night in Peter Lougheed Provincial Park.

Day 2

Plan a leisurely hike to Rawson Lake (pack a fishing pole). Head north, traveling via Spray Lake Provincial Park if you're not put off by unpaved road. In Banff, stay at Tunnel Mountain Campground if you want to walk to town, otherwise head to Two Jack Lake campground.

Day 3

Beat the traffic by rising early for the drive to Lake Louise. Stop at Johnston Canyon for a short walk to a tall waterfall. Snag a spot at the Lake Louise campground before noon, then spend the afternoon visiting local attractions.

Day 4

Rise before dawn to catch Moraine Lake at its most pristine, then begin the trip to Jasper along the Icefields Parkway. Choose to camp en route or continue to the campgrounds spread along the highway south of the town of Jasper.

Day 5

Spend the morning exploring Jasper attractions like Mount Edith Cavell and Maligne Lake, then head back through Lake Louise to Yoho National Park and pitch your tent for the night.

Day 6

Drive to Golden and enjoy lunch at the top of Kicking Horse Mountain Resort. Drive south to Radium Hot Springs. Stay at one of the commercial campgrounds near town or continue on into Kootenay National Park and set up camp there.

Day 7

Before returning to Calgary, make a stop at the Paint Pots, one of Kootenay National Park's most unusual natural wonders.

Highway 40 through Kananaskis Country

BANFF NATIONAL PARK

This 6,641-square-kilometer (2,564-square-mile) national park encompasses some of the world's most magnificent scenery. The snow-capped peaks of the Rocky Mountains form a spectacular backdrop for glacial lakes, fast-flowing rivers, and endless forests. Deer, moose, elk, mountain goats, bighorn sheep, black and grizzly bears, wolves, and cougars inhabit the park's vast wilderness, while the human species is concentrated in the picture-postcard towns of Banff and Lake Louise—two of North America's most famous resorts. Banff is near the park's southeast gate, 128 kilometers (80 miles) west of Calgary. Lake Louise, northwest of Banff along the TransCanada Highway, sits astride its namesake lake, which is regarded as one of the seven natural wonders of the world. The lake is rivaled for sheer beauty only by Moraine Lake, just down the road. Just north of Lake Louise, the Icefields Parkway begins its spectacular course alongside the Continental Divide to Jasper National Park.

One of Banff's greatest draws is the accessibility of its natural wonders. Most highlights are close to the road system, but adventurous visitors can follow an excellent system of hiking trails to alpine lakes, along glacial valleys, and to spectacular viewpoints where crowds are scarce and human impact has been minimal. Summer in the park is busy. In fact, the park receives nearly half of its four million annual visitors in just two months (July and

© ANDREW HEMPSTEAD

HIGHLIGHTS

LOOK FOR ◖ TO FIND RECOMMENDED SIGHTS, ACTIVITIES, DINING, AND LODGING.

◖ **Whyte Museum of the Canadian Rockies:** If you visit only one museum in Banff, make it this one for a snapshot of the park's human history (page 38).

◖ **The Fairmont Banff Springs:** You don't need to book a room here to enjoy the many won-ders of one of the world's great mountain resorts—join a guided tour, enjoy a meal, or simply wander through the grandiose public areas (page 43.).

◖ **Bow Valley Parkway:** This scenic drive be-tween Banff and Lake Louise provides views of abun-dant wildlife and many worthwhile stops (page 46).

◖ **Bourgeau Lake:** A steep trail leads to this lake's rocky shores, populated by colonies of pikas (page 53).

◖ **Lake Louise:** Famous Lake Louise has hypnotized visitors with her beauty for over 100 years. Visitors can rent canoes from the boat-house (page 84).

◖ **Moraine Lake:** If anywhere in the Canadian Rockies qualifies as a Double Must See, it would be this deep-blue body of water surrounded by glaciated peaks (page 85).

◖ **Lake Agnes Trail:** You won't completely es-cape the crowds by hiking this trail from Lake Louise, but you will leave most of them behind (page 87).

◖ **Larch Valley Trail:** This walk is a good in-troduction to hiking in the Canadian Rockies, especially in fall when the larch trees have turned a brilliant gold (page 89).

◖ **Peyto Lake:** Another one of Banff's fa-mous lakes. The main difference is the per-spective from which it is viewed—a lookout high above its shoreline (page 100).

◖ **Mount Assiniboine Provincial Park:** Accessible only on foot or by helicopter, this roadless park is filled with glacier-capped peaks and turquoise lakes (page 107).

August). The rest of the year, crowds outside the town of Banff are negligible. In winter, three world-class winter resorts—Ski Norquay, Sunshine Village, and Lake Louise (Canada's second-largest winter resort)—crank up their lifts. During this low season, hotel rates are reasonable. If you tire of downhill skiing and snowboarding, you can try cross-country skiing, ice-skating, or snowshoeing; take a sleigh ride; soak in a hot spring; or go heli-skiing nearby.

The park is open year-round, although oc-casional road closures occur on mountain passes along the park's western boundary in winter, due to avalanche-control work and snowstorms.

PARK ENTRY

Permits are required for entry into Banff National Park. A **National Parks Day Pass** is adult $9.80, senior $8.30, child $4.90, to a maximum of $20 per vehicle. It is interchangeable between parks and is valid until 4pm the day following its purchase.

An annual **Discovery Pass,** good for entry into national parks and national historic sites across Canada (including two within Banff National Park), is adult $67.70, senior $57.90, child $33.30, to a maximum of $136.40 per vehicle.

All passes can be bought at the eastern park gate on the TransCanada Highway, the park information centers in Banff or Lake Louise, and at campground kiosks. For more information, check online at the Parks Canada website (www.pc.gc.ca).

PLANNING YOUR TIME

If you are planning to visit the Canadian Rockies, it is almost inevitable that your itinerary will include Banff National Park, both for its many and varied outdoor attractions and for its central location. The park can be anything you want it to be, depending on the time of year you visit and what your interests are. The main population center is Banff, which has all the services of a large town, as well as attractions such as the landmark **Fairmont Banff Springs** hotel and the **Whyte Museum of the Canadian Rockies.** The park holds three lakes that you won't want to miss for their scenic beauty: **Lake Louise, Moraine Lake,** and **Peyto Lake.** All three are easily accessible by road but also offer surrounding hiking, and the former two have canoe rentals. Hiking is the park's biggest attraction, and many visitors plan their itinerary around it. I'd suggest mixing it up—choosing from the hikes that reflect your fitness level and combining them with visits to the major natural attractions. For example,

when in the vicinity of Lake Louise, walk the **Lake Agnes Trail,** and while at Moraine Lake, plan on visiting **Larch Valley.** For the more adventurous, **Bourgeau Lake** is a stunning day-hike destination. Keen hikers with more time should also consider including **Mount Assiniboine Provincial Park,** which is renowned for its network of trails.

You can book one accommodation for your entire stay or spend an equal number of nights in Banff and Lake Louise. If you have a family or like the convenience of staying put for your entire vacation, it is practical to book a room in either Banff or Lake Louise and use it as a base—spending your days in the park but also venturing farther afield, with, for example, one day scheduled for Yoho National Park and another for a Canmore/Kananaskis combo.

Unless you're a die-hard skier or snowboarder, summer is definitely the best time of year to visit. The months of July and August are the busiest, with crowds decreasing exponentially in the weeks before and after these two months. June and September are wonderful times to visit the park. Aside from the crowd factor, in June, wildflowers start blooming and wildlife is abundant. September sees temperatures ripe for hiking, and the turning colors are at their peak. In either month, discounted accommodations are a welcome bonus. In May and October-November, the park is at its quietest. Temperatures in any of these three months are generally too cool for hiking (although welcome warm spells are common). The park's three alpine resorts begin opening in December and remain in operation until April or May. While skiing and boarding are the big wintertime draw, plan on expanding your experience by joining a sleigh ride, learning to snowshoe, or heading out for some ice fishing.

THE LAND

The park lies within the main and front ranges of the Rocky Mountains, a mountain

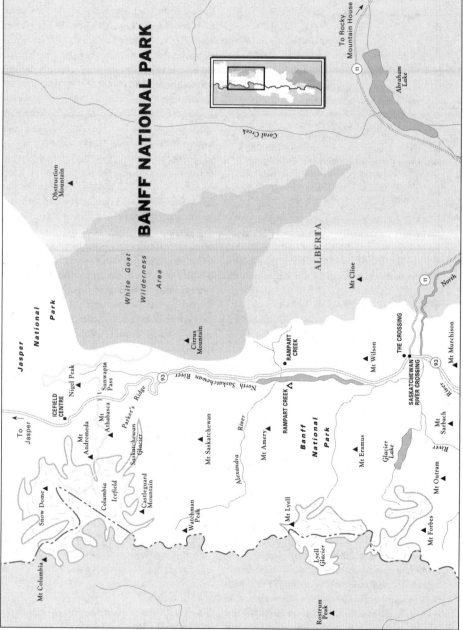

BANFF NATIONAL PARK

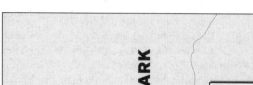

To Rocky Mountain House

Abraham Lake

Coral Creek

Obstruction Mountain

White Goat Wilderness Area

ALBERTA

Mt Cline

North

Jasper National Park

Nigel Peak

Sunwapta Pass

Parker's Ridge

ICEFIELD CENTRE

Mt Andromeda

Mt Athabasca

Saskatchewan Glacier

Cirrus Mountain

RAMPART CREEK

Mt Wilson

THE CROSSING

SASKATCHEWAN RIVER CROSSING

Mt Murchison

North Saskatchewan River

RAMPART CREEK

Banff National Park

Mt Eramus

Glacier Lake

Mt Sarbach

River

Alexandra River

Mt Saskatchewan

Mt Amery

Castleguard Mountain

Columbia Icefield

Snow Dome

To Jasper

Watchman Peak

Mt Lyell

Lyell Glacier

Mt Forbes

Mt Outram

Mt Columbia

Rostrum Peak

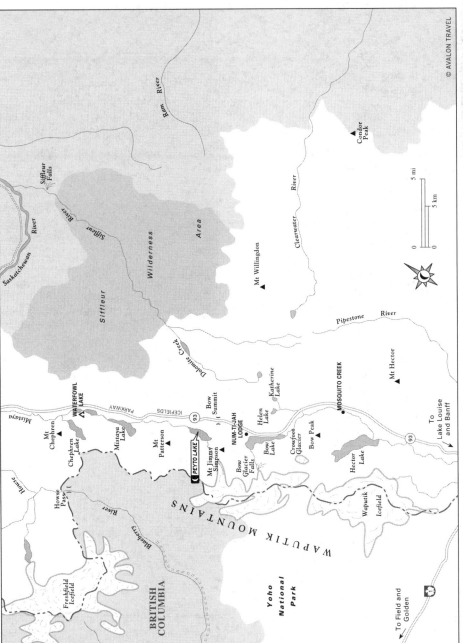

© AVALON TRAVEL

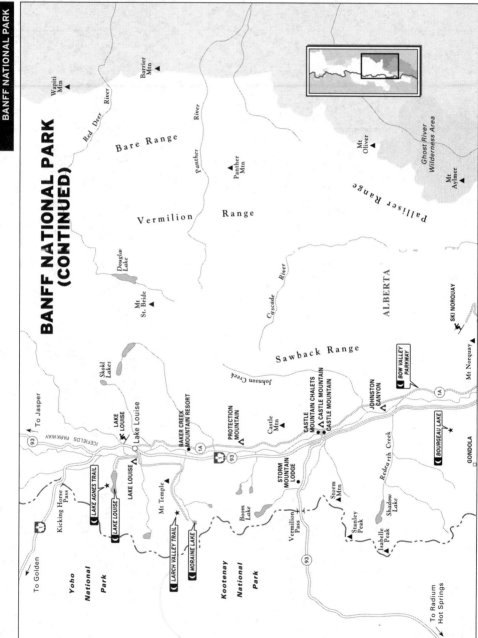

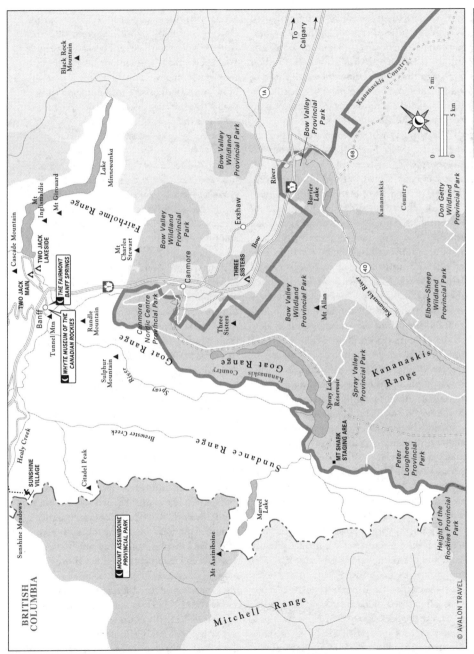

To Calgary

Black Rock Mountain

Lake Minnewanka

Kananaskis Country

5 mi

5 km

0

0

Bow Valley Provincial Park

Bow Valley Wildland Provincial Park

Mt Inglismaldie

Mt Girouard

Cascade Mountain

Fairholme Range

Barrier Lake

Mt Charles Stewart

Bow Valley Wildland Provincial Park

Exshaw

Bow River

Kananaskis Country

Don Getty Wildland Provincial Park

TWO JACK LAKESIDE

TWO JACK MAIN

THE FAIRMONT BANFF SPRINGS

Banff

THREE SISTERS

Canmore

Mt Allan

Elbow-Sheep Wildland Provincial Park

Kananaskis River

WHYTE MUSEUM OF THE CANADIAN ROCKIES

Tunnel Mtn

Rundle Mountain

Canmore Nordic Centre Provincial Park

Bow Valley Wildland Provincial Park

Three Sisters

Goat Range

Kananaskis Country

Goat Range

Kananaskis Range

Sulphur Mountain

Spray River

Spray Valley Provincial Park

Spray Lake Reservoir

Healy Creek

Brewster Creek

Sundance Range

MT SHARK STAGING AREA

SUNSHINE VILLAGE

Citadel Peak

Peter Lougheed Provincial Park

Sunshine Meadows

Marvel Lake

BRITISH COLUMBIA

MOUNT ASSINIBOINE PROVINCIAL PARK

Mt Assiniboine

Height of the Rockies Provincial Park

Mitchell Range

© AVALON TRAVEL

range that extends the length of the North American continent. Although the mountains are composed of bedrock laid down up to one billion years ago, it wasn't until 100 million years ago that forces below the earth's surface transformed the lowland plain of what is now western Canada into the varied, mountainous topography we see today.

The front ranges lie to the east, bordering the foothills. These geologically complex mountains are made up of younger bedrock that has been folded, faulted, and uplifted. The main ranges are older and higher, with the bedrock lying mainly horizontal and not as severely disturbed as the front ranges. Here the pressures have been most powerful; these mountains are characterized by castlelike buttresses and pinnacles and warped waves of stratified rock. Most glaciers are found among these lofty peaks. The spine of the main range is the **Continental Divide.** In Canadian latitudes to the east of the divide, all waters flow to the Atlantic Ocean; those to the west flow into the Pacific.

Since rising above the surrounding plains, these mountains have been eroding. At least four times in the last million years, sheets of ice have covered much of the land. Advancing and retreating back and forth like steel wool across the landscape, they rounded off lower peaks and carved formerly V-shaped valleys into broad U-shaped ones (**Bow Valley** is the most distinctive). Meanwhile, glacial meltwater continued carving ever-deeper channels into the valleys, and rivers changed course many times.

This long history of powerful and even violent natural events over the eons has left behind the dramatic landscape visitors marvel over today. Now forming the exposed sides of many a mountain peak, layers of drastically altered sediment are visible from miles away, especially when accentuated by a particular angle of sunlight or a light fall of snow. **Cirques,** gouged into the mountains by glacial

action, fill with glacial meltwater each spring, creating trademark translucent green lakes that will take your breath away. The wide, sweeping U-shaped valleys scoured out by glaciers past now create magnificent panoramas that will draw you to pull off the road and gasp in awe; open views are easy to come by here, thanks to a climate that keeps the tree line low.

FLORA

Nearly 700 species of plants have been recorded in the park. Each species falls into one of three distinct vegetation zones, based primarily on altitude. Lowest is the montane zone, which covers the valley floor. Above it, the subalpine zone comprises most of the forested area. Highest of all is the alpine zone, where climate is severe and vegetation cover is limited.

Montane-zone vegetation is usually found at elevations below 1,350 meters (4,430 feet) but can grow at higher elevations on sun-drenched, south-facing slopes. Because fires frequently affect this zone, **lodgepole pine** is the dominant species; its tightly sealed cones only open with the heat of a forest fire, thereby regenerating the species quickly after a blaze. **Douglas fir** is the zone's climax species and is found in open stands, such as on Tunnel Mountain. **Aspen** is common in older burn areas, while **limber pine** thrives on rocky outcrops.

Dense forests of **white spruce** and **Engelmann spruce** typify the subalpine zone. White spruce dominates up to 2,100 meters (6,890 feet); above 2,100 meters (6,890 feet) to 2,400 meters (7,870 feet), Engelmann spruce is dominant. In areas affected by fire, such as west of Castle Junction, lodgepole pine occurs in dense stands. **Subalpine fir** grows above 2,200 meters (7,220 feet) and is often stunted by the high winds experienced at such lofty elevations.

The transition from subalpine to alpine is gradual and usually occurs around 2,300 meters (7,550 feet). The alpine has a severe climate, with temperatures averaging below zero.

Low temperatures, strong winds, and a very short summer force alpine plants to adapt by growing low to the ground with long roots. Mosses, mountain avens, saxifrage, and an alpine dandelion all thrive in this environment. The best place to view the brightly colored carpet of **alpine flowers** is at Sunshine Meadows or Parker's Ridge.

FAUNA

Viewing the park's abundant and varied wildlife is one of the most popular visitor activities in Banff. In summer, with the onslaught of the tourist hordes, many of the larger mammals move away from the heavily traveled areas. It then becomes a case of knowing when and where to look for them. Spring and fall are the best times of year for wildlife viewing; the crowds are thinner than in summer, and big-game animals are more likely to be seen at lower elevations. Winter also has its advantages. Although **bears** are hibernating, a large herd of **elk** winters on the outskirts of the town of Banff, **coyotes** are often seen roaming around town, **bighorn sheep** have descended from the heights, and **wolf** packs can be seen along the Bow Valley Corridor.

Small Mammals

One of the first mammals you're likely to come in contact with is the **Columbian ground squirrel,** seen throughout the park's lower elevations. The **golden-mantled ground squirrel,** similar in size but with a striped back, is common at higher elevations or around rocky outcrops. The one collecting Engelmann spruce cones is the **red squirrel.** The **least chipmunk** is striped, but it's smaller than the golden-mantled squirrel. It lives in dry, rocky areas throughout the park.

Short-tailed weasels are common, but **long-tailed weasels** are rare. Look for both in higher subalpine forests. **Pikas** (commonly called rock rabbits) and **hoary marmots** (well

known for their shrill whistles) live among rock slides near high-country lakes; look for them around Moraine Lake and along Bow Summit Loop. **Porcupines** are widespread and are most active at night.

Vermilion Lakes is an excellent place to view the **beaver** at work; the best time is dawn or dusk. **Muskrats** and **mink** are common in all wetlands within the park.

Hoofed Residents

The most common and widespread of the park's hoofed residents are **elk,** which number around 2,800. Starting in 2000, a concerted effort was made to keep them out of Banff's downtown core, but they are still congregating around the outskirts of the town, including up near the Tunnel Mountain campgrounds. They can also be seen along the Bow Valley Parkway. **Moose** were once common around Vermilion Lakes, but competition from an artificially expanded elk population caused their numbers to decline, and now only around 100 live in the park. Look for them at Waterfowl Lakes and along the Icefields Parkway near Rampart Creek.

Mule deer, named for their large ears, are most common in the southern part of the park. Watch for them along the Mount Norquay Road and Bow Valley Parkway. **White-tailed deer** are much less common but are seen occasionally at Saskatchewan River Crossing. A small herd of around 20 **woodland caribou** remains in the Dolomite Pass area and Upper Pipestone Valley and is rarely seen.

It is estimated that the park is home to around 900 **mountain goats.** These nimble-footed creatures occupy all mountain peaks, living almost the entire year in the higher subalpine and alpine regions. The most accessible place to view these high-altitude hermits is along Parker's Ridge in the far northwestern corner of the park. The park's **bighorn sheep** have for the most part lost their fear of

THE ELK OF BANFF NATIONAL PARK

Few visitors leave Banff without having seen elk–a large member of the deer family easily distinguished by its white rump. Though the animals have been reported passing through the park for a century, they've never been indigenous. In 1917, 57 elk were moved to Banff from Yellowstone National Park. Two years later, 20 more were transplanted, and the new herd multiplied rapidly. At that time, coyotes, cougars, and wolves were being slaughtered under a predator-control program, leaving the elk unfettered by nature's population-control mechanisms. The elk proliferated and soon became a problem as they took to wintering in the range of bighorn sheep, deer, moose, and beaver. Between 1941 and 1969, controlled slaughters of elk were conducted in an attempt to reduce the population.

Today, with wolf packs returning to the park, the elk population has stabilized at about 2,800. In summer, look for them in open meadows along the Bow Valley Parkway, along the road to Two Jack Lake, or at Vermilion Lakes.

Each fall, traditionally, hundreds of elk moved into the town itself, but starting in recent years, Parks Canada has been making a concerted effort to keep them away from areas such as the golf course and recreation grounds. The main reason for this is that fall is rutting season, and the libidinal bull elk become dangerous as they gather their harems.

You may still see the odd elk feeding in downtown Central Park or walking proudly down a fairway at the Fairmont Banff Springs Golf Course, but it's more likely you'll spot one while driving along park highways.

---

humans and often congregate at certain spots to lick salt from the road. Your best chance of seeing one of the park's 2,000-2,300 bighorn is at the south end of the Bow Valley Parkway, between switchbacks on Mount Norquay Road, and between Lake Minnewanka and Two Jack Lake.

Wild Dogs and Cats

Coyotes are widespread along the entire Bow River watershed. They are attracted to Vermilion Lakes by an abundance of small game, and many have permanent dens there. **Wolves** had been driven close to extinction by the early 1950s, but today at least four wolf packs have been reported in the park. One pack winters close to town and is occasionally seen on Vermilion Lakes during that period. The **lynx** population fluctuates greatly; look for them in the backcountry during winter. **Cougars** are shy and number fewer than 20 in the park. They are occasionally seen along the front ranges behind Cascade Mountain.

Bears

The exhilaration of seeing one of these magnificent creatures in its natural habitat is unforgettable. From the road you're most likely to see **black bears,** which actually range in color from jet black to cinnamon brown and number around 50. Try the Bow Valley Parkway at dawn or late in the afternoon. Farther north they are occasionally seen near the road as it passes Cirrus Mountain. Banff's 60-odd **grizzly bears** spend most of the year in remote valleys, often on south-facing slopes away from the Bow Valley Corridor. During late spring they are occasionally seen in residential areas, along the Lake Minnewanka loop road, on the golf course, and in the area of Bow Pass.

The chance of encountering a bear face-to-face in the backcountry is remote. To lessen chances even further, you should take some simple precautions: Never hike alone or at dusk. Make lots of noise when passing through heavy vegetation. Keep a clean camp. Read the pamphlets available at all park visitors centers. At the Banff Visitor Centre (224 Banff Ave.), daily trail reports list all recent bear sightings. Report any bears you see to the Warden's Office (403/762-4506).

Reptiles and Amphibians

The **wandering garter snake** is rare and found only near the Cave and Basin, where warm water from the mineral spring flows down a shaded slope into Vermilion Lakes. Amphibians found in the park include the widespread **western toad;** the **wood frog,** commonly found along the Bow River; the rare **spotted frog;** and the **long-toed salamander,** which spawns in shallow ponds and spends the summer under logs or rocks in the vicinity of its spawning grounds.

Birds

Although more than 240 species of birds have been recorded in the park, most are shy and live in heavily wooded areas. One species that definitely isn't shy is the fearless **gray jay,** which haunts all campgrounds and picnic areas. Similar in color, but larger, is the **Clark's nutcracker,** which lives in higher, subalpine forests. Another common bird is the black-and-white **magpie. Ravens** are frequently encountered, especially around campgrounds.

Several species of **woodpecker** live in subalpine forests. A number of species of grouse are also in residence. Most common is the **downy ruffed grouse,** seen in montane forest. The **blue grouse** and **spruce grouse** are seen at higher elevations, as is the **white-tailed ptarmigan,** which lives above the tree line. (Watch for them in Sunshine Meadows or on the Bow Summit Loop.) A colony of **black swifts** in Johnston Canyon is one of only two in the Canadian Rockies.

Good spots to view **dippers** and migrating waterfowl are Hector Lake, Vermilion Lakes, and the wetland area near Muleshoe Picnic Area. A bird blind has been set up below the Cave and Basin but is only worth visiting at dawn and dusk when the hordes of human visitors aren't around. Part of the nearby marsh stays ice free during winter, attracting **killdeer** and other birds.

Although raptors are not common in the park, **bald eagles** and **golden eagles** are present part of the year, and Alberta's provincial bird, the **great horned owl,** lives in the park year-round.

HISTORY

Although the valleys of the Canadian Rockies became ice free nearly 8,000 years ago and native people periodically have hunted in the area since that time, the story of Banff National Park really began with the arrival of the railroad to the area.

The Coming of the Railway

In 1871, Canadian prime minister John A. MacDonald promised to build a rail line linking British Columbia to the rest of the country as a condition of the new province joining the confederation. It wasn't until early 1883 that the line reached Calgary, pushing through to **Laggan,** now known as Lake Louise, that fall. The rail line was one of the largest and costliest engineering jobs ever undertaken in Canada.

Discovery of the Cave and Basin

On November 8, 1883, three young railway workers—Franklin McCabe and William and Thomas McCardell—went prospecting for gold on their day off. After crossing the Bow River by raft, they came across a warm stream and traced it to its source at a small log-choked basin of warm water that had a distinct smell of sulphur. Nearby they detected the source of the foul smell coming from a hole in the ground. Nervously, one of the three men lowered himself into the hole and came across a subterranean pool of aqua-green warm water. The three men had found not gold, but something just as precious—a hot mineral spring that in time

BANFF NATIONAL PARK

WILD BILL PEYTO

These words from a friend sum up Bill Peyto—one of Banff's earliest characters and one of the Canadian Rockies' greatest guides: "rarely speaking—his forte was doing things, not talking about them." In 1886, at the tender age of 18, Ebenezer William Peyto left England for Canada. After traveling extensively, he settled in Banff and was hired as an apprentice guide by legendary outfitter Tom Wilson. Wearing a tilted sombrero, fringed buckskin coat, cartridge belt, hunting knife, and six-shooter, he looked more like a gunslinger than a mountain man.

As his reputation as a competent guide grew, so did the stories. While guiding clients on one occasion, he led them to his cabin. Before entering, Peyto threw stones in the front door until a loud snap was heard. It was a bear trap that he'd set up to catch a certain trapper who'd been stealing his food. One of the guests commented that if caught, the trapper would surely have died. "You're damned right he would have," Bill replied. "Then I'd have known for sure it was him."

In 1900, Peyto left Banff to fight in the Boer War and was promoted to corporal for bravery. This title was revoked before it became official after army officials learned he'd "borrowed" an officer's jacket and several bottles of booze for the celebration. Returning to a hero's welcome in Banff, Peyto established an outfitting business and continued prospecting for copper in Simpson Pass. Although his outfitting business thrived, the death of his wife left him despondent. He built a house on Banff Avenue; its name, "Ain't it Hell," summed up his view of life.

In his later years, he became a warden in the Healy Creek-Sunshine district, where his exploits during the 1920s added to his already legendary name. After 20 years of service he retired, and in 1943, at the age of 75, he passed away. One of the park's most beautiful lakes is named after him, as are a glacier and a popular Banff watering hole (Wild Bill's—a designation he would have appreciated). His face also adorns the large signs welcoming visitors to Banff.

---

would attract wealthy customers from around the world. Word of the discovery soon got out, and the government encouraged visitors to the Cave and Basin as an ongoing source of revenue to support the new railway.

A 2,500-hectare (6,177-acre) reserve was established around the springs on November 25, 1885, and two years later the reserve was expanded and renamed **Rocky Mountains Park.** It was primarily a business enterprise centered around the unique springs and catering to wealthy patrons of the railway. At the turn of the 20th century, Canada had an abundance of wilderness; it certainly didn't need a park to preserve it. The only goal of Rocky Mountains Park was to generate income for the government and the Canadian Pacific Railway (CPR).

A Town Grows

After the discovery of the Cave and Basin

across the Bow River from the railway station (then known as Siding 29), many commercial facilities sprang up along what is now Banff Avenue. The general manager of the CPR (later to become its vice president), William Cornelius Van Horne, was instrumental in creating a hotel business along the rail line. His most recognized achievement was the Banff Springs Hotel, which opened in 1888. It was the world's largest hotel at the time. Enterprising locals soon realized the area's potential and began opening restaurants, offering guided hunting and boating trips, and developing manicured gardens. Banff soon became Canada's best-known tourist resort, attracting visitors from around the world. It was named after Banffshire, the Scottish birthplace of George Stephen, the CPR's first president.

In 1902, the park boundary was again expanded to include 11,440 square kilometers

(4,417 square miles) of the Canadian Rockies. This dramatic expansion meant that the park became not just a tourist resort but also home to existing coal-mining and logging operations and hydroelectric dams. Government officials saw no conflict of interest, actually stating that the coal mine and township at Bankhead added to the park's many attractions. Many of the forests were logged, providing wood for construction, while other areas were burned to allow clear sightings for surveyors' instruments.

After a restriction on automobiles in the park was lifted in 1916, Canada's best-known tourist resort also became its busiest. More and more commercial facilities sprang up, offering luxury and opulence amid the wilderness of the Canadian Rockies. Calgarians built summer cottages, and the town began advertising itself as a year-round destination. As attitudes began to change, the government set up a Dominion Parks Branch, whose first commissioner, J. B. Harkin, believed that land set aside for parks should be used for recreation and education. Gradually, resource industries were phased out. Harkins's work culminated in the National Parks Act of 1930, which in turn led Rocky Mountains Park to be renamed Banff National Park. The park's present boundaries, encompassing 6,641 square kilometers (2,564 square miles), were established in 1964.

Icefields Parkway

Natives and early explorers found the swampy nature of the Bow Valley north of Lake Louise difficult for foot and horse travel. When heading north, they used instead the Pipestone River Valley to the east. Banff guide Bill Peyto led American explorer Walter Wilcox up the Bow Valley in 1896, to the high peaks along the Continental Divide northeast of Lake Louise. The first complete journey along this route was made by Jim Brewster in 1904. Soon after, A. P. Coleman made the arduous journey, becoming a strong supporter for the route aptly known as The Wonder Trail. During the Great Depression of the 1930s, as part of a relief-work project, construction began on what was to become the Icefields Parkway. The road was completed in 1939, and the first car traveled the route in 1940. In tribute to the excellence of the road's early construction, the original roadbed, when upgraded to its present standard in 1961, was followed nearly the entire way.

Town of Banff

For most of its existence, the town of Banff was run as a service center for park visitors by the Canadian Parks Service in Ottawa, a government department with plenty of economic resources but little idea about how to handle the day-to-day running of a midsized town. Any inconvenience this arrangement caused park residents was offset by cheap rent and subsidized services. In June 1988, Banff's residents voted to sever this tie, and on January 1, 1990, Banff officially became an incorporated town, no different than any other in Alberta (except that Parks Canada controls environmental protection within the town of Banff).

Town of Banff

Many visitors planning a trip to the national park don't realize that the town of Banff is a bustling commercial center. The town's location is magnificent. It is spread out along the Bow River, extending to the lower slopes of Sulphur Mountain to the south and Tunnel Mountain to the east. In one direction is the towering face of Mount Rundle, and in the other, framed by the buildings along Banff Avenue, is Cascade Mountain. Hotels and motels line the north end of Banff Avenue, while a profusion of shops, boutiques, cafés, and restaurants hugs the south end. Also at the south end, just over the Bow River, is the Park Administration Building. Here the road forks—to the right is the historic Cave and Basin Hot Springs, to the left the Fairmont Banff Springs and Banff Gondola. Some people are happy walking along the crowded streets or shopping in a unique setting; those more interested in some peace and quiet can easily slip into pristine wilderness just a five-minute walk from town.

SIGHTS AND DRIVES
Banff Park Museum

Although displays of stuffed animals are not usually associated with national parks, the downtown Banff Park Museum (93 Banff Ave., 403/762-1558, 10am-6pm daily mid-May-Sept., 1pm-5pm daily the rest of the year, adult $4, senior $3.50, child $3) provides an insight into the park's early history. Visitors during the Victorian era were eager to see the park's animals without actually having to venture into the bush. A lack of roads and scarcity of large game resulting from hunting meant that the best places to see animals, stuffed or otherwise, were the game paddock, the zoo, and this museum, which was built in 1903. In its early years, the Banff Zoo and Aviary occupied the grounds behind the museum. The zoo kept more than 60 species of animals, including a polar bear. The museum itself was built before the park had electricity, hence the railroad pagoda design using skylights on all levels.

As times changed, the museum was considered outdated; plans for its demolition were put forward in the 1950s. Fortunately, the museum was spared and later restored for the park's 100th anniversary in 1985. While the exhibits still provide visitors with an insight into the intricate workings of various park ecosystems, they are also an interesting link to the park's past. The museum also has a Discovery Room, where touching the displays is encouraged, and a reading room that is stocked with natural history books.

◖ Whyte Museum of the Canadian Rockies

The Whyte Foundation was established in the mid-1950s by local artists Peter and Catharine Whyte to help preserve artistic and historical material relating to the Canadian Rockies. Their museum (111 Bear St., 403/762-2291, 10am-5pm daily, adult $8, senior $5, child free) opened in 1968 and has continued to grow ever since. It now houses the world's largest collection of Canadian Rockies literature and art. Included in the archives are more than 4,000 volumes, oral tapes of early pioneers and outfitters, antique postcards, old cameras, manuscripts, and a large photography collection. The highlight is the photography of Byron Harmon, whose black-and-white studies of mountain geography have shown people around the world the beauty of the Canadian Rockies. The downstairs gallery features changing art exhibitions. The museum also houses the library and archives of the Alpine Club of Canada. On the

© ANDREW HEMPSTEAD

Banff Visitor Centre

grounds are several heritage homes and cabins formerly occupied by local pioneers.

MUSEUM TOURS

The Whyte Museum hosts interesting walking tours during the summer. The most popular of these is the **Heritage Homes Tour,** which allows an opportunity for visitors to take a closer look at the historic residences located in the trees behind the museum, including that of Peter and Catharine Whyte. This tour departs up to five times daily through the summer. The tour is $8 per person, or free with museum admission. On the **Luxton Open House** tour, you can visit the home of a prominent Banff family at your own leisure 1pm-3pm Friday-Sunday in summer. Admission is $8, or free with museum admission.

Cascade Gardens

Across the river from downtown, Cascade Gardens offers a commanding view along Banff Avenue and of Cascade Mountain. The gardens are immaculately manicured, making for enjoyable strolling on a sunny day. The stone edifice in the center of the garden is the **Park Administration Building** (101 Mountain Ave.), which dates to 1936. It replaced a private spa and hospital operated by one of the park's earliest entrepreneurs, Dr. R. G. Brett. Known as Brett's Sanatorium, the original 1886 structure was built to accommodate guests drawn to Banff by the claimed healing qualities of the hot springs' water.

Buffalo Nations Luxton Museum

Looking like a stockade, this museum (1 Birch Ave., 403/762-2388, 11am-6pm daily in summer, 1pm-5pm daily the rest of the year, adult $8.50, senior $6.50, child $3) overlooks the Bow River across from Central Park. It is dedicated to the heritage of the First Nations who once inhabited the Canadian Rockies and adjacent prairies. The museum was developed

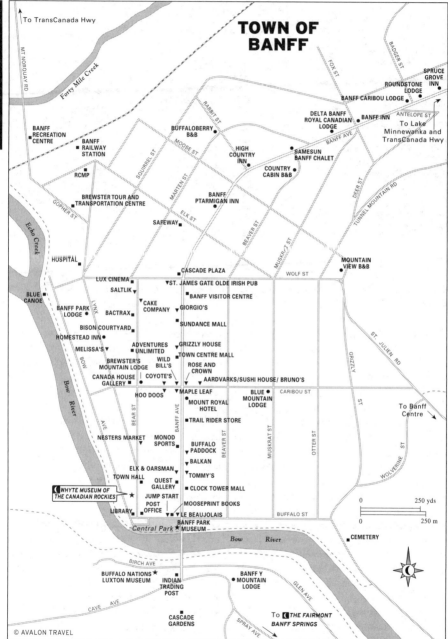

TOWN OF BANFF

To TransCanada Hwy

MT NORQUAY RD

Forty Mile Creek

FOX ST

BADGER ST

SPRUCE GROVE INN

ROUNDSTONE LODGE

BANFF CARIBOU LODGE

RABBIT ST

ANTELOPE ST

DELTA BANFF ROYAL CANADIAN LODGE

BANFF INN

To Lake Minnewanka and TransCanada Hwy

BANFF RECREATION CENTRE

BANFF RAILWAY STATION

BUFFALOBERRY B&B

MOOSE ST

HIGH COUNTRY INN

BANFF AVE

SAMESUN BANFF CHALET

RCMP

SQUIRREL ST

COUNTRY CABIN B&B

DEER ST

GOPHER ST

BREWSTER TOUR AND TRANSPORTATION CENTRE

MARTEN ST

BANFF PTARMIGAN INN

TUNNEL MOUNTAIN RD

SAFEWAY

ELK ST

BEAVER ST

MUSKRAT ST

Echo Creek

HOSPITAL

CASCADE PLAZA

WOLF ST

MOUNTAIN VIEW B&B

BLUE CANOE

LUX CINEMA

SALTLIK

ST. JAMES GATE OLDE IRISH PUB

BANFF VISITOR CENTRE

BANFF PARK LODGE

BACTRAX

CAKE COMPANY

GIORGIO'S

LYNX

BISON COURTYARD

SUNDANCE MALL

HOMESTEAD INN

MELISSA'S

ADVENTURES UNLIMITED

GRIZZLY HOUSE

TOWN CENTRE MALL

BOW

BREWSTER'S MOUNTAIN LODGE

WILD BILL'S

ROSE AND CROWN

ST. JULIEN RD

GRIZZLY ST

CANADA HOUSE GALLERY

COYOTE'S

AARDVARKS/SUSHI HOUSE/ BRUNO'S

Bow River

HOO DOOS

MAPLE LEAF

BLUE MOUNTAIN LODGE

CARIBOU ST

To Banff Centre

MOUNT ROYAL HOTEL

AVE

BEAR ST

TRAIL RIDER STORE

BANFF AVE

NESTERS MARKET

MONOD SPORTS

BUFFALO PADDOCK

BEAVER ST

MUSKRAT ST

OTTER ST

WOLVERINE ST

BALKAN

ELK & OARSMAN

TOMMY'S

TOWN HALL

QUEST GALLERY

CLOCK TOWER MALL

WHYTE MUSEUM OF THE CANADIAN ROCKIES

JUMP START POST OFFICE

MOOSEPRINT BOOKS

LIBRARY

LE BEAUJOLAIS

BANFF PARK MUSEUM

BUFFALO ST

0   250 yds

0   250 m

Central Park

Bow River

CEMETERY

BIRCH AVE

BUFFALO NATIONS LUXTON MUSEUM

INDIAN TRADING POST

BANFF Y MOUNTAIN LODGE

GLEN AVE

CAVE AVE

CASCADE GARDENS

SPRAY AVE

To THE FAIRMONT BANFF SPRINGS

© AVALON TRAVEL

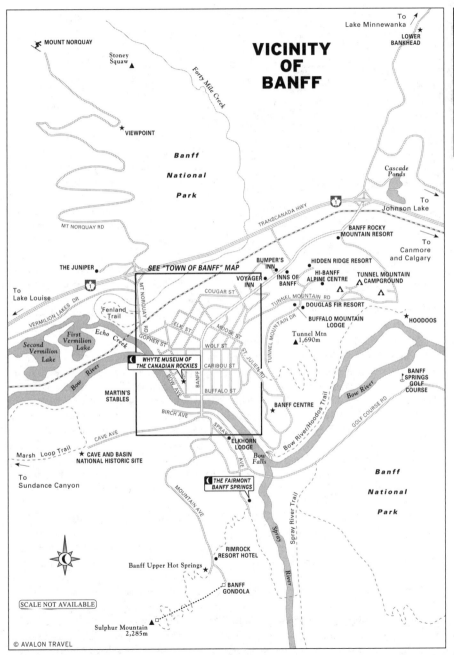

VICINITY OF BANFF

MOUNT NORQUAY

To Lake Minnewanka

LOWER BANKHEAD

Stoney Squaw

Forty Mile Creek

VIEWPOINT

Banff

National

Park

Cascade Ponds

TRANSCANADA HWY

To Johnson Lake

MT NORQUAY RD

BANFF ROCKY MOUNTAIN RESORT

To Canmore and Calgary

THE JUNIPER

SEE "TOWN OF BANFF" MAP

BUMPER'S INN

HIDDEN RIDGE RESORT

VOYAGER INN

INNS OF BANFF

HI-BANFF ALPINE CENTRE

TUNNEL MOUNTAIN CAMPGROUND

To Lake Louise

COUGAR ST

TUNNEL MOUNTAIN RD

DOUGLAS FIR RESORT

VERMILION LAKES DR

Fenland Trail

MT NORQUAY RD

ELK ST

MOOSE ST

BUFFALO MOUNTAIN LODGE

HOODOOS

Echo Creek

GOPHER ST

WOLF ST

TUNNEL MOUNTAIN DR

Tunnel Mtn 1,690m

Second Vermilion Lake

First Vermilion Lake

ST JULIEN RD

WHYTE MUSEUM OF THE CANADIAN ROCKIES

CARIBOU ST

Bow River

BANFF SPRINGS GOLF COURSE

MARTIN'S STABLES

BOW AVE

BANFF

BUFFALO ST

Bow River

BIRCH AVE

BANFF CENTRE

Bow River/Hoodoos Trail

GOLF COURSE RD

CAVE AVE

Marsh Loop Trail

CAVE AND BASIN NATIONAL HISTORIC SITE

SPRAY AVE

ELKHORN LODGE

Bow Falls

Banff

National

Park

To Sundance Canyon

THE FAIRMONT BANFF SPRINGS

MOUNTAIN AVE

Spray River Trail

Spray River

RIMROCK RESORT HOTEL

Banff Upper Hot Springs

BANFF GONDOLA

SCALE NOT AVAILABLE

Sulphur Mountain 2,285m

© AVALON TRAVEL

Whyte Museum of the Canadian Rockies

by prominent local resident Norman Luxton in the early 1900s. At that time it was within the Indian Trading Post, an adjacent gift shop that still stands. The museum contains memorabilia from Luxton's lifelong relationship with the Stoney, including an elaborately decorated tepee, hunting equipment, arrowheads dating back 4,000 years, stuffed animals, original artwork, peace pipes, and traditional clothing. Various aspects of native culture—such as ceremonial gatherings, living in a tepee, and weaving—are also displayed. The Indian Trading Post is one of Banff's more unique gift shops and is definitely worth a browse.

Cave and Basin National Historic Site

At the end of Cave Avenue, this historic site (403/762-1566, 9am-6pm daily in summer, 11am-4pm Mon.-Fri., 9:30am-5pm Sat.-Sun. the rest of the year, adult $4, senior $3.50, child $2.50), which is the birthplace of Banff

National Park and of the Canadian National Parks system, reopened in 2013 after extensive renovations. Here in 1883, three men employed by the Canadian Pacific Railway (CPR) stumbled on the hot springs now known as the Cave and Basin and were soon lounging in the hot water—a real luxury in the Wild West. They built a fence around the springs, constructed a crude cabin, and began the long process of establishing a claim to the site. But the government beat them to it, settling their claims for a few thousand dollars and acquiring the hot springs.

Bathhouses were installed in 1887, and bathers paid $0.10 for a swim. The pools were eventually lined with concrete, and additions were built onto the original structures. Ironically, the soothing minerals in the water that had attracted millions of people to bathe here eventually caused the pools' demise. The minerals, combined with chlorine, produced sediments that ate away at the concrete structure until the pools were deemed unsuitable for swimming in 1993.

Although the pools are now closed for swimming, the center is still one of Banff's most popular attractions. Interpretive displays describe the hows and whys of the springs. A narrow tunnel winds into the dimly lit cave, and short trails lead from the center to the cave entrance and through a unique environment created by the hot water from the springs. Interpretive tours run three times daily in summer.

Banff Upper Hot Springs

These springs (Mountain Ave., 403/762-1515, 9am-11pm daily May-Oct., 10am-10pm Sun.-Thurs. 10am-11pm Fri.-Sat. Oct.-May), toward the Banff Gondola, were first developed in 1901. The present building was completed in 1935, with extensive renovations made in 1996. Water flows out of the bedrock at 47°C (116.6°F) and is cooled to 40°C (104°F) in the main pool. Once considered for privatization,

© ANDREW HEMPSTEAD

the "Cave" at Cave and Basin National Historic Site

the springs are still run by Parks Canada and are popular throughout the year. Swimming is $7.50 adults, $6.50 seniors and children; lockers and towel rental are a couple of dollars extra. Within the complex is **Pleiades Massage & Spa** (403/760-2500), offering a wide range of therapeutic treatments, including massages from $60 for 30 minutes as well as body wraps, aromatherapy, and hydrotherapy.

Banff Gondola

The easiest way to get high above town without breaking a sweat is on this gondola (403/762-2523, 8:30am-9pm daily in summer, shorter hours the rest of the year, closed for two weeks in January, adult $30, child $15). The modern four-person cars rise 700 meters (2,300 feet) in eight minutes to the summit of 2,285-meter (7,500-foot) **Sulphur Mountain.** From the observation deck at the upper terminal, the breathtaking view includes the town, Bow Valley, Cascade Mountain, Lake Minnewanka,

and the Fairholme Range. Bighorn sheep often hang around below the upper terminal. The short **Vista Trail** leads along a ridge to a restored weather observatory. Between 1903 and 1931, long before the gondola was built, Norman Sanson was the meteorological observer who collected data at the station. During this period he made more than 1,000 ascents of Sulphur Mountain, all in the line of duty.

The **Summit Restaurant** (403/762-7486) serves up cafeteria-style food combined with priceless views. Above this eatery is the **Panorama Room** (403/762-7486, June-mid-Oct.), dishing up more of the same, but buffet-style, and the Chinese **Regal View Restaurant** (403/762-7486).

From downtown, the gondola is three kilometers (1.9 miles) along Mountain Avenue. May-October, **Brewster** (403/762-6767) provides shuttle service to the gondola from downtown hotels.

A 5.5-kilometer (3.4-mile) hiking trail to the summit begins from the Upper Hot Springs parking lot. Although it's a long slog, you'll be rewarded with a discounted gondola ride down ($15 one-way).

◖ The Fairmont Banff Springs

On a terrace above a bend in the Bow River is one of the largest, grandest, and most opulent mountain-resort hotels in the world. What better way to spend a rainy afternoon than to explore this turreted 20th-century castle (405 Spray Ave., 403/762-2211, www.fairmont.com), seeking out a writing desk overlooking one of the world's most-photographed scenes and penning a long letter to the folks back home?

"The Springs" has grown with the town and is an integral part of local history. William Cornelius Van Horne, vice president of the CPR, decided that the best way of encouraging customers to travel on his newly completed rail line across the Rockies was to build a series of luxurious mountain accommodations. The largest of these was begun in 1886, as close as possible to Banff's newly discovered hot springs. The location chosen had magnificent views and was only a short carriage ride from the train station. Money was no object, and architect Bruce Price began designing a mountain resort the likes of which the world had never seen. At some stage of construction his plans were misinterpreted, and much to Van Horne's shock, the building was built back to front. The best guest rooms faced the forested slopes of Sulphur Mountain while the kitchen had panoramic views of the Bow Valley.

On June 1, 1888, it opened, the largest hotel in the world, with 250 rooms beginning at $3.50 per night including meals. Water from the nearby hot springs was piped into the hotel's steam baths. Rumor has it that when the pipes blocked, water from the Bow River was used, secretly supplemented by bags of sulphur-smelling chemicals. Overnight, the quiet community of Banff became a destination resort for wealthy guests from around the world, and the hotel soon became one of North America's most popular accommodations. Every room was booked every day during the short summer seasons. In 1903, a wing was added, doubling the hotel's capacity. The following year a tower was added to each wing. Guest numbers reached 22,000 in 1911, and construction of a new hotel, designed by Walter Painter, began that year. The original design—an 11-story tower joining two wings in a baronial style—was reminiscent of a Scottish castle mixed with a French country château. This concrete-and-rock-faced, green-roofed building stood as it did at its completion in 1928 until 1999, when an ambitious multiyear program of renovations commenced. At first, the most obvious change to those who have visited before is the new lobby, moved to a more accessible location, but all rooms have also been refurbished, and many of the restaurants changed or upgraded.

The Canadian Pacific moniker remained part of the Banff Springs's official name until 2000, when the hotel, and all other Canadian Pacific hotels, became part of the Fairmont Hotels and Resorts chain.

Don't let the hotel's opulence keep you from spending time here. Wander through, admiring the 5,000 pieces of furniture and antiques (most of those in public areas are reproductions), paintings, prints, tapestries, and rugs. Take in the medieval atmosphere of Mount Stephen Hall, with its lime flagstone floor, enormous windows, and large oak beams; take advantage of the luxurious spa facility; or relax in one of 12 eateries or four lounges.

The hotel is a 15-minute walk southeast of town, either along Spray Avenue or via the trail along the south bank of the Bow River. **Banff Transit** buses leave Banff Avenue for the Springs twice an hour; $2. Alternatively, horse-drawn buggies take passengers from the Trail Rider Store (132 Banff Ave., 403/762-4551) to the Springs for about $90 for two passengers.

Bow Falls

Small but spectacular Bow Falls is below the Fairmont Banff Springs, only a short walk from downtown. The waterfall is the result of a dramatic change in the course of the Bow River brought about by glaciation. At one time the river flowed north of Tunnel Mountain and out of the mountains via the valley of Lake Minnewanka. As the glaciers retreated, they left terminal moraines, forming natural dams and changing the course of the river. Eventually the backed-up water found an outlet here between Tunnel Mountain and the northwest ridge of Mount Rundle. The falls are most spectacular in late spring when runoff from the winter snows fills every river and stream in the Bow Valley watershed.

To get there from town, cross the bridge at the south end of Banff Avenue, scramble down the grassy embankment to the left, and follow a pleasant trail along the Bow River to a point above the falls. This easy walk is one kilometer (0.6 mile); 20 minutes each way. By car, cross the bridge and follow the Golf Course signs. From the falls, a paved road crosses the Spray River and passes through the golf course.

Banff Centre

On the lower slopes of Tunnel Mountain is Banff Centre, whose surroundings provide inspiration as one of Canada's leading centers for postgraduate students in a variety of disciplines, including Mountain Culture, Arts, and Leadership Development. The Banff Centre opened in the summer of 1933 as a theater school. Since then it has grown to become a prestigious institution attracting artists of many disciplines from throughout Canada. The Centre's **Walter Phillips Gallery** (St. Julien Rd., 403/762-6281, 12:30pm-5pm Wed.-Sun., free) presents changing exhibits of visual arts from throughout the world.

Activities are held on the grounds of the Banff Centre year-round. Highlights include a summer educational program, concerts, displays, live performances, the Playbill Series, the Banff Arts Festival, and Banff Mountain Festivals, to name a few. Call 403/762-6100 for a program, go to the website www.banffcentre. ca, or check the *Crag and Canyon* (published weekly on Wednesday).

Vermilion Lakes

This series of shallow lakes forms an expansive montane wetland supporting a variety of mammals and 238 species of birds. Vermilion Lakes Drive, paralleling the TransCanada Highway immediately west of Banff, provides the easiest access to the area. The level of **First Vermilion Lake** was once controlled by a dam. Since its removal, the level of the lake has dropped. This is the beginning of a long process that will eventually see the area evolve into a floodplain forest such as is found along the Fenland Trail.

The entire area is excellent for wildlife viewing, especially in winter when it provides habitat for elk, coyotes, and the occasional wolf.

Mount Norquay Road

One of the best views of town accessible by vehicle is on this road, which switchbacks steeply to the base of Mount Norquay, the local hangout for skiers and boarders. On the way up are several lookouts, including one near the top where bighorn sheep often graze.

To Lake Minnewanka

Lake Minnewanka Road begins where Banff Avenue ends at the northeast end of town. An alternative to driving along Banff Avenue is to take Buffalo Street, opposite the Banff Park Museum, and follow it around Tunnel Mountain, passing the campground and several viewpoints of the north face of Mount Rundle, rising vertically from the forested valley. This road eventually rejoins Banff Avenue at the Banff Rocky Mountain Resort.

After passing under the TransCanada Highway, **Cascade Falls** is obvious off to the left. The base of the falls can be easily reached in 10 minutes (climbing higher without the proper equipment is dangerous). In winter, these falls freeze, and you'll often see ice climbers slowly making their way up the narrow thread of frozen water. Directly opposite is a turn to **Cascade Ponds,** a popular day-use area where families gather on warmer days to swim, sunbathe, and barbecue.

The next turnout along this road is at **Lower Bankhead.** During the early 1900s, Bankhead was a booming mining town producing 200,000 tons of coal a year. The poor quality of coal and bitter labor disputes led to the mine's closure in 1922. Soon after, all the buildings were moved or demolished.

From the parking lot at Lower Bankhead, a 1.1-kilometer (0.7-mile) interpretive trail leads down through the industrial section

© ANDREW HEMPSTEAD

enjoying a cruise on Lake Minnewanka

of the town and past an old mine train. The town's 1,000 residents lived on the other side of the road at what is now known as **Upper Bankhead.** Just before the Upper Bankhead turnoff, the foundation of the Holy Trinity Church can be seen on the side of the hill to the right. Not much remains of Upper Bankhead. It is now a day-use area with picnic tables, kitchen shelters, and firewood. Through the meadow to the west are some large slag heaps, concealed mine entrances, and various stone foundations.

Lake Minnewanka

Minnewanka (Lake of the Water Spirit) is the largest body of water in Banff National Park. Mount Inglismaldie (2,964 meters/9,720 feet) and the Fairholme Range form an imposing backdrop. The reservoir was first constructed in 1912, and additional dams were built in 1922 and 1941 to supply hydroelectric power to Banff. Even if you don't feel up

to an energetic hike, it's worth parking at the facility area and going for a short walk along the lakeshore. You'll pass a concession selling snacks and drinks, then the tour boat dock, before entering an area of picnic tables and covered cooking shelters—the perfect place for a picnic. Children will love exploring the rocky shoreline and stony beaches in this area, but you should continue farther around the lake, if only to escape the crowds.

Banff Lake Cruise (403/762-3473) is a 90-minute cruise to the far reaches of the lake, passing the Devil's Gap formation. It departs from the dock late May-to early October 3-5 times daily (first sailing at 10am, adult $45, child $20). An easy walking trail leads past a number of picnic spots and rocky beaches to Stewart Canyon. The lake is great for fishing (lake trout to 15 kilograms/33 pounds) and is the only one in the park where motorboats are allowed. The same company operating the tour boats rents aluminum boats with small outboard engines.

From Lake Minnewanka, the road continues along the reservoir wall, passing a plaque commemorating the Palliser Expedition. You'll often have to slow down along this stretch of road for bighorn sheep. The road then descends to **Two Jack Lake** and a small day-use area. Take the turnoff to **Johnson Lake** to access a lakeside trail, good swimming on the warmest days of summer, and picnic facilities with views across to Mount Rundle.

Bow Valley Parkway

Two roads link Banff to Lake Louise. The TransCanada Highway is the quicker route, more popular with through traffic. The other is the more scenic 51-kilometer (32-mile) Bow Valley Parkway, which branches off the TransCanada Highway five kilometers (3.1 miles) west of Banff. Cyclists will appreciate this road's two long, divided sections and low speed limit (60 kph/37 mph). Along this route are several impressive viewpoints, interpretive displays, picnic areas, good hiking, great opportunities for viewing wildlife, a hostel, three lodges, campgrounds, and one of the park's best restaurants. Between March and late June, the southern end of the parkway (as far north as Johnston Canyon) is closed 6pm-9am daily for the protection of wildlife.

As you enter the parkway, you pass the quiet, creekside **Fireside** picnic area, where an interpretive display describes how the Bow Valley was formed. At **Backswamp Viewpoint,** you can look upstream to the site of a former dam, now a swampy wetland filled with aquatic vegetation. Farther along the road is another wetland at **Muleshoe.** This wetland consists of oxbow lakes that were formed when the Bow River changed its course and abandoned its meanders for a more direct path. Across the parkway is a one-kilometer (0.6-mile) trail that climbs to a viewpoint overlooking the valley. (The slope around this trail is infested with wood ticks during late spring/early summer, so be sure to check yourself carefully after hiking in this area.) To the east, **Hole-in-the-Wall** is visible. This large-mouthed cave was created by the Bow Glacier, which once filled the valley. As the glacier receded, its meltwater dissolved the soft limestone bedrock, creating what is known as a solution cave.

Beyond Muleshoe the road inexplicably divides for a few car lengths. A large white spruce stood on the island until it blew down in 1984. The story goes that while the road was being constructed, a surly foreman was asleep in the shade of the tree, and not daring to rouse him, workers cleared the roadway around him. The road then passes through particularly hilly terrain, part of a massive rock slide that occurred approximately 8,000 years ago.

Continuing down the parkway, you'll pass the following sights.

JOHNSTON CANYON

Johnston Creek drops over a series of spectacular waterfalls here, deep within the chasm it has carved into the limestone bedrock. The canyon is not nearly as deep as Maligne Canyon in Jasper National Park—30 meters (100 feet) at its deepest, compared to 50 meters (165 feet) at Maligne—but the catwalk that leads to the lower falls has been built through the depths of the canyon rather than along its lip, making it seem just as spectacular. The lower falls are one kilometer (0.6 mile) from the Bow Valley Parkway, while the equally spectacular upper falls are a further 1.6 kilometers (one mile) upstream. Beyond this point are the **Ink Pots,** shallow pools of spring-fed water. While in the canyon, look for fast-moving black swifts zipping through the air.

SILVER CITY

At the west end of **Moose Meadows,** a small plaque marks the site of Silver City. At its peak, this boomtown had a population of 2,000, making it bigger than Calgary at the time. The city was founded by John Healy, who also founded the notorious Fort Whoop-Up in Lethbridge. During its heady days, five mines were operating, extracting not silver but ore rich in copper and lead. The town had a half dozen hotels, four or five stores, two real-estate offices, and a station on the transcontinental rail line when its demise began. Two men, named Patton and Pettigrew, salted their mine with gold and silver ore to attract investors. After selling 2,000 shares at $5 each, they vanished, leaving investors with a useless mine. Investment in the town ceased, mines closed, and the people left. Only one man refused to leave. His name was James Smith, but he was known to everyone as Joe. In 1887, when Silver City came under the jurisdiction of the National Parks Service, Joe was allowed to remain. He did so and was friendly to everyone, including Stoney natives, Father Albert

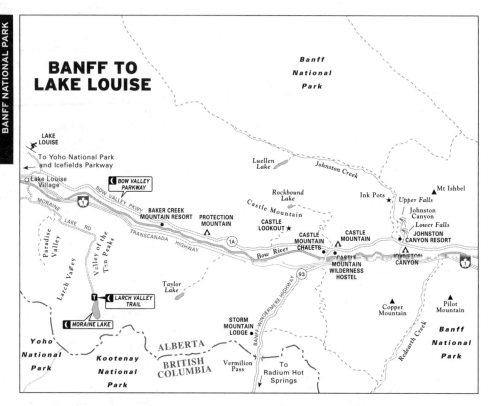

Lacombe (who occasionally stopped by), well-known Banff guide Tom Wilson, and of course the animals who grazed around his cabin. By 1926, he was unable to trap or hunt due to failing eyesight, and many people tried to persuade him to leave. It wasn't until 1937 that he finally moved to a Calgary retirement home, where he died soon after.

CASTLE MOUNTAIN TO LAKE LOUISE

After you leave the former site of Silver City, the aptly named Castle Mountain comes into view. It's one of the park's most recognizable peaks and most interesting geographical features. The mountain consists of very old rock (approximately 500 million years old) sitting atop much younger rock (a mere 200 million years old). This unusual situation occurred as the mountains were forced upward by pressure below the earth's surface, thrusting the older rock up and over the younger rock in places.

The road skirts the base of the mountain, passes Castle Mountain Village (which has gas, food, and accommodations), and climbs a small hill to Storm Mountain Viewpoint, which provides more stunning views and a picnic area. The next commercial facility is **Baker Creek Mountain Resort** (403/522-3761), where the mountain-style restaurant is an excellent spot for a meal. Then it's on to another viewpoint at Morant's Curve, from where Temple Mountain is visible. After passing another picnic area, the Bow Valley Parkway rejoins the TransCanada Highway at Lake Louise.

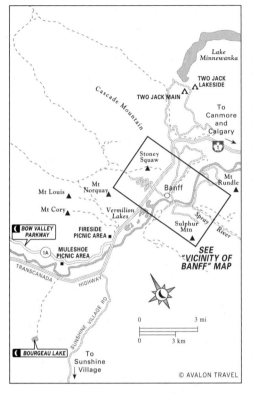

© AVALON TRAVEL

Before attempting any hikes, visit the **Banff Visitor Centre** (224 Banff Ave., 403/762-1550), where staff can advise you on the condition of trails and closures. The best book on hiking in the park is the *Canadian Rockies Trail Guide,* which covers each trail in exacting detail.

If you are planning an overnight trip into the backcountry, you *must* pick up a backcountry camping pass from either of the park information centers before heading out; $10 per person per night or $70 for an annual pass.

Fenland

- Length: 2 kilometers/1.2 miles (30 minutes) round-trip
- Elevation gain: none
- Rating: easy
- Trailhead: Forty Mile Creek Picnic Area, Mount Norquay Road, 300 meters (0.2 mile) north of the rail crossing

If you've just arrived in town, this short interpretive trail provides an excellent introduction to the Bow Valley ecosystem. A brochure, available at the trailhead, explains the various stages in the transition between wetland and floodplain spruce forest, visible as you progress around the loop. This fen environment is prime habitat for many species of birds. The work of beavers can be seen along the trail, and elk are here during winter. This trail is also a popular shortcut for joggers and cyclists heading for Vermilion Lakes.

Tunnel Mountain

- Length: 2.3 kilometers/1.4 miles (30-60 minutes) one-way
- Elevation gain: 300 meters/990 feet
- Rating: easy/moderate
- Trailhead: St. Julien Road, 350 meters (0.2 mile) south of Wolf Street

Accessible from town, this short hike is an easy

HIKING

After experiencing the international thrills of Banff Avenue, most people will want to see the *real* park, which is, after all, the reason that millions of visitors flock here, thousands take low-paying jobs just to stay here, and others become so severely addicted that they start families and live happily ever after here.

Although many landmarks can be seen from the roadside, to really experience the park's personality you'll need to go for a hike. One of the best things about Banff's 80-odd hiking trails is the variety. From short interpretive walks originating in town to easy hikes rewarded by spectacular vistas to myriad overnight backcountry opportunities, Banff's trails offer something for everyone.

climb to one of the park's lower peaks. It ascends the western flank of Tunnel Mountain through a forest of lodgepole pine, switchbacking past some viewpoints before reaching a ridge just below the summit. Here the trail turns northward, climbing through a forest of Douglas fir to the summit (which is partially treed, preventing 360-degree views).

Bow River/Hoodoos

- Length: 4.8 kilometers/3 miles (60-90 minutes) one-way
- Elevation gain: minimal
- Rating: easy
- Trailhead: Bow River Viewpoint, Tunnel Mountain Drive

From a viewpoint famous for its Fairmont Banff Springs outlook, the trail descends to the Bow River, passing under the sheer east face of Tunnel Mountain. It then follows the river a short distance before climbing into a meadow where deer and elk often graze. From this perspective the north face of Mount Rundle is particularly imposing. As the trail climbs, you'll hear the traffic on Tunnel Mountain Road long before you see it. The trail ends at hoodoos, strange limestone-and-gravel columns jutting mysteriously out of the forest. An alternative to returning the same way is to catch the Banff Transit bus from Tunnel Mountain Campground. It leaves every half hour; the trip costs $2.

Sundance Canyon

- Length: 4.4 kilometers/2.7 miles (90 minutes) one-way
- Elevation gain: 100 meters/330 feet
- Rating: easy
- Trailhead: Cave and Basin National Historic Site

Sundance Canyon is a rewarding destination across the river from downtown. Unfortunately,

the first three kilometers (1.9 miles) are along a paved road that is closed to traffic (but not bikes) and hard on your soles. Occasional glimpses of the Sawback Range are afforded by breaks in the forest. Where the paved road ends, the 2.4-kilometer (1.5-mile) Sundance Loop begins. Sundance Creek was once a larger river whose upper drainage basin was diverted by glacial action. Its powerful waters have eroded into the soft bedrock, forming a spectacular overhanging canyon whose bed is strewn with large boulders that have tumbled in.

Spray River

- Length: 12 kilometers/7.4 miles (4 hours) round-trip
- Elevation gain: 70 meters/230 feet
- Rating: easy/moderate
- Trailhead: From the Bow Falls parking lot, cross the Spray River and walk along Golf Course Road to behind the green of the first golf hole on the right-hand side of the road.

This trail follows one of the many fire roads in the park. It is not particularly interesting, but it's accessible from downtown Banff and makes a pleasant way to escape the crowds. From behind the green of the 15th hole on the Stanley Thompson 18, the trail heads uphill into the forest. It follows the Spray River closely—even when not in sight, the river can always be heard. For those so inclined, a river crossing one kilometer (0.6 mile) from the golf course allows for a shorter loop. Continuing south, the trail climbs a bluff for a good view of the Fairmont Banff Springs and Bow Valley. The return journey is straightforward with occasional views, ending at a locked gate behind the Fairmont Banff Springs, a short walk to Bow Falls.

For serious hikers, this trail provides access to the park's rugged and remote southern reaches, but there's another interesting option

SUNSHINE MEADOWS

Sunshine Meadows, straddling the Continental Divide, is a unique and beautiful region of the Canadian Rockies. It's best known as home to Sunshine Village, a self-contained alpine resort accessible only by gondola from the valley floor. But for a few short months each summer, the area is clear of snow and becomes a wonderland for hiking. Large amounts of precipitation create a lush cover of vegetation—over 300 species of wildflowers alone have been recorded here.

From Sunshine Village, trails radiate across the alpine meadow, which is covered in a colorful carpet of fireweed, glacier lilies, mountain avens, white mountain heather, and forget-me-nots (the meadows are in full bloom late July–mid-August). The most popular destination is **Rock Isle Lake,** an easy 2.5-kilometer (1.6-mile) jaunt from the upper village that crosses the Continental Divide while only gaining 100 meters (330 feet) of elevation. Mount Assiniboine (3,618 meters/11,870 feet), known as the "Matterhorn of the Rockies," is easily distinguished to the southeast. Various viewpoints punctuate the descent to an observation point overlooking the lake. From here, options include a loop around Larix Lake and a traverse along Standish Ridge. If the weather is cooperating, it won't matter which direction you head (so long as it's along a formed trail); you'll experience the Canadian Rockies in all their glory.

It's possible to walk the six-kilometer (3.7-mile) restricted-access road up to the meadows, but a more practical alternative is to take the Sunshine Meadows Alpine Shuttle along a road closed to public traffic. This service is operated by **White Mountain Adventures** (403/762-7889 or 800/408-0005, www.sunshinemeadowsbanff.com). Through a June-September season, buses depart Banff at 8:30am daily (adult $55, child $30, round-trip) and the Sunshine Village parking lot on the hour 9am-5pm daily (adult $26, child $15, round-trip). The shuttle returns from the alpine meadow hourly 9:15am-5:30pm, with the 2:30pm and 5:30pm departures continuing to Banff. For $35 extra, you can explore the meadows with a naturalist, who will lead you through all the highlights. Advance reservations are required for both the bus and guided hike. To get to the base of the gondola from Banff, follow the TransCanada Highway nine kilometers (5.6 miles) west to Sunshine Village Road, which continues a similar distance along Healy Creek to the Sunshine Village parking lot.

involving this trail for eager day hikers. It involves arranging a lift to the trailhead of the Goat Creek hike in Spray Valley Provincial Park in Kananaskis Country. From this trailhead, it's 19 kilometers/11.8 miles (six hours) one-way back to Banff down the Spray River watershed on a trail that drops 370 meters (1,210 feet) in elevation. The trail is most popular with mountain bikers and cross-country skiers.

Western Slope of Mount Rundle

- Length: 5.4 kilometers/3.3 miles (2 hours) one-way
- Elevation gain: 480 meters/1,755 feet
- Rating: moderate

- Trailhead: From the Bow Falls parking lot, cross the Spray River and walk along Golf Course Road to behind the green of the first golf hole on the right-hand side of the road.

At 2,950 meters (9,680 feet), Mount Rundle is one of the park's dominant peaks. Climbing to its summit is possible without ropes, but previous scrambling experience is advised. An alternative is to ascend the mountain's western slope along an easy-to-follow trail that ends just over 1,000 vertical meters (3,280 vertical feet) before the summit. The trail follows the Spray River Trail from Golf Course Road, branching off left after 700 meters (0.4 mile). Climbing steadily, it breaks out of the enclosed forest after 2.5 kilometers (1.6 miles). The trail ends in a gully from which the undefined route to the summit begins.

Stoney Squaw

- Length: 2.4-kilometer/1.5-mile loop (1 hour round-trip)
- Elevation gain: 180 meters/590 feet
- Rating: easy
- Trailhead: top of Mount Norquay Road, 6 kilometers (3.7 miles) from town

Looking north along Banff Avenue, Stoney Squaw's 1,884-meter (6,180-foot) summit is dwarfed by Cascade Mountain, directly behind it. To get to the trailhead of a trail that leads to its easily reached summit, follow Mount Norquay Road to a parking lot in front of the resort's day lodge. Immediately to the right of the entrance, a small sign marks the trail. The narrow, slightly overgrown trail passes through a thick forest of lodgepole pine and spruce before breaking out into the open near the summit. The sweeping panorama includes Vermilion Lakes, the Bow Valley, Banff, Spray River Valley, Mount Rundle, Lake Minnewanka, and the imposing face of Cascade Mountain (2,998 meters/9,840 feet). The return trail follows the northwest slope of Stoney Squaw to an old ski run at the opposite end of the parking lot.

Cascade Amphitheatre

- Length: 6.6 kilometers/4.1 miles (2-3 hours) one-way
- Elevation gain: 610 meters/2,000 feet
- Rating: moderate/difficult
- Trailhead: day lodge, top of Mount Norquay Road, 6 kilometers (3.7 miles) from town

This enormous cirque and the subalpine meadows directly behind Cascade Mountain are one of the most rewarding destinations for hiking in the Banff area. The demanding trail begins by passing the day lodge, then skirting the base of several lifts and following an old road to the floor of Forty Mile Valley. Keep right at all trail junctions. One kilometer (0.6 mile) after crossing Forty Mile Creek, the trail begins switchbacking up the western flank of Cascade Mountain through a forest of lodgepole pine. Along the way are breathtaking views of Mount Louis's sheer east face. After the trail levels off, it enters a magnificent U-shaped valley, and the amphitheater begins to define itself. The trail becomes indistinct in the subalpine meadow, which is carpeted in colorful wildflowers during summer. Farther up the valley, vegetation thins out as boulder-strewn talus slopes cover the ground. If you sit still long enough on these rocks, marmots and pikas will slowly appear, emitting shrill whistles before disappearing again.

The most popular route to the summit of 2,998-meter (9,840-foot) Cascade Mountain is along the southern ridge of the amphitheater wall. It is a long scramble up scree slopes and is made more difficult by a false summit; it should be attempted only by experienced scramblers.

C Level Cirque

- Length: 4 kilometers/2.5 miles (90 minutes) one-way
- Elevation gain: 455 meters/1,500 feet
- Rating: moderate
- Trailhead: Upper Bankhead Picnic Area, Lake Minnewanka Road, 3.5 kilometers (2.2 miles) beyond the TransCanada Highway underpass

From a picnic area that sits on the site of an abandoned mining town, the trail climbs steadily through a forest of lodgepole pine, aspen, and spruce to a pile of tailings and broken-down concrete walls. Soon after is a panoramic view of Lake Minnewanka, then the trail reenters the forest before ending in a small cirque with views down the Bow Valley to Canmore and beyond. The cirque is carved into the eastern face of Cascade Mountain, where snow often lingers until July. When the snow melts, the lush soil is covered in a carpet of colorful wildflowers.

Aylmer Lookout

- Length: 12 kilometers/7.5 miles (4 hours) one-way
- Elevation gain: 810 meters/2,660 feet
- Rating: moderate/difficult
- Trailhead: Lake Minnewanka, Lake Minnewanka Road, 5.5 kilometers (3.4 miles) beyond the TransCanada Highway underpass

The first eight-kilometer (five-mile) stretch of this trail follows the northern shore of Lake Minnewanka from the day-use area to a junction. The right fork leads to a campground, while the left climbs steeply to the site of an old fire tower on top of an exposed ridge. The deep-blue waters of Lake Minnewanka are visible, backed by the imposing peaks of Mount Girouard (2,995 meters/9,830 feet) and Mount Inglismaldie (2,964 meters/9,725 feet). Bighorn sheep often graze in this area. From here a trail forks left and continues climbing to the alpine tundra of Aylmer Pass. (Access along this trail is often restricted in summer due to bear activity-check at the visitors center before heading out.)

Cory Pass

- Length: 5.8 kilometers/3.6 miles (2.5 hours) one-way
- Elevation gain: 920 meters/3,020 feet
- Rating: moderate/difficult
- Trailhead: Fireside Picnic Area, Banff end of the Bow Valley Parkway

This strenuous hike has a rewarding objective—a magnificent view of dog-toothed Mount Louis. The towering slab of limestone rises more than 500 meters (1,640 feet) from the valley below. Just over one kilometer (0.6 mile) from the trailhead, the trail divides. The left fork climbs steeply across an open slope to an uneven ridge that it follows before ascending yet another steep slope to Cory Pass—a wild, windy, desolate area surrounded by jagged peaks dominated by Mount Louis. An alternative to returning along the same trail is continuing down into Gargoyle Valley, following the base of Mount Edith before ascending to Edith Pass and returning to the junction one kilometer (0.6 mile) from the picnic area. Total distance for this trip is 13 kilometers (eight miles), a long day considering the steep climbs and descents involved.

◖ Bourgeau Lake

- Length: 7.6 kilometers/4.7 miles (2.5 hours) one-way
- Elevation gain: 730 meters/2,400 feet
- Rating: moderate
- Trailhead: signposted parking lot, TransCanada Highway, 3 kilometers (1.9 miles) west of Sunshine Village Junction

This trail follows Wolverine Creek to a small subalpine lake nestled at the base of an impressive limestone amphitheater. Although the trail is moderately steep, plenty of distractions along the way are worthy of a stop (and rest). Back across the Bow Valley, the Sawback Range is easy to distinguish. As the forest of lodgepole pine turns to spruce, the trail passes under the cliffs of Mount Bourgeau and crosses Wolverine Creek (below a spot where it tumbles photogenically over exposed bedrock). After strenuous switchbacks, the trail climbs into the cirque containing Bourgeau Lake. As you explore the lake's rocky shore, you'll hear the colonies of noisy pikas, even if you don't see them.

Shadow Lake

- Length: 14.3 kilometers/8.9 miles (4.5 hours) one-way
- Elevation gain: 440 meters/1,445 feet
- Rating: moderate
- Trailhead: Redearth Creek Parking Area, TransCanada Highway, 11 kilometers (6.8 miles) west of Sunshine Village Junction

Shadow is one of the many impressive subalpine lakes along the Continental Divide and a popular base for a great variety of day trips. It follows the old Redearth fire road for 11 kilometers (6.8 miles) before forking right and climbing into the forest. The campground is two kilometers (1.2 miles) beyond this junction, and just 500 meters (0.3 mile) farther is **Shadow Lake Lodge.** The lake is nearly two kilometers (1.2 miles) long, and from its southern shore trails lead to Ball Pass, Gibbon Pass, and Haiduk Lake.

Castle Lookout

- Length: 3.7 kilometers/2.3 miles (90 minutes) one-way
- Elevation gain: 520 meters/1,700 feet
- Rating: moderate
- Trailhead: Bow Valley Parkway, 5 kilometers (3.1 miles) northwest of Castle Junction

However you travel through the Bow Valley, you can't help but be impressed by Castle Mountain rising proudly from the forest floor. This trail takes you above the tree line on the mountain's west face to the site of the Mount Eisenhower fire lookout, abandoned in the 1970s and burned in the 1980s. From the Bow Valley Parkway, the trail follows a wide pathway for 1.5 kilometers (0.9 mile) to an abandoned cabin in a forest of lodgepole pine and spruce. It then becomes narrower and steeper, switchbacking through a meadow before climbing through a narrow band of rock and leveling off near the lookout site. Magnificent

panoramas of the Bow Valley spread out before you in both directions. Storm Mountain can be seen directly across the valley.

Rockbound Lake

- Length: 8.4 kilometers/5.2 miles (2.5 hours) one-way
- Elevation gain: 760 meters/2,500 feet
- Rating: moderate/difficult
- Trailhead: Castle Junction, Bow Valley Parkway, 30 kilometers (18.6 miles) west of Banff

This strenuous hike leads to a delightful body of water tucked behind Castle Mountain. For the first five kilometers (3.1 miles), the trail follows an old fire road along the southern flanks of Castle Mountain. Early in the season or after heavy rain, this section can be boggy. Glimpses of surrounding peaks ease the pain of the steady climb as the trail narrows. After eight kilometers (five miles) you'll come to Tower Lake, which the trail skirts to the right before climbing a steep slope. From the top of the ridge, Rockbound Lake comes into view, and the reason for its name immediately becomes apparent. A scramble up any of the nearby slopes will reward you with good views.

MOUNTAIN BIKING

Whether you have your own bike or you rent one from the many bicycle shops in Banff or Lake Louise, cycling in the park is for everyone. The roads to Lake Minnewanka, Mount Norquay, through the golf course, and along the Bow Valley Parkway are all popular routes. Several trails radiating from Banff and ending deep in the backcountry have been designated as bicycle trails. These include Sundance (3.7 km/2.3 mi one-way), Rundle Riverside to Canmore (15 km/9.3 mi one-way), and the Spray River Loop (via Goat Creek; 48 km/30 mi round-trip). Farther afield, other trails are at Redearth Creek, Lake Louise, and in the northeastern reaches of the park near Saskatchewan River Crossing. Before heading into the backcountry, pick up the free *Mountain Biking and Cycling Guide* from the Banff or Lake Louise Visitor Centres. Riders are particularly susceptible to sudden bear encounters. Be alert and make loud noises when passing through heavy vegetation.

Bactrax (225 Bear St., 403/762-8177), **Banff Adventures Unlimited** (211 Bear St., 403/762-4554), and **Banff Springs Ski & Mountain Sports** (Fairmont Banff Springs, 405 Spray Ave., 403/762-5333) rent front- and full-suspension mountain bikes for $10-16 per hour and $40-70 per day. Rates include a helmet, lock, and biking map.

HORSEBACK RIDING

Jim and Bill Brewster led Banff's first paying guests into the backcountry on horseback more than 100 years ago. Today visitors are still able to enjoy the park on this traditional form of transportation.

One of the more popular horseback rides crosses the Spray River.

Warner Guiding & Outfitting (www.horseback.com) offers a great variety of trips. Their main office is downtown in the **Trail Rider Store** (132 Banff Ave., 403/762-4551), although trips depart from either **Martin's Stables** (403/762-2832), behind the recreation grounds on Birch Avenue, or **Banff Springs Corral** (403/762-2848), along Spray Avenue. From Martin's Stables, the one-hour trip departs 9am-6pm daily and takes in a pleasant circuit around the Marsh Loop ($42). A two-hour trip around the Sundance Loop ($75) departs four times daily. Other longer trips include the three-hour Mountain Morning Breakfast Ride, featuring a hearty breakfast along the trail (departs 9am; $112); Explorer Day Ride, a seven-hour ride up the lower slopes of Sulphur Mountain (departs 9am; $210); and the Evening Steak Fry, a three-hour ride with a suitably Western steak and baked bean dinner along the trail (departs 5pm; $108).

In addition to day trips, Warner runs a variety of overnight rides that include lodgings in backcountry lodges or tent camps. The main accommodation is Sundance Lodge, an easy 18-kilometer (10-mile) ride, which has 10 rooms, a large living area, and even hot showers. The shortest option is an overnight trip departing Saturday through the summer for $581 per person. A three-day trip is $866. Four-day ($1,142) and five-day ($1,415) trips split their time between Sundance Lodge and Halfway Lodge, which is farther up the Spray Valley. Rates include horse rental, all meals, and accommodation.

WATER SPORTS
White-Water Rafting

Anyone looking for white-water-rafting action will want to run the **Kicking Horse River,** which flows down the western slopes of the Canadian Rockies into British Columbia.

© ANDREW HEMPSTEAD

rafting on the Bow River

Many operators provide transportation from Banff and Lake Louise.

Rocky Mountain Raft Tours (403/762-3632) offers a one-hour (adult $45, child $20) float trip down the Bow River, beginning just below Bow Falls and ending along the golf course loop road. The three-hour Bow River Safari continues downriver to the park boundary (adult $85, child $40). No rapids are involved, so you'll stay dry.

Canoeing

On a quiet stretch of the Bow River, at the north end of Wolf Street, **Blue Canoe** (403/762-3632 or 403/760-5007; 9am-9pm daily May-Sept., $36 one hour, $20 each additional hour) rents canoes for use on the river, from where it's an easy paddle upstream to the Vermilion Lakes and Forty Mile Creek.

Fishing and Boating

The finest fishing in the park is in Lake Minnewanka, where lake trout as large as 15 kilograms (33 pounds) have been caught. One way to ensure a good catch is through **Banff Lake Cruise** (403/762-3473), which offers fishing trips in a heated cabin cruiser; trolling and downrigging are preferred methods of fishing the lake. A half-day's fishing (3.5 hours) is $395 for one or two persons. The company also rents small aluminum fishing boats with outboard motors for $48 for the first hour, then $24 for every extra hour to a maximum of $125 per day.

Before fishing anywhere in the park, you need a national park fishing license ($10 per day, $35 per year), available from the Banff and Lake Louise Visitor Centres and sport shops throughout the park.

GOLF

One of the world's most scenic golf courses, the **Banff Springs Golf Course** spreads out along the Bow River between Mount Rundle and

Tunnel Mountain. The first course was laid out here in 1911, but in 1928 Stanley Thompson was brought in by the CPR to build what was at the time North America's most expensive course. In 1989, the Tunnel Nine opened (along with a new clubhouse), creating today's 27-hole course.

Fully restored, the course is typical Thompson, taking advantage of natural contours and featuring elevated tees, wide fairways, treacherous fescue grass rough, and holes aligned to distant mountains. From the back markers it is 7,087 yards and plays to a par of 71. The course is not only breathtakingly beautiful, but it's also challenging for every level of golfer. Pick up a copy of the book *The World's Greatest Golf Holes,* and you'll see a picture of the fourth hole on the Rundle 9. It's a par three, over Devil's Cauldron 70 meters (230 feet) below, to a small green backed by the sheer face of Mount Rundle rising vertically more than 1,000 meters (3,280 feet) above the putting surface. Another unique feature of the course is the abundance of wildlife: There's always the chance of seeing elk feeding on the fairways, or coyotes, deer, or bears scurrying across.

Greens fees (including cart and driving range privileges) are $225, discounted to $135 in May and late September-early October. The Tunnel 9 offers the same spectacular challenges as Thompson's original layout but lacks the history; nine holes cost $80. Free shuttle buses run from the Fairmont Banff Springs to the clubhouse. (The original 1911 clubhouse still stands, but it has been replaced by a modern, circular building in the heart of the course.) There you'll find club rentals ($50-65), putting greens, a driving range, a pro shop, two chipping greens (one hidden up in the trees with surrounding bunkers), and a restaurant with a stunning wraparound deck. Booking tee times well in advance is essential; call 403/762-2211.

TOURS
Brewster (403/762-6767 or 800/760-6934, www.brewster.ca) is the dominant tour company in the area. The three-hour Discover Banff bus tour takes in downtown Banff, Tunnel Mountain Drive, the hoodoos, the Cave and Basin, and Banff Gondola (gondola fare included). This tour runs in summer only and departs from the bus depot at 8:30am daily; call for hotel pickup times. Adult fare is $86, children half price. Brewster also runs several other tours. A four-hour tour to Lake Louise departs select Banff hotels daily; $75. In winter this tour departs Tuesday and Friday mornings, runs five hours, and includes Banff sights; $75. During summer, the company also offers tours from Banff to Lake Minnewanka ($76; includes boat cruise) and the Columbia Icefield ($164).

Discover Banff Tours (Sundance Mall, 215 Banff Ave., 403/760-5007 or 877/565-9372, www.banfftours.com) is a smaller company, with smaller buses and more personalized service. Its tour routes are similar to Brewster's: A three-hour Discover Banff tour visits Lake Minnewanka, the Cave and Basin, the Fairmont Banff Springs, and the hoodoos for adult $62, child $38; and a two-hour Evening Wildlife Safari is adult $42, child $25. This company offers a good selection of other tours throughout the year, including a wintertime ice walk in frozen Johnston Canyon (adult $66, child $40).

WINTER RECREATION
From November till May, the entire park transforms itself into a winter playground covered in a blanket of snow. Of Alberta's six world-class winter resorts, three are in Banff National Park. Ski Norquay is a small but steep hill overlooking the town of Banff; Sunshine Village perches high in the mountains on the Continental Divide, catching more than its share of fluffy white powder; and Lake Louise, Canada's

© ANDREW HEMPSTEAD

Historic walking tours visit the homes of local pioneers.

second-largest winter resort, spreads over four distinct mountain faces. Apart from an abundance of snow, the resorts have something else in common—spectacular views, which alone are worth the price of a lift ticket. Although the resorts operate independently, the **Ski Hub** (119 Banff Ave., 403/762-4754, www.skibig3.com, 7am-10pm daily) represents all three and is the place to get information on multiday ticketing and transportation.

Other winter activities in the park include cross-country skiing, ice-skating, snowshoeing, dogsledding, and just relaxing. Crowds are nonexistent, and hotels reduce rates by up to 70 percent (except Christmas holidays)—reason enough to venture into the mountains. Lift and lodging packages begin at $100 per person.

Ski Norquay

Norquay (403/762-4421, www.banffnorquay. com) has two distinct faces—literally and figuratively. There are some great cruising runs and a well-respected ski school, but also the experts-only North American Chair (the one you can see from town), which opens up the famous double-black-diamond Lone Pine run. A magnificent post-and-beam day lodge nestled below the main runs is surrounded on one side by a wide deck that catches the afternoon sun, while holding a cafeteria, restaurant, and bar inside. Lift tickets are adult $74, youth and senior $62, child $32; lift, lesson, and rental packages cost about the same. Hourly passes provide some flexibility (two hours $32, three hours $42, etc). A few runs are lit for night skiing and boarding on Friday evening; adult $28, senior $26, child $15. A shuttle bus makes pickups from Banff hotels for the short, six-kilometer (3.7-mile) ride up to the resort; $8. The season at Norquay usually runs early December-early April.

Sunshine Village

Sunshine Village (403/762-6500 or

THE BREWSTER BOYS

Few guides in Banff were as well known as Jim and Bill Brewster. In 1892, at ages 10 and 12, respectively, they were hired by the Banff Springs Hotel to take guests to local landmarks. As their reputation as guides grew, they built a thriving business. By 1900, they had their own livery and out-fitting company, and soon thereafter they expanded operations to Lake Louise. Their other early business interests included a trading post, the original Mt. Royal Hotel, the first ski lodge in the Sunshine Meadows, and the hotel at the Columbia Icefield.

Today, a legacy of the boys' savvy, Brewster, a transportation and tour company, has grown to become an integral part of many tourists' stays (although it is no longer owned by the Brewster family). The company operates some of the world's most advanced sightseeing vehicles, including a fleet of Ice Explorers on the Columbia Icefield.

Dive, the area is best known for its excellent beginner and intermediate terrain, which covers 60 percent of the mountain. The total vertical rise is 1,070 meters (3,510 feet), and the longest run (down to the lower parking lot) is eight kilometers (five miles). Day passes are adult $84, senior $70, youth $62, child $34, and those younger than six ride free. Two days of lift access and one night's lodging at slopeside Sunshine Inn cost $275 per person in high season—an excellent deal. The inn has a restaurant, lounge, game room, and large outdoor hot tub. Transportation from Banff, Canmore, or Lake Louise to the resort is $18 round-trip; check the website or inquire at major hotels for the timetable.

Rentals and Sales

Each resort has ski and snowboard rental and sales facilities, but getting your gear down in town is often easier. **Abominable Ski & Sportswear** (229 Banff Ave., 403/762-2905) and **Monod Sports** (129 Banff Ave., 403/762-4571) have been synonymous with Banff and the ski industry for decades, and while the **Rude Boys Snowboard Shop** (downstairs in the Sundance Mall, 215 Banff Ave., 403/762-8480) has only been around since the 1980s, it is *the* snowboarder hangout. Other shops with sales and rentals include **Banff Springs Ski & Mountain Sports** (Fairmont Banff Springs, 405 Spray Ave., 403/762-5333), **Ski Hub** (119 Banff Ave., 403/762-4754), **Soul Ski and Bike** (203 Bear St., 403/760-1650), and **Snow Tips** (225 Bear St., 403/762-8177). Basic packages—skis, poles, and boots—are $40-50 per day, while high-performance packages range $55-70. Snowboards and boots rent for $40-60 per day.

877/542-2633, www.skibanff.com) has lots going for it—more than six meters (20 feet) of snow annually (no need for snowmaking up here), wide-open bowls, a season stretching for nearly 200 days (late Nov.-late May), skiing and boarding in two provinces, and the only slopeside accommodations in the park.

The resort has grown up a lot in the last decade as high-speed quads have replaced old chairlifts and opened up new terrain such as Goat's Eye Mountain, and the original gondola was replaced by what is reputed to be the world's fastest gondola. One of Canada's most infamous runs, Delirium Dive, drops off the northeast-facing slope of Lookout Mountain; to ski or board this up-to-50-degree run, you must be equipped with a transceiver, shovel, probe, and partner, but you'll have bragging rights that night at the bar (especially if you've descended the Bre-X line). Aside from Delirium

Cross-Country Skiing

No better way of experiencing the park's winter delights exists than gliding through the landscape on cross-country skis. Many summer hiking trails are groomed for winter

AN ABRIDGED HISTORY OF SKIING IN BANFF NATIONAL PARK

Banff National Park is busiest during summer, but for many visitors from outside North America—especially Europeans and Australians—it is the winter season that they know Banff for. Regardless of its repute, and although winter (Dec.-Apr.) is considered low season, the park remains busy as ski enthusiasts from around the world gather for world-class skiing and boarding. It hasn't always been this way. As recently as the 1960s, many lodgings—including the famous Fairmont Banff Springs—were open only for the summer season.

With winter tourism nonexistent, the first skiers were Banff locals, who would climb local peaks under their own steam. Due mostly to its handy location close to town, a popular spot was **Mount Norquay,** which was skied as early as the 1920s. In 1948, Canada's first chairlift was installed on the mountain's eastern slopes. In the ensuing years, newer and faster lifts have created a convenient getaway that fulfills the needs of locals and visitors alike, who can buzz up for an afternoon of skiing or boarding on slopes that suit all levels of proficiency.

The first people to ski the **Sunshine Meadows** were two local men, Cliff White and Cyril Paris, who became lost in the spring of 1929 and returned to Banff with stories of deep snow and ideal slopes for skiing. In the following years, a primitive cabin was used as a base for overnight ski trips in the area. In 1938 the Canadian National Ski Championships were held here, and in 1942 a portable lift was constructed. The White family was synonymous with the Sunshine area for many years, running the lodge and ski area while Brewster buses negotiated the steep, narrow road that led to the meadows. In 1980, a gondola was installed to whisk skiers and snowboarders six kilometers (3.7 miles) from the valley floor to the alpine village.

The best known of Banff's three resorts is **Lake Louise,** an hour's drive north of town but still within park boundaries. This part of the park also attracted early interest from local skiers, beginning in 1930 when Cliff White and Cyril Paris built a small ski chalet in the Skoki Valley (now operating as Skoki Lodge). The remoteness of this hut turned out to be impractical, so another was built, closer to the road. In 1954, a crude lift was constructed up Larch Mountain from the chalet. The lift had only just begun operation when a young Englishman, Norman Watson (known as the "Barmy Baronet"), who had inherited a fortune, saw the potential for a world-class alpine resort and made the completion of his dream a lifelong obsession. Over the years more lifts were constructed, and two runs—Olympic Men's Downhill and Olympic Ladies' Downhill—were cut in anticipation of a successful bid for the 1968 Winter Olympics (the bid failed).

travel. The most popular areas near town are Johnson Lake, Golf Course Road, Spray River, Sundance Canyon, and upstream from the canoe docks. The booklet *Cross-country Skiing—Nordic Trails in Banff National Park* is available from the Banff Visitor Centre. Weather forecasts (403/762-2088) are posted at both visitors centers.

Rental packages are available from **Snow Tips** (225 Bear St., 403/762-8177) and **Mountain Magic Equipment** (224 Bear St., 403/762-2591). Expect to pay $25-35 per day.

White Mountain Adventures (403/678-4099 or 800/408-0005) offers lessons for $60 per person.

Ice-Skating

Skating rinks are located on the **high school grounds** across from Cascade Plaza and on the golf course side of the **Fairmont Banff Springs.** The latter rink is lit after dark, and a raging fire is built beside it—the perfect place to enjoy a hot chocolate. Early in the season (check conditions first), skating is often possible on **Vermilion Lakes** and **Johnson Lake**. Rent skates from **Banff Springs Ski & Mountain Sports** (Fairmont Banff Springs, 405 Spray Ave., 403/762-5333) for $8 per hour.

Sleigh Rides

Warner Guiding & Outfitting offers sleigh rides ($38 per person) on the frozen Bow River throughout winter. For reservations, call 403/762-4551 or stop by the Trail Rider Store (132 Banff Ave.).

Ice Walks

Between December and late March, Johnston Canyon, a 20-minute drive from Banff along the Bow Valley Parkway, is a wonderland of frozen waterfalls. Two local companies, **Discover Banff Tours** (403/760-5007 or 877/565-9372) and **White Mountain Adventures** (403/678-4099 or 800/408-0005), offer ice walks through the canyon. Both tours reach as far as the Upper Falls and provide guests with ice cleats for their shoes and hot drinks to take the chill off this outdoor activity. Transportation from Banff is included in the rates of $70-75 per person.

Other Winter Activities

Beyond the skating rink below the Fairmont Banff Springs is an unofficial toboggan run; ask at your hotel for sleds or rent them from the sports store at the Fairmont Banff Springs; $6 per hour.

Anyone interested in **ice climbing** must register at the national park desk in the Banff Visitor Centre or call 403/762-1550. The world-famous (if you're an ice climber) Terminator is just outside the park boundary.

If none of these activities appeal to you, head to **Upper Hot Springs** (403/762-1515, 10am-10pm daily, $7.50) for a relaxing soak.

Camping might not be everyone's idea of a winter holiday, but one section of **Tunnel**

Mountain Campground remains open year-round.

INDOOR RECREATION
Swimming and Fitness Facilities

Many of Banff's bigger hotels have fitness rooms, and some have indoor pools. A popular place to swim and work out is in the **Sally Borden Fitness & Recreation Facility** (Banff Centre, St. Julien Rd., 403/762-6450, 6am-11pm daily), which holds a wide range of fitness facilities, a climbing gym, squash courts, a 25-meter-long heated pool, a wading pool, and a hot tub. General admission is $10.50, or pay $4.50 to swim only most evenings. Go to www.banffcentre.ca for a schedule.

Willow Stream Spa

This luxurious spa facility in the Fairmont Banff Springs (405 Spray Ave., 403/762-2211, 6am-10pm daily) is the place to pamper yourself. It sprawls over two levels and 3,000 square meters (0.7 acre) of a private corner of the hotel. The epicenter of the facility is a circular mineral pool capped by a high glass-topped ceiling and ringed by floor-to-ceiling windows on one side and on the other by hot tubs fed by cascading waterfalls of varying temperatures. Other features include outdoor saltwater hot tubs, private solariums, steam rooms, luxurious bathrooms, and separate male and female lounges complete with fireplaces and complimentary drinks and snacks. Numerous other services are offered, including facials, body wraps, massage therapy, salon services, and hydrotherapy. Entry to Willow Stream is included in some package rates for guests at the hotel. Admission is $80 per day, which includes the use of a locker and spa attire, with almost 100 services available at additional cost (most of these include general admission, so, for example, you can spend the day at Willow Stream and receive a one-hour massage for $195).

Other Indoor Recreation

Fairmont Banff Springs (405 Spray Ave., 403/762-2211) has a four-lane, five-pin bowling center; games are $5.75 per person. The **Lux Cinema Centre** (229 Bear St., 403/762-8595) screens new releases for $14 ($10 on Tuesday).

Banff's only waterslide is in the **Douglas Fir Resort** (Tunnel Mountain Dr., 403/762-5591, 4pm-9:30pm Mon.-Fri., 10am-9:30pm Sat.-Sun.). The two slides are indoors, and the admission price of $20 (free for kids younger than age five) includes use of a hot tub and exercise room.

NIGHTLIFE

Like resort towns around the world, Banff has a deserved reputation as a party town, especially among seasonal workers, the après-ski crowd, and young Calgarians. Crowds seem to spread out, with no particular bar being more popular than another or being a place where you can mingle with fellow travelers. Given the location and vacation vibe, drink prices are as high as you may expect, with attitude thrown in for free.

Banff is a nonsmoking town. Also note that the Royal Canadian Mounted Police (RCMP) patrol Banff all night, promptly arresting anyone who even looks like trouble, including anyone drunk or drinking on the streets.

Bars and Lounges

Wild Bill's (upstairs at 201 Banff Ave., 403/762-0333) is named for Banff guide Bill Peyto and is truly legendary. This frontier-style locale attracts the biggest and best bands of any Banff venue, with bookings that vary from local faves to washed-up rockers such as Nazareth; as a general rule, expect alternative music or underground country early in the week and better-known rock or pop Thursday-Sunday. Across the road, the **Maple Leaf** (137 Banff Ave., 403/760-7680) has a stylish space at street level set aside as a bar. The **Elk & Oarsman** (119

Banff Ave., 403/762-4616) serves up beer and more in a clean, casual atmosphere that is as friendly as it gets in Banff. Across the road from Wild Bill's is the **Rose and Crown** (202 Banff Ave., 403/762-2121), serving British beers and hearty pub fare. It also features a rooftop patio and rock-and-roll bands a few nights a week, but there's not much room for dancing. Also down the main drag is **Tommy's** (120 Banff Ave., 403/762-8888), a perennial favorite for young seasonal workers and those who once were and now consider themselves as locals.

Around the corner from Banff Avenue, the **St. James Gate Olde Irish Pub** (207 Wolf St., 403/762-9355) is a large Irish-style bar with a reputation for excellent British-style meals and occasional appearances by Celtic bands.

One block back from Banff Avenue are two excellent choices for a quiet drink. Relative to other town drinking spots, prices at the **Bear Street Tavern** (Bison Courtyard, 221 Bear St., 403/762-2021) are excellent. Add funky surroundings and a sunny courtyard to the mix, and you have an excellent choice for a drink and meal. **Saltlik** (221 Bear St., 403/762-2467) is best known as an upscale (and upstairs) steakhouse. At street level, the lounge opens to a streetside patio.

Around the corner from these two choices is **Melissa's** (218 Lynx St., 403/762-5776), which is a longtime favorite drinking hole for locals. It has a small outdoor patio, a long evening happy hour, a pool table, and multiple TVs.

Hotel Hangouts

Many Banff hotels have lounges open to guests and nonguests alike. They are generally quieter than the bars listed previously and often offer abbreviated menus from adjacent restaurants. For old-world atmosphere, nothing in town comes close to matching the **Sir William Wallace Room,** in the Fairmont Banff Springs (405 Spray Ave., 403/762-2211, 4pm-midnight daily). Another place to enjoy a drink in the park's landmark hotel is the mezzanine-level **Rundle Lounge** (Fairmont Banff Springs, 403/762-2211, noon-1am daily), an open space with views extending down the Bow Valley. Below the hotel is the **Waldhaus Pub** (Fairmont Banff Springs, 403/762-2211, from 11am daily in summer). It has the best deck in town, but it's mainly the haunt of locals coming off the golf course or savvy visitors (such as those who've read this book).

Downtown, the **Mount Royal Hotel** (corner of Banff Ave. and Caribou St., 403/762-3331) has a small lounge off the lobby, while below, accessed from farther up Banff Avenue, is the **Buffalo Paddock** (138 Banff Ave., 403/762-3331), with pool tables. At the opposite end of the style scale is the lounge in the **Voyager Inn** (555 Banff Ave., 403/762-3301), which is worth listing for the fact that it has the cheapest beer in town and drink specials every night (and a liquor store with cheaper prices than downtown).

Nightclubs

Banff has three nightclubs: Cavernous **Aurora** (downstairs in the Clock Tower Mall at 110 Banff Ave., 403/760-5300) was formerly an infamous gathering place known as Silver City, but renovations in the late 1990s added some class to Banff's clubbing scene. It's respectable early in the evening but becomes one obnoxiously loud, overpriced, smoky pickup joint after midnight. In the vicinity, **Sasquatch** (120 Banff Ave., 403/762-4002) is a more intimate space, but equally loud, especially when a celebrity DJ is in town spinning disks. The other option is **Hoo Doos** (at 137 Banff Ave., but enter from Caribou St., 403/762-8434), a stylish setup with similar citylike surroundings.

FESTIVALS AND EVENTS
Spring

Most of the major spring events take place at local winter resorts, including a variety of snowboard competitions that make for great spectator viewing. At Lake Louise, a half-pipe and jump are constructed right in front of the day lodge for this specific purpose. One long-running spring event is the **Slush Cup,** which takes place at Sunshine Village (www.skibanff. com) in late May. Events include kamikaze skiers and boarders who attempt to skim across an almost-frozen pit of water. While winter enthusiasts are at higher elevations, swooshing down the slopes of some of North America's latest-closing resorts, early May sees the Banff Springs Golf Course open for the season.

During the second week of June, the **Banff World Media Festival** (403/678-1216, www. banfftvfest.com) attracts the world's best television directors, producers, writers, and even actors for meetings, workshops, and awards, with many select screenings open to the public. For many delegates, pitching their ideas is what draws them to this event. The main venue is the Fairmont Banff Springs.

Summer

Summer is a time of hiking and camping, so festivals are few and far between. The main event is the **Banff Summer Arts Festival** (403/762-6301 or 800/413-8368, www.banff-centre.ca), a three-week (mid-July-early Aug.) extravaganza presented by professional artists studying at the Banff Centre. They perform dance, drama, opera, and jazz for the public at locations around town. Look for details in the *Crag and Canyon.*

On July 1, Banff kicks off **Canada Day** with a pancake breakfast on the grounds of the Park Administration Building. Then there's a full day of fun and frivolity in both Central and Banff Avenue Parks that includes events such as a stupid pet tricks competition. An impressive parade begins at 5pm, followed by a concert in Central Park and fireworks.

Each summer the national park staff presents an extensive **Park Interpretive Program** at locations in town and throughout the park, including downstairs in the visitors center at 8:30pm daily. All programs are free and include guided hikes, nature tours, slide shows, campfire talks, and lectures. For details, drop by the Banff Visitor Centre (403/762-1550), or look for postings on campground bulletin boards.

Fall

Fall is the park's quietest season, but it's busiest in terms of festivals and events. First of the fall events, on the last Saturday in September, **Melissa's Road Race** (www.melissasroadrace. ca) attracts more than 2,000 runners (the race sells out months in advance) in 10- and 22-kilometer (6- and 14-mile) races.

One of the year's biggest events is the **Banff Mountain Film Festival**, held on the first weekend of November. Mountain-adventure filmmakers from around the world submit films to be judged by a select committee. Films are then shown throughout the weekend to an enthusiastic crowd of thousands. Exhibits and seminars are also presented, and top climbers and mountaineers from around the world are invited as guest speakers.

Tickets to the Banff Mountain Film Festival go on sale one year in advance and sell out quickly. Tickets for daytime shows start at $45 (for up to 10 films). Night shows are from $38, and all-weekend passes cost around $180 (weekend passes with two nights' accommodations and breakfasts start at a reasonable $350). Films are shown in the two theaters of the Banff Centre (St. Julien Rd.). For more information, contact the festival office (403/762-6675); for tickets, contact the Banff Centre box office (403/762-6301 or 800/413-8368, www. banffcentre.ca). If you miss the actual festival, it hits the road on the Best of the Festival World Tour. Look for it in your town, or check out www.banffcentre.ca for venues and dates.

Starting in the days leading up to the film festival, then running in conjunction with it, is the **Banff Mountain Book Festival**, which showcases publishers, writers, and photographers whose work revolves around the world's great mountain ranges. Tickets can be bought to individual events ($16-30), or there's a Book Festival Pass ($130) and a pass combining both festivals ($280).

Winter

By mid-December, lifts at all local winter resorts are open. **Santa Claus** makes an appearance on Banff Avenue at noon on the last Saturday in November; if you miss him there, he usually goes skiing at each of the local resorts on Christmas Day. Events at the resorts continue throughout the long winter season, among them **World Cup Downhill** skiing at Lake Louise in late November. **Snow Days** is a monthlong celebration starting mid-January that features ice sculpting on the frozen lake in front of the Chateau Lake Louise, the Lake Louise Loppet, live theater, a photography competition, and a spelling bee.

SHOPPING

Banff Avenue is renowned for its shops, but in reality has evolved into a continuous stretch of tacky tourist shops and international chains. An exception is **About Canada** (105 Banff Ave., 403/760-2996), which does an excellent job of sourcing Canadian-made gifts.

Canadiana and Clothing

Few companies in the world were as responsible for the development of a country as was the **Hudson's Bay Company** (HBC) in Canada. Founded in 1670, the HBC established trading posts throughout western Canada, many of which attracted settlers, forming the nucleus for towns and cities that survive today, including Alberta's capital, Edmonton. HBC stores continue their traditional role of providing a wide range of goods, in towns big and small across the country. In Banff, the HBC store is at 125 Banff Avenue (403/762-5525).

Another Canadian store, this one famous for its fleeces, sweaters, leather goods, and as supplier to the Canadian Olympic teams, is **Roots** (227 Banff Ave., 403/762-9434). For belts, buckles, and boots, check out the **Trail Rider Store** (132 Banff Ave., 403/762-4551). Also check out the **Rude Boys Snowboard Shop** (215 Banff Ave., 403/762-8480), downstairs in the Sundance Mall, but don't expect to find anything suitable for your grandparents.

Camping and Outdoor Gear

Inexpensive camping equipment and supplies can be found in **Home Hardware** (221 Bear St., 403/762-2080). More specialized needs are catered to at **Monod Sports** (129 Banff Ave., 403/762-4571). Locally owned **Abominable Ski & Sportswear** (229 Banff Ave., 403/762-2905) has a good selection of hiking boots.

Gifts and Galleries

Banff's numerous galleries display the work of mostly Canadian artists. **Canada House Gallery** (201 Bear St., 403/762-3757) features a wide selection of Canadian landscape and wildlife works and native art. The **Quest Gallery** (105 Banff Ave., 403/762-2722) offers a diverse range of affordable Canadian paintings and crafts, as well as more exotic pieces such as mammoth tusks from prehistoric times and Inuit carvings from Nunavut. Browse through native arts and crafts at the **Indian Trading Post** (1 Birch Ave., 403/762-2456), across the Bow River from downtown.

ACCOMMODATIONS AND CAMPING

Finding a room in Banff National Park in summer is nearly as hard as trying to justify its price. By late afternoon, just about every room and campsite in the park will be occupied, and basic hotel rooms start at $120. Fortunately, many alternatives are available. Rooms in private homes begin at around $50

s, $60 d. HI-Banff Alpine Centre has dormitory-style accommodations for under $40 per person per night. Bungalows or cabins can be rented, which can be cost-effective for families or small groups. Approximately 2,400 campsites in 13 campgrounds accommodate campers. Wherever you decide to stay, it is vital to book well ahead during summer and the Christmas holidays. The park's off-season is October-May, and hotels offer huge rate reductions during this period. Shop around, and you'll find many bargains.

All rates quoted are for a standard room in the high season (June-Sept.).

In and Around the Town of Banff

Banff has a few accommodations right downtown, but most are strung out along Banff Avenue, an easy walk from the shopping and dining precinct. Nearby Tunnel Mountain is also home to a cluster of accommodations.

UNDER $50

The only beds in town less than $50 are in dormitories, and therefore, although rates are well less than $50, this is a per-person rate.

HI-Banff Alpine Centre (801 Hidden Ridge Way, 403/762-4123 or 866/762-4122, www.hihostels.ca) is just off Tunnel Mountain Road, three kilometers (1.9 miles) from downtown. This large, modern hostel sleeps 216 in small two-, four-, and six-bed dormitory rooms as well as four-bed cabins. The large lounge area has a fireplace, and other facilities include a recreation room, public Internet access, bike and ski/snowboard workshop, large kitchen, self-service café/bar, and laundry. In summer, members of Hostelling International pay $35 per person per night (nonmembers $39) for a dorm bed or $88 s or d ($96 for nonmembers) in a private room. The rest of the year, dorm beds are $31 (nonmembers $35) and private rooms $84 s or d (nonmembers $92). During July and August, reserve at least one month in advance to be assured of a bed. The hostel is open all day, but check-in isn't until midday. To get there from town, ride the Banff Transit bus ($2), which passes the hostel twice an hour during summer. The rest of the year the only transportation is by cab, about $8 from the bus depot.

A one-time hospital, **Banff Y Mountain Lodge** (102 Spray Ave., 403/762-3560 or 800/813-4138, www.ymountainlodge.com, dorm $33, $88 s, $99 d) has undergone massive renovations to create an excellent, centrally located choice for budget travelers. Facilities include the casual Sundance Bistro (7am-10pm daily), a laundry facility, wireless Internet, and the Great Room—a huge living area where the centerpiece is a massive stone fireplace, with writing desks and shelves stocked with books scattered throughout. Some private rooms have en suites, while family rooms are $135. Rates are reduced outside of summer.

Along the main strip of accommodations and a five-minute walk to downtown is **Samesun Banff** (433 Banff Ave., 403/762-4499 or 877/972-6378, www.samesun.com, dorm $39-41, private $120 s or d). As converted motel rooms, each small dormitory has its own bathroom. Guest amenities include a lounge, wireless Internet, free continental breakfast, and underground parking.

$50-100

Accommodations in this price range are limited to private rooms at HI-Banff Alpine Centre, Banff Y Mountain Lodge, and Samesun Banff, and at a few bed-and-breakfasts. The best value of these is **Mountain View B&B** (347 Grizzly St., 403/760-9353, www.mountainviewbanff.ca, May-Sept., $95-130 s or d), on a quiet residential street three blocks from the heart of downtown. The two guest rooms are simply furnished, each with a double bed, TV, sink, and bar fridge. They share

a bathroom and a common area that includes basic cooking facilities (microwave, toaster, kettle) and opens to a private deck. Off-street parking and a light breakfast round out this excellent choice.

$100-150

(Blue Mountain Lodge (137 Muskrat St., 403/762-5134, www.bluemtnlodge.com, $105-109 s, $129-179 d) is a rambling, older-style lodge with 10 guest rooms, each with a private bath, TV, and telephone. The Trapper's Cabin room is the most expensive, but the gabled ceiling, walls decorated with snowshoes and bearskin, and an electric fireplace create a funky, mountain feel. All guests have use of shared kitchen facilities, a lounge, and Internet access while enjoying an expansive cold buffet breakfast to fuel a day of hiking.

The eight guest rooms at the **Elkhorn Lodge** (124 Spray Ave., 403/762-2299 or 877/818-8488, www.elkhornbanff.ca, from $135) are nothing special, but travelers on a budget who aren't fans of bed-and-breakfasts will find this older lodge suitable. The four small sleeping rooms, each with a bathroom, TV, and coffeemaker, are $135 s or d, while larger rooms with fridges are $195-265. Rates include a light breakfast. It's halfway up the hill to the Fairmont Banff Springs.

Bumper's Inn is at the far end of the motel strip (603 Banff Ave., 403/762-3386 or 800/661-3518, www.bumpersinn.com, $125-140 s or d). The property is best known for its steakhouse, but behind the restaurant are 39 older-style rooms facing a courtyard for $140 s or d (from $75 in winter).

Two blocks off Banff Avenue, the **Homestead Inn** (217 Lynx St., 403/762-4471 or 800/661-1021, www.homesteadinnbanff.com, $129-139 s or d) is a lot closer to downtown than Bumper's. It's a fairly basic hostelry with a faux Tudor exterior, 27 guest rooms, and adjacent good-value restaurant.

$150-200

Some of Banff's private residences have cabins for rent. One of the reasons that 🄲 **Country Cabin Bed & Breakfast** (419 Beaver St., 403/762-3591, www.banffmountaincountry.com, $150 s or d) is the best of these is the quiet location off busy Banff Avenue that is still within easy walking distance of downtown. The log cabin has a separate bedroom, a full bathroom with log and tile features surrounding a jetted tub, and a living area equipped with a fold-out futon and a TV/DVD combo. If you don't feel like dining downtown, you can cook up a storm on the barbecue supplied. Rates are reduced to $95 outside of summer.

The rooms at the **Banff Inn** (501 Banff Ave., 403/762-8844, www.banffinn.com, $179-279 s or d) are no-frills modern in appearance. Each of the 99 rooms has a small log-trimmed balcony, and the facade is Rundlestone (quarried locally and named for Mount Rundle). Pluses include underground heated parking, a day spa, a guest lounge with fireplace and plasma TV, and free continental breakfast.

Spruce Grove Inn (545 Banff Ave., 403/762-3301 or 800/879-1991, www.banffsprucegroveinn.com, $175-285 s or d) is a modern mountain-style lodge where rooms are spacious and a relatively good value (upgrade to a king bed for $205 s or d or a Loft Suite that sleeps four for $235).

Toward downtown from the Spruce Grove is the **High Country Inn** (419 Banff Ave., 403/762-2236 or 800/293-5142, www.banffhighcountryinn.com, from $195 s or d), which has a heated indoor pool, spacious hot tubs, a cedar-lined sauna, and the ever-popular Ticino Swiss/Italian restaurant. All rooms are adequately furnished with comfortable beds and an earthy color scheme. The High Country's Honeymoon Suite ($285) is an excellent value; it features a king-size bed, fireplace, jetted tub, and a large balcony with views to Cascade Mountain.

The **Rundlestone Lodge** (537 Banff Ave., 403/762-2201 or 800/661-8630, www.rundlestone.com, $195-230 s or d) features mountain-style architecture with an abundance of raw stonework and exposed timber inside and out. At street level is a comfortable sitting area centered on a fireplace, as well as an indoor pool, a lounge-style bar, and a restaurant. Furniture and fittings in the 96 rooms are elegant, and all rooms come with high-speed Internet access and a TV/DVD combo. Many rooms have small balconies and gas fireplaces; some are wheelchair accessible.

$200-250

More than 100 years since Jim and Bill Brewster guided their first guests through the park, their descendants are still actively involved in the tourist industry, operating the central and very stylish 🄲 **Brewster's Mountain Lodge** (208 Caribou St., 403/762-2900 or 888/762-2900, www.brewstermountainlodge.com, $235-295 s or d). The building features an eye-catching log exterior with an equally impressive lobby. The Western theme is continued in the 77 upstairs rooms. Standard rooms feature two queen-size beds, deluxe rooms offer a jetted tub and sitting area, and loft suites are designed for families. Packages provide good value here, while off-season rates are slashed up to 40 percent.

The 134-room **Banff Ptarmigan Inn** (337 Banff Ave., 403/762-2207 or 800/661-8310, www.bestofbanff.com, $245 s or d) is a slick, full-service hotel with tastefully decorated rooms, down comforters on all beds, the Meatball Italian restaurant, heated underground parking, wireless Internet, and a variety of facilities to soothe sore muscles, including a spa, whirlpool, and sauna.

The following two accommodations are on Tunnel Mountain Road, a 15-minute downhill walk to town. Although falling in the same price range as many of those on Banff Avenue, all units are self-contained, making them good for families, small groups, or those who want to cook their own meals.

Opened as a bungalow camp in 1946, **Douglas Fir Resort** (403/762-5591 or 800/661-9267, www.douglasfir.com, from $265 s or d) is now a sprawling complex of 133 large condo-style units. Each has a fully equipped kitchen and a living area with fireplace. Other facilities include a hot tub, an exercise room, squash and tennis courts, a grocery store, and a laundry. Infinitely more important if you have children are the indoor waterslides. Check online for packages year-round.

Hidden Ridge Resort (403/762-3544 or 800/661-1372, www.bestofbanff.com, $245-450 s or d) sits on a forested hillside away from the main buzz of traffic. Choose from modern condo-style units to much larger Premier King Jacuzzi Suites. All units have wood-burning fireplaces, wireless Internet, and balconies or patios, and the condos have washer/dryer combos. In the center of the complex is a barbecue area and 30-person outdoor hot tub overlooking the valley.

$250-300

Since opening in 1908, the downtown **Mount Royal Hotel** (138 Banff Ave., 403/762-3331 or 877/442-2623, www.mountroyalhotel.com, $260 s or d) has seen various expansions and a disastrous fire in 1967, which destroyed the original wing. Today guests are offered 135 tastefully decorated rooms and the use of a large health club with hot tub. Also on the premises are a restaurant and small lounge. For a splurge, you won't find better than the one-bedroom suites ($299-429).

The best rooms along the motel strip are at **Delta Banff Royal Canadian Lodge** (459 Banff Ave., 403/762-3307 or 888/778-5050, www.deltahotels.com, from $290 s or d), which features 99 luxuriously appointed rooms, heated underground parking, a lounge, a dining room where upscale Canadian specialties are

the highlight, a spa/pool complex, and a landscaped courtyard.

OVER $300

At **Buffalo Mountain Lodge,** a 15-minute walk from town on Tunnel Mountain Road (Tunnel Mountain Dr., 403/762-2400 or 800/661-1367, www.crmr.com, $339 s or d), you'll notice the impressive timber-frame construction, as well as the hand-hewn construction of the lobby, with its vaulted ceiling and eye-catching fieldstone fireplace. The 108 rooms, chalets, and bungalows all have fireplaces, balconies, large bathrooms, and comfortable beds topped by feather-filled duvets; many have kitchens. And you won't need to go to town to eat—one of Banff's best restaurants, Cilantro Mountain Café (summer only), is on the grounds. Although rack rates start over $300, book in advance and online to pick up summer rates around $250. (The lodge takes its name from Tunnel Mountain, which early park visitors called Buffalo Mountain, for its shape.)

Bed-and-breakfast connoisseurs will fall in love with **Buffaloberry B&B** (417 Marten St., 403/762-3750, www.buffaloberry.com, $335 s or d), a purpose-built lodging within walking distance of downtown. The home itself is a beautiful timber and stone structure, while inside, guests soak up mountain-style luxury in the vaulted living area, which comes complete with a stone fireplace, super comfortable couches, and a library of local books. The spacious rooms come with niceties such as pillow-top mattresses, TV/DVD combos, heated bathroom floors, and bathrobes. Buffaloberry is also the only Banff bed-and-breakfast with heated underground parking.

The 770-room **Fairmont Banff Springs** (405 Spray Ave., 403/762-2211 or 800/257-7544, www.fairmont.com, $469 s or d) is Banff's best-known accommodation. Earlier this century, the hotel came under the ownership of Fairmont Hotels and Resorts, losing its century-old tag as a Canadian Pacific hotel and in the process its ties to the historic railway company that constructed the original hotel back in 1888. Even though the rooms have been modernized, many date to the 1920s, and as is common in older establishments, these accommodations are small (Fairmont rooms are 14.4 square meters/155 square feet). But room size is only a minor consideration when staying in this historic gem. With 12 eateries, four lounges, a luxurious spa facility, a huge indoor pool, elegant public spaces, a 27-hole golf course, tennis courts, horseback riding, and enough twisting, turning hallways, towers, and shops to warrant a detailed map, you'll not be wanting to spend much time in your room. Unless, of course, you are in the eight-room presidential suite. During summer, rack rates for a regular Fairmont room are $469 (s or d), discounted to around $280 the rest of the year. Many summer visitors stay as part of a package—the place to find these is on the website www. fairmont.com. Packages may simply include breakfast, while others will have you golfing, horseback riding, or relaxing in the spa.

On Mountain Avenue, a short walk from the Upper Hot Springs, is **Rimrock Resort Hotel** (403/762-3356 or 888/746-7625, www.rimrockresort.com, $355-455 s or d). The original hotel was constructed in 1903 but was fully rebuilt and opened as a full-service luxury resort in the mid-1990s. Guest amenities include two restaurants, two lounges, a health club, an outdoor patio, and a multistory parking garage. Each of 345 well-appointed rooms is decorated with earthy tones offset by brightly colored fabrics. They also feature picture windows, a king-size bed, a comfortable armchair, a writing desk, two phones, a minibar, and a hair dryer. Since it's set high above the Bow Valley, views for the most part are excellent.

Along the Bow Valley Parkway and Vicinity

The Bow Valley Parkway is the original route between Banff and Lake Louise. It is a beautiful drive in all seasons, and along its length are several accommodations, each a viable alternative to staying in Banff.

UNDER $50

Thirty-two kilometers (20 miles) from Banff along the Bow Valley Parkway, **HI-Castle Mountain** is near several interesting hikes and across the road from a general store with basic supplies. This hostel sleeps 28 in two dorms and has a kitchen, octagonal common room with wood-burning fireplace, hot showers, and bike rentals. Members of Hostelling International pay $24 (nonmembers $28). Make bookings through the association's reservation line (866/762-4122) or book online (www.hihostels.ca). Check-in is 5pm-10pm.

$100-150

Johnston Canyon Resort (403/762-2971 or 888/378-1720, www.johnstoncanyon.com, mid-May-early Oct., $149-314 s or d) is 26 kilometers (16 miles) west of Banff at the beginning of a short trail that leads to the famous canyon. The rustic cabins are older, and some have kitchenettes. On the grounds are tennis courts, a barbecue area, and a general store. Resort dining options are as varied as munching on a burger and fries at the counter of an old-time cafeteria to enjoying pan-fried rainbow trout in a dining room that oozes alpine charm. Basic two-person duplex cabins are $149, two-person cabins with a gas fireplace and sitting area are $189, and they go up in price all the way to $314 for a classic bungalow complete with two bedrooms, cooking facilities, and heritage-style furnishings.

$150-200

Constructed by the Canadian Pacific Railway in 1922, **C Storm Mountain Lodge** (Hwy. 93, 403/762-4155, www.stormmountainlodge. com, early Dec.-mid-Oct., $199-239) features

14 historic cabins restored to their former rustic glory. Each has its original log walls, along with a log bed, covered deck, a wood-burning fireplace, and bathroom with claw-foot tub. They don't have phones or TVs, so there's little to distract you from the past. Off-season deals include a breakfast and dinner package (mid-April-mid-June) for $250 d. Outside, the wilderness beckons, with Storm Mountain as a backdrop. The lodge is at Vermilion Pass, a 25-minute drive from Banff or Lake Louise (head west from the Castle Mountain interchange). The lodge restaurant (7:30am-10:30am and 5pm-9pm daily) is one of my favorite places to eat in the park.

OVER $200

At Castle Junction, 32 kilometers (20 miles) northwest of Banff, is **Castle Mountain Chalets** (403/762-3868 or 877/762-2281, www.castlemountain.com, $255-335 s or d). Set on 1.5 hectares (four acres), this resort is home to a collection of magnificent log chalets. Each has high ceilings, beautifully handcrafted log interiors, at least two beds, a stone fireplace, a full kitchen with dishwasher, a bathroom with hot tub, and satellite TV. At the back of the grounds are several older cabins offered in summer ($190 s or d). Part of the complex is a grocery store, barbecue area, and the only gas between Banff and Lake Louise. The nearest restaurants are at Baker Creek Mountain Resort and Johnston Canyon Resort.

BACKCOUNTRY ACCOMMODATIONS

Brewster's Shadow Lake Lodge (403/762-0116 or 866/762-0114, www.shadowlakelodge.com, mid-June-Sept.) is 14 kilometers (8.7 miles) from the nearest road. Access is on foot or, in winter, on skis. The lodge is near picturesque Shadow Lake, and many hiking trails are nearby. Dating to 1928, the oldest structure has been restored as a rustic yet welcoming dining area, with a woodstove in the kitchen.

Guests overnight in 12 newer, comfortable cabins, while in a separate building are washrooms with showers. The daily rate, including three meals served buffet-style and afternoon tea, is $192 per person per day. The trailhead is along the TransCanada Highway, 19 kilometers (12 miles) from Banff, at the Redearth Creek parking area. In February and March, when access is on cross-country skis, the lodge is open Thursday-Sunday and rates are $140 per person.

Campgrounds

Within Banff National Park, 13 campgrounds hold more than 2,000 sites. Although the town of Banff has five of these facilities with more than 1,500 sites in its immediate vicinity, most fill by early afternoon. The three largest campgrounds are strung out over 1.5 kilometers (0.9 mile) along Tunnel Mountain Road, with the nearest sites 2.5 kilometers (1.6 miles) from town. A percentage of sites at Tunnel Mountain Campground can be reserved through the **Parks Canada Campground Reservation Service** (877/737-3783, www.pccamping.ca), and it's strongly recommended that you do reserve if you require electrical hookups. Although plenty of sites are available for those without reservations, they fill fast each day (especially in July and August). The official checkout time is 11am, so plan on arriving at your campground of choice earlier in the day than this to ensure getting a site. At more popular locations on summer weekends, a line forms, waiting for sites to become vacant. This is especially true at the Banff and Lake Louise campgrounds, which offer powered sites. When the main campgrounds fill, those unable to secure a site will be directed to an overflow area along Minnewanka Lake Road. These provide few facilities and no hookups but cost less. Open fires are permitted in designated areas throughout all campgrounds, but you must purchase a Firewood Permit ($6 per site per night) to burn wood, which is provided at no cost. For general camping information, stop at the Banff Visitor Centre (224 Banff Ave., 403/762-1550) or go to the Parks Canada website, www.pc.gc.ca, and follow the links to Banff National Park.

AROUND THE TOWN OF BANFF

Closest to town is **Tunnel Mountain Campground,** which is three campgrounds rolled into one. The location is a lightly treed ridge east of downtown, with views north to Cascade Mountain and south to Mount Rundle. From town, follow Tunnel Mountain Road east, to beyond the Douglas Fir Resort (which is within walking distance for groceries, liquor, and laundry). If you're coming in off the TransCanada Highway from the east, bypass town completely by turning left onto Tunnel Mountain Road at the Banff Rocky Mountain Resort. Approaching from this direction, the first campground you pass is the park's largest, with 622 well-spaced, relatively private sites ($28 per site), each with a fire ring and picnic table. Other amenities include drinking water, hot showers, and kitchen shelters. This campground has no hookups. It is open mid-May-early September. Less than one kilometer (0.6 mile) farther along Tunnel Mountain Road toward town is a signed turnoff (Hookups) that leads to a registration booth for two more campgrounds. Unless you have a reservation from Parks Canada Campground Reservation Service (877/737-3783, www.pccamping.ca), you'll be asked whether you require an electrical hookup ($32 per site) or a site with power, water, and sewer ($38 per site), then sent off into the corresponding campground. The power-only section (closest to town) stays open year-round, the other mid-May-September. Both have hot showers but little privacy between sites.

Along Lake Minnewanka Road northeast of town are two campgrounds offering fewer services than the others, but with sites that offer more privacy. The pick of the two is **Two Jack Lakeside Campground** (June-mid-Sept., $32 per site), with 80 sites tucked into trees at the south end of Two Jack Lake, an extension of Lake Minnewanka. Facilities include hot showers, kitchen shelters, drinking water, and flush toilets. It's just over six kilometers (3.7 miles) from the TransCanada Highway underpass. The much larger **Two Jack Main Campground** (mid-June-mid-Sept., $22 per site) is a short distance farther along the road, with 381 sites spread throughout a shallow valley. It offers the same facilities as Two Jack Lakeside, sans showers. The overflow camping area ($10) for these and the three Tunnel Mountain campgrounds is at the beginning of the Lake Minnewanka Road loop.

BOW VALLEY PARKWAY

Along Bow Valley Parkway between the town of Banff and Lake Louise are three campgrounds. Closest to Banff is **Johnston Canyon Campground** (early June-mid-Sept., $28 per site), between the road and the rail line, 26 kilometers (16 miles) west of Banff. It is the largest of the three campgrounds, with 140 sites, and has hot showers but no hookups. Almost directly opposite is Johnston Canyon Resort, with groceries and a restaurant, and the beginning of a trail to the park's best-known waterfalls.

Continuing eight kilometers (five miles) toward Lake Louise, **Castle Mountain Campground** (early June-early Sept., $22 per site) is also within walking distance of a grocery store (no restaurant), but it has just 44 sites and no showers. Services are limited to flush toilets, drinking water, and kitchen shelters.

Protection Mountain Campground (July-Aug., $22 per site), a further 14 kilometers (8.7 miles) west and just over 20 kilometers (12.4 miles) from Lake Louise, opens as demand dictates, usually by late June. It offers 89 sites, along with flush toilets, drinking water, and stove-equipped kitchen shelters.

FOOD

Whether you're in search of an inexpensive snack for the family or silver service, you can find it in the town of Banff, which has over 80 restaurants (more per capita than any town or city across Canada). The quality of food varies greatly. Some restaurants revolve solely around the tourist trade, while others have reputations that attract diners from Calgary who have been known to stay overnight just to eat at their favorite haunt. While the quality of food is most people's number one priority when dining out, the level of service (or lack of it) also comes into play in Banff, especially if you are paying big bucks for a fine-dining meal. Getting it all right—good food, top-notch service, and a memorable ambience—in a tourism-oriented town is rare. Which leads to the restaurants I've recommended below, the best of a very varied bunch.

Groceries

Banff has two major grocery stores. In addition to a wide selection of basic groceries, **Nesters Market** (122 Bear St., 403/762-3663, 8am-11pm daily in summer, shorter hours the rest of the year) has a good deli with premade salads and sandwiches, and another deli stocked with meats and cheeses and hot chicken. At the other end of downtown is **Safeway** (318 Marten St., 403/762-5329, 8am-11pm daily).

Cafés and Coffee Shops

Banff's lone bakery is **Wild Flour** (Bison Courtyard, 211 Bear St., 403/760-5074, 7am-6pm daily, $7-10), and it's a good one (albeit a little pricey). Organic ingredients are used whenever possible, and everything is freshly baked daily. The result is an array of healthy

Evelyn's Coffee Bar is one of Banff's favorite cafés.

breads, mouthwatering cakes and pastries, and delicious meat pies. Eat inside or out in the courtyard. **Evelyn's Coffee Bar** (119, 201, and 215 Banff Ave., as well as the corner of Wolf and Bear Streets, 403/762-0352, sandwiches $7) has four central locations pouring good coffee and serving huge sandwiches. The few outside tables at 201 Banff Avenue—on the busiest stretch of the busiest street in town—are perfect for people-watching. The **Cake Company** (220 Bear St., 403/762-8642, 7am-8pm daily, cakes from $4) is another local place serving great coffee and delicious pastries, muffins, and cakes baked daily on the premises. **Jump Start** (206 Buffalo St., 403/762-0332, 7am-6pm daily, $5.50-7), opposite Central Park, has a wide range of coffee concoctions as well as homemade savories and sandwiches.

Cheap Eats

A good place to begin looking for cheap eats is the food court in the lower level of Cascade Plaza (317 Banff Ave.). Here you'll find a juice bar, a place selling pizza by the slice, and **Banff Edo**, which sells simple Japanese dishes for around $9, including a drink. Also downtown is **Barpa Bill's** (223 Bear St., 403/762-0377, 11am-midnight daily, $8-12), a hole-in-the-wall eatery with a couple of indoor tables and a menu of inexpensive Greek dishes. Cash only.

The main reasons for visiting the Banff Centre include attending the many events, exercising at the fitness facility, or wandering through the grounds. Add to this list having a casual meal at **Le Cafe** (Banff Centre, Tunnel Mountain Dr., 403/762-6100, 10am-10pm daily, $6-11), overlooking the swimming pool within the Sally Borden Building. Sandwiches are made to order, or try a minipizza or bowl of steaming soup. In the adjacent Kinnear Centre, **Maclab Bistro** (Banff Centre, Tunnel Mountain Dr., 403/762-6100, 7am-2am daily,

$14-23) is a much larger space with tables spilling outside onto a patio.

Cougar Pete's Cafe in the Banff Alpine Centre (off Tunnel Mountain Rd., 403/762-4122, 7am-1pm and 5pm-10pm, $11-18) offers free wireless Internet and a great outdoor patio. The menu features all the usual café-style dishes, such as a pile of nachos for $11.

Aardvarks (304 Caribou St., 403/762-5500, noon-4am daily) is a late-night pizza hangout.

Family-Style Dining

Children will love the food and parents will love the prices at **Old Spaghetti Factory** (2nd Floor, Cascade Plaza on Banff Ave., 403/760-2779, 11:30am-10pm daily, $9.50-20). The room is casual-rustic, with a few tables spread along a balcony. Sort through a maze of combinations and specials (kids get their own color-in menu), and the most you'll pay for a meal is $20, which includes soup or salad, a side of bread, dessert, and coffee.

Steak

Alberta beef is mostly raised on ranchland east of the park and features prominently on menus throughout town. Finely marbled AAA beef is used in most restaurants and is unequaled in its tender, juicy qualities.

Saltlik (221 Bear St., 403/762-2467, from 11am daily, $23-46) is the perfect choice for serious carnivores with cash to spare.

Considered one of Banff's most fashionable restaurants, the room is big and bold, and the concrete-and-steel split-level interior is complemented by modish wood furnishings. Facing the street, glass doors in the street-level lounge fold back to a terrace for warm-weather dining. The specialty is AAA Alberta beef, finished with grain feeding to enhance the flavor, then flash-seared at 650°C (1,200°F) to seal in the juices, and served with a side platter of seasonal vegetables. Entrées are priced comparable to a city steakhouse, but the cost creeps up as you add side dishes.

Casually Canadian

Of the many Banff drinking holes that offer pub-style menus, **Wild Bill's** (201 Banff Ave., 403/762-0333, 11am-after midnight daily, $14-31) is a standout. It's named for one of Banff's most famed mountain men, and the decor is suitably Western, with a menu to match. The nachos grande ($12.50) with a side of guacamole is perfect to share. Later in the day, flame-grilled T-bone steaks and spit-roasted chicken are traditional favorites. Plan on dining before 9pm to miss the crowd that arrives for the live music.

A town favorite that has faithfully served locals for many years is **Melissa's** (218 Lynx St., 403/762-5511, 7:30am-9:30pm daily, $14-28), housed in a log building that dates from 1928. Lunch and dinner are old-fashioned, casual affairs. Choose from a wide variety of generously sized burgers, freshly prepared salads, and Alberta beef.

Bruno's Café & Grill (304 Caribou St., 403/762-8115, 7am-10pm daily, $12-25), named for Bruno Engler, locally renowned photographer, ski instructor, and mountain man, is a cozy little café with a great mountain ambience and comfortable couches.

Classically Canadian

Sleeping Buffalo Restaurant (Buffalo Mountain Lodge, Tunnel Mountain Rd., 403/762-2400, 7am-10pm daily, $24-37) offers the perfect setting for a moderate splurge. It features a distinctive interior of hand-hewn cedar beams and old-world elegance—complete with stone fireplace and a chandelier made entirely from elk antlers—along with large windows that frame the surrounding forest. The featured cuisine is referred to as Rocky Mountain, reflecting an abundance of Canadian game and seafood combined with native berries and fruits. The least-expensive way to dine on this uniquely Canadian fare is by visiting at lunch and ordering the Rocky Mountain Game Platter, $24 for two people. Dinner entrées include fare like elk sirloin that's given an exotic touch with accompanying quince compote.

The food at **❰ Storm Mountain Lodge** (Hwy. 93, 403/762-4155, 7:30am-9pm daily May-mid-Oct., 5pm-9pm Fri.-Sun. early Dec.-Apr., $25-39) is excellent, but it's the ambience you'll remember long after leaving—an intoxicating blend of historic appeal and rustic mountain charm. The chef uses mostly organic produce with seasonally available game and seafood—bison, venison, wild salmon, and the like—to create tasty and interesting dishes well suited to the I-must-be-in-the-Canadian-wilderness surroundings. Storm Mountain Lodge is a 25-minute drive northwest from Banff; take the TransCanada Highway toward Lake Louise and head west at the Castle Mountain interchange.

Canadian Contemporary

Occupying the prime position on one of Banff's busiest corners is the **Maple Leaf** (137 Banff Ave., 403/760-7680, 11am-11pm daily, $26-42). Take in the dramatic Canadian-themed decor—exposed river stone, polished log work, a two-story interior rock wall, and a moose head (tucked around the corner from the street-level lounge). Some tables surround a busy area by the bar, so try to talk your way into the upstairs back corner. The cooking uses modern styles with an abundance of Canadian game and produce. The lunch menu has a bison burger, along with lighter salads and gourmet sandwiches. Some of Canada's finest ingredients appear on the dinner menu: Stuffed halibut and the bacon-wrapped bison tenderloin are standouts. Treat yourself to a glass of Canadian ice wine to accompany dessert.

Bison Restaurant and Terrace (Bison

Courtyard, Bear St., 403/762-5550, from 5pm daily, $25-38) is an upstairs eatery featuring the very best Canadian ingredients. The interesting decor sees chic-industrial blending with mountain rustic. Tables are inside or out at this upstairs dining room, and almost all have a view of the open kitchen. The food is solidly Canadian, with a menu that takes advantage of wild game, seafood, and Alberta beef.

Juniper Bistro (The Juniper, Norquay Rd., 403/763-6205, 7am-9:30pm daily, $24-39) is well worth searching out for both Canadian cuisine and unparalleled views across town to Mount Rundle and the Spray Valley. The stylish interior may be inviting, but in warmer weather, you'll want to be outside on the patio, where the panorama is most spectacular. The menu blends traditional tastes with Canadian produce. If your taste runs toward seafood, there's grilled calamari as a starter. For those looking for something a little more local,

the elk roast is a good choice. Most breakfasts are under $15, while at lunch, the Taste of the Rockies platter for two ($28) is a treat.

Southwestern

Banff's original bistro-style restaurant, which opened in the early 1990s, is **Coyote's** (206 Caribou St., 403/762-3963, 7:30am-10pm daily, $18-25). Meals are prepared in full view of diners, and the menu emphasizes fresh, health-conscious cooking, with just a hint of Southwestern/Mediterranean style. To start, it's hard to go past the sweet potato and corn chowder, and then choose from mains such as a flank steak marinated in Cajun spices and topped with a generous dab of corn and tomato salsa and warm shrimp and goat cheese enchilada.

European

The **Balkan** (120 Banff Ave., 403/762-3454,

© ANDREW HEMPSTEAD

upstairs at the Bison Restaurant and Terrace

11am-11pm daily, $18-37) is run by a local Greek family, but the menu blends their heritage with the cuisines of Italy, China, and Canada. Select from Greek ribs (pork ribs with a lemon sauce), the Greek chow mein (stir-fried vegetables, fried rice, and your choice of meat), or Greek spaghetti. But the most popular dishes are souvlaki and an enormous Greek platter for two.

Giorgio's (219 Banff Ave., 403/762-5114, lunch and dinner daily, $21-34) has a casual old-world atmosphere. Its chefs prepare as many as 400 meals each afternoon, and the lineup for tables through summer is ever present. Classic pasta dishes start under $25, while fish and meat specialties top out at $34.

■ Ticino (High Country Inn, 415 Banff Ave., 403/762-3848, 5:30pm-10pm daily, $18.50-36) reflects the heritage of the park's early mountain guides, with solid timber furnishings, lots of peeled and polished log work, and old wooden skis, huge cowbells, and an alpenhorn decorating the walls. It's named for the southern province of Switzerland, where the cuisine has a distinctive Italian influence. The Swiss chef is best known for a creamy wild mushroom soup, unique to the region; his beef and cheese fondues; juicy cuts of Alberta beef; and veal dishes. Save room for one of Ticino's sinfully rich desserts. Also of note is the professional service.

You'll think you've swapped continents when you step into **Le Beaujolais** (212 Buffalo St. at Banff Ave., 403/762-2712, lunch daily in summer, from 5pm daily year-round, $32-42), a Canadian leader in French cuisine. With crisp white linens, old-style stately decor, and immaculate service, this elegant room has been one of Banff's most popular fine-dining restaurants for 30 years. Its second-floor location ensures great views of Banff, especially from window tables. The dishes feature mainly Canadian produce, prepared and served with a traditional French flair. Entrées include Alberta pork chop smothered in béarnaise sauce with a side of king crab meat, but the extent of your final tab depends on whether you choose à la carte items or one of the three- and six-course table d'hôte menus ($74 and $95, respectively) —and also on how much wine you consume. Nationalism shows through in the 10,000-bottle cellar, with lots of reds from the Bordeaux and Burgundy regions of France. Reservations are necessary. Within Le Beaujolais, a small area has been set aside as **Café de Paris** (212 Buffalo St. at Banff Ave., 403/762-5365, from 5pm daily, $26-38), a more casual dining experience but with the same views.

If you are staying up on Tunnel Mountain, or even if you're not, **■ Cilantro Mountain Café** (Buffalo Mountain Lodge, 403/760 3008, 11am-11pm daily in summer, $17-30) is an excellent choice for a casual, well-priced meal. You can choose to dine inside the cozy log cabin that holds the main restaurant and open kitchen, or out on the patio. Starters are dominated by seafood options, but the flatbread, baked to order and delivered with choice of dips, is a good choice to share. The thin-crust, wood-fired pizza for one is the highlight, with a small but varied selection of other mains that change as seasonal produce becomes available. Highly recommended if you want a break from Banff Avenue.

Fondue

Even if you've tried exotic meats, you probably haven't had them in a restaurant like the **■ Grizzly House** (207 Banff Ave., 403/762-4055, 11:30am-midnight daily, $18-32), which provides Banff's most unusual dining experience. The decor is, to say the least, eclectic (many say eccentric). Think lots of twisted woods, a motorbike hanging from the ceiling, a melted telephone on the wall. Each table has a phone for across-table conversation, or you can put a call through to your server, the bar, a cab, diners in the private booth, or even those who spend too long in the bathroom. The food is equally unique, and the service is as professional as anywhere in town. The menu hasn't changed in decades, and this doesn't displease anyone. Most dining revolves around traditional Swiss fondues, but with nontraditional dipping meats such as rattlesnake, alligator, shark, ostrich, scallops, elk, and wild boar. Four-course table d'hôte fondue dinners are $44-64 per person, which includes soup or salad, followed by a cheese fondue, then a choice of one of six meat and seafood fondue (or hot rock) choices, and finally a fruity chocolate fondue. The Grizzly House is also open at lunch, when you can sample Canadian game at reduced prices; wild game meat loaf is $14, and an Alberta-farmed buffalo burger is $16.

Asian

At the back of the Clock Tower Mall, **Pad Thai** (110 Banff Ave., 403/762-4911, lunch and dinner daily, $12-18) is a real find. The namesake pad Thai is $11, curries are all around the same price, and delicious spring rolls are $4.50. You can eat in or take out.

A couple of doors off Banff Avenue, **Sushi House Banff** (304 Caribou St., 403/762-2971, lunch and dinner daily, $16-22) is a tiny space with a dozen stools set around a moving miniature railway that has diners picking sushi and other delicacies from a train as it circles the chef, who is loading the carriages as quickly as they empty.

Fairmont Banff Springs

Whether guests or not, most visitors to Banff drop by to see one of the town's biggest tourist attractions, and a meal here might not be as expensive as you think. The hotel itself has more eateries than most small towns—from a deli serving slices of pizza to the finest of fine dining in the Banffshire Club.

If you are in the mood for a snack such as chili and bread or sandwiches to go, head to the lobby level and the **Castle Pantry,** which is open 24 hours daily.

Impressive buffets are the main draw at the **Bow Valley Grill,** a pleasantly laid out dining room that seats 275. Each morning from 6:30am an expansive buffet of hot and cold delicacies, including freshly baked bread and seasonal fruits, is laid out for the masses ($42 per person). Lunch (11:30am-5:30pm daily) offers a wide-ranging menu featuring everything from salads to seafood. Through the busiest months of summer, a lunch buffet (11:30am-2pm Mon.-Fri., 11:30am-4pm Sat., $35) is offered. In summer, evening diners (6pm-9pm) order from a menu that appeals to all tastes, while the rest of the year dinner is offered as a buffet, with a different theme each night. The Sunday brunch (11am-2:30pm, $48) is legendary, with chefs working at numerous stations scattered around the dining area and an enormous spread not equaled for variety anywhere in the mountains. Reservations are required for Sunday brunch (as far in advance as possible) and dinner.

Ensconced in an octagonal room of the Manor Wing, **Castello Ristorante** (6pm-9:30pm Fri.-Tues., $21-36) is a seductive dining room with a modern, upscale ambience. The menu is dominated by Italian favorites, with traditional pastas and specialties such as veal tenderloin. The **Rundle Lounge & Hall** (from 11:30am daily) combines an area filled with comfortable sofas with summer outdoor dining and an upstairs piano bar, where most tables offer views down the Bow Valley. **Grapes** (6pm-9pm daily, $18-26) is an intimate yet casual wine bar noted for its fine cheeses and pâtés. More substantial meals such as fondues are also offered.

The hotel's most acclaimed restaurant is the **Banffshire Club** (6pm-10pm Tues.-Sat., $31-50), which seats just 65 diners. This fine-dining restaurant is a bastion of elegance, which begins as a harp player serenades you through a

© ANDREW HEMPSTEAD

outdoor dining at the Rundle Lounge & Hall

gated entrance. Inside, extravagantly rich wood furnishings, perfectly presented table settings, muted lighting, and kilted staff create an atmosphere as far removed from the surrounding wilderness as is imaginable. Reservations and a jacket are required.

Two restaurants lie within the grounds surrounding the hotel, and both are worthy of consideration. Originally the golf course clubhouse, the **Waldhaus Restaurant** (6pm-9pm daily, closed Apr., $22-33) is nestled in a forested area directly below the hotel. The big room is dominated by dark woods and is warmed by an open fireplace. The menu features German specialties, such as fondues. Below the restaurant is a pub of the same name, with a pub-style dinner menu offered in a casual atmosphere. The **Golf Course Clubhouse** (11:30am-5pm daily in summer, $15-28) is a seasonal restaurant on the golf course proper that serves casual meals throughout the golf season. A shuttle bus runs every

30 minutes between the main hotel lobby and the clubhouse.

For all Fairmont Banff Springs dining reservations, call 403/762-2211.

INFORMATION

Many sources of information are available on the park and its commercial facilities. Once you've arrived, the best place to make your first stop is the **Banff Visitor Centre** (224 Banff Ave., 8am-8pm daily mid-June-Aug., 8am-6pm daily mid-May-mid-June and Sept., 9am-5pm daily the rest of the year). This central complex houses information desks for **Parks Canada** (403/762-1550) and the **Banff/Lake Louise Tourism Bureau** (403/762-0270), as well as a Friends of Banff National Park shop, which stocks a good variety of park-related literature.

National Park Information

On the right-hand side of the **Banff Visitor**

Tourism Information

In the **Banff Visitor Centre,** across the floor from Parks Canada, is a desk for the **Banff/ Lake Louise Tourism Bureau.** This organization represents businesses and commercial establishments in the park. Here you can find out about accommodations and restaurants, and have any other questions answered. To answer the most frequently asked question, the restrooms are downstairs. For general tourism information, contact the Banff/Lake Louise Tourism Bureau office (403/762-8421, www. banfflakelouise.com).

Newspapers

Look for the free *Crag and Canyon* each Wednesday. It's been keeping residents and visitors informed about park issues and town gossip for more than a century. The *Rocky Mountain Outlook* is another free weekly newspaper (Thursday) that offers coverage of mountain life and upcoming events. Both are available on stands at businesses throughout town.

© ANDREW HEMPSTEAD

fondue at the Waldhaus Restaurant

Centre is a row of desks staffed by Parks Canada employees. They will answer all your queries regarding Banff's natural wonders and advise you of trail closures. Anyone planning an overnight backcountry trip should register here and obtain a camping pass ($10 per person per night). Also here, you can pick up park brochures, or wander down the back to peruse park maps, view a free slide show, and watch videos about the park. All questions pertaining to the national park itself can be answered here, or check out the Parks Canada website (www.pc.gc.ca).

The park's **Warden's Office** (403/762-1470) is in the industrial park at the north entrance to town. The **weather office** (403/762-2088) offers updated forecasts. If you want to *see* the weather in Banff, check out the webcam at www.banffgondola.com. Tune in to FM 101.1 or go to www.friendsofbanff.com to listen to Park Radio, which features daily updates and Banff-related programming.

BOOKS AND MAPS

The Canadian Rockies are one of the most written about, and definitely the most photographed, regions in Canada. As a walk along Banff Avenue will confirm, there is definitely no lack of postcards, calendars, and coffee-table books about the area.

Ted (E. J.) Hart, a former director of the Whyte Museum, has authored over a dozen books on the history of the park. **Summerthought Publishing** (www.summerthought.com) is a local company that has been publishing the authoritative *Canadian Rockies Trail Guide* since 1971.

Look for **Gem Trek** (www.gemtrek.com) maps at bookstores and gift shops throughout Banff National Park.

Bookstores

Opposite Central Park and just off Banff

Avenue, **Mooseprint Books and Gifts** (208 Buffalo St., 403/762-3355, 10am-6pm Mon.-Fri., 10am-8pm Sat.-Sun.) is the town's lone independent bookstore. With a welcoming ambience, it stocks just about every book in print about the park, as well as Canadian bestsellers, maps, and gifts such as photographic prints and custom-made jigsaw puzzles.

The **Whyte Museum Shop** (111 Bear St., 403/762-2291, 10am-5pm daily) specializes in regional natural and human history books, and also has a good selection of historic prints.

Banff Public Library

Banff's library (opposite Central Park at 101 Bear St., 403/762-2661, 10am-6pm Mon.-Fri., 11am-6pm Sat., 1pm-4:30pm Sun.) boasts an extensive collection of nonfiction books, many about the park and its environs, which makes it an excellent rainy-day hangout. It also has a large collection of magazines and newspapers. Internet access is free.

SERVICES

The **post office** (9am-5:30pm Mon.-Fri.) is on the corner of Buffalo and Bear Streets opposite Central Park. The general-delivery service here is probably among the busiest in the country, with the thousands of seasonal workers in the area.

Major banks can be found along Banff Avenue and are generally open 10am-4pm Mon.-Thurs., 9am-4:30pm Friday. The **Bank of Montreal** (107 Banff Ave., 403/762-2275) allows cash advances with MasterCard, while the **C.I.B.C.** (98 Banff Ave., 403/762-3317) accepts Visa. **Freya's Currency Exchange** is in the Clock Tower Mall (108 Banff Ave., 403/762-4652).

The only downtown laundry is **Cascade Coin Laundry** (7:30am-10pm daily), on the lower level of the Cascade Plaza. **Chalet Coin Laundry** (8am-10pm daily) is on Tunnel Mountain Road at the Douglas Fir Resort, within walking distance of all Tunnel Mountain accommodations.

Along Banff Avenue you'll find **Banff Camera Shop** (101 Banff Ave., 403/762-3562), with digital imaging capabilities and a full range of equipment.

Mineral Springs Hospital (301 Lynx St., 403/762-2222) has 24-hour emergency service. **Rexall Drug Store,** on the lower level of the Cascade Plaza (317 Banff Ave., 403/762-2245), is open until 9pm daily.

Send and receive email and surf the Internet at most downtown cafés, or head to **Banff Public Library** (101 Bear St., 403/762-2661, 10am-6pm Mon.-Fri., 11am-6pm Sat., 1pm-4:30pm Sun.).

GETTING THERE
From Calgary
International Airport

Calgary International Airport, 128 kilometers (80 miles) east, is the closest airport to Banff National Park. **Brewster** (403/762-6767 or 800/661-1152, www.brewster. ca) shuttles between the airport and Banff National Park twice daily, stopping at Banff, then continuing to Lake Louise. Calgary to Banff is adult $52, child $26. This shuttle delivers guests to all major Banff hotels as well as the **Brewster Tour and Transportation Centre** (100 Gopher St.), a five-minute walk from downtown Banff. The depot has a ticket office, lockers, and a Tim Hortons café. It's open 7:30am-10:45pm daily. The other shuttle company is **Banff Airporter** (403/762-3330 or 888/449-2901, www. banffairporter.com), offering door-to-door service for around the same price. Adjacent desks at the airport's Arrivals level take bookings, but it's best to reserve a seat by booking over the phone or online in advance. The earliest service back to the airport departs Banff at 4:30am.

© ANDREW HEMPSTEAD

Murals of wild animals make public transit buses in Banff very distinctive.

Greyhound

Greyhound (403/762-1092 or 800/661-8747, www.greyhound.ca) offers scheduled service from the Calgary bus depot at 877 Greyhound Way SW, five times daily to the Banff Railway Station and Samson Mall, Lake Louise. Greyhound buses leave Vancouver from the depot at 1150 Station Street, three times daily for the scenic 14-hour ride to the park.

GETTING AROUND

Most of the sights and many trailheads are within walking distance of town. **Banff Transit** (403/760-8294) operates bus service along two routes through the town of Banff: one from the Banff Gondola north along Banff Avenue, the other from the Fairmont Banff Springs to the Tunnel Mountain campgrounds. Mid-May-September, buses run twice an hour between 7am and midnight. October-December, the two routes are merged as one, with buses running hourly midday-midnight. Travel costs $2 per sector.

Cabs around Banff are reasonably priced: flag drop is $4, then it's $2.50 per kilometer. From the Banff bus depot to Tunnel Mountain accommodations will run around $10, same to the Fairmont Banff Springs, more after midnight. Call **Banff Taxi** (403/762-4444).

The days when a row of horse-drawn buggies eagerly awaited the arrival of wealthy visitors at the CPR Station have long since passed, but the **Trail Rider Store** (132 Banff Ave., 403/762-4551) offers visitors rides around town in a beautifully restored carriage ($24 per person for 15 minutes). Expect to pay $58 per carriage for a short loop along the Bow River.

Car Rental

Plan on renting a vehicle before you reach the park. In addition to high pricing for walk-in customers, the main catch is that local companies don't generally offer unlimited mileage. The most you'll get is a free 150 kilometers (93 miles), and then expect to pay 25 cents per

PARKING PROBLEMS (AND HOW TO AVOID THEM)

The downtown core of Banff is busy year-round, but especially so between late June and early September after 10am. If you're staying in a motel along Banff Avenue or on Tunnel Mountain, don't drive into town—walk or catch a Banff Transit bus (ask at your accommodation for a schedule).

If you do drive into downtown, don't let not finding a parking spot on Banff Avenue ruin your holiday. Head to the parking garage at the corner of Bear and Lynx Streets, cross the Bow River and park in the recreation grounds, or cruise for a space along Lynx or Beaver Street.

For travelers with RVs or trailers, finding a downtown parking spot can be a challenge. If you're planning on staying at one of the campgrounds on Tunnel Mountain, check in first, then walk or catch the Roam bus (it departs the campground every 30 minutes; $2) to downtown. If you must bring your rig into town and the few RV-only parking spots at the corner of Lynx and Wolf Streets are taken, there are no options other than the suggestions I give above for regular vehicles.

kilometer thereafter. Agencies and their local contact numbers are **Avis** (Cascade Plaza, 317 Banff Ave., 403/762-3222), **Budget** (Brewster's Mountain Lodge, 208 Caribou St., 403/762-4565), **Enterprise** (corner of Lynx and Caribou Streets, 403/762-2688), and **Hertz** (Fairmont Banff Springs, Spray Ave., 403/762-2027). Reservations for vehicles in Banff should be made well in advance, especially in July and August.

Lake Louise and Vicinity

Lake Louise is 56 kilometers (35 miles) northwest of Banff along the TransCanada Highway, or a little bit longer if you take the quieter Bow Valley Parkway. The hamlet of Lake Louise, composed of a small mall, hotels, and restaurants, is in the Bow Valley, just west of the TransCanada Highway. The lake itself is 200 vertical meters (660 vertical feet) above the valley floor, along a winding four-kilometer (2.5-mile) road. Across the valley is Canada's second-largest winter resort, also called Lake Louise. It's a world-class facility renowned for diverse terrain, abundant snow, and breathtaking views.

When you see the first flush of morning sun hit Victoria Glacier, and the impossibly steep northern face of Mount Victoria reflected in the sparkling, emerald-green waters of Lake Louise, you'll understand why this lake is regarded as one of the world's seven natural wonders. Overlooking the magnificent scene, Fairmont Chateau Lake Louise is without a doubt one of the world's most photographed hotels. Apart from staring, photographing, and videotaping, the area has plenty to keep you busy. Nearby you'll find some of the park's best hiking, canoeing, and horseback riding. Only a short distance away is Moraine Lake, not as famous as Lake Louise but rivaling it in beauty.

From Lake Louise the TransCanada Highway continues west, exiting the park over Kicking Horse Pass (1,647 meters/5,400 feet) and passing through Yoho National Park to Golden. Highway 93, the famous Icefields Parkway, begins one kilometer (0.6 mile) north of the village and heads northwest through the park's northern reaches to Jasper National Park.

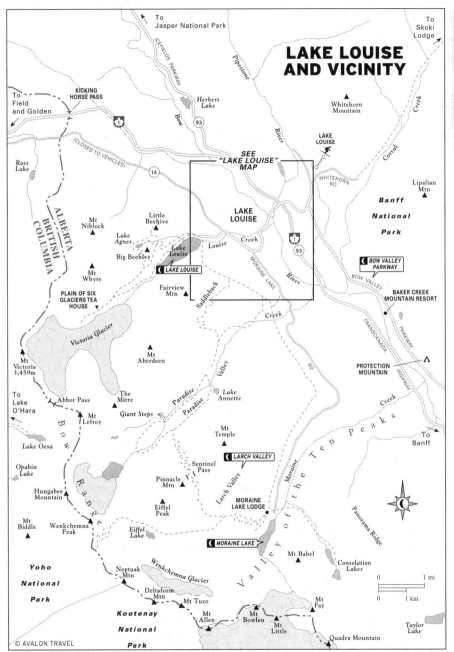

To
Jasper National Park

To
Skoki
Lodge

LAKE LOUISE
AND VICINITY

ICEFIELDS PARKWAY

Pipestone

To
Field
and Golden

KICKING
HORSE PASS

Herbert
Lake

Whitehorn
Mountain

Bow

93

River

Creek

LAKE
LOUISE

(CLOSED TO VEHICLES)

SEE
"LAKE LOUISE"
MAP

Corral

Ross
Lake

1A

WHITEHORN
RD

Lipalian
Mtn

Banff

Mt
Niblock

Little
Beehive

LAKE
LOUISE

National

Lake
Agnes

Big Beehive

Lake
Louise

Louise

Creek

1

93

Park

ALBERTA
BRITISH
COLUMBIA

Mt
Whyte

LAKE LOUISE

MORAINE LAKE

River

BOW VALLEY
PARKWAY

BOW VALLEY

PLAIN OF SIX
GLACIERS TEA
HOUSE

Fairview
Mtn

Saddleback

BAKER CREEK
MOUNTAIN RESORT

Victoria Glacier

Mt
Aberdeen

Creek

TRANS-CANADA

PARKWAY

Mt
Victoria
3,459m

Valley

PROTECTION
MOUNTAIN

HIGHWAY

To
Lake
O'Hara

Abbot Pass

The
Mitre

Mt
Lefroy

Giant Steps

Paradise

Paradise

Lake
Annette

Creek

To
Banff

Bow

Lake Oesa

Mt
Temple

of

the

Ten

Peaks

Opabin
Lake

Sentinel
Pass

LARCH VALLEY

Range

Pinnacle
Mtn

Larch Valley

Hungabee
Mountain

Eiffel
Peak

MORAINE
LAKE LODGE

Moraine

Panorama Ridge

Mt
Biddle

Wenkchemna
Peak

Eiffel
Lake

MORAINE LAKE

Valley

Mt Babel

Consolation
Lakes

0   1 mi

Yoho

Neptuak
Mtn

Wenkchemna Glacier

0   1 km

National

Deltaform
Mtn

Mt Tuzo

Mt
Fay

Park

Kootenay

Mt
Allen

Mt
Bowlen

Mt
Little

Taylor
Lake

National

Quadra Mountain

Park

© AVALON TRAVEL

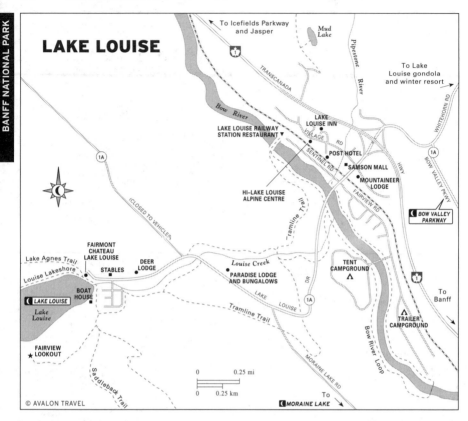

LAKE LOUISE

To Icefields Parkway and Jasper

Mud Lake

Pipestone River

To Lake Louise gondola and winter resort

TRANSCANADA

Bow River

WHITEHORN RD

LAKE LOUISE INN

LAKE LOUISE RAILWAY STATION RESTAURANT ▼

VILLAGE RD

POST HOTEL

SENTINEL RD

SAMSON MALL

HWY

BOW VALLEY PKWY

MOUNTAINEER LODGE

HI-LAKE LOUISE ALPINE CENTRE

FAIRVIEW RD

Tramline Trail

BOW VALLEY PARKWAY

(CLOSED TO VEHICLES)

FAIRMONT CHATEAU LAKE LOUISE

Lake Agnes Trail

Louise Lakeshore

STABLES

DEER LODGE

Louise Creek

TENT CAMPGROUND
∧

PARADISE LODGE AND BUNGALOWS

DR

BOAT HOUSE

LAKE LOUISE

LAKE LOUISE

To Banff

Lake Louise

Tramline Trail

1A

MORAINE LAKE RD

∧ TRAILER CAMPGROUND

Bow River Loop

FAIRVIEW ★ LOOKOUT

Saddleback Trail

0   0.25 mi

0   0.25 km

To
☾ MORAINE LAKE

© AVALON TRAVEL

SIGHTS
☾ Lake Louise

In summer, about 10,000 visitors per day make the journey from the Bow Valley floor up to Lake Louise. By noon the tiered parking lot is often full. An alternative to the road is one of two hiking trails that begin in the village and end at the public parking lot. From here several paved trails lead to the lake's eastern shore. From these vantage points the dramatic setting can be fully appreciated. The lake is 2.4 kilometers (1.5 miles) long, 500 meters (1,640 feet) wide, and up to 90 meters (295 feet) deep. Its cold waters reach a maximum temperature of 4°C (39°F) in August.

Fairmont Chateau Lake Louise is a tourist attraction in itself. Built by the CPR to take the pressure off the popular Banff Springs Resort, the château has seen many changes in the last 100 years, yet it remains one of the world's great mountain resorts. No one minds the hordes of camera-toting tourists who traipse through each day—and there's really no way to avoid them. The immaculately manicured gardens between the château and the lake make an interesting foreground for the millions of Lake Louise photographs taken each year. At the lakeshore boathouse, canoes are rented for $40 per hour.

The snow-covered peak at the back of the lake is **Mount Victoria** (3,459 meters/11,350 feet), which sits on the Continental Divide.

© ANDREW HEMPSTEAD

playing pond hockey in front of the Fairmont Chateau Lake Louise

Amazingly, its base is more than 10 kilometers (6.2 miles) from the eastern end of the lake. Mount Victoria, first climbed in 1897, remains one of the park's most popular peaks for mountaineers. Although the difficult northeast face (facing the château) was first successfully ascended in 1922, the most popular and easiest route to the summit is along the southeast ridge, approached from Abbot Pass.

Moraine Lake

Although less than half the size of Lake Louise, Moraine Lake is just as spectacular and worthy of just as much film. It is up a winding road 13 kilometers (eight miles) off Lake Louise Drive. Its rugged setting, nestled in the Valley of the Ten Peaks among the towering mountains of the main ranges, has provided inspiration for millions of people from around the world since Walter Wilcox became the first white man to reach its shore in 1899. Wilcox's subsequent writings, such as "no scene has given me an equal impression of inspiring solitude and rugged grandeur," guaranteed the lake's future popularity. Although Wilcox was a knowledgeable man, he named the lake on the assumption that it was dammed by a glacial moraine deposited by the retreating Wenkchemna Glacier. In fact, the large rock pile that blocks its waters was deposited by major rockfalls from the Tower of Babel to the south. The lake often remains frozen until June, and the access road is closed all winter. A trail leads along the lake's northern shore, and canoes are rented for $30 per hour from the concession below Moraine Lake Lodge.

Sightseeing Gondola

During summer, the main ski lift at the Lake Louise winter resort (403/522-3555 or 877/253-6888, www.skilouise.com) whisks visitors up the face of Mount Whitehorn to Whitehorn Lodge in either open chairs or enclosed gondola cars. The view from the

"LAKE OF LITTLE FISHES"

During the summer of 1882, Tom Wilson, an outfitter, was camped near the confluence of the Bow and Pipestone Rivers when he heard the distant rumblings of an avalanche. He questioned Stoney Indian guides and was told the noises originated from the "Lake of Little Fishes." The following day, Wilson, led by a native guide, hiked to the lake to investigate. He became the first white man to lay eyes on what he named Emerald Lake. Two years later, the name was changed to Lake Louise, honoring Princess Louise Caroline Alberta, daughter of Queen Victoria.

A railway station known as Laggan was built where the rail line passed closest to the lake, six kilometers (3.7 miles) away. Until a road was completed in 1926, everyone arrived by train. The station's name was changed to Lake Louise in 1913 to prevent confusion among visitors. In 1890, a modest two-bedroom wooden hotel replaced a crude cabin that had been built on the shore of the lake as word of its beauty spread. After many additions, a disastrous fire, and the addition of a concrete wing in 1925, the château of today took shape, minus a convention center that opened in 2004.

top—at an altitude of more than two kilometers (1.2 miles) above sea level, across the Bow Valley, Lake Louise, and the Continental Divide—is among the most spectacular in the Canadian Rockies. Short trails lead through the forests, across open meadows, and, for the energetic, to the summit of Mount Whitehorn, more than 600 vertical meters (1,970 vertical feet) above. Visitors are free to walk these trails, but it pays to join a guided walk if you'd like to learn about the surrounding environment. After working up an appetite (and working off breakfast), head to the teahouse in the Whitehorn Lodge, try the outdoor barbecue, or, back at the base area, enjoy lunch at the **Lodge of the Ten Peaks,** the resort's impressive post-and-beam day lodge. The lift operates 9am-4pm daily May-September, with extended summer hours of 9am-5pm, adult $28, child $14. Ride-and-dine packages are an excellent deal. Pay an extra $2 per person and have a buffet breakfast (8am-11am) included with the gondola ride or $7 extra for the buffet lunch (11:30am-2:30pm). Free shuttles run from Lake Louise accommodations to the day lodge.

HIKING

The variety of hiking opportunities in the vicinity of Lake Louise and Moraine Lake is surely equal to any area on the face of the earth. The region's potential for outdoor recreation was first realized in the late 1800s, and it soon became the center of hiking activity in the Canadian Rockies. This popularity continues today; trails here are among the most heavily used in the park. Hiking is best early or late in the short summer season. Head out early in the morning to miss the strollers, high heels, dogs, and bear bells that you'll surely encounter during the busiest periods.

The two main trailheads are at Fairmont Chateau Lake Louise and Moraine Lake. Two trails lead from the village to the château (a pleasant alternative to driving the steep and busy Lake Louise Drive). Shortest is the 2.7-kilometer (1.7-mile) **Louise Creek Trail.** It begins on the downstream side of the point where Lake Louise Drive crosses the Bow River, crosses Louise Creek three times, and ends at the Lake Louise parking lot. The other trail, **Tramline,** is 4.5 kilometers (2.8 miles) longer but not as steep. It begins behind the railway station and follows the route of a narrow-gauge railway that once transported guests from the CPR line to Chateau Lake Louise.

Bow River Loop

• Length: 7 kilometers/4.3 miles (1.5-2 hours) round-trip
• Elevation gain: minimal
• Rating: easy
• Trailheads: various points throughout Lake Louise village, including behind Samson Mall

This loop follows both banks of the Bow River southeast from the railway station. Used by joggers and cyclists to access various points in the village, the trail also links the railway station to the Lake Louise Alpine Centre, Post Hotel, Samson Mall, both campgrounds, and the Louise Creek and Tramline Trails to Lake Louise. Interpretive signs along its length provide information on the Bow River ecosystem.

Louise Lakeshore

• Length: 2 kilometers/1.2 miles (30 minutes) one-way
• Elevation gain: none
• Rating: easy
• Trailhead: Lake Louise, 4 kilometers (2.5 miles) from TransCanada Highway

Probably the busiest trail in all the Canadian Rockies, this one follows the north shore of Lake Louise from in front of the château to the west end of the lake. Here numerous braided glacial streams empty their silt-filled waters into Lake Louise. Along the trail's length are benches for sitting and pondering what English mountaineer James Outram once described as "a gem of composition and of coloring… perhaps unrivalled anywhere."

Plain of the Six Glaciers

• Length: 5.3 kilometers/3.3 miles (90 minutes) one-way
• Elevation gain: 370 meters/1,215 feet

• Rating: easy/moderate
• Trailhead: Lake Louise

Hikers along this trail are rewarded not only with panoramic views of the glaciated peaks of the main range, but also with a rustic trail's-end teahouse serving homemade goodies baked on a wooden stove. For the first two kilometers (1.2 miles), the trail follows the Louise Lakeshore Trail to the western end of the lake. From there it begins a steady climb through a forest of spruce and subalpine fir. It enters an open area where an avalanche has come tumbling down (now a colorful carpet of wildflowers), then passes through a forested area into a vast wasteland of moraines produced by the advance and retreat of Victoria Glacier. Views of surrounding peaks continue to improve until the trail enters a stunted forest. After switchbacking up through this forest, the trail arrives at the teahouse.

Built by the CPR at the turn of the 20th century, the teahouse operates the same way now as it did then. Supplies are packed in by horse, and all cooking is done in a rustic kitchen. It's open July through early September.

After resting, continue one kilometer (0.6 mile) to the end of the trail on the narrow top of a lateral moraine. From here the trail's namesakes are visible. From left to right, the glaciers are Aberdeen, Upper Lefroy, Lower Lefroy, Upper Victoria, Lower Victoria, and Pope's. Between Mount Lefroy (3,441 meters/11,290 feet) and Mount Victoria (3,459 meters/11,350 feet) is Abbot Pass, where it's possible to make out Abbot Hut on the skyline. When constructed in 1922, this stone structure was the highest building in Canada. The pass and hut are named for Phillip Abbot, who died attempting to climb Mount Lefroy in 1896.

ⒸLake Agnes

• Length: 3.6 kilometers/2.2 miles (90 minutes) one-way

hiking to Plain of the Six Glaciers teahouse

• Elevation gain: 400 meters/1,312 feet
• Rating: moderate
• Trailhead: Lake Louise

This moderately strenuous hike is one of the park's most popular. It begins in front of the château, branching right near the beginning of the Louise Lakeshore Trail. For the first 2.5 kilometers (1.6 miles), the trail climbs steeply, switchbacking through a forest of subalpine fir and Engelmann spruce, crossing a horse trail, passing a lookout, and leveling out at tiny Mirror Lake. Here the old, traditional trail veers right (use it if the ground is wet or snowy), while a more direct route veers left to the Plain of the Six Glaciers. The final elevation gain along both trails is made easier by a flight of steps beside Bridal Veil Falls. The trail ends beside a rustic teahouse overlooking Lake Agnes, a subalpine lake nestled in a hanging valley. The teahouse offers homemade soups, healthy sandwiches, and a wide assortment of teas.

From the teahouse, a one-kilometer (0.6-mile) trail leads to Little Beehive and impressive views of the Bow Valley. Another trail leads around the northern shore of Lake Agnes, climbing to Big Beehive or joining to the Plain of the Six Glaciers Trail, just 3.2 kilometers (two miles) from the château and 2.1 kilometers (1.3 miles) from the teahouse at the end of that trail.

Big Beehive

• Length: 5 kilometers/3.1 miles (2 hours) one-way
• Elevation gain: 520 meters/1,710 feet
• Rating: moderate
• Trailhead: Lake Louise

The lookout atop the larger of the two "beehives" is one of the best places to admire the uniquely colored waters of Lake Louise, more than 500 meters (1,640 feet) directly below. The various trails to the summit have one thing in common: All are steep. But the rewards are worth every drop of sweat along the way. The most popular route follows the Lake Agnes Trail for the first 3.6 kilometers (2.2 miles) to Lake Agnes. From the teahouse, a trail leads to the western end of the lake, then switchbacks steeply up an exposed north-facing ridge. At the crest of the ridge, the trail forks. To the right it descends to the Plain of the Six Glaciers Trail; to the left it continues 300 meters (0.2 mile) to a log gazebo. This trail is not well defined, but scrambling through the large boulders is easy. Across Lake Louise is Fairview Mountain (2,745 meters/9,000 feet), and behind this peak is the distinctive shape of Mount Temple (3,549 meters/11,645 feet). Views also extend up the lake to Mount Lefroy and northeast to the Lake Louise winter resort. Views from the edge of the cliff are spectacular, but be very careful—it's a long, long way down. By returning down the Lake Louise side of the Big Beehive, the loop is 11.5 kilometers (7.1 miles).

Saddleback

- Length: 3.7 kilometers/2.3 miles (90 minutes) one-way
- Elevation gain: 600 meters/1,970 feet
- Rating: moderate
- Trailhead: boathouse, Lake Louise

This trail climbs the lower slopes of Fairview Mountain from beside the boathouse on Lake Louise, ending in an alpine meadow with a view of Mount Temple from across Paradise Valley. Four hundred meters (0.2 mile) from the trailhead, the trail forks. Keep left and follow the steep switchbacks through a forest of Englemann spruce and subalpine fir until reaching the flower-filled meadow. The meadow is actually a pass between Fairview Mountain (to the northwest) and Saddle Mountain (to the southeast). Although most hikers are content with the awesome views from the pass and return along the same trail, it is possible to continue to the summit of Fairview (2,745 meters/9,000 feet), a further climb of 400 vertical meters (1,310 vertical feet). The barely discernible, switchbacking trail to the summit begins near a stand of larch trees above the crest of Saddleback. As you would expect, the view from the top is stupendous; Lake Louise is more than one kilometer (0.6 mile) directly below. This option is for strong, experienced hikers only. From the Saddleback, the trail descends into Sheol Valley, then into Paradise Valley. The entire loop would be 15 kilometers (9.3 miles).

Paradise Valley

- Length: 18 kilometers/11.2 miles (6 hours) round-trip
- Elevation gain: 380 meters/1,250 feet
- Rating: moderate
- Trailhead: Moraine Lake Road, 3.5 kilometers (2.2 miles) from Lake Louise Drive

This aptly named trail makes for a long day hike, but it can be broken up by overnighting at the backcountry campground at the far end of the loop. The trail climbs steadily for the first five kilometers (3.1 miles), crossing Paradise Creek numerous times and passing the junction of a trail that climbs the Sheol Valley to Saddleback. After five kilometers (3.1 miles) the trail divides again, following either side of the valley to form a 13-kilometer (eight-mile) loop. **Lake Annette** is 700 meters (0.4 mile) along the left fork. It's a typical subalpine lake in a unique setting, nestled against the near-vertical 1,200-meter (3,940-foot) north face of snow- and ice-capped **Mount Temple** (3,549 meters/11,645 feet), one of the 10 highest peaks in the Canadian Rockies. This difficult face was successfully climbed in 1966, relatively late for mountaineering firsts. The lake is a worthy destination in itself (allow yourself four hours round-trip from the trailhead). For those completing the entire loop, continue beyond the lake into an open avalanche area that affords views across Paradise Valley. Look and listen for pikas and marmots among the boulders. The trail then passes through Horseshoe Meadow, crosses Paradise Creek, and heads back down the valley. Keep to the left at all trail crossings, and you'll quickly arrive at a series of waterfalls known as the Giant Steps. From the base of these falls, it is eight kilometers (five miles) back to the trailhead.

◖ Larch Valley

- Length: 2.9 kilometers/1.8 miles (60 minutes) one-way
- Elevation gain: 400 meters/1,310 feet
- Rating: moderate
- Trailhead: Moraine Lake, 13 kilometers (8 miles) from Lake Louise Drive

In fall, when the larch trees have turned a magnificent gold and the sun is shining, few spots in the Canadian Rockies can match the beauty of this valley, but don't expect to find much solitude (and don't be too disappointed if the trail is closed in fall—it often is because of wildlife). Although the most popular time for visiting the valley is fall, it is a worthy destination all summer, when the open meadows are filled with colorful wildflowers. The trail begins just past Moraine Lake Lodge and climbs fairly steeply, with occasional glimpses of Moraine Lake below. After reaching the junction of the Eiffel Lake Trail, keep right, passing through an open forest of larch and into the meadow beyond. The range of larch is restricted within the park, and this is one of the few areas where they are prolific. Mount Fay (3,235 meters/10,615 feet) is the dominant peak on the skyline, rising above the other mountains that make up the Valley of the Ten Peaks.

Sentinel Pass

- Length: 5.8 kilometers/3.6 miles (2-3 hours) one-way
- Elevation gain: 725 meters/2,380 feet
- Rating: moderate/difficult
- Trailhead: Moraine Lake

Keen hikers should consider continuing through the open meadows of Larch Valley to Sentinel Pass (2,608 meters/8,560 feet), one of the park's highest trail-accessible passes. The length and elevation gain listed are from Moraine Lake. Once in Larch Valley, you're halfway there and have made over half of the elevation gain. Upon reaching Larch Valley, take the formed trail that winds through the open meadow. After climbing steadily beyond Minnestimma Lakes, the trail switchbacks for 1.2 kilometers (0.7 mile) up a steep scree slope to the pass, sandwiched between Pinnacle Mountain (3,067 meters/10,060 feet) and Mount Temple (3,549 meters/11,645 feet). From the pass most hikers opt to return along the same trail, although with advanced planning it is possible to continue into Paradise Valley and back to the Moraine Lake access

road, a total of 17 kilometers (10.6 miles) one-way.

Eiffel Lake

- Length: 5.6 kilometers/3.5 miles (2 hours) one-way
- Elevation gain: 400 meters/1,310 feet
- Rating: moderate/difficult
- Trailhead: Moraine Lake

Eiffel Lake is small, and it looks even smaller in its rugged and desolate setting, surrounded by the famed Valley of the Ten Peaks. For the first 2.4 kilometers (1.5 miles), follow the Larch Valley Trail, then fork left. Most of the elevation gain has already been made, and the trail remains relatively level before emerging onto an open slope from where each of the 10 peaks can be seen, along with Moraine Lake far below. From left to right the peaks are Fay, Little, Bowlen, Perren, Septa, Allen, Tuzo, Deltaform, Neptuak, and Wenkchemna. The final two peaks are divided by Wenkchemna Pass (2,605 meters/8,550 feet), a further four kilometers (2.5 miles) and 360 vertical meters (1,180 vertical feet) above Eiffel Lake. The lake itself soon comes into view. It lies in a depression formed by a rock slide from Neptuak Mountain. The lake is named for **Eiffel Peak** (3,085 meters/10,120 feet), a rock pinnacle behind it, which with a little imagination could be compared to the Eiffel Tower in Paris.

Consolation Lakes

- Length: 3 kilometers/1.9 miles (1 hour) one-way
- Elevation gain: 65 meters/213 feet
- Rating: easy/moderate
- Trailhead: beside the restrooms at Moraine Lake parking lot

This short trail begins with a crossing of Moraine Creek at the outlet of Moraine Lake and ends at a pleasant subalpine lake. The first section of the trail traverses a boulder-strewn rock pile—the result of rock slides on the imposing Tower of Babel (3,100 meters/10,170 feet)—before entering a dense forest of Engelmann spruce and subalpine fir and following Babel Creek to the lower lake. The wide valley affords 360-degree views of the surrounding jagged peaks, including Mount Temple back down the valley and Mounts Bident and Quandra at the far end of the lakes.

Skoki Lodge

- Length: 14.4 kilometers/8.9 miles (5 hours) one-way
- Elevation gain: 775 meters/2,540 feet
- Rating: moderate/difficult
- Trailhead: end of Fish Creek Road, off Whitehorn Road 1.8 kilometers (1.1 miles) north of Lake Louise interchange

The trail into historic Skoki Lodge is only one of the endless hiking opportunities tucked behind the Lake Louise winter resort, across the valley from all hikes detailed previously. The first four kilometers (2.5 miles) of the trail are along a gravel access road leading to Temple Lodge, part of the Lake Louise winter resort. From here, the trail climbs to Boulder Pass, passing a campground and Halfway Hut, above Corral Creek. The pass harbors a large population of pikas and hoary marmots. The trail then follows the north shore of Ptarmigan Lake before climbing again to Deception Pass, named for its false summit. It then descends into Skoki Valley, passing the Skoki Lakes and eventually reaching Skoki Lodge. Just over one kilometer (0.6 mile) beyond the lodge is a campground, an excellent base for exploring the region.

OTHER SUMMER RECREATION

In Lake Louise, "summer fun" means hiking—and lots of it. You may see small fish swimming along the shore of Lake Louise, but the fishing in this lake and all others in the area is poor due to the super-cold glacial water. Talking of cold water, everyone is invited to take a swim in Lake Louise to celebrate the country's national holiday, **Canada Day** (July 1). You don't need to be Canadian to join in—just brave.

Through summer, **Brewster Adventures** (403/522-3511) offers two-hour horseback rides to the end of **Lake Louise** for $82, half-day rides to **Lake Agnes Teahouse** for $135, and all-day rides up **Paradise Valley,** including lunch, for $285.

WINTER RECREATION

Lake Louise is an immense winter playground, offering one of the world's premier alpine resorts, unlimited cross-country skiing, ice-skating, sleigh rides, and nearby heli-skiing. Between November and May, accommodation prices are reduced by up to 70 percent (except Christmas holidays). Lift and lodging packages begin at $100 per person, and you'll always be able to get a table at your favorite restaurant.

Lake Louise Resort

Canada's answer to U.S. megaresorts such as Vail and Killington is Lake Louise (403/522-3555 or 877/253-6888, www.skilouise.com), which opens in November and operates until mid-May. The nation's second-largest winter resort (behind only Whistler/Blackcomb) comprises 1,700 hectares (4,200 acres) of gentle trails, mogul fields, long cruising runs, steep chutes, and vast bowls filled with famous Rocky Mountain powder.

The resort is made up of four distinct faces. The front side has a vertical drop of 1,000 meters (3,280 feet) and is served by eight lifts, including four high-speed quads and western Canada's only six-passenger chairlift. Resort statistics are impressive: a 990-meter (3,250-foot) vertical rise, 1,700 hectares (4,200 acres) of patrolled terrain, and more than 100 named runs. The four back bowls are each as big as many midsize resorts and are all well above the tree line. Larch and Ptarmigan faces have a variety of terrain, allowing you to follow the sun as it moves across the sky or escape into trees for protection on windy days. Each of the three day lodges has a restaurant and bar. Ski and snowboard rentals, clothing, and souvenirs are available in the Lodge of the Ten Peaks, a magnificent post-and-beam day lodge that overlooks the front face.

Lift tickets per day are adult $89, senior $74, youth $62, and child younger than 12 $28. Free guided tours of the mountain are available three times daily. Inquire at customer service. Free shuttle buses run regularly from Lake Louise accommodations to the hill. From Banff you pay $20 round-trip for transportation to Lake Louise. For information on packages and multiday tickets that cover all three national park resorts, go to www.skibig3.com.

Cross-Country Skiing

The most popular cross-country skiing areas are on Lake Louise, along Moraine Lake Road, and in Skoki Valley at the back of the Lake Louise ski area. For details and helpful trail classifications, pick up a copy of *Cross-Country Skiing-Nordic Trails in Banff National Park* from the Lake Louise Visitor Centre. Before heading out, check the weather forecast at the visitors center or call 403/762-2088. For avalanche reports, call 403/762-1460.

Ice-Skating and Sleigh Rides

Of all the ice-skating rinks in Canada, the one on frozen Lake Louise, in front of the château, is surely the most spectacular. Spotlights allow skating after dark, and on special occasions hot chocolate is served. Skates are available in the château at **Chateau Mountain Sports** (403/522-3628); $10 for two hours.

Brewster Lake Louise Sleigh Rides (403/522-3511) offers rides in traditional horse-drawn sleighs along the shores of Lake Louise beginning from in front of the château. Although blankets are supplied, you should still bundle up. The one-hour ride is $34 per person, $22 for children. Reservations are necessary. The rides are scheduled hourly from 11am on weekends and from 3pm on weekdays, with the last ride between 6 and 9pm.

NIGHTLIFE

The lounge in the **Post Hotel** (200 Pipestone Dr., 403/522-3989) oozes mountain style and upscale charm. It's cozy, quiet, and the perfect place to relax in front of a fire with a cocktail before moving on to the adjacent fine-dining restaurant. Not your scene? Hang out with seasonal workers at the smoky **Lake Louise Grill & Bar** (upstairs in Samson Mall, 403/522-3879), then move across the road with your newfound friends to **Charlie's Pub** (Lake Louise Inn, 403/522-3791) for dancing to recorded music until 2am Up at the Fairmont Chateau Lake Louise (403/522-3511) is **The Glacier Saloon** (from 6pm daily), where on most summer nights a DJ plays music ranging from pop to western.

ACCOMMODATIONS AND CAMPING

In summer, accommodations at Lake Louise are even harder to come by than in Banff, so it's essential to make reservations well in advance. Any rooms not taken by early afternoon will be the expensive ones.

Under $50

With beds for $100 less than anyplace else in the village, the 164-bed **HI-Lake Louise Alpine Centre** (403/522-2200 or 866/762-4122, www.hihostels.ca) is understandably popular. Of log construction, with large windows and high vaulted ceilings, the lodge is a joint venture between the Alpine Club of Canada and Hostelling International Canada. Beyond the reception area is **Bill Peyto's Cafe,** the least-expensive place to eat in Lake Louise. Upstairs is a large timber-frame lounge area and guide's room—a quiet place to plan your next hike or browse through the large collection of mountain literature. Other amenities include Wi-Fi Internet, a laundry, games room, and wintertime ski shuttle. Members of Hostelling International pay $39 per person per night (nonmembers $43) for a dorm bed or $109 s or d ($119 for nonmembers) in a private room. Rates are discounted to $30 for a dorm and $82 s or d for a private room ($35 and $92, respectively, for nonmembers) October-May, including throughout the extremely busy winter season. The hostel is open year-round, with check-in after 3pm In summer and on weekends during the winter season, advance bookings (up to six months) are essential. The hostel is on Village Road, less than one kilometer (0.6 mile) from Samson Mall.

$150-200

Historic **Deer Lodge** (403/410-7417 or 800/661-1595, www.crmr.com, $175-275 s or d) began life in 1921 as a teahouse, with rooms added in 1925. Facilities include a rooftop hot tub with glacier views, game room, restaurant (breakfast and dinner), and bar. The least-expensive rooms are older and don't have phones. Rooms in the $200-250 range are considerably larger, or pay $275 for a heritage-themed Tower Room. Deer Lodge is along Lake Louise Drive, up the hill from the village, and just a five-minute walk from the lake itself.

On the valley floor, **Mountaineer Lodge** (101 Village Rd., 403/522-3844, www.mountaineerlodge.com, May-mid-Oct., $189-239 s or d) offers large, functional guest rooms, many with mountain views and all with Wi-Fi Internet access. On the downside, the rooms have no phones or air-conditioning, and there is no elevator. Rates are halved during the first and last months of the operating season.

$200-250

Aside from the château, the **Lake Louise Inn** (210 Village Rd., 403/522-3791 or 800/661-9237, www.lakelouiseinn.com, from $220 s or d) is the village's largest lodging, with more than 200 units spread throughout five buildings. Across from the lobby, in the main lodge, is a gift shop and an activities desk, and beyond is a pizzeria, restaurant, bar, and indoor pool. Most rates booked online include breakfast.

An excellent option for families and those looking for old-fashioned mountain charm is ◖ **Paradise Lodge and Bungalows** (403/522-3595, www.paradiselodge.com, mid-May-early Oct., $215-345 s or d). This family-operated lodge provides excellent value in a wonderfully tranquil setting. Spread out around well-manicured gardens are 21 attractive cabins in four configurations. Each has a rustic, yet warm and inviting interior, with comfortable beds, a separate sitting area, and an en suite bathroom. Each cabin has a small fridge, microwave, and coffeemaker, while the larger ones have full kitchens and separate bedrooms. Instead of television, children are kept happy with a playground that includes a sandbox and jungle gym. On Wednesday and Sunday nights, a local naturalist presents an outdoor interpretive program for interested guests. The least-expensive cabins, complete with a classic cast-iron stove/fireplace combo, are $245 s or d, or pay $265 for a cabin with a big deck and soaring valley views. Twenty-four luxury suites, each with a fireplace, TV, one or two bedrooms, and fabulous mountain views, start at $290, or $325 with a kitchen. The Temple Suite, with all of the above as well as a large hot tub, is $345. To get there from the valley floor, follow Lake Louise Drive toward the Fairmont Chateau Lake Louise for three kilometers (1.9 miles); the lake itself is just one kilometer (0.6 mile) farther up the hill.

© ANDREW HEMPSTEAD

Baker Creek Mountain Resort is charming.

Over $250

Baker Creek Mountain Resort (403/522-3761, www.bakercreek.com, $265-365 s or d) lies along the Bow Valley Parkway 10 kilometers (6.2 miles) from Lake Louise back toward Banff. Each of the log chalets has a kitchenette, separate bedroom, fireplace, and outside deck (complete with cute wood carvings of bears climbing over the railings). The Trapper's Cabin is a huge space with a log bed, antler chandelier, wood-burning fireplace, double-jetted tub, and cooking facilities. A lodge wing has eight luxurious suites, each with richly accented log work, a deck, a microwave and fridge, and a deluxe bathroom. (Check the website for great off-season deals.) The restaurant here is highly recommended.

Originally called Lake Louise Ski Lodge, the **Post Hotel** (200 Pipestone Dr., 403/522-3989 or 800/661-1586, www.posthotel.com, $375-485 s or d) is one of only a handful of Canadian accommodations that have

been accepted into the prestigious Relaix & Châteaux organization. Bordered to the east and south by the Pipestone River, it may lack views of Lake Louise, but it is as elegant, in a modern, woodsy way, as the château. Each bungalow-style room is furnished with Canadian pine and has a balcony. Many rooms have whirlpools and fireplaces, while some have kitchens. Other facilities include the upscale Temple Mountain Spa, an indoor pool, a steam room, and a library. The hotel has 17 different room types, with 26 different rates depending on the view. Between the main lodge and the Pipestone River are four sought-after cabins, each with a wood-burning fireplace.

At the lake for which it's named, four kilometers (2.5 miles) from the valley floor, is super-luxurious **Moraine Lake Lodge** (403/522-3733 or 877/522-2777, www.morainelake.com, June-Sept., $399-595 s or d). Designed by renowned architect Arthur Erickson, the lodge is a bastion of understated charm, partially obscured from the masses of day-trippers who visit the lake and yet taking full advantage of its location beside one of the world's most-photographed lakes. The decor reflects the wilderness location, with an abundance of polished log work and solid, practical furnishings in heritage-themed rooms. The rooms have no TVs or phones; instead guests take guided nature walks, have unlimited use of canoes, and are pampered with complimentary afternoon tea.

The famously fabulous **Fairmont Chateau Lake Louise** (403/522-3511 or 800/257-7544, www.fairmont.com, from $459), a historic 500-room hotel on the shore of Lake Louise, has views equal to any mountain resort in the world. But all this historic charm and mountain scenery comes at a price. Rooms on the Fairmont Gold Floor come with a private concierge and upgraded everything for a little over $1,000. Official rates drop as low as $250 s or d outside of summer, with accommodation and ski pass packages often advertised for around

© ANDREW HEMPSTEAD

Post Hotel

$250 d. Children younger than 18 sharing with parents are free, but if you bring a pet, it'll be an extra $30.

Backcountry Accommodations

If you're prepared to lace up your hiking boots for a true mountain experience, consider spending time at **Skoki Lodge** (403/256-8473 or 800/258-7669, www.skoki.com, mid-June-late Sept. and mid-Dec.-mid-Apr., $275 pp), north of the Lake Louise ski resort and far from the nearest road. Getting there requires an 11-kilometer (6.8-mile) hike or ski, depending on the season. The lodge is an excellent base for exploring nearby valleys and mountains. It dates to 1931, when it operated as a lodge for local Banff skiers, and is now a National Historic Site. Today it comprises a main lodge, sleeping cabins, and a wood-fired sauna. Accommodations are rustic (propane heat but no electricity) but comfortable, with mostly twin beds in the main lodge and cabins

that sleep up to five. Rates include three meals daily, including a picnic lunch that guests build from a buffet-style layout before heading out hiking or skiing. The dining room and lounge center around a wood-burning fire, where guests come together each evening to swap tales from the trail and mingle with the convivial hosts.

Campgrounds

Exit the TransCanada Highway at the Lake Louise interchange, 56 kilometers (35 miles) northwest of Banff, and take the first left beyond Samson Mall and under the railway bridge to reach **Lake Louise Campground,** within easy walking distance of the village. The campground is divided into two sections by the Bow River but is linked by the Bow River Loop hiking trail that leads into the village along either side of the Bow River. Individual sites throughout are close together, but some privacy and shade are provided by towering lodgepole pines. Just under 200 serviced (powered) sites are grouped together at the end of the road. In addition to hookups, this section has showers and flush toilets; $38. Across the river are 216 unserviced sites, each with a fire ring and picnic table. Other amenities include kitchen shelters and a modern bathroom complex complete with hot showers. These sites cost $34 per night. A dump station is near the entrance to the campground ($8 per use). An interpretive program runs throughout the summer, nightly at 9pm (except Tuesday) in the outdoor theater. Sites can be booked in advance by contacting the **Parks Canada Campground Reservation Service** (877/737-3783, www.pccamping.ca). The many sites available on a first-come, first-served basis fill fast in July and August, so plan on arriving early in the afternoon to ensure a spot. The serviced section of this campground is open year-round, the unserviced section mid-May-September.

FOOD

Other guidebooks encourage readers to "eat at your hotel." Not only is this not helpful, it's misleading. The village of Lake Louise may exist only to serve travelers, but there are good dining options serving all budgets.

Casual

If you don't feel like a cooked breakfast, start your day off at **Laggan's Mountain Bakery** (Samson Mall, 403/552-2017, 6am-8pm daily, lunches $8-12), *the* place to hang out with a coffee and a freshly baked breakfast croissant, pastry, cake, or muffin. The chocolate brownie is delicious (order two slices to save having to line up twice). If the tables are full, order take-out and enjoy your feast on the riverbank behind the mall.

For a casual meal, head to **Bill Peyto's Cafe** in the Lake Louise Alpine Centre (Village Rd., 403/522-2200, 7am-9pm daily, $12-17), where

Bill Peyto's Café is a great value.

© ANDREW HEMPSTEAD

the food is consistent and well priced. A huge portion of nachos is $8, pasta is $12-14, and stir-fries range $12-15.

Across the TransCanada Highway, the **Lodge of the Ten Peaks,** at the base of the Lake Louise winter resort (403/522-3555), is open 7:30am-10:30am daily in summer for a large and varied breakfast buffet that costs a super-reasonable adult $15, child $10. An even better deal is to purchase a breakfast/gondola ride combo for adult $30, child $17 (the gondola ride alone is $28). The buffet lunch (11:30am-2:30pm) is $20, or $35 with the gondola ride.

European

In 1987, the **◖ Post Hotel** (200 Pipestone Dr., 403/522-3989 or 800/661-1586, www.posthotel.com) was expanded to include a luxurious new wing. The original log building was renovated as a rustic, timbered dining room (6:30pm-10pm daily, $31-44) linked to the rest of the hotel by an intimate lounge. Although the dining room isn't cheap, it's a favorite of locals and visitors alike. The chef specializes in European cuisine, preparing several Swiss dishes (such as veal zurichois) to make owner George Schwarz feel less homesick. But he's also renowned for his presentation of Alberta beef, Pacific salmon, and Peking duck. The 32,000-bottle cellar is one of the finest in Canada. Reservations are essential for dinner.

Canadian

One hundred years ago, visitors departing trains at Laggan Station were eager to get to the Chateau Lake Louise as quickly as possible to begin their adventure. Today guests from the château, other hotels, and even people from as far away as Banff are returning to dine in the **◖ Lake Louise Railway Station Restaurant** (200 Sentinel Rd., 403/522-2600, 11:30am-4pm and from 5pm daily, $18-36). Although the menu is not extensive, it puts an emphasis

on creating imaginative dishes with a combination of Canadian produce and Asian ingredients. Lighter lunches include a Caesar salad topped with roasted garlic dressing—perfect for those planning an afternoon hike. In the evening, expect entrées like a memorable pan-seared salmon smothered in basil pesto.

Also well worth the drive is **◖ Baker Creek Bistro** (Baker Creek Mountain Resort, 10 km/6.2 mi from Lake Louise on the Bow Valley Parkway, 403/522-3761, 7am-2pm and 5pm-9:30pm daily, $21-36). Dining is in a small room that characterizes the term "mountain hideaway," in an adjacent lounge bar, or out on a small deck decorated with pots of colorful flowers. The menu isn't large, but dishes feature lots of Canadian game and produce, with favorites like beer-braised bison short ribs and cedar-planked salmon. Also notable is the well-priced wine list.

Fairmont Chateau Lake Louise

Within this famous lakeside hotel is a choice of eateries and an ice-cream shop. For all château dining reservations, call 403/522-1818.

The **Poppy Brasserie** has obscured lake views and is the most casual place for a meal. Breakfasts (7am-10am daily), offered buffet-style ($28 per person), are a little expensive for light eaters. Lunch and dinner (11:30am-9pm daily, $24-38) are à la carte. The **Walliser Stube** (6pm-9pm daily, $31-46) is an elegant two-story wine bar decorated with rich wood paneling and solid oak furniture. It offers a simple menu of German dishes as well as a number of classic fondues. The **Lakeview Lounge** (noon-4pm daily, lunches $16-24) has floor-to-ceiling windows with magnificent lake views. Choose this dining area for lunch or afternoon tea (noon-3pm daily, reservations required, $37 per person, or $45 with a glass of champagne).

The **Fairview Dining Room** (6pm-9pm daily, $35-46) has a lot more than just a fair view. As the château's signature dining room, it enjoys the best views and offers the most elegant setting.

INFORMATION AND SERVICES

Information

Lake Louise Visitor Centre (403/522-3833, 8am-8pm daily mid-June-Aug., 8am-6pm daily mid-May-mid-June and Sept., 9am-4pm daily the rest of the year) is beside Samson Mall on Village Road. This excellent Parks Canada facility has interpretive exhibits, slide and video displays, and staff on hand to answer questions, recommend hikes suited to your ability, and issue camping passes to those heading out into the backcountry. Look for the stuffed (literally) female grizzly and read her fascinating, but sad, story.

Services

A small postal outlet in Samson Mall also serves as a bus depot and car rental agency. Although Lake Louise has no banks, there's a currency exchange in the Fairmont Chateau Lake Louise and a cash machine in the grocery store. The mall also holds a busy laundry (8am-8pm daily in summer, shorter hours the rest of the year). Camping supplies and bike rentals are available from **Wilson Mountain Sports** (403/522-3636).

The closest **hospital** is in Banff (403/762-2222). For the local **RCMP,** call 403/522-3811.

GETTING THERE

Calgary International Airport is the closest airport to Lake Louise. **Brewster** (403/762-6767 or 800/760-6934, www.brewster.ca) and

Banff Airporter (403/762-3330 or 888/449-2901, www.banffairporter.com) offer at least a couple of shuttles per day that continue beyond Banff to Lake Louise from the airport. All charge around the same: $70 each way, with a slight round-trip discount.

Greyhound (403/522-3870) leaves the Calgary bus depot (877 Greyhound Way SW) five times daily for Lake Louise. The fare is less than that charged by Brewster, and the Banff-Lake Louise portion only is around $15. From Vancouver, it's a 13-hour ride to Lake Louise aboard the Greyhound bus.

GETTING AROUND

Samson Mall is the commercial heart of Lake Louise village. If the parking lot out front is full, consider leaving your vehicle across the road behind the Esso gas station, where one area is set aside for large RVs. The campground, alpine center, and hotels are all within easy walking distance of Samson Mall. Fairmont Chateau Lake Louise is a 2.7-kilometer (1.7-mile) walk from the valley floor. The only car-rental agency in the village is **National** (403/522-3870). The agency doesn't have many vehicles; you'd be better off picking one up at Calgary International Airport. **Lake Louise Taxi & Tours** (Samson Mall, 403/522-2020) charges $4.25 for flag drop, then $2.25 per kilometer. From the mall to Fairmont Chateau Lake Louise runs around $20, to Moraine Lake $48, and to Banff $200. **Wilson Mountain Sports** (Samson Mall, 403/522-3636) has mountain bikes for rent from $15 per hour or $45 per day (includes a helmet, bike lock, and water bottle). They also rent camping, climbing, and fishing gear.

Icefields Parkway (Banff)

The 230-kilometer (143-mile) Icefields Parkway, between Lake Louise and Jasper, is one of the most scenic, exciting, and inspiring mountain roads ever built. From Lake Louise it parallels the Continental Divide, following in the shadow of the highest, most rugged mountains in the Canadian Rockies. The first 122 kilometers (76 miles) to Sunwapta Pass (the boundary between Banff and Jasper National Parks) can be driven in two hours, and the entire parkway in four hours. But it's likely you'll want to spend at least a day, probably more, stopping at each of the 13 viewpoints, hiking the trails, watching the abundant wildlife, and just generally enjoying one of the world's most magnificent landscapes. Along the section within Banff National Park are two lodges, three hostels, three campgrounds, and one gas station.

Although the road is steep and winding in places, it has a wide shoulder, making it ideal for an extended bike trip. Allow seven days to pedal north from Banff to Jasper, staying at hostels or camping along the route. This is the preferable direction to travel by bike because the elevation at the town of Jasper is more than 500 meters (1,640 feet) lower than either Banff or Lake Louise.

The parkway remains open year-round, although winter brings with it some special considerations. The road is often closed for short periods for avalanche control. Check road conditions in Banff or Lake Louise before setting out. And be sure to fill up with gas; no services are available between November and April.

SIGHTS AND DRIVES
Lake Louise to Crowfoot Glacier
The Icefields Parkway forks right from the TransCanada Highway just north of Lake Louise. The impressive scenery begins

immediately. Just three kilometers (1.9 miles) from the junction is **Herbert Lake,** formed during the last ice age when retreating glaciers deposited a pile of rubble, known as a **moraine,** across a shallow valley and water filled in behind it. The lake is a perfect place for early-morning or early-evening photography, when the Waputik Range and distinctively shaped **Mount Temple** are reflected in its waters.

Traveling north, you'll notice numerous depressions in the steep, shaded slopes of the Waputik Range across the Bow Valley. The cooler climate on these north-facing slopes makes them prone to glaciation. Cirques were cut by small local glaciers. On the opposite side of the road, **Mount Hector** (3,394 meters/11,130 feet), easily recognized by its layered peak, soon comes into view.

Hector Lake Viewpoint is 16 kilometers (10 miles) from the junction. Although the view is partially obscured by trees, the emerald-green waters nestled below a massive wall of limestone form a breathtaking scene. **Bow Peak,** seen looking northward along the highway, is only 2,868 meters (9,410 feet) high but is completely detached from the Waputik Range, making it a popular destination for climbers. As you leave this viewpoint, look across the northeast end of Hector Lake for glimpses of **Mount Balfour** (3,246 meters/10,650 feet) on the distant skyline.

Crowfoot Glacier
The aptly named Crowfoot Glacier can best be appreciated from a viewpoint 17 kilometers (10.6 miles) north of Hector Lake. The glacier sits on a wide ledge near the top of Crowfoot Mountain, from where its glacial claws cling to the mountain's steep slopes. The retreat of this glacier has been dramatic. Only 50 years ago, two of the claws extended to the base of

the lower cliff. Today they are a shadow of their former selves, barely reaching over the cliff edge.

Bow Lake

The sparkling, translucent waters of Bow Lake are among the most beautiful that can be seen from the Icefields Parkway. The lake was created when moraines deposited by retreating glaciers dammed subsequent meltwater. On still days, the water reflects the snowy peaks, their sheer cliffs, and the scree slopes that run into the lake. You don't need photography experience to take good pictures here! At the southeast end of the lake, a day-use area offers waterfront picnic tables and a trail to a swampy area at the lake's outlet. At the upper end of the lake, you'll find the historic Num-ti-jah Lodge and the trailhead for a walk to Bow Glacier Falls.

The road leaves Bow Lake and climbs to **Bow Summit.** As you look back toward the lake, its true color becomes apparent, and the Crowfoot Glacier reveals its unique shape. At an elevation of 2,069 meters (6,790 feet), this pass is one of the highest points crossed by a public road in Canada. It is also the beginning of the Bow River, the one you camped beside at Lake Louise, photographed flowing through the town of Banff, and fished along downstream of Canmore.

◖ Peyto Lake

From the parking lot at Bow Summit, a short paved trail leads to one of the most breathtaking views you could ever imagine. Far below the viewpoint is Peyto Lake, an impossibly intense green lake whose hues change according to season. Before heavy melting of nearby glaciers begins (in June or early July), the lake is dark blue. As summer progresses, meltwater flows across a delta and into the lake. This water is laden with finely ground particles of rock debris known as rock flour, which

remains suspended in the water. It is not the mineral content of the rock flour that is responsible for the lake's unique color, but rather the particles reflecting the blue-green sector of the light spectrum. As the amount of suspended rock flour changes, so does the color of the lake.

The lake is one of many park landmarks named for early outfitter Bill Peyto. In 1898, Peyto was part of an expedition camped at Bow Lake. Seeking solitude (as he was wont to do), he slipped off during the night to sleep near this lake. Other members of the party coined the name Peyto's Lake, and it stuck.

A farther three kilometers (1.9 miles) along the parkway is a viewpoint from which **Peyto Glacier** is visible at the far end of Peyto Lake Valley. This glacier is part of the extensive **Wapta Icefield,** which straddles the Continental Divide and extends into the northern reaches of Yoho National Park in British Columbia.

Beside the Continental Divide

From Bow Summit, the parkway descends to a viewpoint directly across the Mistaya River from **Mount Patterson** (3,197 meters/10,490 feet). Snowbird Glacier clings precariously to the mountain's steep northeast face, and the mountain's lower, wooded slopes are heavily scarred where rock and ice slides have swept down the mountainside.

As the parkway continues to descend and crosses Silverhorn Creek, the jagged limestone peaks of the Continental Divide can be seen to the west. **Mistaya Lake** is a three-kilometer-long (1.9-mile-long) body of water that sits at the bottom of the valley between the road and the divide, but it can't be seen from the parkway. The best place to view it is from the Howse Peak Viewpoint at Upper Waterfowl Lake. From here the high ridge that forms the Continental Divide is easily distinguishable. Seven peaks can be seen from here, including

© ANDREW HEMPSTEAD

Walk down to the shoreline for a close-up view of Peyto Lake.

Howse Peak (3,290 meters/10,790 feet). At no point along this ridge does the elevation drop below 2,750 meters (9,000 feet). From Howse Peak, the Continental Divide makes a 90-degree turn to the west. One dominant peak that can be seen from Bow Pass to north of Saskatchewan River Crossing is **Mount Chephren** (3,268 meters/10,720 feet). Its distinctive shape and position away from the main ridge of the Continental Divide make it easy to distinguish. (Look for it directly north of Howse Peak.)

To Saskatchewan River Crossing

Numerous trails lead around the swampy shores of **Upper** and **Lower Waterfowl Lakes,** providing one of the park's best opportunities to view moose, who feed on the abundant aquatic vegetation that grows in Upper Waterfowl Lake. Rock and other debris that have been carried down nearby valley systems have built up, forming a wide alluvial fan,

nearly blocking the Mistaya River and creating Upper Waterfowl Lake.

Continuing north is **Mount Murchison** (3,337 meters/10,950 feet), on the east side of the parkway. Although not one of the park's highest mountains, this gray and yellow massif of Cambrian rock comprises 10 individual peaks, covering an area of 3,000 hectares (7,400 acres).

From a parking lot 14 kilometers (8.9 miles) northeast of Waterfowl Lake Campground, a short trail descends into the montane forest to **Mistaya Canyon.** Here the effects of erosion can be appreciated as the Mistaya River leaves the floor of Mistaya Valley, plunging through a narrow-walled canyon into the North Saskatchewan Valley. The area is scarred with potholes where boulders have been whirled around by the action of fast-flowing water, carving deep depressions into the softer limestone bedrock below.

The **North Saskatchewan River** posed

a major problem for early travelers and later for the builders of the Icefields Parkway. This swiftly running river eventually drains into Hudson Bay. In 1989 it was named a Canadian Heritage River. One kilometer (0.6 mile) past the bridge you'll come to a panoramic viewpoint of the entire valley. From here the Howse and Mistaya Rivers can be seen converging with the North Saskatchewan at a silt-laden delta. This is also a junction with Highway 11 (also known as David Thompson Highway), which follows the North Saskatchewan River to Rocky Mountain House and Red Deer. From this viewpoint, numerous peaks can be seen to the west. Two sharp peaks are distinctive: **Mount Outram** (3,254 meters/10,680 feet) is the closer; the farther is **Mount Forbes** (3,630 meters/11,975 feet), the highest peak in Banff National Park (and the sixth highest in the Canadian Rockies).

To Sunwapta Pass

On the north side of the North Saskatchewan River is the towering hulk of **Mount Wilson** (3,261 meters/10,700 feet), named for Banff outfitter Tom Wilson. The Icefields Parkway passes this massif on its western flanks. A pullout just past Rampart Creek Campground offers good views of Mount Amery to the west and Mounts Sarbach, Chephren, and Murchison to the south. Beyond here is the **Weeping Wall,** a long cliff of gray limestone where a series of waterfalls tumbles more than 100 meters (330 feet) down the steep slopes of Cirrus Mountain. In winter this wall of water freezes, becoming a mecca for ice climbers.

After ascending quickly, the road drops again before beginning a long climb to Sunwapta Pass. Halfway up the 360-verticalmeter (1,180-vertical-foot) climb is a viewpoint well worth a stop (cyclists will definitely appreciate a rest). From here views extend down the valley to the slopes of Mount Saskatchewan

and, on the other side of the parkway, Cirrus Mountain. Another viewpoint, farther up the road, has the added attraction of a view of Panther Falls across the valley. A cairn at **Sunwapta Pass** (2,023 meters/6,640 feet) marks the boundary between Banff and Jasper National Parks. It also marks the divide between the North Saskatchewan and Sunwapta Rivers, whose waters drain into the Atlantic and Arctic Oceans, respectively.

HIKING
Helen Lake

- Length: 6 kilometers/3.7 miles (2.5 hours) one-way
- Elevation gain: 455 meters/1,500 feet
- Rating: moderate
- Trailhead: across the Icefields Parkway from Crowfoot Glacier Lookout, 33 kilometers (20 miles) northwest from the junction with the TransCanada Highway

The trail to Helen Lake is one of the easiest ways to access a true alpine environment from the southern end of the Icefields Parkway. The trail climbs steadily through a forest of Engelmann spruce and subalpine fir for the first 2.5 kilometers (1.6 miles) to an avalanche slope, reaching the tree line and the first good viewpoint after three kilometers (1.9 miles). The view across the valley is spectacular, with Crowfoot Glacier visible to the southwest. As the trail reaches a ridge, it turns and descends into the glacial cirque where Helen Lake lies. Listen and look for hoary marmots around the scree slopes along the lakeshore.

For those with the time and energy, it's possible to continue an additional three kilometers (1.9 miles) to Dolomite Pass; the trail switchbacks steeply up a further 100 vertical meters (330 vertical feet) in less than one kilometer (0.6 mile), then descends steeply for a further one kilometer (0.6 mile) to Katherine Lake and beyond to the pass.

Bow Glacier Falls

- Length: 3.4 kilometers/2.1 miles (1 hour) one-way
- Elevation gain: 130 meters/430 feet
- Rating: easy
- Trailhead: Num-ti-jah Lodge, Bow Lake, 36 kilometers (22.3 miles) northwest from the TransCanada Highway

This hike skirts one of the most beautiful lakes in the Canadian Rockies before ending at a narrow but spectacular waterfall. From the parking lot in front of Num-ti-jah Lodge, follow the shore through Willow Flats to a gravel outwash area at the end of the lake. Across the lake are reflected views of Crowfoot Mountain and, farther west, a glimpse of Bow Glacier among the jagged peaks of the Waputik Range. The trail then begins a short but steep climb up the rim of a canyon before leveling out at the edge of a vast moraine of gravel, scree, and boulders. This is the end of the trail, although it's possible to reach the base of Bow Glacier Falls by picking your way through the 800 meters (0.5 mile) of rough ground that remains.

Peyto Lake

- Length: 1.4 kilometers/0.9 mile (30 minutes) one-way
- Elevation loss: 100 meters/330 feet
- Rating: easy
- Trailhead: unmarked pullout, Icefields Parkway, 2.4 kilometers (1.5 miles) north of Bow Summit

Without a doubt, the best place to view Peyto Lake is from a popular viewpoint accessible via a short trail from Bow Summit, 41 kilometers (25.5 miles) along the Icefields Parkway from the TransCanada Highway. The easiest way to access the actual shoreline, though, is along this short trail farther along the highway. A pebbled beach, strewn with driftwood, is the perfect setting for picnicking, painting, or just

admiring the lake's quieter side. Back at the lake lookout, a rough trail drops nearly 300 meters (980 feet) in 2.4 kilometers (1.5 miles) to the lake.

Chephren Lake

- Length: 4 kilometers/2.5 miles (60-90 minutes) one-way
- Elevation gain: 100 meters/330 feet
- Rating: easy
- Trailhead: Waterfowl Lake Campground, Icefields Parkway, 57 kilometers (35 miles) northwest from the TransCanada Highway

This pale-green body of water (pronounced Kef-ren) is hidden from the Icefields Parkway but easily reached. The official trailhead is a bridge across the Mistaya River at the back of Waterfowl Lakes Campground (behind site 86). If you're not registered at the campground, park at the end of the unpaved road running along the front of the campground and walk 300 meters (0.2 mile) down the well-worn path to the river crossing. From across the river, the trail dives headlong into a subalpine forest, reaching a crudely signposted junction after 1.6 kilometers (one mile). Take the right fork. This leads 2.4 kilometers (1.5 miles) to Chephren Lake, descending steeply at the end (this stretch of trail is often muddy). The lake is nestled under the buttresses of Mount Chephren. To the left, farther up the lake, is Howse Peak.

The trail to smaller **Cirque Lake** (4.5 km/2.8 mi from the trailhead) branches left 1.6 kilometers (one mile) along this trail. It is less heavily used, but this lake is popular with anglers for its healthy population of rainbow trout.

Glacier Lake

- Length: 9 kilometers/5.6 miles (2.5-3 hours) one-way
- Elevation gain: 220 meters/770 feet

• Rating: moderate

• Trailhead: an old gravel pit on the west side of the highway, 1 kilometer (0.6 mile) west of Saskatchewan River Crossing

This three-kilometer-long (1.9-mile-long) lake is one of the park's largest lakes not accessible by road. Although not as scenic as the more accessible lakes along the parkway, it's a pleasant destination for a full-day or overnight trip. For the first one kilometer (0.6 mile), the trail passes through an open forest of lodgepole pine to a fancy footbridge across the rushing North Saskatchewan River. From there it climbs gradually to a viewpoint overlooking the Howse River and the valley beyond, then turns away from the river for a long slog through dense forest to Glacier Lake. A primitive campground lies just over 300 meters (0.2 mile) from where the trail emerges at the lake.

Saskatchewan Glacier

• Length: 7.3 kilometers/4.5 miles (2 hours) one-way

• Elevation gain: 150 meters/490 feet

• Rating: moderate

• Trailhead: small parking lot, 35 kilometers (22 miles) northwest of the Saskatchewan River Crossing (just before the highway begins its "Big Bend" up to Sunwapta Pass)

The Saskatchewan Glacier, a tongue of ice from the great Columbia Icefield, is visible from various points along the Icefields Parkway. This hike will take you right to the toe of the glacier. After crossing an old concrete bridge, the trail disappears into the forest to the right, joining an overgrown road and continuing up the valley along the south bank of the river. When the toe of the glacier first comes into sight it looks deceptively close, but it's still a long hike away over rough terrain.

Nigel Pass

• Length: 7.4 kilometers/4.6 miles (2.5 hours) one-way

• Elevation gain: 365 meters/1,200 feet

• Rating: moderate

• Trailhead: Icefields Parkway, 2.5 kilometers (1.6 miles) north of the switchback on the "Big Bend"

Park on the east side of the highway and follow the gravel road to a locked gate. Turn right here and cross Nigel Creek on the bridge. The trail is obvious, following open avalanche paths up the east side of the valley. In a stand of Engelmann spruce and subalpine fir two kilometers (1.2 miles) from the trailhead is an old campsite used first by native hunting parties, then by mountaineers exploring the area around Columbia Icefield. Look for carvings on trees recording these early visitors. From here the trail continues to climb steadily, only increasing in gradient for the last one kilometer (0.6 mile) to the pass. The pass (2,195 meters/7,200 feet) marks the boundary between Banff and Jasper National Parks. For the best view, scramble over the rocks to the left. To the north, the view extends down the Brazeau River Valley, surrounded by a mass of peaks. To the west (left) is Nigel Peak (3,211 meters/10,535 feet), and to the southwest are views of Parker's Ridge and the glaciated peaks of Mount Athabasca.

Parker's Ridge

• Length: 2.4 kilometers/1.5 miles (1 hour) one-way

• Elevation gain: 210 meters/690 feet

• Rating: easy/moderate

• Trailhead: Icefields Parkway, 4 kilometers (2.5 miles) south of Sunwapta Pass

From the trailhead on the west side of the highway, this wide path gains elevation quickly through open meadows and scattered stands of subalpine fir. This fragile environment is easily destroyed, so it's important that you stay on the trail. During the short alpine summer, these meadows are carpeted with red heather, white mountain avens, and blue alpine forget-me-nots. From the summit of the ridge, you look down on the two-kilometer-wide (1.2-mile-wide) Saskatchewan Glacier spreading out below. Beyond is Castleguard Mountain, renowned for its extensive cave system.

ACCOMMODATIONS AND CAMPING

Under $50

North of Lake Louise, four hostels are spread along the Icefields Parkway, two in Banff National Park and two in Jasper National Park. Facilities at all four are limited, and beds should be reserved as far in advance as possible. For reservations, call 778/328-2220 or 866/762-4122, or book online (www.hihostels.ca). The first, 24 kilometers (15 miles) from Lake Louise, is **HI-Mosquito Creek,** which is near good hiking and offers accommodations for 32 in four- and six-bed cabins. Facilities include a kitchen, wood-heated sauna, and a large common room with fireplace. Although the hostel has no showers, guests are permitted to use those at the nearby Lake Louise Alpine Centre. Rates are $24 per night for members of Hostelling International (nonmembers $28). Check-in is 5pm-10pm, and it's open June-March.

HI-Rampart Creek, a further 64 kilometers (40 miles) along the parkway, is nestled below the snowcapped peak of Mount Wilson, with views across the North Saskatchewan River to even higher peaks along the Continental Divide. Like Mosquito Creek, it's near good hiking and has a kitchen and sauna. Its four cabins have a total of 24 bunk beds. Members pay $24 per night (nonmembers $28). It's open nightly May-March. Check-in is 5pm-10pm.

$50-150

The Crossing Resort (403/761-7000, www. thecrossingresort.com, April-Nov., $149-219 s or d) is a large complex 87 kilometers (54 miles) north of Lake Louise and 45 kilometers (28 miles) south of the Columbia Icefield. It's also at the junction of Highway 11, which spurs east along Abraham Lake to Rocky Mountain House and Red Deer. The rooms offer a good combination of size and value but lack the historic charm of those at Num-ti-jah Lodge to the south and the views enjoyed by those at the Columbia Icefield Centre to the north. Each of 66 units has a phone and television. All rates are heavily discounted outside of June-September. In addition to overnight rooms, The Crossing has the only gas between Lake Louise and Jasper, a self-serve cafeteria, a restaurant, a pub, and a supersized gift shop.

Over $150

Pioneer guide and outfitter Jimmy Simpson built 🄲 **Simpson's Num-ti-jah Lodge** (403/522-2167, www.sntj.ca, from $320 s or d), on the north shore of Bow Lake, 40 kilometers (25 miles) north of Lake Louise, as a base for his outfitting operation in 1920. In those days, the route north from Lake Louise was nothing more than a horse trail. The desire to build a large structure when only short timbers were available led to the unusual octagonal shape of the main lodge. Simpson remained at Bow Lake, a living legend, until his death in 1972 at the age of 95. With a rustic mountain ambience that has changed little since Simpson's passing, Num-ti-jah provides a memorable overnight stay. Just don't expect the conveniences of a regular motel. Under the distinctively red, steep-pitched roof of the main lodge are 25 rooms, some that share bathrooms, and there's not a TV or phone in sight. Downstairs, guests soak up the warmth of a roaring log fire while mingling in a comfortable library filled with historic mountain literature. A dining room lined with historic memorabilia is open for breakfast and dinner daily ($18-35).

© ANDREW HEMPSTEAD

Simpson's Num-ti-jah Lodge

Campgrounds

Beyond Lake Louise, the first available camping along the Icefields Parkway is at **Mosquito Creek Campground** (year-round, $21 per site), 24 kilometers (15 miles) from the TransCanada Highway. Don't be perturbed by the name, though; the bugs here are no worse than anywhere else. The 32 sites are nestled in the forest, with a tumbling creek separating the campground from a hostel of the same name. Each site has a picnic table and fire ring, while other amenities include pump water, pit toilets, and a kitchen shelter with an old-fashioned woodstove. If you're camping at Mosquito Creek and want a break from the usual camp fare, consider traveling 17 kilometers (10.6 miles) up the highway to the convivial dining room at Num-ti-jah Lodge (403/522-2167, www.sntj.ca) to feast on Canadian-inspired cuisine in a historic dining room.

Waterfowl Lake Campground (late June-mid-Sept., $27 per site) is 33 kilometers (20 miles) north along the Icefields Parkway from Mosquito Creek. It features 116 sites between Upper and Lower Waterfowl Lakes, with a few sites in view of the lower lake. Facilities include pump water, flush toilets, and kitchen shelters with wood-burning stoves. Rise early to watch the first rays of sun hit Mount Chephren from the shoreline of the lower lake, then plan on hiking the four-kilometer (2.5-mile) trail to Chephren Lake—you'll be first on the trail and back in time for a late breakfast.

Continuing toward Jasper, the Icefields Parkway passes The Crossing, a good place to gas up and buy last-minute groceries before reaching **Rampart Creek Campground** (late June-early Sept., $23 per site), 31 kilometers (19 miles) beyond Waterfowl Lake and 88 kilometers (55 miles) from Lake Louise. With just 50 sites, this campground fills early. Facilities include kitchen shelters, pit toilets, and pump water.

Nearby Parks

◖ MOUNT ASSINIBOINE PROVINCIAL PARK

Named for one of the Canadian Rockies' most spectacular peaks, this 39,050-hectare (96,500-acre), roughly triangular park lies northeast of Radium Hot Springs, sandwiched between Kootenay National Park to the west and Banff National Park to the east. It's inaccessible by road; access is on foot or by helicopter. A haven for experienced hikers, the park offers alpine meadows, lakes, glaciers, and many peaks higher than 3,050 meters (10,000 feet) to explore. The park's highest peak, 3,618-meter (11,870-foot) Mount Assiniboine (seventh highest in the Canadian Rockies), is known as the Matterhorn of the Rockies for its resemblance to that famous Swiss landmark. The striking peak can be seen from many points well outside the boundaries of the park, including Buller Pond in Kananaskis Country and the Sunshine Village winter resort in Banff National Park.

The peak is named for the Assiniboine people, who ventured into this section of the Canadian Rockies many thousands of years before European exploration. The name Assiniboine means "stone boilers," a reference to their preferred cooking method. The mountain was sighted and named by a geological survey team in 1885, but the first ascent wasn't made until 1901.

Lake Magog is the destination of most park visitors. Here you'll find the park's only facilities and the trailheads for several interesting and varied day hikes. One of the most popular walks is along the Sunburst Valley/Nub Ridge Trail. From Lake Magog, small Sunburst Lake is reached in about 20 minutes, then the trail continues northwest a short distance to Cerulean Lake. From this lake's outlet, the trail descends slowly along the Mitchell River

to a junction four kilometers (2.5 miles) from Lake Magog. Take the right fork, which climbs through a dense subalpine forest to Elizabeth Lake, nestled in the southern shadow of Nub Peak. From this point, instead of descending back to Cerulean Lake, plan on taking the Nub Ridge Trail, which climbs steadily for one kilometer (0.6 mile) to a magnificent viewpoint high above Lake Magog. From the viewpoint, it's just less than four kilometers (2.5 miles), downhill all the way, to the valley floor. The total length of this outing is 11 kilometers (6.8 miles), and as elevation gained is only just over 400 meters (1,310 feet), the trail can comfortably be completed in four hours.

Approaching the Park on Foot

Three trails provide access to **Lake Magog,** the park's largest body of water. The most popular comes in from the northeast, starting at the Sunshine Village winter resort in Banff National Park and leading 29 kilometers (18 miles) via Citadel Pass to the lake. Not only is this trail spectacular, but the high elevation of the trailhead (2,100 meters/6,890 feet) makes for a relatively easy approach. Another approach is from the east, in Spray Valley Provincial Park (Kananaskis Country). The trailhead is at the southern end of Spray Lake; take the Mount Shark staging area turnoff 40 kilometers (25 miles) south of Canmore. By the time the trail has climbed the Bryant Creek drainage to 2,165-meter (7,100-foot) Assiniboine Pass, all elevation gain (450 meters/1,480 feet) has been made. At 27 kilometers (16.8 miles), this is the shortest approach, but its elevation gain is greater than the other two trails. The longest and least-used access is from Highway 93 at Simpson River in Kootenay National Park. This trail climbs the Simpson River and Surprise Creek drainages and crosses 2,270-meter (7,450-foot) Ferro Pass to the lake for a total length of 32 kilometers (20 miles).

The Easy Way In

If these long approaches put visiting the park out of your reach, there's one more option: You can fly in by helicopter from the Mount Shark Heliport, at the southern end of Spray Valley Provincial Park, 40 kilometers (25 miles) southwest of Canmore. Flights depart at 12:30pm Wednesday, Friday, and Sunday and cost $160 per person each way, including an 18-kilogram (40-pound) per-person baggage limit. Although **Alpine Helicopters** operates the flights, all bookings must be made through Mount Assiniboine Lodge (call 403/678 2883 8:30am-2:30pm Mon.-Fri., www.assiniboinelodge.com).

If you're planning on hiking into the park, Alpine Helicopters will fly your gear in for $2.25 per pound (0.45 kilogram). This same company, which also operates from a base in Canmore, charges $285 per person for a 30-minute flightseeing trip over the park. For more information, contact Alpine Helicopters (403/678-4802, www.alpinehelicopter.com).

Accommodations

Getting to and staying at **C Mount Assiniboine Lodge** isn't cheap, but the number of repeat guests is testament to an experience that you will never forget. The mountain scenery may take most of the kudos, but the lodge's congenial atmosphere makes the stay equally memorable. Built in 1928 by the CPR, the delightfully rustic lodge is set in a lakeside meadow below its distinctive namesake peak. The main building holds six double rooms that share bathroom facilities and a dining area where hearty meals (included in the rates) are served up communal-style. Scattered in the surrounding trees are six one-room cabins that sleep 2-5 people. Each has

running water and uses propane to heat and light the space. Outhouses and showers are shared. The rate for lodge rooms is $260 per person, while cabin accommodations range $260-420. Children 12 and under are $120. You can reach the lodge on foot or fly in with Alpine Helicopters from a heliport in Spray Valley Provincial Park. The departure days are the same as for campers (Wednesday, Friday, and Sunday); the only difference is that lodge guests pay a little less ($130 each way) and helicopter departures begin at 11:30am Lodge guests flying in may bring 18 kilograms (40 pounds) of gear, plus one pair of skis. If you decide to hike in (or out), the charge for luggage transfers is $2.25 per pound (0.45 kilogram).

The operating season is mid-June to the first weekend of October, and then mid-February to mid-April, for cross-country skiing. There is a minimum stay of two nights. The lodge has no landline phone; for reservations or information call 403/678-2883 (8:30am-2:30pm Mon.-Fri.) or check the website (www.assiniboinelodge.com).

Campgrounds

Lake Magog is the park's main facility area, such as it is. A designated camping area on a low ridge above the lake's west shore provides a source of drinking water, pit toilets, and bear-proof food caches. Open fires are prohibited. Sites are $10 per person per night. No reservations are taken, but even those who visit frequently have told me they've never seen it full. Also at the lake are the **Naiset Huts,** where bunk beds cost $25 per person per night (book through Mount Assiniboine Lodge at 403/678-2883, 8:30am-2:30pm Mon.-Fri., www.assiniboinelodge.com). The cabins contain nothing more than bunk beds with mattresses, so you'll need a stove, cooking utensils, food, a sleeping bag, and your own source of non-gas-powered light.

Information

In addition to the government agency responsible for the park (Ministry of Environment, www.env.gov.bc.ca/bcparks), park information centers in Radium Hot Springs, Lake Louise, and Banff provide information and up-to-date trail conditions.

SIFFLEUR WILDERNESS AREA

This remote region on the Alberta side of the Canadian Rockies lies south of Highway 11, which crosses west-central Alberta between Rocky Mountain House and Saskatchewan River Crossing, in Banff National Park. It is completely protected from any activities that could have an impact on the area's fragile ecosystems. That includes road and trail development: No bridges have been built over the area's many fast-flowing streams, and the few old trails that do exist are not maintained. Elk, deer, moose, cougars, wolverines, wolves, coyotes, black bears, and grizzly bears roam the area's four main valleys, while higher, alpine elevations harbor mountain goats and bighorn sheep.

The main trail into the 41,200-hectare (101,800-acre) wilderness begins from a parking area two kilometers (1.2 miles) south of the Two O'Clock Creek Campground at Kootenay Plains. The area's northeastern boundary is a seven-kilometer (4.3-mile) hike from here. Even if you're not heading right into the wilderness area, the first section of this trail, which passes through Siffleur Falls Provincial Recreation Area to **Siffleur Falls,** is worth walking. The trail crosses the North Saskatchewan River via a swinging bridge, then at the two-kilometer (1.2-mile) mark crosses the Siffleur River, reaching the falls after four kilometers (2.5 miles); allow 70 minutes one-way. These are the official Siffleur Falls, but others lie farther upstream at the 6.2-kilometer (3.9-mile) and 6.9-kilometer (4.3-mile) marks.

Once inside the wilderness area, the trail climbs steadily alongside the Siffleur River and into the heart of the wilderness. Ambitious hikers can continue through to the Dolomite Creek area of Banff National Park, finishing at the Icefields Parkway, seven kilometers (4.3 miles) south of Bow Summit. Total length of this trail is 68 kilometers (42 miles), a strenuous five-day backcountry expedition. Another access point for the area is opposite Waterfowl Lake Campground in Banff National Park. From here it is six kilometers (3.7 miles) up Noyes Creek to the wilderness area boundary; the trail peters out after 4.5 kilometers (2.8 miles) and requires some serious scrambling before descending into Siffleur. This trail—as with all others in the wilderness area—is for experienced hikers only.

Campground

Two O'Clock Creek Campground (May-mid-Oct., $17) lies two kilometers (1.2 miles) from the park's main trailhead in Kootenay Plains Provincial Recreation Area. It is a primitive facility with a picnic shelter, firewood, and drinking water; the 24 sites each have a picnic table and fire pit (firewood $4).

WHITE GOAT WILDERNESS AREA

White Goat comprises 44,500 hectares (110,000 acres) of high mountain ranges, wide valleys, hanging glaciers, waterfalls, and high alpine lakes. It lies north and west of Highway 11, abutting the north end of Banff National Park and the south end of Jasper National Park. The area's vegetation zones are easily recognizable: subalpine forests of Engelmann spruce, subalpine fir, and lodgepole pine; alpine tundra higher up. Large mammals here include a sizable population of bighorn sheep, as well as mountain goats, deer, elk, woodland caribou, moose, cougars, wolves, coyotes, black bears, and grizzly bears.

The most popular hike is the **McDonald Creek Trail,** which first follows the Cline River, then McDonald Creek to the creek's source in the heart of the wilderness area. McDonald Creek is approximately 12 kilometers (7.5 miles) from the parking area on Highway 11, but a full day should be allowed for this section because the trail crosses many streams. From where McDonald Creek flows into the Cline River, it is 19 kilometers (11.8 miles) to the McDonald Lakes, but allow another two full days; the total elevation gain for the hike is a challenging 1,222 meters (4,000 feet). Other hiking possibilities include following the Cline River to its source and crossing Sunset Pass into Banff National Park, 17 kilometers (10.6 miles) north of Saskatchewan River Crossing, or heading up Cataract Creek and linking up with the trails in the Brazeau River area of Jasper National Park.

CANMORE

The town of Canmore lies in the Bow Valley, 103 kilometers (64 miles) west of Calgary, 28 kilometers (17 miles) southeast of Banff, and on the northern edge of Kananaskis Country. Long perceived as a gateway to the mountain national parks, the town is very much a destination in itself these days. Its ideal mountain location and the freedom it enjoys from the strict development restrictions that apply in the nearby parks have made Canmore the fastest-growing town in Canada, with the population having tripled since 1979. The permanent population is 12,500 and there are 5,800 nonpermanent residents (folks who own a home in town but whose permanent address is elsewhere).

The surrounding mountains provide Canmore's best recreation opportunities. Hiking is excellent on trails that lace the valley and mountainside slopes, with many high viewpoints easily reached. Flowing though town, the Bow River offers great fishing, kayaking, and rafting; golfers flock to three scenic courses; and nearby Mount Yamnuska has become the most developed rock-climbing site in the Canadian Rockies. Canmore also hosted the Nordic events of the 1988 Winter Olympic Games and is the home of the Alpine Club of Canada.

PLANNING YOUR TIME

You can include Canmore in your itinerary in a variety of ways. The most obvious one is to make the town a base for your Canadian

HIGHLIGHTS

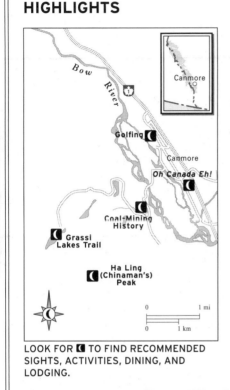

(Coal-Mining History: Explore Canmore's coal-mining history by walking through the residential area west of downtown. Continue up Canmore Creek, past sealed mine entrances, for the full effect (page 116).

(Grassi Lakes Trail: A short walk is required to reach these two lakes, which are natural highlights of the Canmore region (page 117).

(Ha Ling (Chinaman's) Peak: Feeling fit? Follow the trail to this summit for valley views that are unsurpassed (page 117).

(Golfing: The town's three golf courses all offer something a little bit different, but they do have one thing in common—spectacular mountain scenery (page 121).

(Oh Canada Eh!: Slightly tacky, but good fun nevertheless, this dinner theater production at the Cornerstone Theatre brings Canada's best-known symbols to life (page 123).

LOOK FOR **(** TO FIND RECOMMENDED SIGHTS, ACTIVITIES, DINING, AND LODGING.

Rockies vacation. The advantages are less-crowded streets, better-priced accommodations, a choice of family-friendly lodgings, and a central location (Banff is a 15-minute drive to the west and Kananaskis Country is a 40-minute drive southeast). Campers should keep in mind that there are much nicer campgrounds elsewhere in the region. If you decide to stay in Banff instead, there's no reason to relocate to Canmore for a night or two—simply visit the town as part of a day trip (or two).

Regardless of whether or not you stay in Canmore, there's plenty to do in the town itself for one day. Plan on two or more if you enjoy being outdoors. A two-day stay might

include a morning tee time at **Silvertip Golf Resort** or a horseback ride at **Cross Zee Ranch.** After lunch at **Crazyweed Kitchen,** spend the afternoon exploring the main street, the museum, and the historic buildings west of town. The next morning, lace up your hiking boots for the walk to **Grassi Lakes.** Golfers will probably want to squeeze in another round of golf, this time at **Stewart Creek Golf Course,** but there are plenty of other choices—fishing on the Bow River, a rock-climbing lesson, or a helicopter flight-seeing trip. Your two evenings could be spent at *Oh Canada Eh!* at the Cornerstone Theatre and the **Sage Bistro.**

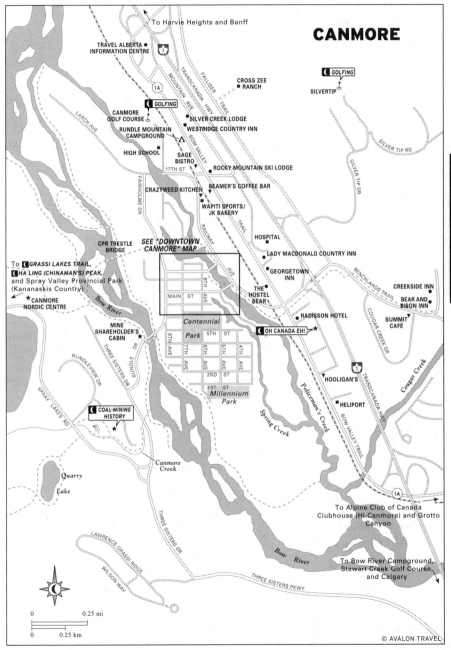

CANMORE

To Harvie Heights and Banff

TRAVEL ALBERTA ■
INFORMATION CENTRE

CROSS ZEE
■ RANCH

☾ GOLFING

SILVERTIP

☾ GOLFING

CANMORE
GOLF COURSE
SILVER CREEK LODGE
RUNDLE MOUNTAIN   WESTRIDGE COUNTRY INN
CAMPGROUND

HIGH SCHOOL   SAGE
BISTRO
17TH ST
ROCKY MOUNTAIN SKI LODGE

CRAZYWEED KITCHEN   BEAMER'S COFFEE BAR

WAPITI SPORTS/
JK BAKERY

HOSPITAL

CPR TRESTLE   SEE "DOWNTOWN
BRIDGE   CANMORE" MAP

LADY MACDONALD COUNTRY INN

To ☾ GRASSI LAKES TRAIL,
☾ HA LING (CHINAMAN'S) PEAK,
and Spray Valley Provincial Park
(Kananaskis Country)

GEORGETOWN
INN

CREEKSIDE INN

★ CANMORE
NORDIC CENTRE

THE
HOSTEL
BEAR

BEAR AND
BISON INN

MAIN   ST

MINE
SHAREHOLDER'S
CABIN

RADISSON HOTEL

SUMMIT
CAFÉ

Centennial
Park   5TH   ST

☾ OH CANADA EH! ★

8TH
AVE

7TH
AVE

6TH
AVE

5TH
AVE

4TH
AVE

2ND   ST

1ST   ST
Millennium
Park

HOOLIGAN'S

HELIPORT

☾ COAL-MINING
HISTORY
★

Canmore
Creek

Quarry
Lake

To Alpine Club of Canada
Clubhouse (HI-Canmore) and Grotto
Canyon

To Bow River Campground,
Stewart Creek Golf Course,
and Calgary

0   0.25 mi

0   0.25 km

© AVALON TRAVEL

CANMORE

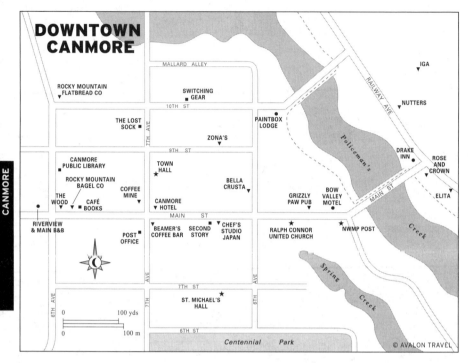

DOWNTOWN CANMORE

MALLARD ALLEY

IGA

ROCKY MOUNTAIN
FLATBREAD CO

SWITCHING
GEAR

NUTTERS

10TH ST

THE LOST
SOCK

PAINTBOX
LODGE

ZONA'S

9TH ST

DRAKE
INN

ROSE
AND
CROWN

CANMORE
PUBLIC LIBRARY

TOWN
HALL

ROCKY MOUNTAIN
BAGEL CO

BELLA
CRUSTA

COFFEE
MINE

THE
WOOD

CAFÉ
BOOKS

CANMORE
HOTEL

GRIZZLY
PAW PUB

BOW
VALLEY
MOTEL

ELITA

MAIN   ST

RIVERVIEW
& MAIN B&B

BEAMER'S
COFFEE BAR

SECOND
STORY

CHEF'S
STUDIO
JAPAN

RALPH CONNOR
UNITED CHURCH

NWMP POST

POST
OFFICE

7TH ST

ST. MICHAEL'S
HALL

0   100 yds

0   100 m

6TH ST

Centennial   Park

© AVALON TRAVEL

THE LAND

Canmore lies in the Bow Valley, flanked by mountains rising up to 1,000 meters (3,280 feet) above the valley floor. To the south and west are the distinctive peaks of the Three Sisters, Mount Lawrence Grassi, impressive Ha Ling Peak (known locally as Chinaman's Peak), and the southeastern extent of Mount Rundle. Across the valley are the Fairholme Range, Mount Lady Macdonald, and Grotto Mountain. Like the rest of the Canadian Rockies, these mountains began as layers of sedimentary rock laid down on the bed of an ancient sea. The seabed was forced upward over millions of years to create today's lofty peaks, whose sedimentary layers give them a distinct appearance. Through the valley flows the braided Bow River, heading eastward and into the Saskatchewan River system. At the north end of town, the river divides in two, leaving downtown Canmore on a low-lying island that is protected from annual spring flooding by dikes of large boulders.

FLORA AND FAUNA

Even though much of the valley floor is developed, large tracts of land are protected by Bow Valley Wildland Provincial Park, making the surrounding area a delight for nature lovers. Lowlands on either side of the Bow River are lined with stands of poplar, while the drier mountainsides support extensive stands of **Douglas fir, Engelmann spruce,** and **lodgepole pine.**

The forested valley floor provides habitat for many larger mammals, including around 100 **elk,** most often sighted on the Canmore Golf Course and along the west side of the Bow River. Other larger mammals present include **white-tailed deer, coyotes, black bears,** and **grizzly bears,** all of which are regularly sighted within town limits. **Bighorn sheep** are common on rocky outcrops above Spray Lakes Road. **Cougars** inhabit the surrounding wilderness but are rarely sighted.

Smaller mammals present in the Bow River and its adjacent sloughs include a healthy population of **beaver,** as well as **muskrat** and **mink. Red** and **Columbian ground squirrels** and **least chipmunks** inhabit the forests around town, while at higher elevations **golden-mantled ground squirrels** and **pikas** find a home.

Birdlife around Canmore is prolific. **Mallard ducks** are a popular attraction on Policeman's Creek in downtown Canmore. Several active **osprey** nests can be seen along the banks of the Bow River; other permanent residents include **great horned owls, jays,** and **ravens.**

HISTORY

The Hudson's Bay Company explored the Bow Valley corridor and attempted, without success, to establish a fur trade with Stoney natives for most of the 1840s. In 1858, an expedition from the east, led by Captain John Palliser, sent back discouraging reports about the climate and prospects of agriculture in the valley. A few decades later the Canadian Pacific Railway (CPR) chose the Bow Valley Corridor as the route through the mountains, and the first divisional point west of Calgary was established in 1883. It was named Canmore for the 11th-century Scottish king Malcolm of Canmore.

Coal Mining

The CPR was delighted to discover that the valley was rich with coal, which it could use in its steam engines. Mining on the lower slopes of the Three Sisters and Mount Rundle commenced in 1886, attracting hundreds of miners and their families. Within a few years numerous mines operated around Canmore. In 1899 the CPR moved its divisional point to Laggan (now Lake Louise), but the mines continued to operate, with the most productive mine located on Canmore Creek. Hotels and businesses were established, and a hospital, North West Mounted Police (NWMP) post, and opera house were built. The Canmore Opera House, reputed to be the only log movie house in the world, still stands and has been relocated to Calgary's Heritage Park.

Many British and European miners were attracted to the area, and the population continued to increase. A small contingent of Chinese miners also lived in Canmore. They didn't stay long, but their memory lives on in the name Chinaman's Peak. A Chinese cook, Ha Ling, was bet $50 that he couldn't climb the peak and return to Canmore in fewer than six hours. He did, and it's been known as Chinaman's Peak ever since. In 1912, the Canadian Anthracite Coal Company relocated its operation from near present-day Banff to the west side of the Bow River, five kilometers (3.1 miles) from the rail line. **Georgetown,** a bustling little village, sprang up beside the mine. Workers enjoyed electricity and running water in cozy cabins along with their own company store, post office, and a school for the kids. Three short years later, markets dried up and the anthracite mine closed. Georgetown was abandoned, and the buildings were barged downstream to Canmore.

Recent Times

A little more than 100 years after mining commenced and less than 30 years after the last mine closed, Canmore experienced its second boom—tourism—which today shows no sign of slowing. When the last of Canmore's mines closed in 1979, the population stood at 3,500; by 2012 that number had more than tripled. Half the current residents have lived in town for fewer than five years.

Canmore is a popular spot for moviemakers; big-budget movies filmed in and around town have included *Shanghai Noon; Grizzly Falls; Mystery, Alaska; The Edge; Wild America; The Last of the Dogmen; Legends of the Fall; Snow Dogs; Open Range;* and the 2006 Brad Pitt film *The Assassination of Jesse James by the Coward Robert Ford.*

Sights and Recreation

Canmore sprawls across both sides of the TransCanada Highway, with downtown Canmore occupying an island in the middle of the Bow River. Although development sprawls in all directions, large tracts of forest remain intact, including along the river, where paths lead beyond built-up areas and into natural areas. The most expansive of these is 32,600-hectare (80,550-acre) **Bow Valley Wildland Provincial Park,** which has been designated in pockets along the valley floor as well as most of the surrounding mountain slopes along both sides of the valley.

SIGHTS

Through booming times, the original core of Canmore, on the southwestern side of the TransCanada Highway, has managed to retain much of its original charm. Many historic buildings line the downtown streets, while other buildings from the coal-mining days are being preserved at their original locations around town. The best way to get downtown from the TransCanada Highway is to take Railway Avenue from Highway 1A and drive down 8th Street, the main drag (parking is easiest one street back along 7th Street, where one parking lot—at 6th Avenue—is designated for RVs).

Downtown

The first building of interest at the east end of the main street is Canmore's original **NWMP post** (609 8th St., 403/678-1955, 9am-6pm daily in summer, noon-4pm Mon.-Fri. the rest of the year, free), built in 1892. It is one of the few such posts still in its original location,

even though at the time of its construction the building was designed as a temporary structure to serve the newly born coal-mining town. The interior is decorated with period furnishings, while out back is a thriving garden filled with the same food crops planted by the post's original inhabitants. The post sits across from Policeman's Creek, a shallow body of water alive with ducks. **Ralph Connor United Church,** a little farther down 8th Street, was built in 1890 and is now a Provincial Historic Site. The church is named for its first reverend, Charles Gordon, who used the pen name Ralph Connor for the 35 books he authored. **Canmore Hotel,** on the corner of 8th Street and 7th Avenue, was built in 1891 (at a time when three hotels already operated) and is still open for thirsty townsfolk and travelers alike.

Around the corner from the hotel, inside the impressive Civic Centre complex, is **Canmore Museum and Geoscience Centre** (902 7th Ave., 403/678-2462, noon-5pm Mon.-Tues., 11am-5pm Wed.-Sun., adult $5, senior and child $3). This facility highlights the region's rich geological history and its importance to the growth of the town and related industries. Geological formations along three local hikes are described, which, along with a small fossil display, microscopes, and computer resources, make this facility an interesting rainy-day diversion.

Coal-Mining History

Several scenic and historic sights lie across the Bow River from downtown, including the remains of various mining operations. To get there, walk south along 8th Avenue for 500

© ANDREW HEMPSTEAD

Canmore's main street is lined with an interesting selection of shops.

meters (0.3 mile) to the Bow River. With a pedestrian-only bridge and paved paths on both sides of the river leading in either direction, this is a good point to stop and get oriented. A pleasant loop can be made by walking north and crossing the river at the old **CPR trestle bridge,** which once served local mines. Follow the trail back downstream, past the **Mine Shareholders' Cabin,** a log structure built in 1914.

In the same vicinity, a trail leads off from Three Sisters Drive up Canmore Creek, passing the remains of a mine site that was first worked in 1891. Beyond the visible coal seam and crumbling concrete foundations is a picturesque waterfall tucked below a residential development. Backtrack 300 meters (0.2 mile) from the end of the trail and climb the wooden steps, crossing Spray Lakes Road to **Quarry Lake.** This small lake lies in an open meadow and is a popular sunbathing and swimming spot.

HIKING

The hiking trails around Canmore are usually passed by in favor of those of its famous neighbors, but some interesting trails do exist. Paved paths around town are suitable for walking, bicycling, and, in winter, skiing. They link Policeman's Creek with the golf course, Nordic center, and Riverview Park on the Bow River.

◖ Grassi Lakes

- Length: 2 kilometers/1.2 miles (40 minutes) one-way
- Elevation gain: 300 meters/980 feet
- Rating: easy/moderate
- Trailhead: Spray Village, beyond the Nordic center, 6 kilometers (3.7 miles) west of downtown off Spray Lakes Road

This historic trail climbs to two small lakes below Chinaman's Peak. From the parking lot just off Spray Lakes Road, take the left fork 150 meters (0.1 mile) along the trail. It climbs steadily to stairs cut into a cliff face before leading up to a bridge over Canmore Creek and to the lakes. Interpretive signs along the trail point out interesting aspects of the Bow Valley and detail the life of Lawrence Grassi, who built the trail in the early 1920s. With Chinaman's Peak as a backdrop, these gin-clear, spring-fed lakes are a particularly rewarding destination. Behind the upper lake, an easy scramble up a scree slope leads to four pictographs (native rock paintings) of human figures. They are on the first large boulder in the gorge. An alternate return route is down a rough access road between the hiking trail and Spray Lakes Road, passing a broken-down log cabin along the way.

◖ Ha Ling (Chinaman's) Peak

- Length: 2.2 kilometers/1.4 miles (90 minutes) one-way
- Elevation gain: 740 meters/2,430 feet
- Rating: moderate/difficult

CANMORE

© ANDREW HEMPSTEAD

one of the two spring-fed Grassi Lakes

- Trailhead: Goat Creek parking lot, Spray Lakes Road, 9 kilometers (5.6 miles) west of Canmore

Ha Ling Peak is the impressive pinnacle of rock that rises high above Canmore to the southwest. While the sheer eastern face is visible from town, this trail winds up the back side of the mountain and ends with stunning views across the Bow Valley. Leaving your vehicle at the Goat Creek Trailhead, cross the road, then walk up to and over the canal to search out the trail, which begins from behind a small work shed. The trail climbs steadily through subalpine forest of Engelmann spruce before breaking out above the tree line, where views north extend down the glacially carved Goat Creek Valley. The trail then forks; the left fork climbs unforgivingly to Chinaman's Peak, but hikers are rewarded with views no less spectacular by continuing to the right along a lightly marked trail that ends at a saddle. On a clear day, the panorama afforded from this viewpoint is worth every painful step. Take care on the return journey; stay high and to the right, and watch for rock cairns and colored flagging to ensure you enter the trees at the right spot.

Cougar Creek

- Length: 9.5 kilometers/6 miles (4 hours) one-way
- Elevation gain: 550 meters/1,800 feet
- Rating: moderate
- Trailhead: corner of Benchlands Trail and Elk Run Boulevard, east side of TransCanada Highway

This unofficial trail follows a valley carved deeply into the Fairholme Range by Cougar Creek. The length and elevation gain listed are to a high ridge on the boundary of Banff National Park. Few hikers reach this point, with most content to turn around within an hour's travel. The first section of trail runs alongside a man-made channel that acts as a

ALPINE CLUB OF CANADA

The Alpine Club of Canada (ACC), like similar clubs in the United States and Great Britain, is a nonprofit mountaineering organization whose objectives include encouraging mountaineering through educational programs, exploring and studying alpine and glacial regions, and preserving mountain flora and fauna.

The club was formed in 1906, mainly through the tireless campaign of its first president, Arthur Wheeler. A list of early members reads like a Who's Who of the Canadian Rockies—Bill Peyto, Tom Wilson, Byron Harmon, Mary Schèffer—names familiar to all Canadian mountaineers. Today the club's membership includes 3,000 alpinists from throughout Canada.

The original clubhouse was near the Banff Springs Hotel, but in 1980 a new clubhouse was built on benchland at the edge of Canmore to serve as the association's headquarters. The club's ongoing projects include operating the Canadian Alpine Centre in partnership with Hostelling International (which calls the property the Lake Louise Alpine Centre), maintaining a system of 20 huts throughout the backcountry of the Canadian Rockies, and publishing the annual *Canadian Alpine Journal—*the country's only record of mountaineering accomplishments.

For further information and membership details, contact the Alpine Club of Canada (403/678-3200, www.alpineclubofcanada.ca).

CANMORE

conduit for runoff in years of high snowfall. It's dry most of summer, but extra care should be taken in spring. Cross just before the mouth of the canyon. From this point, the rough trail crosses the creekbed 10 times in the first three kilometers (1.9 miles) to a major fork. Stay within the left valley, continuing up and around the base of Mount Charles Stewart. From this point the valley walls close in, and it's a steep climb up to the boundary of Banff National Park. On the return journey, continue beyond the parking lot to the Summit Café, where you can relax on the patio with a cool drink.

Mount Lady Macdonald

- Length: 3.5 kilometers/2.1 miles (90 minutes) one-way
- Elevation gain: 850 meters/2,790 feet
- Rating: moderate/difficult
- Trailhead: corner of Benchlands Trail and Elk Run Boulevard, east side of TransCanada Highway

Named for the wife of Canada's first prime minister, this peak lies immediately north of Canmore. Follow Cougar Creek to where the canyon begins and look for a faint trail winding up a grassy bank to the left. Once on the trail, take the steepest option at every fork, then a sharp right 300 meters (0.2 mile) after the trail bursts out into a cleared area. This section is steep, climbing through a rock band to the mountain's southern ridge, which you'll follow the rest of the way. The distance and elevation listed are to an unused helipad below the main summit. It's a steep, unrelenting slog, but views across the Bow Valley are stunning. From this point, the true summit is another 275 vertical meters (900 vertical feet) away, along an extremely narrow ridge that drops away precipitously to the east.

Grotto Canyon

- Length: 2 kilometers/1.2 miles (40 minutes) one-way
- Elevation gain: 60 meters/200 feet
- Rating: easy
- Trailhead: Grotto Pond, Highway 1A, 12 kilometers (7.5 miles) east of Canmore

This is one of the most interesting trails

around Canmore. From Grotto Pond, this trail first follows a power-line road behind the Baymag plant. Then at a signed intersection it takes off through the woods to the mouth of the canyon. No official trail traverses the canyon; hikers simply follow the creekbed through the towering canyon walls. Around 300 meters (0.2 mile) into the canyon, look for pictographs to the left. At the two-kilometer (1.2-mile) mark, the canyon makes a sharp left turn at Illusion Rock, where water cascades through a narrow chasm and into the main canyon. Many hikers return from this point, but through the next section of canyon, the valley opens up, passing hoodoos and a cave. It's 6.5 kilometers (four miles) from the trailhead to the end of the valley, with most of the 680 meters (2,230 feet) of elevation gained in the last two kilometers (1.2 miles).

Heart Creek

- Length: 2 kilometers/1.2 miles (40 minutes) one-way
- Elevation gain: 80 meters/260 feet
- Rating: easy
- Trailhead: Lac des Arcs interchange, TransCanada Highway, 15 kilometers (9.3 miles) east of Canmore

This well-formed trail is signposted from the Lac des Arcs interchange, 15 kilometers (9.3 miles) east of Canmore along the TransCanada Highway. The trail parallels the highway eastward until reaching a fork. The trail to the right follows Heart Creek for just over one kilometer (0.6 mile), crossing the creek seven times on narrow log bridges. It ends at a cleared area below a spot where Heart Creek is forced through a narrow cleft. Those tempted to continue farther can cross the creek, scramble up a steep, forested ridge, then descend the other side to link up with the creek upstream of the gorge. Cross the creek again for views of another narrow chasm.

Heli-Hiking

Heli-hiking is the summer alternative to heli-skiing—a helicopter does the hard work, and you get to hike in a remote, alpine region that would usually entail a long, steep hike to access. **Alpine Helicopters** (403/678-4802, www.alpinehelicopter.com) offers options starting at $489 per person, which includes 10 minutes of flight time and 3-4 hours of hiking. The company is flexible, with ground time and destinations chosen by the clients. Flightseeing (no landing) costs $239 for 25 minutes of air time. The heliport is along Highway 1A south of downtown. Try to book ahead for these trips; they're very popular with travelers staying in Banff, where there is no flightseeing.

OTHER RECREATION
Canmore Nordic Centre

This sprawling complex on the outskirts of Canmore was built for the 1988 Winter Olympic Games. The cross-country skiing and biathlon (combined cross-country skiing and rifle shooting) events were held here, and today the center remains a world-class training ground for Canadian athletes in a variety of disciplines. Even in summer, long after the snow has melted, the place is worth a visit. An interpretive trail leads down to and along the west bank of the Bow River to the barely visible remains of Georgetown, a once-bustling coal-mining town. Many other trails lead around the grounds, and it's possible to hike or bike along the Bow River all the way to Banff. Mountain biking is extremely popular on 70 kilometers (43.5 miles) of trails. Bike rentals are available at **Trail Sports** (below the day lodge, 403/678-6764, 9am-6pm daily, $22 per hour and $55 per day for a front-suspension bike, $28 and $80, respectively, for a full suspension bike). In summer, you can also play disc golf (Frisbees are available at Trail Sports). Snowmaking

CANMORE

© ANDREW HEMPSTEAD

cross-country skiing at the Canmore Nordic Centre

guarantees a ski season running December-late March, with rentals and instruction available through Trail Sports. The day lodge (403/678-2400, 8am-4:30pm daily) has lockers, a lounge area, a café (10am-4pm daily), and an information desk.

Fishing

The **Bow River** has good fishing for brown and brook trout, including right downtown between the old railway bridge and Rundle Drive. Follow Highway 1A east from town to access the best river fishing, as well as **Gap Lake** and **Grotto Pond;** the latter is stocked with rainbow trout. The Bow River is renowned for its rainbow trout fishing. This occurs downstream of Canmore toward Calgary and beyond **Ghost Lake,** which holds healthy populations of lake, rainbow, and brown trout.

For all your fishing needs, head to **Wapiti Sports** (1506 Railway Ave., 403/678-5550), which stocks bait and tackle and sells licenses.

Golfing

As with golfing elsewhere in the Canadian Rockies, book all tee times well in advance, but also try to be flexible, because two of Canmore's three courses offer weekday and twilight discounts. The golfing season in Canmore runs early May-late September.

Silvertip (403/678-1600 or 877/877-5444, www.silvertipresort.com) opened in summer 1998 on a series of wide benches between the valley floor and the lower slopes of Mount Lady Macdonald. It was quickly recognized as one of Canada's finest resort courses, but more tellingly, it boasts a slope rating of 153, the highest of any course in mainland North America. Needless to say, the layout is challenging, with the most distinct feature being an elevation change of 200 meters (660 feet) between the lowest and highest points on the course. Adding to this challenge are narrow, sloping, tree-lined fairways; numerous water hazards; 74 bunkers; and a course length of a frightening 7,300 yards from the back markers. High-season greens fees are $195, which includes a mandatory cart and use of the driving range.

Stewart Creek Golf Club (4100 Stewart Creek Dr., 403/609-6099 or 877/993-4653, www.stewartcreekgolf.com), another newer layout, lies across the valley in the Three Sisters Mountain Village development. It is shorter than Silvertip but still measures more than 7,000 yards from the back tees. The fairways are relatively wide, but positioning of tee shots is important, and the course is made more interesting by hanging greens, greenside exposed rock, and historic mine shafts. Greens fees are $175-195, with twilight rates of $125. These rates include use of a power cart and practice facility.

Canmore Golf & Curling Club (403/678-4785), built in the 1920s as a nine-hole course at the north end of 8th Avenue, has developed into an 18-hole course with a modern clubhouse and a practice facility that includes a driving range. It is an interesting layout, with scenic panoramas and water on some holes. Greens fees are $95.

Horseback Riding

Nestled on a wide bench on the northeastern side of town, **Cross Zee Ranch** (403/678-4171) has been guiding visitors through the valley since the 1950s. From expansive stables, rides pass through thickly wooded areas, along colorful meadows, and to high lookouts. Options include Ranger Ridge and Bone Gully (one hour; $45 per person), Sunny Bench (90 minutes; $60), and the Great Aspens ride (two hours; $75).

Climbing

Hundreds of climbing routes have been laid out around Canmore. **Mount Yamnuska,** which rises 900 meters (2,950 feet) above the valley floor east of town along Highway 1A, is the most developed site. Climbers also flock to **Chinaman's Peak, Cougar Creek,** the area behind **Grassi Lakes,** and **Grotto Canyon.** Canmore is home to many qualified mountain guides.

Yamnuska (403/678-4164 or 866/678-4164, www.yamnuska.com) offers basic rock-climbing courses and instruction for all ability levels on ice climbing, mountaineering, and trekking. A good introduction to rock climbing is the weekend-long Outdoor Rock Intro course, which costs $345. Unique to the company are three-month-long courses that take in all aspects of mountain-oriented skills.

Entertainment and Events

NIGHTLIFE

Canmore doesn't have anywhere near the number of bars that nearby Banff is so famous for, but no one ever seems to go thirsty. **The Wood** (838 8th St., 403/678-3404) has a beer garden that catches the afternoon sun and is especially busy on weekends. At the other end of the main street is the **Drake Inn** (909 Railway Ave., 403/678-5131), with a small outdoor patio and bands most nights. Across the road, at the **Rose and Crown** (749 Railway Ave., 403/678-5168), you'll find a beer garden. All these bars have midweek drink specials, and the latter two have a couple of pool tables.

The **Grizzly Paw Brewing Company** (622 8th St., 403/678-9983) brews its own beer, with six ales produced in-house (look for special winter brews around Christmas). Most are heavy, English-style beers, but the lighter Grumpy Bear Honey Wheat Ale suits most tastes.

Canmore's only nightclub is **Hooligan's**

(Bow Valley Trail, 403/609-2662), but there's live music somewhere in town every weekend.

◖ *OH CANADA EH!*

This musical dinner show (Cornerstone Theatre, 125 Kananaskis Way, off Bow Valley Trail, 403/609-0004 or 800/773-0004) provides a rip-roaring evening of fun and food in a modern building decorated as a cavernous log cabin. It's unashamedly cheesy, but the parade of costumed Canadian characters, such as lumberjacks, natives, Mounties, and even Anne of Green Gables, will keep you laughing as they sing and dance across the floor. The food is surprisingly good, with Canadian favorites such as Alberta beef, salmon, and maple chocolate cake served buffet-style. Performances are nightly through summer at 6:30pm, and the all-inclusive cost is adult $75, senior $69, child 16 and under free.

FESTIVALS AND EVENTS

Canmore's small-town pride lives on through a busy schedule of festivals and events, which are nearly always accompanied by parades of flag-waving kids, free downtown pancake breakfasts, and an evening shindig somewhere in town.

Winter

Throughout the winter months, locals play **hockey** on ponds and rinks scattered throughout the valley. Things get a little more serious at home games of the **Canmore Eagles** (www.canmoreeagles.com), held at the recreation center along 8th Avenue. The New Year is ushered in with **Party on the Pond,** with skating, wagon rides, fireworks, and bonfires on and around the frozen pond beside 10th Street.

Spring

The mid-June celebration **artsPeak Arts Festival** (403/678-6436, www.artspeakcanmore.com) is hosted at venues throughout town, including along the main street. As the name suggests, expect lots of arts-oriented festivities, including workshops, displays, and walking tours.

Summer

Canada Day (July 1) is celebrated with a pancake breakfast, parade, various activities in Centennial Park, and 10:30pm fireworks.

Canmore Nordic Centre hosts a variety of mountain-biking events each summer, highlighted by a stop on the **24 Hours of Adrenalin** tour (416/391-2651, www.24hoursofadrenalin.com), in which 1,500 racers complete as many laps as they can in a 24-hour period, either in teams or as solo riders. For a full listing of mountain-bike races, contact the Nordic center (403/678-2400).

On the Heritage Day long weekend, the first weekend of August, Canmore hosts a **Folk Music Festival** (www.canmorefolkfestival.com), which starts on Saturday and runs through Monday evening. This event, which attracts more than 14,000 fans, features national and international acts performing in Centennial Park, musical workshops, and a free pancake breakfast beside the post office on Heritage Day.

The first Sunday of September is the **Canmore Highland Games** (403/678-9454, www.canmorehighlandgames.ca), a day of dancing, eating, and caber tossing culminating in a spectacular and noisy parade of pipe bands throughout the grounds of Centennial Park; the event attracts more than 10,000 spectators. The grand finale is the *ceilidh,* a traditional Scottish celebration involving loud beer-drinking, foot-stomping music, which takes place under a massive tent set up in the park for the occasion.

Fall

Fall's major gathering is for the **Festival of the Eagles** (www.eaglewatch.ca), held on the middle weekend of October and coinciding with the southbound migration of golden eagles. Viewing scopes are set up at the high school grounds off 17th Street while scheduled events include talks, slide shows, and field trips.

Accommodations and Camping

Canmore's population boom has been mirrored by the construction of new hotels and motels. Most of the newer lodgings are on Bow Valley Trail (Highway 1A). As with all resort towns in the Canadian Rockies, reservations should be made as far in advance as possible in summer.

More than 40 bed-and-breakfasts operate in Canmore. They are all small, family-run affairs, with only one or two rooms (a local town bylaw limits the number of guest rooms in private homes to just two). During summer, they fill every night. For a full list of B&Bs, check the website of the **Canmore/Bow Valley Bed and Breakfast Association** (www.bbcanmore. com) for one that suits your needs.

As you raise your eyebrows over hotel pricing in Canmore, consider two things: (1) Many hotels discount rooms year-round, so use the listed websites to find current deals and packages; and (2) room rates in Canmore are a bargain compared to Banff, just down the road.

Outside the busiest summer period (mid-June–mid-Sept.), room rates are slashed considerably (especially at the more-expensive accommodations); with a little bit of searching, expect to find rates that include two lift tickets (at either the Banff or Kananaskis alpine resorts) for the same price as the room-only rate during summer.

IN AND AROUND THE TOWN OF CANMORE
Under $50
HI-Canmore (403/678-3200, www.hihostels. ca) is an excellent hostel-style accommodation at the base of Grotto Mountain. Affiliated with Hostelling International, the lodge is part of headquarters for the Alpine Club of Canada, the country's national mountaineering organization. In addition to sleeping up to 46 people in seven rooms, it has a kitchen, an excellent library, a laundry room, a bar, a sauna, and a lounge area with a fireplace. Rates are $30 per night for members of Hostelling International or the Alpine Club (nonmembers $36). Private rooms are $60 s or d for members (nonmembers $82). Alpine Club membership is inexpensive and includes a discount at the Lake Louise Alpine Centre. To get here from downtown, follow Bow Valley Trail southeast; it's signposted to the left, 500 meters (0.3 mile) after passing under the TransCanada Highway.

Along the main motel strip, **The Hostel Bear** (1002 Bow Valley Trail, 403/678-1000 or 888/678-1008, www.thehostelbear.com, dorms $32.50, from $90-110 s or d) is a newer building that originally opened as a motel but has been converted to a beautiful facility for budget travelers. It features eye-catching timber and river-stone styling outside and an impressive lobby. Amenities include a large living area with an LCD TV and fireplace, a large modern kitchen, a laundry, wireless Internet, and comfortable beds for 170 guests, with configurations ranging from dorms with privacy curtains to private en suite rooms.

$100-150
With a little over $100 budgeted for a room, it's hard to go past ◖ **Riverview and Main** (918 8th St., 403/678-9777, www.riverviewand-main.ca, $125 s, $145 d), centrally located half a block beyond the end of the downtown core. The rooms are decently sized and brightly

© ANDREW HEMPSTEAD

Rocky Mountain Ski Lodge

decorated, and each has access to a deck. The guest lounge centers on a river-stone, wood-burning fireplace. Rates include a selection of hot and cold breakfast items.

At the edge of Canmore's downtown core is the **Drake Inn** (909 Railway Ave., 403/678-5131 or 800/461-8730, www.drakeinn.com, from $135 s, $149 d). It offers bright and cheerfully decorated motel rooms. Well worth an extra $10 are Creekside Rooms, featuring private balconies overlooking Policeman's Creek. The adjoining bar opens at 7am daily for the best value breakfast in town.

Across the creek from the Drake Inn is the **Bow Valley Motel** (610 8th St., 403/678-5085 or 800/665-8189, www.bowvalleymotel.ca, $120-140 s or d), offering 25 rooms at the north end of the main street. The rooms are far from the cutting edge of modern style, but the location and price are right. On-site is an outdoor hot tub and coin-operated laundry facilities.

Not only can you rent one- and two-bedroom

units with full kitchens at **Rocky Mountain Ski Lodge** (1711 Bow Valley Trail, 403/678-5445 or 800/665-6111, www.rockymtnskilodge.com, from $120 s or d), but there's also plenty of outdoor space for kids to run around, including a small playground. Also on the property is a barbecue and picnic area, a laundry, and wireless Internet. The self-contained suites, some with loft bedrooms, cost from $179.

◪ Creekside Country Inn (709 Benchlands Trail, 403/609-5522 or 866/609-5522, www.creeksidecountryinn.com, $139-199 s or d) is a modern, mountain-style lodge featuring lots of exposed timber. The 12 rooms are elegant in their simplicity; eight have lofts. Facilities include a lounge with roaring log fire, a small exercise room, a whirlpool, and a steam room. Rates include a gourmet continental breakfast that will set you up for the day.

Dominated by exposed log work, the **Canmore Rocky Mountain Inn** (1719 Bow Valley Trail, 403/678-5221 or 800/268-0935, www.canmorerockymountaininn.com, $122-192 s or d) has regularly revamped, air-conditioned rooms, each with a small balcony and fireplace.

$150-200

The quality of accommodations in this category far exceeds that of similarly priced options elsewhere in the Canadian Rockies. If you have up to $200 per night to spend on accommodations, I strongly recommend you consider the first two options, each offering a unique mountain ambience impossible to find in a regular motel.

Silver Creek Lodge (1818 Mountain Ave., 403/678-4242 or 877/598-4242, www.silvercreekcanmore.ca, $158-250 s or d) provides hotel and suite accommodations (one-bedroom with kitchen from $199) within a much larger condominium development. Aside from modern kitchen-equipped rooms, many with mountain views, highlights include the highly

CANMORE

© ANDREW HEMPSTEAD

Each unit at Silver Creek Lodge has a fully-equipped kitchen.

recommended Wild Orchid Asian Bistro, spa services, outdoor hot tubs, and underground parking.

(Lady Macdonald Country Inn (1201 Bow Valley Trail, 403/678-3665 or 800/567-3919, www.ladymacdonald.com, $160-225 s or d) exudes a welcoming atmosphere and offers personalized service not experienced in the larger properties. Its 10 rooms are all individually furnished, with the smallest, the Palliser Room, featuring elegant surroundings and a magnificent wrought-iron bed. The largest of the rooms is the Three Sisters, which has bright, welcoming pastel-colored decor, a king bed, a two-way gas fireplace, a hot tub, and uninterrupted views of its namesake. Rates include a hearty hot breakfast in a country-style breakfast room.

Named for one of the valley's original coal-mining communities, the **(Georgetown Inn** (1101 Bow Valley Trail, 403/678-3439 or 866/695-5955, www.georgetowninn.ca,

$129-219 s or d) is set up as a country inn of times gone by, complete with a pub-style dining room open daily for breakfast, lunch, and dinner. Each of the 20 guest rooms has its own individual charm, with a modern twist on decor that features lots of English antiques. The best value are the Victoria Rooms, each with a separate sitting area and electric fireplace ($159).

With 224 guest rooms, the **Radisson Hotel** (511 Bow Valley Trail, 403/678-3625 or 800/967-9033, www.radisson.com, $189-229 s or d) is Canmore's largest accommodation. Set around landscaped gardens, this complex also features Canmore's only steakhouse (the Sunday brunch is one of the best in the valley), an indoor pool, a fitness facility, and a gift shop. Steeply discounted off-season rates make the Radisson a great deal for nonsummer travel.

(Bear and Bison (705 Benchlands Trail, 403/678-2058, www.bearandbisoninn.com, $179-249 s or d) is an elegant lodging with nine guest rooms in three different themes. Timber and stone surroundings are complemented by rich heritage tones throughout. Each room has a king-size four-poster bed, a jetted tub, a fireplace, and a private balcony or patio. The lounge has a high vaulted ceiling, a welcoming open fire, and panoramic picture windows. Guests also enjoy an inviting library and a private garden complete with an oversized hot tub. Rates include baked goods on arrival, predinner drinks, and a breakfast you will remember for a long time. Outside of summer, rates start at $159-199.

$200-250

 Paintbox Lodge (629 10th St., 403/609-0482 or 888/678-6100, www.paintboxlodge.com, $210-260 s or d) has the same upscale charm as the Bear and Bison but enjoys a more central location, just one block from the main street. The lobby itself—exposed hand-hewn timbers, slate tiles, and unique pieces of mountain-themed art—is an eye-catching gem. The upscale mountain decor continues through the 10 large guest rooms, each lavishly decorated with muted natural colors and a tasteful selection of heritage artifacts. Rooms also boast beds draped with the finest linens, bathrooms anchored by a deep soaking tub, and high-speed Internet access. The more-expensive rooms have fireplaces and balconies.

HARVIE HEIGHTS

Lodging in Harvie Heights, eight kilometers (five miles) west of Canmore and less than one kilometer (0.6 mile) from the entrance to Banff National Park, may seem a little more pricey than Canmore, but most units are self-contained.

$50-100

The least-expensive option at Harvie Heights is a standard motel room at the **Gateway Inn**

(800 Harvie Heights Rd., 403/678-5396 or 877/678-1810, www.gatewayinn.ca, older motel rooms $89-129 s or d, cabins $139-199). Self-contained cabins, each with a kitchenette and adjacent fire pit, are older, but the more expensive ones have three bedrooms; cabins also have a two-night minimum. You'll find a playground, picnic area, and communal fire pit for evening relaxation.

$150-200

Banff Boundary Lodge (1000 Harvie Heights Rd., 403/678-9555 or 877/678-9555, www.banffboundarylodge.com, $179-219 s or d) has less outdoor space than the Gateway Inn but is a newer property. The 42 units each have one or two bedrooms, a comfortable lounge area with TV/DVD, and a full kitchen. Other facilities include an outdoor hot tub, barbecue area, and laundry. Outside of summer, rates drop to around $100, an excellent value.

DEADMAN'S FLATS

Deadman's Flats, seven kilometers (4.3 miles) east of Canmore along the TransCanada Highway, is little more than a truck stop, but it has motels, a bed-and-breakfast, and a 24-hour gas station.

$50-100

The best value of the bunch is the **Big Horn Motel** (403/678-2290 or 800/892-9908, www.bighornmotel.com, $99-209). It offers 27 surprisingly modern, mostly nonsmoking rooms. All have TVs and phones, some have kitchens and balconies, and a couple are wheelchair accessible.

CAMPGROUNDS
Commercial Campgrounds
Along the Bow Valley Trail toward Banff is **Rundle Mountain Campground** (403/678-2131 or 866/678-2267, $28-34 per site), opposite the motel of the same name. It offers

showers, laundry facilities, and hookups, but it's a smaller space with crowded sites.

Other Campgrounds

East of Canmore are three government campgrounds operated by **Bow Valley Campgrounds** (403/673-2163, www.bowvalleycampgrounds.com). Each has pit toilets, kitchen shelters, and firewood for sale at $8 per bundle. None have hookups. **Bow River Campground** (late Apr.-early Sept., unserviced sites $24, powered sites $36) is three kilometers (1.9 miles) east of Canmore at the Three Sisters Parkway overpass; **Three Sisters Campground** (mid-Apr.-Oct., $24 per site) is accessed from Deadman's Flats, a further four kilometers (2.5 miles) east, but it has a pleasant treed setting; while **Lac des Arcs Campground** (late Apr.-mid-Sept., $24 per site) slopes down to the edge of a large lake of the same name seven kilometers (4.3 miles) farther toward Calgary.

Food

The restaurant scene has come a long way in Canmore in the last few years. While you can still get inexpensive bar meals at the many pubs, other choices run the gamut, from the lively atmosphere of dining in the front yard of a converted residence to an upscale French restaurant.

GROCERIES

Sobeys and **Safeway** (both 7am-10pm daily) are large grocery stores on Railway Avenue. Both have in-house bakeries, butchers, and delis, along with a wide selection of fresh seafood.

GOURMET GOODIES

In front of Sobeys, **Nutter's** (900 Railway Ave., 403/678-3335, 9am-7pm Mon.-Fri., 10am-6pm Sat., 11am-6pm Sun.) is chock-full of bulk bins—a great place to stock up for hiking trips.

Downtown, **Bella Crusta** (702 6th Ave., 403/609-3366, 10am-6pm Mon.-Sat.) is the purveyor of the best gourmet pizza in the Bow Valley. Heated slices to go are $6.50, or pay $15-18 for a family-size version and heat it yourself, on a barbecue as the friendly staff recommends.

Away from the downtown core, **JK Bakery** (1514 Railway Ave., 403/678-4232, 7am-5pm Mon.-Sat.) supplies regular and European-style breads to shops and restaurants throughout the Canadian Rockies. A small café out front serves up soups, sandwiches, and pastries, as well as selling gourmet breads over the counter.

Tucked away in an industrial park beyond the south end of Bow Valley Trail is **Valbella Gourmet Foods** (104 Elk Run Blvd., 403/678-3637, 8am-6pm Mon.-Fri., 9am-5pm Sat.). Valbella mainly supplies gourmet meats to Bow Valley restaurants and grocery stores; head there for Canadian specialties such as buffalo, venison, and salmon; fresh cuts of marinated Alberta beef, lamb, chicken, and pork; and cured sausages.

CAFÉS AND COFFEE SHOPS

The **Rocky Mountain Bagel Company** (830 8th St., 403/678-9978, 6:30am-10pm daily) is a popular early-morning gathering spot. With a central location, it's always busy but manages to maintain an inviting atmosphere. It's the perfect place to start the day with a good strong coffee and fruit-filled muffin.

Down one block, **Beamer's Coffee Bar** (737 7th Ave., 403/609-0111, 6:30am-10pm daily) is a smaller space with equally good coffee. Out on the Bow Valley Trail (between Dairy Queen and Boston Pizza) is another **Beamer's**

Coffee Bar (403/678-3988), this one anchored by a long comfortable couch wrapped around a fireplace—the perfect place to relax with one of Beamer's complimentary daily papers or take advantage of the free wireless Internet.

Away from downtown, near where Cougar Creek enters Canmore from the Fairholme Range, is the **Summit Café** (1001 Cougar Creek Dr., 403/609-2120, 6:30am-6pm daily). It features a health-conscious menu including lots of salads, but many people come just to soak up the sun on the outside deck or relax with the daily paper and a cup of coffee.

CONTEMPORARY CANADIAN

Canmore has seen many top-notch restaurants open in the last few years, but one of the originals, **Zona's** (710 9th St., 403/609-2000, 11am-10pm daily, dinner only outside in the summer, $13-19), continues to garner rave reviews. The food is great, and so is the restaurant itself. Earthy tones, hardwood floors, rustic furniture, bamboo blinds, and kiln-fired clay crockery create an inviting ambience unequaled in Canmore. The menu takes its roots from around the world, with an emphasis on healthy eating and freshly prepared Canadian produce. Choose from dishes such as lamb shepherd's pie or vegetarian korma. Zona's also serves homemade lemonade and a wide selection of slightly overpriced wines and beers. A large deck provides much-needed extra seating in summer.

Crazyweed Kitchen (1600 Railway Ave., 403/609-2530, 11:30am-3pm and from 5pm daily, $18-32) dishes up creative culinary fare that gets rave reviews from even cultured Calgarians. From the busy open kitchen, all manner of creative dishes are on offer: beef short ribs in curry, truffle and mushroom gnocchi, and gourmet pizzas. Healthy portions are served at tables inside or out. Also notable

CANMORE

© ANDREW HEMPSTEAD

Crazyweed Kitchen is one of Canmore's most popular restaurants.

is the extensive wine list, with glasses from $8 and bottles from $35.

The innovative Canadian-oriented cuisine and flawless presentation make **Sage Bistro** (1712 Bow Valley Trail, 403/678-4878, 11:30am-10pm daily, $23-36) a longtime Canmore favorite. Mains include familiar favorites with a local twist: bison strip loin smothered in maple blueberry butter, and braised lamb shank with sweet potato fries. Finish up with maple syrup crème brûlée (trust me, you'll love it). The patio is a wonderful place for lunch.

GOURMET PIZZA

Off the top end of Main Street, **Rocky Mountain Flatbread Co.** (838 10th St., 403/609-5508, 11:30am-9:30pm daily, $12-18) is a lovely space of natural tones dominated by a clay wood-fired oven in one corner. The oven is also the main attraction when it comes to the food—gourmet flatbread-style pizzas for under $20. My advice: Start with a bowl of made-from-scratch chicken noodle soup ($6.50), then move on to the chicken, apple, and cherry tomato pizza (the $16.50 size is enough for two people).

ASIAN

Duck down an alleyway off main street to **Chef's Studio Japan** (709 8th St., 403/609-8383, noon-3pm and 4:30pm-10:30pm daily), a Japanese restaurant with a distinctive artsy feel. Seating is at a sushi counter or at regular tables surrounded by original art. The cuisine is not overly inventive, but the portions are generous and the tempura—always a good litmus test—is light and delicate. Educate yourself in the variety of Japanese cooking styles by ordering one of the hot and cold platters designed for sharing between two (from $28).

Wild Orchid Asian Bistro (Silver Creek Lodge, 1818 Mountain Ave., 403/679-2029, daily except Tues. for dinner, call for lunch hours, $15-28) is my favorite Japanese restaurant in the Canadian Rockies. It features all the usual choices, all expertly crafted in the open kitchen, as well as many with a Western twist. Perfect presentation, mountain views, and a large deck add to the appeal.

GLOBAL

The prime location of **Elita** (743 Railway Ave., 403/609-2613, 9am-9pm daily, $14-18) won't become apparent until you climb the steps from busy Railway Avenue to the sun-drenched patio and admire the surrounding mountains. The menu blends simple cooking styles from around the world—a Moroccan chicken salad, Mexican spiced wraps, and Thai curries. Vegetarians and vegans are well cared for.

Information and Services

INFORMATION

The best source of pretrip information (apart from this book, of course) is **Tourism Canmore Kananaskis** (403/678-1295 or 866/226-6673, www.tourismcanmore.com). A **Travel Alberta Information Centre** (403/678-5277, 8am-8pm daily May-Sept., 9am-6pm daily Oct.), just off the TransCanada Highway on the west side of town, provides plenty of information about Canmore and Banff.

The *Rocky Mountain Outlook* and *Canmore Leader* are both filled with local issues and entertainment listings; both weeklies are available free on stands throughout the valley.

The **Canmore Public Library** (950 8th Ave., 403/678-2468) is open 11am-8pm Monday-Thursday, 11am-5pm Friday-Sunday.

At the top end of the main street, **Café Books** (826 Main St., 403/678-0908, 9:30am-8pm daily) stocks an excellent selection of Canadiana, including hiking guides, coffee-table-style pictorials, Rocky Mountain cookbooks, and calendars, as well as nonfiction by local authors. Search out children's books toward the back. With a huge collection of used books, **Second Story** (713 8th St., 403/609-2368, 9am-6pm daily) hasn't been on the second floor since the weight of the books forced a move downstairs to the basement of the same address. Second Story's selection of nonfiction Canadiana is particularly strong.

SERVICES

The **post office** (8:30am-6pm Mon.-Fri.) is on 7th Avenue, beside Rusticana Grocery. **The Lost Sock** laundry (in the small mall on 7th Ave. at 10th St.) is open 24 hours daily and has Internet access. **Canmore Hospital** is along Bow Valley Trail (403/678-5536). For the **RCMP,** call 403/678-5516.

In addition to major hotels, send and receive email and surf the Internet at the following Canmore locations: **Beamer's Coffee Bar** (1702 Bow Valley Trail, 403/678-3988, 7am-10pm daily) and **Canmore Public Library** (700 9th St., 403/678-2468, 11am-8pm Mon.-Thurs., 11am-5pm Fri.-Sun.).

Getting There and Around

GETTING THERE

Canmore is beside the TransCanada Highway (Hwy. 1), 106 kilometers (66 miles) west of Calgary and 22 kilometers (14 miles) east of Banff. Allow just over 1 hour to drive from downtown Calgary and around 1.5 hours from Calgary International Airport.

Banff Airporter (403/762-3330, www.banffairporter.com) offers service between Canmore's Radisson Hotel and Calgary International Airport. The cost from Calgary is around $55 one-way. A desk at the airport's Arrivals level takes bookings, but it's best to reserve a seat by booking over the phone or online in advance.

Greyhound pulls into 701 Bow Valley Trail (403/678-3807, www.greyhound.ca) and offers regular services to Calgary, Banff, and beyond.

GETTING AROUND

The most enjoyable way to get around Canmore is on foot or bike, on the extensive trail network winding throughout the town and on to Banff via the Legacy Trail. **Gear Up** (1302 Bow Valley Trail, 403/678-1636) rents front- and full-suspension mountain bikes, as well as canoes and kayaks. For a cab, call **Apex** (403/609-0030).

CANMORE

KANANASKIS COUNTRY

Lying along the east side of the Continental Divide south of Banff National Park and less than one hour's drive from Calgary, this sprawling 4,250-square-kilometer (1,640-square-mile) area of the Canadian Rockies (pronounced can-AN-a-skiss) has been extraordinarily successful in balancing the needs of the 2.4 million outdoor enthusiasts who visit annually while keeping the region in a relatively natural state. Although the area lacks the famous lakes and glaciated peaks of Banff and Jasper National Parks, the landscape rivals those parks in many ways. As well as the areas set aside for recreation, large tracts of land give full protection to wildlife. Throughout Kananaskis Country, wildlife is abundant, and opportunities for observation of larger mammals are superb.

Kananaskis Country encompasses seven provincial parks, 1,300 kilometers (800 miles) of hiking trails, a complex network of bike paths, areas for horseback riding (and some for ATVs), a world-class 36-hole golf course, boat and bike rentals, and 30 lakes stocked annually with more than 150,000 fish. The downhill-skiing events of the 1988 Winter Olympic Games were held here at the specially developed Nakiska alpine resort, which is now open to the public. Meanwhile, Nordic skiers can glide over hundreds of cross-country skiing trails in the region.

Geographically, Kananaskis Country can

© ANDREW HEMPSTEAD

HIGHLIGHTS

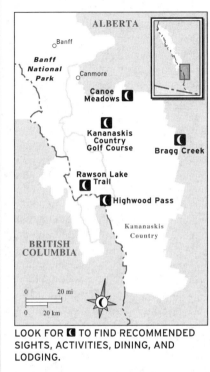

M Canoe Meadows: This is a groovy little spot to make a stop right beside the highway into Kananaskis Country. Even if kayakers aren't doing their stuff down the man-made rapids, the sparkling waters of the Kananaskis River are worth admiring (page 139).

M Kananaskis Country Golf Course: Nongolfers won't be too impressed, but if you do golf and plan on playing just one round in the Canadian Rockies, book a tee time here (page 143).

M Highwood Pass: In Peter Lougheed Provincial Park, you'll find one of the only places in the Canadian Rockies where you can drive to an area of alpine meadows (page 146).

M Rawson Lake Trail: Hikers visit for a variety of reasons—go fishing, to admire the wildflowers, or simply to soak up magnificent mountain scenery. Regardless of your own interests, add this destination to your hiking agenda (page 148).

M Bragg Creek: This picturesque hamlet was discovered years ago by Calgarians. Join them browsing the many galleries and taking lunch at an outdoor café (page 159).

LOOK FOR **M** TO FIND RECOMMENDED SIGHTS, ACTIVITIES, DINING, AND LODGING.

be divided into eight areas, each with its own distinct character: Bow Valley Provincial Park, a small park between the TransCanada Highway and Bow River that extends south along either side of the Kananaskis River; Kananaskis Valley, home to a golf course, ski resort, and the accommodations of Kananaskis Village; Peter Lougheed Provincial Park, which rises from fish-filled lakes to the glaciated peaks of the Continental Divide; Spray Valley Provincial Park, named for a massive body of water nestled below the Continental Divide; Sibbald, an integrated recreation area where horseback riding is permitted; Elbow River Valley and adjacent Sheep River Valley, sections of the foothills that rise to Elbow-Sheep Wildland Provincial Park; and in the far south the Highwood/Cataract Creek area, where the rugged landscape ranges from forested valleys to snow-capped peaks.

The main highway through Kananaskis Country is Highway 40, which branches off the TransCanada Highway 76 kilometers (47 miles) west of Calgary. Other points of access are south of Canmore through the Spray Valley; at Bragg Creek on the region's northeast border; west from Millarville, Turner Valley, and Longview in the southeast; or along the Forestry Trunk Road from the south.

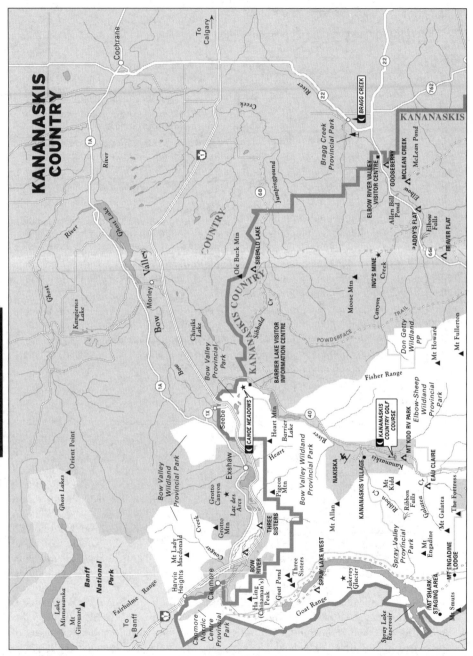

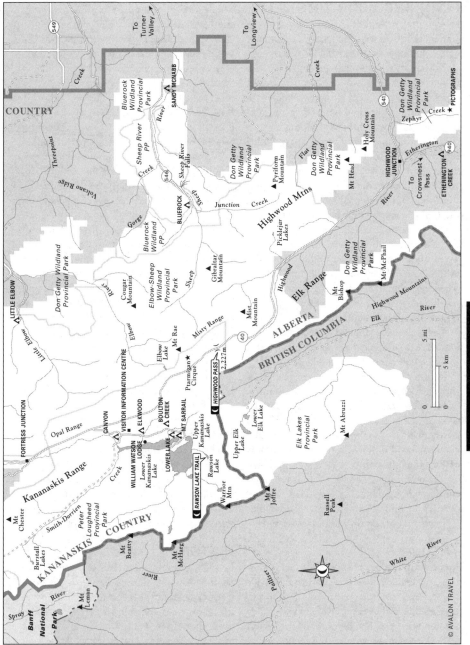

KANANASKIS COUNTRY

© AVALON TRAVEL

PLANNING YOUR TIME

I love planning a camping getaway to Kananaskis Country, especially in summer, when the crowds in Banff can be unbearable—but this is about planning *your* trip. If you're based in Canmore, Banff, or even Calgary, you can easily visit the region in a day, spending your time sightseeing and hiking along Highway 40, then looping back to the TransCanada Highway via Spray Valley Provincial Park. But you should plan to stay longer than a day. If you're camping, you'll be amazed at the number of options (2,300 auto-accessible campsites in 31 campgrounds) and the lack of crowds compared to the national parks. Be warned, though; Calgarians are well aware of this mountain wilderness, and every weekend through summer the region is overrun by urbanites in SUVs and families in minivans. Therefore, plan to arrive during the week, and you'll almost always be assured of a spot. For creature comforts, book a two-night stay at one of the hotels in **Kananaskis Village,** and you'll have time to combine the very best hikes with a round of golf or an extended bike ride.

Information centers are located at each of the main entrances to Kananaskis Country, but the best way to do some pretrip planning is using the website provided by the Alberta government (www.albertaparks.ca). Another good source of online information is **Friends of Kananaskis Country** (www.kananaskis. org), a nonprofit organization that promotes educational programs, is involved in a variety of hands-on projects, and promotes Kananaskis Country in partnership with the government.

THE LAND

Kananaskis Country holds two distinct ecosystems: the high peaks of the Continental Divide to the west and the lower, rolling foothills to the east. The glacier-carved **Kananaskis Valley** separates the two. The Elbow and Sheep River Valleys rise in the west to the front ranges,

which formed around 85 million years ago and have eroded to half their original height. The Main Ranges, which form part of the Continental Divide, are composed of older, erosion-resistant quartzite and limestone, giving them a more jagged appearance.

FLORA AND FAUNA

Kananaskis Country occupies a transition zone between foothills and mountains, and as a result it harbors a wide variety of plant species. In the east, the relatively low-lying Sheep, Elbow, and Sibbald Valleys are dominated by stands of **aspen,** interspersed with open meadows. Climbing gradually to the west, you'll pass through the montane zone, with its forests of **Douglas fir, lodgepole pine, white spruce,** and **balsam poplar,** then enter the subalpine zone, where stands of **Engelmann spruce, subalpine fir,** and occasionally **larch** lead up to the tree line. Above the tree line, which here occurs at around 2,300 meters (7,550 feet), lie the open meadows of the alpine zone. These meadows sleep under a deep cover of snow for most of the year but come alive with color during July when wildflowers bloom. Highwood Pass, along Highway 40, is one of the most accessible areas of alpine terrain in the Canadian Rockies; look for **forget-me-nots, Indian paintbrush,** and **western anemone** along the interpretive trail.

These hills, valleys, and forests are home to an abundance of wildlife, including large populations of **moose, mule deer, white-tailed deer, elk, black bear, bighorn sheep,** and **mountain goat.** Also present, but less likely to be seen, are **wolves, grizzly bears,** and **cougars.**

HISTORY

In 1858, Captain John Palliser bestowed the name Kananaskis on the valley, a pass, and two lakes. Kananaskis was a native who, legend had it, suffered a vicious blow to the head by an enemy but survived. The word itself is thought to mean "the meeting of the water." Aside from

Palliser, the region was visited by many names synonymous with exploration of the Canadian Rockies: David Thompson in 1787 and 1800, Peter Fidler in 1792, and James Sinclair leading Scottish settlers to the Oregon Territory in 1841. Throughout these times, and until recent times, the valley remained mostly uninhabited. Logging took place from 1883, mostly in the foothill valleys of the Elbow and Sheep Rivers. Coal was mined at various sites, including Ribbon Creek, by Kananaskis Village, but never on a large scale. To serve these industries, roads were built, including the Forestry Trunk Road (Highway 40), which traverses the entire foothills parallel to the Continental Divide.

1970s to the Present

During Alberta's oil-and-gas boom of the 1970s, oil revenues collected by the provincial government were placed into the Heritage Savings Trust Fund, from where they were channeled into various projects aimed at improving the lifestyle of Albertans. One lasting legacy of the fund is Kananaskis Country, officially designated by premier Peter Lougheed in 1977 as Kananaskis Country Provincial Recreational Area. The mandate was to accommodate a multitude of uses, including primarily recreational pursuits, but Kananaskis Country also holds 21 active oil and gas leases, 14 grazing permits, and a hydroelectric station on the Kananaskis River. Timber extraction leases have been in place in the region since the 1940s, and their contentious nature surfaced most recently in 2006 when a local company applied to begin harvesting an area west of Bragg Creek.

Since 1977, the provincial government has pumped more than $250 million into Kananaskis Country, with private investors spending a little more than $60 million in that same period. Kananaskis Village was developed in the early 1980s in anticipation of the 1988 Winter Olympic Games.

The first major boundary change since 1977 occurred in early 1996 when Elbow-Sheep Wildland Provincial Park was established; at 76,900 hectares (190,000 acres), it is Alberta's largest provincial park. A couple of years later saw the declaration of Spray Valley Provincial Park, which created a continuous stretch of protection for the Canadian Rockies from Willmore Wilderness Park in the north to Peter Lougheed Provincial Park in the south.

Bow Valley Provincial Park

This provincial park at the north end of Kananaskis Country straddles the TransCanada Highway just west of the Highway 40 junction and extends south to take in a stretch of the Kananaskis River as far south as, and including, Barrier Lake. Most facilities, including two campgrounds and an information center, lie between the TransCanada Highway and the Bow River, at the confluence of the Kananaskis River. The main access point is Highway 1X, which branches north from the TransCanada Highway 80 kilometers (50 miles) west of Calgary and 26 kilometers (16 miles) east of Canmore.

The park protects a small section of the Bow Valley, which was gouged by glaciers during a succession of ice ages, leaving the typical U-shaped glacial valley surrounded by towering peaks. Three vegetation zones are found within the park, but evergreen and aspen forest predominates. The park was originally within the area protected by Banff National Park, but the boundary was moved westward in 1930 to allow development in the Canmore area. The

KANANASKIS COUNTRY

park of today was originally created in 1959 and expanded in 2000.

To the casual motorist driving along the highway, the park seems fairly unspectacular (and is easily missed), but more than 300 species of plants have been recorded, and 60 species of birds are known to nest within its boundaries. The abundance of wildflowers, birds, elk, and smaller mammals can be enjoyed along short interpretive trails.

Popular activities in the park include fishing for brown and brook trout and whitefish in the Bow River, bicycling along the paved trail system, and attending interpretive programs presented by park staff. The main road through the park terminates 12 kilometers (7.5 miles) beyond the information center at a picnic area beside the Bow River.

HIKING

The trails in Bow Valley Provincial Park are short and unassuming. You could hike the entire trail system in a day, but if you choose just one, make it the Many Springs Trail.

Montane Trail

- Length: 2.2 kilometers/1.4 miles (30 minutes) round-trip
- Elevation gain: minimal
- Rating: easy
- Trailhead: Visitor Information Centre off Highway 1X

The Montane Trail begins from behind the main information center and, as the name suggests, traverses montane forest of aspen and towering Douglas fir, skirting an open meadow and several eskers (low ridges left behind by retreating glaciers during the last ice age).

Many Springs Trail

- Length: 2.8 kilometers/1.7 miles (40 minutes) round-trip

- Elevation gain: minimal
- Rating: easy
- Trailhead: Elk Flats day-use area

From the trailhead, this well-formed trail makes a loop around a wetland fed by underground springs. The spring water is relatively warm, creating a microclimate that attracts birds and mammals year-round. Look for orchids around damp areas.

Flowing Water Interpretive Trail

- Length: 1.4 kilometers/0.9 mile (30 minutes) round-trip
- Elevation gain: minimal
- Rating: easy
- Trailhead: Willow Rock Campground, eastern side of Highway 1X

This trail traverses montane forest along a bench above the Kananaskis River and passes a beaver pond. Interpretive panels along the way explain the importance of water and its relationship to the ecosystem.

CAMPGROUNDS

The park holds a number of picnic areas, two large campgrounds, and a grocery store (near the entrance to Bow Valley Campground) with bike rentals and firewood sales. Facilities at the two campgrounds within the park are as good as any in the Canadian Rockies. Both have showers, flush toilets, firewood for sale ($8 per bundle), and kitchen shelters. Continue beyond the information center to reach **Bow Valley Campground** (May-early Oct.), where unserviced sites are $23 and a limited number of sites with power and water are $35. Across Highway 1X, the loop road through **Willow Rock Campground** (Apr.-late Oct.) passes a few powered sites in an open area ($29), then descends to a smattering of well-spaced unserviced sites ($23), some right near the river. This campground also has a coin laundry and playground. For more information, or for reservations at Bow Valley, contact **Bow Valley Park** **Campgrounds** (403/673-2163, www.bowvalleycampgrounds.com).

Kananaskis Valley

This is the most developed area of Kananaskis Country, yet summer crowds are minimal compared to Banff. Highway 40 follows the Kananaskis River through the valley between the TransCanada Highway and Peter Lougheed Provincial Park.

SIGHTS

The following sights are along Highway 40 and are detailed from the TransCanada Highway in the north to Peter Lougheed Provincial Park in the south.

◖ Canoe Meadows

From the TransCanada Highway, 76 kilometers (47 miles) west of Calgary, Highway 40 branches south across open rangeland, entering Kananaskis Country beyond the boundary of the Stoney native reserve. The first worthwhile stop along this route is Canoe Meadows, a large day-use area above the sparkling Kananaskis River. Below the picnic area, white-water enthusiasts use a short stretch of river as a slalom course. Man-made obstacles and gates challenge recreational and racing kayakers, while upstream (around the first bend), the man-made Green Tongue creates a steep wave, allowing kayakers to remain in one spot, spinning and twisting while water rushes past them.

Barrier Lake and Vicinity

South from Canoe Meadows, stop at the **Barrier Lake Visitor Information Centre** (403/673-3985, 9am-6pm daily in summer, 9am-4pm daily the rest of the year) for park information and to browse the small selection of books. Nestled between Highway 40 and

the Kananaskis River, riverside trails lead in both directions, including two kilometers (1.2 miles) downstream to Canoe Meadows. Across the road is Tim Horton's Children's Ranch, set up to help underprivileged kids enjoy summer camp.

The first main body of water Highway 40 passes is **Barrier Lake,** dominated to the south by the impressive peak of Mount Baldy (2,212 meters/7,257 feet). The lake is man-made but still a picture of beauty. From a picnic area at its northern end, an official trail leads across the dam, but just as enjoyable is to walk along the southern lakeshore below the highway. Along its length are stretches of sandy beach, small streams, piles of driftwood, and at the end of the lake a massive scree slope that disappears into the lake.

Opposite Barrier Lake is the **Biogeosciences Institute,** a University of Calgary forestry research station that has been in use since the 1930s. A cabin from this early era still stands, along with a guard's tower put in place during World War II when the facility was used as an internment camp. The cabin is also the starting point for the Forestry Management Interpretive Trail, comprising two interconnected loops that describe the forest and forestry practices.

South to Kananaskis Village and Beyond

After passing a second, lesser-used picnic area at the south end of Barrier Lake, Highway 40 continues south around the base of Mount Baldy and crosses **Wasootch Creek** and another picnic area. The next stop of interest, especially for anglers, is **Mount Lorette Ponds,** a string of five shallow lakes stocked annually

© ANDREW HEMPSTEAD

Kananaskis Village

with rainbow trout. Originally an oxbow in the Kananaskis River, these lakes were artificially deepened when the construction of Highway 40 cut them off from the main flow of the Kananaskis River. Paved paths lead to and around the ponds, passing quiet picnic spots and wheelchair-accessible fishing platforms.

Kananaskis Village lies just off Highway 40, four kilometers (2.5 miles) south of the ponds. The village was the epicenter of action during the 1988 Winter Olympic Games. Developed specially for the games, the village sits on a high bench below Nakiska—where the downhill events of the games were held—and overlooks a golf course. The village comprises two hotels, restaurants, and other service shops set around a paved courtyard complete with waterfalls and trout-stocked ponds.

From the village, it's 15 kilometers (9.3 miles) farther south to the border of Peter Lougheed Provincial Park. Just beyond the village is **Wedge Pond.** Originally dug as a gravel pit during golf course construction, it is now filled with water and encircled by a one-kilometer (0.6-mile) trail offering fantastic views across the river to towering 2,958-meter (9,700-foot) Mount Kidd.

HIKING
Prairie View

- Length: 6.5 kilometers/4 miles (2-2.5 hours) one-way
- Elevation gain: 420 meters/1,380 feet
- Rating: moderate
- Trailhead: north end of Barrier Lake, Highway 40

This trail provides a variety of options; the most straightforward leads to a high viewpoint atop McConnell Ridge. To get started, cross the Barrier Dam, take the right fork at the first junction, and go left at the second. From this point the trail climbs steadily along an old fire lookout road to the summit, where views extend south

© ANDREW HEMPSTEAD

looking down to Barrier Lake from Prairie View Trail

across Barrier Lake to Mount Baldy. The actual site of the fire lookout is one kilometer (0.6 mile) farther and 80 vertical meters (260 vertical feet) from the main trail along the ridge. The additional climb to the lookout is well worth the effort; you'll be rewarded with views across Bow Valley to Mount Yamnuska and east across the prairies to Calgary. Back on the main trail, at the 6.5-kilometer (four-mile) mark, you'll come to Jewell Pass, a major trail junction. The options from this point are to descend along Jewell Creek to the shore of Barrier Lake, passing picturesque Jewell Falls (14 km/8.7 mi round-trip from the parking lot; allow four hours), or to continue north into the Quaite Valley and to the Heart Creek trailhead in the Bow Valley (a further 8 km/five mi one-way).

Baldy Pass

• Length: 4.5 kilometers/2.8 miles (1.5-2 hours) one-way

• Elevation gain: 520 meters/1,710 feet
• Rating: moderate
• Trailhead: Highway 40, 3 kilometers (1.9 miles) south of Barrier Lake

This trail traverses Elbow-Sheep Wildland Provincial Park to a 1,990-meter (6,530-foot) divide separating the Kananaskis River and Jumpingpound Creek watersheds. Cross Highway 40 from the unmarked parking lot, entering the woods at the marked trailhead. After 500 meters (0.3 mile), at a marked intersection, the trail enters a usually dry watercourse, which it follows the entire way to the pass. Only the last 500 meters (0.3 mile) are particularly steep, across an avalanche slope. An even better view than that afforded at the pass can be had by following the northern ridge from the pass. It's a steep scramble, though, gaining as much elevation in one kilometer (0.6 mile) as the whole trail gains between the trailhead and pass.

Ribbon Falls

- Length: 9 kilometers/5.6 miles (3 hours) one-way
- Elevation gain: 335 meters/1,100 feet
- Rating: moderate
- Trailhead: upper parking lot at Ribbon Creek, off Kananaskis Village access road

Moderate elevation gain and a well-formed trail make this one of the more popular day hikes in the Kananaskis Valley. Following Ribbon Creek through a narrow valley between Mount Kidd and Ribbon Peak, it passes chunks of iron from an old logging camp and the remains of two abandoned log cabins. Beyond the second cabin, the trail enters Dipper Canyon, dotted with pools of water, then climbs across an avalanche slope to a lookout over Ribbon Falls.

Two kilometers (1.2 miles) beyond the falls is Ribbon Lake, but reaching it requires some rock-climbing skills. From the falls, the trail

The trail to Ribbon Falls follows Ribbon Creek.

© ANDREW HEMPSTEAD

switchbacks up a scree slope to a sheer cliff face. Three lengths of chain and a series of narrow ledges need to be negotiated to reach the cliff top, and then it's a straightforward hike through a subalpine forest to the lake.

Mount Allan (Centennial Ridge)

- Length: 11 kilometers/6.8 miles (4-5 hours) one-way
- Elevation gain: 1,350 meters/4,430 feet
- Rating: difficult
- Trailhead: upper parking lot at Ribbon Creek

This is the highest maintained trail in the Canadian Rockies and one of the few that actually reach a mountaintop. Its final destination is the summit of Mount Allan, on whose slopes the Nakiska ski area lies. From the marked trailhead, it branches to the right, through the Hidden Ski Trail, then left through an open meadow that was the site of the Ribbon Creek Coal Mine. Then the fun starts: The trail gains 610 meters (2,000 feet) of elevation in the next two kilometers (1.2 miles). At the end of this climb, the trail arrives atop Centennial Ridge and at the top of the Olympic Platter, starting point for the Men's Downhill at the 1988 Winter Olympic Games. It follows the ridge past a group of intriguing 25-meter-high (82-foot-high) hoodoos known as the Rock Garden, passes a false summit, and then, finally, reaches the top of 2,990-meter (9,810-foot) Mount Allan.

Galatea Creek

- Length: 5.9 kilometers/3.7 miles (2 hours) one-way
- Elevation gain: 425 meters/1,390 feet
- Rating: moderate
- Trailhead: Highway 40, 10 kilometers (6.2 miles) south of Mount Kidd RV Park

Galatea Creek flows from high in the

Kananaskis Range through a narrow valley bordered to the north by Mount Kidd and to the south by Fortress Ridge. From Highway 40, the trail descends to the Kananaskis River, crossing via a long suspension bridge. Take the left fork once across the river. The trail is easy to follow as it parallels the north bank of Galatea Creek beneath the sheer southern wall of Mount Kidd. It traverses a wide avalanche slope before reaching the final steep ascent to tree-encircled Lillian Lake, which is stocked with rainbow trout. Behind the lake's backcountry campground, a trail continues two kilometers (1.2 miles) to Upper Galatea Lake.

OTHER RECREATION

In Kananaskis Village, **Kananaskis Outfitters** (403/591-7000) rents sporting equipment, including mountain bikes (from $15 per hour, $45 per day), canoes and kayaks ($55 per day), and various downhill and cross-country skiing

© ANDREW HEMPSTEAD

Nakiska is a world-class ski resort.

equipment. **Inside Out Experience** (403/949-3305 or 877/999-7238) runs three-hour rafting trips on the Kananaskis River below Barrier Dam for $75 per person.

◖ Kananaskis Country Golf Course

Regularly voted "Best Value in North America" by *Golf Digest,* this 36-hole layout (403/591-7272 or 877/591-2525, www.kananaskisgolf.com) is bisected by the Kananaskis River and surrounded by magnificent mountain peaks. It comprises two 18-hole courses: **Mount Kidd,** featuring undulating terrain and an island green on the 197-yard fourth hole, and **Mount Lorette.** Both courses measure more than 7,000 yards from the back markers. The course opened in 1983 at a cost of almost $1 million per hole. The bunkers alone—filled with pure white silica from British Columbia—cost $350,000. Renowned golf-course architect Robert Trent Jones Sr., who designed the layout, described the Kananaskis River Valley as "the best spot I have ever seen for a golf course." After marveling at the surrounding mountains, few will disagree with his statement. Just don't let the 142 sand traps, water that comes into play on more than half the holes, or the large rolling greens distract you. Greens fees are $100 (Albertan residents pay $80), and a cart is an additional $17 per person. Golfers enjoy complimentary valet parking and use of the driving range, a restaurant and bar with awesome mountain views, and a well-stocked golf shop.

Nakiska

The winter resort of Nakiska (403/591-7777, www.skinakiska.com; for accommodation reservations, call 800/258-7669) was built to host the alpine skiing events of the 1988 Winter Olympic Games but is now open to the public. Great cruising and fast fall-line skiing on runs cut specially for racing will satisfy the intermediate-to-advanced crowd. The Bronze chairlift accesses a novice area below the main area. The area has a total of 28 runs and a vertical rise of 735 meters (2,410 feet). Lift tickets are adult $74, senior and student $60, child $34. Kids ages five and younger ski free. Packages are offered in adjacent Kananaskis Village, as well as Canmore, 56 kilometers (35 miles) to the northwest and linked by shuttle Tuesday and Friday through the winter season.

Cross-Country Skiing

The most accessible of Kananaskis Country's 200 kilometers (124 miles) of cross-country trails are in the Ribbon Creek area. Most heavily used are those radiating from Kananaskis Village and those around the base of Nakiska. Most trails are easy to intermediate, including a five-kilometer (3.1-mile) track up Ribbon Creek. Rentals are available in the Village Trading Post in Kananaskis Village.

ACCOMMODATIONS AND CAMPING
Kananaskis Village

This modern mountain village 90 kilometers (56 miles) from Calgary was built for the 1988 Winter Olympic Games. It was again in the world spotlight when eight of the world's most politically powerful men met here during the G8 Summit in June 2002. In an attempt to prevent anarchy experienced at previous summits, the Canadian government decided on a wilderness destination, the first time the summit had ever taken place outside of a city. The actual summit was accompanied by Canada's largest-ever security operation, leaving world leaders to discuss economic growth, global poverty, sustainable development, and peace and security without interruption.

Kananaskis Village is home to 412-room **Delta Lodge at Kananaskis** (403/591-7711 or 866/432-4322, www.deltahotels.com, from $250 s or d), part of an upscale Canadian hotel chain. It offers three distinct types of

rooms in three buildings surrounding a cobbled courtyard. In the main lodge are 251 moderately large Delta rooms, many with mountain views, balconies, and fireplaces. Connected by a covered walkway are 70 Signature Club (a Delta designation) rooms, each boasting elegant Victorian-era charm, a mountain view, a luxurious bathroom complete with bathrobes, oversized beds, and many extras, such as CD players. Guests in this wing also enjoy a private lounge and continental breakfast. Rooms in Mount Kidd Manor combine natural colors with dramatic contemporary styling; some are bedroom lofts with gas fireplaces, kitchenettes, large bathrooms, and sitting rooms. Outdoor seating from various eateries spills into the courtyard, and biking and hiking trails radiate out in all directions. All in all, a good place to base yourself for an overnight hotel stay.

Other Accommodations and Camping

A magnet for families, **Ⓒ Sundance Lodges** (403/591-7122, www.sundancelodges.com, mid-May–late Sept.) is also a wonderful option for travelers looking to try camping or who want something a little more adventurous than a regular motel room. Campsites cost $29 per night, with rentals including tents, camp stoves, sleeping bags, and utensil kits available for minimal charge. Next up are the tepees ($57–83), 12 of them, each with colorfully painted canvas walls rising from wooden floors. Inside are mattresses, a heater, and a lantern. Finally, you can stay in one of 18 Trapper Tents ($85 s or d), with similar interior fittings but larger and with a canvas-covered awning over a picnic table. When you tire of hiking and biking on surrounding trails, return to the lodge for fishing in a man-made pond, horseshoes, badminton, and volleyball. Other amenities include a general store, hot showers, a laundry, and Internet access. Sundance sits beside the

Kananaskis River, just off Highway 40, 22 kilometers (13.7 miles) south of the TransCanada Highway. **Mount Kidd RV Park** (403/591-7700, www.mountkiddrv.com, unserviced sites $32.50, hookups $41-48, booking fee $10) is the finest RV park in all the Canadian Rockies. It's nestled below the sheer eastern face of Mount Kidd in a forest of spruce and lodgepole pine, along Highway 40 south of Kananaskis Village and the golf course, and 26 kilometers (16 miles) from the TransCanada Highway. The campground's showpiece is the Campers Center (yes, the American spelling). Inside is the main registration area and all the usual bathroom facilities as well as a game room, a lounge, groceries, a concession area, and a laundry room. Outside are two tennis courts, picnic areas by the river, and many paved biking and hiking trails. The combination of amenities and the mountain location—unequaled anywhere in the Canadian Rockies—makes this an extremely popular campground.

Those who can survive without such luxuries should continue 6.5 kilometers (four miles) south beyond Mount Kidd RV Park to **Eau Claire Campground** (mid-May-early Sept., $22 per site), operated by Kananaskis Camping (403/591-7226, www.kananaskiscountrycampgrounds.com). Facilities are limited to 50 sites (those on the outside of the loop afford the most privacy), each with a picnic table and fire pit, along with pump water, pit toilets, and a playground. No reservations are taken, but the website posts up-to-date vacancy numbers.

Other options for campers are to continue south along Highway 40 into Peter Lougheed Provincial Park or take Highway 68 east from Barrier Lake to Sibbald Lake.

FOOD

The Delta Lodge (403/591-7711) contains three restaurants, a deli, and two bars. For a warm, relaxed atmosphere, head to the **Bighorn Lounge** (from 11am daily), near the arcade's main entrance. It features a bistro-style menu highlighted by a wide variety of appetizers perfect for sharing, such as cheese platters. **Obsessions Deli** (from 8am daily, $8-14) serves up light snacks, including healthy sandwiches and rich, handmade truffles. Also in the arcade is the **Fireweed Grill** (6am-10pm daily, $15-32), with a casual Western-style atmosphere, floor-to-ceiling windows, and an adjoining outdoor patio used during summer. Breakfast is served buffet-style daily until 10am **Seasons Steakhouse** (6pm-9:30pm Tues.-Sat. June-Oct., $24-41), in the Signature Club wing, is the village's most elegant restaurant.

INFORMATION

A short distance along Highway 40 from Highway 1 (but north of Barrier Lake), **Barrier Lake Visitor Information Centre** (403/673-3985, 9am-6pm daily in summer, 9am-4pm daily the rest of the year) is a good place to start your trip into Kananaskis Country. A small information booth located near the main entrance to Kananaskis Village operates through the months of summer.

Peter Lougheed Provincial Park

This park is a southern extension of the Kananaskis Valley and protects the upper watershed of the Kananaskis River. It is contained within a high mountain valley and dominated by two magnificent bodies of water: **Upper** and **Lower Kananaskis Lakes.** To the west and south is the Continental Divide and British Columbia, while to the north is Spray Valley Provincial Park and to the east is Elbow-Sheep Wildland Provincial Park. Originally named Kananaskis Provincial Park, it was renamed in 1986 after Peter Lougheed (pronounced LAW-heed). Lougheed was the Albertan premier who, with the help of oil-money-based Heritage Savings Trust Fund, began the development of Kananaskis Country as a multiuse recreation area. The 500-square-kilometer (193-square-mile) wilderness area is the second-largest provincial park in Alberta. Captain John Palliser passed by the Kananaskis Lakes in 1858, summing up the beauty of the lakes by writing "We came upon a magnificent lake, hemmed in by mountains, and studded by numerous islets, very thickly wooded. This lake, about four miles long and one-and-a-half miles wide, receives water from the glacier above, and is a favorite place of resort to the Kootenie Indians."

Highway 40 is the main route through the park. The most important intersection to make note of is five kilometers (3.1 miles) along Highway 40 from the park's north boundary. At this point, Kananaskis Lakes Road branches off to the west, accessing Upper and Lower Kananaskis Lakes. These two lakes are the center of boating and fishing in the park, and opportunities abound for hiking and camping nearby.

◗ HIGHWOOD PASS

In the southeastern corner of the park, Highway 40 climbs to Highwood Pass (2,227 meters/7,310 feet), the highest road pass in Canada. On the way up to the pass, a pleasant detour is Valley View Trail, a five-kilometer (3.1-mile) paved road whose route higher up the slopes of the Opal Range allows views across the entire park to the Continental Divide. The pass itself is right at the tree line, making it one of the most accessible alpine areas in all the Canadian Rockies. Simply step out of your vehicle and follow the interpretive trails through the **Highwood Meadows.** In the vicinity, the **Rock Glacier Trail,** two kilometers (1.2 miles) north of Highwood Pass, leads 150 meters (0.1 mile) to a unique formation of moraine rock.

From the pass, Highway 40 descends into the Highwood/Cataract Creek areas of Kananaskis Country (Highwood Junction is 35 km/22 mi from the pass). Note: The road over Highwood Pass passes through a critical wildlife habitat, and in this regard it is closed December-mid-June.

HIKING

The park offers several interesting interpretive trails and more strenuous hikes. Most trailheads are along Kananaskis Lakes Road, a paved road that leads off Highway 40 to Upper and Lower Kananaskis Lakes. Many trails feature interpretive signs; others require an interpretive booklet available from the Visitor Information Centre. **Rockwall Trail,** from the Visitor Information Centre, and **Marl Lake Trail,** from Elkwood Campground, are wheelchair accessible and barrier free, respectively. These are some of the park's more popular interpretive and day hikes:

Boulton Creek

- Length: 4.9 kilometers/3 miles (90 minutes) round-trip

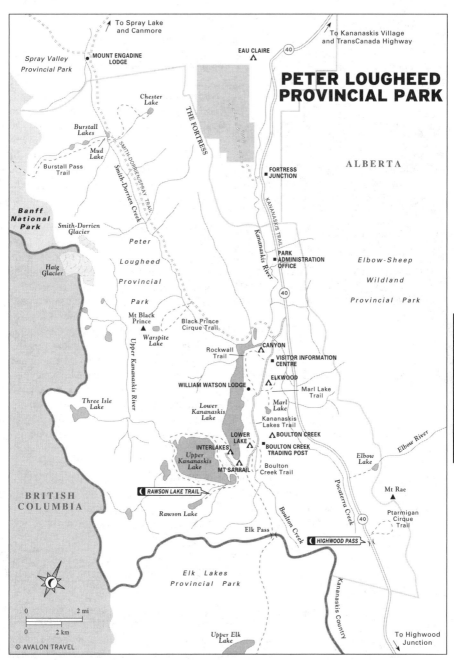

To Spray Lake
and Canmore

To Kananaskis Village
and TransCanada Highway

EAU CLAIRE
Λ

40

Spray Valley
Provincial Park

MOUNT ENGADINE
LODGE

PETER LOUGHEED
PROVINCIAL PARK

Chester
Lake

THE FORTRESS

Burstall
Lakes

Mud
Lake

SMITH-DORRIEN/SPRAY TRAIL

Burstall Pass
Trail

Smith-Dorrien Creek

FORTRESS
JUNCTION

ALBERTA

Banff
National
Park

Smith-Dorrien
Glacier

Peter

Lougheed

Provincial

Park

KANANASKIS TRAIL

Kananaskis River

PARK
ADMINISTRATION
OFFICE

Elbow-Sheep

Wildland

Provincial   Park

40

Haig
Glacier

Mt Black
Prince ▲

Black Prince
Cirque Trail

Warspite
Lake

Upper Kananaskis River

Rockwall
Trail

CANYON Λ

VISITOR INFORMATION
CENTRE

ELKWOOD Λ

Marl Lake
Trail

WILLIAM WATSON LODGE

Three Isle
Lake

Lower
Kananaskis
Lake

Marl
Lake

Kananaskis
Lakes Trail

LOWER
LAKE Λ

Λ BOULTON CREEK

INTERLAKES Λ

Upper
Kananaskis
Lake

MT SARRAIL Λ

BOULTON CREEK
TRADING POST

Boulton
Creek Trail

Elbow River

Elbow
Lake

BRITISH
COLUMBIA

◖ RAWSON LAKE TRAIL ▸

Rawson Lake

Boulton Creek

Pocaterra Creek

Mt Rae ▲

40

Ptarmigan
Cirque
Trail

Elk Pass

◖ HIGHWOOD PASS ▸

Elk   Lakes
Provincial   Park

Kananaskis Country

0   2 mi

0   2 km

© AVALON TRAVEL

Upper Elk
Lake

To Highwood
Junction

KANANASKIS COUNTRY

© ANDREW HEMPSTEAD

Rawson Lake

- Elevation gain: minimal
- Rating: easy
- Trailhead: Boulton Bridge, Kananaskis Lakes Road, 10 kilometers (6.2 miles) from Highway 40

A booklet, available at the trailhead or at the Visitor Information Centre, corresponds with numbered posts along this interpretive trail. The highlighted stops emphasize the valley's human history. After a short climb from a riverside parking lot below the Boulton Creek Trading Post, the trail reaches a cabin built in the 1930s as a stopover for forest-ranger patrols. The trail then follows a high ridge and loops back along the other side of the creek to the trailhead.

◖ Rawson Lake

- Length: 3.5 kilometers/2.2 miles (1.5 hours) one-way
- Elevation gain: 305 meters/1,000 feet

- Rating: moderate
- Trailhead: Upper Lake day-use area, Kananaskis Lakes Road, 13 kilometers (8 miles) from Highway 40

This picturesque subalpine lake is one of the most rewarding half-day hiking destinations in Kananaskis Country. It sits in a high cirque and is backed by a towering yet magnificently symmetrical headwall, so it's easy to spend an hour or two soaking up your surroundings once you reach the end of the trail. Snow lies along the trail well into July, and the lake doesn't open for fishing until July 15, but it is nevertheless a popular destination throughout summer.

Make your way to the farthest parking lot at Upper Lake (through the middle of the main parking lot) and begin the trek by taking the Upper Kananaskis Lake Circuit Trail. Sarrail Creek Falls is passed at the one-kilometer (0.6-mile) mark, 150 meters (0.1 mile) before the Rawson Lake cutoff. Taking the uphill option, you're faced with almost two kilometers (1.2 miles) of switchbacks. The trail then levels out, with boardwalks constructed over boggy sections of trail, suddenly emerging at the lake's outlet. Continue around the southern shore, past an intriguing elevated outhouse, to small meadows and slopes of scree that disappear into the lake.

Elbow Lake

- Length: 1.3 kilometers/0.8 mile (30 minutes) one-way
- Elevation gain: 135 meters/440 feet
- Rating: easy
- Trailhead: Elbow Pass day-use area, Highway 40, 13 kilometers (8 miles) south of Kananaskis Lakes Road

The official trail is a wide road that climbs quickly into the bowl holding shallow Elbow Lake. The lake is a popular spot, especially for summer picnics; campsites are spread around

© ANDREW HEMPSTEAD

Elbow Lake

the south shore. An interesting side trip is to Rae Glacier, a small glacier on the north face of Mount Rae. The trail starts on the east shore of the lake, gaining 400 meters (1,310 feet) of elevation in just over two kilometers (1.2 miles).

Elbow Lake is the source of the Elbow River, which flows eastward through Elbow-Sheep Wildland Provincial Park and into the foothills. The short hiking trail from Highway 40 up to the lake is part of a much longer historic route that ran between the two valleys and is still passable for backcountry adventurers.

The trailhead for this steep interpretive walk is across the road from the parking lot at Highwood Pass. A booklet, available at the trailhead or at the Visitor Information Centre, corresponds with numbered posts along the trail. As you climb into the alpine zone, magnificent panoramas unfold. Along the trail you are likely to see numerous small mammals. Columbian ground squirrels, pikas, least chipmunks, and hoary marmots are all common. At higher elevations, the meadows are home to bighorn sheep, mountain goats, and grizzly bears.

Ptarmigan Cirque

- Length: 5.6 kilometers/3.5 miles (2 hours) round-trip
- Elevation gain: 230 meters/750 feet
- Rating: moderate
- Trailhead: Highwood Pass, Highway 40, 17 kilometers (10.6 miles) south of Kananaskis Lakes Road

Warspite Lake

- Length: 2.1 kilometers/1.3 miles (40 minutes) one-way
- Elevation gain: 100 meters/330 feet
- Rating: easy
- Trailhead: Mount Black Prince day-use area, Smith-Dorrien/Spray Trail, 8 kilometers (5 miles) from Kananaskis Lakes Road

BEAT THE CAMPING CROWD

Every weekend throughout summer, thousands of Calgarians flee the city for the mountains. Kananaskis Country–and Peter Lougheed Provincial Park in particular–is the most popular destination. With little more than 500 campsites–many offered on a first-come, first-served basis–campgrounds fill fast. This isn't usually a problem during the week, but by lunchtime Friday, enthusiastic Calgarians are busy setting up camp for the weekend, and by midafternoon all sites will be filled. (Some folks head out on Thursday, stake a spot by paying for three nights' camping, head back to Calgary, then return

after work on Friday). The official checkout time is 11am, but plan on arriving earlier than this to secure a site. When every campground is full, a sign at the junction of Highway 40 and Kananaskis Lakes Road directs campers to the Pocaterra day-use area, where overflow camping costs $8. Another option is to continue up and over Highwood Pass to the more remote campgrounds detailed under Highwood/Cataract Creek.

Reservations are taken for some campgrounds annually from May 1 onwards. Use the website www.reserve.albertaparks.ca and have your credit card at hand.

This easily reached lake is away from the busiest part of the park, making it an uncrowded yet worthwhile jaunt (also known as the **Black Prince Cirque Trail,** although officially ending well before the actual cirque). Numbered posts along the trail correspond to a booklet available at the trailhead or at the Visitor Information Centre. The trail begins by climbing steadily to an area that was logged in the early 1970s. It then winds up through a forest of Engelmann spruce and subalpine fir, crossing Warspite Creek and emerging at the forest-encircled lake. An unmarked route continues along the north shoreline, then climbs unrelentingly before entering Black Prince Cirque, which was formed by ancient glacial action. Each spring the cirque fills with water, forming small, emerald-green lakes. It's an additional three kilometers (1.9 miles) each way from Warspite Lake to the cirque.

Burstall Pass

- Length: 7.4 kilometers/4.6 miles (2.5 hours) one-way
- Elevation gain: 480 meters/1,575 feet
- Rating: moderate/difficult
- Trailhead: Mud Lake, Smith-Dorrien/

Spray Trail, 20 kilometers (12.4 miles) from Kananaskis Lakes Road

From Mud Lake (a popular fishing hole), this trail begins with a three-kilometer (1.9-mile) climb up an old logging road to Burstall Lakes. After traversing some willow flats, it begins climbing again through heavy forest and across avalanche paths to a large cirque. The final ascent to the pass is a real slog, but the view across the Upper Spray Valley (which is in Banff National Park) is worth it.

OTHER RECREATION

Hiking is the most popular activity in the park but by no means the only one. The **Bike Trail,** a 20-kilometer (12.4-mile) paved trail designed especially for bicycles, begins behind the Visitor Information Centre and follows Lower Kananaskis Lake all the way to Mount Sarrail Campground. Many other trails are designated for mountain-bike use; inquire at the Visitor Information Centre (403/591-6344). **Boulton Creek Trading Post** (403/591-7678) rents mountain bikes; $12 per hour, $45 per day.

Fishing is fair in Upper and Lower Kananaskis Lakes, where trout and whitefish tease anglers. A nightly interpretive program takes place in campground amphitheaters throughout the park. Look for schedules posted on bulletin boards or check with the Visitor Information Centre.

In winter and spring, Highwood Pass is closed to traffic, but Highway 40 entering the park from the north is cleared, and cross-country skiing is excellent.

ACCOMMODATIONS AND CAMPING
William Watson Lodge

This special facility by Lower Kananaskis Lake (403/591-7227, www.williamwatsonlodgesociety.com) is available to persons with disabilities and seniors. It provides a wide range of barrier-free facilities, including hiking trails, a picnic area, and a stocked trout pond. Guests stay in either a campground or one of 22 barrier-free cabins, and they must supply their own bedding and food. The main lodge has a kitchen, lounge, library, laundry room, and a sundeck with gas barbecues. Disabled guests may bring up to three family members or friends. The cost is $14-28 per person per night. Reservations are essential and can be made up to four months in advance by Albertans and, space permitting, up to two months in advance by non-Albertans.

Campgrounds

Within Peter Lougheed Provincial Park are six auto-accessible campgrounds that hold 507 sites. They're linked by bicycle and hiking trails. Firewood is available at each campground for $8 per bundle. These campgrounds are operated by **Kananaskis Camping Inc.** (403/591-7226, www.kananaskiscountrycampgrounds.com), whose website is a wealth of information and includes vacancy reports, updated at 10am daily through summer.

The following campgrounds are listed from north to south along Kananaskis Lakes Road, from Highway 40 to the end of the road.

Canyon Campground (mid-June-early Sept., $20 per site) comprises two distinct types of camping at the northern end of Lower Kananaskis Lake, just over four kilometers (2.5 miles) along Kananaskis Lakes Road from Highway 40. An open meadow provides pull-through sites suited to RVs and trailers (Loop B), while up the hill off to the right, sites are protected by a forest of spruce and fir. Between the two loops is the trailhead for a 1.2-kilometer (0.7-mile) hiking path that traverses the Kananaskis Canyon. Another trail leads across Kananaskis Lakes Road to the nearby information center (the trailhead is beside Site 37). Each of 51 sites has a picnic table and fire pit, which along with pit toilets and tap water are the limit of facilities.

Just over one kilometer (0.6 mile) south of the information center (and on the same side of the road), **Elkwood Campground** (mid-May-early Sept., $23 per site) is the largest of the park's campgrounds, with 130 sites. It offers showers ($1 for five minutes) along each of four loops, flush toilets, a playground, and an interpretive amphitheater.

Boulton Creek Campground (May-Oct., $24-35 per site) has coin-operated showers just beyond the registration gate (complete with rack for those who have a bike), flush toilets, and an interpretive amphitheater. A few of the 118 sites have power, and the campground is within walking distance of a restaurant and grocery store. Boulton Creek is the only campground that takes reservations; book through Kananaskis Camping Inc. (403/591-7226, www.kananaskiscountrycampground.com).

Immediately beyond Boulton Creek Campground, turn right to access **Lower Lake Campground** (mid-May-early Oct., $22 per site), with 98 sites spread along three loops. Some sites (along Loop B) come close to the lake but are not within sight. Each private site has a picnic table and fire pit, while campers share pit toilets and two playgrounds. Eight sites are set away from the road—perfect for

KANANASKIS COUNTRY

tent campers who don't mind a short walk. Boulton Creek Trading Post is a short walk up and over Kananaskis Lakes Road from Loop A.

Mount Sarrail Campground (mid-June-early Sept., $22 per site), at the southern end of Upper Kananaskis Lake, 2.5 kilometers (1.6 miles) beyond Lower Lake Campground, is for tenters only. It's described as a walk-in campground, but some of the 44 sites are right by the main parking lot. It has pit toilets, pump water, and bear-proof food caches.

Finally, where Kananaskis Lakes Road branches left to the upper lake and right to the lower lake is an unpaved one-way road through **Interlakes Campground** (mid-May-early Oct., $22 per site), which loops back along the shore of Lower Kananaskis Lake before rejoining Kananaskis Lakes Road. It has 48 sites, many with lake views and some accessible enough to pull through a large RV or trailer. Facilities are basic: pump water, picnic tables, fire pits, and pit toilets, but if you score one of the lakeside sites, you'll be in prime position for a magnificent sunrise.

INFORMATION AND SERVICES

At the excellent **Visitor Information Centre** (4 km/2.5 mi along Kananaskis Lakes Road from Hwy. 40, 403/591-6322; 9am-5pm daily in summer, 9:30am-4:30pm daily the rest of the year), exhibits catalog the natural and cultural history of the park through photographs, videos, and hands-on displays, and a great display tells the story about the bears of Kananaskis Country. The knowledgeable staff hides hordes of literature under the desk, but you have to ask for it. Also ask them to put a movie or slide show on in the theater; most revolve around the park. The movie *Bears and Man* is a classic 1970s flick dealing with public attitude toward bears—one of the first documentaries to do so. A large lounge area that overlooks the valley to the Opal Range is used mainly in winter by cross-country skiers but is always open for trip planning or relaxing.

Boulton Creek Trading Post

Located along Kananaskis Lakes Road, 10 kilometers (6.2 miles) south of Highway 40, this busy hub is the park's only commercial center (9am-6pm mid-May-mid-Oct., extended to 10pm in July and Aug.). It sells groceries, basic camping supplies, fishing tackle and licenses, propane, and firewood. The store also rents bikes. Next door is an unremarkable family-style restaurant serving up pasta, burgers, and the like. A cooked breakfast is $10 (although the restaurant does not open until 9am). It also has an ice-cream window and serves coffee.

Spray Valley Provincial Park

The creation of 35,800-hectare (88,460-acre) Spray Valley Provincial Park in 2001 provided the final link in continuous protection between bordering Peter Lougheed Provincial Park in the south and Willmore Wilderness Park beyond the northern reaches of Jasper National Park in the north. To the west lies the remote and rarely traveled south end of Banff National Park, while to the north is the Bow Valley and Canmore. The park's dominant feature is **Spray Lake Reservoir,** a 26-kilometer-long (16-mile-long) body of water that is an integral part of a massive hydroelectric scheme. The Spray Development began in 1948 with construction of a road between Canmore and the Spray River. The next stage was damming the river, creating a reservoir of approximately 2,000 hectares (5,000 acres), then diverting its course through Whiteman's Pass and using the water flow as it drops into the Bow River to

© ANDREW HEMPSTEAD

Spray Lake

generate hydroelectric power. The water drops a total of 300 vertical meters (1,000 vertical feet) and passes through three power plants, which combined generate enough electricity to power a city of 100,000.

SMITH-DORRIEN/ SPRAY TRAIL

The Smith-Dorrien/Spray Trail (known as Spray Lakes Road from the Canmore end) is the only road through the park. This 60-kilometer (37-mile) unpaved (and often dusty) road links Peter Lougheed Provincial Park in the south to Canmore in the north. From the south, the road climbs up the Smith-Dorrien Creek watershed, passing Mud Lake and entering Spray Valley Provincial Park just south of Mount Engadine Lodge. Around three kilometers (1.9 miles) farther north is **Buller Pond** (on the west side of the road), from where the distinctive "Matterhorn" peak of Mount Assiniboine can be seen on a clear day. The road then parallels

the eastern shoreline of Spray Lake for more than 20 kilometers (12.4 miles), passing three lakefront picnic areas. The mountains that rise steeply to the east are the same ones visible to the *west* driving along the Kananaskis Valley. They rise to a high point of 3,121 meters (10,240 feet) at **Mount Sparrowhawk** (opposite the picnic area of the same name), which was roundly recommended as having better slopes than the barely adequate Mount Allan for hosting the downhill-skiing events of the 1988 Winter Olympics. In the end, its remote location killed the idea and any development was spared, except for a few lakeside picnic tables across the road. Beyond the north end of Spray Lake, the road passes **Goat Pond** and the Goat Creek trailhead, then descends steeply into the Bow Valley and Canmore.

The obvious loop—south from the TransCanada Highway along Highway 40 to Peter Lougheed Provincial Park, then north through Spray Valley Provincial Park to

© ANDREW HEMPSTEAD

Buller Pond

ski trails and quickly reaching the muddy shoreline of the lake, which is known for excellent cutthroat trout fishing. Dedicated anglers stop here; most other hikers cross the lake's outlet and continue 900 meters/0.6 mile (allow 20 minutes one-way) to a delightful spring that bursts from the forested slopes of Mount Shark and flows along a riverbed carpeted in moss.

Jakeroy Glacier

- Length: 4 kilometers/2.5 miles (1.5-2 hours) one-way
- Elevation gain: 600 meters/1,970 feet
- Rating: moderate/difficult
- Trailhead: Spray Lake West Campground

This small, hidden glacier is nestled in the shadow of the Goat Range. Reaching it entails some route finding, but the rewards are ample. To get to the trailhead, follow the campground access road for 1.5 kilometers (0.9 mile) beyond the end of the dam wall and park where it crosses a small creek (opposite Site 17). At the No Camping sign on the upstream side of the road, search out the trail that disappears into a forest of lodgepole pine. The trail parallels the creek for much of the way, making a minimal elevation gain through a moss-carpeted valley, until emerging in an open area where the creek flows through a willow-choked meadow. The headwall and hanging valley are now in clear view straight ahead. Continue a little farther, crossing the creek below a waterfall. From this point onward, the trail becomes indistinct, climbing steeply up the scree slope between the cliff face and the tree line. Most of the elevation gain is made in this last one kilometer (0.6 mile). The final steep pitch is through a forest of Engelmann spruce and larch into a hanging valley. A moraine running along the left side of the valley affords the best views of the glacier.

Canmore and back along the TransCanada Highway to Highway 40—is 150 kilometers (93 miles); allow at least three hours for the entire loop.

HIKING
Watridge Lake

- Length: 3.5 kilometers/2.2 miles (1 hour) one-way
- Elevation gain: 50 meters/165 feet
- Rating: easy
- Trailhead: Follow the Smith-Dorrien/Spray Trail 40 kilometers (25 miles) south from Canmore, then head 5 kilometers (3.1 miles) west to the Mount Shark staging area.

Most of the hiking in Spray Valley Provincial Park requires some route finding; Watridge Lake is the exception and is open to mountain bikes. The trail begins from behind the information board at the entrance to the main parking lot, skirting a maze of cross-country

© ANDREW HEMPSTEAD

the view from Mount Engadine Lodge

Goat Creek

- Length: 19 kilometers/11.8 miles (6 hours) one-way
- Elevation loss: 370 meters/1,210 feet
- Rating: easy/moderate
- Trailhead: Smith-Dorrien/Spray Trail, 9 kilometers (5.6 miles) west of Canmore

With prearranged transportation, this is an easy trail that gives hikers a real sense of achievement—walking from Kananaskis Country to downtown Banff. Beginning from the north end of the Spray Valley Provincial Park, the trail closely parallels Goat Creek for nine kilometers (5.6 miles) to the confluence of the Spray River, which it then follows all the way to the grounds of the famous Fairmont Banff Springs. This is also a good trail for mountain biking or cross-country skiing. It's downhill all the way.

ACCOMMODATIONS AND CAMPING

The Spray Valley had long been the target of developers, but the creation of a park put an end to proposed heli-skiing and boat tour operations. Existing facilities for visitors include a lodge, a campground, three picnic areas, and a heli-pad used as a staging area for flights into nearby Mount Assiniboine Provincial Park.

Lodge

Although a number of backcountry lodges are scattered throughout the Canadian Rockies, **Mount Engadine Lodge** (403/678-4080, www.mountengadine.com, late June-mid-Oct. and late Dec.-Mar., from $200 s, $420-450 d) is the only one accessible by public road. Technically, this means it's not a true "backcountry" lodge, but it has the feel of one, and, besides, most people don't even know it's there as they speed past on unpaved Smith-Dorrien/Spray Trail. It comprises luxurious rooms in the main lodge and two cabins set on a ridge overlooking an open meadow and small creek. The main lodge has a dining room, a comfortable lounge area with two stone fireplaces, and a beautiful sundeck holding a hot tub. Breakfast is served buffet-style, lunch can be taken at the lodge or packed for a picnic, and dinner is served in multiple courses of hearty European specialties. All meals are included in the nightly rates. Mount Engadine Lodge is 40 kilometers (25 miles) southwest of Canmore, at the turnoff to the Mount Shark staging area.

Campground

As the name suggests, **Spray Lake West Campground,** the only campground in the park, spreads out along the western shoreline of Spray Lake. Many of the 50-odd sites are private, but facilities are limited to picnic tables, fire pits, and pit toilets. Sites cost $22 per night, with firewood an additional $8 per bundle. It's open from when the snow clears (usually mid-May) to early September.

Sibbald

This small area in the north of Kananaskis Country protects the rolling foothills that descend to the rich grazing land west of Calgary. Access is along partly paved Highway 68, which branches south off the TransCanada Highway 17 kilometers (10.6 miles) west of the Cochrane intersection. Access is also possible from the west, off Highway 40 two kilometers (1.2 miles) south of the Barrier Lake Visitor Information Centre. From the east, Highway 68 climbs through the Jumpingpound Creek watershed to **Jumpingpound Demonstration Forest,** 18 kilometers (11.2 miles) from the highway. The forest is circled by a 10-kilometer (6.2-mile) driving tour, with signs identifying species in the surrounding forest. It also passes a portable sawmill, a small picnic area, and a wetland. Meanwhile, Highway 68 continues westward, passing a turnoff to **Sibbald Lake,** the Ole Buck Loop and Deer Ridge Circuit Trails, a picnic area, and a campground. It then crosses a low divide (look for impressive beaver ponds on the south side of the road) and descends through a narrow valley to Highway 40, the main route through Kananaskis Country. The only other road in Sibbald is the 35-kilometer (22-mile) Powderface Trail, a rough,

unsealed road (usually passable by two-wheel drive) that leads south from west of Sibbald Lake to Highway 66 through the Elbow River Valley.

Fishing is a popular activity in Sibbald. Sibbald Lake is stocked with rainbow trout and gets busy. To the west, **Sibbald Meadows Pond** is a quieter body of water, also stocked with fish and surrounded by reeds.

HIKING
Ole Buck Loop

- Length: 4.4 kilometers/2.7 miles (90 minutes) round-trip
- Elevation gain: 170 meters/560 feet
- Rating: easy/moderate
- Trailhead: Sibbald Lake day-use area

This trail makes a loop around the south-facing slopes of Ole Buck Mountain, which rises to the northeast of Sibbald Lake. From the Sibbald Forestry Exhibit, follow a trail between the lake and campground for one kilometer (0.6 mile). The Ole Buck Loop Trail branches to the left at this point, crossing Bateman Creek, from where the 2.4-kilometer (1.5-mile) loop begins. Views from high points along the trail extend south to Moose Mountain.

Deer Ridge Circuit

- Length: 6 kilometers/3.7 miles (2 hours) round-trip
- Elevation gain: 210 meters/690 feet
- Rating: easy/moderate
- Trailhead: Sibbald Lake day-use area

Take the trail south, following the access road for 150 meters (0.1 mile), then skirt the south shore of Moose Pond to a trail junction. The left fork is the Eagle Hill Trail, while the trail to the right climbs steadily up Deer Ridge. A short spur from the ridge leads to a lookout with views south to Moose Mountain. Returning to the main trail, turn left, descending along the north face of the ridge and back to the trailhead.

CAMPGROUNDS

Sibbald Lake Campground (mid-May-mid-Oct., $27 per site) lies within easy walking distance of Sibbald Lake and is signposted off Highway 68, 24 kilometers (15 miles) west of the TransCanada Highway and 12 kilometers (7.5 miles) east of Highway 40. It contains 134 sites spread along five loops (Loop E comes closest to the lake) winding through a mixed forest of aspen, spruce, and lodgepole pine. Amenities include pit toilets, picnic tables, fire rings, and drinkable well water. Equestrian campers can park and camp at **Dawson Equestrian Campground,** a short distance from Highway 68 along the Powderface Trail. This is a staging area for many horse trails.

INFORMATION

The closest information center in Sibbald is **Barrier Lake Visitor Information Centre** (2 km/1.2 mi north of the Hwy. 68/Hwy. 40 junction, 403/673-3985, 9am-6pm daily June-mid-Sept., 9am-4pm daily the rest of the year).

Elbow River Valley and Vicinity

The Elbow River has its source at Elbow Lake, among the high peaks of Elbow-Sheep Wildland Provincial Park. As it cuts east through the foothills, the Elbow River Valley gradually opens up, exiting Kananaskis Country near the picturesque hamlet of **Bragg Creek** and continuing its eastward flow, draining into the Bow River within the Calgary city limits. (The "elbow" for which the river was named by David Thompson in 1814 occurs at what is now Glenmore Reservoir, the source of Calgary's drinking water.)

The main access is Elbow Falls Road (Highway 66) west from Bragg Creek. It enters Kananaskis Country after eight kilometers (five miles), at the Elbow River Valley Visitor Centre. Close to the eastern boundary lie two good fishing spots: **McLean Pond** and **Allen Bill Pond.** Both are stocked with rainbow trout. Moose Mountain, home to a fire lookout since 1929, can be seen north of the highway. Continuing west, there is six-meter-high (20-foot-high) **Elbow Falls,** the highest road-accessible waterfall in Kananaskis Country. Just before the falls, an unpaved road leads north to **Ing's Mine,** where a small coal mine operated 1915-1920. Beyond the falls, the road first ascends through an area charred by a 1981 wildfire, and then descends to its end at a camping spot and picnic area, 42 kilometers (26 miles) from Bragg Creek.

HIKING
Sulphur Springs

- Length: 2 kilometers/1.2 miles (40 minutes) one-way
- Elevation gain: 200 meters/656 feet

- Rating: easy/moderate
- Trailhead: Sulphur Springs Creek, Highway 66

Park at Sulphur Springs Creek (just east of Paddy's Flat Campground) and follow the north bank of the small creek upstream, veering left at the cutline to reach the springs. Fed by sulphur-rich water, the springs were diverted through an iron casing in the 1930s.

Paddy's Flat

- Length: 2.2 kilometers/1.4 miles (30 minutes) round-trip
- Elevation gain: minimal
- Rating: easy
- Trailhead: Loop B, Paddy's Flat Campground, 20 kilometers (12.4 miles) west of Bragg Creek

This interpretive trail passes through a forest of lodgepole pine interspersed with white spruce, aspen, and, along a spring-fed creek, poplar, before looping back around and following the Elbow River downstream, back to the trailhead. Numbered posts correspond with a brochure available at the beginning of the trail.

Moose Mountain

- Length: 7 kilometers/4.3 miles (2.5-3 hours) one-way
- Elevation gain: 670 meters/2,200 feet
- Rating: moderate/difficult
- Trailhead: 7 kilometers (4.3 miles) along an unmarked gravel road that spurs north of Highway 66, 700 meters (0.4 mile) west of Paddy's Flat Campground

Rising to an elevation of 2,438 meters (8,000 feet), Moose Mountain is the dominant peak in the Elbow River Valley area. Its summit provides 360-degree views over the entire region. From 500 meters (0.3 mile) before a gate across the road, the trail follows an old fire-lookout road for four kilometers (2.5 miles),

climbing steadily just below the ridgeline. It then descends before climbing again into an open meadow. Here begins the relentless slog to the domelike lower summit, from where it's another 100 vertical meters (330 vertical feet), via switchbacks or a direct climb up a ridge, to the upper summit and fire lookout.

Little Elbow

- Length: 2.5 kilometers/1.6 miles (50 minutes) one-way
- Elevation gain: minimal
- Rating: easy
- Trailhead: Forget-me-not Pond, near the end of Highway 66

This interpretive trail explores a short stretch of the Little Elbow River, just before its confluence with the Elbow River. From Forget-me-not Pond, the trail passes between the road and the river, then continues upstream, looping past interpretive boards that describe the river and the mammals that live along its length.

CAMPGROUNDS

Five campgrounds, with a combined 551 sites, lie along the Elbow River Valley. The most developed of the five is **McLean Creek Campground,** 12 kilometers (7.5 miles) west of Bragg Creek and just south of Highway 66, by McLean Creek. At the campground entrance is the Camper Centre, with groceries, coin showers, and firewood ($8 per bundle). As in all campgrounds in Kananaskis Country, each of the 170 sites has a picnic table and fire pit. Unpowered sites are $26 per night, powered sites $34. The other campgrounds and their distances from Bragg Creek are **Gooseberry** (10 km/6.2 mi), **Paddy's Flat** (20 km/12.4 mi), **Beaver Flat** (30 km/18.6 mi), and, at the end of the road, **Little Elbow** (50 km/31 mi). The latter has facilities for campers with horses. Each of these campgrounds has only basic facilities—pit toilets and hand-pumped drinking water—but, still, sites are $24 per night. As at McLean Creek, firewood is available at $8 per bundle. McLean Creek is open year-round, while the other four campgrounds begin opening in mid-May and close between early September and the end of October.

INFORMATION

Elbow Valley Visitor Information Centre (403/949-4261, 9:30am-4:30pm Mon.-Thurs., 9am-5pm Fri.-Sun. May-Sept., weekends only the rest of the year) is at the entrance to Kananaskis Country, 10 kilometers (6.2 miles) west of Bragg Creek on Highway 66.

BRAGG CREEK

Bragg Creek is a rural hamlet nestled in the foothills of the Canadian Rockies, 40 kilometers (25 miles) west of Calgary. It lies on the edge of Kananaskis Country, at the entrance to the Elbow River Valley. The town and its quiet, tree-lined streets are a far cry from the hustle

and bustle of nearby Canmore and Banff, providing an ideal retreat to kick back and do some golfing, dining, and relaxing in one of the mountains' true gems.

The **Stoney Trail,** a native trading route that passed through the area, had been in use for generations when the first white people arrived in the early 1880s. The first settlers were farmers, followed by Calgarians who built weekenders in town. Today many of Bragg Creek's 1,000 residents commute daily to nearby Calgary. The ideal location and quiet lifestyle have attracted artists and artisans. The town claims to have more painters, potters, sculptors, and weavers than any similarly sized town in Alberta.

Sights and Recreation

Arriving along Highway 22 from either the north or south, you'll be greeted upon arrival in Bragg Creek by a slightly confusing four-way-stop intersection with a treed triangle of

KANANASKIS COUNTRY

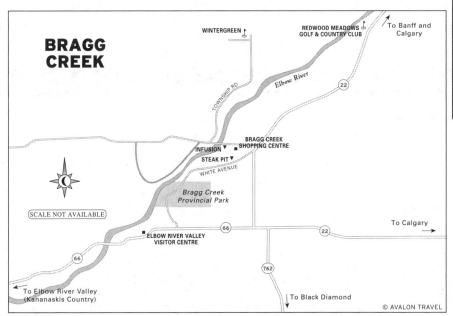

© AVALON TRAVEL

land in the middle. Take the option along the north (right) side of the distinctive polished-log Bragg Creek Trading Post II to access the main shopping center, a Western-themed collection of basic town services interspersed with craft shops and cafés. White Avenue, also known as **Heritage Mile** and originally the main commercial strip, has more of the same and leads through an appealing residential area. This road continues southwest to 122-hectare (300-acre) **Bragg Creek Provincial Park**, a day-use area alongside the Elbow River. With a basket of goodies from one of Bragg Creek's many food outlets, leave the main parking lot behind to enjoy a picnic lunch on a riverside picnic table.

Wintergreen Golf & Country Club (403/949-3333), six kilometers (3.7 miles) north of town from the west side of the Elbow River, is an immaculately manicured golf course with water hazards on 14 of the 18 holes. Greens fees are $72 midweek and $95 on weekends, which includes use of an excellent practice facility.

Food

Bragg Creek Shopping Centre holds a wide variety of eateries as well as most services, including a gas station, bakery, grocery store, and post office. Around the corner, at the main intersection, is the **Cinnamon Spoon** (Bragg Creek Trading Post II, 403/949-4110, 6am-5pm daily; $5.50-9), with the best coffee in town, as well as pastries, cakes, smoothies, and sandwiches made to order. Beyond Bragg Creek Shopping Centre, **Infusion** (23 Balsam Ave., 403/949-3898, 11am-10pm daily, $18-38) presents a menu of French and Asian cooking styles. Favorites include lightly battered salmon with basil and curry sauce and any of the Alberta beef dishes.

The **Steak Pit** (43 White Ave., 403/949-3633, from 11:30am daily, $22-36) has been a longtime local favorite. The decor is early Canadian, yet realistic and elegant. The dining room, decorated with hand-hewn cedar furniture, is only a small part of the restaurant, which also has a café and lounge. Eating here isn't cheap but *is* comparable to Calgary restaurants. The menu sets out to prove great steaks don't need fancy trimmings, and it does so with the best cuts of Alberta beef and great spuds.

Sheep River Valley

The Sheep River Valley lies immediately south of the Elbow River Valley, in an area of rolling foothills between open ranchlands to the east and the high peaks bordering **Elbow-Sheep Wildland Provincial Park** to the west. Access is from the town of **Turner Valley** (take Sunset Boulevard west from downtown), along Highway 546. The Kananaskis Country boundary lies 25 kilometers (15.5 miles) west of Turner Valley through rolling ranching land, from which point the highway follows the Sheep River for another 21 kilometers (13 miles) to its confluence with Bluerock Creek.

A short distance west of the entrance to Kananaskis Country is Sandy McNabb Campground and various interpretive trails. Continuing along Highway 546, the road enters **Sheep River Provincial Park**. Originally set aside in 1973 as Sheep River Wildlife Sanctuary, the park protects the winter range of bighorn sheep. The sheep spend the summer farther up the valley, and for hundreds of years they have migrated down to the open slopes alongside the Sheep River each fall. Sheep are the most common large mammal in the valley; explorer David Thompson reported that the natives also named the valley for its sheep (*itou-kai-you* in their language). At Bighorn day-use

© ANDREW HEMPSTEAD

Sheep River Falls

area, a short trail leads to a viewpoint of open meadows that are critical winter habitat for approximately 200 sheep. **Sheep River Falls,** a short distance before the end of the road, is reached by a short walk.

HIKING
Price's Camp

• Length: 5 kilometers/3.1 miles (1.5 hours) one-way

• Elevation gain: 50 meters/164 feet

• Rating: easy/moderate

• Trailhead: Sandy McNabb day-use area, Highway 546

Although the trail itself is easy, it requires fording the Sheep River, is reached through a maze of cutlines and old logging roads, and can be muddy after rainfall. If all that hasn't put you off, wade across the river upstream of Coal Creek to reach the trailhead. Head west (to the right), following a grassy bench along the river,

from which the trail enters a forest of lodgepole pine. When the trail crosses March Creek, head 300 meters (0.2 mile) up the north bank of the creek to this abandoned logging camp, a pleasant destination for a picnic lunch.

Foran Grade Ridge

• Length: 2.5 kilometers/1.6 miles (50 minutes) one-way

• Elevation gain: 190 meters/620 feet

• Rating: easy/moderate

• Trailhead: unmarked pullout 1.5 kilometers (0.9 mile) west of the winter closure gate at Sandy McNabb day-use area

Climbing steadily from Highway 546, this trail traverses an open field and passes through an aspen forest before reaching the high point of the ridge. From here, views extend up the Sheep River Valley all the way to the Opal Range. The distance given is to this first vantage point. An alternative to returning along the same route is to continue along the ridge for another 2.5 kilometers (1.6 miles), then descend the west side of the ridge to Windy Point Creek, which the trail follows downstream to Highway 40. Either walk back to the trailhead along the highway or cross the road and link up with a trail running through the valley floor for a total trail length of 11 kilometers (6.8 miles).

CAMPGROUNDS

Along Highway 546 are two campgrounds. **Sandy McNabb Campground** (May-mid-Oct., $22 per site) is the first you'll come to, a short walk from the river right by the entrance to Kananaskis Country. It's named for an Albertan oilman who made an annual pilgrimage to this spot with his family. Each of the 98 sites has a picnic table and fire pit (firewood is $8 per bundle). Other facilities are limited to pit toilets and hand-pumped water.

At the end of Highway 546, 21 kilometers (13 miles) farther west, is **Bluerock Campground** (mid-May-mid-Oct., $22 per site), where some of the 66 sites are set aside for equestrian campers. This campground has similar services to Sandy McNabb.

Both facilities are operated by **High Country Camping** (403/591-7226, www.campingalberta.com). All sites are filled on a first-come, first-served basis.

Highwood/Cataract Creek

The Highwood/Cataract Creek areas stretch from Peter Lougheed Provincial Park to the southern border of Kananaskis Country. This is the least-developed area in Kananaskis Country. The jagged peaks of the Highwood Mountains are its most dominant feature; high alpine meadows among the peaks are home to bighorn sheep, elk, and grizzlies. Lower down, spruce and lodgepole pine forests spread over most of the valley, giving way to grazing lands along the eastern flanks. Higher elevations, including along the Continental Divide, are protected by **Don Getty Wildland Provincial Park.**

The main access from the north is along Highway 40, which drops 600 vertical meters (1,970 feet) in the 35 kilometers (22 miles) between **Highwood Pass** and **Highwood Junction.** From the east, Highway 541 west from Longview joins Highway 40 at Highwood Junction. A lesser-used access is Highway 532, which branches west from Highway 22 about 37 kilometers (23 miles) south of Longview. This unpaved road passes Indian Graves Campground, then begins a steep climb to **Plateau Mountain,** high above the tree line and

with stunning views back across to Porcupine Hills. The main summer activities in this area of Kananaskis Country are hiking, horseback riding, climbing, and fishing. Winter use is primarily by snowmobilers.

HIKING

Only a few formal hiking trails are signposted. The rest are traditional routes that aren't well traveled; many require river crossings.

Picklejar Lakes

- Length: 4.2 kilometers/2.6 miles (90 minutes) one-way
- Elevation gain: 470 meters/1,540 feet
- Rating: moderate
- Trailhead: Lantern Creek day-use area (not Picklejar day-use area), 3 kilometers (1.9 miles) south of the Mist Creek day-use area, Highway 40

The name of these lakes was coined by early anglers, who claimed fishing them was as "easy as catching fish in a pickle jar." The name stuck, and it's still mostly anglers who are attracted to

© ANDREW HEMPSTEAD

the top of Plateau Mountain

the four lakes. They lie at the southern end of Elbow-Sheep Wildland Provincial Park. To access the trail, cross the road from Lantern Creek day-use area and walk up the hill 100 meters (330 feet). The trail is unmarked but easy to follow as it passes through a lightly forested area and open meadows to a ridge above Picklejar Creek. Descend and cross the creek, following its north bank up a steep, open slope, or stay high and right across a scree slope to reach the pass at 2,180 meters (7,150 feet). The first lake is 300 meters (0.2 mile) beyond the pass. The trail continues past two more lakes before ending at the fourth, which is the largest and has incredibly clear water. A lightly marked trail encircles the fourth lake.

Zephyr Creek

- Length: 4.5 kilometers/2.8 miles (90 minutes) one-way

- Elevation gain: 180 meters/590 feet

- Rating: moderate

- Trailhead: Sentinel day-use area, east of Highwood Junction along Highway 541

The walk itself along Zephyr Creek is easy enough, but the trail commences only after a difficult ford of the Highwood River from Highway 541. From the picnic area, descend and wade across the river to an old logging road. Turn right, then keep left, climbing slowly into the valley through which Zephyr Creek flows. The trail crosses the creek twice before reaching a small cairn marking the entrance into Painted Creek Valley. Where the valley walls close in, 800 meters (0.5 mile) from Zephyr Creek, pictographs can be found on the rocky canyon wall, one meter (three feet) up from the ground.

CAMPGROUNDS

All three campgrounds in the Highwood/ Cataract Creek areas are south of Highwood Junction. **Etherington Creek** (May-Nov., $20 per site) is seven kilometers (4.3 miles) south of

© ANDREW H MPSTEAD

one of the Picklejar Lakes

including water, pit toilets, firewood, fire pits, and picnic tables.

Continuing south, along Highway 532 up and over Plateau Mountain Ecological Reserve, is 16-site **Indian Graves Campground** (mid-May-mid-Sept., $22 per site).

INFORMATION AND SERVICES

Highwood House (Highwood Junction, 9am-5pm Fri.-Sun. May-June, 9am-8pm daily July-Sept., 9:15am-5pm weekends only Oct.-Apr.) has gas and a grocery store. Also at the junction is **Highwood Ranger Station** (403/558-2151, 10am-6pm Thurs.-Mon. late June-early Sept.).

GETTING THERE AND AROUND

Kananaskis Country is not served by any form of public transportation, nor are there guided tours. Instead, drive your own vehicle or a rental and head west from Calgary or east from Banff along the TransCanada Highway. The main access point is equidistant from both (around 50 minutes), from where Highway 40 heads south to the parks and places detailed above.

the junction, while **Cataract Creek** (mid-May-early Sept., $20) is five kilometers (3.1 miles) farther south. Both offer primitive facilities,

KOOTENAY NATIONAL PARK AND VICINITY

Shaped like a lightning bolt, this narrow 140,600-hectare (347,300-acre) park lies on the British Columbia side of the Canadian Rockies. The park's northern section is bordered by Banff National Park; Mount Assiniboine Provincial Park lies to the east and Yoho National Park to the north. Highway 93, extending for 94 kilometers (58 miles) through the park, provides spectacular mountain vistas. Along the route you'll find many short and easy interpretive hikes, scenic viewpoints, hot springs, picnic areas, and roadside interpretive exhibits. The park isn't particularly noted for its day-hiking opportunities, but backpacker destinations such as Kaufmann Lake and the Rockwall rival almost any other area in the

Canadian Rockies. Even if you never leave the highway, the scarred hillsides from wildfires that swept through the park in 2001 and 2003 will be obvious. The fires jumped the highway in places, burned bridges and information booths, and forced the closure of some trails due to the danger of falling trees; check at local information centers for the latest updates.

Kootenay has the fewest services of the four contiguous mountain national parks. Day-use areas, a gas station and lodge, and three campgrounds are the only roadside services inside the park. The small service town of Radium Hot Springs, at the junction of Highways 93 and 95 near the park's west gate, has a permanent population of well under 1,000 but offers

HIGHLIGHTS

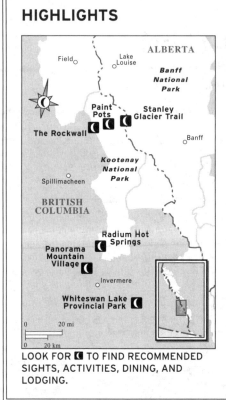

(Paint Pots: These naturally occurring ponds make a colorful stop along Highway 93 (page 170).

(Radium Hot Springs: After a long day hiking, the best recipe for soothing aching muscles is a soak in these mineral waters, located just outside the town of the same name (page 171).

(Stanley Glacier Trail: Although it takes around 90 minutes to reach the end of this trail, the stunning views are worth every step (page 172).

(The Rockwall: This is the domain of serious hikers, but those willing to make the effort are rewarded with one of the most awe-inspiring geological formations in all the Canadian Rockies (page 173).

(Panorama Mountain Village: This self-contained resort offers something for everyone—golfing, hiking, and biking in summer and world-class skiing and boarding in winter (page 182).

(Whiteswan Lake Provincial Park: This one is for keen anglers—one of the best fishing spots in all the Canadian Rockies (page 183).

LOOK FOR (TO FIND RECOMMENDED SIGHTS, ACTIVITIES, DINING, AND LODGING.

a range of accommodations, cafés and restaurants, gas stations, and grocery stores. Radium and the surrounding Columbia River Valley is covered in its own section at the end of this chapter. The park is open year-round, although you should check road conditions in winter, when avalanche-control work and snowstorms can close Highway 93 for short periods.

PLANNING YOUR TIME

Just one road passes through Kootenay National Park, and you can travel from one end to the other in under two hours. But plan to spend at least a full day in the park. Traveling from Banff to Invermere, an itinerary may look

like this: Leave Banff early in the morning and be the first on the trail to **Stanley Glacier.** Make stops at **Marble Canyon** and the **Paint Pots,** then enjoy a late lunch at one of the many riverside picnic areas along the Vermilion River. Spend the afternoon leisurely making your way up and over the park's two highway passes before stopping for a soak at **Radium Hot Springs.**

Because of the limited services, most visitors either camp out or stay in the Columbia River Valley. That said, the three park accommodations I've recommended are all excellent choices for overnight stays.

If your schedule isn't rushed, I recommend

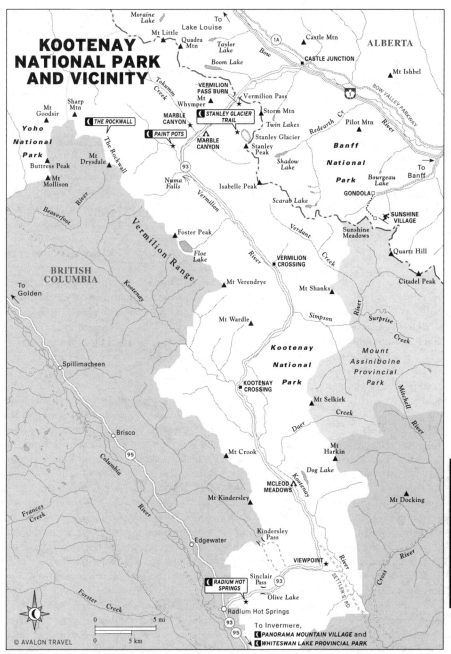

KOOTENAY
NATIONAL PARK
AND VICINITY

Moraine Lake
Mt Little
Lake Louise
To
Quadra Mtn
Mt Little
Taylor Lake
Boom Lake
Bow
1A
Castle Mtn
CASTLE JUNCTION
ALBERTA
Mt Ishbel
BOW VALLEY PARKWAY

Mt Goodsir
Sharp Mtn
Tokumm Creek
VERMILION PASS BURN
Mt Whymper
Vermilion Pass
Storm Mtn

Yoho
National
Park
THE ROCKWALL
MARBLE CANYON
STANLEY GLACIER TRAIL
PAINT POTS
MARBLE CANYON
Twin Lakes
Redearth Cr
Pilot Mtn
River

The Rockwall
Stanley Glacier
Stanley Peak

Banff

Buttress Peak
Mt Drysdale
Shadow Lake

National
Mt Mollison
Numa Falls
Vermilion
Isabelle Peak
Park
Bourgeau Lake
GONDOLA
To Banff

River
Beaverfoot
Scarab Lake
Verdant
Sunshine Meadows
Quartz Hill
SUNSHINE VILLAGE

Foster Peak
Vermilion Range
Floe Lake
River
VERMILION CROSSING
Creek
Citadel Peak

BRITISH
COLUMBIA
Kootenay
Mt Verendrye
Mt Shanks
River
Surprise Creek

To Golden
Mt Wardle
Simpson

Kootenay
Mount
Assiniboine
Provincial
Park

National
Spillimacheen
KOOTENAY CROSSING
Park
Mt Selkirk
Creek
Mitchell River

Brisco
95
Daer
Mt Crook
Mt Harkin
Dog Lake

Columbia
River
MCLEOD MEADOWS
Kootenay

Frances Creek
Mt Kindersley
Mt Docking

Edgewater
Kindersley Pass
River

VIEWPOINT
River
Cross River
SETTLER'S RD

Forster Creek
RADIUM HOT SPRINGS
Sinclair Pass
93
Olive Lake

Radium Hot Springs
93
95
To Invermere,
PANORAMA MOUNTAIN VILLAGE and
WHITESWAN LAKE PROVINCIAL PARK

0   5 mi
0   5 km
© AVALON TRAVEL

PARK ENTRY

Permits are required for entry into Kootenay National Park. A **National Parks Day Pass** is adult $9.80, senior $8.30, child $4.90, up to a maximum of $20 per vehicle. It can also be used in Banff National Park and beyond, if that is your direction of travel, and is valid until 4pm the day following its purchase. A **Discovery Pass,** good for entry into all Canadian national parks for one year from purchase, is adult $67.70, senior $57.90, child $33.30, up to a maximum of $136.40 per vehicle. Both types of pass are available from the western park gate, park information centers, and campground kiosks. For more information, check the Parks Canada website (www.pc.gc.ca).

spending a couple of days in the Columbia Valley, golfing at Radium Hot Springs, fishing at **Whiteswan Lake Provincial Park,** or skiing and boarding at **Panorama Mountain Village.** The atmosphere in the valley is more relaxed than in Banff and prices are cheaper, but more importantly for families, you'll find plenty of things to do.

THE LAND

Kootenay National Park lies on the western side of the Continental Divide, straddling the Main and Western ranges of the Canadian Rockies. As elsewhere in the Canadian Rockies, the geology of the park is complex. Over the last 70 million years, these mountains have been pushed upward—folded and faulted along the way—by massive forces deep beneath the earth's surface. They've also been subject to erosion that entire time, particularly during the ice ages, when glaciers carved U-shaped valleys and high cirques into the landscape. These features, along with glacial lakes and the remnants of the glaciers themselves, are readily visible in the park today. The park protects the upper

headwaters of the **Vermilion** and **Kootenay Rivers,** which drain into the Columbia River south of the park.

FLORA

In the lowest areas of the park, in the Kootenay River Valley, **Douglas fir** and **lodgepole pine** find a home. Along the upper stretches of the Vermilion River Valley, where the elevation is higher, **Engelmann spruce** thrive, while immediately above lie forests of **subalpine fir.** The tree line in the park is at around 2,000 meters (6,560 feet) above sea level. This is the alpine zone, where low-growing species such as **willow** and **heather** predominate. For a short period each summer, these elevations come alive with color as **forget-me-nots, avens,** and **avalanche lilies** flower. Of special interest is the interpretive trail through Vermilion Pass Burn, where fire destroyed 2,400 hectares (5,930 acres) of forest in 1968. Lodgepole pine is the dominant species here. The area affected by the more recent wildfires is an excellent place to see the natural regeneration process at work.

FAUNA

Large mammals tend to remain in the Kootenay and Vermilion River Valleys. **White-tailed deer, mule deer, moose, black bears,** and **elk** live year-round at these lower elevations, as do **bighorn sheep,** which can be seen at mineral licks along Highway 93. The most common large mammal present in Kootenay is the **mountain goat,** but these flighty creatures stay at high elevations, feeding in alpine meadows throughout summer. **Grizzlies** number around 10 within the park; they range throughout the backcountry and occasionally are sighted in spring high on roadside avalanche slopes.

HISTORY

Although their traditional home was along the river valley to the south, the indigenous Kootenay people regularly came to this area to enjoy the hot springs—a meeting place for mountain and Plains bands. Natives called the springs Kootemik (place of hot water). Early European visitors warped Kootemik into Kootenay and applied the name to the local residents. The natives traveled as far east as the Paint Pots area, to collect ocher for ceremonial painting purposes.

In 1905 Randolph Bruce, an Invermere businessman, persuaded the Canadian government and Canadian Pacific Railway (CPR) to build a road linking the Columbia River Valley to the prairie transportation hub of Calgary so that western produce could get out to eastern markets. Construction of the difficult **Banff-Windermere Road** began in

1911. But with three mountain ranges to negotiate and deep, fast-flowing rivers to cross, the money ran out after completion of only 22 kilometers (13.6 miles). To get the highway project going again, the provincial government agreed to hand over an eight-kilometer-wide (five-mile-wide) section of land along both sides of the proposed highway to the federal government. In return, the federal government agreed to finance completion of the highway. Originally called the Highway Park, the land became known as Kootenay National Park in 1920. The highway was finally completed in 1922, and the official ribbon-cutting ceremony was held at Kootenay Crossing in 1923; a plaque marks the spot.

Sights and Recreation

ROAD-ACCESSIBLE SIGHTS

The eastern access to Kootenay National Park is Highway 93 (also known as the Banff-Windermere Road), which branches west from the TransCanada Highway at **Castle Mountain Junction,** 29 kilometers (18 miles) northwest of Banff and 27 kilometers (16.8 miles) southeast of Lake Louise. From this point, Highway 93 climbs steadily for six kilometers (3.7 miles) to the Continental Divide, crossing it at an elevation of 1,640 meters (5,650 feet). The divide marks the border between Kootenay National Park to the west and Banff National Park to the east.

West from the Continental Divide

Immediately west of the divide is the **Vermilion Pass Burn.** Lightning started the fire that roared through this area in 1968, destroying thousands of hectares of trees. Lodgepole pine, which requires the heat of a fire to release its seeds, was the first plant species to sprout up through the charred ground. More than 40 years later, effects of the devastating fire are still

obvious. Along the short **Fireweed Trail** you'll see the growth of a new forest on the floor of the old. **Mount Storm** (3,161 meters/10,370 feet) is the distinctive peak to the east.

Beyond the Vermilion Pass Burn pullout, the devastation caused by a more recent fire (2003) becomes apparent. Also started by lightning, it began as a number of fires, which came together to cross the highway, burn entire watersheds, and extend high up the surrounding mountains to the extent of the tree line.

Marble Canyon

Be sure to stop and take the enjoyable self-guided trail, one kilometer (0.6 mile) each way, which leads along this ice-carved, marble-streaked canyon and through the remains of a forest destroyed by wildfires in 2003. The walk takes only about 30 minutes or so, yet as one of several interpretive plaques says, it takes you back more than 500 million years.

From the parking lot, the trail follows a fault in the limestone and marble bedrock through Marble Canyon, which has been

KOOTENAY NATIONAL PARK

below Numa Falls

the ocher in the early 1900s and shipped it to paint manufacturers in Calgary.

Several much longer hiking trails lead off the Paint Pots trail, including one of many routes to the Rockwall.

Along the Vermilion River

From the Paint Pots, the highway parallels the glacial-fed Vermilion River for 30 kilometers (19 miles). The first worthwhile stop is **Numa Falls,** where the Vermilion River tumbles over exposed bedrock. Continuing downstream, extensive devastation along the southwestern flanks of Mount Shanks is the result of fire started by a lightning strike. The fire destroyed more than 4,000 hectares (9,884 acres) of forest over a two-month period starting in July 2001.

Vermilion Crossing holds the only commercialism in the heart of the park, but compared to neighboring Banff, the development is minuscule. Here you'll find the **Kootenay Park Lodge** complex, which includes cabin accommodations, a restaurant, a general store, and an official park information center (open mid-May–mid-Oct.). Across the road from the lodge is a riverside picnic area.

Continuing south, the highway passes two signposted mineral licks (watch for bighorn sheep, mountain goats, and moose), then climbs to a viewpoint for **Hector Gorge.** A pleasant picnic area along this stretch of highway is beside **Wardle Creek.**

Kootenay Valley

As you continue to climb from the Vermilion River and pass small, green Kootenay Pond, your eyes will revel in views of milky green rivers, lush grassy meadows, tree-covered hills, and craggy, snowcapped peaks; keep your eyes peeled for mountain goats. The highway then descends to cross the Kootenay River at **Kootenay Crossing.** This was where the official ribbon-cutting ceremony opening the Banff-Windermere Road took place in 1923.

eroded to depths of 37 meters (130 feet) by fast-flowing Tokumm Creek. As the canyon narrows, water roars down through it in a series of falls. The trail ends at a splendid viewpoint where a natural rock arch spans a gorge. Marble Canyon is also the trailhead for the Kaufmann Lake Trail.

◖ Paint Pots

A scenic one-kilometer (0.6-mile) trail (20 minutes each way) leads over the Vermilion River to this unique natural wonder: three circular ponds stained red, orange, and mustard yellow by oxide-bearing springs. The natives, who believed that animal spirits resided in these springs, collected ocher from around the pools. They mixed it with animal fat or fish oil and then used it in ceremonial body and rock painting. The ocher had a spiritual association and was used in important rituals. Europeans, seeing an opportunity to "add to the growing economy of the nation," mined

© ANDREW HEMPSTEAD

Numa Falls is along the Vermilion River.

Today you'll find a roadside historical exhibit, hiking trails, and a warden's station. The following stretch of highway passes through an area of high wildlife concentration. Black bears, elk, deer, moose, coyotes, and, in winter, wolves are all regular visitors to cleared areas along the highway.

After passing McLeod Meadows Campground and a riverside picnic area inhabited by a healthy population of chirpy Columbian ground squirrels, Highway 93 climbs to a pullout that affords panoramic views of the entire valley and across to the Mitchell and Vermilion ranges.

West from Sinclair Pass

Beyond the Kootenay Valley viewpoint, Highway 93 tops out at 1,486 meters (4,875 feet) atop **Sinclair Pass.** Just beyond the pass, tiny **Olive Lake** is worth a stop. With outlets that flow in opposite directions and into two different watersheds, the lake is geologically

interesting, but for the younger set, spotting brook trout from the viewing platform will prove more attention-grabbing.

From Olive Lake, it's a steep 12-kilometer (7.5-mile) descent along Sinclair Creek to the park's western boundary and the town of Radium Hot Springs. Just after the halfway point is the only road tunnel in the Canadian Rockies. After you emerge from the tunnel, a parking lot on the south side of the road provides the perfect viewing point for sheer red cliffs that form the high point of the Redwall Fault. Through this fracture in the Earth's crust, mineral springs have been bubbling to the surface for thousands of years, staining the rock with red-colored iron oxide.

◖ Radium Hot Springs

This soothing attraction (250/347-9485, 9am-11pm daily in summer, noon-9pm daily the rest of the year) lies inside the park but just three kilometers (1.9 miles) northeast of the town of the same name, which is outside the park boundary. It was discovered many centuries ago by the Kootenay people, who, like today's visitors, came to enjoy the odorless mineral water that gushes out of the Redwall Fault at 44°C (111°F). Englishman Roland Stuart purchased the springs for $160 in 1890 and built rough concrete pools to contain the water. Development continued when a visiting millionaire—impressed by the improvement in his paralysis after soaking in the springs—contributed more money to the project. Originally known as Sinclair Hot Springs, after an early settler, the springs' name was changed to Radium in 1915 for the high level of radioactivity in the water. With the declaration of Kootenay National Park in 1922, ownership reverted to the government.

Today the water is diverted from its natural course into the commercial pools, including one that is Canada's largest. Steep cliffs tower directly above the hot pool, whose waters are

KOOTENAY NATIONAL PARK

© ANDREW HEMPSTEAD

Make time to stop for a soak at Radium Hot Springs.

colored a milky blue by dissolved salts, which include calcium bicarbonate and sulfates of calcium, magnesium, and sodium. The hot pool (39°C/97°F) is particularly stimulating in winter, when it's edged by snow and covered in steam—your head is almost cold in the chill air, but your submerged body melts into oblivion. Admission is adult $7 (or swim all day for $10), senior and child $5.75 (day pass $7.85). Towel and locker rentals are available, as are spa services. If you're camping at the park's Redstreak Campground, you can reach the complex on foot.

Sinclair Canyon

From the hot springs, Highway 93 passes through narrow Sinclair Canyon, descending quickly to the town of Radium Hot Springs. The canyon was eroded by the fast-flowing waters of Sinclair Creek, but not enough for a two-lane highway. But that was nothing a stick of dynamite couldn't fix. In addition to artificially widening the canyon, road builders constructed the highway over the top of the creek where it flows through the narrow gap. Small parking lots above and below the canyon provide an opportunity to pull over and walk through the canyon.

HIKING

Some 200 kilometers (124 miles) of trails lace Kootenay National Park. Hiking opportunities range from short interpretive walks to challenging treks through remote backcountry. All trails start from Highway 93 on the valley floor, so you'll be facing a strenuous climb to reach the park's high alpine areas, especially those in the south. For this reason, many hikes require an overnight stay in the backcountry. The following hikes are listed from east to west.

🄲 Stanley Glacier

- Length: 4.2 kilometers/2.6 miles (90 minutes) one-way
- Elevation gain: 350 meters/1,150 feet
- Rating: moderate
- Trailhead: Highway 93, 7 kilometers (4.4 miles) west of the Continental Divide

Although this glacier is no more spectacular than those alongside the Icefields Parkway just a few minutes' drive away, the sense of achievement of traveling on foot makes this trail well worth the effort. From Highway 93, the trail crosses the upper reaches of the Vermilion River, then begins a steady climb through an area burned by devastating fires in 1968. After two kilometers (1.2 miles), the trail levels off and begins winding through a massive U-shaped glacial valley, crossing Stanley Creek at the 2.4-kilometer (1.5-mile) mark. In open areas, fireweed, harebells, and yellow columbine carpet the ground. To the west, the sheer face of Mount Stanley rises 500 meters (1,640 feet) above the forest.

The trail officially ends atop the crest of a moraine after 4.2 kilometers (2.6 miles), with distant views to Stanley Glacier. It's possible (and worthwhile) to continue 1.3 kilometers (0.8 mile) to the tree-topped plateau visible higher up the valley. After reaching the top of the first moraine beyond the official trail end, take the left fork, which switchbacks up and over another crest before making a steady ascent through slopes of loose scree to the plateau. Surprisingly, once on the plateau, you'll find a gurgling stream, a healthy population of marmots, and incredible views west to Stanley Glacier and north back down the valley. Be especially careful on the return trip—it's extremely easy to lose your footing on the loose rock.

Kaufmann Lake

- Length: 15 kilometers/9.3 miles (5 hours) one-way
- Elevation gain: 570 meters/1,870 feet
- Rating: moderate
- Trailhead: Highway 93, Marble Canyon parking lot

This is an overnight backpack trip to a beautiful lake in the extreme north end of the park. The trail follows Tokumm Creek the entire distance, passing through a forest of lodgepole pine before entering an open meadow and crossing many small waterways. Most of the elevation gain is made in the final two kilometers (1.2 miles), as the trail switchbacks up to the glacial cirque holding Kaufmann Lake. The exquisite lake is surrounded by peaks jutting as high as 3,400 meters (11,150 feet). Two campgrounds lie at the end of the trail.

◖ The Rockwall

- Length: 54 kilometers/33.6 miles (3 days) round-trip
- Elevation gain: 760 meters/2,490 feet
- Rating: moderate/difficult
- Trailhead: various points along Highway 93

This is one of the classic hikes in all the Canadian Rockies. The Rockwall is a 30-kilometer-long (18.6-mile) east-facing escarpment that rises more than 1,000 meters (3,280 feet) from an alpine environment. Four different routes provide access to the spectacular feature; each begins along Highway 93 and traverses a steep valley to the Rockwall's base.

The most popular trail starts at the Paint Pots and follows Helmet Creek 12 kilometers (7.5 miles) to spectacular 365-meter (1,200-foot) Helmet Falls. A further 2.4 kilometers (1.5 miles) takes you to the beginning of the Rockwall trail and a campground, the first of five along the route. The trail then follows the Rockwall in a southeasterly direction for 30 kilometers (18.6 miles), passing magnificent glaciers, waterfalls, and lakes before ending at Floe Lake, 10.4 kilometers (6.5 miles) from the highway.

The Tumbling Creek and Numa Creek drainages provide alternate access routes to the Rockwall and require similar elevation gains. The elevation gain noted here is for the initial climb from the highway; along the route, ascents are made to four additional passes, with elevation gains ranging 280-830 meters (920-2,720 feet).

Hikers will need to make arrangements for shuttle transportation between the beginning and end of this route—about 13 kilometers (eight miles) apart—or allow extra time to hike back. As elsewhere in the park, all hikers spending the night in the backcountry must register and pick up a permit ($8 per person per night) at either of the park information centers.

Floe Lake

- Length: 10.4 kilometers/6.5 miles (3.5 hours) one-way

- Elevation gain: 730 meters/2,395 feet
- Rating: moderate/difficult
- Trailhead: Highway 93, 8 kilometers (5 miles) north of Vermilion Crossing

Of all the lakes in Kootenay National Park, this would have to be the most beautiful. Unfortunately, reaching it requires a strenuous day trip or an overnight expedition. From Highway 93, the trail crosses the Vermilion River then begins its long ascent of the Floe Creek watershed, passing through a forest of lodgepole pine and making many long switchbacks before leveling off 400 meters (1,310 feet) before the lake. Nestled in a glacial cirque, the gemlike lake's aquamarine waters reflect the Rockwall, a sheer limestone wall rising 1,000 meters (3,280 feet) above the far shore. In fall, stands of stunted larch around the lakeshore turn brilliant colors, adding to the incredible beauty.

Dog Lake

- Length: 2.6 kilometers/1.6 miles (40 minutes) one-way
- Elevation gain: 80 meters (260 feet)
- Rating: easy
- Trailhead: McLeod Meadows Picnic Area, Highway 93

Dog Lake is no *Mona Lisa,* but it is a popular and easily reached destination, especially for those staying in McLeod Meadows Campground (if you're not camping, park at the picnic area 500 meters/0.3 mile to the south). The trail first crosses the wide Kootenay River by footbridge. Then it hops a low ridge over to the shallow lake, which is fringed by marshes at the north end.

Kindersley Summit

- Length: 10 kilometers/6.2 miles (4 hours) one-way
- Elevation gain: 1,050 meters/3,445 feet

- Rating: difficult
- Trailhead: Highway 93, 2 kilometers (1.2 miles) west of Sinclair Pass

The elevation gain on this strenuous day hike will be a deterrent for many, but views from the summit will make up for the pain endured along the way. From Highway 93, the trail climbs through a valley for about three kilometers (1.9 miles), then switchbacks up across several avalanche paths and through more forest before emerging at an alpine meadow on Kindersley Pass. The final two-kilometer (1.2-mile) slog gets you higher, to an elevation of 2,400 meters (7,870 feet) at Kindersley Summit, a saddle between two slightly higher peaks. This is where the scenery makes the journey worthwhile. You'll enjoy views west to the Purcell Mountains, east to the Continental Divide, and, most spectacularly, north over the Kootenay River Valley. An alternate return route to the valley floor follows Sinclair Creek down from Kindersley Summit. This cuts two kilometers (1.2 miles) off the return distance.

Juniper Trail

- Length: 3.2 kilometers/2 miles (1 hour) round-trip
- Elevation gain: 90 meters/295 feet
- Rating: easy
- Trailhead: Highway 93, uphill from the west park gate

Named for the abundance of juniper along one section, this trail traverses a variety of terrain in a relatively short distance. You'll pass Sinclair Creek, an avalanche slope, and a lookout offering views of Windermere Valley and the Purcell Mountains. Beginning on the north side of the road just inside the park boundary, this trail rejoins the highway 1.5 kilometers (0.9 mile) farther into the park. There you can retrace your steps back to the start or return along the highway via Sinclair Canyon.

Accommodations and Camping

Accommodations within the park are limited, but all of the three recommendations below are good ones. If you feel the need to be in town, Radium Hot Springs has inexpensive motels.

$50-100

The only lodging in the heart of the park is **Kootenay Park Lodge** (403/762-9196, www.kootenayparklodge.com, mid-May-late Sept., $100-195 s or d), a cabin complex at Vermilion Crossing, 65 kilometers (40 miles) from Radium Hot Springs. Although no railway passes through the park, the 1923 lodge was one of many built by the CPR throughout the Canadian Rockies. It consists of a main lodge with restaurant, 12 cabins, a store, and an official park information center. The most basic cabins each have a bathroom, small fridge, and coffeemaker, with rates rising to $195 for the newer Vermilion Cabins with a separate bedroom and a fireplace. Utensil and cooking kits are $10 per stay.

OVER $150

The well-kept **☾ Cross River Wilderness Centre** (403/271-3296 or 877/659-7665, www.crossriver.ca, $188 per person including meals) has a real sense of privacy and of being well away from the well-worn tourist path of Highway 93. And it is—tucked in a riverside setting 15 kilometers (9.3 miles) down Settler's Road, which branches off the highway 114 kilometers (71 miles) from Banff and 32 kilometers (20 miles) from Radium Hot Springs. The smart, spacious cabins are equipped with wood-burning fireplaces, log beds draped in down duvets, toilets, and sinks. Showers are located in the main building, along with the main lounge, cooking facilities, a dining area, and a deck. As you can imagine, the atmosphere is convivial, with the cabins attracting outdoorsy types who want to enjoy the Canadian Rockies in their natural state—without room service and fine dining. Highly recommended.

☾ Nipika Mountain Resort (250/342-6516 or 877/647-4525, www.nipika.com, $205 s or $290 d) offers the same wilderness experience as the Cross River cabins and is in the same vicinity—along Settler's Road, which branches off Highway 93 114 kilometers (71 miles) from Banff and 32 kilometers (20 miles) from Radium Hot Springs. Sleeping up to eight people, the seven cabins are larger than those at Cross River and have full en suite bathrooms and kitchens with wood-burning stoves. The cabins are modern but were constructed in a very traditional manner—the logs were milled on-site, and construction is dovetail notching. Guests bring their own food and spend their days hiking, fishing, and wildlife-watching. In winter, an extensive system of trails is groomed for cross-country skiing.

CAMPGROUNDS

The park's largest camping area is **Redstreak Campground** (mid-May-mid-Oct.), on a narrow plateau in the extreme southwest (vehicle access from Highway 93/95 on the south side of Radium Hot Springs township), which holds 242 sites, showers, and kitchen shelters. In summer, free slide shows and talks are presented by park naturalists five nights a week and typically feature topics such as wolves, bears, the park's human history, or the effects of fire. Trails lead from the campground to the hot springs, town, and a couple of lookouts. Unserviced sites are $29, hookups $37-40. Fire permits cost $8 per site per night. A limited number of sites can be reserved through the Parks Canada Campground Reservation Service (877/737-3783, www.pccamping.ca).

The park's two other campgrounds lie to the

north of Radium Hot Springs along Highway 93. Both offer fewer facilities (no hookups or showers). The larger of the two is **McLeod Meadows Campground,** beside the Kootenay River 27 kilometers (16.8 miles) from Radium Hot Springs. Facilities include flush toilets, kitchen shelters, and a fire pit and picnic table at each of the 98 sites. **Marble Canyon,** across the highway from the natural attraction of the same name, offers 61 sites and similar facilities. Both are open late June-early September, and all sites cost $24. No reservations are taken at these two campgrounds.

Hikers planning overnight trips in the backcountry must register at either of the park information centers and pick up a backcountry camping pass ($10 per person per night, or $70 for a season pass).

Information and Transportation

Kootenay National Park Visitor Centre (250/347-9615, 9am-7pm daily in summer, 9am-5pm daily in spring and fall) is outside the park in the town of Radium Hot Springs, at the base of the access road to Redstreak Campground. Here you can collect a free map with hiking trail descriptions, find out about trail closures and campsite availability, get weather forecast, browse through a gift shop, buy park passes and fishing licenses, and register for overnight backcountry trips.

The other source of park information is at **Kootenay Park Lodge,** at Vermilion Crossing (summer only). It's worth noting that this is the only privately operated official information center in any Canadian national park—a reflection on the folks running this lodge.

For further park information, contact the park superintendent (P.O. Box 220, Radium Hot Springs, BC V0A 1M0, 250/347-9615) or check the Parks Canada website (www. pc.gc.ca). For park road conditions, call 403/762-1450.

GETTING THERE AND AROUND
Kootenay National Park is not served by public transportation, nor do any of the Banff tour companies include the park on their itineraries. The vast majority of visitors arrive by vehicle. Visitors can either base themselves in the village of Radium Hot Springs, 132 kilometers (82 miles) southwest of the town of Banff, or make the journey from Banff itself.

Radium Hot Springs and Vicinity

The small service center of Radium Hot Springs (pop. 900) sits at the southwest entrance to Kootenay National Park, 103 kilometers (64 miles) southwest of Castle Mountain Junction (Banff National Park). Its setting is spectacular; most of the town lies on benchlands above the Columbia River, from which the panoramic views take in the Canadian Rockies to the east and the Purcell Mountains to the west. As well as providing accommodations and other services for park visitors and highway travelers, Radium is a destination in itself for many travelers. The town is just three kilometers (two miles) from the hot springs for which it is named and boasts a wildlife-rich wetland on its back doorstep, two excellent golf courses, and many other recreational opportunities.

SIGHTS AND RECREATION
Columbia River Wetland

Radium sits in the Rocky Mountain Trench, which has been carved over millions of years by the Columbia River. From its headwaters south of Radium, the Columbia flows northward through a 180-kilometer-long (110-mile-long) wetland to Golden, continuing north for a similar distance before reversing course and flowing south into the United States. The wetland nearby Radium holds international significance, not only for its size (26,000 hectares/64,250 acres), but also for the sheer concentration of wildlife it supports. More than 100 species of birds live among the sedges, grasses, dogwoods, and black cottonwoods surrounding the convoluted banks of the Columbia. Of special interest are blue herons in large numbers and ospreys in one of the world's highest concentrations.

The wetland also lies along the Pacific Flyway, so particularly large numbers of ducks, Canada geese, and other migratory birds gather here in spring and autumn. The northbound spring migration is celebrated with the **Wings over the Rockies** (www.wingsovertherockies.org), which is held in the second week of May. The festival features ornithologist speakers, field trips on foot and by boat, workshops, and events tailored especially for children, all of which take place in Radium and throughout the valley. At any time of year, use the festival website to source the valley's best birding spots.

Golfing

The Columbia River Valley supports many golf courses and is marketed around western Canada as a golfing destination. Aside from the excellent resort-style courses and stunning Canadian Rockies scenery, golfers here enjoy the area's mild climate. Warm temperatures allow golfing as early as March and as late as October—a longer season than is typical at other mountain courses.

The 36-hole **Radium Resort** is a highlight of golfing the Canadian Rockies, comprising two very different courses. One of them, the 6,767-yard, par 72 **Springs Course** (250/347-6200 or 800/667-6444), is generally regarded as one of British Columbia's top 10 resort courses. It lies between the town and steep cliffs that descend to the Columbia River far below. Immaculately groomed fairways following the land's natural contours, near-perfect greens, and more than 70 bunkers filled with imported sand do little to take away from the surrounding mountainscape. Greens fees are $115 for 18 holes (discounted to $85 Mon.-Thurs.). The resort's second course, the **Resort Course** (250/347-6266 or 800/667-6444), is much shorter (5,306 yards from the tips) but tighter and still challenging. It is nestled in the shadow of the Rockies to the south of Radium, circling the resort's other facilities, which include accommodations, tennis courts, and many other exercise facilities. Greens fees are $65. Both courses have club and cart rentals, with the Springs Course also home to a driving range and teaching academy.

Other Recreation

While golfing is the big draw at Radium, the village is also a base for **Kootenay River Runners** (4983 Hwy. 93, 250/347-9210 or 800/599-4399), who offer white-water rafting trips for $90 for a half-day trip and $138 for a full day. Transportation and wet suits are provided, and the full-day trip includes lunch. This company also offers a more relaxing evening float through the Columbia River wetland in large and stable voyageur canoes, which depart at 5:30pm daily; the cost is adult $49, child $35.

ACCOMMODATIONS AND CAMPING

Radium, with a population of just 900, has more than a dozen motels, an indication of

KOOTENAY NATIONAL PARK

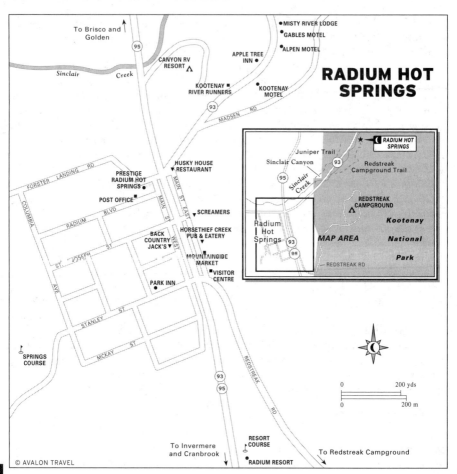

its importance as a highway stop for overnight travelers. Those that lie along the access road to Kootenay National Park come alive with color through summer as each tries to outdo the others with floral landscaping. When booking any of these accommodations, ask about free passes to the hot pools.

Under $50

At the top end of the motel strip, closest to the national park, **⬤ Misty River Lodge** (5036 Hwy. 93, 250/347-9912, www.radiumhostel. bc.ca, dorm beds $26, $60-85 d, breakfast $8 per person) provides an excellent base for travelers on a budget. Also known as Radium Hot Springs International Hostel, this converted motel has 11 beds in dormitories and private rooms that include a room that combines valley views with a full kitchen. Amenities include a communal kitchen, a lounge, and a big deck with even bigger views to the distant Purcell Mountains. You can also rent bikes and canoes.

$50-100

Kootenay Motel (250/347-9490 or 877/908-2020) is along Highway 93, up the hill from the junction of Highway 95. The rooms are nothing special (but air-conditioned) and rent from $70 s, $78 d, $10 extra for a kitchenette. Also on-site is a barbecue area and pleasant gazebo.

Up the hill a little and across the road is **Apple Tree Inn** (Hwy. 93, 250/347-9565 or 800/350-1511, www.appletreeinnbc.com, Apr.-Oct., $80-140 s or d), with a pleasant outdoor barbecue area.

Continuing toward the national park entrance, there is the **Gables Motel** (5058 Hwy. 93, 250/347-9866 or 877/387-7007, www.gablesmotel.ca, $79-129 s or d), where each of the 17 smallish rooms has mountain views and is well furnished.

Several older motels lie in the quiet residential streets west of Highways 93/95. One of these, the **Park Inn** (4873 Stanley St., 250/347-9582 or 800/858-1155, www.parkinn.bc.ca, $85-115 s or d), has rates that remain reasonable even though it undergoes regular revamps. It features an indoor pool and a covered barbecue area. Some units have kitchenettes and separate bedrooms.

While the rustic ambience of **Addison's Bungalows** (250/346-6888 or 800/794-5024, www.addisonsbungalows.com, Mar.-mid-Oct., $97-169 s or d) hasn't changed for generations, the surrounding scenery has. Originally located opposite the town's hot springs, the cabins were moved in 2001 to improve habitat for resident bighorn sheep. Today you'll find them just south of Brisco, 27 kilometers (17 miles) north of town along Highway 95. Each of the eight cabins has a small kitchen, bathroom, stone fireplace, deck, TV, and wireless Internet.

Over $100

In the middle of the motel strip is the **Alpen Motel** (Hwy. 93, 250/347-9823 or 888/788-3891, www.alpenmotel.com, $119-139 s or d), which arguably has the best and brightest flowers out front. The air-conditioned rooms are the best along the strip, which is reflected in the price (but hot springs passes are included).

Three kilometers (1.9 miles) south of town, **Radium Resort** (250/347-9311 or 800/667-6444, www.radiumresort.com) is surrounded by an 18-hole golf course and holds a wide variety of facilities, including a health club, indoor pool, restaurant, and lounge. Guest rooms overlook the golf course and are linked to the main lodge building by a covered walkway. Regular motel rooms range $175-210 s or d, while kitchen-equipped condos sleeping up to six people start at $265 per night. Check the website or call for specials (rooms are often sold for around $120, even in the middle of summer). Additionally, golf, ski, and spa packages lower rates considerably, especially before and after summer's peak season.

Prestige Radium Hot Springs (7493 Main St. W., 250/347-2300 or 877/737-8443, www.prestigeinn.com, $185-245 s or d) sits at the town's main intersection. Facilities include a fitness room, indoor pool, gift shop, spa services, an Italian restaurant, and a lounge bar.

Campgrounds

Within Kootenay National Park, but accessed from in town off Highways 93/95, is **Redstreak Campground** (mid-May-mid-Oct., unserviced sites $27, hookups $35-39, fire permits $8 per site per night), which has 242 sites, showers, and kitchen shelters. A limited number of sites can be reserved through the Parks Canada Campground Reservation Service (877/737-3783, www.pccamping.ca). The closest commercial camping is at **Canyon RV Resort** (5012 Sinclair Creek Rd., 250/347-9564, www.canyonrv.com, Apr.-Oct., $36-46 per site), nestled in its own private valley immediately north of the Highway 93/95 junction. Treed sites are spread along both sides of a pleasant creek,

Radium Resort

© ANDREW HEMPSTEAD

and all facilities are provided, including a playground and laundry.

Perfectly described by its name, **Dry Gulch Provincial Park** (250/422-3003, May-mid-Oct., $21 per site) offers 26 sites four kilometers (2.5 miles) south of town. Typical of provincial park camping, each site has a picnic table and fire pit but no hookups. Reservations are not taken.

FOOD

The town of Radium Hot Springs holds several good choices for a food break. For breakfast, head to the **Springs Course** restaurant (Stanley St., 250/347-9311, 7am-9pm daily Apr.-Oct., $13-25), at the golf course on the west side of the highway. The view from the deck, overlooking the Columbia River and Purcell Mountains, is nothing short of stunning. The food is good and remarkably inexpensive; in the morning, for example, an omelet with three fillings, hash browns, and toast is just $12.

Back in town, **Back Country Jack's** (Main St. W., 250/347-0097, 11am-11pm daily, $12-18) is decorated with real antiques and real hard bench seats in private booths. There's a wide variety of platters to share, including Cowboy Caviar (nachos and baked beans) and a surprisingly good barbecued chicken soup. For a main, the half-chicken, half-ribs and all the extras for two ($34) is a good deal. Across the road, **Horsethief Creek Pub and Eatery** (Main St. E., 250/347-6400, lunch and dinner daily, $14-24) serves up similar fare in more modern surroundings. Both places have a few outdoor tables.

As always, **Husky House Restaurant** (250/347-9811, 7am-11pm daily, $9.50-17), at the corner of Highways 93 and 95, serves a solid menu of no-frills North American fare at reasonable prices. Just around the corner is **Screamer's,** the place to hang out with an ice cream on a hot summer afternoon. The ice cream here has been researched many times, most often when returning from camping trips in the Columbia Valley. Also along this strip is **Mountainside Market,** with an excellent choice of groceries and an in-house deli and butcher.

The restaurant at the **Radium Resort** (3 km/1.9 mi south of town, 250/347-6268, breakfast, lunch, and dinner daily) caters mostly to golfers throughout the day and resort guests in the evening, but everybody is welcome. Enjoy lunch on the outdoor patio for around $15, or dine on sea bass smothered with a fruit-filled salsa for $28 in the evening. Buffets are offered on Wednesday (usually pasta) and Saturday (roast beef) nights from 6pm ($31 per person).

INFORMATION

On the east side of the highway, just south of the Highway 93/95 junction, is the **Radium Hot Springs Visitor Info Centre** (250/347-9331 or 800/347-9704, www.radiumhotsprings.com). This building is also home to the national park information center. It's open weekdays in spring and fall and 9am-7pm daily in the busier summer months.

NORTH FROM RADIUM ALONG HIGHWAY 95

From Radium, Highway 95 follows the Columbia River north for 105 kilometers (65 miles) to Golden, from where the TransCanada Highway heads east, through Yoho National Park and across the Continental Divide to Banff National Park. Between Radium and Golden are several small, historic towns worthy of a stop. The first is **Edgewater,** where a farmers market is held each Saturday. Continuing north is **Brisco,** gateway to the mountaineering mecca of **Bugaboo Provincial Park.** Named for a member of the 1859 Palliser expedition, Brisco was founded on the mining industry and later grew as a regional center for surrounding farmland. Brisco General Store is a throwback to those earlier times, selling just about

everything. Nearby **Spillimacheen** ("white water" to the natives) sits at the confluence of the Spillimacheen River and Bugaboo Creek.

SOUTH ALONG HIGHWAY 93/95

The highway south from Radium takes you 140 kilometers (87 miles) to the city of Cranbrook, which sits on Highway 3, a major transprovincial route across the southern portion of British Columbia. This highway accesses four provincial parks: **Whiteswan, Top of the World, Elk Lakes,** and **Height of the Rockies.**

Invermere

The commercial center of the Columbia River Valley is Invermere (pop. 3,500), on the shoreline of Lake Windermere 15 kilometers (nine miles) south of Radium. The population swells threefold throughout summer as vacation homes in Invermere and surrounding lakeside communities fill with a mostly Albertan influx of visitors who come for the water sports, the swimming, and the holiday atmosphere.

Off the Invermere access road, toward Wilmer, a small plaque marks the site of **Kootenae House.** Established by David Thompson in 1807, it was the first trading post on the Columbia River. The valley's first permanent settlement, known as Athalmer, was alongside the outlet of Lake Windermere, but continual flooding led to the town's expansion on higher ground. The old town site is now a popular recreation area, where a pleasant grassy area dotted with picnic tables runs right down to a sandy beach and the warm, shallow waters of the lake. It's on the left as you travel along the Invermere access road. As you approach the town itself, consider a stop at **Windermere Valley Museum** (622 3rd St., 250/342-9769, 11am-4pm Mon.-Fri. in summer, donation), where the entire history of the valley is contained in seven historic buildings.

Invermere holds limited accommodations,

but it has plenty of eateries, grocery stores, and gas stations. On a Saturday morning in downtown Invermere, you'll find all sorts of goodies at the outdoor **market,** which happens right on the main street. Farther down the hill, the **Quality Bakery** (888/681-9977, 7:30am-6pm Mon.-Sat., daily in summer) lives up to its name with a huge range of ultra-healthy sandwiches and not-so-healthy cakes and pastries. The town's most upscale dining room is **Strand's** (up the hill from the main street at 818 12th St., 250/342-6344, 5pm-9pm daily, $24-38). It's contained in a restored 1912 heritage house set on landscaped gardens, with diners seated in small, intimate rooms. The immaculately presented seasonal menu often includes delicacies such as trout, salmon, and venison that are served with a wide selection of vegetables.

Back out on the highway, at the south side of the town turnoff, is the **Invermere Visitor Info Centre** (250/342-2844, www.adventurevalley. com, 9am-5pm daily July-Aug.).

◀ Panorama Mountain Village

Panorama, in the Purcell Mountains immediately west of Invermere, is a year-round self-contained resort comprising a redeveloped base area, a residential subdivision, an open-air gondola to move visitors between the two main villages, a year-round water park, and a resort-style golf course. **Greywolf Golf Course** (250/341-4100) is a challenging 7,140 yards from the back tees, with water coming into play on 14 of the 18 holes, including the signature sixth hole, the Cliffhanger, which requires an accurate tee shot across a narrow canyon to a green backed by towering cliffs. Greens fees are $149, dropping to $99 for twilight rates booked seven days out. Also during the warmer months, there are chairlift rides (noon-5pm, $21), mountain biking ($45 per day for unlimited chairlift rides), white-water rafting, inflatable-kayak trips down Toby Creek, and

horseback riding. In the village itself you'll find tennis, a climbing wall, and an extensive complex of hot pools.

Skiing first put Panorama on the map, mainly because the resort boasts the third-highest vertical rise of all North American winter resorts (1,200 meters/3,940 feet), behind only Whistler/Blackcomb, also in British Columbia, and Big Sky, Montana. Despite the impressive relief, Panorama offers slopes suitable for all levels of expertise. Lift tickets are adult $72, senior $64, child $38.

The village is also home to **R.K. Heli-Ski** (250/342-3889 or 800/661-6060, www.rkheliski.com), which operates out of its own heliplex, complete with a lounge and restaurant. The company is one of the few heli ski operations that specializes in day trips, which cost from $690 per person.

Accommodations in Panorama Mountain Village are all relatively new but vary greatly in size and amenities. Rooms are booked through the resort's main switchboard (250/342-6941 or 800/663-2929, www.panoramaresort.com), as can all summer activities. Outside of the resort's marketing department, summer is still thought of as the off-season, and there are some great summer deals to be had, such as two nights' accommodation, breakfasts, and unlimited use of the chairlift for $90 per person per night.

TOP OF THE WORLD PROVINCIAL PARK

This wild and remote 8,790-hectare (21,720-acre) park lies beyond Whiteswan Lake Provincial Park, a rough 52 kilometers (32 miles) from Highway 93/95 (turn off the Whiteswan Lake access road at Alces Lake). You can't drive into the park, but it's a fairly easy six-kilometer (3.7-mile) walk from the end of the road to picturesque **Fish Lake,** the park's largest body of water. The trail climbs alongside the pretty Lussier River to the lake, which is encircled with Engelmann spruce and surrounded by peaks up to 2,500 meters (8,200 feet) high. The hike to the lake gains just over 200 vertical meters (660 vertical feet) and makes a good day trip. Trails from the lake lead to other alpine lakes and to a viewpoint that allows a good overall perspective on the high plateau for which the park is named. Fish Lake is productive for cutthroat and Dolly Varden trout.

Campgrounds and Information

Bring everything you'll need, because there are no services within the park. Camping is possible at one of four designated areas for $5 per person, or you can stay in the large cabin nestled in trees beside Fish Lake ($15 per person). For park information and trail conditions, contact **BC Parks** (www.env.gov.bc.ca/bcparks).

◖ WHITESWAN LAKE PROVINCIAL PARK

Access to this popular British Columbia park is from Highway 93/95, 50 kilometers (31 miles) south of Radium Hot Springs and 28 kilometers (17.4 miles) north of Skookumchuck. From a signed turnoff, an unpaved logging road takes off east into the mountains, leading first to 1,994-hectare (4.930-acre) Whiteswan Lake Provincial Park, then to Top of the World Provincial Park. The road climbs steadily from the highway, entering Lussier Gorge after 11 kilometers (6.8 miles). Within the gorge, a steep trail leads down to **Lussier Hot Springs.** Two small pools have been constructed to contain the odorless hot (43°C/110°F) water as it bubbles out of the ground and flows into the Lussier River. Within the park itself, the road closely follows the southern shorelines of first **Alces Lake,** then the larger **Whiteswan Lake.** The two lakes attract abundant birdlife; loons, grebes, and herons are all common. They also attract anglers, who come for great rainbow

trout fishing. Both lakes are stocked and have a daily quota of two fish per person.

Campgrounds

The main road skirts the lakes and passes four popular campgrounds. The sites are $17 per night and fill on a first-come, first-served basis. All sites come with a picnic table and fire grate. There are no hookups or showers.

HEIGHT OF THE ROCKIES PROVINCIAL PARK

This long and narrow, 68,000-hectare (134,000-acre) park protects a 50-kilometer-long (31-mile-long) section of the Canadian Rockies, including a 25-kilometer-long (15.5-mile-long) stretch bordering the Continental Divide. The park lies entirely in British Columbia, bordered by Elk Lakes and Peter Lougheed Provincial Parks to the east and Banff National Park at its narrow northern reaches. It is accessible only on foot and is not a destination for the casual day-tripper. Mountains dominate the landscape, with 26 peaks—some of which remained unnamed until recently—rising over the magical 10,000-foot (3,050-meter) mark. They lie in two distinct ranges: the **Royal Group** in the north and the **Italian Group** in the south. The dominant peak is 3,460-meter (11,350-foot) **Mount King George,** in the Royal Group, which is flanked by massive hanging glaciers on its north- and east-facing slopes. Mountain goats thrive on all the massifs, while the remote valleys are home to high concentrations of elk and grizzly bears.

The park can be reached from two directions. Neither is signposted, so before setting out for the park, pick up a good map of the area at a local information center or Forest Service office. The following directions are intended only as a guide.

Connor Lake is the most popular destination in the south of the park. It is reached by passing through Whiteswan Lake Provincial Park, then continuing along a rough logging road that parallels the White River to its upper reaches. (The most important intersection to watch for is 11 km/6.8 mi from Whiteswan Lake; stay right, immediately crossing the river.) At the end of the road, a tortuous 72 kilometers (45 miles) from Highway 93/95, is a small area set aside for tents and horse corrals. From this trailhead, it's an easy walk up Maiyuk Creek and over a low ridge to Connor Lake, where you'll enjoy great views of the Italian Group to the north and Mount Forsyth to the southwest.

Small **Queen Mary Lake** lies in the western shadow of the impressive Royal Group. It is generally the destination only of those on horseback or mountaineers continuing into the Royal Group. To get there, turn off Highway 93/95 at Canal Flats and follow a logging road up the Kootenay River watershed. For the first 48 kilometers (30 miles), the road follows the Kootenay itself. Then it turns westward and climbs along the south side of the Palliser River 35 kilometers (21.7 miles) farther to road's end. From this point, it's a 12-kilometer (7.5-mile) hike up a forested valley, with numerous creek crossings, to the lake.

Campgrounds

Primitive campgrounds lie on the shores of **Connor** and **Queen Mary Lakes** ($5 per person). An eight-person cabin sits at the north end of Connor Lake. Beds are offered on a first-come, first-served basis for $15 per person per night.

YOHO NATIONAL PARK AND VICINITY

Yoho, a Cree word of amazement, is a fitting name for this 131,300-hectare (324,450-acre) national park in British Columbia on the western slopes of the Canadian Rockies. The TransCanada Highway bisects the park on its run between Lake Louise (Alberta) and Golden (British Columbia). Banff National Park borders Yoho to the east, while Kootenay National Park lies immediately to the south.

Yoho is the smallest of the four contiguous Canadian Rockies national parks, but its wild and rugged landscape holds spectacular waterfalls, extensive ice fields, a lake to rival those in Banff, and one of the world's most intriguing fossil beds. In addition, you'll find some of the finest hiking in all Canada on the park's 300-kilometer (186-mile) trail system.

Within the park are four lodges, four campgrounds, and the small railway town of Field, where you'll find basic services. The park is open year-round, although road conditions in winter can be treacherous, and occasional closures occur on Kicking Horse Pass. The road out to Takakkaw Falls is closed through winter, and it often doesn't reopen until mid-June.

PLANNING YOUR TIME

Yoho National Park is a gem of a destination, well worth visiting even for just a day. If you do make the park a day trip from Banff, you'll have enough time to drive to **Takakkaw Falls,**

HIGHLIGHTS

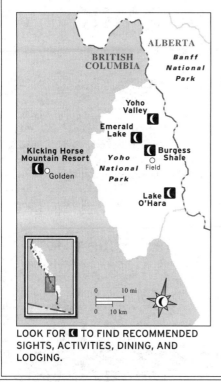

0 10 mi
0 10 km

LOOK FOR ■ TO FIND RECOMMENDED SIGHTS, ACTIVITIES, DINING, AND LODGING.

■ Yoho Valley: The valley doesn't become snow free until June, but when it does, the access road passes natural wonders such as Takakkaw Falls and opens up excellent hikes (page 190).

■ Emerald Lake: You can hike, canoe, fish, or simply soak up the mountain scenery (page 190).

■ Lake O'Hara: Quite simply, magical. Access is limited by a quota system, so take heed of the reservation information and be prepared for a day of hiking you will always remember (page 191).

■ Burgess Shale: The hiking is strenuous along a restricted-access trail, but because this is one of the world's most important paleontological sites, the trek is a once-in-a-lifetime experience (page 194).

■ Kicking Horse Mountain Resort: I've ridden each of the gondolas in the Canadian Rockies, and this one, near Golden, is my favorite for unbeatable top-of-the-world views (page 201).

hike the loop trail around **Emerald Lake,** and enjoy lunch in between at one of the restaurants I recommend. Organized tours from Banff and Lake Louise follow a similar itinerary—a good option if you don't have a vehicle (children will love being on the bus as it negotiates the road to Takakkaw Falls). The highlight of a visit to Yoho is **Lake O'Hara,** one of the most special places in the Canadian Rockies. Unlike at the region's other famous lakes, you can't simply drive up to O'Hara. Instead, you must make advance reservations for a shuttle bus that trundles up a restricted-access road to the lake.

The summer tourist season in Yoho is shorter than in the other national parks. Emerald Lake doesn't become ice free until early June, and the road to Takakkaw Falls remains closed until mid-June. While July and August are the prime months to visit, September is also pleasant, both weather- and crowd-wise. Lake O'Hara doesn't become snow free until early July, but the best time to visit is the last week of September, when the forests of larch have turned a brilliant gold color.

The last part of this chapter covers the town of **Golden,** which lies beyond the park's western boundary. Here, the highlight is summer gondola rides at **Kicking Horse Mountain Resort.** The more adventurous can take a white-water

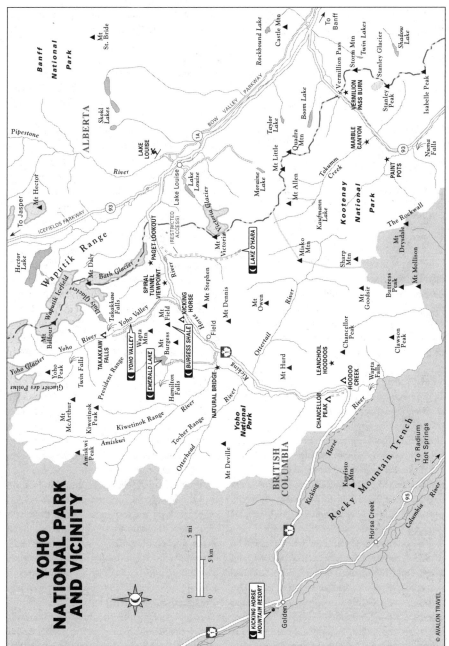

© AVALON TRAVEL

PARK ENTRY

Unless you're traveling straight through and not stopping, a permit is required for entry into Yoho National Park. A **National Parks Day Pass** is adult $9.80, senior $8.30, child $4.90, up to a maximum of $20 per vehicle. It can be used in the other national parks and is valid until 4pm the day following its purchase. The **Discovery Pass,** good for entry into Yoho and all of Canada's national parks for one year from purchase, is adult $67.70, senior $57.90, child $33.30, to a maximum of $136.40 per vehicle. Both types of pass are available from the Field Visitor Centre and at campground kiosks. For more information on passes, go to the Parks Canada website (www.pc.gc.ca).

rafting trip down the Kicking Horse River or go mountain biking. Including Golden with the highlights of Yoho National Park makes for a very long day trip; an overnight stay either in the park or in Golden will give you two days to enjoy both at a relaxed pace.

THE LAND

The park extends west from the Continental Divide to the western main ranges of the Rocky Mountains. The jagged peaks along this section of the Continental Divide—including famous Mount Victoria, which forms the backdrop for Lake Louise—are some of the park's highest. But the award for Yoho's loftiest summit goes to 3,562-meter (11,686-foot) **Mount Goodsir,** west of the Continental Divide in the Ottertail Range.

The park's only watershed is that of the **Kicking Horse River,** which is fed by the Wapta and Waputik Icefields. The Kicking Horse, wide and braided for much of its course through the park, flows westward, joining the mighty Columbia River at Golden. The park has many individual geological features of interest, including **Takakkaw and Twin Falls,** **Natural Bridge, Leanchoil Hoodoos, Emerald Lake,** and **Lake O'Hara.**

FLORA

Elevations within the park cover a range of more than 2,500 meters (8,200 feet), making for distinct vegetation changes and more than 600 recorded species of plants. **Douglas fir** is the climax species at lower elevations, but **lodgepole pine** dominates areas affected by fire. **Western red cedar, hemlock,** and the delightful **calypso orchid** can be found in the damp eastern shoreline of Emerald Lake. At higher elevations, where temperatures are lower and precipitation is higher, the familiar subalpine forests of **Engelmann spruce** and **subalpine fir** thrive. The northernmost extent of **larch** exists around Lake O'Hara. Larch is a conifer (evergreen), but its needles turn a stunning orange in fall—a photographer's delight. Above the tree line, where wind and rain have deposited soil, wildflowers such as **heather, Indian paintbrush,** and **arnica** create a carpet of color for a few short weeks in midsummer.

FAUNA

The animals for which Yoho is best known are fossilized in beds of shale and have been dead for more than 500 million years. But they still create great interest for the role their remains have played in our understanding of life on earth in prehistoric times.

Large mammals are not as common in Yoho as in the other parks of the Canadian Rockies, simply because the terrain is so rugged. Valleys are inhabited by **mule deer, elk, moose, black bears,** and a wide variety of smaller mammals. **Porcupines** are common along Yoho Valley Road. The park has a healthy population of **grizzly bears,** but sightings are relatively rare because the grizzly tends to remain in remote valleys far from the busy TransCanada Highway corridor. Much of the park is above the tree line; here noisy **marmots** and **pikas** find a home, along with an estimated 400 **mountain goats.** More than 200 bird species have been recorded within the park.

HISTORY

The Kootenay and Shuswap tribes of British Columbia were the first humans to travel through the rugged area that is now the national park. It's believed the men hid their families in the mountains before crossing over to the prairies to hunt buffalo and to trade with other tribes. On their return, they set up seasonal camps along the Kicking Horse River to dry the buffalo meat and hides. They used a more northern route than that taken by travelers today, crossing the divide at Howse Pass and descending to the Kootenay Plains beyond the present-day junction of Highways 93 and 11.

The first Europeans to explore the valley of the Kicking Horse River were members of the 1858 Palliser Expedition, which set out to survey the west and report back to the British government on its suitability for settlement. The party approached from the south, climbing the Kootenay and Vermilion watersheds of present-day Kootenay National Park before descending to Wapta Falls. It was here that the unfortunate expedition geologist, Dr. James Hector, inadvertently gave the Kicking Horse River its name. While walking his horse over rough ground, he was kicked unconscious and took two hours to come to, by which time, so the story goes, other members of his party had begun digging his grave.

Guided by outfitter Tom Wilson, Major A. B. Rogers (for whom Rogers Pass to the west is named) surveyed Kicking Horse Pass in 1881. His favorable report to the Canadian Pacific Railway (CPR) led to this route being chosen for the much-awaited transcontinental railway. The railbed was laid in 1884, and its grade was terribly steep; the first train to attempt the run suffered a brake failure and derailed, killing three workers. In 1909, after dozens more wrecks and derailments, the CPR rerouted the steepest section of the line through the Spiral Tunnels. The highway now follows the original rail grade.

The small township of Field started as a railway maintenance depot at the bottom of treacherous Big Hill. In 1886 the CPR opened Mount Stephen House in Field, both to encourage visitors to this side of the mountains and as a dining stop for customers of the railway. The CPR then built lodges at several natural attractions in the area, including **Emerald Lake Lodge** in 1902, **Lake O'Hara Lodge** in 1913, and **Wapta Lodge Bungalow Camp** in 1921.

As in adjacent Banff, the coming of the railway was a prime catalyst in the formation of Yoho National Park. Upon the opening of the railway line in 1886, 2,600 hectares (6,425 acres) of land around the base of Mount Stephen were set aside as Mount Stephen Park Reserve, Canada's second national park. In 1901 the reserve was expanded, and after three further boundary changes, the park of today came into being in 1930. Mining of lead, zinc, and silver continued until 1952, and today remnants of the Monarch and Kicking Horse Mines can still be seen on the faces of Mount Stephen and Mount Field, respectively.

Sights and Recreation

ROAD-ACCESSIBLE SIGHTS

As with all other parks of the Canadian Rockies, you don't need to travel deep into the backcountry to view the most spectacular features—many are visible from the roadside.

The following sights are listed from east to west, starting at the park boundary (the Continental Divide).

Spiral Tunnel Viewpoint

The joy CPR president William Van Horne felt upon completion of his transcontinental rail line in 1886 was tempered by massive problems along a stretch of line west of Kicking Horse Pass. Big Hill was less than five kilometers (3.1 miles) long, but its gradient was so steep that runaway trains, crashes, and other disasters were common. A trail from Kicking Horse Campground takes you past the remains of one of those doomed trains.

Nearly 25 years after the line opened, railway engineers and builders finally solved the problem. By building two spiral tunnels down through two kilometers (1.2 miles) of solid rock to the valley floor, they lessened the grade dramatically, and the terrors came to an end. Today the TransCanada Highway follows the original railbed. Along the way is a viewpoint with interpretive displays telling the fascinating story of Big Hill.

◖ Yoho Valley

Fed by the Wapta Icefield in the far north of the park, the **Yoho River** flows through this spectacularly narrow valley, dropping more than 200 meters (660 feet) in the last kilometer (0.6 mile) before its confluence with the Kicking Horse River. The road leading up the valley passes the park's main campground, climbs a *very* tight series of switchbacks (watch for buses reversing through the middle section), and emerges at **Upper Spiral Tunnel Viewpoint,** which offers a different perspective on the aforementioned tunnel. A further 400 meters (0.2 mile) along the road is a pullout for viewing the confluence of the Yoho and Kicking Horse Rivers—a particularly impressive sight as the former is glacier-fed and therefore silty, while the latter is lake-fed and clear.

Yoho Valley Road ends 14 kilometers (8.7 miles) from the main highway at **Takakkaw Falls,** the most impressive waterfall in the Canadian Rockies. The falls are fed by the Daly and Des Poilus Glaciers of the Waputik Icefield, which straddles the Continental Divide. Meaning "wonderful" in the language of the Cree, Takakkaw tumbles 254 meters (830 feet) over a sheer rock wall at the lip of the Yoho Valley, creating a spray bedecked by rainbows. It can be seen from the parking lot, but it's well worth the easy 10-minute stroll over the Yoho River to appreciate the sight in all its glory.

Natural Bridge

Three kilometers (1.9 miles) west of Field is the turnoff to famous Emerald Lake. On your way out to the lake, you'll first pass another intriguing sight. At Natural Bridge, two kilometers (1.2 miles) down the road, the Kicking Horse River has worn a narrow hole through a limestone wall, creating a bridge. Over time, the bridge will collapse and, well, won't be such an intriguing sight anymore. A trail leads to several viewpoints. You'll probably see people clambering over the top of the bridge, but resist the urge to join them—it's dangerous and not recommended.

◖ Emerald Lake

Outfitter Tom Wilson stumbled on stunning

© ANDREW HEMPSTEAD

Natural Bridge

Emerald Lake while guiding Major A. B. Rogers through the Kicking Horse River Valley in 1881. He was led to the lake by his horse, which had been purchased from natives. He later surmised that the horse had been accustomed to traveling up to the lake, meaning that the horse's former owners must have known about the lake before the white man arrived.

One of the jewels of the Canadian Rockies, the beautiful lake is surrounded by a forest of Engelmann spruce, as well as many peaks more than 3,000 meters (9,840 feet) high. It is covered in ice most of the year but comes alive with activity for a few short months in summer when hikers, canoeists, and horseback riders take advantage of the magnificent surroundings. **❰ Emerald Lake Lodge** (250/343-6321 or 800/663-6336, www.crmr.com) is the grandest of Yoho's accommodations, offering a restaurant, café, lounge, and recreation facilities for both guests and nonguests.

❰ LAKE O'HARA

Nestled in a high bowl of lush alpine meadows, Lake O'Hara, 11 kilometers (6.8 miles) from the nearest public road, is surrounded by dozens of smaller alpine lakes and framed by spectacular peaks permanently mantled in snow. As if that weren't enough, the entire area is webbed by a network of hiking trails established during the 20th-century by luminaries such as Lawrence Grassi. Trails radiate from the lake in all directions; the longest is just 7.5 kilometers (4.7 miles), making Lake O'Hara an especially fine hub for day hiking. What makes this destination all the more special is that a quota system limits the number of visitors.

Book the Bus

It's possible to walk to Lake O'Hara, but most visitors take the shuttle bus along a road closed to the public. The departure point is a signed parking lot 15 kilometers (9.3 miles) east of Field and three kilometers (1.9 miles) west of the Continental Divide. Buses for day visitors depart between mid-June and early October at 8:30am and 10:30am, returning at 2:30pm, 4:30pm, and 6:30pm To book a seat, call the dedicated reservations line (250/343-6433). Reservations are taken up to three months in advance, but as numbers are limited, you will need to call *exactly* three months prior to be assured of a seat; even then, you should call as early in the day as possible. Phone lines are open 8am-4pm Monday-Friday April-May and 8am-4pm daily June-September. The reservation fee is $12 per booking, and the bus fare is $15 per person round-trip. The procedure is simple enough, but to be assured a seat, it's important you get it right: For example, to visit on September 25 (when the larch are at their colorful peak), start dialing at 8am on June 25 (with a credit card ready). Reservations are only required for the inbound shuttle; outgoing buses fill on demand.

All times—bus departures and reservation

YOHO NATIONAL PARK

center hours—are mountain standard time (the same time zone as Banff).

Other Considerations

After the 20-minute bus trip to the lake, day hikers are dropped off at **Le Relais,** a homely log shelter where books and maps are sold, including the recommended *Lake Louise and Yoho Gem Trek* map. Hot drinks and light snacks are served—something to look forward to at the end of the day, as this is also the afternoon meeting place for the return trip.

Several overnight options are available at the lake, including the **Elizabeth Parker Hut** (403/678-3200, www.alpineclubofcanada.ca), **Lake O'Hara Lodge** (250/343-6418, www. lakeohara.com), and a campground (reservations for camping are made in conjunction with the shuttle bus), but each should be booked well in advance.

Lake O'Hara Shoreline

- Length: 2.8 kilometers/1.7 miles (40 minutes) one-way
- Elevation gain: minimal
- Rating: easy
- Trailhead: warden's cabin, across from Le Relais

Most people use sections of this easy loop around Lake O'Hara to access the trails, but it is an enjoyable walk in its own right, especially in the evening. Across from Le Relais, behind the warden's cabin, interpretive boards lay out the various options throughout the valley and explain local history. Heading in a clockwise direction from this point, the trail crosses Cataract Creek, the lake's outlet, then passes along the north shoreline, crossing gullies, and then reaching Seven Veil Falls at the 1.2-kilometer (0.7-mile) mark. Traversing the cool, damp, southern shoreline, the trail passes branches to the Opabin Plateau and a short detour to Mary Lake. Lake O'Hara Lodge is

passed at the 2.4-kilometer (1.5-mile) mark, from where it's a short stroll back along the road to Le Relais.

Lake Oesa

- Length: 3 kilometers/1.9 miles (1 hour) one-way
- Elevation gain: 240 meters/790 feet
- Rating: easy/moderate
- Trailhead: Shoreline Trail, 800 meters (0.5 mile) beyond Cataract Creek

With the Continental Divide peaks of Mount Victoria (3,464 meters/11,365 feet) and Mount Lefroy (3,423 meters/11,230 feet) as a backdrop, this small aqua-colored lake surrounded by talus slopes is one of the area's gems. All the elevation gain is made in the first 2.4 kilometers (1.5 miles), as the trail switchbacks to a ledge overlooking Lake O'Hara. The trail then levels out, passing three small bodies of water before climbing over a low rise and entering the cirque in which Lake Oesa lies.

Opabin Plateau Circuit

- Length: 5.9 kilometers/3.7 miles (2 hours) round-trip
- Elevation gain: 250 meters/820 feet
- Rating: easy/moderate
- Trailhead: Shoreline Trail

Separated from Lake Oesa by 2,848-meter (9,344-foot) Mount Yukness, this plateau high above the tree line dotted with small lakes is one of the most picturesque destinations in the Canadian Rockies. The time quoted is an absolute minimum because it's easy to spend an entire day exploring the alpine plateau and scrambling around the surrounding slopes. Two trails lead up to the plateau, which itself is laced with trails. The most direct route is the Opabin Plateau West Circuit, which branches right from the Shoreline Trail 300 meters (0.2 mile) beyond Lake O'Hara Lodge.

It then passes Mary Lake, climbs steeply, and reaches the plateau in a little less than two kilometers (1.2 miles). Opabin Prospect is an excellent lookout along the edge of the plateau. From this point, take the right forks to continue to the head of the cirque and Opabin Lake. This section of trail passes through a lightly forested area of larch that comes alive with color the second week of September. From Opabin Lake, the East Circuit traverses the lower slopes of Yukness Mountain, passing Hungabee Lake, then descending steeply to Lake O'Hara and ending back along the Shoreline Trail 600 meters (0.4 mile) east of Lake O'Hara Lodge.

Lake McArthur

- Length: 3.5 kilometers/2.2 miles (80 minutes) one-way
- Elevation gain: 300 meters/980 feet
- Rating: easy/moderate
- Trailhead: Le Relais

A personal favorite, this trail leads to the largest and (in my opinion) most stunning body of water in the Lake O'Hara area. Beginning from behind Le Relais, the trail passes through an open meadow and the Elizabeth Parker Hut; stay left to reach Schèffer Lake after 1.6 kilometers (one mile). At a junction beyond that lake, the left fork leads to Lake McArthur and the right fork to McArthur Pass. The lake option climbs steeply for 800 meters (0.5 mile), then levels out and traverses a narrow ledge before entering the Lake McArthur Cirque. (Stay high, even if trails descending into the McArthur Valley look like they offer an easier approach.) After leveling off, the trail enters the alpine zone and quickly reaches its maximum elevation and the first views of Lake McArthur. Backed by Mount Biddle and the Biddle Glacier, the deep-blue lake and colorful alpine meadows are an unforgettable panorama.

Odaray Highline

- Length: 2.6 kilometers/1.6 miles (1 hour) one-way
- Elevation gain: 280 meters/920 feet
- Rating: easy/moderate
- Trailhead: Le Relais

For a panoramic overview of the Lake O'Hara area with a minimum of energy output, it's hard to beat this trail, which ends atop the Odaray Plateau west of the lake. This trail passes through an important wildlife corridor, and a voluntary program to limit use—and therefore human interference—is in place. Check with park staff for the latest access restrictions. From Le Relais, follow the Lake McArthur Trail to Schèffer Lake as detailed previously, then take the right fork, which climbs gently toward McArthur Pass. Just before the pass, take the right fork. From this point, it's a steep one kilometer (0.6 mile) up to the lofty perch below Odaray Mountain.

Cathedral Basin

- Length: 7.5 kilometers/4.7 miles (2.5 hours) one-way
- Elevation gain: 300 meters/980 feet
- Rating: moderate
- Trailhead: Lake O'Hara Campground

The trail out to Cathedral Basin is the longest in the Lake O'Hara area, yet it's still an easy day trip for most people. Reach the trailhead from Le Relais by walking the short distance back down the access road or by following Cataract Creek downstream from behind the warden's cabin. From the campground the trail heads northwest, crossing Morning Glory Creek at the 2.4-kilometer (1.5-mile) mark, then passing Linda Lake. The final ascent to Cathedral Basin makes a wide loop through an area of ancient rock slides. From this point, the magnificent panorama of the Lake O'Hara area and the backdrop of the Continental Divide are laid out to the southeast.

BURGESS SHALE

High on the rocky slopes above Field is a layer of sedimentary rock known as the Burgess Shale, which contains what are considered to be the world's finest fossils from the Cambrian period. The site is famous worldwide because it has unraveled the mysteries of a major stage of evolution.

In 1909, Smithsonian Institution paleontologist Charles Walcott was leading a pack train along the west slope of Mount Field, on the opposite side of the valley from the newly completed Spiral Tunnel, when he stumbled across these fossil beds. Encased in the shale, the fossils here are of marine invertebrates about 510 million years old. Generally, fossils are the remains of vertebrates, but at this site some freak event—probably a mudslide—suddenly buried thousands of soft-bodied animals (invertebrates), preserving them by keeping out the oxygen that would have decayed their delicate bodies. Walcott excavated an estimated 65,000 specimens from the site. Today paleontologists continue to uncover perfectly preserved fossils here—albeit in far fewer numbers than in Walcott's day. They've also uncovered additional fossil beds, similar in makeup and age, across the valley, on the north face of Mount Stephen.

Reaching the Two Sites

Protected by UNESCO as a World Heritage Site, the two research areas are open only to those accompanied by a licensed guide. The **Burgess Shale Geoscience Foundation** (250/343-6006 or 800/343-3006, www. burgess-shale.bc.ca) guides trips to both sites between July and mid-September. The access to **Walcott's Quarry** is along a strenuous 10-kilometer (6.2-mile) trail that gains 760 meters (2,500 feet) in elevation. Trips

leave Friday-Monday at 8am from the trading post at the Field intersection, returning around 6:30pm; $120 per person. Trips to the **Mount Stephen Fossil Beds** depart Saturday and Sunday at 8:30am, returning at around 4:30pm; $90 per person. The trail to the Mount Stephen beds gains 760 meters (2,500 feet) of elevation in three kilometers (1.9 miles). The trails to both sites are unrelenting in their elevation gain—you must be fit to hike them. Reservations are a must.

EMERALD LAKE HIKES
Emerald Lake Loop

- Length: 5.2 kilometers/3.2 miles (1.5 hours) round-trip
- Elevation gain: minimal
- Rating: easy
- Trailhead: Emerald Lake parking lot, 9 kilometers (5.6 miles) from Highway 1

One of the easiest yet most enjoyable walks in Yoho is around the park's most famous lake. The trail encircles the lake and can be hiked in either direction. The best views are from the western shoreline, where a massive avalanche has cleared away the forest of Engelmann spruce. Across the lake from this point, Mount Burgess can be seen rising an impressive 2,599 meters (8,530 feet). Traveling in a clockwise direction, beyond the avalanche slope, the trail to Emerald Basin veers off to the left, and at the 2.2-kilometer (1.4-mile) mark, a small bridge is crossed. Views from this point extend back across the lodge to the Ottertail Range. Beyond the lake's inlet, the vegetation changes dramatically. A lush forest of towering western red cedar creates a canopy, protecting moss-covered fallen trees, thimbleberry, and bunchberry extending to the water's edge. Just over one kilometer (0.6 mile) from the bridge, the trail divides: The left fork leads back to the parking lot via a small forest-encircled pond, or continue straight ahead through the grounds of Emerald Lake Lodge. Park staff lead a guided hike around the lake every Saturday morning, departing at 10am from the parking lot trailhead.

Hamilton Falls

• Length: 800 meters/0.5 mile (20 minutes) one-way
• Elevation gain: 60 meters/200 feet
• Rating: easy
• Trailhead: information kiosk, Emerald Lake parking lot

The trail to these falls begins from the Emerald Lake parking lot, down the hill from the bridge to the lodge. It's an easy walk through a forest of Engelmann spruce and subalpine fir to a viewpoint at the base of the falls. A little farther along, the trail begins switchbacking steeply and offers even better views of the cascade.

The trail continues beyond the waterfall to **Hamilton Lake,** which lies in a small glacial cirque a steep 880 vertical meters (2,890 feet) above Emerald Lake. Total distance from Emerald Lake to Hamilton Lake is 5.5 kilometers/3.4 miles (2.5 hours) one-way.

Emerald Basin

• Length: 4.5 kilometers/2.8 miles (1.5-2 hours) one-way
• Elevation gain: 280 meters/920 feet
• Rating: easy/moderate
• Trailhead: Emerald Lake Loop, 1.5 kilometers (0.9 mile) from the parking lot

The trail to the delightful Emerald Basin begins from the west shore of Emerald Lake, from where it's a steady three-kilometer (1.9-mile) climb through a subalpine forest to the basin, which, chances are, you'll have to yourself. The most impressive sight awaiting you there is the south wall of the President Range, towering 800 vertical meters (2,625 feet) above.

YOHO VALLEY HIKES

The valley for which the park is named lies north of the TransCanada Highway. As well as the sights discussed previously, it provides many fine opportunities for serious day hikers to get off the beaten track. The following day hikes begin from different trailheads near the end of the road up Yoho Valley. In each case, leave your vehicle in the Takakkaw Falls parking lot.

Twin Falls

• Length: 8 kilometers/5 miles (2.5 hours) one-way
• Elevation gain: 300 meters/980 feet
• Rating: moderate
• Trailhead: Takakkaw Falls parking lot, 14 kilometers (8.7 miles) from Highway 1

This trail takes over where the road through the Yoho Valley ends, continuing in a northerly direction up the Yoho River to Twin Falls, passing many other waterfalls along the way. At spectacular Twin Falls, water from the Wapta Icefield divides in two before plunging off an 80-meter-high (262-foot-high) cliff. Mother Nature may work in amazing ways, but sometimes she needs a helping hand—or so the CPR thought. In the 1920s, the company dynamited one of the channels to make the falls more symmetrical. **Twin Falls Chalet** was built below the falls by the CPR in 1923 and today offers hikers light snacks through the middle of the day.

Iceline

• Length: 6.4 kilometers/4 miles (2.5 hours) one-way
• Elevation gain: 690 meters/2,260 feet
• Rating: moderate/difficult
• Trailhead: HI-Yoho (Whiskey Jack Hostel)

The Iceline is one of the most spectacular day hikes in the Canadian Rockies. The length given is from HI-Yoho to the highest point

© ANDREW HEMPSTEAD

YOHO NATIONAL PARK

The Iceline Trail offers impressive valley and glacier views.

along the trail (2,250 meters/7,380 feet). (Day hikers are asked to leave their vehicles across the road from the hostel, in the Takakkaw Falls parking lot.) From the hostel, the trail begins a steep and steady one-kilometer (0.6-mile) climb to a point where two options present themselves: The Iceline Trail is to the right, and Yoho Lake is to the left. After another 20 minutes of walking, the Iceline Trail option enters its highlight—a four-kilometer (2.5-mile) traverse of a moraine below Emerald Glacier. Views across the valley improve as the trail climbs to its crest and passes a string of small lakes filled with glacial meltwater. Many day hikers return from this point, although officially the trail continues into Little Yoho River Valley. Another option is to continue beyond Celeste Lake and loop back to Takakkaw Falls and the original trailhead, a total distance of 18 kilometers (11.2 miles).

Yoho Lake

- Length: 3.7 kilometers/2.3 miles (1.5 hours) one-way
- Elevation gain: 300 meters/990 feet
- Rating: moderate
- Trailhead: HI-Yoho (Whiskey Jack Hostel)

The trail to Yoho Lake, which can be combined with the Iceline Trail, officially begins along the hostel access road, but hikers are asked to leave their vehicles across the road in the Takakkaw Falls parking lot. It leads 3.7 kilometers (2.3 miles) to picturesque, spruce-encircled Yoho Lake, where you find picnic tables and campsites. Options from this point include continuing to Yoho Pass (below the tree line), from where it's 5.5 kilometers (3.4 miles) and an elevation loss of 530 meters (1,740 feet) down to Emerald Lake; six kilometers (3.7 miles) and an elevation gain of 300 meters (985 feet) to spectacular Burgess Pass; or 2.4 kilometers (1.5 miles) north, with moderately steady elevation, to an intersection with the Iceline Trail.

HIKES IN OTHER AREAS OF THE PARK

The hikes detailed as follows are along the TransCanada Highway.

Paget Lookout

- Length: 3.5 kilometers/2.2 miles (90 minutes) one-way
- Elevation gain: 520 meters/1,700 feet
- Rating: moderate
- Trailhead: Wapta Lake picnic area (not signposted), 5 kilometers (3.1 miles) west of the Continental Divide

The trail to this viewpoint is moderately strenuous but worthwhile for the panorama of the Kicking Horse River Valley. The first section of trail traverses a forest of Engelmann spruce. Then the trail breaks out above the tree line just below the lookout, the site of

TAKAKKAW FALLS

Much discussion is made of which is Canada's highest waterfall. Della Falls, on Vancouver Island, also in British Columbia, is 440 meters (1,440 feet) high, but its drop is broken by a ledge. Takakkaw Falls is considerably lower, at 254 meters (830 feet), but the drop is unbroken, which, officially, makes it Canada's highest. There is one thing of which there is no doubt: Takakkaw Falls will leave you breathless, much as it did famous alpinist Sir James Outram and everyone who has viewed the spectacle since.

The torrent, issuing from an icy cavern, rushes tempestuously down a deep, winding chasm till it gains the verge of the unbroken cliff, leaps forth in sudden wildness for a hundred and fifty feet, and then in a stupendous column of pure white sparkling water, broken by giant jets descending rocketlike and wreathed in volumed spray, dashes upon the rocks almost a thousand feet below, and, breaking into a milky series of cascading rushes for five hundred feet more, swirls into the swift current of the Yoho River.

Sir James Outram, In the Heart of the Canadian Rockies

an abandoned fire tower. As an alternative, branch right 1.4 kilometers (0.9 mile) along the trail and continue 1.6 kilometers (one mile) to milky **Sherbrooke Lake,** which is fed by the Waputik Icefield.

Hoodoo Trail

- Length: 3 kilometers/1.9 miles (60-90 minutes) one-way
- Elevation gain: 460 meters/1,510 feet
- Rating: moderate
- Trailhead: Hoodoo Creek Campground, 23 kilometers (14.3 miles) southwest of Field

Hoodoos are found in varying forms throughout the Canadian Rockies, but this outcrop, officially known as the **Leanchoil Hoodoos,** is among the most impressive. Hoodoos are formed by the erosion of relatively soft rock from beneath a cap of harder, more weather-resistant rock. Although these examples require some effort to reach, their intriguing appearance makes the trip worthwhile. The first half of the trail, through a decommissioned campground, is relatively flat, leaving all the elevation gain to be made in the last, painful 1.5 kilometers (0.9 mile).

Wapta Falls

- Length: 2.4 kilometers/1.5 miles (45 minutes) one-way
- Elevation loss: minimal
- Rating: easy
- Trailhead: 1.8 km (1.1 miles) along an unmarked road 25 kilometers (15.5 miles) west of Field and 5 kilometers (3.1 miles) east of park boundary

In the park's extreme southwestern corner, this trail follows an old fire road for one kilometer (0.6 miles), then narrows for an easy stroll through thick forest to a viewpoint above these 30-meter-high (100-feet-high) falls on the Kicking Horse River. A steep, switchbacking descent leads 500 meters (0.3 mile) to a viewpoint downstream of the base of the falls.

BOATING AND FISHING

No river or stream in this area is particularly well known for fishing, mainly because most of the water is glacially derived and therefore heavily silt-laden. Species present in the park's lakes and rivers include Dolly Varden and rainbow, lake, and cutthroat trout. A national park **fishing permit** costs $10 daily or $35 annually.

Emerald Lake Canoe Rentals (250/343-6000, 9am-8pm daily June-Sept.), in a small boat shed on the shore of Emerald Lake, rents canoes and small boats for $30 per hour, $45 for two hours, or $80 all day. Fishing in Emerald Lake isn't world-class, but there are some trout in the waters, and Emerald Lake Canoe Rentals offers a range of fishing tackle for rent or sale.

WINTER RECREATION

The TransCanada Highway through the park is open year-round, but facilities are only open June-mid-September. Some of the trails at higher elevations are impassable until July. Wintertime attracts cross-country skiers who happily slide along the Yoho Valley to frozen Takakkaw Falls or follow the Lake O'Hara trails.

Practicalities

ACCOMMODATIONS AND CAMPING

The park provides a variety of options, all well priced in comparison to Banff. Some travelers make Yoho a base for an entire Canadian Rockies vacation, traveling to Banff (just over an hour's drive east) or Golden (under an hour west) for supplies and civilized diversions.

Under $50

Marvel at the wonder of Takakkaw Falls from the deck at **HI-Yoho National Park** (Yoho Valley Rd., 403/760-7580 or 866/762-4122, www.hihostels.ca, late June-Sept., members $24, nonmembers $27), also known as Whiskey Jack Hostel, which offers basic dormitory accommodation for up to 27 guests, who have use of a communal kitchen and showers. Check-in is 5pm-11pm.

In downtown Field, **⟨ Fireweed Hostel** (313 Stephen Ave., 250/343-6999 or 877/343-6999, www.fireweedhostel.com, dorms $40, $125 d, two-bedroom suite $160) is one of the few private backpacker lodges in the Canadian Rockies—and it's a good one. It's a modern, purpose-built building with solid bunk beds topped by pillow-top mattresses, a beautiful lounge with log fireplace and LCD TV, and a modern well-equipped kitchen.

At Lake O'Hara is the **Elizabeth Parker Hut,** one of over a dozen rustic accommodations

scattered throughout the Canadian Rockies that is owned and operated by the Alpine Club of Canada (403/678-3200, www.alpineclubof-canada.ca). What stands this accommodation apart from the other Alpine Club properties is its accessibility—just a short walk from the shuttle bus drop-off point at Lake O'Hara. (To book a seat on the bus, call the reservations line at 250/343-6433 three months in advance. Seats are limited.) Guests bring their own bedding and food, and sleep in dorm-style beds. The rate is $45 per person per night ($30 for Alpine Club members). Most beds are filled via a lottery system that requires registration by November 1 for the following summer; see the website for details.

$150-200

In the hamlet of Field is the simple yet elegant **Kicking Horse Lodge** (100 Centre St., 250/343-6303, www.trufflepigs.com, $170-260 s or d), which offers 14 well-furnished rooms and the highly recommended Truffle Pigs Bistro. Outside of summer, rooms are discounted as low as $120—a great alternative to higher-priced Lake Louise for winter visitors.

The streets of Field are lined with private homes offering reasonably priced overnight accommodations in rooms of varying privacy and standard. One of the better choices is the **Alpine Guesthouse** (313 2nd Ave.,

250/343-6878, www.alpineguesthouse.ca), with a modern two-bedroom suite—complete with a kitchen, cable TV, outdoor patio, and private entrance for $195 per night (as low as $95 in winter). Like everywhere else in Field, it's within walking distance of the general store and Truffle Pigs Bistro.

Don't be put off by the dull redbrick exterior of the **Canadian Rockies Inn** (Stephen St., 250/343-6046 or 877/343-6046, www.canadianrockiesinn.com, $180 s or d), housed within what was once the local police station, for inside the rooms are spacious and filled with contemporary styling. Each unit has a fridge and coffeemaker.

Over $200

Emerald Lake Lodge (250/343-6321 or 800/663-6336, www.crmr.com, from $345 s or d) is a gracious, luxury-class accommodation along the southern shore of one of the Canadian Rockies' most magnificent lakes. The original lodge was built in 1902 in the same tradition as the Fairmont Chateau Lake Louise and Fairmont Banff Springs—as a playground for wealthy railway travelers. No original buildings remain (although the original framework is used in the main building); instead guests lap up the luxury of richly decorated duplex-style units and freestanding cabins. Each spacious unit is outfitted in a heritage theme and has a wood-burning fireplace, private balcony, luxurious bathroom, comfortable bed topped by a plush duvet, and in-room coffee. Other lodge amenities include a hot tub and sauna, swimming pool, restaurant, lounge, and café. Guests can also go horseback riding, or go boating and fishing on Emerald Lake.

Comprising upscale cabins set alongside the Kicking Horse River, **Cathedral Mountain Lodge** (250/343-6442 or 866/619-6442, www.cathedralmountain.com, mid-May-Sept., $289-389 s or d) lies one kilometer (0.6 mile) along Yoho Valley Road from the TransCanada Highway. In recent years, the original cabins have been replaced by fancy log chalets, with modern amenities and plenty of space to spread out. Each has a log bed topped by a down duvet, stone fireplace, bathroom with soaker tub and bathrobes, and private deck. Rates include a continental breakfast and naturalist program. Within a magnificent timber-frame building in the center of the complex is a stylish restaurant and lounge.

Spending a night at **Lake O'Hara Lodge** (250/343-6418, www.lakeohara.com, mid-June-early Oct.) is a special experience, and one that draws familiar faces year after year. On a practical level, it allows hikers not equipped for overnight camping the opportunity to explore one of the finest hiking destinations in all the Canadian Rockies at their leisure. The 15 one-bedroom cabins, each with a private bathroom, are spread around the lakeshore, while within the main lodge are eight rooms, most of which are twins and share bathrooms. Rates of $460 s, $595 d for a room in the main lodge (shared bathrooms) and $860-865 d for a cabin include all meals, taxes, gratuities, and transportation. As the lodge is located 13 kilometers (eight miles) from Highway 1, guests arrive by a shuttle bus that departs from a parking lot three kilometers (1.9 miles) west of the Continental Divide and 15 kilometers (nine miles) east of Field. Between February and April, the eight rooms in the main lodge are available for cross-country skiers for $337.50 per person, inclusive of meals and ski tours.

Campgrounds

Unlike neighboring Banff and Jasper, no reservations are taken for camping in Yoho's vehicle-accessible campgrounds. All sites have a picnic table and fire ring, with a fire permit costing $8 (includes firewood). When all campgrounds are filled, campers are directed to overflow areas.

The park's main camping area is **Kicking Horse Campground** (mid-May-early Oct.,

$28 per site), five kilometers (3.1 miles) northeast of Field along the road to Takakkaw Falls. Facilities include coin showers ($1), flush toilets, and kitchen shelters. Back toward the TransCanada Highway, **Monarch Campground** (mid-June-early Sept., $17.60 per site) offers more-limited facilities and less-private walk-in tent sites; **Hoodoo Creek Campground** (mid-June-Aug., $22 per site), along the TransCanada Highway, 23 kilometers (14 miles) southwest of Field, provides 30 sites among the trees and facilities that include flush toilets, hot water, kitchen shelters, and an interpretive program.

At the end of the road up the Yoho Valley, **Takakkaw Falls Campground** (July-Sept., $18 per site) is designed for tent campers only. Park at the end of the road and load up the carts with your gear for a pleasant 400-meter (0.2-mile) walk along the valley floor. No showers are provided, and the only facilities are pit toilets and picnic tables.

Just below **Lake O'Hara,** alongside the access road, is a delightful little campground surrounded by some of the region's finest hiking. Each of 30 sites has a tent pad, fire pit, and picnic table, while other facilities include pit toilets, two kitchen shelters with woodstoves, and bear-proof food caches. Reservations for sites are made in conjunction with the bus trip along the restricted-access road from Highway 1 to Lake O'Hara; for bus information call the dedicated reservations line at 250/343-6433. (Reservations for the bus are limited and must be made three months in advance.) Even though access is aboard a bus, you should treat the trip as one into the backcountry; passengers are limited to one large or two small bags, and no coolers or fold-up chairs are permitted on board the shuttle. Camping is $10 per person per night, the bus costs $15 per person round-trip, and the reservation fee is $12 per booking. Three to five sites are set aside for bookings made the previous day, but as with the shuttle,

they fill within minutes of the reservation line opening.

FOOD

In downtown Field, **[Truffle Pigs Bistro** (Kicking Horse Lodge, 250/343-6303, dinner daily, also breakfast and lunch in summer, $19-32) is one of those unexpected finds that makes traveling such a joy. In the evening this place really shines, with dishes as adventurous as smoked Alaskan salmon tiramisu and as simple as Albertan-raised beef served with baby potatoes and grilled tomato.

Overlooking an arm of Emerald Lake, **[Cilantro on the Lake** (250/343-6321, 11am-9pm daily mid-June-Sept., $25-39) is a casual café featuring magnificent views from tables inside an open-fronted, log chalet-style building or out on the lakefront deck. The menu is varied—you can sit and sip a coffee or have a full lunch or dinner. Starters—such as thick and creamy corn and potato chowder—are all less than $12, while mains range to $39. The café is part of **Emerald Lake Lodge,** which also includes a more formal but historically attractive dining room where dinner dishes such as grilled caribou with raspberry black pepper sauce ($36) are served daily from 6pm. This restaurant is also open year-round for breakfast and lunch, or choose the more casual lounge bar and sink into one of the comfy couches with an abbreviated but still appealing menu.

INFORMATION

The main source of information about the park is the **Field Visitor Centre** on the TransCanada Highway at Field (250/343-6783, 9am-8pm daily in summer, 9am-4pm daily the rest of the year). Inside you'll find helpful staff, information boards, interpretive panels, and a Friends of Yoho bookstore. This is also the place to pick up backcountry camping permits, buy topographical maps, and find out schedules for campground interpretive programs.

For more information, write Yoho National Park, P.O. Box 99, Field, BC V0A 1G0; or surf the Internet to the **Parks Canada** website (www.pc.gc.ca). For park road conditions, call 403/762-1450; for avalanche reports, call 403/762-1460.

GETTING THERE AND AROUND

Transportation to and around the park is limited. Most visitors arrive in their own vehicles, allowing just over an hour to travel between the town of Banff and the village of Field along the TransCanada Highway. **Greyhound** (403/762-6767, www.greyhound.ca) stops in Field daily on its route between Banff and Golden, from where it continues west to Vancouver. **Brewster** (403/762-6767, www.brewster.ca) offers a nine-hour Mountain Lakes and Waterfalls Tour of the park, departing Banff daily at 8:30am (summer only). This tour takes in both the Yoho Valley and Emerald Lake, as well as Lake Louise. The cost is adult $109, child $55.

Golden

From the western boundary of Yoho National Park, the TransCanada Highway meanders down the beautiful Kicking Horse River Valley to the town of Golden (pop. 4,400), at the confluence of the Kicking Horse and Columbia Rivers. As well as being a destination in itself, Golden makes a good central base for exploring the region or as an overnight stop on a tour through the Canadian Rockies that takes in the national parks on the western side of the Continental Divide.

Although Golden is an industrial town through and through—with local mines and huge logging operations that include a lumber mill that opened in 1999—it also has a reputation for local outdoor-recreation opportunities, most notably for its four-season resort, whitewater rafting down the Kicking Horse River, golfing the fairways of one of the region's best courses, and hang gliding.

SIGHTS AND RECREATION

Take Highway 95 off the TransCanada Highway, and you'll find yourself in the old section of town, a world away from the commercial strip along the main highway. There's not really much to see in town, although you may want to check out the small museum on 14th Street. The 8.8-kilometer (5.5-mile) **Rotary Loop** is a paved walking and biking trail that leads across the river from downtown via an impressive timber-frame pedestrian bridge, then upstream across Highway 95 (10th Ave. S) to the campground.

The **Columbia River Wetland,** which holds international significance not only for its size (26,000 hectares/64,250 acres) but also for the sheer concentration of wildlife it supports, extends as far north as Golden. One easily accessible point of the wetland is **Reflection Lake,** on the southern outskirts of Golden. Here you'll find a small shelter with a telescope for viewing the abundant birdlife.

◖ Kicking Horse Mountain Resort

Summer or winter, as you descend into Golden from Yoho National Park, it's easy to make out the ski slopes of Kicking Horse Mountain Resort (250/439-5400 or 866/754-5425, www.kickinghorseresort.com) across the valley.

The resort's eight-person detachable Golden Eagle Express gondola transports visitors high into the alpine mid-June–September in just 18 minutes. The 360-degree panorama at the summit is equal to any other

YOHO NATIONAL PARK

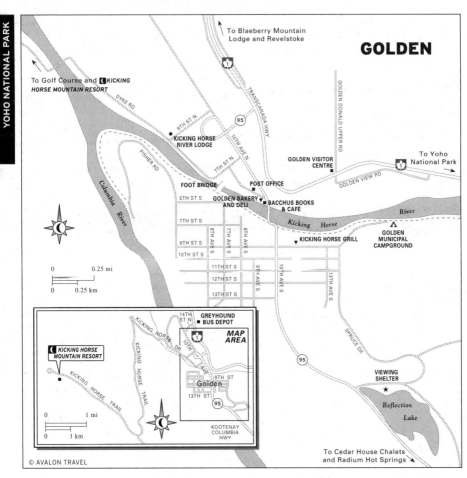

accessible point in the Canadian Rockies, with the Purcell Mountains immediately to the west and the Columbia Valley laid out below. Graded hiking trails lead from the upper terminal through a fragile, treeless environment, while mountain bikers revel in a challenging descent in excess of 1,000 meters (3,280 feet). A single gondola ride is adult $27, senior $26, child $13.50. Mountain bikers pay $42.50 for a full-day pass, with rent-and-ride packages costing $95 for the full day, including a full-suspension bike. The gondola operates through the warmer months 10:30am-5:30pm daily.

With a vertical rise of 1,260 meters (4,130 feet), 45 percent of terrain designated for experts, lots of dry powder snow, and minimal crowds, Kicking Horse has developed a big reputation since opening for the 2000-2001 winter season. In addition to the 3.5-kilometer-long (2.2-mile-long) gondola, four other lifts transport skiers and boarders to hidden bowls and to a high point of 2,450 meters (8,040 feet), giving the resort North America's second-highest vertical rise (1,260 meters/4,135 feet). Lifts operate mid-December-early April, and tickets are adult $74, senior $64, child $38. Facilities in the base lodge include rentals, a cafeteria, and a ski school, while the summit restaurant is also open daily for lunch and Friday and Saturday for dinner.

To get to Kicking Horse, follow the signs from Highway 1 into town and take 7th Street North west from 10th Avenue North; it's over the Columbia River and 13 kilometers (eight miles) uphill from this intersection.

White-Water Rafting

Anyone looking for white-water-rafting action will want to run the Kicking Horse River. The rafting season runs mid-May-mid-September, with river levels at their highest in late June. The Lower Canyon, immediately upstream of Golden, offers the biggest thrills, including a three-kilometer (1.9-mile) stretch of continuous rapids. Upstream of here the river is tamer but still makes for an exciting trip, while even farther upstream, near the western boundary of Yoho National Park, it's more of a float—a good adventure for the more timid visitor. The river is run by several companies, most of which offer the option of half-day ($60-80) or full-day ($100-150) trips. The cost varies with inclusions such as transportation from Banff and lunch.

Alpine Rafting (250/344-6778 or 888/599-5299, www.alpinerafting.com) offers trips ranging from a family-friendly float to the excitement of descending the Lower Canyon. They operate from a signposted base 25 kilometers (15.5 miles) east of Golden, where there is also primitive camping. Other local companies include **Wet 'n' Wild Adventures** (250/344-6546 or 800/668-9119, www.wetnwild.bc.ca) and **Glacier Raft Company** (250/344-6521, www.glacierraft.com). From Lake Louise, **Wild Water Adventures** (403/522-2211 or 888/647-6444, www.wildwater.com) leads half-day trips

down the river for $93, including a narrated bus trip to their purpose-built RiverBase put-in point 27 kilometers (17 miles) east of Golden. Departures are from Lake Louise at 8:15am and 1:30pm The full-day trip ($139) is broken up by a riverside lunch. **Canadian Rockies Rafting** (403/678-6535 or 877/226-7625, www.rafting.ca) operates on the river from Banff while **Hydra River Guides** (403/762-4554 or 800/644-8888, www.raftbanff.com) is a Banff-based company that also runs the river.

Other Summer Recreation

Golden Golf and Country Club (250/344-2700 or 866/727-7222, www.golfgolden.com) is a challenging 18-hole course in a forested section of the valley through town and to the north. This course is generally in excellent condition, with water coming into play on many holes—including the signature 11th and 12th holes along Holt Creek—and numerous streams and lakes to catch wayward shots. Greens fees are $75, or there's a $50 twilight rate.

Adventurous souls are drawn to Golden for its thermals, perfect for hang gliding and paragliding, and to the steep face of Jubilee Mountain, a renowned sport-climbing destination. Cowboys descend on town the first weekend of September for the **Golden Rodeo.**

ACCOMMODATIONS AND CAMPING

You can stay in one of the regular motels lining the highway, but don't. Instead, choose one of the unique mountain lodgings that surround the town.

Under $50

Kicking Horse River Lodge (801 9th St. N., 250/439-1112 or 877/547-5266, www.khrl.com, dorm beds $36, $125-240 s or d) epitomizes the new wave of lodging in the Canadian Rockies. It is a modern, riverfront log building with amenities that include high-speed

Internet, a living area with a large-screen TV, and a café (summer only) with outdoor seating overlooking the Columbia River.

$50-100

Blaeberry Mountain Lodge (1680 Moberly School Rd., 250/344-5296, www.blaeberry-mountainlodge.bc.ca) is on a 62-hectare (150-acre) property among total wilderness. Rooms are in the main lodge or self-contained cabins, with plenty of activities available to guests. Standard rooms with shared bathroom are $105 s or d, and the large cabins, which feature a separate bedroom and full kitchen, are $145. The three-bedroom cottage is $360 for up to four people. Breakfast and dinner are offered for $15 and $39, respectively. Blaeberry is nine kilometers (5.6 miles) north of Golden along Highway 1, then seven kilometers (4.3 miles) farther north along Moberly School Road.

Over $100

South of town, **Cedar House Chalets** (735 Hefti Rd., 250/290-0001, www.cedar-housechalets.com, $215-290 s or d) are spacious one- to three-bedroom cabins with full kitchens, wood-burning fireplaces, wireless Internet, barbecues, and hot tubs—with the bonus of an excellent on-site restaurant.

Of the accommodations at the base of Kicking Horse Mountain Resort, **Copper Horse Lodge** (250/344-7644 or 877/544-7644, www.copperhorselodge.com, $195-245 s or d including breakfast) comes highly recommended. Guest rooms are outfitted in earthy yet stylish color schemes and include bathrobes, Internet access, and TV/DVD combos. Other amenities include a restaurant, lounge, and outdoor hot tub.

Campgrounds

Continue south through the old part of town over the Kicking Horse River and take 9th Street South east at the traffic lights to reach

Golden Municipal Campground (250/344-5412, www.goldenmunicipalcampground.com, $24-32 per site). It's a quiet place, strung out along the river and two kilometers (1.2 miles) from downtown along a riverfront walkway. Facilities include picnic shelters, hot coin-operated showers, wireless Internet, and 72 sites (32 with power hookups) with fire pits. Adjacent is a recreation center with a swimming pool and fitness facility.

FOOD

Kicking Horse Mountain Resort

At an elevation of 2,347 meters (7,700 feet), **Eagle's Eye** is the crowning glory of Kicking Horse Mountain Resort (250/439-5400 or 866/754-5425, lunch daily, dinner weekends only, $28-42) and is Canada's highest restaurant. Access is by gondola from the resort's base village, 13 kilometers (eight miles) west of downtown Golden. As you'd expect, the views are stunning and are set off by a stylish timber and stonework interior, including a floor-to-ceiling fireplace and a wide wraparound deck protected from the wind by glass paneling. Dinner choices are more adventurous than lunch, but the food remains distinctly Canadian.

Downtown

Start your day with the locals at the **Golden Bakery & Deli** (419 9th Ave., 250/344-2928, 6:30am-6pm Mon.-Sat.), where the coffee is always fresh and the faces friendly. Baked goodies include breads, pastries, cakes, and meat pies, with inexpensive daily specials displayed on a blackboard in a seated section off to the side of the main counter.

Bacchus Books & Cafe (409 9th Ave., 250/344-5600, 9am-5:30pm Mon.-Sat., 10am-4pm Sun., lunches $7.50-11) has an upstairs café offering a breakfast and lunch menu filled with healthy, inexpensive meals.

Constructed of rough-cut logs complete with

© ANDREW HEMPSTEAD

Golden Visitor Centre

bulging burls, the **Kicking Horse Grill** (1105 9th St. S., 250/344-2330, from 5:30pm daily, $14-29) is one of Golden's finest restaurants. The menu changes with the seasons but always offers distinctly international dishes ranging from paella to sushi.

South of Golden

A five-minute drive south of Golden off Highway 95, the **Cedar House Restaurant** (735 Hefti Rd., 250/344-4679, 5pm-10pm daily, $23-34) is a good choice for wonderfully flavored food that takes advantage of seasonal Canadian produce, including vegetables organically grown on the property. The soup of the day is a good way to get things going, then

choose between mains such as prawn risotto or grilled Alberta beef tenderloin. The dining room is in a log building, but on warmer evenings you'll want to be outside on the patio.

INFORMATION AND SERVICES

While accommodations, fast-food restaurants, and gas stations line the TransCanada Highway, downtown Golden holds other basic services, including the **post office** (502 9th Ave.). Ninth Avenue also holds outdoor equipment shops and **Bacchus Books & Cafe** (409 9th Ave., 250/344-5600, 9am-5:30pm Mon.-Sat., 10am-4pm Sun.), offering a wide selection of new and used books, with plenty of local reading and detailed maps of the Columbia Valley.

The year-round **Golden Visitor Centre** is ensconced in an architecturally striking building beside the highway before it descends into town from the east (111 Golden Upper Donald Rd., 250/344-7125 or 800/622-4653, www.tourismgolden.com, 9am-4pm daily, until 8pm in summer). Interpretive displays describe the valley and everything there is to do and see, while outside a short walking trail leads to a lookout.

GETTING THERE AND AROUND

Golden is on the TransCanada Highway, 134 kilometers (83 miles) west of the town of Banff and 713 kilometers (443 miles) east of Vancouver. **Greyhound** buses (250/344-2917, www.greyhound.ca) stop four times daily in Golden, utilizing the Husky gas station as a depot.

For a cab, call **Mount 7 Taxi** (250/344-5237).

JASPER NATIONAL PARK

Snowcapped peaks, vast ice fields, beautiful glacial lakes, soothing hot springs, thundering rivers, and the most extensive backcountry trail system of any Canadian national park make Jasper a stunning counterpart to its sister park, Banff. Lying on the Albertan side of the Canadian Rockies, Jasper protects the entire upper watershed of the Athabasca River, extending to the Columbia Icefield (and Banff National Park) in the south. To the east are the foothills, to the west the Continental Divide (which marks the Alberta-British Columbia border) and Mount Robson Provincial Park. Encompassing 10,900 square kilometers (4,208 square miles), Jasper is a haven for wildlife; much of its wilderness is traveled only by wolves and grizzlies.

The park's most spectacular natural landmarks can be admired from two major roads. The Yellowhead Highway runs east-west from Edmonton through the park to Mount Robson Provincial Park. The Icefields Parkway, regarded as one of the world's great mountain drives, runs north-south, connecting Jasper to Banff. At the junction of these two highways is the park's main service center—the town of Jasper. With half the population of Banff, its setting—at the confluence of the Athabasca and Miette Rivers, surrounded by rugged, snowcapped peaks—is a little less dramatic, though still beautiful. But the town is also less commercialized than Banff and its streets a little

HIGHLIGHTS

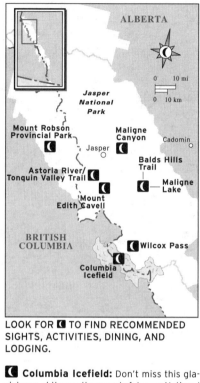

LOOK FOR ◖ TO FIND RECOMMENDED SIGHTS, ACTIVITIES, DINING, AND LODGING.

◖ **Columbia Icefield:** Don't miss this glacial area at the southern end of Jasper National Park. Take the Ice Explorer tour to get a close-up view of this natural wonder (page 214).

◖ **Wilcox Pass:** Escape the crowds lingering around the Icefield Centre on this hike, where the panorama of the Columbia Icefield is laid out in all its glory (page 218).

◖ **Maligne Canyon:** Easy access makes this attraction extremely popular. Visit before 9am to miss the tour-bus crowd (page 225).

◖ **Maligne Lake:** The most famous body of water in Jasper National Park. And for good reason-it's simply stunning. Take a tour boat to Spirit Island or hike the Lake Trail (Mary Schäffer Loop) along the lake's eastern shore (page 226).

◖ **Mount Edith Cavell:** Although this peak is visible from various points within the park, no vantage point is as memorable as that from its base, reachable by road from Highway 93A. For a neck-straining view, take the Cavell Meadows Trail (page 228).

◖ **Bald Hills Trail:** The vast majority of visitors to Maligne Lake don't travel past the lake's shoreline. Go beyond the ordinary on this trail, which provides stunning views of the whole Maligne Valley from alpine meadows (page 232).

◖ **Astoria River/Tonquin Valley Trail:** A trail up the Astoria River leads to the Tonquin Valley, one of the park's most spectacular sights. If you aren't equipped for backcountry camping, consider riding in on horseback and staying at one of two wilderness lodges (page 233).

◖ **Mount Robson Provincial Park:** Mount Robson rises high above lush forests and rushing waterfalls in this beautiful park to the west of Jasper (page 252).

quieter—a major plus for those looking to get away from it all.

Many of the park's campgrounds are accessible by road, while others dot the backcountry. Hiking is the number one attraction, but fishing, boating, downhill skiing and snowboarding, golfing, horseback riding, and white-water rafting are also popular. The park is open year-round, although road closures do occur on the Icefields Parkway during winter months due to avalanche-control work and snowstorms.

PLANNING YOUR TIME

It's a cliché, but backcountry enthusiasts could spend a full summer exploring Jasper and still not see everything. If you're planning to visit Jasper, I'm assuming you *do* enjoy the outdoors—hiking, fishing, watching wildlife, and

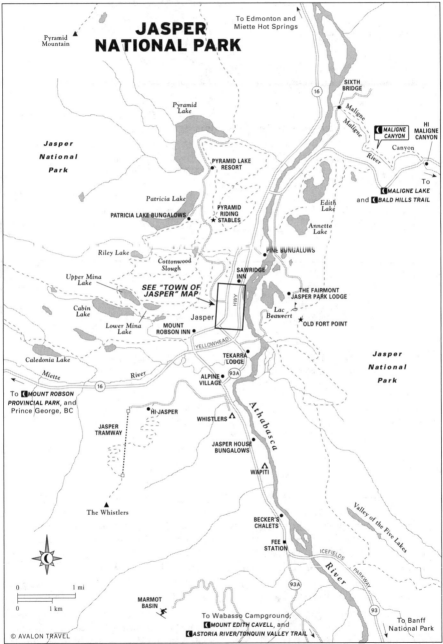

JASPER NATIONAL PARK

To Edmonton and
Miette Hot Springs

Pyramid
Mountain

SIXTH
BRIDGE

16

Pyramid
Lake

Maligne

MALIGNE
CANYON

HI
MALIGNE
CANYON

Jasper
National
Park

Maligne

PYRAMID LAKE
RESORT

Canyon

River

To
MALIGNE LAKE
and BALD HILLS TRAIL

Patricia Lake

PYRAMID
RIDING
STABLES

Edith
Lake

PATRICIA LAKE BUNGALOWS

Annette
Lake

Riley Lake

PINE BUNGALOWS

Cottonwood
Slough

SAWRIDGE
INN

Upper Mina
Lake

SEE "TOWN OF
JASPER" MAP

THE FAIRMONT
JASPER PARK LODGE

Cabin
Lake

HWY

Lac
Beauvert

Lower Mina
Lake

MOUNT
ROBSON INN

Jasper

OLD FORT POINT

YELLOWHEAD

Caledonia Lake

TEKARRA
LODGE

Jasper
National
Park

Miette

River

16

93A

ALPINE
VILLAGE

To MOUNT ROBSON
PROVINCIAL PARK, and
Prince George, BC

HI-JASPER

WHISTLERS

Athabasca

JASPER
TRAMWAY

JASPER HOUSE
BUNGALOWS

WAPITI

The Whistlers

Valley of the Five Lakes

BECKER'S
CHALETS

FEE
STATION

ICEFIELDS

PARKWAY

River

93A

0   1 mi

0   1 km

MARMOT
BASIN

To Wabasso Campground,
MOUNT EDITH CAVELL, and
ASTORIA RIVER/TONQUIN VALLEY TRAIL

93

To Banff
National Park

© AVALON TRAVEL

PARK ENTRY

Permits are required for entry into the park. A **National Parks Day Pass** is adult $9.80, senior $8.30, child $4.90, up to a maximum of $20 per vehicle. It can also be used in neighboring Banff National Park if you're traveling down the Icefields Parkway and is valid until 4pm the day following its purchase. An annual **Discovery Pass**–good for entry into all of Canada's national parks and historic sites–is adult $67.70, senior $57.90, child $33.30, up to a maximum of $136.40 per vehicle.

Both types of pass can be purchased at the park information center, at the booth along the Icefields Parkway a few kilometers south of the town of Jasper, and at campground kiosks. If you're traveling north along the Icefields Parkway, you'll be required to stop and purchase a park pass just beyond Lake Louise (Banff National Park). The Parks Canada website (www.pc.gc.ca) has detailed pass information.

the like—but maybe not with a backpack full of provisions strapped to your back. Keeping this in mind, I'd recommend spending four days in the park. The best choices for accommodations are the summer-only cabin complexes, so book for three nights and spend your days exploring natural attractions such as **Mount Edith Cavell, Maligne Canyon, Maligne Lake,** and adjacent **Mount Robson Provincial Park.** If you're traveling up from Lake Louise, plan on spending the first day along the **Icefields Parkway,** arriving at the **Columbia Icefield** before the crowds. If your time in Jasper is limited to two days and one night, you should have enough time to visit each of the natural attractions I mark as must-see sights, walk a couple of the shorter trails, and even squeeze in a rafting trip or golf game.

Jasper is delightful in winter. You can spend your time doing all the same activities as in Banff, but without the pizzazz of Banff Avenue and the crowds of the Lake Louise

and Sunshine Village ski resorts. Most of the wintertime action revolves around skiing and boarding at **Marmot Basin,** but you can also try cross-country skiing or snowshoeing, walk through an ice canyon, and take a sleigh ride. In the evening, you can kick back in front of a roaring fire knowing that you're paying a lot less for lodging than you would be in Banff.

THE LAND

Although the peaks of Jasper National Park are not particularly high, they are among the most spectacular along the range's entire length. About 100 million years ago, layers of sedimentary rock—laid down here up to a billion years ago—were forced upward, folded, and twisted under tremendous pressure into the mountains seen today. The land's contours were further altered during four ice ages that began around one million years ago. The last ice age ended about 10,000 years ago, and the vast glaciers began to retreat. A remnant of this final sheet of ice is the huge Columbia Icefield; covering approximately 325 square kilometers (125 square miles) and up to 400 meters (1,300 feet) deep, it's the most extensive ice field in the Rocky Mountains. As the glaciers retreated, piles of rock melted out and were left behind. Meltwater from the glaciers flowed down the valleys and was dammed up behind the moraines. **Maligne Lake,** like many other lakes in the park, was created by this process. The glacial silt suspended in the lake's waters produces amazing emerald, turquoise, and amethyst colors; early artists who painted these lakes had trouble convincing people that their images reflected reality.

In addition to creating the park's gem-like lakes, the retreating glaciers carved out the valleys that they ever-so-slowly flowed through. The Athabasca River Valley is the park's largest watershed, a typical example of a U-shaped, glacier-carved valley. The Athabasca River flows north through the valley into the

Mackenzie River system and ultimately into the Arctic Ocean. The glacial silt that paints the park's lakes is also carried down streams into the Athabasca, giving the river a pale green milky look. Another beautiful aspect of the park's scenery is its abundance of waterfalls. They vary from the sparkling tumble of Punchbowl Falls, where Mountain Creek cascades down a limestone cliff into a picturesque pool, to the roar of Athabasca Falls, where the Athabasca River is forced through a narrow gorge.

FLORA

Elevations in the park range from 980 meters (3,215 feet) to more than 3,700 meters (12,140 feet). That makes for a wide range of resident plant life. Only a small part of the park lies in the montane zone. It is characterized by stands of **Douglas fir** (at its northern limit) and **lodgepole pine,** while **balsam poplar, white birch,** and **spruce** also occur. Savanna-like grasslands occur on drier sites in valley bottoms. Well-developed stretches of montane can be found along the floors of the Athabasca and Miette River Valleys, providing winter habitat for larger mammals such as elk.

The subalpine zone, heavily forested with evergreens, extends from the lower valley slopes up to the tree line at an elevation of around 2,200 meters (7,220 feet). The subalpine occupies 40 percent of the park's area. The dominant species in this zone is lodgepole pine, although **Engelmann spruce, subalpine fir, poplar,** and **aspen** also grow here. The park's extensive stands of lodgepole pine are inhabited by few large mammals because the understory is minimal. Wildflowers are common in this zone and can be found by the roadside, in clearings, or on riverbanks.

Timberline here lies at an elevation of 2,050-2,400 meters (6,275-7,870 feet) above sea level. Above this elevation is the alpine zone, where the climate is severe (the average yearly temperature is below freezing), summer is brief, and only a few stunted trees survive. The zone's plant species grow low to the ground, with extensive root systems to protect them during high winds and through the deep snow cover of winter. During the short summer, these open slopes and meadows are carpeted with a profusion of flowers such as **golden arnicas, bluebells, pale columbines,** and red and yellow **paintbrush.** Higher still are brightly colored **heather, buttercups,** and **alpine forget-me-nots.**

FAUNA

Wildlife is abundant in the park and can be seen throughout the year. During winter, many larger mammals move to lower elevations where food is accessible. February and March are particularly good for looking for animal tracks in the snow. By June, most of the snow cover at lower elevations has melted, the crowds haven't arrived, and animals can be seen feeding along the valley floor. In fall, tourists move to warmer climates, the rutting season begins, bears go into hibernation, and a herd of elk moves into downtown Jasper for the winter.

While the park provides ample opportunities for seeing numerous animals in their natural habitat, it also leads to human-animal encounters that are not always positive. For example, less than 10 percent of the park is made up of well-vegetated valleys. These lower areas are essential to the larger mammals for food and shelter but are also the most heavily traveled by visitors. Game trails used for thousands of years are often bisected by roads, and hundreds of animals are killed each year by speeding motorists. Please drive slowly in the park.

Campground Critters

Several species of small mammals thrive around campgrounds, thanks to an abundance of humans who are careless with their food.

Columbian ground squirrels are bold and will demand scraps of your lunch. **Golden-mantled ground squirrels** and **red squirrels** are also common. The **least chipmunk** (often confused with the golden-mantled ground squirrel thanks to similar stripes) can also be seen in campgrounds; they'll often scamper across your hiking trail, then sit boldly on a rock waiting for you to pass.

Aquatic Species

Beavers are common between the town of Jasper and the park's east gate. Dawn and dusk are the best times to watch these intriguing creatures at work. Wabasso Lake, a 2.6-kilometer (1.6-mile) hike from the Icefields Parkway, was created by beavers; their impressive dam has completely blocked the flow of Wabasso Creek. Also common in the park's wetlands are **mink** and **muskrat;** search out these creatures around the lakes on the benchland north of the town of Jasper.

Ungulates

Five species of deer inhabit the park. The large-eared **mule deer** is commonly seen around the edge of the town or grazing along the north end of the Icefields Parkway. **White-tailed deer** can be seen throughout the park. A small herd of **woodland caribou** roams throughout the park; they are most commonly seen during late spring in the Opal Hills or along a signposted stretch of the Icefields Parkway. The town of Jasper is in the home range of about 500 **elk,** which can be seen most of the year around town or along the highway northeast and south of town. **Moose,** although numbering fewer than 100 in all of Jasper, can occasionally be seen feeding on aquatic plants along the major drainage systems.

In summer, **mountain goats** browse in alpine meadows. A good place for goat watching is Goat Lookout on the Icefields Parkway.

Unlike most of the park's large mammals, these sure-footed creatures don't migrate to lower elevations in winter but stay sheltered on rocky crags where wind and sun keep the vegetation snow free. Often confused with the goat is the darker **bighorn sheep.** The horns on the males of this species are thick and often curl 360 degrees. Bighorns are common in the east of the park at Disaster Point and will often approach cars. An estimated 2,500 bighorn reside in the park.

Bears

Numbering around 80 within Jasper National Park, **black bears** are widespread and occasionally wander into campgrounds looking for food. They are most commonly seen along the Icefields Parkway in spring, when they first come out of hibernation. **Grizzly bears** are occasionally seen crossing the Icefields Parkway at higher elevations early in summer. For the most part they remain in remote mountain valleys, and if they do see, smell, or hear you, they'll generally move away. Read *Keep the Wild in Wildlife* before setting out into the woods; the pamphlet is available at information centers throughout the park.

Reclusive Residents

Several of the park's resident species keep a low profile, usually out of sight of humans. Populations of the shy and elusive **lynx** fluctuate with that of their primary food source, the snowshoe hare. The largest of the big cats in the park is the **cougar** (also called the mountain lion), a solitary carnivore that inhabits remote valleys. Jasper's **wolves** are one of the park's success stories. After being driven to near extinction, the species has rebounded. Five packs now roam the park, but they keep to the deep wilderness rarely traveled by people. While not common in the park, **coyotes** can be seen in cleared areas alongside the roads, usually at dawn and dusk.

Other Mammals

The **pine marten** is common but shy; look for them in subalpine forests. The **short-tailed weasel**—a relative of the marten—is also common, while the **long-tailed weasel** is rare. At higher elevations, look for **pikas** in piles of fallen rock. **Hoary marmots** live near the upper limits of vegetation growth, where their shrill warning whistles carry across the open meadows; The Whistlers area, accessed by tramway, supports a healthy population of these noisy creatures.

Birds

The extensive tree cover in the lower valleys hides many species of birds, making them seem less abundant than they are; 240 species have been recorded. The two you're most likely to see are the **gray jay** and **Clark's nutcracker,** which regularly joins picnickers for lunch. Also common are black-and-white **magpies,** raucous **ravens,** and several species of **ducks,** which can be seen around lakes in the Athabasca River Valley. Harlequin ducks nest in the park during early summer. A stretch of the Maligne River is closed during this season to prevent human interference.

The colony of **black swifts** in Maligne Canyon is one of only two in Alberta. Their poorly developed legs make it difficult for them to take off from their nests in the canyon walls—they literally fall before becoming airborne. High alpine slopes are home to **white-tailed ptarmigan,** a type of grouse that turns white in winter. Also at this elevation are flocks of **rosy finches** that live under overhanging cliffs. In subalpine forests, the songs of **thrushes** and the tapping of **woodpeckers** can be heard.

At dusk, **great horned owls** swoop silently through the trees, their eerie call echoing through the forest. **Golden eagles** and **bald eagles** can be seen soaring high above the forests, and 15 pairs of **ospreys** are known to nest

in the park, many along the Athabasca River between town and the east park gate.

HISTORY

In the summer of 1810, David Thompson, one of Canada's greatest explorers, became the first white man to enter the Athabasca River Valley. The following winter, when Thompson was making the first successful crossing of Athabasca Pass, some of his party remained in the Athabasca River Valley and constructed a small supply depot northeast of the present town. Other trading posts were built along the Athabasca River, including one that became known as Jasper House, for the clerk Jasper Haws. This particular post was first established in 1813, then moved to the shore of Jasper Lake in 1829.

By 1865, with the fur trade over and the Cariboo goldfields emptying along routes easier than passing through what is now Jasper National Park, the Athabasca River Valley had very few permanent residents. One settler was Lewis Swift, who in 1892 made his home in the abandoned buildings of Jasper House, farming a small plot of land beside the Athabasca River. "Old Swift" became known to everyone, providing fresh food and accommodations for travelers and generating many legendary tales, such as the day he held the Grand Trunk Pacific Railway at gunpoint until they agreed to reroute the line away from his property.

In 1907, aware that the coming of the railway would mean an influx of settlers, the federal government set aside 5,000 square miles as Jasper Forest Park, buying all the land, save for the parcel owned by Lewis Swift. A handful of Metis homesteaders continued to live in the valley, but the land on which they lived was leased. The threat of oversettlement of the valley had been abated, but as a designated forest park, mining and logging were still allowed.

MARY SCHÄFFER

In the early 1900s, exploration of mountain wilderness areas was considered a man's pursuit; however, one spirited and tenacious woman entered that domain and went on to explore areas of the Canadian Rockies that no white man ever had.

Mary Sharples was born in 1861 in Pennsylvania and raised in a strict Quaker family. She was introduced to Dr. Charles Schäffer on a trip to the Rockies, and in 1889 they were married. His interest in botany drew them back to the Rockies, where Charles collected, documented, and photographed specimens until his death in 1903. Mary also became adept at these skills. After hearing Sir James Hector (the geologist on the Palliser Expedition) reciting tales of the

mountains, her zest to explore the wilderness returned. In 1908, Mary, guide Billy Warren, and a small party set out for a lake that no white man had ever seen but that the Stoney knew as Chaba Imne (Beaver Lake). After initial difficulties, they succeeded in finding the elusive body of water now known as Maligne Lake. In Mary's words, "There burst upon us the finest view any of us have ever beheld in the Rockies." In 1915, Mary married Billy Warren, continuing to explore the mountains until her death in 1939. Her successes as a photographer, artist, and writer were equal to any of her male counterparts, but she is best remembered for her unwavering love of the Canadian Rockies—her "heaven of the hills."

JASPER NATIONAL PARK

Mining and a Link to the Outside World

In 1908, Jasper Park Collieries staked claims in the park. By the time the railway came through in 1911, mining activity was centered at Pocahontas (near the park's east gate), where a township was established and thrived. During an extended miners' strike, the men spent their spare time constructing log pools at Miette Hot Springs, which were heavily promoted to early park visitors. The mine closed in 1921, and many families relocated to Jasper, which had grown from a railway camp into a popular tourist destination. By this time the park boundaries had changed dramatically. In 1911, the park had been reduced to two-thirds its original size, then in 1914 enlarged to include Maligne Lake and Columbia Icefield, then enlarged yet again in 1928 to take in Sunwapta Pass. Today's borders were set in 1930, when Jasper was officially designated a national park.

And what of Old Swift? Well, after working as the park's first game warden, he hung onto his land until 1935. The government of the day made various offers, but Swift ended up selling to a wealthy Englishman who operated a dude

ranch on the site until finally selling the land to the government in 1962.

Jasper Grows

In 1911, a construction camp was established for the Grand Trunk Pacific Railway near the present site of downtown Jasper. When the northern line was completed, visitors flocked into the remote mountain settlement, and its future was assured. The first accommodation for tourists was 10 tents on the shore of Lac Beauvert that became known as Tent City. In 1921, the tents were replaced and the original Jasper Park Lodge was constructed. By the summer of 1928, a road was completed between Edmonton and Jasper, and a golf course was built. As the number of tourists to the park continued to increase, existing facilities were expanded. In 1940 the Icefields Parkway was completed, linking Jasper to Banff and making the park more accessible.

Town of Jasper

The modern infrastructure of Jasper began developing in the 1960s, but until 2002 the town site was run from Ottawa by Parks

Canada. Jasper is now officially incorporated as a town, with locally elected residents serving as mayor and council members. Decisions made by the council must still balance the needs of living in a national park but also represent locals who call the park home. On the surface, obvious visible changes of this autonomy are a new emergency services building, a new wastewater treatment plant, and improvements to an ever-increasing downtown parking problem. One thing hasn't changed, and that's the basic premise of the town's existence: More than 50 percent of Jasper's 5,200 residents work in the hospitality industry, serving the needs of two million visitors annually.

Icefields Parkway (Jasper)

Sunwapta Pass (2,040 meters/6,690 feet), four kilometers (2.5 miles) south of the Columbia Icefield, marks the boundary between Banff and Jasper National Parks.

The following sights along the Icefields Parkway are detailed from south to north, from the Icefield Centre to the town of Jasper, a distance of 105 kilometers (65 miles). The scenery along this stretch of road is no less spectacular than the other half through Banff National Park, and it's easy to spend at least a full day en route.

No gas is available along this stretch of the Icefields Parkway. The nearest gas stations are at Saskatchewan River Crossing (Banff National Park) and in the town of Jasper, 150 kilometers (93 miles) apart, so keep your tank topped up to be safe.

◖ COLUMBIA ICEFIELD

The largest and most accessible of 17 glacial areas along the Icefields Parkway is the 325-square-kilometer (125-square-mile) Columbia Icefield, beside the Icefields Parkway at the south end of the park, 105 kilometers (65 miles) south from Jasper and 132 kilometers (82 miles) north from Lake Louise. It's a remnant of the last major glaciation that covered most of Canada 20,000 years ago, and it has survived because of its elevation at 1,900-2,800 meters (6,230-9,190 feet) above sea level, cold temperatures, and heavy snowfalls. From the main body of the ice cap, which sits astride the Continental Divide, six glaciers creep down three main valleys. Of these, **Athabasca Glacier** is the most accessible and can be seen from the Icefields Parkway; it is one of the world's few glaciers that you can drive right up to. It is an impressive 600 hectares (1,480 acres) in area and up to 100 meters (330 feet) deep. The speed at which glaciers advance and retreat varies with the long-term climate. Athabasca Glacier has retreated to its current position from across the highway, a distance of more than 1.6 kilometers (one mile) in a little more than 100 years. Currently it retreats up to two meters (six feet) per year. The rubble between the toe of Athabasca Glacier and the highway is a mixture of rock, sand, and gravel known as **till**, deposited by the glacier as it retreats.

The ice field is made more spectacular by the impressive peaks that surround it. **Mount Athabasca** (3,491 meters/11,450 feet) dominates the skyline, and three glaciers cling to its flanks. **Dome Glacier** is also visible from the highway; although part of the Columbia Icefield, it is not actually connected. Instead it is made of ice that breaks off the ice field 300 meters (980 feet) above, supplemented by large quantities of snow each winter.

Exploring the Icefield

From the Icefields Parkway, an unpaved road leads down through piles of till left by the

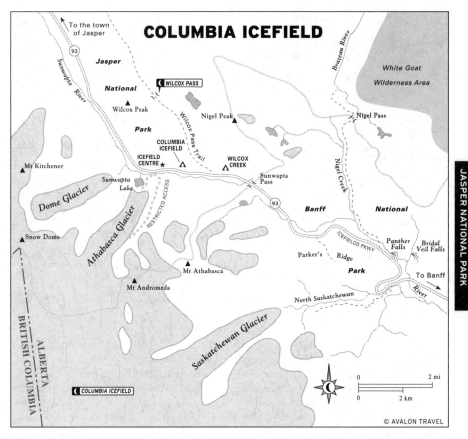

COLUMBIA ICEFIELD

To the town of Jasper

Jasper

National

Park

WILCOX PASS

Wilcox Peak

Nigel Peak

Nigel Pass

White Goat
Wilderness Area

COLUMBIA
ICEFIELD

ICEFIELD
CENTRE

WILCOX
CREEK

Mt Kitchener

Sunwapta
Lake

Dome Glacier

Snow Dome

Athabasca Glacier

RESTRICTED ACCESS

Sunwapta
Pass

Banff

National

Panther
Falls

Bridal
Veil Falls

Parker's   Ridge

Park

To Banff

Mt Athabasca

Mt Andromeda

North Saskatchewan

Saskatchewan Glacier

ALBERTA
BRITISH COLUMBIA

COLUMBIA ICEFIELD

0   2 mi
0   2 km

© AVALON TRAVEL

Sunwapta River   Brazeau River   Nigel Creek   ICEFIELDS PKWY   River

JASPER NATIONAL PARK

retreating Athabasca Glacier to a parking area beside Sunwapta Lake. An interesting alternative is to leave your vehicle beside the highway and take the 1.6-kilometer (one-mile) hiking trail through the lunarlike landscape to the parking area. From this point, a short path leads up to the toe of the glacier. (Along the access road, look for the small markers showing how far the toe of the glacier reached in years past; the farthest marker is across the highway beside the stairs leading up to the Icefield Centre.)

The ice field can be dangerous for unprepared visitors. Like all glaciers, the broken surface of the Athabasca is especially hazardous because snow bridges can hide its deep crevasses. The crevasses are uncovered as the winter snows melt. The safest way to experience the glacier firsthand is on specially developed vehicles with balloon tires that can travel over the crevassed surface. These Ice Explorers are operated by **Brewster** (780/852-6550, www.explorerockies.com). The 90-minute tour of Athabasca Glacier includes time spent walking on the surface of the glacier. The tour, which begins with a bus ride from the Icefield Centre, costs adult $50, child $25, and operates 9am-5pm mid-April-mid-October (try to plan your tour for before 10am or after 3pm, after the tour buses have

© ANDREW HEMPSTEAD

Take an Ice Explorer onto the Columbia Icefield.

departed for the day). The ticketing office is on the main floor of the Icefield Centre (no reservations are taken), with the surrounding area resembling an airport departure lounge—check the television screens for departure times and ensure you make your way to the correct gate. Early in the season, the glacier is still covered in a layer of snow and is therefore not as spectacular as during the summer. If you're in Banff or Jasper without transportation, consider Brewster's day trip to the Columbia Icefield, which lasts nine hours and costs adult $170, child $85, including the Ice Explorer excursion.

Icefield Centre

The magnificent Icefield Centre is nestled at the base of Mount Wilcox, overlooking the Athabasca Glacier. The building is as environmentally friendly as possible: Lights work on motion sensors to reduce electricity, some water is reused, suppliers must take their packaging with them after deliveries, and the entire building freezes in winter.

The center is the staging point for Ice Explorer tours, but before heading out onto the ice field, don't miss the **Glacier Gallery** on the lower floor. This large display area details all aspects of the frozen world, including the story of glacier formation and movement. The centerpiece is a scaled-down fiberglass model of the Athabasca Glacier, which is surrounded by hands-on displays and audiovisual presentations.

Back on the main floor of the center you'll find a Parks Canada desk (780/852-6288)—a good source of information for northbound visitors—Ice Explorer ticketing desk, restrooms, and the obligatory gift shop.

Upstairs you'll find the cavernous **Columbia Café,** with snacks and hot drinks to go on the right and an overpriced cafeteria-style restaurant to the left. Both are open 9am-6pm daily. Across the hallway is the **Glacier Dining Room,** open 7am-10am daily for a breakfast buffet, reopening 6pm-9:30pm for ordinary Chinese-Canadian fare (mains range $19-34). The only redeeming feature of these dining options has nothing to do with the food—the view from both inside and out on the massive deck is stupendous. (For northbound travelers, my advice is to pick up lunch at Laggan's Mountain Bakery in Lake Louise.)

The Icefield Centre also holds a limited number of hotel rooms (Glacier View Inn, 780/852-6550 or 877/423-7433, www.explorerockies.com, $229-289 s or d). Check-in is on the main level.

The entire Icefield Centre closes down for the winter in mid-October, reopening the following year in mid-April. During summer, the complex (including display area) is open 9am-10pm daily, with reduced hours outside of July and August.

COLUMBIA ICEFIELD TO THE TOWN OF JASPER

Sunwapta Lake, at the toe of the Athabasca Glacier, is the source of the **Sunwapta River,** which the Icefields Parkway follows for 48 kilometers (30 miles) to Sunwapta Falls.

Immediately north of Icefield Centre is an unheralded pullout where few travelers stop, but which allows for an excellent panorama of the area away from the crowds. Across the glacial-green Sunwapta River is a wasteland of till and a distinctive terminal moraine left behind by the retreating **Dome Glacier.** Between the Dome and Athabasca Glaciers is 3,459-meter (11,350-foot) **Snow Dome.**

Eight kilometers (five miles) north from the Icefield Centre, the road descends to a viewpoint for **Stutfield Glacier.** Most of the glacier is hidden from view by a densely wooded ridge, but the valley floor below its toe is littered with till left by the glacier's retreat. The main body of the Columbia Icefield can be seen along the

cliff top high above, and south of the glacier you can see Mount Kitchener.

Six kilometers (3.7 miles) farther down the road is **Tangle Ridge,** a grayish-brown wall of limestone over which Beauty Creek cascades. At this point the Icefields Parkway runs alongside the Sunwapta River, following its braided course through the **Endless Range,** the eastern wall of a classic glacier-carved valley.

Sunwapta Falls

A further 41 kilometers (25 miles) along the road, a 500-meter (0.3-mile) spur at Sunwapta Falls Resort leads to Sunwapta Falls. Here the Sunwapta River changes direction sharply and drops into a deep canyon. The best viewpoint is from the bridge across the river, but it's also worth following the path on the parking lot side of the river downstream along the rim of the canyon. Two kilometers (1.2 miles) downstream, the river flows into the much-wider Athabasca Valley at the Lower Falls.

Goat Lookout

After following the Athabasca River for 17 kilometers (11 miles), the road ascends to a lookout with picnic tables offering panoramic river views. Below the lookout is a steep bank of exposed glacially ground material containing natural deposits of salt. The local mountain goats spend most of their time on the steep slopes of Mount Kerkeslin, to the northeast, but occasionally cross the road and can be seen searching for the salt licks along the roadside or riverbank, trying to replenish lost nutrients.

Athabasca Falls

Nine kilometers (5.6 miles) beyond Goat Lookout and 32 kilometers (20 miles) south of Jasper, the Icefields Parkway divides when an old stretch of highway (Highway 93A) crosses the Athabasca River and continues along its west side for 25 kilometers (15.5 miles) before rejoining the parkway seven kilometers

Athabasca Falls

body of water is ringed by a band of cliffs (popular with locals in summer as a cliff-diving spot), but many private (unofficial) picnic spots line its western shoreline.

Two kilometers (1.2 miles) north of the Horseshoe Lake parking lot are a couple of lookouts with sweeping views across the Athabasca River to **Athabasca Pass,** used by David Thompson on his historic expedition across the continent. To the north of the pass lies Mount Edith Cavell. From this lookout it is 26 kilometers (16 miles) to the town of Jasper.

HIKING

For those who aren't comfortable hiking in remote areas, the trails branching off the Icefields Parkway can be somewhat intimidating. If that sounds like you, consider one of the shorter walks not detailed below, such as to Horseshoe Lake.

◖ Wilcox Pass

- Length: 4 kilometers/2.5 miles (90 minutes) one-way
- Elevation gain: 340 meters/1,115 feet
- Rating: moderate
- Trailhead: Wilcox Creek Campground, 3 kilometers (1.9 miles) south of the Icefield Centre

Views of the Columbia Icefield from the Icefields Parkway pale in comparison with those achieved along this trail, on the same side of the valley as the Icefield Centre. This trail was once used by northbound outfitters because, 120 years ago, Athabasca Glacier covered the valley floor and had to be bypassed. Beginning from the Wilcox Creek Campground access road, the trail climbs through a stunted forest of Engelmann spruce and subalpine fir to a ridge with panoramic views of the valley, Mount Athabasca, and the Athabasca Glacier. Ascending gradually from there, the trail enters a fragile environment of alpine meadows. From these meadows and the

(4.3 miles) south of the town. At the southern end of this loop, the Athabasca River is forced through a narrow gorge and over a cliff into a cauldron of roaring water below. As the river slowly erodes the center of the riverbed, the falls will move upstream. Trails lead from a day-use area to various viewpoints above and below the falls. The trail branching under Highway 93A follows an abandoned river channel before emerging at the bottom of the canyon. Facilities at Athabasca Falls include picnic tables and restrooms.

Continuing North to Jasper

Take Highway 93A beyond Athabasca Falls to reach Mount Edith Cavell, or continue north along the Icefields Parkway to access the following sights. The first worthwhile stop along this route is **Horseshoe Lake,** reached along a 350-meter (0.2-mile) trail from a parking lot three kilometers (1.9 miles) north of Athabasca Falls. The southern end of this delightful little pass, most hikers return along the same trail (the distance quoted), although it is possible to continue north, descending to the Icefields Parkway at Tangle Ridge, 11.5 kilometers (7.1 miles) along the road from the trailhead.

Fortress Lake

- Length: 24 kilometers/15 miles (7-8 hours) one-way
- Elevation gain: minimal
- Rating: moderate
- Trailhead: Sunwapta Falls, 58 kilometers (36 miles) south of the town of Jasper

The trail to this seldom-visited lake straddling the Continental Divide gains little elevation, making it popular with mountain-bike riders experienced in backcountry travel. After crossing the canyon below Sunwapta Falls, the trail meanders along the east bank of the Athabasca River for 15 kilometers (9.3 miles), then crosses it. Beyond the main bridge you'll need to ford the braided Chaba River, then continue southwest along the river flats for six kilometers (3.7 miles) to the east end of Fortress Lake. The lake lies within British Columbia in **Hamber Provincial Park.** Its shores are difficult to traverse because they lack established trails. At the end of the trail, **Fortress Lake Wilderness Retreat** (250/344-2639, www.fortresslake.com) provides cabin accommodations, mostly for anglers who fly in by helicopter from Golden, but hikers are also welcome.

Geraldine Lakes

- Length: 5 kilometers/3.1 miles (2 hours) one-way
- Elevation gain: 410 meters/1,350 feet
- Rating: moderate
- Trailhead: Geraldine Fire Road, off Highway 93A, 1 kilometer (0.6 mile) from Athabasca Falls

The first of the four Geraldine Lakes is an easy

looking across to the Athabasca Glacier from the Wilcox Pass Trail

© ANDREW HEMPSTEAD

JASPER NATIONAL PARK

two-kilometer (1.2-mile) hike from the end of the 5.5-kilometer (3.4-mile) Geraldine Fire Road. The forest-encircled lake reflects the north face of Mount Fryatt (3,361 meters/11,030 feet). The trail continues along the northwest shore, climbs steeply past a scenic 100-meter-high (330-foot-high) waterfall, and traverses some rough terrain where the trail becomes indistinct; follow the cairns. At the end of the valley is another waterfall. The trail climbs east of the waterfall to a ridge above the second of the lakes, five kilometers (3.1 miles) from the trailhead. Although the trail officially ends here, it does continue to a campground at the south end of the lake. Two other lakes, accessible only by bushwhacking, are farther up the valley.

Valley of the Five Lakes

- Length: 2.3 kilometers/1.4 miles (40 minutes) one-way

JASPER NATIONAL PARK

HIKING IN JASPER NATIONAL PARK

The 1,200 kilometers (745 miles) of hiking trails in Jasper are significantly different from those in the other mountain national parks. The park has an extensive system of interconnecting backcountry trails that, for experienced hikers, can provide a wilderness adventure rivaled by few areas on the face of the earth. For casual day hikers, on the other hand, opportunities are more limited.

Most trails in the immediate vicinity of the town have little elevation gain and lead through montane forest to lakes. The trails around Maligne Lake, at the base of Mount Edith Cavell, and along the Icefields Parkway have more rewarding objectives and are more challenging. These are covered in detail throughout the chapter. The most popular trails for extended backcountry trips are the **Skyline Trail,** between Maligne Lake Road and Maligne Lake

(44.5 km/27.6 mi, three days each way); the trails to **Amethyst Lakes** in the Tonquin Valley (19 km/11.8 mi, one day each way) and **Athabasca Pass** (50 km/31 mi, three days each way), which was used by fur traders for 40 years as the main route across the Canadian Rockies; and the **South Boundary Trail,** which traverses a remote section of the front ranges into Banff National Park (160 km/100 mi, 10 days each way).

Before setting off on any hikes, whatever the length, go to the **park information center** in downtown Jasper or the Parks Canada desk in the Icefield Centre along the Icefields Parkway for trail maps, trail conditions, and trail closures, or to purchase a copy of the *Canadian Rockies Trail Guide* by Brian Patton and Bart Robinson.

- Elevation gain: 60 meters/200 feet
- Rating: easy
- Trailhead: Icefields Parkway, 10 kilometers (6.2 miles) south of the town of Jasper

These lakes, nestled in an open valley, are small but make a worthwhile destination. From the trailhead, 10 kilometers (6.2 miles) south of town along the Icefields Parkway, the trail passes through a forest of lodgepole pine, crosses a stream, and climbs a ridge from where you'll have a panoramic view of surrounding peaks. As the trail descends to the lakes, turn left at the first intersection to a point between two of the lakes. These lakes are linked to Old Fort Point by a tedious 10-kilometer (6.2-mile) trail through montane forest.

ACCOMMODATIONS AND CAMPING

The two lodges and two hostels along the parkway proper are covered in this section. There are also several accommodations along the Icefields Parkway but within close proximity to the town of Jasper.

Under $50

Reservations for the two hostels can be made by contacting HI-Canada (778/328-2220 or 866/762-4122, www.hihostels.ca). At both facilities, check-in is 5pm-11pm, but the main lodges are open all day.

HI-Beauty Creek (May-Sept., members $24, nonmembers $27), 17 kilometers (10.5 miles) north of the Columbia Icefield and 144 kilometers (90 miles) north from Lake Louise, is nestled in a small stand of Douglas fir between the Icefields Parkway and the Sunwapta River. Each of its separate 12-bed male and female cabins has a woodstove and propane lighting. A third building holds a kitchen and dining area. There are no flush toilets or showers.

Farther north is the equally rustic **HI-Athabasca Falls** (closed Tues. Oct.-Apr. and all of Nov., members $24, nonmembers $27), 32 kilometers (20 miles) south of the town of Jasper and 198 kilometers (123 miles) north from Lake Louise. It is larger than the one at Beauty Creek and has electricity. Athabasca Falls is only a few minutes' walk away.

Over $200

Historic **Sunwapta Falls Rocky Mountain Lodge** (780/852-4852 or 888/922-9222, www. sunwapta.com, May-mid-Oct., $229-379 s or d) is 55 kilometers (34 miles) south of the town of Jasper and within walking distance of the picturesque waterfall for which it is named. It features 52 comfortable motel-like units, with either two queen beds or one queen bed and a fireplace; some have balconies. In the main lodge is a lunchtime self-serve restaurant popular with passing travelers. In the evening, this same room is transformed into a restaurant featuring simply prepared Canadian game and seafood in the $24-36 range and a delectable wild berry crumble for $8.50.

Glacier View Inn (780/852-6550 or 877/422-2623, www.explorerockies.com, May-Sept., $229-289 s or d), the top story of Columbia Icefield Centre, lies in a stunning location high above the tree line and overlooking the Columbia Icefield, 105 kilometers (65 miles) south of the town of Jasper and 132 kilometers (82 miles) north of Lake Louise. It features 29 standard rooms, 17 of which have glacier views, and 3 larger, more luxurious corner rooms. All units have satellite TV and phones. In May and the last two weeks of September, rates start at $150. (For the view alone, the more expensive rooms are well worth the extra $20.) Because of the remote location, dining options are limited to the in-house café and restaurant. The **Glacier**

Dining Room opens at 7am daily for a breakfast buffet, reopening 6pm-9:30pm for dinner. On the same level is a cafeteria-style café and a snack bar. All food outlets are designed around the basic needs of passing highway travelers.

Campgrounds

Aside from Whistlers and Wapiti Campgrounds at the top end of the Icefields Parkway near the town of Jasper, there are five campgrounds along this stretch of highway. All sites fill on a first-come, first-served basis.

Wilcox Creek and **Columbia Icefield Campgrounds** are within two kilometers (1.2 miles) of each other at the extreme southern end of the park, just over 100 kilometers (62 miles) south of the town of Jasper and around 125 kilometers (78 miles) north of Lake Louise. Both are primitive facilities with pit toilets, cooking shelters, and fire rings; all sites are $16. Smallish sites at Columbia Icefield Campground are set in a stunted subalpine forest of aspen and spruce, with views extending across to the Athabasca Glacier. Immediately to the south, Wilcox Creek offers larger sites, better suited to RVs and trailers, but with no hookups.

Jonas Creek, Honeymoon Lake, and **Mount Kerkeslin Campgrounds** are all within a 50-kilometer (31-mile) stretch continuing north. All cost $17 per night and have primitive facilities (no hookups or showers).

JASPER NATIONAL PARK

Town of Jasper

JASPER NATIONAL PARK

At the top end of the Icefields Parkway, 280 kilometers (174 miles) north of Banff and a 3.5-hour drive west of the provincial capital, Edmonton, the town of Jasper is the service center of the park.

With all the things to do and see in the surrounding wilderness, it's amazing how many people hang out in town. July and August are especially busy; much-needed improvements to the parking situation have had little impact on the traffic—try for a parking spot in the lot along the railway line. The best way to avoid the problem is to avoid town during the middle of the day. The park information center, on Connaught Drive, is the only real reason to be in town. The shaded park in front of the center is a good place for people-watching, but you may get clobbered by a wayward Hacky Sack. Connaught Drive, the town's main street, parallels the rail line as it curves through town. Also along this road you'll find the bus depot, rail terminal, restaurants, motels, and a parking lot. Behind Connaught Drive is Patricia Street (one-way eastbound), which has more restaurants and services and leads to a string of hotels on Geikie Street. Behind this main core are rows of neat houses—much less pretentious than those in Banff—and all the facilities of a regular town, including a library, school, civic center, post office, museum, swimming pool, and hospital.

SIGHTS AND DRIVES
Downtown
At the back of town is the excellent **Jasper-Yellowhead Museum and Archives** (400 Bonhomme St., 780/852-3013, 10am-5pm daily mid-June-Sept., 10am-5pm Thurs.-Sun. the rest of the year, adult $6, senior and child $5), as unstuffy as any museum could

possibly be and well worth a visit even for non-museum types. The main gallery features colorful, modern picture boards with exhibits that take visitors along a timeline of Jasper's human history through the fur trade, the coming of the railway, and the creation of the park. Documentaries are shown on demand in a small television room. The museum also features extensive archives, including hundreds of historical photos, manuscripts, documents, maps, and videos.

The Den (corner of Connaught Dr. and Miette Ave., 780/852-3361, 9am-10pm daily), in the darkened bowels of the Whistlers Inn, is a throwback to a bygone era, when displays of stuffed animals were considered the best way to extol the wonders of nature. "See animals in their natural setting" cries museum advertising, but the shrubbery looks suspiciously like fake Christmas trees, and the bull elk seems to be screaming, "Get me out of here!" Yep, they even charge you for it—exchange $4 for a token at the Whistlers's reception desk.

Patricia and Pyramid Lakes
A winding road heads through the hills at the back of town to these two picturesque lakes, formed when glacial moraines dammed shallow valleys. The first, to the left, is Patricia; the second, farther along the road, is Pyramid, backed by **Pyramid Mountain** (2,765 meters/9,072 feet). Both lakes are popular spots for picnicking, fishing, and boating. Boat rentals are available at **Pyramid Lake Boat Rentals** (780/852-4900), across the road from the lake in the Coast Pyramid Lake Resort. Canoes, rowboats, paddleboats, and kayaks are $35 for the first hour and $25 for each additional hour. The resort also rents motorboats for $60 per hour. From the resort, the road continues around the lake to a bridge, which leads to an

To Pyramid
Lake

To Hwy 16

To
◀MALIGNE CANYON
and
Miette Hot Springs

TONQUIN PRIME
RIB VILLAGE ▼

TONQUIN
INN ●

TONQUIN
INN

JUNIPER   ST

**TOWN OF
JASPER**

CONNAUGHT DR

PYRAMID LAKE RD

Pyramid Benchland Trail

BEAR HILL
LODGE ●

16

ASPEN   AVE

BONHOMME ST

GEIKIE ST

PATRICIA ST

YELLOWHEAD HWY

Athabasca River

JASPER NATIONAL PARK

N

★ JASPER-
YELLOWHEAD
MUSEUM

■ ACTIVITY
CENTRE

■ JASPER AQUATIC
CENTRE

CEDAR AVE

BEAR'S PAW BAKERY

PALISADES ▼ ■

▼ JASPER PIZZA PLACE

ASTORIA
HOTEL ●

To Mina
Lakes

TOTEM SKI SHOP ■

SOURCE FOR ■
SPORTS

■ JASPER CAMERA & GIFT

PARK
INFROMATION
CENTRE ■

■ EVERST
OUTDOOR
STORE

ELM   AVE

LIBRARY ■

POST
OFFICE ■

WHISTLERS
INN
●

LA
FIESTA ▼

RAIL STATION
■

ATHABASCA HOTEL ●

CHABA
THEATRE ■

MALIGNE   AVE

OUR NATIVE LAND ■

■ BAREFOOT IN THE PARK

HOSPITAL ■

ON-LINE SPORT ■
& TACKLE

THE
OTHER
PAW ▼

▼ CANTONESE
RESTAURANT

SYRAHS ▼

CAFÉ MONDO ▼

SOMETHING ELSE
RESTAURANT

MALIGNE TOURS ■
OFFICE

▼ FIDDLE RIVER

MIETTE   AVE

FREEWHEEL CYCLE ▼

CONNAUGHT
SQUARE

NUTTER'S ▼

SOFT ROCK
▼ CAFÉ

PINE   AVE

L & W RESTAURANT ▼

VILLA
CARUSO

To Icefields Parkway, Banff
(Banff National Park) and
Prince George, BC

To Old Fort Point

0   200 yds

0   200 m

© AVALON TRAVEL

JASPER NATIONAL PARK

© ANDREW HEMPSTEAD

Pyramid Lake

island popular with picnickers. The road ends at the quieter end of the lake.

Jasper Tramway

This tramway (780/852-3093, 9am-8pm daily in summer, shorter hours late Apr.-June and Sept.-mid-Oct., closed the rest of the year, adult $31, child 6-15 $16) climbs more than 1,000 vertical meters (3,280 feet) up the steep north face of **The Whistlers,** named for the hoary marmots that live on the summit. The tramway operates two 30-passenger cars that take seven minutes to reach the upper terminal, during which time the conductor gives a lecture about the mountain and its environment. From the upper terminal, a 1.4-kilometer (0.9-mile) trail leads to the 2,470-meter (8,104-foot) true summit. The view is breathtaking; to the south is the Columbia Icefield, and on a clear day you can see Mount Robson (3,954 meters/12,970 feet)—the highest peak in the Canadian

Rockies—to the northwest. Free two-hour guided hikes leave the upper terminal for the true summit at 10am, 11am, 2pm, and 3pm daily. You should allow two hours on top and, on a clear summer's day, two more hours in line at the bottom. The tramway is three kilometers (1.9 miles) south of town on Highway 93 (Icefields Parkway), and then a similar distance up Whistlers Road.

Edith and Annette Lakes

These two lakes along the road to The Fairmont Jasper Park Lodge—across the Athabasca River from town—are perfect for a picnic, swim, or pleasant walk. They are remnants of a much larger lake that once covered the entire valley floor. The lakes are relatively shallow; therefore, the sun warms the water to a bearable temperature for swimming. In fact, they have the warmest waters of any lakes in the park. The 2.5-kilometer (1.6-mile) **Lee Foundation Trail** encircles Lake Annette and is wheelchair

JASPER NATIONAL PARK

Jasper Tramway

golf clubhouse; you're welcome to walk around the resort, play golf, dine in the restaurants, and, of course, browse through the shopping promenade—even if you're not a registered guest. On the lakeshore in front of the lodge is a boat rental concession; canoes and kayaks can be rented for $25 per 30 minutes. From the main lodge, a walking trail follows the shoreline of Lac Beauvert through the golf course, linking up with other trails at Old Fort Point. To walk from town will take one hour.

【 Maligne Canyon

Maligne Lake, one of the world's most photographed lakes, lies 48 kilometers (30 miles) southeast of Jasper. It's the source of the **Maligne River,** which flows northward to Medicine Lake and then disappears underground, eventually emerging downstream of Maligne Canyon. The river was known to the natives as Chaba Imne (River of the Great Beaver), but the name by which we know it today was coined by a missionary. After his horses were swept away by its swift-flowing waters in 1846, he described the river as being *"la traverse maligne."* Driving up the Maligne River Valley to the lake is a 600-million-year-old lesson in geology that can be appreciated by anyone.

accessible. Between the two lakes is a large picnic area with a playground.

The Fairmont Jasper Park Lodge

Accommodations are not usually considered sights, but then this is the Rockies, where grand railway hotels attract as many visitors as the more legitimate natural attractions. The Fairmont Jasper Park Lodge has been the premier accommodation in the park since it opened in 1921. Back then it was a single-story structure, reputed to be the largest log building in the world. It burned to the ground in 1952 but was rebuilt. Additional bungalows were erected along Lac Beauvert ("beautiful green lake" in French), forming a basis for today's lodge. Rows of cabins radiate from the main lodge, which contains restaurants, lounges, and the town's only covered shopping arcade. Today up to 900 guests can be accommodated in 446 rooms. A large parking area for non-guests is located on Lodge Road, behind the

As the Maligne River drops into the Athabasca River Valley, its gradient is particularly steep. The fast-flowing water has eroded a deep canyon out of the easily dissolved limestone bedrock. The canyon is up to 50 meters (165 feet) deep, yet so narrow that squirrels often jump across. At the top of the canyon, opposite the teahouse, you'll see large potholes in the riverbed. These potholes are created when rocks and pebbles become trapped in what begins as a shallow depression; under the force of the rushing water, they carve jug-shaped hollows into the soft bedrock.

To get here, head northeast from town and turn right onto Maligne Lake Road. The canyon access road veers left 11 kilometers (6.8 miles) from Jasper.

An interpretive trail winds down from the parking lot, crossing the canyon six times. The most spectacular sections of the canyon can be seen from the first two bridges, at the upper end of the trail. In summer, a teahouse operates at the top of the canyon. To avoid the crowds at the upper end of the canyon, an alternative would be to park at Sixth Bridge, near the confluence of the Maligne and Athabasca Rivers, and walk *up* the canyon. The **Maligne Valley Shuttle** (780/852-3370) stops at the canyon eight times daily along its run between 627 Patricia Street in downtown Jasper and Maligne Lake; fare is $15 one-way from town. In winter, guided tours of the frozen canyon are an experience you'll never forget.

Medicine Lake

From the canyon, Maligne Lake Road climbs to Medicine Lake, which does a disappearing act each year. The water level fluctuates due to a network of underground passages that emerge downstream in Maligne Canyon. At the northwest end of the lake, beyond where the outlet should be, the riverbed is often dry. In fall, when runoff from the mountains is minimal, the water level drops, and by November the lake comprises a few shallow pools. Natives believed that spirits were responsible for the phenomenon, hence the name.

◖ Maligne Lake

At the end of the road, 48 kilometers (30 miles) from town, is Maligne Lake, the largest glacier-fed lake in the Canadian Rockies and second largest in the world. The first paying visitors were brought to the lake in the 1920s, and it has been a mecca for camera-toting tourists from around the world ever since. Once at the lake, activities are plentiful. But other than taking in the spectacular vistas, the only thing you

won't need your wallet for is hiking one of the numerous trails in the area.

The most popular tourist activity at the lake is a 90-minute narrated cruise on a glass-enclosed boat up the lake to oft-photographed **Spirit Island.** Cruises leave in summer every hour on the hour 10am-5pm, with fewer sailings in May and September; adult $55, child $27.50. Many time slots are booked in blocks by tour companies; therefore, reservations are suggested. Rowboats and canoes can be rented at the Boat House, a provincial historic site dating to 1929, for $30 per hour or $90 per day. Double sea kayaks go for $35 per hour and $100 per day. The lake also has excellent trout fishing; guided fishing tours are available.

All commercial operations to and around the lake are operated by **Maligne Tours** (616 Patricia St., 780/852-3370 or 866/625-4463, www.malignelake.com), based in downtown Jasper. At the lake itself, in addition to the cruises and boat rentals, Maligne Tours operates a souvenir shop and large café with a huge area of tiered outdoor seating overlooking the lake. At the adjacent Maligne Lake Chalet, which has been meticulously restored, the company serves a comprehensive afternoon tea (2pm-4:30pm daily July-Aug., $32), with the most sought after tables enjoying lake views.

The **Maligne Valley Shuttle** runs from the Maligne Tours office and from various hotels out to the lake 3-4 times daily mid-May-late September. The first shuttle leaves for the lake each morning at 8:30am; $40 round-trip.

East Along Highway 16

From Jasper, it's 50 kilometers (31 miles) to the park's eastern boundary along Highway 16, following the Athabasca River the entire way. Beyond the turnoff to Maligne Lake, Highway 16 enters a wide valley flanked to the west by The Palisade and to the east by the Colin Range. The valley is a classic montane environment, with open meadows and forests of

© ANDREW HEMPSTEAD

JASPER NATIONAL PARK

Oft-photographed Spirit Island is the turn-around point for tour boats on Maligne Lake.

Douglas fir and lodgepole pine. After crossing the Athabasca River, 20 kilometers (12.4 miles) from Jasper, the highway parallels **Jasper Lake,** which is lined by sand dunes along its southern edge. At the highway, a plaque marks the site of **Jasper House** (the actual site is on the opposite side of the river). The next worthwhile stop is **Disaster Point,** four kilometers (2.5 miles) farther north. This is a great spot for viewing bighorn sheep, which gather at a mineral lick, an area of exposed mineral salts. Disaster Point is on the lower slopes of Roche Miette, a distinctive 2,316-meter-high (7,600-foot-high) peak that juts out into the Athabasca River Valley. Across the highway, the braided Athabasca River is flanked by wetlands alive with migrating birds in the spring and fall.

Miette Hot Springs Road branches south from the highway 43 kilometers (27 miles) east of Jasper. This junction marks the site of **Pocahontas,** a coal-mining town in existence between 1910 and 1921. The mine itself was high above the township, with coal transported to the valley floor by cable car. All buildings have long since been removed, but a short interpretive walk leads through the remaining foundations. One kilometer (0.6 mile) along Miette Hot Springs Road, a short trail leads to photogenic **Punchbowl Falls.** Here Mountain Creek cascades through a narrow crevice in a cliff to a pool of turbulent water.

Miette Hot Springs

After curving, swerving, rising, and falling many times, Miette Hot Springs Road ends 18 kilometers (11 miles) from Highway 16 at the warmest springs in the Canadian Rockies (780/866-3939, 10:30am-9pm daily mid-May-mid-Oct., extended to 8:30am-10:30pm daily in summer). In the early 1900s, these springs were one of the park's biggest attractions. In 1910, a packhorse trail was built up the valley, and the government constructed a bathhouse. The original hand-hewn log structure was replaced in the

Soak away your cares at Miette Hot Springs.

© ANDREW HEMPSTEAD

JASPER NATIONAL PARK

1930s with pools that remained in use until new facilities were built in 1985. Water that flows into the pools is artificially cooled from 54°C (128°F) to a soothing 39°C (100°F). A newer addition to the complex is a smaller, cool plunge pool. Admission is adult $6.75 for a single swim ($9.25 for the day) while seniors and children pay $5.25 ($7.75 for the day).

Many hiking trails begin from the hot springs complex; the shortest is from the picnic area to the source of the springs (allow five minutes each way). Overlooking the pools is a café, while a restaurant and lodging are just down the hill.

◀ Mount Edith Cavell

This 3,363-meter (11,033-foot) peak is the most distinctive and impressive in the park. Known to natives as the "White Ghost" for its snowcapped summit, the mountain was given its official name in honor of a British nurse who was executed for helping prisoners of war escape German-occupied Belgium during World War I. The peak was first climbed that same year; today the most popular route to the summit is up the east ridge (to the left of the summit). The imposing north face (facing the parking lot) has been climbed but is rated as an extremely difficult climb.

GETTING A CLOSER LOOK

For those less adventurous, several vantage points, including downtown Jasper and the golf course, provide good views of the peak. But the most impressive place to marvel at the mountain is from directly below the north face. A 14.5-kilometer (nine-mile) road winds up the Astoria River Valley from Highway 93A, ending right below the face. This steep, narrow road has many switchbacks. Trailers must be left in the designated area at the bottom. Highway 93A was the original Icefields Parkway, following the southeast bank of the Athabasca River. The route has now been bypassed by the more direct one on the other side of the river.

From the parking lot at the end of the road, you must strain your neck to take in the magnificent sight of the mountain's 1,500-meter (4,920-foot) north face and **Angel Glacier,** which lies in a saddle on the mountain's lower slopes. On warm days, those who are patient may be lucky enough to witness an avalanche tumbling from the glacier, creating a roar that echoes across the valley. From the parking area, the **Path of the Glacier Trail** (one hour round-trip) traverses barren moraines deposited by the receding Angel Glacier and leads to some great viewpoints.

HIKING AROUND THE TOWN OF JASPER
Pyramid Benchland

• Length: 7 kilometers/4.3 miles (2 hours) round-trip

- Elevation gain: 120 meters/400 feet
- Rating: easy
- Trailhead: Jasper-Yellowhead Museum, Pyramid Lake Road

Numerous official and unofficial hiking trails weave across the benchland immediately west of the town of Jasper. From the far corner of the parking lot beside the museum, a well-marked trail climbs onto the benchland. Keep right, crossing Pyramid Lake Road, and you'll emerge on a bluff overlooking the Athabasca River Valley. Bighorn sheep can often be seen grazing here. If you return to the trailhead from here, you will have hiked seven kilometers (4.3 miles). The trail continues north, disappearing into the montane forest until arriving at Pyramid Lake. Various trails can be taken to return to town; get a map at the park information center before setting out.

Mina Lakes

- Length: 2.5 kilometers/1.6 miles (50 minutes) one-way
- Elevation gain: 70 meters/230 feet
- Rating: easy
- Trailhead: Jasper-Yellowhead Museum, Pyramid Lake Road

Lower and Upper Mina Lakes lie on the benchland immediately west of the town of Jasper. The trailhead is the same as the Pyramid Lake Loop, except instead of keeping right, you'll need to take the first left fork (signposted as Route 8 to Cabin Creek West), which climbs up onto the bench, then crosses a treeless 100-meter-wide (328-foot-wide) corridor, cleared to act as a firebreak for the town. Cabin Lake Road passes along the firebreak, leading west (left) to man-made Cabin Lake and east (right) to Pyramid Lake Road. Continuing straight ahead, the trail climbs gradually through a typical montane forest of lodgepole pine, Douglas fir, and poplar before emerging at Lower Mina

Lake. After a further 500 meters (0.3 mile) and just beyond the end of Lower Mina Lake, the upper lake and a pebbly stretch of beach are reached. The distance given above is to this point, but with a map in hand, it's possible to continue along the shore of the upper lake; two kilometers (1.2 miles) beyond the end of the lake the trail forks—looping back along Cabin Lake Road via Cabin Lake to the left and to Riley Lake to the right.

Patricia Lake Circle

- Length: 5-kilometer/3.1-mile loop (90 minutes round-trip)
- Elevation gain: minimal
- Rating: easy
- Trailhead: 2 kilometers (1.2 miles) along Pyramid Lake Road

This trail begins across the road from the riding stables on Pyramid Lake Road. It traverses a mixed forest of aspen and lodgepole pine—prime habitat for larger mammals such as elk, deer, and moose. The second half of the trail skirts Cottonwood Slough, where you'll see several beaver ponds. Unlike the name suggests, this trail doesn't encircle Patricia Lake, but instead just passes along a portion of its southern shoreline.

The Palisade

- Length: 11 kilometers/6.8 miles (4 hours) one-way
- Elevation gain: 850 meters/2,790 feet
- Rating: difficult
- Trailhead: the end of Pyramid Lake Road, 8 kilometers (5 miles) from town

The destination of this strenuous hike is the site of an old fire lookout tower atop a high ridge between the Athabasca River Valley and Pyramid Mountain. From the locked gate at the end of Pyramid Lake Road, the trail crosses Pyramid Creek after one kilometer (0.6 mile), then climbs steadily for the entire distance along a forest-enclosed fire road (take the right fork at the 7.5-km/4.7-mi mark). Once at the end of the trail, it's easy to see why this site was chosen for the lookout; the panorama extends down the valley and across Jasper Lake to Roche Miette (2,316 meters/7,600 feet).

Old Fort Point

- Length: 6.5-kilometer/4-mile loop (2 hours round-trip)
- Elevation gain: 60 meters/200 feet
- Rating: easy
- Trailhead: Take Highway 93A south from downtown, follow the first left after crossing Highway 16, and park across the Athabasca River.

Old Fort Point is a distinctive knoll above the Athabasca River, to the east of town. Although it is not likely that a fort was ever located here, the first fur-trading post in the Rockies, Henry House, was just downstream. It's easy to imagine fur traders and early explorers climbing to this summit for 360-degree views of the Athabasca and Miette Rivers. From the parking lot beyond the single-lane vehicle bridge over the Athabasca River, climb the wooden stairs, take the trail to the top of the knoll, and then continue back to the parking lot along the north flank of the hill.

The Whistlers

- Length: 8 kilometers/5 miles (3 hours) one-way
- Elevation gain: 1,220 meters/4,000 feet
- Rating: difficult
- Trailhead: 3 kilometers (1.9 miles) along Whistlers Road from Highway 93

This steep ascent, the park's most arduous day hike, is unique in that it passes through three distinct vegetation zones in a relatively short distance. (For the less adventurous, Jasper Tramway (780/852-3093) traverses the same route described here.) From the trailhead on Whistlers Road, immediately below the hostel, the trail begins climbing and doesn't let up until you merge with the crowds getting off the tramway at the top. The trail begins in a montane forest of aspen and white birch, climbs through a subalpine forest of Engelmann spruce and alpine fir, then emerges onto the open, treeless tundra, which is inhabited by pikas, hoary marmots, and a few hardy plants. Carry water with you, because none is available before the upper tramway terminal.

HIKING IN THE MALIGNE LAKE AREA

Maligne Lake, 48 kilometers (30 miles) from the town of Jasper, provides more easy hiking with many opportunities to view the lake and explore its environs. To get there, take Highway 16 east for four kilometers (2.5 miles) from town and turn south on Maligne Lake Road. The first three hikes detailed are along the access road to the lake; the others leave from various parking lots at the northwest end of the lake.

Providing transportation to the lake, the **Maligne Valley Shuttle** (780/852-3370) runs from 616 Patricia Street and from some hotels out to the lake up to four times daily; $32.10 one-way.

Maligne Canyon

- Length: 3.7 kilometers/2.3 miles (90 minutes) one-way
- Elevation gain: 125 meters/410 feet
- Rating: moderate
- Trailhead: turnoff to Sixth Bridge, 2.5 kilometers (1.6 miles) along Maligne Lake Road from Highway 16

Maligne Canyon is one of the busiest places in the park, yet few visitors hike the entire length of the canyon trail. By beginning from the lower end of the canyon, at the confluence of the Maligne and Athabasca Rivers, you'll avoid starting your hike alongside the masses, and you'll get to hike downhill on your return (when you're tired). To access the lower end of the canyon, follow the one-kilometer (0.6-mile) spur off Maligne Lake Road to Sixth Bridge. Crowds will be minimal for the first three kilometers (1.9 miles) to Fourth Bridge, where the trail starts climbing. By the time you get to Third Bridge, you start encountering adventurous hikers coming down the canyon, and soon thereafter you'll meet the real crowds—high heels, bear bells, and all. Upstream of here the canyon is deepest and most spectacular.

Watchtower Basin

- Length: 10 kilometers/6.2 miles (3.5 hours) one-way
- Elevation gain: 630 meters/2,070 feet
- Rating: moderate/difficult
- Trailhead: Maligne Lake Road, 24 kilometers (15 miles) from Highway 16

Watchtower is a wide, open basin high above the crowds of Maligne Lake Road. All the elevation gain is made during the first six kilometers (3.7 miles) from Maligne Lake Road, through a dense forest of lodgepole pine and white spruce. As the trail levels off and enters the basin, it continues to follow the west bank of a stream, crossing it at kilometer 10 (mile 6.2) and officially ending at a campground. To the west and south, the **Maligne Range** rises to a crest three kilometers (1.9 miles) beyond the campground. From the top of this ridge, at the intersection with the Skyline Trail, it is 17.5 kilometers (11 miles) northwest to Maligne Canyon, or 27 kilometers (17 miles) southeast to Maligne Lake. By camping at Watchtower Campground, day trips can be made to a small lake in the basin or to highlights of the Skyline Trail such as the Snowbowl, Curator Lake, and Shovel Pass.

Jacques Lake

- Length: 12 kilometers/7.5 miles (3-3.5 hours) one-way
- Elevation gain: 100 meters/330 feet
- Rating: moderate
- Trailhead: Beaver Lake Picnic Area, 28 kilometers (17.4 miles) from Highway 16 along Maligne Lake Road

The appeal of this trail, which begins from the southeast end of Medicine Lake, is its lack of elevation gain and the numerous small lakes it skirts as it travels through a narrow valley. On either side, the severely faulted mountains of the Queen Elizabeth Ranges rise steeply above the valley floor, their strata tilted nearly vertical.

Lake Trail (Mary Schäffer Loop)

- Length: 3.2-kilometer/2-mile loop (1 hour round-trip)
- Elevation gain: minimal
- Rating: easy
- Trailhead: Boat House, Maligne Lake

This easy, pleasant walk begins from beside the Boat House, following the eastern shore of Maligne Lake through an open area of lakeside picnic tables to a point known as **Schäffer Viewpoint,** named for the first white person to see the valley. Across the lake are the aptly named Bald Hills, the Maligne Range, and, to the southwest, the distinctive twin peaks of Mount Unwin (3,268 meters/10,720 feet) and Mount Charlton (3,217 meters/10,550 feet). After dragging yourself away from the spectacular panorama, continue along a shallow bay before following the trail into a forest of spruce and subalpine fir, then looping back to the middle parking lot.

Opal Hills

- Length: 8.2-kilometer/5.1-mile loop (3 hours round-trip)

- Elevation gain: 455 meters/1,500 feet
- Rating: moderate
- Trailhead: north corner, upper parking lot, Maligne Lake

This trail begins from behind the information board in the corner of the parking lot, climbing steeply for 1.5 kilometers (0.9 mile) to a point where it divides. Both options end in the high alpine meadows of the Opal Hills; the trail to the right is shorter and steeper. Once you are in the meadow, the entire Maligne Valley can be seen below.

◖ Bald Hills

- Length: 5.2 kilometers/3.2 miles (2 hours) one-way
- Elevation gain: 495 meters/1,620 feet
- Rating: moderate
- Trailhead: picnic area at the end of Maligne Lake Road

This trail follows an old road for its entire distance to the site of a fire lookout that has long since been removed. The sweeping view takes in the jade-green waters of Maligne Lake, the Queen Elizabeth Ranges, and the twin peaks of Mount Unwin and Mount Charlton. The Bald Hills extend for seven kilometers (4.3 miles), their highest summit not exceeding 2,600 meters (8,530 feet). A herd of caribou summers in the hills, although are rarely seen. On the return journey, make the short detour to Moose Lake (see below).

Moose Lake

- Length: 1.4 kilometers/0.9 mile (30 minutes) one-way
- Elevation gain: minimal
- Rating: easy
- Trailhead: picnic area at the end of Maligne Lake Road

This trail begins 200 meters (0.1 mile) along

the Bald Hills Trail, spurring left along the Maligne Pass Trail (signposted). One kilometer (0.6 mile) along this trail, a rough track branches left, leading to Moose Lake—a quiet body of water where moose are sometimes seen. To return, continue along the trail as it descends to the shore of Maligne Lake, a short stroll from the picnic area.

HIKING NEAR MOUNT EDITH CAVELL

Cavell Road begins from Highway 93A, 13 kilometers (eight miles) south from the town of Jasper, and winds through a subalpine forest, ascending 300 meters (980 feet) in 14.5 kilometers (nine miles). Trailheads are located at the end of the road (Cavell Meadows Trail and a short interpretive trail) and across from the hostel two kilometers (1.2 miles) from the end (Astoria River/Tonquin Valley Trail). A third trailhead is on Marmot Basin Road where it crosses Portal Creek (Maccarib Pass Trail).

Cavell Meadows

- Length: 4 kilometers/2.5 miles (1.5 hours) one-way
- Elevation gain: 380 meters/1,250 feet
- Rating: moderate
- Trailhead: parking lot at the end of Cavell Road, 27.5 kilometers (17 miles) south of town

This trail, beginning from the parking lot beneath Mount Edith Cavell, provides access to an alpine meadow and panoramic views of Angel Glacier. The trail begins by following the paved Path of the Glacier Trail, then branches left, climbing steadily along a rocky ridge and then through a subalpine forest of Engelmann spruce and then stunted subalpine fir to emerge facing the northeast face of Mount Edith Cavell and Angel Glacier. The view of the glacier from this point is nothing less than awesome, as the ice spills out of a cirque, clinging to a 300-meter-high (984-foot-high) cliff face. The trail continues to higher viewpoints and an alpine meadow that, by mid-July, is filled with wildflowers.

⬛ Astoria River/Tonquin Valley

- Length: 19 kilometers/11.8 miles (6-7 hours) one-way
- Elevation gain: 450 meters/1,480 feet
- Rating: moderate
- Trailhead: opposite the hostel on Cavell Road

From Cavell Road, this trail descends through a forest on the north side of Mount Edith Cavell for five kilometers (3.1 miles), then crosses the Astoria River and begins a long ascent into spectacular Tonquin Valley. Amethyst Lakes and the 1,000-meter (3,280-foot) cliffs of the Ramparts first come into view after 13 kilometers (eight miles). At the 17-kilometer (10.5-mile) mark, the trail divides. To the left it climbs into Eremite Valley, where there is a campground. The right fork continues, following the Astoria River to Tonquin Valley, Amethyst Lakes, and a choice of four campgrounds.

Maccarib Pass

- Length: 21 kilometers/13 miles (7-8 hours) one-way
- Elevation gain: 730 meters/2,400 feet
- Rating: moderate/difficult
- Trailhead: 6.5 kilometers (4 miles) up Marmot Basin Road

This trail is slightly longer and gains more elevation than the trail along the Astoria River but is more spectacular. It strikes out to the southwest, following Portal Creek for a short distance, then passes under Peveril Peak before making a steep approach to Maccarib Pass, 12.5 kilometers (7.8 miles) from the trailhead.

The full panorama of the Tonquin Valley can be appreciated as the path gradually descends from the pass. At Amethyst Lakes it links up with the Astoria River Trail, and many options for day hikes head out from campgrounds at the lakes.

OTHER SUMMER RECREATION

Several booking agents represent the many recreation-tour operators in Jasper. **Jasper Adventure Centre** (604 Connaught Dr., 780/852-5595 or 800/565-7547, www.jasperadventurecentre.com), in the lobby of the Chaba Theatre, takes bookings for all of the following activities, as well as for accommodations and transportation to various points in the park and beyond. **Maligne Tours** (616 Patricia St., 780/852-3370) operates all activities in the Maligne Lake area, including the famous lake cruise.

Mountain Biking

Cycling in the park continues to grow in popularity: The ride between Banff and Jasper, along the Icefields Parkway, attracts riders from around the world. In addition to the paved roads, many designated unpaved bicycle trails radiate from the town. One of the most popular is the Athabasca River Trail, which begins at Old Fort Point and follows the river to a point below Maligne Canyon. Cyclists are particularly prone to sudden bear encounters; make noise when passing through heavily wooded areas. The brochure *Mountain Biking Trail Guide* lists designated trails and is available from the information center and all local sport shops. Rental outlets include **Source for Sports** (406 Patricia St., 780/852-3654), **Freewheel Cycle** (618 Patricia St., 780/852-3898), **Vicious Cycle** (630 Connaught Dr., 780/852-1111), and the **Activity Centre** at The Fairmont Jasper Park Lodge (780/852-5708). Expect to pay $10-15 per hour or $28-50 for any 24-hour period, which includes a helmet and lock.

Horseback Riding

On the benchlands immediately behind the town of Jasper is **Jasper Riding Stables** (Pyramid Lake Rd., 780/852-7433, early May–early Oct.). The stables offer one-, two-, and three-hour guided rides for $38, $65, and $92, respectively. The one-hour trip follows a ridge high above town, providing excellent views of the Athabasca River Valley. **Skyline Trail Rides** (The Fairmont Jasper Park Lodge, 780/852-4215, mid-May–mid-Oct.) offers a 1.25-hour guided ride around Lake Annette ($40 per person) and a two-hour ride along the Valleyview Trail ($65 per person).

Overnight pack trips consist of 4–6 hours of riding per day, with a few nights spent at a remote mountain lodge where you can hike, boat, fish, or ride. Rates start at $200 per person per day for meals, accommodation, and a horse, of course. For details, contact **Skyline Trail Rides** (780/852-4215 or 888/852-7787, www.skylinetrail.com) or **Tonquin Valley Adventures** (780/852-1188, www.tonquinadventures.com).

White-Water Rafting

Within the park, the **Athabasca** and **Sunwapta Rivers** are run by a half dozen outfitters, while across the border in British Columbia, the **Fraser River** is another option for a guided rafting trip. On the Athabasca River, the Mile 5 Run is an easy two-hour float that appeals to all ages. Farther upstream, some operators offer a trip that begins from below Athabasca Falls, on a stretch of the river that passes through a narrow canyon; this run takes three hours. The boulder-strewn rapids of the Sunwapta and Fraser Rivers offer more thrills and spills—these trips are for the more adventurous and last 3–4 hours. Most companies offer a choice of rivers and provide transportation to and from downtown hotels. Expect to pay $65-75 for trips on the Athabasca

and $85-95 for the Sunwapta and Fraser. The following companies run at least two of three rivers: **Maligne Rafting Adventures** (780/852-3370 or 866/625-4463), **Rocky Mountain River Guides** (780/852-3777 or 866/952-3777), and **White Water Rafting** (780/852-7238 or 800/557-7238). **Jasper Raft Tours** (780/852-2665 or 888/553-5628) specialize in family-friendly trips, floating a 16-kilometer (10-mile) stretch of the Athabasca River in large, stable inflatable rafts; adult $64, child $24.

Fishing

Fishing in the many alpine lakes, for rainbow, brook, Dolly Varden, cutthroat, and lake trout, as well as pike and whitefish, is excellent. Many outfitters offer guided fishing trips. Whether you fish with a guide or by yourself, you'll need a national park fishing license ($10 per day, $35 per year), available from the park information center or **On-line Sport & Tackle** (600 Patricia St., 780/852-3630). Maligne Lake is the most popular fishing hole; in 1980, a 10-kilogram (22-pound) rainbow trout was caught in its deep waters.

At Maligne Lake, guided fishing trips are offered from the Boat House by **Maligne Tours** (780/852-3370, 8:30am-6:30pm daily June-Aug.). The half-day trip is $199 per person for two people, and the full-day trip is $299 per person for two people.

Currie's Guiding (780/852-5650, www.curriesguidingjasper.com) offers trips to Maligne Lake (full day $285 per person) and to Talbot Lake, a shallow body of water east of town renowned for its pike fishing. Rates include equipment and instruction. **Source for Sports** (406 Patricia St., 780/852-3654) and **On-line Sport & Tackle** (600 Patricia St., 780/852-3630) sell and rent fishing tackle and also have canoe and boat rentals.

Golf

The world-famous **The Fairmont Jasper**

Park Lodge Golf Course (780/852-6090) was designed by renowned golf-course architect Stanley Thompson. The course opened in 1925, after 200 men had spent an entire year clearing trees and laying out the holes to Thompson's design. Today it is consistently ranked as one of the top 10 courses in Canada. The 18-hole, 6,670-yard course takes in the contours of the Athabasca River Valley as it hugs the banks of turquoise-colored Lac Beauvert. It is a true test of accuracy, and with holes named The Maze, The Bad Baby, and The Bay, you'll need lots of balls. Greens fees for 18 holes vary with the season: $225 mid-June-September, $160 mid-May-mid-June, and $125 in early May and from October 1 through closing (usually mid-October). These rates are discounted for Canadian residents. A power cart is $40 per round. Golfing after 5pm is discounted to just over $100—a great deal during the long days of June and July. Other facilities include a driving range, club rentals ($50-60), a restaurant, and a lounge.

Tours

Brewster (780/852-3332, www.explorerockies.com) offers a four-hour Discover Jasper tour taking in Patricia and Pyramid Lakes, Maligne Canyon, and Jasper Tramway (ride not included in fare). It departs at 8:30am daily April-October from the railway station; $65. **Maligne Tours** (616 Patricia St., 780/852-3370, www.malignelake.com) schedules a variety of tours, including a six-hour trip to Maligne Lake ($95, includes cruise). **Jasper Adventure Centre** (604 Connaught Dr., 780/852-5595, www.jasperadventurecentre.com), in the Chaba Theatre, operates several well-priced tours, including the following: Mount Edith Cavell (departs 2pm, three hours, $65), Maligne Valley (departs 8:30am, five hours, $95, including boat tour), and Miette Hot Springs and wildlife (departs 6pm, four hours, $72). Similarly priced tours take in historic sites and local wildlife.

Indoor Recreation

The **Jasper Aquatic Centre** (401 Pyramid Lake Rd., 780/852-3663) has an Olympic-size swimming pool; admission $5.80. The **Jasper Activity Centre** (780/852-3381), next door, has squash courts, indoor and outdoor tennis courts, a climbing wall, a weight room, and an indoor skate park; admission $7.50.

WINTER RECREATION

Winter is certainly a quiet time in the park, but that doesn't mean there's a lack of things to do. Marmot Basin offers world-class alpine skiing; many snow-covered hiking trails are groomed for cross-country skiing; portions of Lac Beauvert and Pyramid Lake are cleared for ice-skating; horse-drawn sleighs travel around town; and Maligne Canyon is transformed into a magical, frozen world. Hotels reduce rates by 40-70 percent through winter, and many offer lodging and lift tickets for around $100 per person.

Marmot Basin

The skiing at Marmot Basin (780/852-3816 or 866/952-3816, www.skimarmot.com) is highly underrated. A huge injection of cash in recent years has meant even better facilities are offered, with the Canadian Rockies Express being the longest detachable quad in Alberta. Lifts now take skiers and boarders into Charlie's Basin, a massive powder-filled bowl, and to the summit of Eagle Ridge, which accesses open bowls and lightly treed glades of two other mountain faces. Local Joe Weiss saw the potential for skiing in the basin in the 1920s and began bringing skiers up from the valley. A road was constructed from the highway in the early 1950s, and the first paying skiers were transported up to the slopes in a snowcat. The first lift, a 700-meter (2,300-foot) rope tow, was installed on the Paradise face in 1961, and the area has continued to expand ever since. Marmot Basin has nine lifts servicing 680 hectares (1,675 acres) of terrain with a vertical rise of 900 meters (2,940 feet). The longest run is 5.6 kilometers (3.5 miles). Marmot doesn't get the crowds of the three alpine resorts in Banff National Park, so lift lines are uncommon. The season runs early December-late April. Lift tickets are adult $78, senior and child $64. (Throughout Jasper in January celebrations, adult tickets are just $52.) Rentals are available at the resort or in town at **Totem Ski Shop** (408 Connaught Dr., 780/852-3078).

Cross-Country Skiing

For many people, traveling Jasper's hiking trails on skis is just as exhilarating as on foot. An extensive network of 300 kilometers (185 miles) of summer hiking trails is designated for skiers, with around 100 kilometers (62 miles) groomed. The four main areas of trails are along Pyramid Lake Road, around Maligne Lake, in the Athabasca Falls area, and at Whistlers Campground. A booklet available at the park information center details each trail and its difficulty. Weather forecasts and avalanche-hazard reports are also posted here.

Rental packages are available from **Source for Sports** (406 Patricia St., 780/852-3654), the rental shop at **The Fairmont Jasper Park Lodge** (780/852-3433), and **Totem Ski Shop** (408 Connaught Dr., 780/852-3078), offering rentals, repairs, and sales.

Maligne Canyon

By late December, the torrent that is the Maligne River has frozen solid. Where it cascades down through Maligne Canyon, the river is temporarily stalled for the winter, creating remarkable formations through the deep limestone canyon. **Jasper Adventure Centre** (306 Connaught Dr., 780/852-5595) offers exciting three-hour guided tours into the depths of the

canyon throughout winter, at 10am, 2pm, and 7pm daily; adult $60, child $30.

ENTERTAINMENT AND EVENTS

Cinema

The **Chaba Theatre** (604 Connaught Dr., 780/852-4749) shows first-run movies in its two theaters.

Nightlife

The most popular nightspot in town is the **Atha-B** (510 Patricia St., 780/852-3386, minimal cover charge), in the Athabasca Hotel, where bands play some nights. It gets pretty rowdy with all the seasonal workers, but it's still enjoyable. This hotel also has a large lounge and a bar with a pool table and a popular 5pm-7pm happy hour. **Pete's Club** (upstairs at 614 Patricia St., 780/852-6262) has a jam on Tuesday night and bands playing Friday-Sunday. The music varies—it could be blues, rock, or Celtic. The **De'd Dog Bar and Grill** (404 Connaught Dr., 780/852-3351), in the Astoria Hotel, is a large, dimly lit sports bar with pool tables and plenty of locals drinking copious amounts of beer, especially during the 5pm-7pm happy hour. Right downtown, the **Whistle Stop Pub** (105 Miette Ave., 780/852-3361), in the Whistlers Inn, has a great atmosphere, with a classic wooden bar and memorabilia everywhere.

Escape the typical bar scenes at the **Downstream Bar** (620 Connaught Dr., 780/852-9449), which opens at 4pm and has live music Friday and Saturday. You don't need to be a guest of Jasper's finest hotel, The Fairmont Jasper Park Lodge (780/852-3301), to enjoy the ambience of its three lounges: the **Emerald Lounge** has comfortable indoor seating and a long outdoor terrace overlooking Lac Beauvert; **Tent City** is a sports-style bar with a relaxed atmosphere and two pool tables; and **Palisade's** is a winter-only bar attracting the après-ski crowd each evening. Most of Jasper's other large hotels, including the Amethyst Lodge, Jasper Inn, and Marmot Lodge, also have lounges.

Festivals and Events

Summer is prime time on the park's events calendar. **Canada Day** (July 1) celebrations begin with a pancake breakfast and progress to a flag-raising ceremony (in front of the information center) and a parade along Connaught Drive. Live entertainment and a fireworks display end the day. The **Jasper Heritage Rodeo** (www. jasperheritagerodeo.com), on the second weekend of August, dates from 1926 and attracts pro cowboys from across Canada. Apart from the traditional rodeo events, the fun includes a mechanical bull, a children's rodeo, pancake breakfasts, the ever-popular stick-pony parade, and the crowning of Miss Rodeo Jasper. Most of the action takes place in the arena at the Jasper Activity Centre, behind town on Pyramid Lake Road.

On the other side of the calendar, winter is not totally partyless—**Jasper in January** (www.jasperinjanuary.com) is a two-week celebration that includes fireworks, special evenings at local restaurants, a chili cook-off, discounted lift tickets at Marmot Basin, and all the activities associated with winter.

Park Interpretive Program

Parks Canada offers a wide range of interpretive talks and hikes throughout summer. Each summer evening in the **Whistlers Campground Theatre,** a different slide show and movie program is shown. The theater is near the shower block. The **Wabasso Campfire Circle** takes place each Saturday night just before dusk; hot tea is supplied while various speakers talk about wildlife in the park. Wabasso Campground is along Highway 93A approximately 16 kilometers (10 miles) south of town.

Many different guided hikes are offered (all free) throughout summer; check bulletin boards at the park information center and campgrounds, or call 780/852-6176.

SHOPPING

Jasper certainly doesn't provide the shopping experience found in Banff, but several interesting shops beckon on rainy days. **Our Native Land** (601 Patricia St., 780/852-5592) is a large shop chock-full of arts and crafts produced by artisans from throughout western Canada. Search out everything from moose-hide moccasins to masks (check out the musk ox head near the back of the store). It also stocks Inuit soapstone carvings from the Canadian Arctic. **Bearfoot in the Park** (606 Connaught Dr., 780/852-2221) features a good cross-section of Canadiana, including books and locally made soaps.

Within 200 meters (660 feet) of the information center is **Source for Sports** (406 Patricia St., 780/852-3654), **Totem Ski Shop** (408 Connaught Dr., 780/852-3078), and **Everest Outdoor Stores** (414 Connaught Dr., 780/852-5902), each with a good stock of camping gear and other outdoor equipment.

ACCOMMODATIONS AND CAMPING
In and Around Town

In summer, motel and hotel rooms here are expensive. Most of the motels and lodges are within walking distance of town and have indoor pools and restaurants. Luckily, alternatives to staying in $200-plus hotel rooms do exist. The best of these are the lodges scattered around the edge of town. Open in summer only, each offers a rustic yet distinct style of accommodation in keeping with the theme of staying in a national park. Additionally, many private residences have rooms for rent in summer; three hostels are close to town; and there's always camping in the good ol' outdoors.

Unless otherwise noted, accommodations

JASPER NATIONAL PARK

PRIVATE-HOME ACCOMMODATIONS

At last count, Jasper had almost 100 residential homes offering accommodations. They often supply nothing more than a room with a bed, but the price is right at $60-120 s or d. Use of a bathroom is usually shared with other guests or the family; few have kitchens, and only a few supply light breakfast. In most cases, don't expect too much with the lower-priced choices. The positive side, apart from the price, is that your hosts are usually knowledgeable locals, and downtown is only a short walk away. For a full listing that includes the facilities at each approved property and an online availability page, visit the **Jasper Home Accommodation Association** website (www.stayinjasper.com).

The park information center has a board listing private-home accommodations with rooms available for the upcoming night. Most have signs out front, so you could cruise the residential streets (try Connaught, Patricia, and Geikie) looking for a Vacancy sign, but checking at the information center is easier.

discussed here are within walking distance of downtown Jasper. Rates quoted are for a standard room in summer. Outside the busy June-September period, most lodgings reduce rates drastically (ask also about ski packages during winter).

UNDER $50

Staying in hostels isn't for everyone, but it's the only type of accommodation in the park that comes close to falling into this price category.

Hostelling International-Canada operates five hostels in Jasper National Park, but none right in downtown Jasper. Reservations are highly recommended at all hostels during July and August. Make these by calling 778/328-2220 or 866/762-4122, online at www.hihostels.ca, or through other major hostels such as those in Lake Louise, Banff, Calgary, or Edmonton.

On the road to the Jasper Tramway, seven kilometers (4.3 miles) south from town off the Icefields Parkway, is **HI-Jasper,** which has 84 beds in men's and women's dorms, a large kitchen, a common room, showers, a laundry, public Internet access, an outdoor barbecue area, and mountain-bike rentals. Members of Hostelling International pay $28 (nonmembers $32). Private rooms are $67 and $75 s or d, respectively. In the summer months, this hostel fills up every night. The front desk is open noon-midnight daily. Cab fare between downtown Jasper and the hostel is around $30.

HI-Maligne Canyon (Maligne Lake Rd., June-Sept., members $24, nonmembers $28) is beside the Maligne River and a short walk from the canyon. Although rustic, it lies in a beautiful setting. The 24 dorm beds are in two cabins; other amenities include electricity, a kitchen, and a dining area. Check-in is 5pm-11pm.

■ **HI-Mount Edith Cavell** (mid-June-mid-Oct., members $24, nonmembers $28) offers a million-dollar view for the price of a dorm bed. It's 13 kilometers (eight miles) up Cavell Road off Highway 93A, and because of the location there's usually a spare bed. Opposite the hostel are trailheads for hiking in the Tonquin Valley, and it's just a short walk to the base of Mount Edith Cavell. The hostel is rustic (no showers and only pit toilets) but has a kitchen, dining area, and outdoor wood sauna. Check-in is 5pm-11pm.

$50-100

The cheapest motel-style units at **Patricia Lake Bungalows** (780/852-3560 or 888/499-6848, www.patricialakebungalows.com, May-mid-Oct., $99-325 s or d), beside the lake of the same name, a five-minute drive north from

Jasper along Pyramid Lake Road, just fall into this price range (from $99 per night), but it is worth paying extra for a freestanding unit. Comfortable but older cottages with kitchens and TV start at $200 s or d, rising to $225 for those with either a lake view or fireplace. Suites ($200-275) are a good value in relation to similar-sized rooms elsewhere in town. The newest units ($285-325) are in a complex called The Grove. These have separate bedrooms and a balcony or patio with barbecue. Other resort amenities include a barbecue area and an outdoor hot tub.

$100-150

If you're simply looking for somewhere to rest your head, consider Jasper's least expensive hotel rooms at the downtown **Athabasca Hotel** (510 Patricia St., 780/852-3386 or 877/542-8422, www.athabascahotel.com, from $105 s or d). This historic three-story brick building dates to 1928, replacing the original structure of the same name, which was the town's first hotel. The cheapest of its 61 rooms share bathrooms and are above a noisy bar, but the price is right. This hotel also has more expensive rooms, each with a vaguely Victorian decor and private bathrooms (from $160 s or d).

$150-200

The following accommodations all offer a true Canadian Rockies experience, relative to hotels in similar price ranges.

With a variety of cabin layouts and a central location, (**Bear Hill Lodge** (100 Bonhomme St., 780/852-3209, www.bearhilllodge.com, $189-414 s or d) makes a great base camp for travelers who want the cabin experience within walking distance of downtown services. The original cabins are basic, but each has a TV, bathroom, gas fireplace, and coffee-making facilities ($189 s or d). Chalet Rooms are larger and more modern, and each has a wood-burning fireplace but no kitchen ($189). Colin

Rooms are more spacious still; each has a jetted tub, gas fireplace, and limited cooking facilities ($225). Units are discounted 40 percent during the first and last months of operation. Breakfasts ($9 per person) feature a wide selection of freshly baked items, fruit, and cereals. Other amenities include a jetted tub, a barbecue area, laundry facilities, and Internet access.

Typifying a bungalow camp of the 1950s, **Pine Bungalows** (780/852-3491, www.pinebungalows.com, May-mid-Oct., $160-220 s or d) lies on a secluded section of the Athabasca River opposite the northern entrance to town. The least expensive units are wooden cabins with kitchens and fireplaces (most cabins face the river, but numbers 1 and 3 enjoy the best views), while more modern two-bedroom log cabins are $220. A three-night minimum applies in July and August.

One of the least expensive of a string of lodges immediately south of downtown is **Jasper House Bungalows** (4 km/2.5 mi south along the Icefields Parkway, 780/852-4535, www.jasperhouse.com, May-mid-Oct., $160-260 s or d). It comprises 56 cedar log cabins, each with a TV and coffeemaker (those at the upper end of the price range are fully self-contained and overlook the river). Basic but woodsy motel-style units are $160 s or d with a kitchenette. Also on-site is an old-style rustic restaurant open through the summer season for a breakfast buffet and à la carte dinner.

Farther south along the Icefields Parkway, (**Becker's Chalets** (780/852-3779, www.beckerschalets.com, May-mid-Oct., $165-255 s or d) is spread along a picturesque bend of the Athabasca River, six kilometers (3.7 miles) south of town. This historic lodging took its first guests more than 50 years ago and continues to be a park favorite for many guests who make staying here an annual ritual. Moderately priced chalets, each with a kitchenette, gas fireplace, and double bed, are an excellent deal ($160, or $190 for those on the riverfront).

JASPER NATIONAL PARK

Deluxe log duplexes featuring all the modern conveniences, including color TV, start at a reasonable $195 s or d and go up to $380 for a unit that sleeps eight. Also available are a few one-bed sleeping rooms ($120). Becker's also boasts one of the park's finest restaurants.

A short distance south along Highway 93A from downtown, at the junction with the Icefields Parkway three kilometers (1.9 miles) south of town, is **K** **Alpine Village** (780/852-3285, www.alpinevillagejasper.com, late Apr.-mid-Oct., $190-320 s or d). This resort is laid out across well-manicured lawns, and all buildings are surrounded by colorful gardens of geraniums and petunias. After a day exploring the park, guests can soak away their cares in the outdoor hot pool or kick back on a row of Adirondack chairs scattered along the Athabasca River, directly opposite the resort. The older sleeping cabins have been renovated ($190 s or d, $225 with a kitchen and fireplace),

while the 2009 Deluxe Bedroom Suites feature open plans, stone fireplaces, luxurious bathrooms, and decks with private forested views ($290 s or d). The Deluxe Family Cabins ($320) sleep up to five, with two beds in an upstairs loft, a fireplace, and a full kitchen.

$200-250

The lure of **Tekarra Lodge** (Hwy. 93A, 1.6 km/1 mi south from downtown, 780/852-3058 or 888/962-2522, www.tekarralodge.com, mid-May-early Oct., $225-325 s or d) is its historic log cabins and forested setting on a plateau above the confluence of the Miette and Athabasca Rivers. Each cabin has been totally modernized yet retains a cozy charm, with comfortable beds, fully equipped kitchenettes, wood-burning fireplaces, and smallish but adequate bathrooms. The spacious Tekarra Cabins are best suited for small families. An on-site restaurant is open for breakfast

The woodsy cabins at Alpine Village are a delight.

© ANDREW HEMPSTEAD

"SUMMER-ONLY" LODGING

The earliest tourists to Jasper came by train, but as the automobile gained popularity in the 1920s, accommodations were built specifically to cater to visitors who arrived by motor vehicle. Typically, these "bungalow camps" consisted of a cluster of cabins set around a central lodge where meals were served and—with no need for the railway—were spread throughout the park. This type of accommodation remains in various forms today, a popular alternative for those who don't need the luxuries associated with hotels and the services of downtown Jasper. They are generally only open May-early October.

rentals (across the road), an interpretive program, a fitness center, and a large barbecue area make the resort a good choice for families.

Hotel choices barely over the $200 mark include the **Tonquin Inn** (100 Juniper St., 780/852-4987 or 800/661-1315, www.tonquininn.com, $215-370 s or d), with an outdoor hot tub, laundry facilities, a steakhouse restaurant, and a sunny lounge bar; and **Maligne Lodge** (780/852-3143 or 800/661-1315, www.malignelodge.com, $210-270 s or d), also with an indoor pool. These places are worth considering outside of summer, when the cabin accommodations are closed and rates are discounted substantially, sometimes by more than 60 percent.

On Connaught Drive southwest of downtown, **Mount Robson Inn** (780/852-3327 or 800/587-3327, www.mountrobsoninn.com, from $220 s or d) has 78 rooms, each air-conditioned and with coffeemakers, alarm clocks, high-speed Internet, and hair dryers—in other words, you could be staying in a generic city hotel. On the plus side, the suites here are a good deal (relative to other Jasper accommodations); each holds two separate bedrooms, a full bathroom with additional outside vanity, and a fireplace (from $280 per unit).

The **Sawridge Inn** (82 Connaught Dr., 780/852-5111 or 888/729-7343, www.sawridgejasper.com, $245-345 s or d) offers 154 air-conditioned rooms built around a large atrium and indoor pool. Rates are reduced up to 60 percent outside of the busiest mid-June-September period.

$250-350

Chateau Jasper (96 Geikie St., 780/852-5644 or 800/661-1315, www.chateaujasper.com, from $290 s or d) is one of Jasper's nicest lodgings. Guest rooms are spacious and elegantly finished with maple furnishings and low ceilings that give them a cozy feel. Bathrooms are particularly well equipped, with guests also

(7:30am-11am) and dinner (5pm-11pm). Other amenities include bike rentals and a laundry room. From the lodge, hiking trails lead along the Athabasca River in both directions as well as over the river to the golf course and The Fairmont Jasper Park Lodge.

This is the price range that most downtown Jasper hotel rooms fall within. Right downtown is the **Astoria Hotel** (404 Connaught Dr., 780/852-3351 or 800/661-7343, www.astoriahotel.com, $217-235 s or d). This European-style lodging was built in 1924 and kept in the same family since. Rooms are brightly furnished, and each has a fridge, TV, and VCR. Outside of summer, these same rooms cost from $120. Note that there is no elevator in this four-story hotel.

Near the end of Pyramid Lake Road, north from downtown, are the sprawling, impossible-to-miss grounds of **Pyramid Lake Resort** (780/852-4900 or 888/852-7737, www.mpljasper.com, $235-345 s or d), the only lodging away from town (besides The Fairmont Jasper Park Lodge) that offers motel-style accommodations. Plenty of water-based activities and enjoying the use of plush bathrobes. The classy in-house dining room, Silverwater Grill, offers a good-value breakfast buffet ($14) and dinner (mains $16-32).

OVER $350

◖ The Fairmont Jasper Park Lodge

(780/852-3301 or 800/257-7544, www.fairmont.com, from $385 s or d) lies along the shore of Lac Beauvert across the Athabasca River from downtown. This is the park's original resort and its most famous. It's a sprawling property, with plenty of activities. The best known of these is the golf course, but guests also enjoy walking trails, horseback riding, canoeing, tennis, and swimming in an outdoor heated pool that remains open year-round. The main lodge features stone floors, carved wooden pillars, and a high ceiling. This building contains multiple restaurants and lounges, an activity booking desk, a fitness room, a games room, and Jasper's only covered shopping arcade. The 441 rooms vary in configuration and are linked by paths and greenspace. All have coffeemakers, TVs, telephones, and Internet access. The least expensive Fairmont Rooms are smallish, hold two twin beds, and offer limited views. Also away from the lake are larger Deluxe Rooms; each has a patio or balcony. Junior Suites have a distinct country charm, and each has either a sitting room and balcony or patio with lake views. Moving up to the more expensive options, Lakeview Suites overlook Lac Beauvert and are backed by the 18th fairway of the golf course. Each features a patio or balcony, a fireplace, and two TVs.

The various historic cabins provide The Fairmont Jasper Park Lodge's premier accommodations. Starting from $1,100 per night, they are priced beyond the reach of most travelers but are mentioned here simply because they are among the most exclusive guest rooms in all of Canada. They have hosted true royalty (Queen Elizabeth) and movie royalty (Marilyn Monroe, during the filming of *River of No Return*). The smallest is the secluded and cozy Athabasca Cottage, while my favorite is the historically charming Point Cabin. Built in 1928, this cabin features five en suite bedrooms, a kitchen with outdoor barbecue, lake views, and a massive living area anchored by a stone fireplace.

Most guests don't pay the summer rack rates quoted here. The cost of lodging is usually included in one of the plethora of packages offered. Outside of summer, The Fairmont Jasper Park Lodge becomes a bargain, with rooms with lake views (remember, it'll be frozen in winter) for less than $200.

East of Town

Two accommodations east of the town of Jasper but still within the park boundary are open in summer only.

$100-150

Miette Hot Springs Resort (780/866-3750, www.mhresort.com, May-Sept., $100-150 s or d) is within walking distance of the park's only hot springs, 18 kilometers (11 miles) from Highway 16 and 61 kilometers (38 miles) from town. Motel units are slightly less than the bungalows, which have cooking facilities. Guest facilities include a covered barbecue area, restaurant, and laundry room.

Located at the site of a once-bustling coal-mining town, **Pocahontas Cabins** (780/866-3732 or 800/852-7737, www.mpljasper.com, May-Sept., $110-325 s or d) is at the bottom of the road that leads to Miette Hot Springs, 43 kilometers (27 miles) east of Jasper along Highway 16. Sleeping-room cabins start at $110 s or d, or pay $140 for a kitchen-equipped unit. Settler's Cabins, with separate bedrooms, are $195 s or d. Best of all are the newer log cabins, completed in 2012. Each is equipped with a full kitchen, separate bedroom, TV, and fireplace. You can dine at the well-priced

© ANDREW HEMPSTEAD

JASPER NATIONAL PARK

relaxing in the Point Cabin at The Fairmont Jasper Park Lodge

restaurant (open for breakfast, lunch, and dinner) or pick up supplies in Jasper and cook up a storm in the shaded barbecue area.

Hinton

This medium-size town lies along Highway 16, approximately 19 kilometers (12 miles) east of the park gate and 69 kilometers (43 miles) east of the town of Jasper. Staying here provides an inexpensive alternative to staying in the park. The strip of motels, restaurants, fast-food places, and gas stations along Highway 16 is the place to start looking for a room.

$50-100

The best value is **Pines Motel** (709 Gregg Ave., 780/865-2624, www.pines-motel.com, $79 s, $89-109 d), with 22 regularly revamped rooms adjacent to the local golf course. Each room has a microwave, fridge, and coffeemaker.

The dowdy-looking **Big Horn Motel** (485 Gregg Ave., 780/865-1555, $99-129 s or d),

beside the Husky gas station, has surprisingly good rooms, some larger than others.

$100-150

Holiday Inn Hinton (393 Gregg Ave., 780/865-3321 or 877/660-8550, www.holidayinn.com, from $119 s, $129 d) has everything you'd expect from a Holiday Inn—reliable rooms, a restaurant, a fitness room, and kid-friendly extras like PlayStation.

Backcountry Accommodations

Two backcountry lodges are southwest of Jasper in the spectacular Tonquin Valley. Accessible only on foot or horseback or, in winter, by skiing, both lodges are open to hikers (with advance reservations); most guests stay as part of a package that includes horseback riding.

Dating to 1939, **Tonquin Amethyst Lake Lodge** (780/852-1188, www.tonquinadventures.com) was extensively upgraded in the early 1990s. Private cabins have wood-burning heaters, twin log beds with thick blankets, oil lanterns, and a spectacular view. Tonquin Adventures offers a number of well-priced packages, including riding into the lodge on horses, accommodations, three hearty ranch-style meals, and use of small boats and fishing gear (three days, $795; four days, $1,050; five days, $1,295). The rate for walk-in hikers is $179 pp per night. Rates are reduced in winter, when guests ski in under their own power. Regardless of the season, getting there involves a 19-kilometer (11.8-mile) journey from a trailhead opposite HI-Mount Edith Cavell.

Nearby **Tonquin Valley Backcountry Lodge** (780/852-3909, www.tonquinvalley.com) offers a similar setup, with most guests arriving by horseback on a prearranged ride from the nearest road. In this case, the departure point is along Marmot Basin Road, from a parking lot at Portal Creek. Rates for hikers are $170 per person per night, with a five-night package—inclusive of horse rental—costing $1,375 per person.

Guest Ranch

The mountain retreat ◖ **Black Cat Guest Ranch** (780/865-3084 or 800/859-6840, www.blackcatguestranch.ca, $110 s or d) lies on the eastern edge of the park, surrounded by mountain wilderness. All 16 rooms have private baths and views of the mountains. Horseback riding is available during the day (June-September), and in the evening guests relax in the large living room or hot tub. Meals packages are adult $51, child $34. To get to the ranch, follow Highway 16 for 19 kilometers (12 miles) beyond the east gate, head north along Highway 40 for six kilometers (3.7 miles), turn left to Brule and continue for 11 kilometers (6.8 miles), and then turn right and follow the signs.

Campgrounds

Most campgrounds in Jasper begin opening in mid-June, and all but Wapiti are closed by mid-October. All campsites have a picnic table and fire ring, with a fire permit costing $8 (includes firewood). A percentage of sites in the most popular campgrounds can be reserved through the Parks Canada Campground Reservation Service (877/737-3783, www.pccamping.ca) for a nominal fee. If you're traveling in July or August, know which dates you'll be in Jasper, and require electrical hookups, it is strongly advised to take advantage of this service. Whistlers and Wapiti are the only two campgrounds with powered sites, and therefore they're in great demand. A line usually forms well before the official check-out time of 11am.

Unlike neighboring Banff National Park, Jasper's 10 campgrounds combine to handle all but the busiest summer nights. And on the rare occasion all campsites fill, campers are directed to overflow areas. These are glorified parking lots with no designated sites, but fees are reduced ($12 per unit).

NEAR THE TOWN OF JASPER

Whistlers Campground, at the base of Whistlers Road, three kilometers (1.9 miles) south of town, has 781 sites, making it the largest campground in the Canadian Rockies. It is divided into four sections; prices vary with the services available: walk-in sites $22.50, unserviced sites $27.40, powered sites $32.30, full hookups $38.20. Washrooms and streetlights are spread throughout, while each section has showers, playgrounds, and a nightly interpretive program. Whistlers is open May-mid-October.

Two kilometers (1.2 miles) farther south along the Icefields Parkway is **Wapiti Campground,** which offers 366 sites and has showers; unserviced sites $27.40, powered sites $32.30. This is the park's only campground open year-round, with serviced winter camping $21.50 per night.

Sites at **Wabasso Campground,** along

© ANDREW HEMPSTEAD

Whistlers Campground

Highway 93A approximately 16 kilometers (10 miles) south of town, are set among stands of spruce and aspen; $21.50 per night.

EAST ALONG HIGHWAY 16
East of town, off Highway 16, are two smaller, more primitive campgrounds. **Snaring River Campground,** 17 kilometers (11 miles) from Jasper on Celestine Lake Road, is $15.70 (overflow camping is $10.50); **Pocahontas Campground,** 45 kilometers (28 miles) northeast, is $21.50. Both are open mid-May-early September.

FOOD
It's easy to get a good, or even great, meal in Jasper. Connaught Drive and Patricia Street are lined with cafés and restaurants. Considering this is a national park, menus are reasonably well priced. You should expect hearty fare, with lots of beef, game, and a surprisingly good selection of seafood.

Coffeehouses and Cafés
You'll smell the wonderful aroma of freshly baked bread even before entering **Bear's Paw Bakery** (4 Cedar Ave., 780/852-3233, 6am-6pm daily, lunches under $10). The European-style breads (the muesli loaf is a delight) are perfect for a picnic lunch, but not as tempting as the cakes and pastries. The freshly brewed coffee and oversized scones help make this my favorite Jasper café. Operated by the same owners, **The Other Paw** (610 Connaught Dr., 780/852-2253, 7am-6pm daily) has a slightly more contemporary feel, but more of the same great baked goods, as well as delicious salads.

With a couple of tables spilling onto the side-walk, **Café Mondo** (616 Patricia St., 780/852-9676, 8am-8pm daily, until 9pm in summer, $7.50-11) is a popular hangout for locals each morning, but where this place shines is the pizza by the slice and freshly made salads throughout the day.

Nutter's (622 Patricia St., 780/852-5844, 9am-6pm daily in summer) is a good pre-hiking stop, with a wide choice of goodies in bulk bins.

Casual and Family-Style Dining
The ubiquitous family-style restaurant is alive and well in Jasper. One of the originals is the **L&W Restaurant** (corner of Patricia St. and Hazel Ave., 780/852-4114, breakfast, lunch, and dinner daily, $11-18.50). It features a small outside patio and plenty of greenery that brings to life an otherwise ordinary restaurant—a good place to take the family for an affordable meal.

You won't be dazzled by the surroundings at **Palisades** (Cedar Ave., 780/852-5222, 4pm-9:30pm daily and 8:30am-11:30am for breakfast in summer, $15-28), but the wide-ranging menu appeals to families: inexpensive vegetarian choices, pastas and pizza, Greek specialties less than $20, a massive T-bone steak, and a $6 kids' menu.

Bear's Paw Bakery

© ANDREW HEMPSTEAD

Pizza lovers congregate at **Jasper Pizza Place** (402 Connaught Dr., 780/852-3225, from 11am daily, $15-27). It's a large and noisy restaurant with bright furnishings, a concrete floor, exposed heating ducts, and walls lined with photos from Jasper's earliest days. Regular thick-crust pizzas are available all day, but it's not until 5pm, when the wood-fired oven begins producing thin-crust pizzas with adventurous toppings, that this place really shines.

On the same side of town as Jasper Pizza Place is Jasper's oldest restaurant, **Papa George's** (Astoria Hotel, 406 Connaught Dr., 780/852-3351, 7am-10pm daily, $14-22), which has been dishing up hearty fare to park visitors since 1925. The setting is old-fashioned, with east-facing windows taking in the panorama of distant mountain peaks.

Steak

Most restaurants feature Alberta beef prominently, but it's a specialty at these two places.

Prime Rib Village (Tonquin Inn, 100 Juniper St., 780/852-4966, from 5pm daily, $27-36) has been a longtime Jasper favorite. Charbroiled steaks and hearty servings of prime rib top out the menu, but the prime rib sandwich ($21), with a plate-load of extras, will fill any carnivorous cravings for a few dollars less. This restaurant also offers a surprisingly good selection of seafood.

◀ Villa Caruso (640 Connaught Dr., 780/852-3920, 11am-midnight daily, $20-39) is a steakhouse with a modern mountain vibe. The upstairs location—request a balcony table if the weather's warm—allows great views across the valley. The menu features a wide variety of Alberta beef dishes, including a massive 16-ounce T-bone for $39. But there's a lot more than steak on offer, including chicken, seafood, and pasta dishes.

Seafood

Fiddle River Restaurant (upstairs at 620

Connaught Dr., 780/852-3032, 5pm-10pm daily, $24-39) is a long way from the ocean and not particularly coastal in feel, but it offers a wide variety of seafood. The strikingly rustic decor matches dark polished wood with forest-green furnishings, and large windows provide mountain views (reservations are needed for windowside tables). Trout, arctic char, red snapper, ahi tuna, and halibut all make regular appearances on the blackboard menu.

European

Syrahs (606 Patricia St., 780/852-4559, 5pm-9:30pm daily, $24-37) is an elegantly casual eatery offering a wide range of uncomplicated dishes using Canadian game and produce prepared with Swiss-influenced cooking styles. Start with venison sausage strudel, then choose between dishes such as banana- and pine nut-crusted rack of lamb or cheese fondue for two. Syrahs also has one of Jasper's most impressive wine lists. Also notable at Syrahs is the staff, who seem experienced and knowledgeable.

For standard Greek fare, head to **Something Else Restaurant** (621 Patricia St., 780/852-3850, 11am-11pm daily, $15-21). Portions are generous, service is friendly, the prices are right, and you'll find plenty of alternatives if the Greek dishes don't appeal to you.

Miss Italia Ristorante (610 Patricia St., 780/852-4002, breakfast, lunch, and dinner daily, $15-21), upstairs in the Patricia Centre Mall, features bright and breezy interior decor with tables also set on a narrow terrace bedecked in pots of colorful flowers. Cooked breakfasts (from 8am) are $7-12. The rest of the day, look for pastas made fresh, baked fillet of Atlantic salmon, and souvlaki with a side of salad and pita bread. Check out the daily specials before ordering—they are taken from the regular menu but discounted a couple of bucks and come with soup or salad.

Directly behind the park information center, **La Fiesta** (504 Patricia St., 780/852-0404,

noon-11pm daily, $19-29) is a small eatery where the Mediterranean meets Mexico. It offers a tapas-style menu of Mexican dishes ranging $7.50-13, as well as adventurous delights such as cinnamon-chili chicken served with roasted orange jus. This is also the best place in town for a martini.

Asian

The **Cantonese Restaurant** (608 Connaught Dr., 780/852-3559, noon-10pm daily, $9.50-14) is the place to go for Chinese; set five-course menus for two start at just $35.

Denjiro (410 Connaught Dr., 780/852-3780, 5pm-11:30pm daily, $16-22) features a traditional sushi bar and tatami booths for eating the Japanese cuisine; combination dinners average $22 per person.

The Fairmont Jasper Park Lodge

Jasper's premier accommodation, across the river from downtown, offers a choice of casual or elegant dining in a variety of restaurants and lounges. Across from the reception area is a dedicated dining reservation desk, staffed 11am-8pm daily in summer, or call 780/852-6052. Reservations are required for the Edith Cavell and Moose's Nook dining rooms. Families appreciate the fact that children five and under eat free.

Downstairs in the shopping arcade, **Meadows Restaurant** is a casual room open for a breakfast buffet 7am-11am daily (continental $24, full breakfast $32), and then 6pm-9pm Wednesday-Sunday in the summer only. The turnover of food is quick, meaning everything remains fresh. Request a table away from the buffet for a quieter dining experience.

The **Emerald Lounge** (11:30am-10pm daily, $22-37) takes pride of place in the expansive lobby of the main building. Table settings of various configurations are spread throughout the room while also sprawling out and along the **Emerald Outdoor Patio,** from where views

© ANDREW HEMPSTEAD

Dining at Moose's Nook Northern Grill is an authentic Canadian experience.

over picturesque Lac Beauvert to distant mountains are uninterrupted. Both lunch and dinner menus feature imaginative modern Canadian cuisine, but with dinner (from 5:30pm) being decidedly more expensive. At lunch, salads can be made into a full meal by adding extras such as smoked salmon and slices of chicken breast, or stick to mains such as bison burger.

The elegantly rustic 🄲 **Moose's Nook Northern Grill** (6pm-9pm daily, $31-44) is a good place to enjoy traditional Canadian fare, such as grilled wild boar chops, whiskey-flamed arctic char, or a char-grilled Albertan rib eye steak. Be sure to leave room for dessert—the chestnut-crusted cheesecake smothered in maple syrup is incredible.

Cavell's Restaurant & Terrace (breakfast and dinner daily, $22-44) serves up what is generally regarded as the finest food in Jasper. Its stylish wooden furniture contrasts with the white linens and large, bright windows overlooking Lac Beauvert and the mountains

beyond. With an emphasis on local produce and Canadian game and seafood, the classic cuisine is served with a European flair.

From 7am throughout the golf season, light breakfasts, drinks, and snacks are served at **First Cup,** in the golf clubhouse opposite the first tee. Between 10am and 5pm, the smell of sizzling steaks served from a barbecue out front of the clubhouse wafts across the grounds. Expect to pay $7-13 for burgers, wraps, and the like.

Other Hotel Dining

Most of the larger accommodations have restaurants. In general, they open for breakfast and dinner only, with a cold or cooked buffet complementing an à la carte dinner menu. **Walter's Dining Room** (Sawridge Hotel, 82 Connaught Dr., 780/852-5111, 6am-10:30am and 6pm-9:30pm daily, $19-36) is a cut above the rest and reasonably priced. Surrounded by the greenery of a four-story atrium, the setting is relaxed but elegant. The menu features contemporary preparations using Canadian ingredients such as Alberta beef and salmon. You could start with the duck terrine with sweet apricots, followed by salmon simmered in a chardonnay and fennel broth, spending a little more than $40 for the two courses. The adjacent lounge has the same pleasant setting and a smaller, less-expensive menu.

One block back from the Sawridge Hotel is the Jasper Inn and its **Inn Restaurant** (98 Geikie St., 780/852-4461, breakfast and dinner daily, $18-33), with a fine sheltered courtyard complete with an outdoor fireplace and heat lamps for those cooler evenings. As is usually the case in hotel restaurants, the menu is of wide appeal, presenting pastas, beef dishes, and seafood, such as a halibut burger with sweet potato fries.

Outside Downtown

With so many dining choices in downtown Jasper, it's easy to ignore the many fine restaurants scattered elsewhere in the park.

One of Jasper's best restaurants, **Becker's Gourmet Restaurant** (780/852-3535, 8am-11am and 5:30pm-9pm daily May-mid-Oct., $22-38) is six kilometers (3.7 miles) out of town to the south along the Icefields Parkway, but well worth the short drive. From this cozy dining room, where the atmosphere is intimate, or the adjacent enclosed conservatory, the views of Mount Kerkeslin and the Athabasca River are inspiring. This restaurant is a throwback to days gone by, with an ever-changing menu of seasonal game and produce that includes a wild game platter. A menu staple is the pesto-crusted rack of lamb. For dessert, the strawberry shortcake is a delight. The breakfast buffet costs $16.

Back toward town from Becker's, on Highway 93A, is the dining room of historic **Tekarra Lodge** (780/852-4624, 8am-11am and 5:30pm-9:30pm daily mid-May-early

Oct., $28-43). The setting may be mountain-style rustic, but the cooking appeals to modern preferences with combinations like prosciutto-wrapped chicken with pear and smoke gouda.

You'll probably want to eat at the **Treeline Restaurant** (780/852-3093, 10am-5pm daily late Apr.-mid-Oct., 9am-8pm daily July-Aug., $14-21) just for the view—it's high above town at the upper terminal of the Jasper Tramway. The dishes are simple and relatively inexpensive, with burgers for around $14 and limited mains mostly under $20.

INFORMATION
Park Information Centre

The residence of Jasper's first superintendent, a beautiful old stone building dating to 1913, is now used by Parks Canada as the park information center (Connaught Dr., 780/852-6176, www.pc.gc.ca, 8:30am-7pm daily in summer, 9am-4pm daily the rest of the year), right downtown. The staff provides general information on the park and can direct you to hikes in the immediate vicinity. Also within the building is the **Parks Canada Trail Office** (780/852-6177), which handles questions for those going into the backcountry and issues the relevant passes. **Tourism Jasper** (780/852-6236, www.jasper.travel) also has a desk in the building, and the friendly staff never seem to tire of explaining that all the rooms in town are full. As well as providing general information on the town, they have a large collection of brochures on activities, shopping, and restaurants. Also in the building is the **Friends of Jasper National Park** outlet (780/852-4767), selling maps, books, bear spray, and souvenirs. Look for notices posted out front with the day's interpretive programs.

Other Sources of Information

Jasper's weekly newspaper, *The Fitzhugh,* is available throughout town and is free.

© ANDREW HEMPS-EAD

Park Information Centre

The official Town of Jasper website (www. jasper-alberta.com), with lists of current events, weather conditions, and loads of helpful links, is also worth checking out.

Jasper National Park Radio is on the AM band at 1490. For weather conditions in the park, call 780/852-6176.

Books and Bookstores

Housed in Jasper's historic Royal Canadian Mounted Police detachment building and a 2012 extension, **Jasper Municipal Library** (500 Robson St., 780/852-3652, 10am-8pm Mon.-Thurs., 10am-5pm Fri.-Sat.) holds just about everything ever written about the park.

Head to the **Friends of Jasper National Park** store (780/852-4767) in the park information center or the **museum** for a good selection of books on the park's natural and human history. A larger selection of literature, including lots of western Canadiana, can be found at **Jasper Camera and Gift** (412 Connaught

Dr., 780/852-3165, 9am-9pm daily in summer, shorter hours the rest of the year).

SERVICES

The **post office** (502 Patricia St., 780/852-3041, 9am-5:30pm Mon.-Fri.) is behind the park information center. Mail to be picked up here should be addressed General Delivery, Jasper, AB T0E 1E0. **More Than Mail** (632 Connaught Dr., 780/852-3151, 9am-10pm daily) offers a wide range of communication services, including regular post, public Internet access, fax and copying facilities, a work area for laptops, international calling, and office supplies.

The two **laundries** on Patricia Street are open 6am-11pm daily and offer **showers** that cost $2 for 10 minutes (quarters).

The **hospital** (780/852-3344) is at 518 Robson Street. For the **RCMP,** call 780/852-4848.

All hotels and motels as well as most lodges

have wireless Internet access. Send and receive email and surf the Internet at the following Jasper locations: **Jasper Municipal Library** (500 Robson St., 780/852-3652, 10am-8pm Mon.-Thurs., 10am-5pm Fri.-Sat.), **More Than Mail** (632 Connaught Dr., 780/852-3151, 9am-10pm daily), **Soft Rock Café** (632 Connaught Dr., 780/852-5850, 8am-10pm daily).

GETTING THERE

Jasper is linked to the outside world by road and rail. Alberta's capital, Edmonton, is 364 kilometers (226 miles) to the east along a wide, mostly-twinned highway. Heading south along the Icefields Parkway, Banff is 287 kilometers (178 miles) and Calgary is 406 kilometers (252 miles). From Vancouver, Jasper is 781 kilometers (486 miles) to the northeast; allow eight hours.

Getting to Jasper by public transportation is easy, although the closest airport handling domestic and international flights is at Edmonton, a four-hour drive to the east. The **VIA Rail station** and the **bus depot** (used by both Greyhound and Brewster) are in the same building, central to town at 607 Connaught Drive. The building is open 24 hours daily in summer (7:30am-10:30pm Mon.-Sat., 7:30am-11am and 6:30pm-10:30pm Sun. the rest of the year). Lockers are available for $1 per day. Car-rental agencies and a café are here, too.

Rail

Jasper is on the Canadian route, the only remaining transcontinental passenger rail service in the country. Trains run either way three times weekly. To the west the line divides, going to both Prince Rupert and Vancouver; to the east it passes through Edmonton and all points beyond. For all rail information, contact **VIA Rail** (800/561-8630, www.viarail.ca). Another rail option is offered by **Rocky Mountaineer Vacations** (604/606-7245 or 877/460-7245, www.rockymountaineer.com). This company operates a luxurious summer-only rail service between Vancouver and Jasper, with an overnight in Kamloops (British Columbia).

Bus

Greyhound buses (780/852-332 or 800/661-8747, www.greyhound.ca) depart Jasper for all points in Canada (except Banff), including Vancouver (three times daily, 12-13 hours, $142 one-way), Edmonton (five times daily, 4.5 hours, $67 one-way) with connections to Calgary, and Prince Rupert (once daily, 18 hours, $198 one-way).

The main carrier up the Icefields Parkway from Calgary and Banff is Banff-based **Brewster** (780/852-3332 or 866/606-6700, www.brewster.ca). This company operates a shuttle between Calgary International Airport daily May-October ($134 each way). Between December and April, **Sun Dog Tours** (780/852-4056 or 888/786-3641, www.sundogtours.com) operates a skier shuttle between Calgary and Jasper once daily in each direction. Sample fares to Jasper are from Calgary, $128; from Banff, $69; and from Lake Louise, $58.

GETTING AROUND

The **Maligne Valley Shuttle** (780/852-3370) runs out to Maligne Lake mid-May-September, 3-4 times daily ($40 round-trip) from its depot at 616 Patricia Street. Stops are made at Maligne Canyon and HI-Maligne Canyon. Other pickup points include the Jasper Inn and The Fairmont Jasper Park Lodge.

Rental cars start at $60 per day, including 150 kilometers (93 miles) free. The following companies have local agencies, and their local numbers are **Avis** (780/852-3970), **Budget** (780/852-3222), **Hertz** (780/852-3888), and **National** (780/852-1117).

Cabs in town are not cheap. Most drivers will take you on a private sightseeing tour or to trailheads if requested; try **Jasper Taxi** (780/852-3600 or 780/852-3146).

JASPER NATIONAL PARK

Other Parks Near Jasper

Two parks adjoining Jasper National Park are well worth visiting if you have the time. To the west, across the Continental Divide, Mount Robson Provincial Park is named for the Canadian Rockies' highest mountain and is best-known by hikers for the Berg Lake Trail. More remote is Willmore Wilderness Park, northeast of Jasper, where most travel is by horseback.

◖ MOUNT ROBSON PROVINCIAL PARK

At the northern end of the Canadian Rockies, spectacular 224,866 hectare (555,650-acre) Mount Robson Provincial Park was created in 1913 to protect a vast wilderness of steep canyons and wide forested valleys; icy lakes, rivers, and streams; and rugged mountain peaks permanently blanketed in snow and ice. The park lies along the Continental Divide in British Columbia, adjacent to Jasper National Park, and shelters the headwaters of the Fraser River, one of British Columbia's most important waterways. Towering over the park's western entrance is magnificent 3,954-meter (12,970-foot) **Mount Robson,** the highest peak in the Canadian Rockies.

Highway 16 splits the park in two, and many sights of interest are visible from the highway. But you'll have to leave the car behind to experience one of the park's biggest draws; the famous Berg Lake Trail is strictly for hikers.

Getting There and Around

Mount Robson Provincial Park is west of the town of Jasper along Highway 16. From the park boundary at Yellowhead Pass it is 62 kilometers (39 miles) west to the visitor center. No public transportation serves the park, so you will need your own vehicle.

Flora and Fauna

The elevation differences within the park are as great as anywhere else in the Canadian Rockies, making for a great variety of flora and fauna. The main service center lies in a forested valley at an elevation of just 840 meters (2,750 feet), right in the heart of the montane. The oft-photographed view of Mount Robson from the visitors center is framed by a stand of trembling aspen across a cleared meadow, but the most common tree at this elevation is **Douglas fir,** which covers the valley floor. **Western red cedar** and **hemlock** thrive in damp sections of the park. As in the rest of the Canadian Rockies, the subalpine zone is dominated by **Engelmann spruce** and, at higher elevations, **subalpine fir.** The alpine zone in the park begins at around 2,300 meters (7,550 feet).

In spring, **black bears** are often seen feasting on dandelions by the roadside, but their larger relative, the **grizzly,** rarely makes an appearance in the busy valley through which Highway 16 winds. **Elk, moose,** and **mountain goats** are also present, as are many smaller critters. More than 170 bird species have been identified, with the rare **harlequin duck** a special joy to watch as it passes through the park each spring.

History

Local Shuswap natives called Mount Robson *Yuh-hai-has-hun* (Mountain of the Spiral Road) for its layered appearance. Historians guess that the peak's European name honors a member of the Hudson's Bay Company, although details of the christening have been lost to history.

Mountaineers were attracted to the challenge of climbing Mount Robson in the early 1900s; the first official ascent took place in 1913 (the same year the park as we know it today was created). Led by Swiss guide Conrad Kain, the first ascent party was made up of members of the Alpine Club of Canada. Although this was the first official summit climb, the summit had been attempted four years earlier by the Reverend George Kinney and friends. Kinney thought he'd made the summit, but he was climbing the summit ridge in a heavy fog; a cairn and a message recording the names of the members of Kinney's climbing team were later found on the ridge about 100 vertical meters (320 vertical feet) from the top.

Roadside Sights

Highway 16 enters the park from the east at 1,066-meter (3,500-foot) **Yellowhead Pass,** on the British Columbia-Alberta border. It's the lowest highway pass over the Continental Divide. From the divide, it's 60 kilometers (37.2 miles) to the park's western boundary and the visitors center. Just west of the divide, a rest area beside picturesque **Portal Lake** is a good introduction to the park.

Continuing westward, the highway passes long, narrow **Yellowhead Lake** at the foot of 2,458-meter (8,060-foot) **Yellowhead Mountain,** then crosses the upper reaches of the Fraser River. The Moose River drains into the Fraser River at **Moose Marsh,** a good spot for watching wildlife at the southeast end of **Moose Lake.** Moose often feed here at dawn and dusk, and waterfowl are present throughout the day.

Continuing west, the highway parallels Moose Lake; waterfalls on the lake's far side create a photogenic backdrop. As the road descends steeply to a wide, open section of the valley, it passes the main facility area, where you'll find a visitors center, campgrounds, a gas station, and a restaurant. On a clear day, the panorama from this lump of commercialism is equal to any sight in British Columbia. The sheer west face of Mount Robson slices skyward just seven kilometers (4.3 miles) away across a flower-filled meadow. This is as close as you can get to the peak in your car.

If you're approaching the park from the west,

you'll see Mount Robson long before you reach the park boundary (provided the weather is cooperating). It's impossible to confuse this distinctive peak with those that surround it—no wonder it's known as the Monarch of the Canadian Rockies.

Berg Lake Trail

- Length: 19.5 kilometers/12 miles (8 hours) one-way
- Elevation gain: 725 meters/2,380 feet
- Rating: moderate/difficult
- Trailhead: 2 kilometers (1.2 miles) north of Mount Robson Visitor Centre

This is the most popular overnight hike in the Canadian Rockies, but don't let the crowds put you off—the hike is well worth it. Beautiful aqua-colored Berg Lake lies below the north face of Mount Robson, which rises 2,400 meters (7,880 feet) directly behind the lake. Glaciers on the mountain's shoulder regularly calve off into the lake, resulting in the icebergs that give the lake its name.

The trail begins by following the Robson River 4.5 kilometers (2.8 miles) through dense subalpine forest to glacially fed **Kinney Lake.** There the trail narrows, crossing the fast-flowing river at the eight-kilometer (five-mile) mark and climbing alongside it. The next four kilometers (2.5 miles), through the steep-sided Valley of a Thousand Falls, are the most demanding, but views of four spectacular waterfalls ease the pain of the 500-vertical-meter (1,640-vertical-foot) climb. The first glimpses of Mount Robson come soon after reaching the head of the valley, from where it's one kilometer (0.6 mile) farther to the outlet of Berg Lake, 17.5 kilometers (10.9 miles) from the trailhead. The first of three lakeside campgrounds is two kilometers (1.2 miles) from this point.

While the panorama from the lake is stunning, most hikers who have come this far will want to spend some time exploring the area.

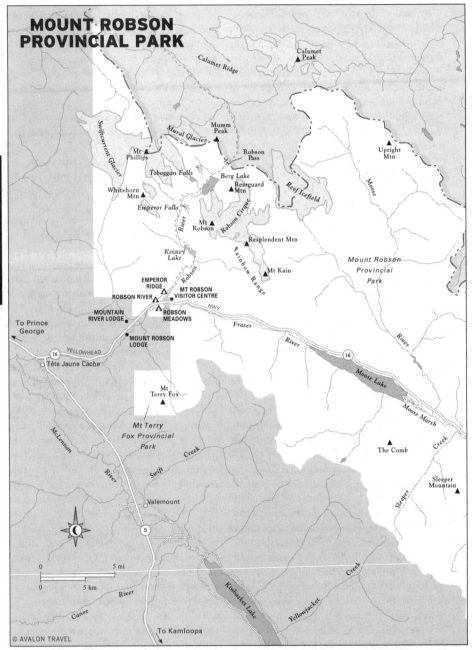

MOUNT ROBSON PROVINCIAL PARK

Calumet Ridge

Calumet Peak

Mumm Peak

Mural Glacier

Swiftcurrent Glacier

Robson Pass

Upright Mtn

Mt Phillips

Moose

Toboggan Falls

Berg Lake

Reef Icefield

Whitehorn Mtn

Rearguard Mtn

Robson Cirque

Emperor Falls

River

Mt Robson

Resplendent Mtn

Kinney Lake

Rainbow Range

Mt Kain

Mount Robson Provincial Park

EMPEROR RIDGE

Robson

ROBSON RIVER

MT ROBSON VISITOR CENTRE

MOUNTAIN RIVER LODGE

ROBSON MEADOWS

HWY

To Prince George

Fraser

River

River

MOUNT ROBSON LODGE

YELLOWHEAD

16

16

Tête Jaune Cache

Moose Lake

Mt Terry Fox

Moose Marsh

Mt Terry Fox Provincial Park

McLennan

Creek

The Comb

Creek

River

Swift

Creek

Sleeper Mountain

Valemount

Sleeper

5

0   5 mi

0   5 km

River

Creek

Kinbasket Lake

Canoe

River

Yellowjacket

To Kamloops

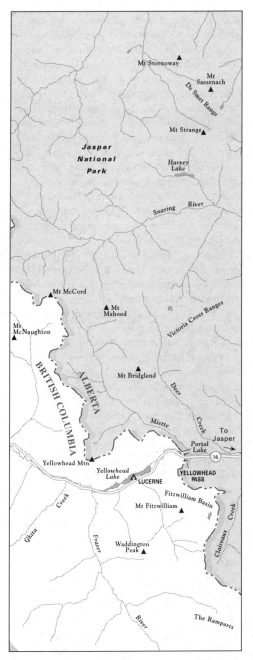

From the north end of the lake, trails lead to Toboggan Falls and more mountain views, to the head of Robson Glacier, and to Robson Pass, which opens up the remote northern reaches of Jasper National Park.

CAMPGROUNDS

It's possible to traverse the trail's first section and return the same day; to get all the way to Berg Lake and back, you'll need to stay in the backcountry overnight. Along the route seven primitive campgrounds hold 75 campsites, including three campgrounds along the lakeshore. Reservations for these sites can be made up to three months in advance by calling the BC Parks' Discover Camping hotline (604/689-9025 or 800/689-9025); the booking fee is $6.42 per night to a maximum of $19.26. Book early, because the quota fills quickly. Upon arrival in the park, all overnight hikers must then check in at the visitors center and pay a camping fee of $10 per person per night.

If the uphill walk in seems too ambitious, contact **Robson Helimagic** (250/566-4700 or 877/454-4700, www.robsonhelimagic.com), which makes helicopter drop-offs at Robson Pass from Valemount every Monday and Friday; $229 per person (minimum four).

Other Hikes in the Park

Aside from the popular trail to Berg Lake, the park holds only two other established trails. The shortest ascends the slopes of 2,458-meter (8,060-foot) **Yellowhead Mountain.** From the trailhead across the rail line at Yellowhead Lake, it's a steady climb through subalpine forest to the first viewpoint at the one-kilometer (0.6-mile) mark. Another three kilometers (1.9 miles) and an elevation gain of 720 meters (2,060 feet) bring you to flower-filled meadows and panoramic views extending east to the Continental Divide and west to the Selwyn Range. Allow two hours each way for this hike.

The other option is the 13-kilometer

(eight-mile) **Fitzwilliam Basin Trail,** which requires an overnight stay in the backcountry. Elevation gain is 950 meters (3,120 feet), so it's a demanding trail. From the trailhead on the south side of Highway 16, three kilometers (1.9 miles) east of Lucerne Campground, the trail climbs steadily for six kilometers (3.7 miles) to the confluence of Rockingham and Fitzwilliam Creeks. Although easy to follow, the remaining seven kilometers (4.3 miles) along the northern slopes of 2,911-meter (9,550-foot) Mount Fitzwilliam are rough going. After ascending a steep ridge, the trail all but disappears, but many camping spots can be found in the wide lake-filled basin.

Accommodations

The park has no indoor accommodations, but two lodges lie just outside the park's western boundary, and motel accommodations are available 42 kilometers (26 miles) to the southwest in Valemount.

Mountain River Lodge (4 km/2.5 mi west of the visitors center, 250/566-9899, www.mtrobson.com) is in a delightful setting right alongside the Fraser River. The main lodge holds four guest rooms, each with a different character, a balcony, and a private bathroom. The smallest of the rooms (with twin beds and a private bathroom down the hall) is $110 s or d, while the other three are $135; rates include a cooked breakfast. Self-contained cabins cost $159-179 s or d per night, with breakfast available at an extra charge.

One kilometer (0.6 mile) west of Mountain River Lodge is **Mount Robson Lodge** (250/566-4821 or 888/566-4821, www.mountrobson-lodge.com, May-Oct., $79-139 s or d), with 18 freestanding cabins; the more expensive ones have kitchens, or eat at the small café.

Campgrounds

Within the park, four auto-accessible campgrounds are open May-mid-September, with another just outside the park boundary. Three of these are park operated. Closest to the visitors center (and my favorite) is **Robson River Campground** (250/566-4811, where numerous trails lead down to the river for the classic upstream view of Mount Robson. It's also only a short walk to the visitors center and a café. Across the highway is the larger **Robson Meadows Campground** (250/566-4811), with 125 sites on a spiral road system that centers on an outdoor theater that hosts evening interpretive programs throughout the summer. A number of sites at Robson Meadows can be reserved through www.discovercamping.ca. Both campgrounds have flush toilets and showers but no hookups; $21 per site.

Beside the east end of Yellowhead Lake (swimming for the brave), 50 kilometers (31 miles) from the visitors center, is the more rustic **Lucerne Campground** (250/566-4811, $17 per site). Facilities include drinking water, pit toilets, and picnic tables.

Emperor Ridge Campground (250/566-8438, mid-May-late Sept., $18 per site) is a small commercial facility right behind the visitors center that offers hot showers but no hookups.

Robson Shadows Campground, part of Mount Robson Lodge (250/566-4821 or 888/566-4821, www.mountrobsonlodge.com, May-Oct., $25 per site), is farthest from the visitors center (5 km/3.1 mi west) but has unobstructed views of the distinctive peak, with a riverside location as a bonus. It also has showers but no hookups.

Information

At the park's western entrance, **Mount Robson Visitor Centre** (250/566-9174, www.env.gov.bc.ca/bcparks, 8am-8pm daily mid-June-mid-Sept., 8am-5pm daily mid-May-mid-June and mid-Sept.-mid-Oct.) features informative natural-history slide shows, an evening interpretive program, and trail reports updated daily.

The center stocks the brochure *Mount Robson Provincial Park,* which provides sufficient information if you're only driving through the park. Hikers and climbers can pick up more detailed trail descriptions and maps at the center.

WILLMORE WILDERNESS PARK

* **Visit in conjunction with:** Jasper National Park

Willmore Wilderness Park is a northern extension of Jasper National Park. It lies south and west of Grande Cache, a small town on Highway 40 between Hinton and Grande Prairie. The 460,000-hectare (1,137,000-acre) wilderness area is divided roughly in half by the Smoky River. The area west of the river is reached from Sulphur Gates. The east side is far less traveled—the terrain is rougher and wetter. The park is accessible only on foot, horseback, or, in winter, on skis. It is totally undeveloped; the trails that do exist are not maintained and in most cases are those once used by trappers.

The park is made up of long, green ridges above the tree line and, farther west, wide passes and expansive basins along the Continental Divide. Lower elevations are covered in lodgepole pine and spruce, while at higher elevations the cover changes to fir. The diverse wildlife is one of the park's main attractions; white-tailed and mule deer, mountain goats, bighorn sheep, moose, elk, caribou, and black bears are all common. The park is also home to wolves, cougars, and grizzly bears.

Park Access and Travel

The easiest way to access the park is from Sulphur Gates Provincial Recreation Area, six kilometers (3.7 miles) north of Grande Cache on Highway 40, and then a similar distance along a gravel road to the west. Those not planning a trip into the park can still enjoy the cliffs

at **Sulphur Gates** (formerly known as Hell's Gate), which is only a short walk from the end of the road. These 70-meter (230-foot) cliffs are at the confluence of the Sulphur and Smoky Rivers. The color difference between the glacial-fed Smoky River and spring-fed Sulphur River is apparent as they merge.

One of the most popular overnight trips from Sulphur Gates is to **Clarke's Cache,** an easy 16-kilometer (10-mile) hike to the remains of a cabin where trappers once stored furs before taking them to trading posts farther afield. A good option for a day trip for fit hikers is to the 2,013-meter (6,600-foot) summit of **Mount Stearn** from a trailhead 3.5 kilometers (2.2 miles) along the access road to Sulphur Gates. The trail begins by climbing alongside a stream through montane, then subalpine forest, and then through open meadows before reentering the forest and forking and rejoining. The official trail then climbs steeply and continuously to Lightning Ridge (10 km/6.2 mi one-way), but an easier summit is reached by heading up through the grassed slopes to a summit knob, 6.5 kilometers (four miles) and 1,000 vertical meters (3,280 vertical feet) from the road; allow 6-6.5 hours for the round-trip.

Practicalities

Anyone planning an extended trip into the park should be aware that no services are available, most trails are unmarked, and certain areas are heavily used by horse packers. **High Country Vacations** (780/827-3246 or 877/487-2457, www.horsebacktherockies.com) offers pack trips into the park; expect to pay around $240 per person per day, all-inclusive, for a 10-day trip.

GRANDE CACHE

This town of 4,300, the most remote in the Canadian Rockies, is at the gateway to Willmore Wilderness Park and is surrounded by total wilderness, offering endless

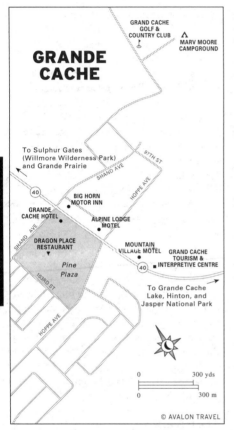

opportunities for hiking, canoeing, kayaking, fishing, and horseback riding. It perches on the side of Grande Mountain above the Smoky River, which flows from its source in Jasper National Park through Willmore Wilderness Park, eventually joining the Peace River and draining into the Arctic Ocean.

The first Europeans to explore the area were fur trappers and traders, who cached furs near the site of the present town before taking them to major trading posts. At one point there was a small trading post south of town in the vicinity of the Pierre Gray Lakes; its remains are still visible. Grande Cache is a planned town. Construction started in 1969 in response to a need for services and housing for miners and their families working at a new coal mine. The town was developed 20 kilometers (12.4 miles) south of the mine to maintain a scenic environment.

Sights and Recreation

For great views of the surrounding area, consider climbing **Grande Mountain,** along a trail that has 800 meters (2,400 feet) of elevation gain and takes around three hours one way. It's a steep trail, gaining 730 meters (2,400 feet) of elevation in 3.5 kilometers (2.1 miles), but from the summit, the view across the Smoky River Valley to the Rocky Mountains is spectacular. The trail follows a power line the entire way to the peak and is easy to follow. To get to the trailhead, head northwest of town one kilometer (0.6 mile) and turn right at the cemetery gate. Park, walk along the road to the power line, veer right, and start the long slog to the summit. **Grande Cache Lake,** five kilometers (3.1 miles) south of town, has good swimming, canoeing, and fishing; rainbow and brook trout, whitefish, and arctic grayling are commonly caught.

In recent years, Grande Cache has placed itself on the calendar of extreme ultra-marathoners the world over as host of the early August **Canadian Death Race** (www.canadiandeathrace.com). The footrace takes place along a super-demanding 125-kilometer (78-mile) course, which summits three peaks.

Accommodations and Camping

Room rates in this mountain hideaway are surprisingly inexpensive, but because fewer than 250 rooms are available in the whole town, reservations should be made in advance. On the highway through town, the **Big Horn Motor Inn** (780/827-3744 or 888/880-2444, www.bighorninn.com, $75 s, $85 d) is the best value. Each of 37 rooms has a small fridge and wireless Internet, and some have kitchenettes.

A laundry room and a restaurant are on the premises. Also along the highway is the similarly priced **Alpine Lodge Motel** (780/827-2450). If you're looking for something a little different, consider a stay at ◖ **Sheep Creek Back Country Lodge & Cabins** (780/831-1087, www.sheepcreek.net, June-late Sept., $125-200 s or d), which is accessed by a short walking trail and a suspension bridge from 24 kilometers (15 miles) north of town. It attracts an eclectic array of guests—anglers, hunters, mountain bikers—but everyone is welcome. Each rustic cabin has a simple kitchen, bedroom, deck, chemical toilet, and gravity-fed shower. A communal fridge/freezer is located in the main building. Guests bring their own food and towels.

The only camping right in town is at **Marv Moore Campground** (780/827-2404, May-late Sept., tents $25, powered sites $30), which has semiprivate, well-shaded sites and showers, kitchen shelters, a laundry, and firewood. It's at the north end of town on Shand Avenue beside the golf course. Four forestry campgrounds are at regular intervals along Highway 40; of special note for its scenic location is the one at the south end of **Sulphur Gates Provincial Recreation Area** (west off Hwy. 40 north of town, May-Oct., $15 per site), which makes a good base for exploring adjacent Willmore Wilderness Park. It has just 10 sites.

Food

On a clear day, the view from the **Family Restaurant** (Grande Cache Hotel, 780/827-3377, breakfast, lunch, and dinner daily, $13-19) is worth at least the price of a coffee. Soup and sandwich lunch specials are approximately $10, and pizza and pasta dishes start at $13. At the back of Grande Cache Hotel is **Rockies Bar and Grill** (780/827-3377), with a regular bar menu and occasional live music. Across the plaza is **Dragon Place Restaurant** (780/827-3898, 11am-10pm daily, $10.50-17). This is your quintessential small-town Chinese restaurant, with big portions of all the usual westernized Chinese favorites.

Information and Services

The excellent **Grande Cache Tourism & Interpretive Centre** (780/827-3300 or 888/827-3790, www.grandecache.ca, 9am-6pm daily in summer, 9am-5pm Mon.-Sat. the rest of the year) is a great source of park information.

The **post office** is in the plaza, as is a **laundry** (beside IGA). **Home Hardware,** in the Pine Plaza, stocks camping and fishing gear.

WATERTON LAKES NATIONAL PARK

Everybody traveling to this small, rugged 526-square-kilometer (203-square-mile) park does so by choice; tucked away in the extreme southwestern corner of Alberta, the park is not on a major highway or on the way to anywhere else. It's bounded to the north and east by the rolling prairies covering southern Alberta; to the south by the U.S. border and Glacier National Park in Montana; and to the west by the Continental Divide, which forms the Alberta-British Columbia border. The natural mountain splendor, a chain of deep glacial lakes, large and diverse populations of wildlife, an unbelievable variety of day hikes, and a changing face each season make this park a gem that shouldn't be missed on any trip to the Canadian Rockies.

The route to Waterton is almost as scenic as the park itself. From whichever direction you arrive, the transition from prairie to mountains is abrupt, almost devoid of the foothills that characterize other areas along the eastern slopes of the Canadian Rockies. Between the park gate and the small township of Waterton, two roads penetrate the mountains to the west. One ends at a large glaciated lake, the other at a spectacular canyon. The town is a smaller version of those in Banff and Jasper. Like those towns, Waterton holds a grand hotel built by the railway, a golf course, and a wide range of services, but the atmosphere here is very different.

© ANDREW HEMPSTEAD

HIGHLIGHTS

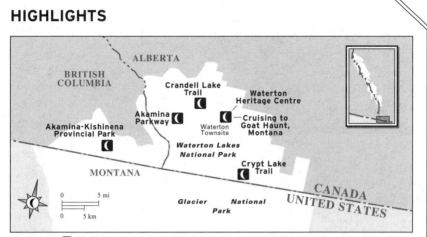

LOOK FOR (TO FIND RECOMMENDED SIGHTS, ACTIVITIES, DINING, AND LODGING.

(**Waterton Heritage Centre:** This is a good place to learn about the park's natural history (page 266).

(**Akamina Parkway:** You'll want to take all the scenic drives detailed in this chapter, but this one gets the nod as a must-see attraction. Why? Because when you reach the end of the road, you can rent a canoe and paddle out onto magnificent Cameron Lake (page 268).

(**Crypt Lake Trail:** This hike is undoubtedly the most spectacular trail in the park (page 271).

(**Crandell Lake Trail:** If the Crypt Lake

Trail is a little beyond you, or if you have a family in tow, plan on hiking up the easy incline to this lake instead (page 271).

(**Cruising to Goat Haunt, Montana:** Taking a tour boat along Upper Waterton Lake and across the border to Montana has been the most popular activity in the park for over 50 years—and for around $30 you can do it, too (page 273).

(**Akamina-Kishinena Provincial Park:** Accessible on foot from Waterton, expand your hiking schedule by planning trips to Wall and Forum Lakes (page 282).

PLANNING YOUR TIME

Chances are, if you're planning on visiting Waterton Lakes, you're not the same type of traveler who thinks a trip to Banff entails staying at Best Western and eating at McDonald's—instead you're looking to experience the natural wonders of the Canadian Rockies without the crowds and commercialism.

The vast majority of visitors arrive in July and August. As with the other parks of the Canadian Rockies, June and September are

fine times to visit, but as crowds are smaller here, avoiding high summer isn't as much of an issue. Many businesses, including accommodations, close between October and April, although basic services are still available. Cross-country skiing enthusiasts will love winter in the park, but don't expect much else in the way of recreation.

Simply because of the out-of-the-way location, you'll want to spend at least one day in the park, but it's preferable to stay two or more. With two days and one night scheduled, plan

WATERTON LAKES

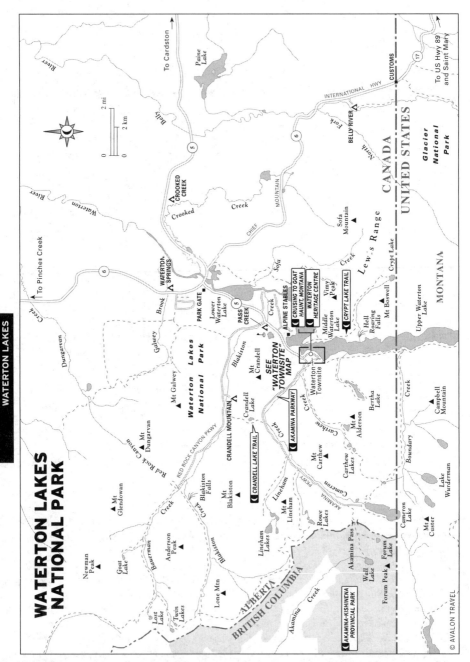

WATERTON LAKES NATIONAL PARK

© AVALON TRAVEL

on joining the boat cruise to **Goat Haunt** on one day and spending the second day exploring the two main roads, including the **Akamina Parkway** to Cameron Lake. This still allows time to walk some shorter trails. If you're an enthusiastic hiker, add a third day to your itinerary and hike either the trail to **Crypt Lake** or head across the provincial border on foot to **Akamina-Kishinena Provincial Park.**

If your tour of the Canadian Rockies originates south of the border and you're traveling by road, I highly recommend leaving Waterton Lakes until the end of your trip—the slower pace and solitude will create a pleasant ending for your travels.

THE LAND
Geology

Major upheavals under the earth's surface approximately 85 million years ago forced huge plates of rock upward and began folding them over each other. One major sheet, known as the Lewis Overthrust, forms the backbone of Waterton's topography as we see it today. It slid up and over much younger bedrock along a 300-kilometer (186-mile) length extending north to Bow Valley.

About 45 million years ago, this powerful uplift ceased and the forces of erosion took over. About 1.9 million years ago, glaciers from the sheet of ice that once covered most of Alberta crept through the mountains. As these thick sheets of ice advanced and retreated with climatic changes, they gouged out valleys such as the classically U-shaped Waterton Valley. The three Waterton Lakes are depressions left at the base of the steep-sided mountains after the ice had completely retreated 11,000 years ago. The deepest is 150 meters (500 feet). Cameron Lake, at the end of the Akamina Parkway, was formed when a moraine—the pile of rock that accumulates at the foot of a retreating glacier—dammed Cameron Creek. From the lake, Cameron Creek flows through a glaciated valley before dropping into the much deeper Waterton Valley at Cameron Falls, behind the town of Waterton. The town itself sits on an alluvial fan composed of silt and gravel picked up by mountain streams and deposited in Upper Waterton Lake.

Climate

Climate plays an active role in creating the park's natural landscape. This corner of the province tends to receive more rain, snow, and wind—much more wind—than other parts of Alberta. These factors, combined with the park's varied topography, create an environment where more than half the known species in Alberta have been recorded. Wind is the most powerful presence in the park. Prevailing winds from the south and west bring Pacific weather over the divide, creating a climate similar to that experienced farther west. These warm fronts endow the region with **chinooks**—dry winds that can raise temperatures in the park by up to 40°C (104°F) in 24 hours.

One of the nicest aspects of the park is that it can be enjoyed in all seasons. Summer is great

---

PARK ENTRY

Visitors to Waterton Lakes National Park are required to stop at the park gate and buy a permit. A **National Parks Day Pass** is adult $8, senior $7, child $4, to a maximum of $20 per vehicle, and is valid until 4pm the day following its purchase. An annual pass for entry to the park is adult $39, senior $34, child $20, to a maximum of $98 per vehicle.

If you're traveling to national parks beyond Waterton, a better deal is the annual **Discovery Pass,** good for entry into all of Canada's national parks and historic sites; adult $68, senior $58, child $34, or $137 per vehicle. These passes can be purchased at any park gate; check www.pc.gc.ca for more information.

for the sunny windless days, fall for the wildlife viewing, winter for the solitude, and spring for the long days of sunlight as the park seems to be waking up from its winter slumber. Be aware, however, that many of the park's best sights and hiking trails lie at high elevations; some areas may be snowed in until mid-June.

FLORA

Botanists have recorded 1,200 species of plants growing within the park's several different vegetation zones. In the park's northeastern corner, near the park gate, a region of prairies is covered in semiarid vegetation such as **fescue grass.** As Highway 5 enters the park it passes Maskinonge Lake, a wetlands area of marshy ponds where aquatic plants flourish. Parkland habitat dominated by **aspen** is found along the north side of Blakiston Valley and near Belly River Campground, while montane forest covers most mountain valleys and lower slopes. This montane zone is dominated by a high canopy of **lodgepole pine** and **Douglas fir** shading a forest floor covered with wildflowers and berries. An easily accessible section of this habitat is along the lower half of Bertha Lake Trail; an interpretive brochure is available at the Waterton Visitor Centre.

Above the montane forest is the subalpine zone, which rises as far as the timberline. These distinct forests of **larch, fir, Engelmann spruce,** and **whitebark pine** can be seen along the Carthew Lakes Trail. On the west-facing slopes of Cameron Lake are mature groves of subalpine trees up to 400 years old; this oldest growth in the park has managed to escape fire over the centuries. Blanketing the open mountain slopes in this zone is bear grass, which grows up to one meter (three feet) in height and is topped by a bright blossom often likened to a lighted torch. Above the tree line is the alpine zone, where harsh winds and short summer seasons make trees a rarity. Only **lichens**

and **alpine wildflowers** flourish at these high altitudes. Crypt Lake is a good place for viewing this zone.

FAUNA

Wildlife viewing in the park requires patience and a little know-how, but the rewards are ample, as good as anywhere in the Canadian Rockies. **Elk** inhabit the park year-round. A large herd gathers by Entrance Road in late fall, wintering on the lowlands. By early fall, many **mule deer** are wandering around town. **Bighorn sheep** are often seen on the north side of Blakiston Valley or on the slopes above the Waterton Visitor Centre; occasionally they end up in town. **White-tailed deer** are best viewed along Red Rock Canyon Parkway. The park has a small population of **moose,** occasionally seen in low-lying wetlands. **Mountain goats** rarely leave the high peaks of the backcountry, but from Goat, Crypt, or Bertha Lake you might catch a glimpse of one high above you.

The most common predators in the park are the **coyotes,** which spend their summer days chasing ground squirrels around the prairie and parkland areas. For its size, Waterton has a healthy population of **cougars,** but these shy, solitary animals are rarely seen. About 50 **black bears** live in the park. They spend most of the summer in the heavily forested montane regions. During August and September, scan the slopes of Blakiston Valley, where the bears can often be seen feasting on saskatoon berries before going into winter hibernation. Much larger than black bears are **grizzlies,** which roam the entire backcountry but are rarely encountered. Larger even still are **bison.** Although these prairie dwellers never lived in the mountains, they would have grazed around the eastern outskirts of what is now the park. A small herd is contained in the **Bison Paddock,** just before the park gate.

Golden-mantled ground squirrels live on the Bear's Hump and around Cameron Falls.

© ANDREW HEMPSTEAD

Deer are a common sight throughout Waterton townsite.

Columbian ground squirrels are just about everywhere. **Chipmunks** scamper about on Bertha Lake Trail. The best time for viewing **beavers** is at dawn and dusk along the Belly River. **Muskrats** can be seen on the edges of Maskinonge Lake eating bulrushes. **Mink** also live at the lake but are seen only by those with patience.

Two major flyways pass the park, and during September-November, many thousands of waterfowl stop on Maskinonge and Lower Waterton Lakes. On a power-line pole beside the entrance to the park is an active **osprey** nest—ask staff to point it out for you. Waterton Heritage Centre has a great little free checklist for birders listing the 250 species recorded within park boundaries.

HISTORY

Evidence found within the park suggests that the Kootenay people who lived west of the park made trips across the Continental Divide 8,000-10,000 years ago to hunt bison on the plains and fish in the lakes. They camped in the valleys during winter, taking shelter from the harsh weather. But by about 1,500 years ago, they were spending more time in the west and crossing the mountains only a few times a year to hunt bison. By the 1700s, the Blackfoot—with the help of horses—had expanded their territory from the Battle River throughout southwestern Alberta. They patrolled the mountains on horseback, making it difficult for the Kootenay hunting parties to cross. But their dominance was short-lived. With the arrival of guns and the encroaching homesteads of early settlers, Blackfoot tribes retreated to the east, leaving the Waterton Lakes Valley uninhabited.

Oil City

Kootenai Brown, the valley's first permanent settler, first noticed beads of oil floating on Cameron Creek. He and a business partner siphoned it from the water's surface, bottled it, and sold it in Fort Macleod and Cardston. This discovery created much interest among the oil-starved entrepreneurs of Alberta, who formed the Rocky Mountain Development Company to do some exploratory drilling. At this stage the park was still a forest reserve; the trees were protected, but prospecting and mining were still allowed. A rough road was constructed through the Cameron Creek Valley, and in September 1901 the company struck oil at a depth of 311 meters (1,020 feet). It was the first producing oil well in western Canada and only the second in the country. In the resulting euphoria, a town site named Oil City was cleared and surveyed, a bunkhouse and dining hall were constructed, and the foundations for a hotel were laid. The boom was short-lived. Drilling rigs kept breaking down, and the flow of oil soon slowed to a trickle. A monument along the Akamina Parkway stands at the site of the well, and a little farther up the road at a roadside marker, a trail leads through thick undergrowth to the town site. All that remains are the ill-fated hotel's foundations and some depressions in the ground.

Waterton-Glacier International Peace Park

After becoming the valley's first permanent resident in 1869, Kootenai Brown began promoting the beauty of the area to the people of Fort Macleod. One of his friends, local rancher F. W. Godsal, began lobbying the federal government to establish a reserve. In 1895 an area was set aside as a forest reserve. Shortly after Montana's Glacier National Park was created in 1910, the Canadian government changed the name of the reserve to Waterton Lakes Dominion Park; it was later redesignated a national park. Many people followed in the footsteps of Kootenai Brown, and a small town named Waterton grew up on the Cameron Creek delta. The town had no rail link, so unlike Banff and Jasper—its famous mountain neighbors to the north—it didn't draw large crowds of tourists. Nevertheless, it soon became a popular summer retreat with a hotel, restaurant, and dance hall. The Great Northern Railway decided to operate a bus service from its Montana rail line to Jasper, with a stop at Waterton. This led to the construction of the **Prince of Wales Hotel.**

Boat cruises from the hotel across the international boundary were soon the park's most popular activity. This brought the two parks closer together, and in 1932, after much lobbying from Rotary International members on both sides of the border, the Canadian and U.S. governments agreed to establish Waterton-Glacier International Peace Park, the first of its kind in the world. The parks are administered separately but cooperate in preserving this pristine mountain wilderness through wildlife management, search-and-rescue operations, and interpretive programs. Peace Park celebrations take place each year, and the **Peace Park Pavilion** by the lake is dedicated to this unique bond. In 1979, UNESCO declared the park a **Biosphere Reserve,** only the second such reserve in Canada. In 1995, the park's importance was further recognized when UNESCO declared Waterton-Glacier International Peace Park a World Heritage Site.

Sights and Drives

Hiking is definitely the reason most visitors are drawn to Waterton, but there are plenty of other activities to fit in between hikes or for all family members. The scenic drives described below are highly recommended activities, as is the boat cruise across the border to Goat Haunt, Montana, in Glacier National Park.

Make your first stop the **Waterton Visitor Centre** (403/859-5133), on the slight rise before the road descends to the village.

WATERTON HERITAGE CENTRE

The only official man-made "sight" is the Waterton Heritage Centre (117 Waterton Ave., 403/859-2624, 10am-5pm daily May-June and Sept., 10am-8pm daily July and Aug.). This small museum contains exhibits telling the story of the park's natural and human history, including a section of aspen in which a trapper carved his initials over 100 years ago. It also holds a selection of paintings and woodcarvings created by local artists as well as a selection

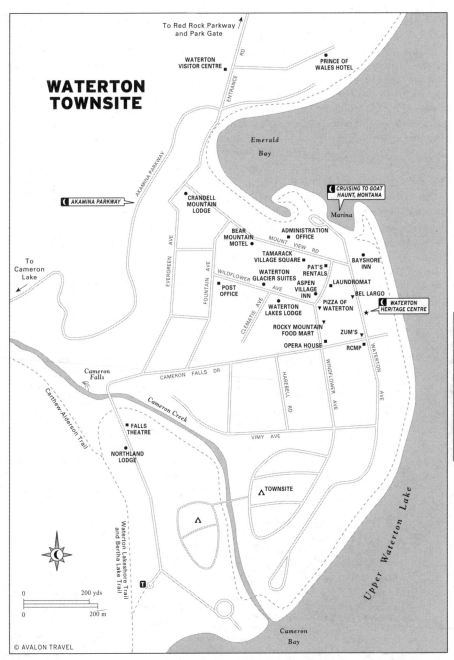

WATERTON
TOWNSITE

To Red Rock Parkway
and Park Gate

WATERTON
VISITOR CENTRE

PRINCE OF
WALES HOTEL

ENTRANCE RD

Emerald

Bay

AKAMINA PARKWAY

CRUISING TO GOAT
HAUNT, MONTANA

AKAMINA PARKWAY

CRANDELL
MOUNTAIN
LODGE

Marina

BEAR
MOUNTAIN
MOTEL

ADMINISTRATION
OFFICE

MOUNT VIEW RD

BAYSHORE
INN

TAMARACK
VILLAGE SQUARE

PAT'S
RENTALS

EVERGREEN AVE

FOUNTAIN AVE

WILDFLOWER AVE

WATERTON
GLACIER SUITES

POST
OFFICE

ASPEN
VILLAGE
INN

LAUNDROMAT

BEL LARGO

To
Cameron
Lake

CLEMATIS AVE

WATERTON
LAKES LODGE

PIZZA OF
WATERTON

WATERTON
HERITAGE CENTRE

ROCKY MOUNTAIN
FOOD MART

ZUM'S

WATERTON AVE

Cameron
Falls

OPERA HOUSE

RCMP

CAMERON FALLS DR

HAREBELL RD

WINDFLOWER AVE

Carthew-Alderson Trail

Cameron Creek

FALLS
THEATRE

NORTHLAND
LODGE

VIMY AVE

Waterton Lakeshore Trail
and Bertha Lake Trail

TOWNSITE

Upper Waterton Lake

0   200 yds

0   200 m

Cameron
Bay

© AVALON TRAVEL

WATERTON LAKES

of local interest books. The heritage center is operated by the Waterton Natural History Association, which runs a variety of educational programs.

From the heritage center, wander south along the lakeshore to a large picnic area and the trailhead for the **Waterton Lakeshore Trail,** or north to the **International Peace Park Pavilion** and stunning views across Emerald Bay to the Prince of Wales Hotel.

◀ AKAMINA PARKWAY

This road, snow free May-October, starts in the town site and switchbacks up into the Cameron Creek Valley, making an elevation gain of 400 meters (1,310 feet) before ending after 16 kilometers (10 miles) at Cameron Lake. The viewpoint one kilometer (0.6 mile) from the junction of the park road is on a tight curve, so park off the road. From this lookout, views extend over the town site and the **Bear's Hump,**

The Red Rock Canyon Parkway leads through wildflower meadows.

which was originally part of a high ridge that extended across the lake to Vimy Peak (glacial action ultimately wore down the rest of the ridge). This section of the road is also a good place to view bighorn sheep. Between here and Cameron Lake are several picnic areas and stops of interest, including the site of Alberta's first producing oil well and, a little farther along the road, the site of **Oil City,** the town that never was.

Cameron Lake, at the end of the road, is a 2.5-kilometer-long (1.6-mile-long) subalpine lake that reaches depths of more than 40 meters (130 feet). It lies in a large cirque carved out about 11,000 years ago by a receding glacier. Mount Custer, at the southern end of the lake, is in Montana. Waterton has no glaciers, but Herbst Glacier on Mount Custer can be seen from here. To the west (right) of Custer is **Forum Peak** (2,225 meters/7,300 feet), whose summit cairn marks the boundaries of Alberta, Montana, and British Columbia.

Beside the lakeshore are enclosed information boards and a concession stand (7:30am-7:30pm daily June-Aug.) selling light snacks and renting kayaks ($28 s, $30 d per hour) as well as canoes, rowboats, and paddleboats (all $30 for the first hour, $20 for additional hours). A narrow trail leads along the lake's west shoreline, ending after 1.5 kilometers (0.9 mile) at a viewing platform surrounded by cow parsnip; allow 30 minutes each way. Take notice of bear warnings for this trail, as it ends in prime grizzly habitat.

RED ROCK CANYON PARKWAY

The best roadside wildlife viewing within the park is along this 13-kilometer (eight-mile) road that starts near the golf course and finishes at **Red Rock Canyon.** It is generally open May-October, depending on snow cover. The transition between rolling prairies and mountains takes place abruptly as you travel up the

Blakiston Valley. Black bears (and very occasionally grizzly bears) can be seen feeding on saskatoon berries along the open slopes to the north. **Mount Blakiston** (2,920 meters/9,580 feet), the park's highest summit, is visible from a viewpoint three kilometers (1.9 miles) along the road. The road passes interpretive signs, picnic areas, and Crandell Mountain Campground. At the end of the road is Red Rock Canyon, a water-carved gorge where the bedrock, known as argillite, contains a high concentration of iron. The iron oxidizes and turns red when exposed to air—the rock literally rusts. A short interpretive trail leads along the canyon.

CHIEF MOUNTAIN INTERNATIONAL HIGHWAY

This 25-kilometer (15.5-mile) highway, part of Highway 6, borders the eastern boundaries of the park and joins it to Glacier National Park in Montana. It starts east of the park gate at **Maskinonge Lake** and climbs for seven kilometers (4.3 miles) to a viewpoint where many jagged peaks and the entrance to Waterton Valley can be seen. The road then rounds **Sofa Mountain,** which still bears the scars from a wildfire that swept up its lower slopes in 1998.

To the south, the distinctive peak is **Chief Mountain,** which has been separated from the main mountain range by erosion. The road then passes the Belly River Campground and climbs to the **border crossing** of Chief Mountain. Hours of operation at this port of entry are 9am-6pm daily mid-May-end of May and early September-end of September, 7am-10pm daily June-early September. When the post is closed, you must use the Carway/Piegan port of entry (7am-11pm daily year-round). It's on Alberta Highway 2 south of Cardston (or on U.S. Highway 89 north of St. Mary in Montana, depending on your direction of travel).

From the border, it's 50 kilometers (31 miles) to St. Mary and the spectacular Going-to-the-Sun Highway through **Glacier National Park.** Stop by the park's **St. Mary Visitor Center** (406/888-7800, 8am-5pm daily mid-May-June and Sept.-mid-Oct., 8am-9pm daily July and Aug.). A good source of pretrip information is the official park website (www.nps.gov/glac). If you are crossing the border into Canada from the south, your initial impression of the park will be misleading, as this section lacks the high peaks and impressive lakes farther west, near the town site.

Recreation

HIKING

You can soak up the park's beauty along the scenic drives, but you'll be cheating yourself if you don't walk at least one trail. While the park does have its fair share of uphill slogs, don't be too daunted by the surrounding mountains—there are also some pleasant walks that everyone can enjoy, including the trail along Cameron Lake.

Although the park is relatively small, its trail system is extensive; 224 kilometers (140 miles) of well-maintained trails lead to alpine lakes

and lofty summits affording spectacular views. One of the most appealing aspects of hiking in Waterton is that with higher trailheads than other parks in the Canadian Rockies, the tree line is reached quickly. Most of the lakes can be reached in a few hours. Once you've finished hiking the trails in Waterton, you can cross the international border and start on the 1,200 kilometers (746 miles) of trails in Glacier National Park.

The eight hikes detailed comprise only a small cross section of Waterton's extensive trail system. The popular *Canadian Rockies Trail Guide,* sold in local stores, includes a chapter detailing all hikes. Government topographic maps (one map covers the entire park) are available at the Waterton Heritage Centre, but the best map for hikers is the Gem Trek version, also widely available. If you are planning to stay overnight in the backcountry, you must obtain a permit ($10 per person per night) from Waterton Visitor Centre or the park administration office.

Bear's Hump

• Length: 1.2 kilometers/0.7 mile (40 minutes) one-way
• Elevation gain: 225 meters/740 feet
• Rating: moderate
• Trailhead: Waterton Visitor Centre

This is one of the most popular short hikes in the park, and although steep, it affords panoramic views of the Waterton Valley. From the back of the visitors center parking lot, the trail switchbacks up the northern flanks of the Bear's Hump, finishing at a rocky ledge high above town. From this vantage point, the sweeping view extends north and east across the prairies and south along Upper Waterton Lake to Glacier National Park.

Bertha Lake

• Length: 5.8 kilometers/3.6 miles (2 hours) one-way
• Elevation gain: 460 meters/1,510 feet
• Rating: moderate
• Trailhead: south side of the town site along Evergreen Avenue

Bertha Lake is a popular destination with day hikers and campers alike. For the first 1.5 kilometers (0.9 mile), moderate elevation gain is made to a lookout point and the junction of the Waterton Lakeshore Trail. Then the trail branches right and levels off

for just over one kilometer (0.6 mile) to **Lower Bertha Falls.** While many casual hikers turn around at this point, you should plan on continuing to the final destination. It's uphill all the way, as the trail crosses an old avalanche slope before switchbacking up through a subalpine forest to its maximum elevation on a ridge above the hanging valley in which Bertha Lake lies. Filtered views of **Upper Bertha Falls** provide an excuse for a break along the way. From the trail's high point, it's a short walk down to the lakeshore, from where you can continue along either shoreline or just relax under the trees with a picnic lunch. The lake itself is beautiful, both for its dark turquoise coloring and backdrop of mountain peaks.

Waterton Lakeshore

• Length: 14 kilometers/8.7 miles (4 hours) one-way
• Elevation gain: minimal
• Rating: moderate
• Trailhead: south side of the town site along Evergreen Avenue

This trail follows the heavily forested western shores of Upper Waterton Lake across the international boundary to **Goat Haunt, Montana,** linking up with more than 1,200 kilometers (746 miles) of trails in Glacier National Park. Many hikers take the Waterton Shoreline Cruise Company's **MV International** (403/859-2362, June-Sept. only, $18) one way and hike the other. Starting from town, the first 1.5 kilometers (0.9 mile) climb steadily to a lookout point high above the lake, then the hike branches left off the Bertha Lake Trail, descending to Bertha Bay. The boat dock at Boundary Bay, six kilometers (3.7 miles) from town, is a good place for lunch. Hikers heading south and planning to camp in Glacier National Park must register at the Waterton Visitor Centre.

Crypt Lake

- Length: 8.7 kilometers/5.4 miles (3-4 hours) one-way
- Elevation gain: 680 meters/2,230 feet
- Rating: moderate/difficult
- Trailhead: Crypt Landing; access is by boat. The **Crypt Lake Shuttle** (403/859-2362, June-Sept., $20 round-trip) leaves the marina at 9am and 10am daily for Crypt Landing; return trips depart at 4pm and 5:30pm.

This is one of the most spectacular day hikes in Canada. Access to the trailhead on the eastern side of Upper Waterton Lake is by boat. The trail switchbacks for 2.5 kilometers (1.6 miles) past a series of waterfalls and continues steeply up to a small green lake before reaching a campground. The final ascent to Crypt Lake from the campground causes the most problems, especially for those who suffer from claustrophobia or acrophobia. A ladder on the cliff face leads into a natural tunnel that you must crawl through on your hands and knees. The next part of the trail is along a narrow precipice with a cable for support. The lake at the end of the trail, nestled in a hanging valley, is no disappointment. Its dark green waters are rarely free of floating ice, and the steep walls of the cirque rise more than 500 meters (1,640 feet) above the lake on three sides. The international boundary is at the southern end of the lake. A good way to avoid the crowds on this trail is to camp at the dock and set out before the first boat arrives in the morning.

Crandell Lake

- Length: 2.4 kilometers/1.5 miles (40 minutes) one-way
- Elevation gain: 120 meters/395 feet
- Rating: easy
- Trailhead: Crandell Campground, Red Rock Canyon Parkway

This easy hike to a subalpine lake is popular with campers staying at Crandell Campground. Alternatively, the trailhead can be reached by noncampers along the Canyon Church Camp access road.

The lake can also be accessed from a trailhead seven kilometers (4.3 miles) west of town along the Akamina Parkway. This trail is shorter (0.8 km/0.5 mi) and follows a wagon road that was cut through the valley to Oil City.

Goat Lake

- Length: 6.7 kilometers/4.2 miles (2 hours) one-way
- Elevation gain: 500 meters/1,640 feet
- Rating: moderate
- Trailhead: end of Red Rock Canyon Parkway, 18 kilometers (11.2 miles) from Waterton town site

The first hour of walking from the trailhead at Red Rock Canyon follows the Snowshoe Trail along **Bauerman Creek** before branching to the right and climbing switchbacks through a mixed forest. The steep gradient evens out as the trail enters the Goat Lake cirque. After the uphill slog, the lake is a welcome sight, its emerald-green waters reflecting the towering headwalls that surround it. Look for the lake's namesake on the open scree slopes west of the lake.

Carthew-Alderson

- Length: 20 kilometers/12.4 miles (6-7 hours) one-way
- Elevation gain: 650 meters/2,130 feet
- Rating: moderate/difficult
- Trailhead: end of Akamina Parkway, 16 kilometers (10 miles) from Waterton town site

This hike linking the end of the Akamina Parkway to Waterton town site can be completed in one long day or done with an overnight stop at Alderson Lake, 13 kilometers

KOOTENAI BROWN

John George Brown was born in England in the 1840s and reputedly educated at Oxford University. He joined the army and went to India, later continuing to San Francisco. Then, like thousands of others, he headed for the Cariboo goldfields of British Columbia, quickly spending any of the gold he found. After a while he moved on, heading east into Waterton Valley, where his party was attacked by a band of Blackfoot. He was shot in the back with an arrow and pulled it out himself. For a time he worked with the U.S. Army as a Pony Express rider. One day he was captured by Chief Sitting Bull, stripped, and tied to a stake until his fate could be decided, but he managed to escape during the night with his scalp intact. Brown acquired his nickname through his close association with the Kootenay (today's preferred spelling) people, hunting buf-falo and wolves with them until the animals had all but disappeared.

Brown married in 1869 and built a cabin by Upper Waterton Lake, becoming the valley's first permanent resident. Even though he had been toughened by the times, he was a conservationist at heart. When a reserve was set aside in 1895, Brown was employed as its first warden. In 1911, the area was declared a national park, and Brown, age 71, was appointed its superintendent. He continued to push for an expansion of park boundaries until his final retirement at age 75. He died a few years later. His final resting place is along the lakeshore—fitting for one of Canada's most celebrated mountain men. Look for the signed trail along the park access road; it's a five-minute walk from the road.

(eight miles) from the trailhead. The trail leads through most of the climatic zones of the park and offers some of the best scenery to be had on any one hike. Transportation to the trailhead can be arranged through **Tamarack Outdoor Outfitters** (Mount View Rd., 403/859-2378, $15 one-way), which operates a hiker shuttle service to this and other trailheads in the park. From the Cameron Lake parking lot, the trail climbs four kilometers (2.5 miles) to **Summit Lake,** a worthy destination in itself. The trail then forks to the left and climbs steeply to Carthew Ridge. After rising above the tree line and crossing a scree slope, the trail reaches its highest elevation of 2,310 meters (7,580 feet) at **Carthew Summit.** The views from here are spectacular, even more so if you scramble up to one of Mount Carthew's lower peaks. To the north is a hint of prairie, to the southeast the magnificent bowl-shaped cirque around Cameron Lake. To the south, the Carthew Lakes lie directly below, while glaciated peaks in Montana line the horizon. From

this summit, the trail descends steeply to the Carthew Lakes, reenters the subalpine forest, and emerges at **Alderson Lake,** which is nestled under the headwalls of Mount Alderson. The trail then descends through the Carthew Creek Valley and finishes at Cameron Falls in the town site.

Vimy Peak

- Length: 12 kilometers/7.5 miles (5 hours) one-way
- Elevation gain: 825 meters/2,700 feet
- Rating: moderate
- Trailhead: Chief Mountain International Highway, 0.5 kilometer (0.3 mile) from the Highway 5 junction

Vimy Peak overlooks the town site from across Upper Waterton Lake. It was once part of a ridge that extended across the Waterton Valley and was worn down by the relentless forces of glacial action. The initial six-kilometer (3.7-mile) stretch is along the eastern bank of Lower Waterton Lake through forest and grassland.

WATERTON LAKES

The trail then continues along the lake to Bosporus Landing opposite the town or climbs steeply to Vimy Peak (2,379 meters/7,805 feet). The Vimy Peak Trail actually ends at a basin short of the summit, which is still a painfully steep 40-minute scramble away.

OTHER RECREATION
▮ Cruising to Goat Haunt, Montana

This is the most popular organized activity in Waterton. From the marina in downtown Waterton town site, **Waterton Shoreline Cruise Company** (403/859-2362) runs scheduled cruises across the international boundary to Goat Haunt, Montana, at the southern end of Upper Waterton Lake. The 45-minute trip along the lakeshore passes spectacular mountain scenery and usually wildlife. A half-hour stopover is made at Goat Haunt, which lies in a remote part of Glacier National Park and consists of little more than a dock and interpretive displays. You can return on the same boat or go hiking and return later in the day. If you are planning an overnight hike from here, you are required to register at the Waterton Visitor Centre before heading out on the lake. Another popular option is to take an early boat trip and walk back to town on the **Waterton Lakeshore Trail,** which takes about four hours. Departures are twice daily early May-June and September-early October and four times daily in July and August (first departure at 10am). Remember, you are crossing into another country on this cruise, so correct documentation is required, including for U.S. citizens. Early and late in the season, the border crossing is closed, and therefore the cruise doesn't include a landing. Tickets cost $40 round-trip (children are half price), and you'll need to book ahead in summer. The same company operates a regular shuttle service to the Crypt Lake trailhead for $20 round-trip.

Fishing

Fishing in the lakes is average, with most anglers chasing brook and rainbow trout, pike, and whitefish. A national park fishing license is required and can be obtained from the Waterton Visitor Centre or any of the administration offices. The license costs $10 for a single day or $35 for an annual permit.

Windsurfing

Winds of up to 70 kph (45 mph) attract hardcore windsurfers throughout summer and into fall. The winds are predominantly south to north, providing fast runs across Upper Waterton Lake from the beach at Cameron Bay. The lake is deep, keeping the water temperature low and making a wet suit necessary. Read the warning signs at the beach before heading out.

Scuba Diving

On any given summer day, scuba divers can be seen slipping into the frigid waters of **Emerald Bay.** A steamer was scuttled in the bay in 1918. It had been used to haul logs and as a tearoom but now sits on the lake's floor, attracting divers who find it a novelty to explore a sunken ship so far from the ocean. No equipment rental is available in the park. The closest is at **Awesome Adventures** (314 11th St. S., 403/328-5041) in Lethbridge, where you can also get your tanks filled. Full gear rental is $75 per day, $105 for the weekend, including air fills. Through this shop, certification courses and field trips to Waterton Lakes are organized throughout the summer. Stop in on your way to the park for a rundown on all the dives, or ask at the Waterton Visitor Centre.

Golfing

The rolling fairways and spectacular mountain backdrop of **Waterton Lakes Golf Course** (403/859-2114) can distract even the most serious golfer's attention. The 18-hole

The MV *International* cruises across the border to Montana.

© ANDREW HEMPSTEAD

course, designed by Stanley Thompson and dating to 1929, is not particularly long (6,103 yards) or difficult, but the surrounding mountains and unhurried pace of play make for a pleasant environment. The course is four kilometers (2.5 miles) north of the town site on the main access road and is open June–early October. A round of golf costs $49. Club rentals are $9-25, and a power cart is an additional $34 per round. At the end of your round, plan on relaxing at the clubhouse over a light meal and cold drink.

Horseback Riding

Just off the main park access road before town is **Alpine Stables** (403/859-2462), which offers hour-long trail rides (starting on the hour 9am-5pm) for $35. Two-hour rides cost $60 and pass through prime wildlife-viewing habitat. The three-hour ride, costing $80, takes in the bison paddock, while eight hours in the saddle opens up possibilities such as a climb to the summit

of Vimy Peak ($145). These longer rides leave on demand, so call ahead to make a reservation.

Winter Recreation

Winter is a quiet time in the park. Traffic on the roads is light, the Prince of Wales Hotel sits empty, the snowcapped peaks and abundant big game provide plenty of photographic opportunities, and a few trails are maintained for cross-country skiing. The main access road is plowed regularly, and the Akamina Parkway is cleared to allow access to ski trails. Skiing in the park is usually possible December-March, but conditions can change dramatically. Cold arctic fronts scream down from the north, and chinook winds from the west can raise temperatures by up to 20°C (68°F) in an hour. Ski trails are set on weekends, and the ski-touring opportunities are endless. Trails in the backcountry are not marked. Groups should carry avalanche beacons, be capable of self-rescue, and register with the warden before setting out.

Ice climbing, snowshoeing, and backcountry winter camping are also popular. Winter camping is possible at Pass Creek, where you'll find a kitchen shelter, woodstove, and pit toilets. Three accommodations stay open year-round and offer all-inclusive winter packages. Gas may or may not be available in winter.

Obtain trail information and weather forecasts at the park administration office (Mount View Rd., 403/859-2224, 8am-4pm Mon.-Fri. year-round). For information regarding backcountry skiing conditions and avalanche danger, contact the **Canadian Avalanche Association** (250/837-2435, www.avalanche.ca).

Entertainment and Events

Roasting marshmallows at your campsite, sitting around a roaring fire at your lodge, listening to a park interpretive program, or going for a moonlit walk along the lakeshore—these are the best ways to spend your evenings, and they can all be yours at no charge.

Interpretive programs typically begin in late June and run through to the first weekend of September. The subject matter changes from year to year, but you can rely on interesting, interactive topics that mix learning with fun. Presentations at the **Falls Theatre** (in town, across the road from Cameron Falls) and at Crandell Theatre (Crandell Campground) usually begin nightly at 8pm, with guest speakers appearing at the Falls Theatre Saturday night. Ask at the Waterton Visitor Centre (403/859-5133) for a printed schedule.

Waterton's few bars and lounges are all affiliated with lodgings. **Wolf's Den Lounge** (Waterton Lakes Lodge, corner of Windflower Ave. and Cameron Falls Rd., 403/859-2151) is more modern and has big-screen TVs and bands on high-season weekends. Being the biggest and most central bar in town, the **Thirsty Bear Saloon** (Bayshore Inn, Waterton Ave., 403/859-2211, 11am-2am daily) gets crowded with young seasonal workers. It pours happy hour 3pm-6pm daily, and a band plays two or three nights a week. In the Prince of Wales Hotel, the staid **Windsor Lounge** (403/859-2231) has panoramic views across the lake and live entertainment most summer nights. **Waterton Lakes Opera House** (309 Windflower Ave., 403/859-2466) shows movies daily at 7:30 and 9:30pm.

Accommodations and Camping

If you're camping, grab a campsite as early in the day as possible. If you're staying in an accommodation, you'll find them all within Waterton town site and within walking distance of everywhere. Upon arrival in town, if it's too early to check in, spend some time exploring the downtown core and lakefront on foot.

HOTELS, MOTELS, AND LODGES

Waterton has a limited number of accommodations. Most start opening in May and by mid-October are closed, with only the hostel, Crandell Mountain Lodge, and Waterton Glacier Suites open year-round. All accommodations are within the town site, so walking to the marina and shops isn't a problem.

Finding a room on short notice shouldn't be

WATERTON LAKES

too difficult in May, June, and September, but for July and August call as early as possible.

$50-100

One block from the main street, the **Bear Mountain Motel** (208 Mount View Rd., 403/859-2366, www.bearmountainmotel. com, mid-May-Sept., $99 s or d, with kitchenette from $139) is an older park-at-your-door 34-unit motel with basic furnishings and no phones.

$100-150

Northland Lodge (Evergreen Ave., 403/859-2353, www.northlandlodgecanada.com, early May-early Oct., $135-215) is a converted house that backs onto wilderness. It was built in 1929 by Louis Hill, who also built the Prince of Wales Hotel. Cameron Falls and downtown Waterton are both just a short walk away. It features nine guest rooms, a large lounge with a TV and fireplace, wireless Internet, and a large balcony. The two rooms that share a bathroom are $135 s or d, while all others have en suites. Some have fridges; rates include tea, coffee, and muffins in the morning.

 ◖**Crandell Mountain Lodge** (Mount View Rd., 403/859-2288 or 866/859-2288, www. crandellmountainlodge.com, $145-240) is a centrally located country-style inn. The lodge has seen many changes since it first opened in 1940 with shared bathrooms and wood-heated water. Today each of the 17 rooms has a private bath and is beautifully finished with smart furnishings (no phones), and out back is a private garden area. Two rooms are wheelchair accessible. The smallest rooms are $145 s or d, most—with a choice of fireplace or kitchenette—are $175, and the largest suites are $240. Rates are reduced around 30 percent mid-September-early June.

$150-200

For families, **Aspen Village Inn** (111 Windflower Ave., 403/859-2255 or 888/859-8669, www.theaspenvillageinn.com, May-mid-Oct., $155-250 s or d) is an excellent choice. For starters, the rooms are super spacious, but there's also a playground and a picnic area. Grown-ups aren't forgotten—the outdoor hot tub is the perfect place to soak weary bones. Accommodations are in two wings and multiroom cottages. The latter range from one bedroom, no kitchen to three bedrooms and a kitchen. Lodge rooms are also offered in different configurations, such as, for example, a two-bedroom kitchen-equipped unit ($250).

At the **Bayshore Inn** (Waterton Ave., 403/859-2211 or 888/527-9555, www.bayshoreinn.com, early May-early Oct., $199-282 s or d), you're paying for a prime waterfront location rather than a memorable room. On-site amenities include a hot tub, restaurant, café, and pub. For the first and last months of the season, the Bayshore offers excellent meal-inclusive packages for the same price as their summertime, room-only rates.

Over $200

 ◖**Waterton Glacier Suites** (Windflower Ave., 403/859-2004 or 866/621-3330, www. watertonsuites.com, $232-292 s or d) is open year-round and provides excellent value. Each of 26 units features stylish, modern decor that hints at Western, is air-conditioned, and offers a fridge and microwave. Options include two-bedroom suites ($232), units with a jetted tub and fireplace ($272), and spacious loft units ($292). Off-season rates range $109-169.

Modern **Waterton Lakes Lodge** (corner of Windflower Ave. and Cameron Falls Rd., 403/859-2151 or 866/985-6343, www.watertonlakeslodge.com, Apr.-Oct., $205-285 s or d) is on a 1.5-hectare (3.7-acre) site in the heart of town. All 80 rooms are large and modern, and each has mountain-themed decor and mountain views. In-room amenities include air-conditioning, a TV/VCR combination, Internet access, and a coffeemaker. The complex also holds the Waterton Health Club (free entry for guests), a tiered restaurant, a small café, and a lounge with big-screen TVs. Check the website for steeply discounted off-season rates.

Waterton's best-known landmark is the **Prince of Wales Hotel** (403/236-3400 or 406/892-2525, www.glacierparkinc.com, mid-May–mid-Sept., $234-299 s or d), a seven-story gabled structure built in 1927 on a hill overlooking Upper Waterton Lake. It was another grand mountain resort financed by the railway, except, unlike those in Banff and Jasper, it had no rail link and has always been U.S.-owned. It was built as part of a chain of first-class hotels in Glacier National Park and is still owned by the company that controls those south of the border. Early guests were transported to the hotel by bus from the Great Northern Railway in Montana. After extensive restoration inside and out, the hotel has been returned to its former splendor, best appreciated by standing in the lobby area and gazing out across the lake and up into the exposed timber-frame ceiling. Off the lobby you'll find a restaurant, lounge, and gift shop. Rates for the smallest (and they're small) value rooms are $235 s or d; standard rooms start at $290. The opulence and history of this hotel are unequaled in Waterton, but don't expect the facilities of a similarly priced city hostelry: Rooms have no television, and value rooms on the upper floors have no elevator access.

CAMPGROUNDS

If you want to enjoy the warm summer nights of southern Alberta, you will find several options for camping within and around the park.

Park Campgrounds

Waterton Lakes National Park has three campgrounds holding 391 campsites. Reservations are taken for some sites at the main Townsite Campground through the **Parks Canada**

Campground Reservation Service (877/737-3783, www.pccamping.ca). The three campgrounds detailed below are open only in summer. The rest of the year, camping is allowed at the Pass Creek day-use area, along the park access road.

The most popular camping spot—thanks to a central location and top-notch amenities—is the **Townsite Campground** (mid-Apr.–mid-Oct.), within walking distance of the lake, trailheads, restaurants, and shops. Many of its more than 238 sites have power, water, and sewer hookups. The campground also offers showers and kitchen shelters. Walk-in tent sites are $23, unserviced sites $28, hookups $39. The quota of unreserved sites fills quickly each day (especially in July and August), so to ensure a spot, try to time your arrival before check-out time (11am).

The 129 sites at **Crandell Campground** (mid-May–early Sept., $23 per site), 10 kilometers (6.2 miles) from the town site on Red Rock Canyon Parkway, are sprinkled through a lightly forested area of the valley bottom. This campground has flush toilets and kitchen shelters but no hookups. Pleasant Crandell Lake is an easy 2.4-kilometer (1.5-mile) walk from the southwest corner of the campground.

Belly River Campground (mid-May–early Sept., $17 per site), 26 kilometers (16 miles) from the town site along Chief Mountain International Highway, is the smallest (24 sites) and most primitive of the park's developed campgrounds. Located beside a shallow, slow-moving body of water, facilities are limited to pit toilets, a kitchen shelter, and drinking water.

Campfires are not allowed at the Townsite Campground, but at the other two facilities, an $8 fire permit includes unlimited wood.

Waterton also holds 12 backcountry campgrounds. Each has pit toilets, a cook shelter, and a water supply. Open fires are discouraged and are prohibited during periods of high fire danger; check with a warden. If you are planning to camp in the backcountry, you must obtain a Wilderness Use Permit from the Waterton Visitor Centre or the administration office. Permits are $10 per person per night. Half of all sites can be reserved in advance. If your planned backcountry itinerary takes you over the border, ask at the information center about border-crossing regulations.

Commercial Campgrounds

You're a little way from the action at the commercial campgrounds outside the park, but the wider range of facilities (especially if you have a young family) and the peace of mind in being able to reserve a site with hookups make them a viable alternative.

Waterton Springs Campground (3 km/1.9 mi north of the park gate on Hwy. 6, 403/859-2247 or 866/859-2247, www.watertonspringscamping.com, late May-Sept., tent sites $18, hookups $20-35) centers around a large facility building holding modern bathrooms, a lounge, a general store, and a laundry room. Also on-site is a playground and a fishing pond stocked with rainbow trout. Some sites are a fair walk from the main bathrooms.

On Highway 5, six kilometers (3.7 miles) east of the park gate, is **Crooked Creek Campground** (403/653-1100, May-Sept., $25-29), operated by the not-for-profit Waterton Natural History Association. The sites are close together, so it's best suited to RVs.

Family fun is the order of the day at the ❰ **Great Canadian Barn Dance Campground** (Wynder Rd., Hill Spring, 403/626-3407 or 866/626-3407, www.greatcanadianbarndance.com, May-Oct., unserviced sites $28, hookups $32-38), a converted farm lying 40 minutes along rural roads from the park. As the name suggests, the action revolves around a Saturday evening barn dance, held in an authentic barn. A casual roast beef dinner is included in the admission of adult $42, child $12.50. Although the facility is busiest on weekends, you can camp through the week, with activities such as swimming and canoeing to keep the young ones happy. To get there from Waterton, head 18 kilometers (11 miles) east on Highway 5, 21 kilometers (13 miles) north on Highway 800, and then 1.6 kilometers (one mile) east on Highway 505 to Wynder Road.

Food

When it's time to eat, the park offers everything from meals to fit the most austere budget to fine dining. Unless you're planning a meal at the Prince of Wales, the dress code in park restaurants is casual.

If you plan on cooking your own food, stock up before you get to the park. Groceries are available at the **Rocky Mountain Food Mart** (Windflower Ave., 403/859-2526, 8am-10pm daily) while **Tamarack Outdoor Outfitters** (Mount View Rd., 403/859-2378, 8am-8pm daily) has light snacks and lunches for hikers and picnickers.

CAFÉS AND CHEAP EATS

Waterton has a smattering of coffee shops and small cafés. **Waterton Bagel & Coffee Co.** (in the theater building on the corner of Windflower Ave. and Cameron Falls Dr., 403/859-2211, 7am-9:30pm daily) brews up the best coffee in town.

Pizza of Waterton (305 Windflower Ave., 403/859-2660, 5pm-10pm Mon.-Fri., noon-10pm Sat.-Sun.) dishes up the best—okay, the only—pizza in town. It's actually pretty good, piled high with toppings of your choice. A 12-inch (good for two) costs $25, beer is $6, and there's a choice of wines for under $28 per bottle. Eat inside, at the picnic tables out front, or take your order back to your campsite.

AFTERNOON TEA

Afternoon tea is a tradition at the landmark **Prince of Wales Hotel** (403/859-2231, 2pm-5pm daily, $38), but it's an overpriced one. Still, it's popular, especially with the tour-bus crowd that stays at the hotel as an extension of a tour through adjacent Glacier National Park. Sure, it's tasty and memorable—think finger sandwiches, pastries and cakes, tea, coffee, and other beverages served up on white linen at tables with the best view in town—but it's not cheap.

RESTAURANTS

Along the main street, the selection of places to eat is varied, but none are outstanding. If you're looking for a decent family restaurant, **Zum's** (116 Waterton Ave., 403/859-2388, 8am-9pm daily, $18-35) is a good choice. The burgers are tasty and come in all forms (including with buffalo patties) for around $10, with fries extra. The dinner menu includes varied preparations of chicken, seafood, and beef for $16-33. Wash it all down with a milk shake ($6).

Bel Lago (113 Waterton Ave., 403/859-2213, 11am-10pm daily, $21-33) offers satisfying pastas and traditional Italian dishes such as osso bucco, with as many tables outside as in.

The **Kootenai Brown Dining Room** (Bayshore Inn, 403/859-2211, 7am-10pm daily,

$21-32) has predictable hotel dining, with a menu to suit all tastes. The lake views through the dining room windows make this place that much more enjoyable. In July and August, a breakfast buffet costs $18.

The big windows at the **Royal Stewart Dining Room** (403/859-2231, 11:30am-2pm and 5pm-9:30pm daily in summer, $27-40), a formal restaurant in the Prince of Wales Hotel, allow you to gaze down along Upper Waterton Lake while soaking up an old-world elegance unequaled in the park. A simple breakfast buffet every morning (6:30am-10am, $21 per person) is worth attending for the views alone. The rest of the day, the menu is mostly old-fashioned, but with choices like charbroiled pork chop smothered in a Saskatoon berry and gorgonzola sauce, no one complains. Prices are similar to any big-city restaurant of the same standard—for dinner, expect to pay around $120 for two without alcoholic drinks and tip. If you are going to splurge, do it here.

OUTSIDE THE PARK

You'll pass **Twin Butte Country General Store** (Hwy. 6, 16 km/10 mi north of the park entrance, 403/627-4035, 10am-8pm daily, $9-22) on the road between Pincher Creek and the park. Rather than just a general store as the name suggests, it is home to a friendly little café serving up inexpensive Mexican dishes and local specialties such as elk burgers.

WATERTON LAKES

Information and Services

On the main access road opposite the Prince of Wales Hotel, the **Waterton Visitor Centre** (403/859-5133, 9am-5pm daily May and early Sept., 9am-8pm daily June-Aug.) provides general information on the park, sells fishing licenses, and issues Wilderness Use Permits. The park's administration office on Mount View Road (403/859-2224, 8am-4pm weekdays year-round) offers the same services as the visitors center. For more information on the park, write to Superintendent, Waterton Lakes National Park, Waterton Park, AB T0K 2M0. The Parks Canada website is www.pc.gc.ca. For general tourist information, the local chamber of commerce website, www.mywaterton.com, provides plenty of current information and links to accommodations.

BOOKS AND MAPS

Tamarack Outdoor Outfitters (Mount View Rd., 403/859-2378, 8am-8pm daily) has a section devoted to books, with field and recreation guides dominating. The **Waterton Natural History Association,** based in the Waterton Heritage Centre (117 Waterton Ave., 403/859-2624, 10am-5pm daily May and Sept., 10am-8pm daily July-Aug.), stocks every book ever written about the park (except this one), as well as many titles pertaining to western Canada in general.

Although the free park maps handed out at the Waterton Visitor Centre suffice for hiking any of the trails detailed in this book, I highly recommend picking up the Gem Trek map, which puts the varied topography in perspective and helps identify natural features of note.

SHOPPING AND SERVICES

The numerous tourist-oriented gift shops along Waterton Avenue are worth browsing through when the weather isn't cooperating. **Tamarack Outdoor Outfitters** (Mount View Rd., 403/859-2378, 8am-8pm daily) is a five-generation family business that stocks a little of everything. Here you'll find a good range of outdoor clothing and equipment, fishing tackle, books, a currency exchange, and picnic supplies.

Waterton has no banks, but travelers checks are accepted at most businesses, and **ATMs** are scattered throughout town.

The **post office** is beside the fire station on Fountain Avenue. A **laundry** on Windflower Avenue is open 8am-10pm daily.

The closest **hospitals** are in Cardston (403/653-4411) and Pincher Creek (403/627-3333). The park's 24-hour emergency number is 403/859-2636. For the **RCMP,** call 403/859-2244.

WATERTON LAKES

Getting There and Around

GETTING THERE

Waterton Lakes National Park is in the far southwest corner of Alberta, a three-hour drive south from Calgary along Highway 2 and around four hours from Banff. The nearest city (and airport) is Lethbridge, 140 kilometers (87 miles) to the northeast. The airport at Lethbridge is served by Air Canada's regional connector and has Budget, Hertz, and National rental cars. The closest **Greyhound** buses come to the park is Pincher Creek, 50 kilometers (31 miles) away. From the depot (1015 Hewetson St., 403/627-2716), a cab to the park (call **Crystal Taxi,** 403/627-4262) will run around $100 each way.

GETTING AROUND

Tamarack Outdoor Outfitters (Mount View Rd., 403/859-2378, www.watertonvisitorservices.com) operates hiker shuttle services to various trailheads within the park. Cameron Lake, the starting point for the Carthew-Alderson Trail (which ends back in town), is a popular drop-off point; $15 one-way. You could take one of these shuttles, then return on the bus later in the day if driving the steep mountain roads doesn't appeal to you. The company also offers a shuttle along the Chief Mountain International Highway.

Pat's (Mount View Rd., 403/859-2266) rents mountain bikes for $10 for the first hour, then $7 per hour thereafter, to a maximum of $45 per day. Motorized scooters are $35 per hour or $135 per day.

© ANDREW HEMPSTEAD

Rent a bike to explore the Waterton townsite and lakeshore.

WATERTON LAKES

Nearby Parks

◖ AKAMINA-KISHINENA PROVINCIAL PARK

Bordering Waterton Lakes National Park (Alberta) and Glacier National Park (Montana, United States), this remote tract of 10,922 hectares (27,000 acres) protects the extreme southeastern corner of British Columbia. The park is named for its two main waterways, which flow southward into Montana from the Flathead Basin. This was the main reason for the park's creation, because now, alongside Waterton Lakes National Park, entire watersheds of Glacier National Park are protected.

The landscape has changed little in thousands of years, since the Kootenay rested in the open meadows beside Kishinena Creek before crossing the Continental Divide to hunt bison on the prairies. The park supports a healthy population of grizzly bears, along with other endangered species such as wolverines, wolves, and lynx.

The only access is on foot from one of two trailheads. The longer option is from the end of an unsealed road that leaves Highway 3 at 16 kilometers (10 miles) south of Fernie, British Columbia. The road leads 110 kilometers (68 miles) into the Flathead River Valley, where trails climb along Kishinena then Akamina Creek into the park.

Access from Waterton Lakes National Park

The most popular and easiest access to the park is by hiking trail from the Akamina Parkway in Waterton Lakes National Park (Alberta). The signposted trailhead is 15 kilometers (9.3 miles) along this road from Waterton town site. From the parkway, the trail gains 110 meters (360 feet) of elevation in 1.5 kilometers (0.9 mile) before reaching the boundary of the park high atop the Continental Divide. After a further

700 meters (0.4 mile), the trail divides. The closest of two subalpine bodies of water, **Forum Lake,** is 2.2 kilometers (1.4 miles) to the left up a tedious ascent of Forum Creek. Colorful meadows surround the lake's outlet, while a layered headwall provides a stunning backdrop. Allow 1.5 hours for this 4.4-kilometer (2.7-mile) hike. Nestled below Akamina Ridge, **Wall Lake** is straight ahead from the junction, 2.7 kilometers (1.7 miles). This trail gains only minimal elevation and passes Akamina Creek Campground.

Campgrounds

The park's only facility is **Akamina Creek Campground,** accessible on foot 2.4 kilometers (1.5 miles) from the Akamina Parkway along the trail to Wall Lake. In a forest of Engelmann spruce, each of 10 sites has a picnic table and fire pit; $6 per night.

BEAUVAIS LAKE PROVINCIAL PARK

Located just north of Waterton (access is via a 20-kilometer (12.4-mile) road heading southwest from Pincher Creek, Beauvais Lake Provincial Park is a wilderness area with a rich history of early settlement. Foundations of buildings are all that remain of the first homesteaders' efforts to survive in what was then a remote location. The park's most famous settler was James Whitford, one of General Custer's scouts at the famous Battle of Little Bighorn. He is buried at Scott's Point, accessed from the end of the road along the lake's north side. Most of the 18-kilometer (11.2-mile) network of hiking trails are at the other end of the lake, including a short walk to a beaver pond. The lake is also good for boating and is stocked annually with rainbow and brown trout. The main campground (403/382-4097, $17-23 per site), at the lake's western end, is open year-round. It's fairly primitive (pit toilets, no showers), with just a few powered sites. If you're tent camping, continue beyond the summer cabins to a group of roadside walk-in sites.

ELK LAKES PROVINCIAL PARK

This park encompasses more than 17,000 hectares (42,000 acres) of rugged wilderness along the British Columbia side of the Canadian Rockies. The park lies adjacent to the southern border of Peter Lougheed Provincial Park in Alberta, but the only road access is from Highway 3, more than 120 kilometers (75 miles) to the south. Head north for 35 kilometers (22 miles) from Sparwood, between Cranbrook and the Alberta border, on a paved road to **Elkford,** then take an unpaved forestry road 67 kilometers (42 miles) farther north into the park.

The end of the road, where you'll find a kiosk with a park map and up-to-date trail conditions, is the park's main trailhead. From this point, it's an easy one kilometer (0.6 mile) to **Lower Elk Lake** and then another kilometer beyond the end of the lake to **Upper Elk Lake.** At the lower lake, a narrow trail climbs to a lookout. Aside from the long drive in, the ratio of effort to reward in reaching these lakes is unmatched in the Canadian Rockies. The stunningly beautiful upper lake is surrounded by steep snowcapped peaks, and several avalanche paths end right at water's edge. Fishing in the lower lake is productive for Dolly Varden and cutthroat trout.

Information and Services

The park has no facilities. The nearest town is Elkford (pop. 2,200), a small coal-mining community 67 kilometers (42 miles) south. The community has few services, but there's a small **municipal campground** within walking distance of downtown (www.elkfordcampground.com, $23 with hookups). The **Elkford Visitor Info Centre** (Front St., 250/865-4614 or 877/355-9453, www.tourismelkford.ca) is a good source of park information.

WATERTON LAKES

CALGARY

Calgary's nickname, Cowtown, is cherished by the city's one million residents, who prefer that romantic vision of their beloved home to the city's more modern identity as a world energy and financial center. The city's rapid growth, from a North West Mounted Police (NWMP) post to a large and vibrant metropolis in little more than 100 years, can be credited largely to the effects of resource development, particularly oil and natural gas.

Once run by gentlemen who had made their fortunes in ranching, Calgary is still an important cattle market. But the oil and gas bonanzas of the 1940s, 1950s, and 1970s changed everything. The resources discovered throughout western Canada brought enormous wealth and growth to the city, turning it into the headquarters for a burgeoning energy industry. With the city's rapid growth comes all the problems plaguing major cities around the world, with one major exception—the distinct lack of manufacturing and industrial sites means there is little pollution.

Downtown is a massive cluster of modern steel-and-glass skyscrapers, the legacy of an explosion of wealth in the 1970s, with cranes once again making their appearance as new commercial projects totaling over $1 billion are currently under construction. Set in this futuristic mirage on the prairie are banks, insurance companies, investment companies, and the head offices of hundreds of oil companies. But not

HIGHLIGHTS

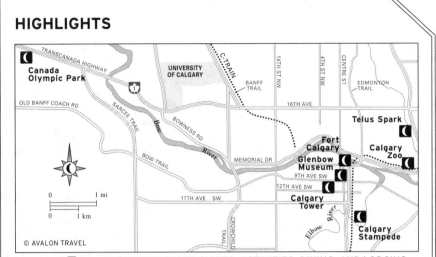

© AVALON TRAVEL

LOOK FOR ◖ TO FIND RECOMMENDED SIGHTS, ACTIVITIES, DINING, AND LODGING.

◖ **Calgary Tower:** It's not the city's tallest building, but from the observation deck you get a wonderful idea of Cowtown's layout, making this a great first stop on your sightseeing itinerary (page 291).

◖ **Glenbow Museum:** One of Canada's finest private museums, the Glenbow is renowned for its coverage of native history, and the new *Mavericks* display will entrance even non-museum types (page 294).

◖ **Telus Spark:** If it's indoor weather (or even if it's not), this bright, modern museum is the place to spend time with younger children (page 294).

◖ **Fort Calgary:** The site of Calgary's original riverside settlement has risen from the past to provide an insight into the hardships of the city's earliest residents (page 295).

◖ **Canada Olympic Park:** Follow in the footsteps of Eddie the Eagle and the Jamaican bobsled team at the site of the 1988 Winter Olympic Games (page 296).

◖ **Calgary Zoo:** Yes, you'll see all the usual suspects (hippos, kangaroos, gorillas), but also a wide range of Canadian mammals—including some you don't want to meet in the wild (page 297).

◖ **Calgary Stampede:** Few cities in the world are associated as closely with a festival as Calgary is with the Stampede, a 10-day, early July celebration of everything cowboy (page 303).

forgetting its roots, the city sets aside all the material success it's achieved as a boomtown each July to put on the greatest outdoor show on earth—the Calgary Stampede, a Western extravaganza second to none.

PLANNING YOUR TIME

For the vast majority of visitors arriving by air, Calgary International Airport is their first stop in Alberta, and it's straight off to the mountain national parks of Banff and Jasper. But even with a week in Alberta, it's worth scheduling a day in Calgary—maybe to settle in upon arrival, or to relax the day before flying out. Two major attractions within walking distance of downtown hotels are the **Calgary Tower** and the **Glenbow Museum,** both easily visited in a casual morning. With children in tow, replace

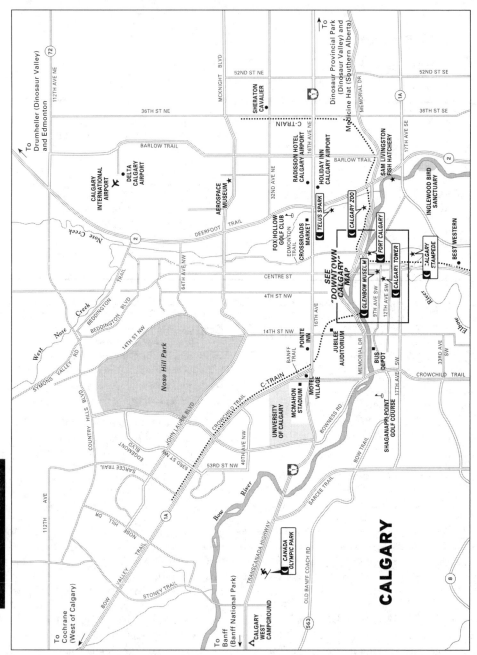

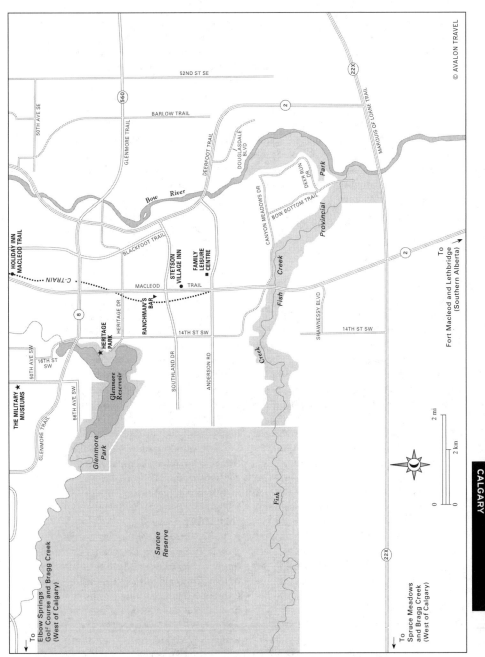

© AVALON TRAVEL

52ND ST SE

BARLOW TRAIL

GLENMORE TRAIL

50TH AVE SE

560

DEERFOOT TRAIL

DOUGLASDALE BLVD

2

22X

MARQUIS OF LORNE TRAIL

Bow River

CANYON MEADOWS DR

DEER RUN DR

BOW BOTTOM TRAIL

Provincial Park

HOLIDAY INN
MACLEOD TRAIL

BLACKFOOT TRAIL

C-TRAIN

STETSON
VILLAGE INN

FAMILY
LEISURE
CENTRE

Fish Creek

2

To
Fort Macleod and Lethbridge
(Southern Alberta)

MACLEOD

TRAIL

SHAWNESSY BLVD

8

HERITAGE DR

RANCHMAN'S
BAR

14TH ST SW

14TH ST SW

HERITAGE
PARK

SOUTHLAND DR

ANDERSON RD

50TH AVE SW

16TH ST
SW

66TH AVE SW

Glenmore
Reservoir

Creek

THE MILITARY
MUSEUMS

GLENMORE TRAIL

Glenmore
Park

Sarcee
Reserve

Fish

2 mi

2 km

0

0

CALGARY

To
Elbow Springs
Golf Course and Bragg Creek
(West of Calgary)

To
Spruce Meadows
and Bragg Creek
(West of Calgary)

22X

the tower with the fun of **Telus Spark.** After lunch at a steakhouse such as Hy's, you can learn about the city's earliest history at **Fort Calgary** and then cross the river to see some of Canada's iconic wildlife at the **Calgary Zoo.** Sports fans won't want to miss **Canada Olympic Park,** either on your second day in the city or on the way to or from the mountains.

Attending the **Calgary Stampede** is a vacation in itself for tens of thousands of visitors each year, but you will want to plan ahead by making accommodation reservations and getting tickets well in advance. Even if you're not a rodeo fan, if your itinerary has you in Calgary in early July, plan to visit the Stampede grounds for the day (no advance tickets required), just to say you've experienced the Greatest Outdoor Show on Earth.

HISTORY

In addition to being one of Canada's largest cities, Calgary is also one of the youngest; at 140 years old, it has a heritage rather than a history. Native Blackfoot people moved through the area approximately 2,000 years ago, but they had no particular interest in the direct vicinity of what is now Calgary. Approximately 300 years ago, Sarcee and Stoney natives moved down from the north and commenced continual warring between tribes. White settlers first arrived in the late 1700s. David Thompson wintered in the area, then the Palliser Expedition passed by on its way west to the Rockies. But it wasn't until the late 1860s that any real activity started. Buffalo had disappeared from the American plains, and as hunters moved north, so did the whiskey traders, bringing with them all the problems associated with this illegal trade.

Fort Calgary

The NWMP established a post at Fort Macleod soon after they came west to quell the whiskey trade. In 1875, a second fort was established on a terrace at the confluence of the Bow and Elbow Rivers. Inspector J. F. Macleod, who took over command of the fort in 1876, coined the name Calgary. It comes from Calgary Bay, a remote village on the Isle of Mull in Scotland said to translate from Gaelic as "garden on the cove."

The Coming of the Railway

For many years, the Canadian Pacific Railway had planned to build a northern route across the continent through Edmonton and Yellowhead Pass. But eventually the powers in the east changed their minds and decided on a southern route through Kicking Horse Pass. This meant that the line passed right through Fort Calgary. In 1883, a station was built on an alluvial plain between the Bow and Elbow Rivers. A town site was laid out around it, settlers streamed in for free land, and nine years after the railway arrived, Calgary acquired city status—something that had taken its northern rival, Edmonton, more than 100 years to obtain.

In 1886, a major fire destroyed most of the town's buildings. City planners decreed that all new structures were to be built of sandstone, which gave the fledgling town a more permanent look. The many sandstone buildings still standing today—the Palliser Hotel, the Hudson's Bay Company store, and the courthouse, for example—are a legacy of this early bylaw.

Ranching

An open grazing policy, initiated by the Dominion Government, encouraged ranchers in the United States to drive their cattle from overgrazed lands to the fertile plains around Calgary. Slowly, a ranching industry and local beef market developed. The first large ranch was established west of Calgary, and soon many NWMP retirees, English aristocrats, and wealthy American citizens had invested in nearby land. Calgary's first millionaire was Pat Burns, who developed a meatpacking empire that still thrives today. Linked to international markets by rail and sea, Calgary's fortunes continued to rise with those of the ranching industry, receiving only a minor setback in 1905 when Edmonton was declared the provincial capital. During the first 10 years of the 20th century, the city's population increased 1,000 percent, and rail lines were built in all directions, radiating from the city like enormous spokes. Immigration slowed, and the economy spiraled downward as the effects of World War I were felt.

Oil

The discovery of oil at Turner Valley in Calgary's backyard in 1914 signaled the start of an industry that was the making of modern Calgary. The opening of an oil refinery in 1923 and further major discoveries nearby transformed a medium-size cow town into a world leader in the petroleum and natural-gas industries. At its peak, the city was the headquarters of more than 400 related companies. Calgary became Canada's fastest-growing city, doubling its population between 1950 and 1975. During the worldwide energy crisis of the 1970s, oil prices soared. Although most of the oil was extracted from farther afield, the city boomed as a world energy and financial center. Construction in the city center during this period was never-ending, as many corporations from around the world moved their headquarters to Alberta. During this period, Calgary had Canada's highest per capita disposable income and was home to more Americans than any other Canadian city. Much of the wealth obtained from oil and gas was channeled back into the city, not just for office towers but also for sporting facilities, cultural centers, and

parks for citizens and visitors alike to enjoy. During the early 1980s, the province was hit by a prolonged downturn in the oil market. But good fortune prevailed when the International Olympic Committee announced that Calgary had been awarded the **1988 Winter Olympic Games.** Life was injected into the economically ravaged city, construction started anew, and the high-spirited Calgarians were smiling once again.

Today and the Future

Calgary has been Canada's fastest-growing city since the late '90s. The population has increased by more than 25 percent since 1996, with current estimates having the city grow another 25 percent to 1.25 million people in the next decade. Even with $4 billion currently slated for new infrastructure, the city is struggling to address the needs of this expansion, which includes new schools, hospitals, and a ring road planned to eventually encircle the entire city. Much of the land in and around downtown has been rezoned for multifamily dwellings, with the area south of downtown seeing massive redevelopment and controversial plans in place for the East Village project immediately east of downtown. City limits continue to expand at a phenomenal rate—especially in the northwest, north, and south—with new suburbs, housing estates, and commercial centers extending as far as the eye can see. But Calgary is still a small town at heart, enjoying tremendous civic and public support. Many of the city's self-made millionaires bequeath their money to the city, and residents in the thousands are always willing to volunteer their time at events such as the Calgary Stampede. This civic pride makes the city a great place to live and an enjoyable destination for the millions of tourists who visit each year.

CALGARY

Sights

ORIENTATION

The TransCanada Highway (Highway 1) passes through the city north of downtown and is known as **16th Avenue North** within the city limits. Highway 2, Alberta's major north-south highway, becomes **Deerfoot Trail** as it passes through the city. Many major arteries are known as **trails,** named for their historical significance, not, as some suggest, for their condition. The main route south from downtown is **Macleod Trail,** a 12-kilometer (7.5-mile) strip of malls, motels, restaurants, and retail stores. If you enter Calgary from the west and are heading north to the airport or Edmonton, a handy bypass to take is **Stoney Trail,** which joins Highway 2 north of the city.

The street-numbering system is divided into four quadrants. At first it can be more confusing than the well-meaning city planner intended, but after initial disorientation, the system soon proves its usefulness. Basically, the four quadrants are geographically named—northwest, northeast, southwest, and southeast. Each street address has a corresponding abbreviation tacked onto it (NW, NE, SW, and SE). The north-south division is the Bow River. The east-west division is at Macleod Trail, and north of the downtown at Centre Street. Streets run north to south and avenues from east to west. Both streets and avenues are numbered progressively from the quadrant divisions (e.g., an address on 58th Avenue SE is on the 58th street south of the Bow River, is east of Macleod Trail, and is on a street that runs east to west). Things don't get any easier in the many new subdivisions that dominate the outer flanks of the city. Many street names are *very* similar to one another, so check whether you want, for example, Mackenzie Lake Bay, Mackenzie Lake Place, Mackenzie Lake Road, or Mackenzie Lake Avenue. Fill the gas tank, pack a hearty lunch, and good luck!

DOWNTOWN

The downtown core is a mass of modern steel-and-glass high-tech high-rises built during the oil boom of the 1970s and early 1980s. Calgary's skyline was transformed during this period, and many historic buildings were knocked down to make way for a wave of development that slowed considerably during the 1990s. The last few years have seen a subtle change in direction, with developers incorporating historic buildings in new projects, especially along Stephen Avenue Walk. The best way to get around is on foot or on the C-train, which is free along 7th Avenue.

Crisscrossing downtown is the Plus 15 walkway system, a series of interconnecting, enclosed sidewalks elevated at least 4.5 meters (15 feet—hence the name) above road level. In total, 47 bridges and 12 kilometers (7.5 miles) of public walkway link downtown stores, four large malls, hotels, food courts, and office buildings to give pedestrians protection from the elements. All walkways are well marked and wheelchair accessible. The following sights can be visited separately or seen on a walking tour (in the order presented).

Stephen Avenue Walk

The traditional center of the city is 8th Avenue, between 1st Street SE and 3rd Street SW—a traffic-free zone known as Stephen Avenue Walk. This bustling, tree-lined pedestrian mall has fountains, benches, cafés, restaurants, and souvenir shops. In summer, the mall is full with shoppers and tourists, and at lunchtime, thousands of office workers descend from the buildings above. Many of Calgary's earliest sandstone buildings still stand along the mall on the block between 1st and 2nd Streets SW. On the corner of 1st Street SW is the **Alberta Hotel,** one of the city's most popular meeting places until Prohibition in 1916.

◖ Calgary Tower

Ninth Avenue, south of the mall, has banks, some of Calgary's best hotels, parking stations, the Telus Convention Centre, the Glenbow Museum, and one of the city's most famous landmarks, the Calgary Tower (101 9th Ave., at the corner of Centre St., 403/266-7171, 9am-9pm daily, until 10pm in summer, adult $16, senior $14, child $11). Built in 1968 (and known then as the Husky Tower), this 190-meter (620-foot) tower dominated the skyline until 1985, when the nearby Petro-Canada towers went up. Although it's now only Calgary's fourth-tallest building, the ride to the top is a worthwhile introduction to the city. The Observation Terrace affords a bird's-eye view of the Canadian Rockies and the ski-jump towers at Canada Olympic Park to the west; the Olympic Saddledome (in Stampede Park) to the south; and the city below, literally—a glass floor allows visitors to stand right over the top of 9th Avenue. The nonreflective window glass is perfect for photography; binoculars are available for guest use; and audio-visual terminals describe the sights below. The tower also houses two restaurants, a snack bar, and a gift shop.

Olympic Plaza and Vicinity

This downtown park at the east end of Stephen Avenue Walk (on the corner of 2nd St. SE), which is filled with office workers each lunch hour, was used during the 1988 Winter Olympic Games for the nightly medal-presentation ceremonies. Plaques here commemorate medal winners, and the bricks on the ground are inscribed by members of the public who helped sponsor the Olympics by "purchasing"

individual bricks before the Games. In summer, outdoor concerts are held here, and in winter, the shallow wading pool freezes over and is used as an ice-skating rink. Across 2nd Street SE from the plaza is **City Hall,** built in 1911. It still houses some city offices, although most have moved next door to the modern **Civic Complex.**

Back across 2nd Street SE is the **Epcor Centre for the Performing Arts,** incorporating two of Calgary's historic sandstone buildings. The complex houses three theaters and the 2,000-seat **Jack Singer Concert Hall,** home to the city's orchestra.

In front of the Education Building on 1st Street SE (between 5th and 6th Avenues) are the **Armengol Structures**—expressionless, raceless, humanlike forms with outstretched arms.

Chinatown

At the east end of town on 3rd Avenue is a small Chinatown of approximately 2,000 residents. Chinese immigrants came to Calgary in the 1880s to work on the railroads and stayed to establish food markets, restaurants, and import stores. Chinatown has seen its share of prejudice, from marauding whites gaining revenge for an outbreak of smallpox to bungling city bureaucrats who demanded that the streets be narrow and signs be in Chinese to give the area an authentic look. The **Calgary Chinese Cultural Centre** (197 1st St. SW, 403/262-5071, 9am-9pm daily, free) is one of the largest such centers in Canada. It's topped by a grand central dome patterned in the same style as the Temple of Heaven in Beijing. The centerpiece of its intricate tile work is a glistening golden dragon hanging 20 meters (66 feet) above the floor. Head up to the 3rd floor for the best views, passing a mural along the way. At street level is a store selling traditional Chinese medicines, and on the lower level is

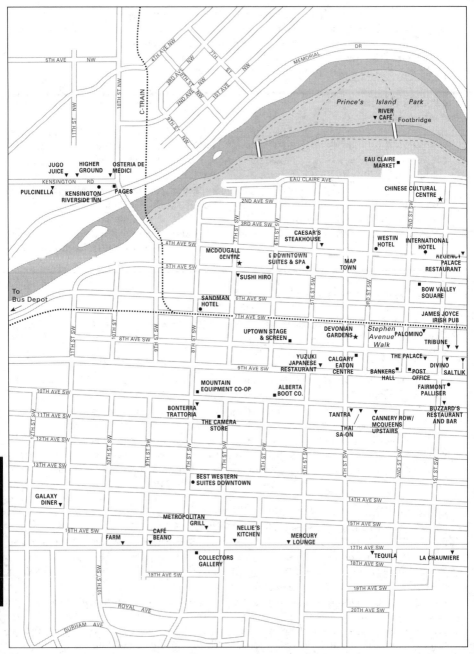

CALGARY

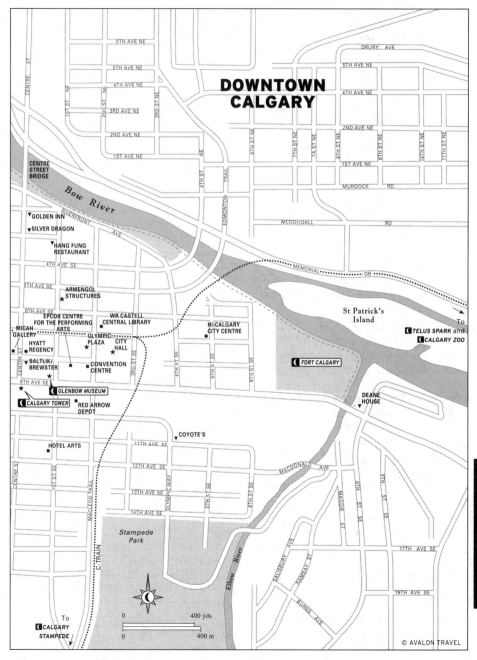

DOWNTOWN CALGARY

CALGARY

© AVALON TRAVEL

MIDNAPORE

The last rest stop for early travelers along the Macleod Trail, linking Fort Macleod to Fort Calgary, was just south of Fish Creek. A trading post and crude cabins constituted the town. The post office opened and was manned by a postmaster with dubious reading skills. One of the first parcels he received was addressed to Midnapore, India, and had been misdirected through him. Fear of losing his job kept him from asking too many questions, and as the community had no official name, he directed that all mail to this post be addressed to Midnapore. The name stuck, and a suburb of Calgary came to have the same name as an Indian city on the opposite side of the world.

a small museum and gallery (11am-5pm daily, adult $5, senior and child $2.50) displaying the cultural history of Calgarians of Chinese descent. One of the museum's most intriguing pieces is the world's oldest known seismograph, which dates to AD 132.

West on First Avenue

Eau Claire Market, at the north end of 3rd Street SW, is a colorful indoor market filled with stalls selling fresh fruit from British Columbia, seafood from the Pacific, Alberta beef, bakery items, and exotic imports. Under the same roof are specialty shops, an IMAX and regular theaters, and nine restaurants.

The northern limit of downtown is along the Bow River, where picturesque **Prince's Island Park** is linked to the mainland by a bridge at the end of 3rd Street SW. Jogging paths, tables, and grassy areas are scattered among the trees on this man-made island. To the east is **Centre Street Bridge,** guarded on either side by large (restored) stone lions. For a good view of the city, cross the bridge and follow the trail along the cliff to the west.

MUSEUMS

◖ Glenbow Museum

Adjacent to Stephen Avenue Walk, this excellent museum (130 9th Ave. SE, 403/268-4100, 9am-5pm Mon.-Sat., noon-5pm Sun., adult $17, senior $13, child $10) chronicles the entire history of western Canada through three floors of informative exhibits and well-displayed artifacts. The museum's permanent collections of contemporary and Inuit art, as well as special exhibitions from national and international collections, are on the 2nd floor. The 3rd-floor "Niitsitapiisinni: Our Way of Life" gallery is the best part of the museum. Developed under the watchful eye of Blackfoot elders, it details the stories and traditions of native peoples through interpretive panels and displays of ceremonial artifacts, jewelry, and a full-size tepee. The 3rd floor also presents "Mavericks: An Incorrigible History of Alberta," telling the story of prominent Albertans from various eras in local history—the fur trade, the NWMP, pioneering settlers, ranching, and the oil industry.

◖ Telus Spark

The main displays at this science center (220 St. Georges Dr. NE, 403/817-6800, www.sparkscience.ca, 9am-4pm Sun.-Fri., 9am-5pm Sat., adult $20, senior $18, child $14) are kid oriented, but that's not a bad thing. It's a wonderful facility chockablock with hands-on science exhibits. Learn about the natural world in Earth & Sky, learn about technology in Energy & Innovation, and then get creative in the Open Studio. Part of Telus Spark is the Creative Kids Museum, where it's sensory overload—children ages 10 and under can build a structure using oversized wooden blocks, hone their painting skills, make music, and explore the climbing structure.

Aerospace Museum

This museum (beside McKnight Blvd. at 4629

© ANDREW HEMPSTEAD

Stephen Avenue Walk

McCall Way NE, 403/250-3752, 10am-4pm daily, adult $10, senior $7, child $5) traces the history of aviation in Canada through a large collection of aircraft scattered around the grounds, including a restored Sopwith triplane from World War I. Inside the main building is the *Silver Dart,* Canada's first airplane; one of North America's largest collections of aircraft engines; uniforms; photographs dating back to the flight of one of Calgary's first airplanes, the *West Wind,* in 1914; and a gift store packed with flight-related literature.

Military Museums of Calgary

Combining former naval and regiments museums, as well as galleries devoted to the Canadian Air Force, this facility (4520 Crowchild Trail SW, 403/974-2850, 9am-5pm Mon.-Fri., 9:30am-4pm Sat.-Sun., adult $10, senior $5, child $4) is Canada's largest military museum. Highlights include the history of four regiments and the importance of Canada's

navy, which was the Allies' third-largest navy in 1945. On display are three fighter aircraft that flew from the decks of aircraft carriers, as well as uniforms, models, flags, photographs, and a memorial to those who lost their lives in the Korean War.

HISTORIC PARKS
◖ Fort Calgary

In 1875, with the onset of a harsh winter, the newly arrived NWMP built Fort Calgary at the confluence of the Bow and Elbow Rivers in fewer than six weeks. The original fort was replaced by a more permanent brick building in 1914, but this was later demolished. After much work, the 16-hectare (40-acre) site has been transformed into a two-part historic park (750 9th Ave. SE, 403/290-1875, 9am-5pm daily, adult $12, senior $11, child $7). Most of the focus is on the interpretive center, housing a replica of 1888 barracks, complete with volunteer Royal Canadian Mounted Police veterans on hand to answer questions. Inside, the lives of Canada's famous "Mounties," the legacy of natives, hardy pioneers, and the wild frontier they tamed are all brought to life through convincingly costumed interpreters. Various shops and businesses from Calgary's earliest days, including an entire 1930s streetscape, are inside. Beside the barracks is an exact replica of the original fort, built using tools and techniques that are more than 120 years old. History comes alive through a variety of activities and programs, including carpenters at work, a room especially for kids that is filled with games of a bygone era, a museum shop styled on an old Hudson's Bay Company store, and a canteen selling meals that I imagine are more appealing than those the original officers enjoyed. To get to Fort Calgary, either walk along the river from downtown or hop aboard bus #1 (Forest Lawn) or #14 (East Calgary) from 7th Avenue.

CALGARY

© ANDREW HEMPSTEAD

Prince's Island Park is linked to downtown by a pedestrian bridge.

Heritage Park

This 27-hectare (66-acre) park (1900 Heritage Dr. SW, 403/268-8500, 10am-5pm daily mid-May-Aug., 9:30am-5pm Sat.-Sun. only Sept.-early Oct., adult $20, senior $16, child $15, an extra $10 per person for unlimited rides) is beside the Glenbow Reservoir southwest of downtown. Gasoline Alley is an indoor exhibit showcasing the history of vehicles. Behind here, more than 100 buildings and exhibits help recreate an early 20th-century pioneer village. Many of the buildings have been moved to the park from their original locations. Highlights include a Hudson's Bay Company fort, a two-story outhouse, a working blacksmith's shop, an 1896 church, a tepee, and an old schoolhouse with original desks. A boardwalk links stores crammed with antiques, and horse-drawn buggies carry passengers along the streets. You can also ride in authentic passenger cars pulled by a steam locomotive or enjoy a cruise in a paddle wheeler on the reservoir. A traditional bakery sells cakes and pastries, and full meals are served in the Wainwright Hotel. To get there from downtown, take the C-train to Heritage Station and transfer to bus #502 (weekends only).

◖ CANADA OLYMPIC PARK

The 1988 Winter Olympic Games are remembered for many things, but particularly a bobsled team from Jamaica, the antics of English plumber/ski-jumper "Eddie the Eagle," and most of all for their success. This 95-hectare (235-acre) park (403/247-5452, www.winsportcanada.ca) on the south side of the TransCanada Highway on the western outskirts of the city is the legacy Calgarians get to enjoy year-round. It was developed especially for the Paralympics and the ski-jumping, luge, bobsled, and freestyle skiing events of the games. Now the park offers activities year-round, including tours of the facilities, luge rides, summer ski-jumping, and sports

CALGARY

training camps. In winter, the beginner/intermediate runs are filled with locals who are able to hit the snow as early as November with the help of a complex snowmaking system. Many ski-jumping, bobsled, and luge events of national and international standard are held here throughout the winter.

Canada Sports Hall of Fame

This Hall of Fame devoted to Canada's best athletes (10am-5pm Tues.-Sun., adult $12, senior $10, child $8) features 12 galleries highlighting the achievements of over 50 sporting stars. As you may expect, the center is dominated by winter-sport athletes from all disciplines, but there are also tributes to Calgarians such as "Doc" Seaman, who contributed millions of dollars to minor hockey development.

Ski-Jumping, Luge, and Bobsled Facilities

Visible from throughout the city are the 70- and 90-meter (230- and 295-foot) ski-jump towers, synonymous with the Winter Olympic Games. These two jumps are still used for national and international competitions and training. A glass-enclosed elevator rises to the observation level. The jump complex has three additional jumps of 15, 30, and 50 meters (49, 98, and 164 feet), which are used for junior competitions and training. All but the 90-meter (295-foot) jump have plastic-surfaced landing strips and are used during summer.

At the western end of the park are the luge and bobsled tracks. A complex refrigeration system keeps the tracks usable even on relatively hot days (up to 28°C/80°F). At the bottom of the hill is the Ice House, home to the National Sliding Centre, the world's only year-round facility where athletes can practice their dynamic starts for luge, bobsled, and skeleton. Self-guided tours (10am-5pm daily mid-May-Sept.) cost $20 per person.

OTHER PARKS
◖ Calgary Zoo

The Calgary Zoo (1300 Zoo Rd. NE, 403/232-9300, 9am-5pm daily year-round, adult $21, senior $19, child $13) is one of Canada's finest zoos. It was established in 1920 near the heart of downtown on St. Georges Island and has become noted for its realistic simulation of animal habitats. In Destination Africa, giraffes tower over a huge glass-walled pool that provides a home to two hippos, with sunken stadium seating allowing visitors a fish-eye view of the hippos' often-relaxing day. Other highlights include a section on Australia's nocturnal animals (lights are turned on at night, reversing night and day and allowing visitors to watch nocturnal animals during their active periods), exotic mammals such as lions and tigers, and conservatories filled with tropical flowers, butterflies, and birds. One of the largest display areas is Canadian Wilds, devoted to the mammals you may or may not see on your travels through Alberta. In the Prehistoric Park section, the world of dinosaurs is brought to life with full-size replicas set amid plantlife and rock. The main parking lot is off Memorial Drive east of downtown, or jump aboard the 202 Whitehorn C-train running east along 7th Avenue.

Stampede Park

Best known for hosting the Calgary Stampede, these grounds south of downtown (at 17th Ave. and 2nd St. SE) are used for many activities and events year-round. In the center of the park is the saddle-shaped 18,800-seat **Saddledome,** which boasts the world's largest cable-suspended roof and is one of Calgary's most distinctive structures. It was used for hockey and figure-skating events during the 1988 Winter Olympic Games and is now home to the National Hockey League (NHL) Calgary Flames. "The Dome" is constantly in use for concerts, trade shows, and entertainment events. The **Grain Academy Museum** on the

CALGARY

Plus 15 level of the **Roundup Centre** (403/263-4594, 10am-4pm Mon.-Fri., free) is a museum cataloging the history of cereal-based agriculture in the province through working models and hands-on displays. Take the C-train from downtown to Victoria Park/Stampede or Stampede/Erlton.

Sam Livingston Fish Hatchery

Pearce Estate Park, a pleasant spot for a picnic, is home to this hatchery (403/297-6561, 10am-4pm Mon.-Fri., 1pm-5pm Sat.-Sun. in summer, weekdays only the rest of the year, free). The facility produces approximately 2.5 million trout per year, which are used to stock 300 lakes and rivers throughout the province. A self-guided tour (grab a brochure at the main office) leads through the hatchery, from the incubation room to holding tanks and an area containing various displays and a theater. To reach the park and hatchery, take 17th Avenue east from the city and turn north onto 17th Street SE.

Inglewood Bird Sanctuary

More than 250 species of birds have been noted in this 32-hectare (79-acre) park on the bank of the Bow River, east of downtown. The land was originally owned by a member of the NWMP and was established as a park in 1929. Walking trails are open year-round, but before heading out, it's worth dropping by the interpretive center (2425 9th Ave. SE, 403/221-4500, 10am-5pm daily May-Sept., 10am-4pm Tues.-Sun. Oct.-Apr., donation) to learn more about the urban ecosystem and to pick up a bird list. To get there, take 9th Avenue SE to Sanctuary Road and follow the signs to a parking area on the south bank of the river.

Fish Creek Provincial Park

At the southern edge of the city, this 1,170-hectare (2,900-acre) park is one of the largest urban parks in North America. Three geographical regions meet in the area, giving the park a diversity of habitat. Stands of aspen and spruce predominate, but a mixed-grass prairie, as well as balsam, poplar, and willow, can be found along the floodplains at the east end of the park. The ground is colorfully carpeted with over 350 recorded species of wildflowers, and wildlife is abundant. Mule deer and ground squirrels are common, and white-tailed deer, coyotes, beavers, and the occasional moose are also present. An interpretive trail begins south of Bow Valley Ranch and leads through a grove of balsam and poplar to a shallow, conglomerate cave. An information display is located on the west side of Macleod Trail overlooking the site of Alberta's first woolen mill. The easiest access to the heart of the park is to turn east on Canyon Meadows Drive from Macleod Trail, then south on Bow River Bottom Trail.

DINOSAUR VALLEY

© ANDREW HEMPSTEAD

Royal Tyrrell Museum

East of Calgary, the Red Deer River has carved a deep valley through the otherwise featureless prairie, and in doing so has unearthed one of the world's most significant paleontological resources through an area known as the Badlands or Dinosaur Valley. Before charging out into the badlands, it is important to understand that the two major dinosaur destinations, the town of **Drumheller** and **Dinosaur Provincial Park,** are not close to each other. It is possible to visit each separately on a day trip from Calgary, but to visit both destinations in one day is a little much.

The highlight of a visit to the town of Drumheller, just over an hour's drive northeast of Calgary, is the **Royal Tyrrell Museum** (North Dinosaur Trail, 403/823-7707 or 888/440-4240, www.tyrrellmuseum.com, 9am-9pm daily mid-May-Aug., 10am-5pm Tues.-Sun. the rest of the year, adult $12, senior $10, youth $8), the world's largest museum devoted entirely to paleontology. It integrates display areas with fieldwork done literally on the doorstep, with specimens transported to the museum for re-

search and cataloging. Even for those visitors with little or no interest in dinosaurs, it's easy to spend half a day in the massive complex. The museum holds more than 80,000 specimens, including 50 full-size dinosaur skeletons, the world's largest such display.

At Dinosaur Provincial Park, 200 kilometers (124 miles) east of Calgary, you'll discover one of the world's most important dinosaur fossil beds. Thirty-five species of dinosaurs have been unearthed here, along with the skeletal remains of crocodiles, turtles, fish, lizards, frogs, and flying reptiles. Not only is the diversity of specimens great, but so is the sheer volume; more than 300 museum-quality specimens have been found. Protected as a UNESCO World Heritage Site, the park has a small field station (403/378-4342, 9am-4pm daily Apr.-mid-May, 8:30am-7pm daily mid-May-Aug., 9am-4:30pm daily Sept, 9am-4pm weekdays the rest of the year, adult $5, senior $3.50, child $2.50), but the best way to learn about the area is on a guided walk or bus tour.

CALGARY

Sports and Recreation

The **City of Calgary** (403/268-2489, www.calgary.ca) operates a wide variety of recreational facilities, including swimming pools and golf courses, throughout the city. They also run a variety of excursions, such as canoeing and horseback riding, as well as inexpensive courses ranging from fly-tying to rock climbing.

WALKING AND BIKING

A good way to get a feel for the city is by walking or biking along the 210 kilometers (130 miles) of paved trails within the city limits. The trail system is concentrated along the Bow River as it winds through the city; other options are limited. Along the riverbank, the trail passes through numerous parks and older neighborhoods to various sites such as Fort Calgary and Inglewood Bird Sanctuary. From Fort Calgary, a trail passes under 9th Avenue SE and follows the Elbow River, crossing it several times before ending at Glenmore Reservoir and Heritage Park. Ask at tourist information centers for a map detailing all trails. The ski slopes at **Canada Olympic Park** (west of downtown along the TransCanada Hwy., 403/247-5452) are the perfect place to hone your downhill mountain-bike skills. Full-suspension-bike rental is $48 for two hours or $75 for a full day, while a day pass for the chairlift is $35.

SWIMMING AND FITNESS CENTERS

The **City of Calgary** (403/268-2489) operates eight outdoor pools (open June-early Sept.) and 12 indoor pools (open year-round). Facilities at each vary. Admission at indoor pools includes the use of the sauna, hot tub, and exercise room. Admission to all pools is adult $7.50-10.50, around half price for seniors and kids.

The **YMCA** (101 3rd St. SW, 403/269-6701,

5:30am-10pm Mon.-Fri., 7am-7pm Sat.-Sun., $14) is a modern fitness center beside Eau Claire Market at the north end of downtown. All facilities are first-class, including an Olympic-size pool, a weight room, an exercise room, a jogging track, squash courts, a hot tub, and a sauna.

The large **Family Leisure Centre** (11150 Bonaventure Dr. SE, 403/278-7542, 9am-9pm daily) has a lot more to offer than just swimming. The entry fee of adult $12.80, child $7.40 includes use of regular pools as well as a giant indoor waterslide, a wave pool, and even a skating rink.

AMUSEMENT PARKS

Calaway Park (10 km/6.2 mi west of city limits along the TransCanada Hwy., 403/240-3822, 10am-7pm Sat.-Sun. May-June, 10am-7pm daily July-Aug., 11am-6pm Sat.-Sun. Sept.-mid-Oct.) is western Canada's largest outdoor amusement park, with 27 rides including a double-loop roller coaster. Other attractions include an enormous maze, Western-themed minigolf, a zoo for the kids, a trout-fishing pond, live entertainment in the Western-style Showtime Theatre, and many eateries. Admission including most rides is $38 for ages 7-49, $29 ages 3-6 and 50 and over.

WINTER RECREATION

When Calgarians talk about going skiing or snowboarding for the day, they are usually referring to the five world-class winter resorts in the Rockies, a one- to two-hour drive to the west. The city's only downhill facilities are at **Canada Olympic Park** (403/247-5452), which has three chairlifts and a T-bar serving a vertical rise of 150 meters (500 feet). Although the slopes aren't extensive, on the plus side are a long season (mid-Nov.-late Mar.), night skiing (weeknights until 9pm), extensive lodge facilities including rentals, and excellent teaching staff. Lift tickets can be purchased on an hourly basis ($37 for four hours) or for a full day ($49). Seniors pay just $20 for a full day on the slopes.

SPECTATOR SPORTS
Hockey
There's no better way to spend a winter's night in Calgary than by attending a home game of the **Calgary Flames** (403/777-2177, www.calgaryflames.com, from $58), the city's NHL franchise. On these nights, the Saddledome in Stampede Park fills with 20,000 hockey fans who follow every game with a passion. No matter whether the team is winning or losing, the atmosphere is electric. After a prolonged slump (they last won the Stanley Cup in 1989), they are now one of the most competitive NHL franchises. The regular season runs October-April, and games are usually held in the early evening (7pm weeknights, 8pm Sat., 6pm Sun.).

Football
The **Stampeders** (403/289-0205, www.stampeders.com, $34-90) are Calgary's franchise in the Canadian Football League (CFL), an organization similar to the U.S. NFL. Although the team's popularity fluctuates with its performance, crowd levels remain high through even the longest losing streaks. Near the end of the season, weather can be a deciding factor in both the games' results and attendance. At kick-off in the Stampeders' final game of 1993, the temperature was -20°C (-4°F) and -33°C (-27°F) with the windchill, but more than 20,000 Calgarians braved the weather to attend. The season runs July-November. Home games are played at the 35,500-seat **McMahon Stadium** (1817 Crowchild Trail NW). From downtown, take the C-train to Banff Trail Station.

Entertainment and Events

Ffwd (www.ffwdweekly.com) is a free weekly magazine available throughout the city. It lists theater events, cinema screenings, and art displays, and keeps everyone abreast of the local music scene. Tickets to major concerts, performances, and sporting events are available in advance from **Ticketmaster** (403/777-0000, www.ticketmaster.ca).

THE ARTS
Art Galleries
It may put a dent in Calgary's cow town image, but the city does have a remarkable number of galleries displaying and selling work by Albertan and Canadian artisans. Unfortunately, they are not concentrated in any one area, and most require some effort to find. Renowned for its authentic native art, **Micah Gallery** is the exception. It's right downtown on Stephen Avenue Walk (110 8th Ave. SW, 403/245-1340). A cluster of galleries lies along 9th Avenue SE. Most affordable is **Galleria Arts & Crafts** (907 9th Ave. SE, 403/270-3612), with two stories of shelf space stocked with paintings, etchings, metal sculptures, jewelry, and wood carvings.

Theater
Calgary's Western image belies a cultural diversity that goes further than being able to get a few foreign beers at the local saloon. In fact, the city has 10 professional theater companies, an opera, an orchestra, and a ballet troupe. The main season for performances is September-May.

   Alberta Theatre Projects (403/294-7402, www.atplive.com, $24-70) is a well-established company based in the downtown Epcor Centre for the Performing Arts (220 9th Ave. SE). Usual performances are of contemporary material. Also based at the Epcor Centre for the Performing Arts is **Theatre Calgary** (403/294-7440, www.theatrecalgary.com). **Lunchbox Theatre** (115 9th Ave. SE, 403/265-4292, www.lunchboxtheatre.com, adult $20, senior $17), in a custom-built theater at the base of the Calgary Tower, runs especially for the lunchtime crowd September-early May. For adult-oriented experimental productions, consider a performance by **One Yellow Rabbit** (Epcor Centre for the Performing Arts, 225 8th Ave. SE, 403/264-3224, www.oyr.org).

Music and Dance

Calgary Opera (403/262-7286, www.calgaryopera.com, $28-96) performs in a restored church (corner 13th Ave. and 7th St. SW) October-April. The 2,000-seat Jack Singer Concert Hall at the Epcor Centre for the Performing Arts is home to the **Calgary Philharmonic Orchestra** (403/571-0270, www.cpo-live.com), one of Canada's top orchestras. **Alberta Ballet** (403/245-4549, www.albertaballet.com) performs at locations throughout the city.

Cinemas

Many major shopping malls—including Eau Claire Market, closest to downtown—have a **Cineplex** cinema. For information, call the 24-hour film line (403/263-3166) or check the website (www.cineplex.com). Over the Bow River from downtown, the 1935 **Plaza Theatre** (1133 Kensington Rd. NW, Kensington, 403/283-2222, www.theplaza.ca) shows everything from mainstream to Hindi.

NIGHTLIFE
Country-Music Bars

With a nickname like Cowtown, it's not surprising that some of Calgary's hottest nightspots play country music. **Ranchman's** (9615

Macleod Trail SW, 403/253-1100) is *the* place to check out first, especially during Stampede Week. Some of country's hottest stars have played this authentic honky-tonk. Food is served at a bar out front all day, then at 7pm the large dance hall opens with a band keeping the crowd boot-scootin' most nights. The hall is a museum of rodeo memorabilia and photographs, with a chuck wagon hanging from the ceiling. On the south side of the railway tracks from downtown is hip **Cowboys** (1088 Olympic Way SE, 403/265-0699). The crowd is urban-slick, but when country music plays, the fancy-dancing crowd seems to know every word. Both of these bars are open for lunch and offer a quiet atmosphere through the afternoon.

Other Bars and Dance Clubs

Options for a quiet drink include lounge bars in major downtown hotels. Of these, the **Sandstone Lounge** (Hyatt Regency, 700 Centre St., 403/717-1234) stands out for its central location (off Stephen Avenue Walk), classy surroundings, and extensive drink selection. **Raw Bar** (Hotel Arts, 119 12th Ave. SW, 403/266-4611, 11am-9pm daily) is as exotic as it gets in Calgary—a cabana-like setting around an outdoor pool. Back on Stephen Avenue Walk, in an old bank building, **James Joyce Irish Pub** (114 8th Ave. SW, 403/262-0708) has Guinness on tap and a menu of traditional British dishes. Nearby is **Ceilis** (803 8th Ave. SW, 403/265-1200), an Irish pub with over 60 beers on tap.

Downtown in a grandly restored theater, **The Palace** (218 8th Ave. SW, 403/263-9980) has a large dance floor and big-time lighting and sound systems. **Mercury Lounge** (550 17th Ave. SW, 403/229-0222) attracts a young, hip crowd for its cocktail-bar ambience—the perfect pre-nightclub hangout. For many Mercury patrons, the next stop is **Tequila** (219 17th Ave. SW, 403/209-2215), where a DJ spins house and hip-hop for a young party crowd. Also within walking distance is the **Metropolitan Grill** (880 16th Ave. SW, 403/802-2393), where the over-25 crowd gravitates to the outdoor patio on warm summer nights. Glitzy **355 Mansion** (355 10th Ave. SW, 403/264-0202) attracts the beautiful, high-end crowd but remains welcoming.

FESTIVALS AND EVENTS
Fall
In October, hockey and skiing and snowboarding fever hits the city as the **NHL Calgary Flames** start their season and the first snow flies. Late September-early October sees screenings of movies during the **Calgary International Film Festival** (403/283-1490, www.calgaryfilm.com) at the historic Plaza Theater in Kensington and at the Globe Theatre and Cineplex at Eau Claire Market. This is followed by **Wordfest** (403/237-9068, www.wordfest.com), where authors talk about their books, workshops are given, and many readings take place at venues throughout the city and in Banff. As Halloween approaches, a good place for kids is the Calgary Zoo (403/232-9300, www.calgaryzoo.org), where there are **Boo at the Zoo** celebrations after dark through late October.

Winter
Although severely curtailed by the weather, Calgarians enjoy the winter with the opening of the theater, ballet, and opera seasons. National and international ski-jumping, luge, and bobsledding events are held at **Canada Olympic Park** November-March.

Spring
Calgary International Children's Festival (403/294-7414, www.calgarychildfest.org) is the third week of May. Events include theater, puppetry, and performances by musicians from around the world. It's held in the Epcor Centre

for the Performing Arts and Olympic Plaza. Olympic Plaza comes alive with the sights, sounds, and tastes of the Caribbean in the first week of June for **Carifest** (403/774-1300, www.carifestcalgary.com).

Summer
Few cities in the world are associated as closely with an event as Calgary is with the **Calgary Stampede** (403/261-0101 or 800/661-1260, www.calgarystampede.com). Held each summer in July, the Stampede features an outdoor rodeo and chuck wagon races, as well as a gigantic midway with numerous attractions and displays. A grandstand show with fireworks caps off each day.

Canada Day is celebrated on July 1 in Prince's Island Park, Fort Calgary, the zoo, and Heritage Park. The **Calgary Folk Music Festival** (403/233-0904, www.calgaryfolkfest.com), during the last weekend of July, is an indoor and outdoor extravaganza of Canadian and international performers that centers on Prince's Island Park. The first full week of August, and also at this downtown riverfront park, is **Afrikadey!** (403/234-9110, www.afrikadey.com), with performances and workshops by African-influenced musicians and artists, and screenings of African-themed films.

◖ Calgary Stampede
Every July, the city's perennial rough-and-ready cow town image is thrust to the forefront when a fever known as Stampede hits town. For 10 days, Calgarians let their hair down—business leaders don Stetsons, bankers wear boots, half the town walks around in too-tight denim outfits, and the rate of serious crime drops. Nine months later, maternity hospitals report a rise in business. For most Calgarians, it is known simply as The Week (always capitalized). The Stampede is many things to many people but is certainly not for the cynic. It is a

CALGARY

celebration of the city's past—of endless sunny days when life was broncos, bulls, and steers, of cowboys riding through the streets and saloons on every corner. But it is not just about the past. It's the cow town image Calgarians cherish and the frontier image that visitors expect. On downtown streets, everyone is your neighbor. Flapjacks and bacon are served free of charge around the city; normally staid citizens shout "Yahoo!" for no particular reason; Indians ride up and down the streets on horseback; and there's drinking and dancing until dawn every night.

The epicenter of the action is **Stampede Park,** immediately south of the city center, where more than 100,000 people converge each day. The park hosts the world's richest outdoor rodeo and the just-as-spectacular chuck wagon races, where professional cowboys from all over the planet compete to share $1.6 million over 10 days. But Stampede Park offers a lot more than a show of cowboy skills. The gigantic midway takes at least a day to get around: A staggering number of attractions, displays, and free entertainment cost only the price of gate admission; and a glittering grandstand show, complete with fireworks, ends each day's shenanigans.

HISTORY

Early in the 20th century, Guy Weadick, an American cowpoke, got the idea that people would pay to see traditional cowboy skills combined with vaudeville showmanship. In 1912, with the backing of local businessmen, Weadick put on a show billed as The Last and Best Great Western Frontier Days, a reference to the fact that many Albertans thought the local cattle industry was near its end. An estimated 60,000 people lined the streets for the parade, and 40,000 attended each day of rodeo events. This turnout was amazing, considering that barely more than 65,000 people lived in Calgary at the time.

The highlight of the event was on the final day, when Tom Three Persons, a little-known Blood Indian rider from southern Alberta, rode the legendary bronc Cyclone for eight seconds to collect the world-championship saddle and $1,000.

The following year, Weadick took the show to Winnipeg. Then World War I intervened, and not until 1919 was the Calgary show revived with Weadick at the helm. In the era of popular Hollywood westerns, Weadick convinced moviemakers down south that the event was worthy of screening. In 1925, *Calgary Stampede* was released, putting the city on the map. As it turned out, the inaugural show wasn't the first and last, but rather the beginning of an annual extravaganza that is billed, and rightly so, as The Greatest Outdoor Show on Earth.

STAMPEDE PARADE

Although Stampede Park opens on Thursday evening for **Sneak-a-Peek** (an event that alone attracts approximately 40,000 eager patrons), Stampede Week officially begins Friday morning with a spectacular parade through the streets of downtown Calgary. The approximately 150 floats include close to 4,000 parade participants and 700 horses, and the procession takes two hours to pass any one point. It features an amazing array of floats, each cheered by the 250,000 people who line the streets up to 10 deep. The loudest "Yahoos" are usually reserved for Alberta's oldest residents, Stampede royalty, and members of Calgary's professional sports teams, but this is the Stampede, so even politicians and street sweepers elicit enthusiastic cheers.

The parade proceeds west along 6th Avenue from 2nd Street SE, then south on 10th Street SW and east on 9th Avenue. Starting time is 9am, but crowds start gathering at 6am, and you'll be lucky to get a front-row spot much after 7am.

SPRUCE MEADOWS

It is somewhat ironic that a city known around the world for its rodeo is also home to the world's premier show-jumping facility, **Spruce Meadows** (Spruce Meadows Way, 403/974-4200, www.sprucemeadows.com). The 120-hectare (300-acre) facility, with a wonderfully refined atmosphere, comprises six grassed outdoor rings, two indoor arenas, seven stables holding 700 horse stalls, 90 full-time employees (and many thousands of volunteers), and its own television station that broadcasts worldwide.

Spruce Meadows hosts a packed schedule of tournaments that attract the world's best riders and up to 40,000 spectators a day. The four big tournaments are the **National,** the first week of June; **Canada One,** the last week of June; the **North American,** the first week of July; and the **Masters,** the first week of September. The Masters is the world's richest show-jumping tournament, with $1 million up for grabs on the Sunday afternoon ride-off.

In Europe, the world of show-jumping can be very hoity-toity. At Spruce Meadows, the atmosphere couldn't be more different, which makes it a wonderful place to spend a day—even for non-horse lovers. The pomp and ceremony associated with the sport is present—it's just not obvious to the casual observer. Instead visitors spread out picnic lunches on grassy embankments, wander through the stables, and watch the superstars of the sport up close and personal. During the major tournaments, browsing through the on-site agricultural fair, arts and crafts booths, and a large marketplace promoting Alberta attractions will round out a busy day of following the competitions from ring to ring.

General admission is free. Except on the busiest of days, this will get you a prime viewing position at any of the rings. The exception is tournament weekends, when covered reserved seating ($28-45) is the best way to watch the action. To get to Spruce Meadows on tournament weekends, take the C-train south to Fish Creek-Lacombe Station, from which bus transfers to the grounds are free. By car, take Macleod Trail south to Highway 22X and turn right toward the mountains along Spruce Meadows Way.

RODEO

The pinnacle of any cowboy's career is walking away with the $100,000 winner's check on the last day of competition in the Calgary Stampede. For the first eight days, 20 of the world's best cowboys and cowgirls compete in two pools for the right to ride on the final Sunday. Saturday is a wild-card event. On each of the 10 days, the rodeo starts at 1:30pm. Although Stampede Week is about a lot more than the rodeo, everyone loves to watch this event. Cowboys compete in bronc riding, bareback riding, bull riding, calf roping, and steer wrestling, and cowgirls compete in barrel racing. Bull fighting and nonstop chatter from hilarious rodeo clowns keep the action going between the more traditional rodeo events.

CHUCK WAGON RACES

The **Rangeland Derby** chuck wagon races feature nine heats each evening starting at 8pm. At the end of the week, the top four drivers from the preliminary rounds compete in a $100,000 dash-for-the-cash final. Chuck wagon racing is an exciting sport anytime, but at the Stampede the pressure is intense as drivers push themselves to stay in the running. The grandstand in the infield makes steering the chuck wagons through an initial figure eight difficult, heightening the action before they burst onto the track for what is known as the Half Mile of Hell to the finish line. The first team across the finish line does not always win the race; drivers must avoid 34 penalties, ranging from 1-10 seconds, which are added to their overall time.

CALGARY

RODEO EVENTS

The rodeo is made up of six traditional events, three of which are judged on points and three of which are timed.

BAREBACK RIDING

In this event, the rider doesn't use a saddle or reins. He is cinched to a handhold and a leather pad attached to the horse's back. The idea is to stay on the wildly bucking horse for eight seconds. As the cowboy leaves the chute, he must keep both spurs above the horse's shoulders until the horse's front hooves hit the ground. Riders are judged on style and rhythm, which is achieved by spurring effectively and remaining in control. The cowboy is disqualified if he doesn't last eight seconds, if he loses a stirrup, or if he touches the animal with his hand. Scores are given out of 100, with a maximum of 50 points allotted for the horse's power and bucking pattern, and a maximum of 50 awarded to the rider for his control and spurring action. Scores above 85 are usually good enough to win.

SADDLE BRONC RIDING

This event differs from bareback riding in that the horse is saddled and the rider, rather than being cinched to the animal, hangs onto a rein attached to the halter. Again, both spurs must be above the horse's shoulders until after the first jump. Bronc riding is one of the classic rodeo events and, when performed properly, is a joy to watch. Riders are judged by spurring action and are disqualified for falling before eight seconds have elapsed. The highest score ever achieved in this event was a 95 by Australian Glenn O'Neill at the Innisfail Rodeo in 1996.

BULL RIDING

Traditionally the last event in a rodeo, bull riding is considered to be the most exciting eight seconds in sports. The cowboy must hang onto a 1,800-pound bull for the required eight seconds with as much control as possible. No spurring is required (for obvious reasons), although if he gets the chance to do so, it earns the cowboy extra points. Disqualification occurs if the cowboy's loose hand touches either himself or the animal, or if he doesn't last eight seconds, which is the case more often than not. Like in bareback riding, the cowboy has one hand

cinched to the animal in a handhold of braided rope. Riders are tied so tightly to the animal that if they are bucked off on the side away from their riding hand, they often become "hung up" and are dragged around like a rag doll until rescued by a rodeo clown. Scores are given out of 100; because of the difficulty of bull riding, just staying on for eight seconds ensures a good ride, but look for a score of around 85 to win.

CALF ROPING

This timed event has its roots in the Old West, when calves had to be roped and tied down to receive a brand or medical treatment. The calf is released from a chute and followed closely by a mounted cowboy. The cowboy must lasso the calf, dismount, race to the animal, and tie a "pigging string" around any three of its legs. The cowboy then throws his hands into the air to signal the end of his run. After remounting his horse, the cowboy rides forward, slackening the rope. He's disqualified if the calf's legs don't remain tied for six seconds. The fastest time wins, with a 10-second penalty for breaking the gate. Any time under eight seconds is good.

STEER WRESTLING

Also known as "bull-dogging," this timed event is for the big boys. The steer, which may weigh up to five times as much as the cowboy, jumps out of the chute, followed closely by a "hazer" (mounted cowboy) who rides alongside, jumps off his horse at full speed, and slides onto the steer's back, attempting to get hold of its horns. The cowboy slows down by digging his feet into the ground, using a twisting motion to throw the steer to the ground. The fastest time wins. Look for a winning score under four seconds (the world record is 2.2 seconds).

BARREL RACING

This is the only rodeo event for women. Riders must guide their horses around three barrels, set in a cloverleaf pattern, before making a hat-flying dash to the finish line. To do this requires great skill and an excellent relationship between the cowgirl and her horse. The fastest time wins, and there's a five-second penalty for knocking down a barrel. An average winning time is around 15 seconds.

OTHER HIGHLIGHTS

The cavernous **Roundup Centre** holds various commercial exhibits and demonstrations (plenty of free samples); Kitchen Theatre, showcasing Calgary's culinary scene; and a Western Showcase of art and photography. At the front of the Roundup Centre is **Stampede Corral,** where you might find dog shows, the Calgary Stampede Show Band, or a talent show for seniors. A **midway** takes center stage on the western edge of the park with the thrills and spills of rides, such as the reverse bungee, drawing as many spectators as paying customers.

Agricultural displays are situated in the center of Stampede Park. **Centennial Fair** is an outdoor stage with children's attractions such as duck races and magicians. In the **Agricultural Building** livestock is displayed, and the World Blacksmith's Competition and horse shows take place next door in the **John Deere Show Ring.**

At the far end of Stampede Park, across the Elbow River, is **Indian Village.** Here, members of the five nations who signed Treaty Seven 100 years ago—the Blackfoot, Blood, Piegan, Sarcee, and Stoney—set up camp for the duration of the Stampede. Each tepee has its own colorful design. Behind the village is a stage where native dance competitions are held.

Once you've paid gate admission, all entertainment (except the rodeo and chuck wagon races) is free. Well-known Canadian performers appear at the outdoor **Coca-Cola Stage** 11am-midnight. **Nashville North** is an indoor venue with a bar, live country acts, and a dance floor; it's open until 2am.

TICKETS

Advance tickets for the afternoon rodeos and evening chuck wagon races/grandstand shows go on sale the year before the event (usually sometime in September), with the best seats selling out well in advance. The grandstand is divided into sections, each with a different price tag. The best views are from the "A" section, closest to the infield yet high enough not to miss all the action. To either side are the "B" and "C" sections, also with good views. Above the main level is the Clubhouse level, divided into another four sections all enclosed by glass and air-conditioned. These seats might not have the atmosphere of the lower or higher levels, but they are protected from the elements, and patrons have access to a bar, full-service restaurant, and lounge area. Ticket prices for the first eight days of rodeo competition range $45-85. The evening chuck wagon races/grandstand shows run $52-94. Tickets for the final two days of competition are an extra few dollars. Tickets to both the rodeos and chuck wagon races/grandstand shows include general admission to Stampede Park. Order tickets by phone (403/269-9822 or 800/661-1767) or online (www.calgarystampede.com) starting early October the year prior.

If you didn't purchase your tickets in advance, you'll need to pay the $18 **general admission** at the gate. Then, once on the grounds, you can purchase "rush seating" tickets for the afternoon's rodeo (adult $20, child $10) or the chuck wagon race/grandstand show (adult $24, child $12) 90 minutes prior to showtime from the booths in front of the grandstand. You'll only have access to either an area of the infield with poor views or seats well away from the action.

INFORMATION

Check either of Calgary's daily newspapers for a pull-out section with results of the previous day's competition and a schedule of events on the grounds and around town. At Stampede Park, a schedule and maps are available at distinctive **Howdy Folk Chuckwagons,** topped with cowboy hats and staffed by friendly volunteers.

Contact the Calgary Stampede office at

403/261-0101 or 800/661-1260, www.calgary-stampede.com.

GETTING THERE AND PARKING
The C-train runs at least every 10 minutes east-bound along 7th Avenue downtown to one of two Stampede stations ($2.75 one-way). Many hotels and campgrounds run shuttle services to downtown for the Friday parade and then to Stampede Park for the rest of the week; expect to pay $20 round-trip per person.

If you decide to drive, parking close to the grounds is possible, but the roads can be chaotic. Many local residents turn their gardens into parking lots—most stand out on the road waving at you as if to say that their month's rent depends on the $25-35 parking fee. The official parking lots throughout the area immediately north of Stampede Park usually charge $20 per day in the morning, rising as high as $40 in the afternoon, depending on how busy they are.

Shopping

PLAZAS AND MALLS
The largest shopping center downtown is **Calgary Eaton Centre,** on Stephen Avenue Walk at 4th Street SW. This center is linked to other plazas by the Plus 15 walkway system. Other downtown shopping complexes are **Eau Claire Market,** at the entrance to Prince's Island Park, where the emphasis is on fresh foods and trendy boutiques; **TD Square,** at 7th Avenue and 2nd Street SW; and **The Bay,** part of Alberta's history with its link to the Hudson's Bay Company. **Uptown 17** is a strip of more than 400 retail shops, restaurants, and galleries along 17th Avenue SW. **Kensington,** across the Bow River from downtown, is an eclectic mix of specialty shops.

MARKETS
At **Crossroads Market** (1235 26th Ave. SE, 403/291-5208, 9am-5pm Fri.-Sun.), you'll find rows and rows of local seasonal produce, as well as prepared foods like the well-researched Simple Simon Pies. Crossroads is also known for its arts and crafts.

CAMPING GEAR AND WESTERN WEAR
Mountain Equipment Co-op (830 10th Ave. SW, 403/269-2420) is Calgary's largest

camping store. This massive outlet boasts an extensive range of high-quality clothing, climbing and mountaineering equipment (including a climbing wall), tents, sleeping bags, kayaks and canoes, books and maps, and other accessories. The store is a cooperative owned by its members, similar to the American REI stores, except that to purchase anything you must be a member (a once-only $5 charge). To order a copy of the co-op's mail-order catalog, call 800/663-2667. Across the road, a similar supply of equipment is offered at **Coast Mountain Sports** (817 10th Ave. SW, 403/264-2444). The selection may be smaller than at MEC, but many name-brand items are perpetually sale priced.

Alberta Boot Co. (614 10th Ave. SW, 403/263-4605), within walking distance of downtown, is Alberta's only Western-boot manufacturer. This outlet shop has thousands of pairs for sale in all shapes and sizes, all made from leather. Boots start at $250 and go all the way up to $1,700 for alligator hide. You'll find **Lammle's Western Wear** outlets in all the major malls and downtown on Stephen Avenue Walk. Another popular Western outfitter is **Riley & McCormick,** also on Stephen Avenue Walk (220 8th Ave. SW, 403/262-1556) and at the airport.

BOOKSTORES

For topographic, city, and wall maps, as well as travel guides and atlases, **Map Town** (400 5th Ave. SW, 403/266-2241 or 877/921-6277, www.maptown.com, 7:30am-5:30pm Mon.-Fri., 10am-5pm Sat.) should have what you're looking for. Tech-savvy travelers will be impressed by the selection of GPS units and related software, as well as the scanning service, which allows you to have topo maps sent directly to your email inbox.

The suburb of Kensington, immediately northwest of downtown, is home to **Pages** (1135 Kensington Rd. NW, 403/283-6655, 10am-5:30pm Mon.-Sat., until 9pm Thurs.-Fri., and noon-5pm Sun.), which offers a thoughtful selection of Canadian fiction and nonfiction titles.

Indigo Books & Music has a couple of dozen stores across Calgary under their various brands, including **Chapters** in Chinook Centre (6455 Macleod Trail, 403/212-0090) and another farther south (9631 Macleod Trail, 403/212-1442), and the **Indigo** store in Signal Hill Centre (Sarcee Trail SW, 403/246-2221). The company also operates stores in major malls and Calgary International Airport under the IndigoSpirit name.

USED BOOKS

Fair's Fair (1609 14th St. SW, 403/245-2778, from 10am daily) is the biggest of Calgary's secondhand and collector bookstores. Surprise, surprise, it's remarkably well organized, with a solid collection of well-labeled Canadiana filling more than one room. Fair's Fair has another large outlet in Inglewood (907 9th Ave. SE, 403/237-8156). On the north side of downtown, **Aquila Books** (826 16th Ave. NW, 403/282-5832) is a real gem, with one of the world's best collections of antiquarian Canadian Rockies and mountaineering books.

Accommodations and Camping

Accommodations in Calgary vary from campgrounds, a hostel, and budget motels to a broad selection of high-quality hotels catering to top-end travelers and business conventions. Most downtown hotels offer drastically reduced rates on weekends—Friday and Saturday nights might be half the regular room rate. During Stampede Week, prices are higher than the rest of the year, and accommodations are booked months in advance. Rates quoted below are for a double room in summer, but outside of Stampede Week.

The bed-and-breakfast scene in Calgary is alive and well. Most are located off the main tourist routes. The **Bed & Breakfast Association of Calgary** (www.bbcalgary.com) represents around 40 of these homes offering rooms to visitors. The association doesn't offer a reservation service (although they do offer a handy online availability calendar), but is simply a grouping of properties that meet certain standards.

DOWNTOWN
Under $50

Part of the worldwide Hostelling International organization, **HI-Calgary City Centre** (520 7th Avenue SE, 403/670-7580 or 888/762-4122, www.hihostels.ca) is an excellent choice for budget travelers, both for its convenient location and wide variety of facilities. It has 94 beds, most in eight-bed dormitories, but there are a couple of private rooms. Other amenities include a fully equipped kitchen, laundry facilities, a large common room, Internet kiosks, free wireless Internet, bike rental, an outdoor barbecue, a game room, a snack bar, lockers, and free parking. Members of Hostelling International pay $32 for a dorm bed ($36 for nonmembers) or $75-81 s or d ($83-89 for nonmembers) in the private rooms. It's one block east of the City Hall C-train station.

$50-100

The most central bed-and-breakfast is **Inglewood B&B** (1006 8th Ave. SE, 403/262-6570, www.inglewoodbedandbreakfast.com, $100-165 s or d), named for the historic neighborhood in which it lies. Its location is excellent—close to the river and Stampede Park, as well as a 10-minute stroll from downtown. The three rooms within this modern Victorian-style home each have private bathrooms, and rates include a cooked breakfast of your own choosing.

$150-200

A few blocks west of the downtown shopping district, but linked by the C-train, you'll find the 301-room **Sandman Hotel** (888 7th Ave. SW, 403/237-8626 or 800/726-3626, www.sandmanhotels.com, $175-245 s or d). This full-service property features an indoor pool, a family-style restaurant, and large, attractive rooms

Across the railway tracks from downtown, the **Best Western Plus Suites Downtown** (1330 8th St. SW, 403/268-6900 or 800/981-2555, www.bestwesternsuitescalgary.com, $190 s or d) features 123 self-contained units, each with contemporary styling, a kitchen, and air-conditioning. Rates include full breakfast and parking.

$200-250

◖ Hotel Arts (119 12th Ave. SW, 403/266-4611 or 800/661-9378, www.hotelarts.ca, $249-436 s or d) is a newish 12-story, 188-room accommodation on the south side of the railway tracks, within easy walking distance of Stampede Park. The rooms are contemporary-slick, with 42-inch LCD flat-screen TVs,

cordless phones, high-speed Internet access, luxurious bathrooms, and plush beds with goose-down duvets. Downstairs is a fitness room, an outdoor heated pool surrounded by a beautiful patio, a restaurant, and a lounge.

The **International Hotel Suites Calgary** (220 4th Ave. SW, 403/265-9600 or 800/661-8627, www.internationalhotel.ca, $245-295 s or d) features 250 one- and two-bedroom suites, an indoor pool, a fitness room, and a restaurant.

$250-300

When I spend the night in Calgary on business, I try to stay somewhere different every time (in the name of research). But when it's a special occasion, it's difficult to beat the ◖ **Kensington Riverside Inn** (1126 Memorial Dr. NW, Kensington, 403/228-4442 or 877/313-3733, www.kensingtonriversideinn.com, $299-369 s or d), surprisingly the city's only boutique hotel. Why? From the moment I'm tempted by a homemade cookie from the jar at the reception to the moment I slide between the Egyptian cotton sheets that top out ultra-comfortable mattresses, the inn has a captivating atmosphere that is unlike any other city accommodation. Each of the 19 guest rooms has a slightly different feel (from bold contemporary to warmly inviting) and layout (some have a private balcony, others have a gas fireplace or jetted tub), but it's in-room niceties such as heated towel racks or a quiet hour spent in the central living room with evening hors d'oeuvres that make the inn super special. A coffee tray and morning paper left by your door, followed by a gourmet breakfast served in the downstairs Chef's Table dining room, are included in the rates. The inn is across the Bow River from downtown in Kensington, one of Calgary's hippest neighborhoods.

Over $300

One block north from the Calgary Tower is the

Kensington Riverside Inn

☾ Hyatt Regency Calgary (700 Centre St., 403/717-1234 or 800/492-8804, www.calgary. hyatt.com, $319-469 s or d). Incorporating a historic building along Stephen Avenue Walk in its construction, this 21-story hotel features an indoor swimming pool, a refined lounge, over 500 pieces of original art, and a renowned restaurant specializing in Canadian cuisine. The hotel's Stillwater Spa is the premier spa facility in Calgary—spend any time here, and you'll forget you're in a city hotel. The up-to-date guest rooms won't take your breath away, but they have a wide range of amenities and luxurious bathrooms.

Calgary's best-known hotel, the gracious **Fairmont Palliser** (133 9th Ave. SE, 403/263-0520 or 866/540-4477, www.fairmont.com, from $429 s or d) was built in 1914 by the Canadian Pacific Railway for the same clientele as the company's famous properties in Banff and Jasper. The rooms may seem smallish by modern standards, and the hotel lacks certain recreational facilities, but the elegance and character of the grande dame of Calgary accommodations are priceless. The cavernous lobby has original marble columns and staircases, a magnificent chandelier, and solid-brass doors that open onto busy 9th Avenue. As you'd expect, staying at the Palliser isn't cheap, but it's a luxurious way to enjoy the city.

MACLEOD TRAIL

A string of hotels along Macleod Trail south of downtown picks up highway traffic as it enters the city. Most midpriced chains are represented, with the following just a sampling.

$100-150

Most of the chain motels along Macleod Trail fall into this price category. Book in advance or online to pick up rates around $100 a night.

Southernmost of the motels on Macleod Trail is the 34-room **Stetson Village Inn** (10002 Macleod Trail SW, 403/271-3210 or

CALGARY

Hyatt Regency Calgary

888/322-3210, www.stetsoninn.ca, $115 s or d), an older-style place tucked between shopping malls. Local calls are free, and the adjoining restaurant is open daily for breakfast and dinner. The rates could be lower (and they are in winter—$79 s or d), but it's a prime spot for getting out of the city to begin your exploration of southern Alberta.

The **Best Western Calgary Centre Inn** (3630 Macleod Trail SW, 403/287-3900 or 877/287-3900, www.bwcalgarycentre.com, $149-169 s or d) may be close to the geographical center of the city, but it's not downtown as the name suggests. Each of the rooms is decorated in a bright and breezy color scheme and comes stocked with amenities such as a hair dryer and coffeemaker. On the premises are an indoor pool and a fitness center. Rates include continental breakfast.

A few blocks farther south, with a C-train station on its back doorstep, stands **Holiday Inn Macleod Trail** (4206 Macleod Trail SW, 403/287-2700 or 800/661-1889, www.holidayinn.com, $149 s or d), where the 150 rooms were last renovated in 2009. Facilities here include a large indoor pool, a restaurant, and a lounge.

MOTEL VILLAGE

Motel Village is Calgary's main concentration of moderately priced motels. The "village" is not an official designation, just a dozen motels bunched together on a single block bordered by 16th Avenue NW, Crowchild Trail, and Banff Trail. From the adjacent Banff Trail station, downtown is a short, safe ride away on the C-train.

$100-150

The **Comfort Inn** (2369 Banff Trail NW, 403/289-2581 or 800/228-5150, www.comfortinncalgary.com, $139-179 s or d) combines a wide range of amenities with reasonable rates to be my pick of Motel Village accommodations.

All rooms have a simple yet snazzy contemporary look, along with high-speed Internet, a coffeemaker, a hair dryer, and an ironing facility, and a national paper is delivered to your door each morning. Other features include an indoor pool and waterslide complex. Rates include a light breakfast.

Best Western Village Park Inn (1804 Crowchild Trail NW, 403/289-0241, www. bestwesternalberta.com, $145 s or d) features 159 spacious rooms well equipped for business and leisure travelers, and a huge atrium containing a lounge with an adjoining restaurant (6:30am-11pm) and a swimming pool.

WEST OF DOWNTOWN

This area, known as 16th Avenue NW within city limits, has a string of inexpensive motels lining the TransCanada Highway heading west from the city toward the Canadian Rockies, but none are a particularly good value.

$150-200

Directly opposite Canada Olympic Park is the **Four Points by Sheraton Calgary West** (8220 Bow Ridge Crescent NW, 403/288-4441 or 877/288-4441, www.fourpointscalgarywest. com, $169-195 s or d), a real standout for motel accommodations on this side of the city. The 150 rooms are big and bright, and each has a balcony (ask for one with a view of Canada Olympic Park). Along with city-hotel luxuries like room service, other amenities include an indoor pool and waterslide, a fitness center, the Mountain Oasis Retreat spa facility, and a restaurant (breakfast around $12) and lounge. Check the hotel website for rates well under $150 and for suites for less than the rack rate. Some packages include airport shuttles—perfect if you're renting from Hertz, which has a desk in the lobby.

Across the road from the Sheraton is **Sandman Hotel & Suites** (125 Bow Ridge Crescent NW, 403/288-6033 or 800/726-3626, www.sandmanhotels.com, $185 s or d). It features spacious modern rooms, an indoor pool, a fitness room, and a 24-hour Denny's restaurant.

NORTHEAST (AIRPORT)

Many hotels lie in the northeast section of the city at varying distances from Calgary International Airport. All of those detailed below have airport shuttles, and most can be contacted directly by courtesy phone from the airport. If you're reading this book, chances are you're flying into Calgary. If not, and you're planning on flying out of Calgary, it's worth knowing that these same hotels may let you leave a vehicle with them free of charge until your return *and* use their shuttle service simply for staying overnight.

$100-150

Check hotel websites listed below for rooms around the $100 mark, or take the easy way out and book your stay at the no-frills **Pointe Inn** (1808 19th St. NE, 403/291-4681 or 800/661-8164, www.pointeinn.com, $100 s or d). Facilities include a launderette, a restaurant, and a lounge. Request a nonsmoking room.

$150-200

Holiday Inn Calgary Airport (1250 McKinnon Dr. NE, 403/230-1999 or 800/465-4329, www.holidayinn.com, $165-195 s or d) is a little farther from the airport than the other choices, but since there's a free shuttle, that is of little consequence. The rooms are exactly what you expect from Holiday Inn, the restaurant has surprisingly good city views, and the indoor pool is the perfect place to refresh yourself after a long flight.

Similarly priced is the **Radisson Hotel Calgary Airport** (2120 16th Ave. NE, 403/291-4666 or 800/395-7046, www.radisson.com, $178-278 s or d), which features 185 comfortable rooms, a large lobby filled with

CALGARY

greenery and comfortable seating, an indoor pool, a fitness center, spa services, a restaurant, and a lounge.

Over $200

⟨ Delta Calgary Airport (403/291-2600 or 888/492-8804, www.deltahotels.com, $279 s or d) is the only accommodation right at the airport. The main terminal is linked to the hotel lobby by a walkway that leads into an expansive atrium and restaurant. The medium-size rooms come with luxuries like down duvets and plush bathrobes, each has a writing desk, and most importantly, they are well sound-proofed. Premier Rooms, which are the same size as regular rooms, come with upgraded furnishings for a few bucks extra. Hotel amenities include two restaurants, a lounge, an indoor pool, and a business center.

CAMPGROUNDS

No camping is available within the Calgary city limits, although campgrounds can be found to the east and west along the TransCanada Highway.

West

The only Calgary campground with an outdoor swimming pool is **⟨ Calgary West Campground** (221 101st St. SW, 403/288-0411 or 888/562-0842, www.calgarycamp-ground.com, mid-Apr.-mid-Oct., unserviced sites $34, hookups $40-46), on a north-facing hill a short way west of Canada Olympic Park. In addition to the pool, modern facilities include showers, a laundry room, a game room, and a grocery store. Around 320 sites are laid out on terraces, so no one misses out on the views.

Calaway Park (10 km/6.2 mi west of the city limits, 403/249-7372, www.calawaypark.com, mid-May-Aug., tent sites $28, hookups $32-38) is farther out along the TransCanada Highway. It offers a large, open camping area. Trees are scarce, but on clear days the view of the Canadian Rockies is spectacular.

East

Mountainview Farm Campground, three kilometers (1.9 miles) east of the city limits on the TransCanada Highway (403/293-6640, www.calgarycamping.com, tent sites $38, hookups $40-45) doesn't have a view of the mountains, but it does have minigolf and hay rides. The sites are very close together. Facilities include showers, a grocery store, and a laundry room.

Food

Calgary may lack the cultural trappings that Alberta's capital, Edmonton, boasts, but it gives that city a run for its money in the restaurant department. Southwest of downtown, along 17th Avenue and 4th Street, a once-quieter part of the city has been transformed into a focal point for Calgary's restaurant scene, with cuisine to suit all tastes. Familiar North American fast-food restaurants line Macleod Trail south of the city center.

DOWNTOWN

All of the major high-rise buildings have plazas with inexpensive food courts, coffeehouses, and cappuccino bars—the perfect places for people-watching. Local suits all have their own favorite haunts, but only two places really stand out to me as trying that little bit harder to be different and to please at the same time. Both are owned by the same company, Sunterra, which started out as a family farm before moving into processing, then retail. **Sunterra Village Marché** (Plus 15 Level, TransCanada Tower, 450 1st St.

CALGARY

SW, 403/262-8240, 6am-8pm Mon.-Fri.) is set up to represent a French streetscape, complete with a patisserie, carvery, salad counter, deli, wine bar, and juice joint. Meals can be packaged to go, but plan on "eating in" at a wide variety of seating styles, including outdoors. **Sunterra Marché** (Plus 15 Level, Bankers Hall, 855 2nd St. SW, 403/269-3610, 6:30am-6:30pm Mon.-Wed., 6:30am-8pm Thurs.-Fri., 9:30am-5:30pm Sat.) has a much smaller selection but the same high quality of gourmet-to-go lunches.

Eau Claire Market and Vicinity

At the entrance to Prince's Island Park, this expansive indoor market has a large food court and several restaurants. In the food court (daily until 9pm), you'll find a great seafood outlet, a bakery, international food places such as the Italian **Prego Cucina Italiana** (403/233-7885), and an outlet of the local coffee chain **Good Earth Café** (403/237-8684).

Outside the market's western entrance is **Joey Tomato's** (200 Barclay Parade SW, 403/263-6336, from 11am daily, $17-26), a bistro-style chain restaurant serving moderately priced Italian favorites. Last time I visited, the pork ribs were as juicy as they come. This place is a big hit with the lunchtime and after-work crowd, especially the large outdoor section on summer afternoons.

Across from Joey Tomato's, you'll find **1886 Buffalo Café** (187 Barclay Parade SW, 403/269-9255, 6am-3pm Mon.-Fri., 7am-3pm Sat.-Sun., breakfasts $9-15). Named for the year it was built, it's at least 100 years older than other buildings in the neighborhood. This restaurant oozes an authentic Old Calgary ambience. Inexpensive breakfasts attract the most interesting group of diners, but the place is busy all day. Portions are generous, coffee refills are free, and when you've finished your meal, ask to see the museum downstairs.

Steak

Caesar's Steak House (512 4th Ave. SW, 403/264-1222, 11am-midnight Mon.-Fri., 4:30pm-midnight Sat., $28-52) opened in 1972 and is still going strong. The elegant room is decorated in a Roman-style setting with dark woods, leather seating, and dim lighting—just what you expect from a steakhouse. Although the menu includes ribs and seafood, it's juicy prime cuts of Alberta beef that this place is known for.

Striving hard to be the flashiest steakhouse in town, **Saltlik** (101 Stephen Ave. Walk, 403/537-1160, lunch and dinner daily, $17-34) stretches the rules when it comes to tradition—it's big, bold, and brassy, the exact opposite of Caesar's.

Tribune (118 Stephen Ave. Walk, 403/269-3160, 11am-10pm Mon.-Thurs., 11am-11pm Fri., 4pm-11pm Sat., $19-37) has the same urban-slick setting as Saltlik, which is right across the road. Prices are similar, and while steak is the big draw, the menu covers all bases, with mains as simple as tomato penne. The best cuts of Alberta beef with a side of seasonal vegetables are a reasonable $29.

You don't need to spend a fortune to dig into a juicy steak at **Buzzards Restaurant & Bar** (140 10th Ave. SW, 403/264-6959, 11am-11pm Mon.-Fri., 5pm-11pm Sat., $14-28), easily found by its barn-board porch and the broken-down wagon out front. Choices range from bison burgers for $14 to elk striploin for $28, and it wouldn't be a complete meal at Buzzard's without sharing a platter of prairie oyster fritters ($12.50) to start.

Canadian

Thomsons (112 Stephen Ave. Walk, 403/537-4449, 6:30am-1:30pm and 5pm-9:30pm daily, $22-36) is in a historic sandstone building cleverly integrated with the modern Hyatt Regency, but it's not aimed at the hotel crowd. First off, the buffet breakfast ($20) is as good as it gets,

CALGARY CUISINE

© ANDREW HEMPSTEAD

Deane House

Calgary has grown up (and out) so much in the last decade that defining the local cuisine is almost impossible. Steakhouses such as **Caesar's** were long the mainstay, and happily they still thrive. In the last decade, it's been joined by dozens of top-class restaurants that specialize in giving Canadian produce a modern makeover, with **Farm, Divino, Tribune,** and **Saltlik** leading the way. A few old diners survive; those such as the **Galaxy,** off trendy 17th Avenue SW, and **Peter's Drive-In,** along the TransCanada Highway, have been amazingly popular since the 1960s. But in both cases, you could be eating anywhere in North America. **Buzzard's** is what everyone wants to think Calgary used to be like, but it is about as authentic as downtown bankers wearing blue jeans for Stampede. While you can't go wrong eating at any of these places, two other restaurants stand out for top-notch food and a distinctive I-must-be-in-Calgary ambience.

Built in 1906 for the superintendent of Fort Calgary, **Deane House** (806 9th Ave., 403/269-7747, 11am-3pm Tues.-Fri., 9am-2pm Sat.-Sun.) is a casual dining room surrounded by carefully tended gardens that re-create those laid out 100 years ago. The menu offers a wide choice of simple, healthy lunchtime fare, all under $20 (Alberta beef is the exception), making it the perfect place to head after spending the morning at adjacent Fort Calgary.

In the far south of the city, **The Ranche** (off Bow Bottom Trail SE, 403/225-3939, 11:30am-2pm and 5pm-9pm Mon.-Thurs., 11:30am-2pm and 5pm-10pm Fri., 5pm-10pm Sat., 10:30am-2pm and 5pm-9pm Sun., $24-39) is a beautifully restored Victorian mansion that was the headquarters of the Bow Valley Ranch in the late 1880s. While the surroundings are old-style stately, the food is anything but, with elk, caribou, buffalo, and beef (from the owner's ranch) combined with organic vegetables and local ingredients to create an imaginative menu that is among the best in the city. Expect to pay $14-28 for a lunch entrée. For Sunday brunch, the eggs Benedict with smoked elk ham ($17) is an easy choice.

1886 Buffalo Café, beside Eau Claire Market

with omelets made to order and real maple syrup to douse your pancakes. The rest of the day, the menu is dominated by Canadian game and seafood. Maybe start with PEI mussels in traditional ale, then choose from something as Canadian as grilled arctic char, or splurge on the Alberta beef tenderloin. Just make sure to leave room for the smoothest crème brûlée in the city.

Walk north from Eau Claire Market to reach the ◖ **River Café** (Prince's Island Park, 403/261-7670, 11am-10pm Mon.-Fri., 10am-10pm Sat.-Sun., $26-49), a cozy, rustic dining room that will surprise you with some of Calgary's finest cooking. More of a restaurant than a café, it features extensive use of produce and ingredients sourced from across Canada. Standouts include buffalo, top-quality Alberta beef, and salmon dishes, with the latter often incorporating maple syrup. Lunch mains range $17-24 (including a delicious smoked trout flatbread), while weekend brunch ranges $11-19.

Had a bad experience dining in a revolving restaurant? Haven't we all. Hopefully your meal at the **Sky 360** (101 9th Ave. SW, 403/508-5822, 11am-2pm and 5pm-10pm daily, $23-42) atop the Calgary Tower will be memorable for more than just the view. A full rotation takes one hour. Expect healthy, modern cooking that uses lots of Canadian produce, with lunchtime sandwiches, such as maple-smoked chicken with apple chutney, for under $20. In the evening, the butternut squash soup is a good way to start, before moving on to mains such as braised pork chop with Digby scallops.

Seafood

Yes, Calgary is a long way from the ocean, but it nonetheless has a few excellent seafood restaurants. Across the railway tracks from downtown are two of the best: **Cannery Row** (317 10th Ave. SW, 403/269 8889) and, directly upstairs, **McQueens Upstairs** (403/269-4722). Cannery Row is a casual affair, with an open

CALGARY

kitchen, an oyster bar, and the ambience of a San Francisco seafood restaurant. Dishes such as grilled swordfish, jambalaya, and blackened snapper are mostly under $20. The menu at McQueens Upstairs is more sophisticated and varied. Dinner entrées start at $24 and rise to over $40 for fresh lobster. Both restaurants are open Monday-Friday for lunch and daily for dinner, and have weekend evening entertainment (blues or jazz at McQueens).

Within the Hyatt Regency building, the sophisticated ambience of **Catch** (100 Stephen Ave. Walk, 403/206-0000, 11:30am-1:30pm Mon.-Fri., 5:30pm-9:30pm Mon.-Sat., $34-50) is as big an attraction as the menu of seasonal seafood that is flown in daily from both of Canada's coasts. The main level is an oyster bar, where you can sample a variety of shucked oysters with an extensive choice of drinks, while more formal dining is upstairs in the main room.

Asian

Chinatown, along 2nd and 3rd Avenues east of Centre Street, naturally has the best assortment of Chinese restaurants. **Hang Fung Restaurant** (119 3rd Ave. SE, 403/269-4646, lunch and dinner daily, $7.50-14), tucked behind a Chinese grocery store of the same name, doesn't try to be anything it's not. Chinese locals come here for simple inexpensive meals, mostly under $10. Just as inexpensive is **Golden Inn Restaurant** (107 2nd Ave. SE, 403/269-2211, from 4pm daily, $10-18), which is popular with the local Chinese as well as with professionals, and late-shift workers appreciate its long hours (open until 4am). The menu features mostly Cantonese-style deep-fried food. For a Chinese buffet, head to the cavernous **Regency Palace Restaurant** (328 Centre St. SE, 403/777-2288, lunch Mon.-Fri. and dinner daily, $12-17).

Yuzuki Japanese Restaurant (510 9th Ave. SW, 403/261-7701, lunch weekdays, dinner daily, $13-19) is a good downtown eatery where the most expensive lunch item is the assorted sushi for $16, which comes with miso soup. More upscale is **Sushi Hiro** (727 5th Ave. SW, 403/233-0605, 11:30am-2pm Mon.-Fri., 5pm-11pm Mon.-Sat., $14-22). Sushi choices change regularly but generally include red salmon, yellowtail, sea urchin, and salmon roe. The tempuras ($14-16) are also excellent. If you sit at the oak-and-green-marble sushi counter, you'll be able to ask the chef what's best.

Tucked away across the railway tracks from downtown is **Thai Sa-On** (351 10th Ave. SW, 403/264-3526, dinner nightly, $12-20), a small space that's big on the tastes of Thailand. The menu offers a great variety of red and green curries, but I tried the red snapper—medium spiced, baked, and served whole—and couldn't have been happier. The prices? For downtown dining, the food is ridiculously inexpensive, with a whole steamed fish with garlic-lime sauce costing just $20.

KENSINGTON

Across the Bow River from downtown lies the trendy suburb of Kensington, which is home to several coffeehouses and restaurants. One of the nicest cafés is **Higher Ground** (1126 Kensington Rd. NW, 403/270-3780, 7am-10pm Mon.-Fri., 8am-midnight Sat., 8am-11pm Sun.), a specialty coffee shop with a few window-front tables and wireless Internet. Head to **Jugo Juice** (1154 Kensington Crescent NW, 403/270-0120, 7am-close Mon.-Sat., 8am-close Sun.) and enjoy freshly squeezed juices and a great variety of healthy smoothies outside along a narrow sidewalk.

The casual, two-story **Pulcinella** (1147 Kensington Crescent NW, 403/283-1166, 11:30am-11pm Mon.-Sat., 11:30am-10pm Sun., $15-27) has the most traditional pizza you will find in Alberta, right down to an oven constructed of stone imported from the slopes of Mount Vesuvius. Pizzas have perfectly formed crusts and chunky ingredients, many of which have been imported from the mother country.

When you enter **Sultan's Tent** (4 14th St., 403/244-2333, 5pm-11pm Wed.-Sun., $18-28.50), a server appears with a silver kettle and basin filled with orange-blossom-scented water with which to wash your hands. It's all part of Moroccan custom and part of the fun. The restaurant features swinging lanterns, richly colored tapestries hanging from the walls, piped-in Arabic music, and, most important, delicious Moroccan delicacies. If you're hungry, try the Sultan's Feast ($55), a five-course dinner.

A few blocks toward the city, Kensington's busiest intersection offers a bunch of eateries, including another Italian restaurant, **Osteria de Medici** (201 10th St. NW, 403/283-5553, 11am-11pm Mon.-Sat., 4pm-10pm Sun., $21-36). Although still traditional, the atmosphere is more refined and the menu more adventurous than Pulcinella, but service is friendly and prices not as high as they could be.

UPTOWN 17TH AVENUE

The area immediately south of downtown offers a diverse choice of dining options. The major concentrations of restaurants are along 17th Avenue SW, as well as south for a couple of blocks along 4th Street.

For gourmet coffees, hot chocolate made with locally made chocolate, and exotic teas, join the crowds at **Café Beano** (1613 9th St. SW, 403/229-1232, 7am-11pm daily).

Restaurants

Typifying the modern wave of slow food is **[FARM** (1006 17th Ave. SW, 403/245-2276, 11:30am-2pm and from 5pm daily, $12-25), where the emphasis is on local, seasonal ingredients prepared in simple and tasty ways. Many diners concentrate on the meats and cheeses

FARM is one of Calgary's best restaurants.

CALGARY

© ANDREW HEMPSTEAD

listed on a large chalkboard hanging on the back wall before moving on to house specialties such as a killer BLT salad. The room itself is appealing, with stools along the open kitchen allowing diners to watch their meals being prepared by the friendly kitchen staff.

Few restaurants in the city have been as popular over multiple decades as **Chianti** (1438 17th Ave. SW, 403/229-1600, lunch Mon.-Fri., dinner daily, $15-26). More than 20 well-prepared pasta dishes are featured on the menu, and all the pasta is made daily on the premises. Among many specialties are an antipasto platter and Salmone Cappesante, baked salmon with scallops and mango in a creamy coconut

and curry sauce. Most regular pasta entrées are less than $20. The restaurant is dark and noisy in typical Italian style. The owner often sings with an accordionist on weekends.

Closer to downtown, **Bonterra Trattoria** (1016 8th St. SW, 403/262-8480, 11:30am-2:30pm Mon.-Fri., 5pm-10pm daily, $17-44) has a stylish dining room with a vaulted ceiling and lots of exposed woodwork. Tables out on the Mediterranean-style patio are in great demand through summer. The menu is modern Italian, with pastas from $17 and the pan-seared halibut a worthwhile splurge at $32. The nationalistic wine list has only a few bottles under $40, but many are available by the glass.

Information and Services

Information Centers

Tourism Calgary (403/263-8510 or 800/661-1678, www.tourismcalgary.com) promotes the city to the world. The organization also operates two Visitor Information Centres. The one that greets visitors arriving by air is across from Carousel 4 at **Calgary International Airport** (403/735-1234, 6am-11pm daily year-round). The other is right downtown, at the base of the **Calgary Tower** (101 9th Ave. SW, 403/750-2362, 9am-7pm daily in summer, 9am-5pm daily the rest of the year).

Libraries

The Calgary Public Library's 18 branch libraries are scattered throughout the city. The largest is **W. R. Castell Central Library** (616 Macleod Trail SE, 403/260-2600, www.calgarypubliclibrary.com, 9am-8pm Mon.-Thurs., 9am-5pm Fri., 10am-5pm Sat., noon-5pm Sun.). Four floors of books, magazines, and newspapers from around the world are enough to keep most people busy on a rainy afternoon.

Post and Internet

The downtown **post office** is at 207 9th Avenue SW. All city libraries provide free Internet access, while almost all hotels have either wireless or modem Internet access. Alternatively, head to **Cyber Center** (1602 Centre St. NE, 403/398-3528, 8am-7pm daily) for some online surfing.

Banks

In the heart of downtown, **Calforex** (228 8th Ave. SW, 403/290-0330) exchanges foreign currency and lets you wire international payments. Most major banks carry U.S. currency and can handle basic foreign-exchange transactions.

Photography

I've been trusting my photographic needs to **The Camera Store** (802 11th Ave. SW, 403/234-9935, 9am-6pm Mon.-Fri., 9am-5pm Sat.) for many years. They have knowledgeable service and sales divisions, with the latter up to speed on the latest digital and video technology.

Emergency Services

For medical emergencies, call 911 or contact **Foothills Hospital** (1403 29th Ave. NW, 403/670-1110) or **Rockyview General Hospital** (7007 14th St. SW, 403/943-3000). Across 16th Avenue to the north from Foothills Hospital, the **Alberta Children's Hospital** (2888 Shaganappi Trail NW, 403/955-7211) is difficult to miss with its colorfully modern exterior. For the **Calgary Police,** call 911 in an emergency or 403/266-1234 for nonurgent matters.

Getting There and Around

GETTING THERE

The vast majority of visitors arrive either by road or touch down at Calgary International Airport. For those driving, it is 1,061 kilometers (653 miles) to Calgary from Vancouver and 3,471 kilometers (2,157 miles) from Toronto. For travelers from the United States, the most direct route from the border is Highway 4 then 3 then 2, originating at Coutts, from where it is 274 kilometers (170 miles) via Lethbridge to downtown.

Air

Calgary International Airport (airport code YYC; www.calgaryairport.com) is within the city limits northeast of downtown. It is served by more than a dozen scheduled airlines and used by seven million passengers each year (Canada's fourth-busiest airport). Arrivals is on the lower level, where passengers are greeted by White Hat volunteers who are dressed in traditional Western attire and answer visitors' questions about the airport, transportation, and the city. Across from the baggage carousels are an information desk and a bank of interactive computer terminals linked to hotels and other tourist services. The desks for all major rental-car outlets are across the road.

A cab to downtown runs approximately $45, or take the **Calgary Transit** bus (403/262-1000, www.calgarytransit.com) to downtown for $8 one-way. This service runs every 30 minutes 5am-midnight daily.

Air Canada, WestJet, and several U.S. airlines fly into Calgary; click through the links on the airport website for details.

Bus

The **Greyhound** bus depot (850 16th St. SW, 403/265-9111 or 800/661-8747, www.greyhound.ca) is two blocks away from the C-train stop ($2.75 into town), or you can cross the overhead pedestrian bridge at the terminal's southern entrance and catch a transit bus (same price). To walk the entire distance to town would take 20 minutes. A cab from the bus depot to downtown runs $15, to HI-Calgary City Centre $20. The depot is cavernous. It has a restaurant, an ATM, information boards, and lockers large enough to hold backpacks ($3). Greyhound buses connect Calgary daily with Edmonton (3.5 hours), Banff (2 hours), Vancouver (15 hours), and all other points within the province. No seat reservations are taken. Just turn up, buy your ticket, and hop aboard. If you buy your ticket seven days in advance, discounts apply. If you plan to travel extensively by bus, the Discovery Pass is a good deal.

From their offices near the Calgary Tower, **Red Arrow** (205 9th Ave. SE, 403/531-0350, www.redarrow.ca) shuttles passengers between Calgary and downtown Edmonton, with some services continuing to Fort McMurray in northern Alberta.

GETTING AROUND

Like major cities around the world, locals complain about the road system, but in reality,

CALGARY

driving is relatively uncomplicated, especially as new sections of the long-awaited ring road are completed, including a section in the northwest that makes traveling between Banff and the Calgary International Airport a lot quicker.

Bus

Calgary Transit (403/262-1000, www.calgarytransit.com) goes just about everywhere in town by combining two light-rail lines with extensive bus routes. Buses are adult $2.75, child $2—deposit the exact change in the box beside the driver and request a transfer (valid for 90 minutes). A day pass, which is valid for unlimited bus and rail travel, is adult $8.50, child $5.75. The best place for information and schedules is the **Calgary Transit Customer Service Centre** (244 7th Ave. SW, 10am-5pm Mon.-Fri.).

C-Train

C-train, the light-rail transit (LRT) system, has three lines that total 60 kilometers (37 miles) of track and over 40 stations. All lines converge on 7th Avenue, running parallel for the entire distance through downtown. From here, the 202 (also known as Whitehorn) runs past the zoo and the Max Bell Theatre to suburban Saddletowne. The West LRT, which was completed in 2013, has six stations extending west as far as 69th Street. The other line 201/starts in the northwest at Crowchild station, with stops at the university and Banff Trail (Motel Village). On the south side of the city, stations include two for Stampede Park and a bunch along Macleod Trail before ending in the far south of the city at Somerset-Bridlewood.

C-train travel is free along 7th Avenue and $2.75 to all other destinations.

Passengers with Disabilities

All C-trains and stations are wheelchair accessible. Low-floor buses are employed on many bus routes; call ahead for a schedule. **Calgary Handi-bus** (403/276-8028, www.calgaryhandibus.com) provides wheelchair-accessible transportation throughout the city.

Taxi

The flag charge for a cab in Calgary is $3.75, and it's around $1.60 for every kilometer. Passengers departing Calgary International Airport by cab pay a $4 surcharge. Taxi companies include **Advance** (403/777 1111), **Associated Cabs** (403/299-1111), **Checker/Yellow Cabs** (403/299-9999), and **Mayfair** (403/255-6555).

Car Rental

If you're planning on starting your Alberta travels from Calgary and need a rental car, make reservations as far in advance as possible to secure the best rates. Rentals beginning from the airport incur additional charges, so consider renting from downtown or from one of the many hotels that have representatives based in their lobbies.

Rental agencies and their local numbers include **Avis** (403/269-6166), **Budget** (403/226-1550), **Discount** (403/299-1224), **Economy** (403/291-1640), **Enterprise** (403/263-1273), **Hertz** (403/221-1676), **National** (403/221-1690), **Rent-A-Wreck** (403/287-9703), and **Thrifty** (403/262-4400).

BACKGROUND

The Land

The Rocky Mountains rise from the dense forests of central Mexico and run north through the U.S. states of New Mexico, Colorado, Wyoming, and Montana. Continuing north across the 49th parallel (the U.S.-Canada border), the range forms a natural border between the Canadian provinces of British Columbia and Alberta. Mountainous British Columbia is Canada's westernmost province, extending to the Pacific Ocean, while Alberta, to the east, is mostly prairie. The provincial boundary is the Continental Divide, an imaginary line that runs along the Rockies' highest peaks.

Although it is a subjective matter, perhaps most would agree that this particular stretch of the Rocky Mountains—the Canadian Rockies—is the most spectacular segment. North of British Columbia and Alberta, the Rockies descend to their northern terminus in the boreal forests of northern Canada.

The Canadian Rockies are relatively low compared to other well-known mountain ranges of the world; the highest peak, Mount Robson, tops out at 3,954 meters (12,970 feet). Running parallel to the mountains along their eastern edge is a series of long, rolling ridges

© ANDREW HEMPSTEAD

known as the foothills. To the west is the Rocky Mountain Trench, a long, wide valley that in turn is bordered to the west by various subranges of the Columbia Mountains.

GEOLOGY

The Rocky Mountains began rising 75 million years ago, making them relatively young compared to the world's major mountain ranges. But to fully appreciate the geology of the Rockies, you must look back many hundreds of millions of years, to the Precambrian era. At this time, about 700 million years ago, the Pacific Ocean covered most of the western provinces and states. The ocean advanced, then receded, several times over the next half billion years. Each time the ocean flooded eastward it deposited layers of silt and sand on its bed—layers that built up with each successive inundation. Starting approximately 550 million years ago, the oceans began to come alive with marine invertebrates and the first crustaceans. As these creatures died and sank to the ocean floor, they added to the layers of sediment. Over time, the ever-increasing sediment load compressed the underlying layers into sandstone, shale, and quartzite.

Birth of the Rockies

Some 200 million years ago, the stability of the ocean floor began wavering along the West Coast of North America, culminating 75 million years ago as two plates of the earth's crust collided. According to plate tectonics theory, the earth's crust is broken into several massive chunks (plates) that are always moving and occasionally bump into each other. This isn't something that happens overnight; a plate may move only a few centimeters over thousands of years. In the case of the Rockies, the Pacific Plate butted into the North American Plate and was forced beneath it. The land at this subduction zone was crumpled and thrust upward, creating the Rocky

Mountains. Layers of sediment laid down on the ocean floor over the course of hundreds of millions of years were folded, twisted, and squeezed; great slabs of rock broke away, and in places older strata were pushed on top of younger. By the beginning of the Tertiary period, around 65 million years ago, the present form of mountain contours was established and the geological framework of the mountains was in place.

The Ice Ages

No one knows why, but around one million years ago the world's climate cooled a few degrees. Ice caps formed in Arctic regions and slowly moved south over North America and Eurasia. These advances, followed by retreats, occurred four times.

The final major glaciation began moving south 35,000 years ago. A sheet of ice up to 2,000 meters (6,560 feet) deep covered all but the highest peaks of the Rocky Mountains. The ice scoured the terrain, destroying all vegetation as it crept slowly forward. In the mountains, these rivers of ice carved hollows, known as **cirques,** into the slopes of the higher peaks. They rounded off lower peaks and reamed out valleys from their preglacier V shape to the trademark, postglacial U shape. The retreat of this ice sheet, beginning around 12,000 years ago, also radically altered the landscape. Rock and debris that had been picked up by the ice on its march forward melted out during the retreat, creating high ridges known as lateral and terminal **moraines.** Many of these moraines blocked natural drainages, resulting in the formation of lakes. Meltwater drained into rivers and streams, incising deep channels into the sedimentary rock of the plains. Today, the only remnants of this ice age are the scattered ice fields along the Continental Divide, including the 325-square-kilometer (125-square-mile) Columbia Icefield.

FOOTHILLS ERRATICS TRAIN

During the last ice age, a sheet of ice up to 1,000 meters (3,280 feet) thick crept southward across the area that is now Jasper National Park. A landslide deposited hundreds of large quartzite boulders atop the ice, which continued moving south, carrying the boulders with it. Many thousands of years later, as temperatures warmed and the ice melted, the boulders were deposited far from their source, creating what geologists call an "erratics train"–a string of glacially deposited rocks that in this case extends 650 kilometers (400 miles) south through Alberta. The largest of these boulders–the world's largest erratic, weighing an estimated 18,000 tons–lies just beyond the foothills, seven kilometers (4.3 miles) west of Okotoks. The name is difficult to forget; it's called the **Big Rock.**

Waterways

Water in its various forms has had a profound effect on the appearance of the Canadian Rockies. In addition to the scouring action of the glaciers, flowing water in rivers and streams has, over the millennia, deeply etched the landscape. The process continues today.

The flow of water is directly related to **divides,** or high points of land that dictate the direction of water flow. The dominant divide in the Canadian Rockies, and indeed North America, is the Continental Divide. The natural boundary created by this divide forms the Alberta-British Columbia border, while other, less obvious divides form borders of many parks of the Canadian Rockies. The five national parks are classic examples of this scenario. The divides forming the boundaries of Banff National Park encompass the entire upper watershed of the **Bow River.** The Bow flows southward through the park, then heads east out of the mountains and into the Saskatchewan River system, whose waters continue east to Hudson Bay and the Atlantic Ocean. The Bow River is fed by many lakes famed for their beauty, including the **Bow, Louise,** and **Moraine.** To the south, the rivers of Kananaskis Country and Waterton Lakes National Park also drain into the Saskatchewan River system.

The boundary between Jasper and Banff National Parks is an important north-south divide. The **Columbia Icefield,** a remnant of the last ice age, lies on either side of this divide. Runoff from the south side of the ice field flows south into the Saskatchewan River system, while runoff from the north side forms the upper headwaters of the **Athabasca River** system. The Athabasca flows north through Jasper National Park and into the Mackenzie River system, which continues north to the Arctic Ocean. All water draining off the western slopes of the Continental Divide ends up in the Pacific Ocean via two major river systems: the **Columbia** and the **Fraser.** The mighty Columbia makes a wide northern loop before heading south into the U.S. state of Washington and draining into the Pacific Ocean. Along the way it picks up the waters of the **Kootenay River,** which begins high in Kootenay National Park and makes a lazy loop south through Montana and Idaho before joining the Columbia at Castlegar, British Columbia, and the **Kicking Horse River,** which flows down from the divides that form the borders of Yoho National Park. The **Fraser River,** the longest river entirely within British Columbia, begins in the high reaches of Mount Robson Provincial Park.

CLIMATE

More than any other factor, prevailing moisture-laden westerlies blowing across British Columbia from the Pacific Ocean dictate the climate of the Canadian Rockies. The cold heights of the mountain peaks wring the winds dry, making for clear, sunny skies in southern Alberta; Calgary gets up to 350 hours of sunshine in June alone—good news, unless you're a farmer. In winter, the dry winds blasting down the eastern slopes of the Rockies can raise temperatures on the prairies by up to 40°C (104°F) in 24 hours. Called **chinooks,** these desiccating blows are a phenomenon unique to Alberta.

Elevation and, to a lesser degree, latitude are two other factors affecting the climate within the mountain ecosystem. Elevations vary from 800 meters (2,600 feet) above sea level at Radium Hot Springs to 1,500 meters (4,920 feet) at Lake Louise to 3,954 meters (12,970 feet) at the summit of Mount Robson. As a general rule, temperatures fall 5°C (9°F) for every 1,000 meters (3,280 feet) of elevation gained. Another interesting phenomenon occurring in the Canadian Rockies is the **temperature inversion,** in which a layer of warm air sits on top of a cold air mass. During these inversions, high- and low-country roles are reversed; prairie residents can be shivering and bundling up, while their mountain fellows are sunning themselves in short sleeves.

The Seasons

Summer in the mountains is short, but the days are long. With up to 17 hours of daylight around the summer solstice of June 21, this is an ideal time for travel and camping out. The months on either side of summer are ideal for touring, especially September, when rainfall is minimal. Winter is cold, but the skiing and snowboarding are fantastic.

January is usually the coldest month, when Banff's average temperature is -10°C (14°F). In winter, extended spells of -30°C (-22°F) are not uncommon anywhere in the mountains, and temperatures occasionally drop below -40°C (-40°F). The coldest temperature recorded was -52°C (-62°F), in Lake Louise on January 25, 1950. Severe cold weather is often accompanied by sunshine; the cold is a dry cold, unlike the damp cold experienced in coastal regions. Cold temperatures and snow can be expected through mid-March.

Although March, April, and May are, more or less, the official months of spring, snow often falls in May, many lakes may remain frozen until June, and snow cover on higher mountain hiking trails remains until early July. During this period of the year, the mountains are often affected by low-pressure weather patterns from the southeast, creating continuous days of rain, especially in the south.

Things warm up in summer. July is the hottest month, with Banff, Jasper, and Canmore's average daytime temperature topping out above 23°C (73°F) and Radium Hot Springs and Golden enjoying average daytime highs of 29°C (84°F) and 27°C (81°F), respectively. On hot days, the temperature can hit 30°C (86°F) along lower-elevation valleys. Again, because of the dryness of the air, these temperatures are more bearable here than in coastal regions experiencing the same temperatures.

By late September, the mountain air begins to have a distinct chill. October brings the highest temperature variations of the year; the thermometer can hit 30°C (86°F) but also dip as low as -20°C (-4°F). Mild weather can continue until early December, but generally the first snow falls in October, and by mid-November winter has set in.

CHINOOK WINDS

On many days in the dead of winter, a distinctive arch of clouds forms in the sky over the southwestern corner of Alberta as a wind peculiar to the Canadian Rockies swoops down over the mountains. The warm wind, known as a *chinook* (snow eater), can raise temperatures by up to 20°C (68°F) in an hour and up to 40°C (104°F) in a 24-hour period. The wind's effect on the snowpack is legendary. One story tells of a backcountry skier who spent the better part of a day traversing to the summit of a snow-clad peak on the front range of the Canadian Rockies. As he rested and contemplated skiing down, he realized that the slope had become completely bare!

Chinooks originate over the Pacific Ocean when warm, moist air is pushed eastward by prevailing westerlies. The air pressure of these winds is less than at lower elevations, and, therefore, as the air moves down the front ranges of the Canadian Rockies, it is subjected to increased pressure. This increasing of the air pressure warms the winds, which then fan out across the foothills and prairies. The "chinook arch" is formed as the clear air clashes with the warmer cloud-laden winds. The phenomenon is most common in southern Alberta but occurs to a lesser degree as far north as the Peace River Valley. Pincher Creek, the gateway to Waterton Lakes National Park, experiences about 35 chinooks each winter.

Flora

Botanists divide the Canadian Rockies into three distinct vegetation zones (also called **biomes**): montane, subalpine, and alpine. The boundaries of these zones are determined by several factors, the most important being altitude. Latitude and exposure are also factors, but less so. Typically, within any 1,500 meters (4,920 feet) of elevation change, you'll pass through each of the three zones. These changes can be seen occurring most abruptly in Waterton Lakes National Park. Conifers (evergreens) predominate in the montane and subalpine, whereas above the tree line, in the alpine, only low-growing hardy species survive.

MONTANE

The foothills, along with most major valleys below an elevation of about 1,500 meters (4,920 feet), are primarily cloaked in montane forest. **Aspen, balsam poplar,** and **white spruce** thrive here. **Lodgepole pine** is the first species to emerge after fire. Its hard seed cones are sealed by a resin that is melted only at high temperatures. When fire races through the forest, the resin melts and the cones release their seeds. The lodgepole is named for its straight, slender trunk, which natives used as a center pole for tepees. On dry, south-facing slopes, **Douglas fir** is the climax species. Where sunlight penetrates the forest, such as along riverbanks, flowers like **lady's slipper, Indian paintbrush,** and **saxifrage** are common. Large tracts of **fescue grassland** are common at lower elevations. The montane forest holds the greatest diversity of life of any vegetation zone and is prime winter habitat for larger mammals. But this is the habitat where most development occurs and therefore is often much changed from its natural state.

SUBALPINE

Subalpine forests occur where temperatures are lower and precipitation higher than in the montane. In the Canadian Rockies, this is generally 1,500-2,200 meters (4,920-7,220 feet) above sea level. The upper limit of the

© ANDREW TEMPSTEAD

Indian paintbrush is common along riverbanks.

subalpine zone is the tree line. Approximately half the flora of the mountains falls within this zone. The climax species are **Engelmann spruce** and **subalpine fir** (recognized by its spirelike crown), although extensive forests of **lodgepole pine** occur in areas that have been scorched by fire in the last 100 years. Before lodgepole pines take root in fire-ravished areas, fireweed blankets the scorched earth. At higher elevations, stands of **larch** are seen. Larches are deciduous conifers—unlike those of other evergreens, their needles turn a golden-orange color each fall, producing a magnificent display for photographers.

ALPINE

The alpine zone extends from the tree line to mountain summits. The upper limit of tree growth in the Canadian Rockies varies between 1,800-2,400 meters (5,900-7,900 feet) above sea level, dropping progressively to the north until it meets the treeless tundra of the Arctic. Vegetation at these high altitudes occurs only where soil has been deposited. Large areas of alpine meadows burst with color for a short period each summer as **lupines, mountain avens, alpine forget-me-nots, avalanche lily, moss campion,** and a variety of **heathers** bloom.

Fauna

One of the biggest attractions of the Canadian Rockies is the abundance of wildlife, especially large mammals such as elk, moose, bighorn sheep, and bears, which are all widespread and easily viewed throughout the mountains.

THE DEER FAMILY
Mule Deer and White-Tailed Deer

Mule deer and white-tailed deer are similar in size and appearance. Their color varies with the season but is generally light brown in summer, turning dirty gray in winter. While both species are considerably smaller than elk, the mule deer is a little stockier than the white-tailed deer. The mule deer has a white rump, a white tail with a dark tip, and large mulelike ears. It inhabits open forests along valley floors. Waterton town site has a healthy population of mule deer. The white-tailed deer's tail is dark on top, but when the animal runs, it holds its tail erect, revealing an all-white underside. Whitetails frequent thickets along the rivers and lakes of the foothills. They are most common on the British Columbia side of the Continental Divide.

Elk

The elk, or **wapiti,** is the most widespread and common of the larger mammals living in the Canadian Rockies. It has a tan body with a dark-brown neck, dark-brown legs, and a white rump. This second-largest member of the deer family weighs 250-450 kilograms (550-1,000 pounds) and stands 1.5 meters (five feet) at the shoulder. Beginning each spring, stags grow an impressive set of antlers, covered in what

© ANDREW HEMPSTEAD

Elk are the most common large mammals in the Canadian Rockies.

is known as velvet. The velvet contains nutrients that stimulate antler growth. By fall, the antlers have reached their full size and the velvet is shed. Rutting season takes place between August and October; listen for the shrill bugles of the stags serenading the females. During the rut, randy males will challenge anything with their antlers and can be dangerous. The stags shed their antlers each spring, but don't relax too much because, also in spring, females protecting their young can be equally dangerous. Large herds of elk live in and around the towns of Banff and Jasper, often nonchalantly wandering along streets and feeding on tasty plants in residential gardens.

Moose

The giant of the deer family is the moose, an awkward-looking mammal that appears to have been designed by a cartoonist. It has the largest antlers of any animal in the world, stands up to 1.8 meters (six feet) at the shoulder, and weighs up to 500 kilograms (1,100 pounds). Its body is dark brown, and it has a prominent nose, long spindly legs, small eyes, big ears, and an odd flap of skin called a bell dangling beneath its chin. Apart from all that, it's good-looking. Each spring the bull begins to grow palm-shaped antlers that by August will be fully grown. Moose are solitary animals preferring marshy areas and weedy lakes, but they are known to wander to higher elevations searching out open spaces in summer. They forage in and around ponds on willows, aspen, birch, grasses, and all aquatic vegetation. They are not particularly common in the Canadian Rockies, numbering around 400. Although they may appear docile, moose will attack humans if they feel threatened.

Caribou

Small populations of caribou inhabit the backcountry of Jasper National Park, including the Bald Hills near Maligne Lake. They are also occasionally spotted from the Icefields Parkway south of Sunwapta Falls. Native people named the animal *caribou* (hoof scraper) for the way in which they feed in winter, scraping away snow with their hooves. Caribou are smaller than elk and have a dark brown coat with creamy patches on the neck and rump. Both sexes grow antlers, but those of the females are shorter and have fewer points. On average males weigh 180 kilograms (400 pounds), females 115 kilograms (250 pounds). Like the elk, they breed in fall, with the males gathering a harem.

BEARS

The two species of bears present in the mountains—black bears and grizzlies—can be differentiated by size and shape. Grizzlies are larger than black bears and have a flatter, dish-shaped face and a distinctive hump of muscle behind their neck. Color is not a reliable way to tell them apart. Black bears are not always black. They can be brown or cinnamon, causing them to be confused with the brown-colored grizzly.

Black Bears

If you spot a bear feeding beside the road, chances are it's a black bear. These mammals are widespread throughout all forested areas of the Canadian Rockies. Their weight varies considerably, but males average 150 kilograms (330 pounds) and females 100 kilograms (220 pounds). Their diet is omnivorous, consisting primarily of grasses and berries but supplemented by small mammals. They are not true hibernators, but in winter they can sleep for up to a month at a time before changing position. During this time, their heartbeat drops to 10 beats per minute, their body temperature drops, and they lose up to 30 percent of their body weight. Females reach reproductive maturity after five years; cubs, usually two, are born in late winter, while the mother is still asleep.

© ANDREW HEMPSTEAD

Grizzly bears often cause traffic jams.

Grizzly Bears

Grizzlies, second largest of eight recognized species of bears worldwide (only polar bears are larger), have disappeared from most of North America but are widespread throughout the Canadian Rockies, numbering around 300 in the region. Grizzlies are only occasionally seen by casual observers; most sightings occur in alpine and subalpine zones, although sightings at lower elevations are not unusual, especially when snow falls early or late. The bears' color ranges from light brown to almost black, with dark tan being the most common. On average, males weigh 200-350 kilograms (440-770 pounds). The bears eat small and medium-size mammals, and berries in fall. Like black bears, they sleep through most of the winter. When they emerge in early spring, the bears scavenge carcasses of animals that succumbed to the winter, until the new spring vegetation becomes sufficiently plentiful. Females first give birth at four years old, and then every three years, with cubs remaining with their mother for 2-3 years.

WILD DOGS AND CATS
Coyotes

The coyote is often mistaken for a wolf when in fact it is much smaller, weighing up to only 15 kilograms (33 pounds). It has a pointed nose and a long, bushy tail. Its coloring is a mottled mix of brown and gray, with lighter-colored legs and belly. The coyote is a skillful and crafty hunter, preying mainly on rodents. Coyotes have the remarkable ability to hear the movement of small mammals under the snow, allowing them to hunt these animals without actually seeing them. They are often seen patrolling the edges of highways and crossing open meadows in low-lying valleys.

Wolves

Wolves that inhabit the Canadian Rockies are larger than coyotes and larger than the wolves

WILDLIFE AND YOU

An abundance of wildlife is one of the biggest draws of the Canadian Rockies. To help preserve this precious resource, obey fishing and hunting regulations and use common sense.

Do not feed the animals. Many animals may seem tame, but feeding them endangers yourself, the animal, and other visitors, as animals become aggressive when looking for handouts (even the smallest critters, such as squirrels).

Store food safely. When camping, keep food in your vehicle or out of reach of animals. Just leaving it in a cooler isn't good enough.

Keep your distance. Although it's tempting to get close to wildlife for a better look or a photograph, it disturbs the animal and, in many cases, can be dangerous.

Drive carefully. The most common cause of premature death for larger mammals is being hit by vehicles.

measure up to 1.5 meters (five feet) long. The average male weighs 75 kilograms (165 pounds) and the female 40-55 kilograms (90-120 pounds). Cougars are versatile hunters whose acute vision takes in a peripheral span in excess of 200 degrees. They typically kill a large mammal such as an elk or deer every 12-14 days, eating part of it and caching the rest. Their diet also includes chipmunks, ground squirrels, snowshoe hares, and occasionally porcupines. Their athletic prowess puts Olympians to shame. They can spring forward more than 8 meters (26 feet) from a standstill, leap 4 meters (13 feet) into the air, and safely jump from a height of 20 meters (65 feet).

The cougar is a solitary animal with distinct territorial boundaries. This limits its population density, which in turn means that its overall numbers are low. They are most common in the foothills along the eastern slopes of the Canadian Rockies.

Lynx

The elusive lynx is identifiable by its pointy black ear tufts and an oversized tabby cat appearance. The animal has broad, padded paws that distribute its weight, allowing it to float on the surface of snow. It weighs up to 10 kilograms (22 pounds) but appears much larger because of its coat of long, thick fur. The lynx, uncommon but widespread throughout the region, is a solitary creature that prefers the cover of subalpine forests, feeding mostly at night on snowshoe hares and other small mammals.

OTHER LARGE MAMMALS
Mountain Goats

The remarkable rock-climbing ability of these nimble-footed creatures allows them to live on rocky ledges or near-vertical slopes, safe from predators. They also frequent the alpine meadows and open forests of the Canadian Rockies, where they congregate around natural salt licks. The goats stand one meter (3.2 feet) at the

of eastern Canada. They weigh up to 60 kilograms (132 pounds), stand up to one meter (3.2 feet) high at the shoulder, and resemble large huskies or German shepherds. Their color ranges from snow white to brown or black; those in the Canadian Rockies are, most often, shades of gray. They usually hunt in packs of up to eight members, traveling, hunting, and resting together, and adhering to a hierarchical social order. As individuals, they are complex and intriguing, capable of expressing happiness, humor, and loneliness.

Once the target of a relentless campaign to exterminate the species, the wolf has made an incredible comeback in the Canadian Rockies; today about 120 wolves roam the region.

Cougars

Rarely encountered by casual hikers, cougars (known in other parts of North America as mountain lions, pumas, or catamounts)

WILDLIFE VIEWING: THE BEST SPOTS

Where's the best place to view animals? This is probably the most common question posed by visitors to the Canadian Rockies. While a precise answer is impossible—this isn't a zoo, after all—noting a couple of general rules of thumb can make your chances of observation more likely. Spring is the best time for viewing wildlife from the roadside; larger mammals come down into the valleys in winter and stay through spring, moving back up to higher elevations as the snow melts. Mammals are most active at dawn and dusk, which are great times of day for scanning the landscape for movement.

In most cases, all species listed below are widespread in their particular habitat throughout the Canadian Rockies. The locations listed below for each species are simply the ones that will give you the best chance of seeing that species.

- **Beaver:** Athabasca River wetlands, Jasper National Park
- **Bighorn sheep:** Radium Hot Springs, just outside Kootenay National Park
- **Bison:** Buffalo Paddock, Waterton Lakes National Park
- **Black bear:** Icefields Parkway, Banff and Jasper National Parks
- **Caribou:** Bald Hills, Jasper National Park
- **Cougar:** forested valleys around Canmore
- **Coyote:** along Highway 16, east of the town of Jasper, Jasper National Park
- **Elk:** around the outskirts of Banff and Jasper towns
- **Grizzly bear (stuffed):** Lake Louise Visitor Centre, Banff National Park
- **Human beings:** Banff Avenue, Banff National Park
- **Lynx:** Vermilion Pass, Kootenay National Park
- **Marmot:** end of Stanley Glacier Trail, Kootenay National Park
- **Moose:** Peter Lougheed Provincial Park, Kananaskis Country
- **Mountain goat:** Icefields Parkway south of Athabasca Falls, Jasper National Park
- **Mule deer:** Waterton town site, Waterton Lakes National Park
- **Porcupine:** Yoho Valley Road, Yoho National Park
- **White-tailed deer:** Sheep River Valley, Kananaskis Country
- **Wolf:** Bow Valley Parkway, Banff National Park

shoulder and weigh 65-130 kilograms (140-290 pounds). Both sexes possess a peculiar beard, or rather, goatee. Both sexes have horns. It is possible to determine the sex by the shape of the horns; those of the female grow straight up before curling slightly backward, whereas those of the male curl back in a single arch. The goats shed their thick coats each summer, making them look ragged, but by fall they've regrown a fine, new white woolen coat.

Bighorn Sheep

Bighorn sheep are some of the most distinctive mammals of the Canadian Rockies. Easily recognized by their impressive horns, they are often seen grazing on grassy mountain slopes or at salt licks beside the road. The color of their coat varies with the season; in summer it's a brownish-gray with a cream-colored belly and rump, turning lighter in winter. Fully grown males can weigh up to 120 kilograms (270 pounds), while females generally weigh around 80 kilograms (180 pounds). Both sexes possess horns, rather than antlers like members of the deer family. Unlike antlers, horns are not shed each year and can grow to astounding sizes. The horns of rams are larger than those of ewes and curve up to 360 degrees.

The spiraled horns of an older ram can measure longer than one meter (3.2 feet) and weigh as much as 15 kilograms (33 pounds). During the fall mating season, a hierarchy is established among the rams for the right to breed ewes. As the males face off against each other to establish dominance, their horns act as both a weapon and a buffer against the head butting of other rams. The skull structure of the bighorn, rams in particular, has become adapted to these head-butting clashes, keeping the animals from being knocked unconscious.

Bighorn sheep are particularly tolerant of humans and often approach parked vehicles; although they are not especially dangerous, as with all mammals, you should not approach or feed them.

Bison

Before the arrival of Europeans, millions of bison roamed the North American plains, with some entering the valleys of the Canadian Rockies to escape harsh winters. Several factors contributed to their decline, including combined presence of explorers, settlers, and natives. By the 1800s they were wiped out, and since then a couple of attempts at reintroduction have taken place, including the release of a small herd in Jasper National Park. (No one has sighted them for many years.) Today, your best chance of viewing these shaggy beasts is in Waterton Lakes National Park, where a small herd is contained in the buffalo paddock.

SMALL MAMMALS
Beavers

One of the animal kingdom's most industrious mammals is the beaver. Growing to a length of 50 centimeters (20 inches) and tipping the scales at around 20 kilograms (44 pounds), it has a flat, rudderlike tail and webbed back feet that enable it to swim at speeds up to 10 kph (6 mph). The exploration of western Canada can be directly attributed to the beaver, whose pelt was in high demand in fashion-conscious Europe in the early 1800s. The beaver was never entirely wiped out from the mountains, and today the animals can be found in almost any forested valley with flowing water. Beavers build their dam walls and lodges of twigs, branches, sticks of felled trees, and mud. They eat the bark and smaller twigs of deciduous plants and store branches under water, near the lodge, as a winter food supply.

Squirrels

Several species of squirrel are common in the Canadian Rockies. The **golden-mantled ground squirrel,** found in rocky outcrops of subalpine and alpine regions, has black stripes along its sides and looks like an oversized chipmunk. Most common is the **Columbian ground squirrel,** which lives in burrows, often in open grassland. It is recognizable by its reddish legs, face, and underside, and a flecked, grayish back. The bushy-tailed **red squirrel,** the bold chatterbox of the forest, leaves telltale shelled cones at the base of conifers. Another member of the species, the nocturnal **northern flying fox,** glides through the montane forests of mountain valleys but is rarely seen.

Hoary Marmots

High in the mountains, above the tree line, hoary marmots are often seen sunning themselves on boulders in rocky areas or meadows. They are stocky creatures, weighing 4-9 kilograms (9-19 pounds). When danger approaches, these large rodents emit a shrill whistle to warn their colony. Marmots are active only for a few months each summer, spending up to nine months a year in hibernation.

Porcupines

This small, squat animal is easily recognized by its thick coat of quills. It eats roots and leaves but is also known as being destructive around wooden buildings and vehicle tires. Porcupines are common and widespread throughout all forested areas, but they're hard to spy because they feed most often at night.

Other Rodents

Widespread throughout western Canada, **muskrats** make their mountain home in the waterways and wetlands of all low-lying valleys. They are agile swimmers, able to stay submerged for up to 12 minutes. They grow to a length of 35 centimeters (18 inches), but the best form of identification is the tail, which is black, flat, and scaly. Closely related to muskrats are **voles,** which are often mistaken for mice. They inhabit grassed areas of most valley floors.

Shrews

A member of the insectivore family, the **furry shrew** has a sharp-pointed snout and is closely related to the mole. It must eat almost constantly because it is susceptible to starvation within only a few hours of its last meal. Another variety present throughout the region, the **pygmy shrew** is the world's smallest mammal; it weighs just four grams (0.1 ounces).

Pikas

Pikas, like rabbits, are lagomorphs, which are distinguished from rodents by a double set of incisors in the upper jaw. The small, grayish pika is a neighbor to the marmot, living among the rubble and boulders of scree slopes above timberline.

Weasels

The weasel family, comprising 70 species worldwide, is large and diverse, but in general, all members have long, slim bodies and short legs, and all are carnivorous and voracious eaters, consuming up to one-third of their body weight each day. Many species can be found in the Canadian Rockies, including the **wolverine,** largest of the weasels worldwide, weighing up to 20 kilograms (44 pounds). Known to natives as *carcajou* (evil one), the wolverine is extremely powerful, cunning, and cautious. This solitary creature inhabits forests of the subalpine and lower alpine regions, feeding on any available meat, from small rodents to the carcasses of larger mammals. Rarely sighted by humans, the wolverine is a true symbol of the wilderness.

The **fisher** has the same habitat as the wolverine but is much smaller, reaching just five kilograms (11 pounds) in weight and growing up to 60 centimeters (24 inches) in length. This nocturnal hunter preys on small birds and rodents, but reports of fishers bringing down small deer have been made. Smaller still is the **marten,** which lives most of its life in the trees of the subalpine forest, preying on birds, squirrels, mice, and voles. Weighing just one kilogram (2.2 pounds) is the **mink,** once highly prized for its fur. At home in or out of water, it feeds on muskrats, mice, voles, and fish. Mink numbers in the Canadian Rockies are low.

As well as being home to the largest member of the weasel family, the region also holds the smallest—the **least weasel** (the world's smallest carnivore), which grows to a length of just 20 centimeters (8 inches) and weighs a maximum of 60 grams (2 ounces). Chiefly nocturnal, it feeds mostly on mice and lives throughout open wooded areas, but it is not particularly common.

REPTILES AND AMPHIBIANS

Two species of snake, the **wandering garter snake** and the **red-sided garter snake** (North America's northernmost reptile), are found at lower elevations in the Canadian Rockies. **Frogs** are also present; biologists have noted two different species, which are also present at the lower elevations in the Canadian Rockies.

FISH

The lakes and rivers of the Canadian Rockies hold a variety of fish, most of which belong to the trout and salmon family and are classed as coldwater species—that is, they inhabit waters where the temperature ranges 4-18°C (39-64°F). The predominant species, the **rainbow trout,** is not native to the mountains; it was introduced from more northern Canadian watersheds as a sport fish and is now common throughout lower-elevation lakes and rivers. It has an olive green back and a red strip running along the center of its body. Only three species of trout are native to the mountains. One of these, the **bull trout,** is Alberta's provincial fish. Throughout the mid-1900s, this truly native Canadian trout was perceived as a predator of more favored introduced species and was mostly removed. Today, what was once the most widespread trout east of the Continental Divide is confined to the headwaters of the Canadian Rockies' river systems and is classed as a threatened species. While the bull trout has adapted to the harsh conditions of its reduced habitat, its continuing struggle for survival can be attributed to many factors, including a scarcity of food and a slow reproductive cycle. Bull trout grow to 70 centimeters (27 inches) in length and weigh up to 10 kilograms (22 pounds).

The **lake trout,** which grows to 20 kilograms (44 pounds), is native to large, deep lakes throughout the mountains. Identified by a silvery gray body and irregular white splotches along its back, this species grows slowly, taking up to 8 years to reach maturity and living up to 25 years. Named for a bright red dash of color that runs from below the mouth almost to the gills, the **cutthroat trout** is native to southern Alberta's mountain streams, but it has been introduced to high-elevation lakes and streams on both sides of the Canadian Rockies. The **brown trout,** introduced from Europe in 1924, is found in the Bow and Red Deer Rivers and some slower streams in the eastern zones of Kananaskis Country. Its body is a golden brown color, and it is the only trout

with both black and red spots. The **brook trout** is a colorful fish identified by a dark-green back with pale-colored splotches and purple-sheened sides. It is native to eastern Canada but was introduced to the mountains as early as 1903 and is now widespread throughout lakes and streams on the Alberta side of the Continental Divide. **Golden trout** were introduced to a few mountain lakes around 1960 as a sport fish. They are a smallish fish, similar in color to rainbow trout.

The **mountain whitefish** (commonly but incorrectly called arctic grayling by Albertan anglers) is a light-gray fish native to most lower-elevation lakes and rivers of the Canadian Rockies. Also inhabiting the region's waters are **arctic grayling** and **Dolly Varden** (named for a colorful character in a Charles Dickens story).

BIRDS

Bird-watching is popular in the mountains, thanks to the approximately 300 resident bird species and the millions of migratory birds that pass through each year. All it takes is a pair of binoculars, a good book detailing species, and patience. Dense forests hide many species, making them seem less common than they actually are. The Columbia River wetland, between Radium Hot Springs and Golden, lies on the Pacific Flyway and is a major bird-watching area.

Raptors

A wide variety of raptors are present in the Canadian Rockies—some call the mountains home year-round, while others pass through during annual spring and fall migrations. **Golden eagles** migrate across the Canadian Rockies, heading north in spring to Alaska and crossing back over in fall en route to Midwest wintering grounds. Golden eagles—more than 10,000 of them annually—soar high above the mountains on thermal drafts. **Bald eagles** also soar over the Canadian Rockies during annual

© ANDREW HEMPSTEAD

Ospreys are widespread but not common.

hovering up to 50 meters (160 feet) above water, watching for movement, then diving into the water, thrusting their legs forward and collecting prey in their talons.

Distinct from all previously listed species is a group of raptors that hunts at night. Best known as owls, these birds are rarely seen because of their nocturnal habits but are widespread throughout forested areas of the mountains. Most common is the **great horned owl,** identified by its prominent "horns," which are actually tufts of feathers. Also present are the **snowy owl** and, in the north of the region, the **great gray owl,** the largest of the owls, which grows to a height of 70 centimeters (27.6 inches).

Other Birds

Bird-watchers will be enthralled by the diversity of eastern and western bird species in the Canadian Rockies. Widespread are **magpies, sparrows, starlings, grouse, ravens,** and **crows. Blackbirds, finches, thrushes, hummingbirds, woodpeckers, flycatchers,** and 28 species of **warblers** are common in forested areas. **Ptarmigan** are common in open meadows above the tree line. A popular campground visitor, the cheeky **gray jay** is similar in appearance to the curious **Clark's nutcracker.**

migrations; mature birds can be distinguished from below by their white head and tail (immature birds resemble the dark-brown-colored golden eagle). **Ospreys** spend summers in the region, nesting high up in large dead trees, on telephone poles, or on rocky outcrops, but always overlooking water. They feed on fish,

History

THE EARLIEST INHABITANTS

Human habitation of the Canadian Rockies began at the end of the last ice age, approximately 11,000 years ago. The descendants of the people who migrated from northeast Asia across a land bridge spanning the Bering Strait had fanned out across North America, and as the receding ice cap began to uncover the land north of the 49th parallel, groups of people moved northward with it, in pursuit of large mammals at the edge of the melting ice mass.

The mountain landscape then was far different than it is today. Forests were nonexistent; the retreating ice had scoured the land, and most of the lower valleys were carpeted in tundra.

The following gives an overview of the people and their cultures. To learn more, plan on visiting Banff's **Buffalo Nations Museum.**

The Kootenay

The Kootenay (other common spellings include Kootenai, Kootenae, and Kutenai) were the first human beings to enter the Canadian Rockies. Once hunters of buffalo on the great American plains, they were pushed westward by fierce enemies. As the ice cap melted, they moved north, up the western edge of the Rocky Mountains. This migration was by no means fast—perhaps only 40 kilometers (25 miles) in each generation—but about 10,000 years ago the first Kootenay arrived in the Columbia River Valley. They were hunters and gatherers, wintering along the Columbia and Kootenay River Valleys, then moving to higher elevations during the warmer months. Over time they developed new skills, learning to fish the salmon-rich rivers using spears, nets, and simple fish weirs. The Kootenay were a serious people with few enemies. They mixed freely with the Shuswap and treated the earliest explorers, such as David Thompson, with respect. They regularly traveled east over the Rockies to hunt—to the wildlife-rich Kootenay Plains or farther south to the Great Plains in search of bison. But as the fearsome Blackfoot extended their territory westward to the foothills of present-day Alberta, the Kootenay made fewer trips onto the plains. By the early 1700s, they had been driven permanently back to the west side of the Continental Divide.

The Shuswap

The Shuswap make up only a small chapter in the human history of the Canadian Rockies, although they traveled into the mountains on and off for many thousands of years. They were a tribe of Salish people who, as the Kootenay did farther east, moved north, then east, with the receding ice cap. By the time the Kootenay had moved into the Kootenay River Valley, the Salish had fanned out across most of southwestern and interior British Columbia, following the salmon upstream as the glacial ice receded. Those who settled along the upper reaches of the Columbia River became known as the Shuswap. They spent summers in the mountains hunting caribou and sheep, put their fishing skills to the test each fall, then wintered in pit houses along the Columbia River Valley. The descendants of these people live on the Kinbasket Shuswap Reserve, just south of Radium Hot Springs.

The Stoney

The movement of humans into the mountains from the east was much more recent. Around 1650, the mighty Sioux nation began splintering, with many thousands moving north into present-day Canada. Although these immigrants called themselves Nakoda (people), other tribes called them Assiniboine (people who cook with stones) because their traditional cooking method was to heat stones in a fire, place the hot stones in a rawhide or birchbark basket with water, and cook meat and vegetables in the hot water. The white people translated *Assiniboine* as Stone People, or Stoney for short.

Slowly, generation after generation, smaller groups of the Stoney moved westward along the Saskatchewan River system, allying themselves with the Cree but keeping their own identity. They pushed through the Blackfoot territory of the plains and reached the Rockies' foothills about 200 years ago. There they split into bands, moving north and south along the foothills and penetrating the wide valleys where hunting was productive. They lived in small family-like groups and developed a lifestyle different from that of the Plains Indians, diversifying their skills and becoming less dependent on buffalo. Moving with the seasons, they gathered berries in fall and became excellent hunters of mountain animals. They traveled over the mountains to trade with the Shuswap but rarely ventured onto the plains, home of the warlike Peigan, Blackfoot, and Blood bands of the Blackfoot Confederacy.

DAVID THOMPSON

One of Canada's greatest explorers, David Thompson was a quiet, courageous, and energetic man who drafted the first comprehensive and accurate map of western Canada. He arrived in Canada from England as a 14-year-old apprentice clerk for the Hudson's Bay Company. With an inquisitive nature and a talent for wilderness navigation, he quickly acquired the skills of surveying and mapmaking. Natives called him Koo-koo-sint, which translates as "the man who looks at stars."

Between 1786 and 1812, Thompson led four major expeditions into western Canada—the first for the Hudson's Bay Company and the last three for its rival, the North West Company. The longest and most important one was the last, during which he traveled up and crossed the Continental Divide at **Howse Pass.** After descending into the Columbia River Valley, he established Kootenae House on Lake Windermere, using this outpost for a five-year odyssey of exploration of the entire Columbia River system. In the process, he discovered **Athabasca Pass,** which for the next 40 years was the main route across the Canadian Rockies to the Pacific Ocean.

In 1813, Thompson began work on a master map covering the entire territory controlled by the North West Company. The map was four meters (13 feet) long and two meters (seven feet) wide, detailing more than 3.9 million square kilometers (1.5 million square miles). On completion it was hung out of public view in the council hall of a company fort in the east. Years later, after his death in 1857, the map was discovered, and Thompson became recognized as one of the world's greatest land geographers.

The Stoney were a steadfast yet friendly people. Alexander Henry the Younger reported in 1811 that the Stoney, "although the most arrant horse thieves in the world, are at the same time the most hospitable to strangers who arrive in their camps."

As the great buffalo herds were decimated, the Stoney were affected less than the Plains Indians, but the effect of white settlers' intrusion on their lifestyle was still apparent. The missionaries of the day found their teachings had more effect on the mountain people than on those of the plains, so they intensified their efforts on the Stoney. Rev. John McDougall gained their trust and in 1873 built a small mission church by the Bow River at Morleyville. When the Stoney were presented with Treaty 7 in 1877, they chose to locate their reserve around the Morleyville church. Abandoning their nomadic lifestyle, they quickly became adept at farming; unlike the Plains Indians, who relied for their survival on government rations, the Stoney were almost self-sufficient on the reserve.

EUROPEAN EXPLORATION AND SETTLEMENT

In 1670, the British government granted the Hudson's Bay Company the right to govern Rupert's Land, roughly defined by all the land that drained into Hudson Bay. A vast area of western Canada, including present-day Manitoba, Saskatchewan, Alberta, Northwest Territories, and Nunavut, fell under that definition. The land was rich in fur-bearing mammals, which both the British and the French sought to exploit for profit. The Hudson's Bay Company first built forts around Hudson Bay and encouraged Indians to bring furs to the posts. But soon, French fur traders based in Montreal began traveling west to secure furs, forcing their British rivals to do the same. On one such trip, Anthony Henday became the first white man to view the Canadian Rockies when, on September 11, 1754, he climbed a ridge above the Red Deer River near present-day Innisfail. Henday returned to the east the following spring, bringing canoes loaded with furs and providing reports of snowcapped peaks.

In 1792, Peter Fidler became the first in a long succession of Europeans to actually enter the mountains. The following year Alexander Mackenzie became the first man to cross the continent, traveling the Peace and Fraser river watersheds to reach the Pacific Ocean. Mackenzie's traverse was long and difficult, so subsequent explorers continued to seek an easier route farther south. In 1807, David Thompson set out from Rocky Mountain House, traveling up the North Saskatchewan River to Howse Pass, where he descended to the Columbia River. He established a small trading post near Windermere Lake, but warring Peigan and Kootenay natives forced him to search out an alternate pass to the north. In 1811, he discovered Athabasca Pass, which was used as the main route west for the next 50 years.

In 1857, with the fur trade in decline, the British government sent Captain John Palliser to investigate the agricultural potential of western Rupert's Land. During his three-year journey, he explored many of the watersheds leading into the mountains, including one trip up the Bow River and over Vermilion Pass into the area now encompassed by Kootenay and Yoho National Parks.

The Dominion of Canada

By the 1860s, some of the eastern provinces were tiring of British rule, and a movement was abuzz to push for Canadian independence. The British government, wary of losing Canada as it had lost the United States, passed legislation establishing the Dominion of Canada. At that time, the North-West Territories, as Rupert's Land had become known, was a foreign land to those in eastern Canada; life out west was primitive with no laws, and no outpost held more than a couple of dozen residents. But in an effort to solidify the Dominion, the government bought the North-West Territories back from the Hudson's Bay Company in 1867.

In 1871, British Columbia agreed to join the Dominion as well, but only on the condition that the federal government build a railway to link the fledgling province with the rest of the country.

The Coming of the Railway

The idea of a rail line across the continent, replacing canoe and cart routes, was met with scorn by those in the east, who saw it as unnecessary and uneconomical. But the line pushed westward, reaching Winnipeg in 1879 and what was then Fort Calgary in 1883.

Many routes across the Continental Divide were considered by the Canadian Pacific Railway, but Kicking Horse Pass, surveyed by Major A. B. Rogers in 1881, got the final nod. The line and its construction camps pushed into the mountains, reaching Siding 29 (known today as Banff) early in the fall of 1883, Laggan (Lake Louise) a couple of months later, then crossing the divide and reaching the Field construction camp in the summer of 1884. The following year, on November 7, 1885, the final spike was laid, opening up the lanes of commerce between British Columbia and the rest of Canada. In 1914, rival company Grand Trunk Pacific Railway completed a second rail line across the Rockies, to the north through what is now Jasper National Park.

PARKS AND TOURISM
The Parks of Today Take Shape

In 1883, three Canadian Pacific Railway (CPR) workers stumbled on hot springs at the base of Sulphur Mountain, near where the town of Banff now lies. This was the height of the Victorian era, when the great spa resorts of Europe were attracting hordes of wealthy clients. With the thought of developing a similar-style resort, the government designated a 2,600-hectare (6,425-acre) reserve around the hot springs, surveyed a town site, and encouraged the CPR to build a world-class hotel there.

In 1887, Rocky Mountains Park was officially created, setting aside 67,300 hectares (166,300 acres) as a "public park and pleasure ground for the benefit, advantage, and enjoyment of the people of Canada." The park was later renamed Banff. It was Canada's first national park and only the third national park in the world.

Across the Continental Divide to the west, the railway passed by a small reserve that had been created around the base of Mount Stephen. This was the core of what would become Yoho National Park, officially dedicated in 1901. In anticipation of a flood of visitors to the mountains along the more northerly Grand Trunk Pacific Railway, Jasper Forest Park was established in 1907 (renamed Jasper National Park in 1930). Kootenay National Park was created to protect an eight-kilometer-wide (five-mile-wide) strip of land on either side of the Banff-Windermere Road, which was completed in 1922. Of the five national parks in the Canadian Rockies, Waterton Lakes National Park was the only one created purely for its aesthetic value. It was established after tireless public campaigning by local resident John George "Kootenai" Brown, who also became the park's first superintendent.

The First Tourists Arrive

In the era the parks were created, the Canadian Rockies region was a vast wilderness accessible only by rail. The parks and the landscape they encompassed were seen as economic resources to be exploited rather than as national treasures to be preserved. Logging, hunting, and mining were permitted inside park boundaries; all but Kootenay National Park had mines operating within them for many years (the last mine, in Yoho National Park, closed in 1952). To help finance the rail line, the CPR began encouraging visitors to the mountains by building grand mountain resorts: Mount Stephen House in 1886, the Banff Springs Hotel in 1888, a lodge at Lake Louise in 1890, and Emerald Lake Lodge in 1902. Knowledgeable locals, some of whom had been used as guides and outfitters during railway construction, offered their services to the tourists the railway brought. Tom Wilson, "Wild" Bill Peyto, Jim and Bill Brewster, the Otto Brothers, and Donald "Curly" Phillips are synonymous with this era, and their names grace everything from pubs to mountain peaks.

Early Mountaineering

Recreational mountaineering has been popular in the Canadian Rockies for more than 100 years. Reports of early climbs on peaks around Lake Louise spread, and by the late 1880s the area had drawn the attention of both European and American alpinists. Many climbers were inexperienced and ill equipped, but first ascents were nevertheless made on peaks that today are still considered difficult. In 1893, Walter Wilcox and Samuel Allen, two Yale schoolmates, spent the summer climbing in the Lake Louise area, making two unsuccessful attempts to reach the north peak of Mount Victoria. The following summer they made first ascents of Mount Temple and Mount Aberdeen, extraordinary achievements considering their lack of experience and proper equipment. Accidents were sure to happen, and they did. During the summer of 1896, P. S. Abbot slipped and plunged to his death attempting to climb Mount Lefroy. In doing so, he became North America's first mountaineering fatality. Following this incident, Swiss mountain guides were employed by the CPR to satisfy the climbing needs of wealthy patrons of the railway and make the sport safer. During the period of their employment, successful climbs were made of Mount Victoria, Mount Lefroy, and Mount Balfour.

In 1906, Arthur O. Wheeler organized the Alpine Club of Canada, which was instrumental in the construction of many trails and backcountry huts still in use today. In 1913,

Swiss guide Conrad Kain led a group of the club's members on the successful first ascent of Mount Robson, the highest peak in the Canadian Rockies. By 1915, most of the other major peaks in the range had been climbed as well.

Changing Times

One major change that occurred early on was the shift from railroad-based to automobile-based tourism. Until 1913, motorized vehicles were banned from the mountain parks, allowing the CPR a monopoly on tourists. Wealthy visitors to the mountains came in on the train and generally stayed in the CPR's own hotels for weeks on end and often for the entire summer. The burgeoning popularity of the automobile changed all this; the motor-vehicle ban was lifted, and road building went ahead full steam. Many of the trails that had been built for horseback travel were widened to accommodate autos, and new roads were built: from Banff to Lake Louise in 1920, to Radium Hot Springs in 1923, and to Golden in 1930. The Icefields Parkway was finally completed in 1940. Visitor numbers increased, and facilities expanded to keep pace. Dozens of bungalow camps were built specially for those arriving by automobile. Many were built by the CPR, far from their rail line, including in Kootenay National Park and at Radium Hot Springs. Lodges were also built deep in the backcountry, including at Mount Assiniboine and Lake O'Hara.

Another major change that has occurred over the last 90 years is in the way the complex human-wildlife relationship in the parks has been managed. Should the relationship be managed to provide the visiting public the best viewing experience, or rather to provide the wildlife with the most wild and natural environment possible? Today the trend favors the wildlife, but early in the history of the Canadian Rockies' parks, the operating strategy clearly favored the visitor. The Victorian concept of wildlife was that it was either good or evil. Although an early park directive instructed superintendents to leave nature alone, it also told them to "endeavor to exterminate all those animals which prey upon others." A dusty century-old philosophy, perhaps, but as recently as the 1960s, a predator-control program led to the slaughter of nearly every wolf in the park. Seventy years ago, you could view a polar bear on display behind the Banff Park Museum. Only 50 years ago, hotels were taking guests to local dumps to watch bears feeding on garbage. Creating a balance between growth and its impact on wildlife is today's most critical issue in the Canadian Rockies. Many high-traffic areas are fenced, with passes built over and under the highway for animal movement. Development in the national park towns of Banff and Jasper is strictly regulated, unlike areas outside the parks, such as Canmore and the Columbia River Valley, where development continues unabated.

Amazingly enough, throughout unsavory sagas of the 20th century and ever-increasing human usage, the Canadian Rockies have remained a prime area for wildlife viewing and will hopefully continue to be so for a long time to come.

ESSENTIALS

Getting There

For international travelers, Vancouver and Calgary are the main gateways to the Canadian Rockies. From these two cities, as well as points across Canada, scheduled train and bus services pass through the region year-round.

AIR

The closest city to the Canadian Rockies is **Calgary,** Alberta, 128 kilometers (80 miles) east of Banff. **Vancouver,** British Columbia's largest city, is a major gateway to the mountains for international travelers. It lies on Canada's West Coast, 830 kilometers (515 miles) west of Banff. **Edmonton,** 360 kilometers (224 miles) east of Jasper, also has an international airport. Even though Vancouver is a lot farther from the Canadian Rockies than Calgary, it is a popular starting point, as the trip across British Columbia by rail, bus, or car is spectacular.

Air Canada

Canada's national airline, Air Canada (604/688-5515 or 888/247-2262, www.air-canada.com) is one of the world's largest airlines. It offers direct flights to Calgary and Vancouver from all major Canadian cities, as

AIR TAXES

The Canadian government collects a variety of "departure taxes" on all flights originating from Canada. These taxes are generally not in the advertised fare, but they will all be included in the ticket purchase price. First up is the **Air Travellers Security Charge**, $5-10 each way for flights within North America and $25 round-trip for international flights. **NAV Canada** also dips its hand in your pocket, collecting $10-25 per flight for maintaining the country's navigational systems. All major Canadian airports charge an **Airport Improvement Fee** to all departing passengers, with Vancouver and Calgary charging $20 and $25, respectively, per passenger. You'll also need to pay this fee from your original departure point, and if connecting through Toronto, another $4 is collected. And, of course, the above taxes are taxable, with the Canadian government collecting the 5 percent goods and services tax. While there is no bright side to paying these extras, it is made easy for consumers, with airlines lumping all the charges together and into the ticket price.

well as from Los Angeles, San Francisco, Las Vegas, Denver, Phoenix, Houston, Chicago, Washington, D.C., New York, and Orlando.

From Europe, Air Canada flies directly from London and Frankfurt to Vancouver and Calgary, and from other major European cities via Toronto. From the South Pacific, Air Canada operates flights from Sydney and in alliance with Air New Zealand from Auckland and other South Pacific islands to Vancouver. Asian cities served by direct Air Canada flights to Vancouver include Beijing, Nagoya, Osaka, Seoul, Shanghai, Taipei, and Tokyo. Air Canada's flights originating in the South American cities of Buenos Aires, São Paulo, Lima, and Bogotà are routed through Toronto, where you'll need to change planes for either Calgary or Vancouver.

WestJet

Similar in concept to Southwest Airlines, WestJet (604/606-5525 or 800/538-5696, www.westjet.com) has daily flights to its Calgary hub, as well as to Vancouver and Edmonton from across Canada as far east as St. John's, Newfoundland.

From the United States

Air Canada offers the most flights into Calgary

and Vancouver from the United States, but one or both of the cities are also served by the following U.S. carriers: **Alaska Airlines** (800/252-7522, www.alaskaair.com) from Anchorage and Los Angeles; **American Airlines** (800/433-7300, www.aa.com) from Chicago and Dallas; **Continental Airlines** (800/231-0856, www.continental.com) from its Houston hub and New York (Newark); **Delta** (800/221-1212, www.delta.com), with summer-only flights from Atlanta and Salt Lake City; **Northwest Airlines** (800/225-2525, www.nwa.com) from Detroit, Indianapolis, Memphis, and Minneapolis; and finally **United Airlines** (800/241-6522, www.united.com) from Chicago, Denver, San Francisco, and Seattle.

From Europe

In addition to Air Canada's flights from London to Calgary and Vancouver, **British Airlines** (800/247-9297, www.britishairlines.com) also flies this route daily. Air Canada flights between Vancouver and Continental Europe are routed through Toronto. **Lufthansa** (800/563-5954, www.lufthansa.com) has a daily flight between Frankfurt and Vancouver.

From Australia and New Zealand

Qantas (604/279-6611, www.qantas.com.

au) flies to Vancouver from Sydney; flights originating in Melbourne and Brisbane are routed through Los Angeles. **Air New Zealand** (800/663-5494, www.airnewzealand.com) operates in alliance with Air Canada to either Calgary or Vancouver, with a variety of interesting options, including stops in South Pacific destinations like Nandi (Fiji). **Air Pacific** (800/227-4446, www.airpacific.com) offers flights from points throughout the Pacific to Honolulu and then on to Vancouver.

From Asia

Vancouver is the closest West Coast gateway to Asia, being more than 1,200 kilometers (746 miles) closer to Tokyo than Los Angeles. This and the city's large Asian population mean that it is well served by carriers from across the Pacific. In addition to Air Canada's multiple Asian destinations, Vancouver is served by: **Air China** (800/685-0921, www.airchina.com) from Beijing; **ANA** (888/422-7533, www.ana.co.jp) from Osaka and Tokyo in affiliation with Air Canada; **Cathay Pacific** (604/606-8888, www.cathaypacific.com) twice daily from Hong Kong; **Japan Airlines** (800/525-3663, www.jal.co.jp) from Tokyo; **Korean Air** (800/438-5000, www.koreanair.com) from Seoul; **Philippine Airlines** (800/435-9725, www.philippineairlines.com) from Manila; and **Singapore Airlines** (800/663-3046, www.singaporeair.com) from Singapore via Seoul. For the short hop between Vancouver and Calgary on Air Canada, expect to pay around $150 extra each way.

RAIL

The original transcontinental line passed through Banff, crossing the Continental Divide at Kicking Horse Pass and continuing to Vancouver via Rogers Pass. But this form of transportation, which opened up the Canadian Rockies to tourists, began to fade with the advent of efficient air services, and the last scheduled services on this line ended in 1991. Government-run VIA Rail provides coast-to-coast rail service using a more northerly route that passes through Jasper National Park. At Jasper, the westbound transcontinental line divides, with one set of tracks continuing west to Prince Rupert via Prince George and the other heading southwest to Vancouver. Another, more luxurious, option is the privately run Rocky Mountaineer, with summer service to Banff and Jasper from Vancouver.

VIA Rail

Government-run VIA Rail (416/366-8411 or 888/842-7245, www.viarail.ca) provides passenger-train service right across Canada. The *Canadian* is a thrice-weekly service between Toronto and Vancouver via Winnipeg, Saskatoon, Edmonton, Jasper, and Kamloops. Service is provided in two classes of travel: Economy features lots of leg room, reading lights, pillows and blankets, and a Skyline Car complete with bar service, while Silver and Blue is more luxurious, featuring sleeping rooms, daytime seating, all meals, a lounge and dining car, and shower kits for all passengers. At Jasper, the westbound transcontinental line divides, with one set of tracks continuing slightly north to Prince Rupert. Along this route, the train makes three trips per week. It is a daytime-only service, with passengers transferred to Prince George accommodations for an overnight stay. It also offers Economy and Touring Class.

If you're traveling anywhere in western Canada from the eastern provinces, the least-expensive way to travel is on a **Canrailpass**, which allows seven one-way trips anywhere on the VIA Rail system within any given 21-day period. During high season (June 1-Oct. 15) the pass is adult $1,159, senior (over 60) and child $1,043. The rest of the year the fare is adult $725, senior and child $653.

On regular fares, discounts of 25-40 percent

CUTTING FLIGHT COSTS

Ticket structuring for air travel has traditionally been so complex that finding the best deal required some time and patience (or a good travel agent), but the process has become much easier in recent years. Air Canada leads the way, with streamlined ticketing options that are easy to understand.

The first step when planning your trip to the Canadian Rockies is to contact the airlines that fly to Vancouver or Calgary and search out the best price they have for the time of year you wish to travel. **Air Canada** (www.aircanada.com) has a streamlined fare structure that makes it easy to find the fare that serves your needs and budget. Also look in the travel sections of major newspapers—particularly in weekend editions—where budget fares and package deals are frequently advertised. While the Internet has changed the way many people shop for tickets, having a travel agent whom you are comfortable dealing with—who takes the time to call around, does some research to get you the best fare, and helps you take advantage of any available special offers or promotional deals—is an invaluable asset in starting your travels off on the right foot.

Within Canada, **Travel Cuts** (866/246-9762, www.travelcuts.com) and **Flight Centre** (888/967-5302, www.flightcentre.ca), both with offices in all major cities, including Halifax, consistently offer the lowest airfares available, with the latter guaranteeing the lowest. Flight Centre offers a similar guarantee from its U.S. offices (866/967-5351, www.flightcentre.us), as well as those in the United Kingdom (tel. 0870/499-0040, www.flightcentre.co.uk), Australia (tel. 13/31-33, www.flightcentre.com.au), and New Zealand (tel. 0800/24-35-44, www.flightcentre.co.nz). In London, **Trailfinders** (194 Kensington High St., Kensington, tel. 020/7938-3939, www.trailfinders.com) always has good deals to Canada and other North American destinations. Reservations can be made directly through airline or travel agency websites, or use the services of an Internet-only company such as **Travelocity** (www.travelocity.com) or **Expedia** (www.expedia.com).

When you have found the best fare, open a **frequent flyer** membership affiliated with the airline—**Air Canada** (www.aeroplan.com) has a very popular reward program that makes rewards easily obtainable.

---

apply to travel in all classes October-June. Those over 60 and under 18, as well as students under 25, receive an additional 10 percent discount that can be combined with other seasonal fares. Check for advance-purchase restrictions on all discount tickets.

Rocky Mountaineer

Rocky Mountaineer Vacations (604/606-7245 or 877/460-3200, www.rockymountaineer.com) runs a luxurious rail trip between Vancouver and Banff or Jasper, through the spectacular interior mountain ranges of British Columbia. Travel is during daylight hours only so you don't miss anything. Trains depart in either direction in the morning (every second or third day), overnighting at Kamloops. One-way

travel in RedLeaf Service, which includes light meals, nonalcoholic drinks, and Kamloops accommodations, costs $959 per person d from Vancouver to either Banff or Jasper and $1,059 from Vancouver to Calgary. SilverLeaf is a step up in quality, with a glass-domed car allowing a wide range of viewing opportunities. Prices in SilverLeaf are $1,259 per person d from Vancouver to either Banff or Jasper and $1,389 from Vancouver to Calgary. GoldLeaf Service is the ultimate in luxury. Passengers ride in a two-story glass-domed car, eat in a separate dining area, and stay in Kamloops's most luxurious accommodations. GoldLeaf costs $2,099 per person d from Vancouver to Banff or Jasper and $2,299 to Calgary. Outside of high season (mid-Apr.-May and the first two weeks of Oct.), all fares are reduced a few hundred dollars. Trains terminate in Vancouver off Terminal Avenue at 1755 Cottrell Street (behind Pacific Central Station).

BUS
Greyhound

Greyhound (403/762-1092 or 800/661-8747, www.greyhound.ca) serves areas throughout Canada and the United States. Travel by Greyhound is simple—just roll up at the depot and buy a ticket. No reservations are necessary. Greyhound bus depots are always close to downtown and generally link up with local public transportation. Always check for any promotional fares that might be available at the time of your travel. Regular-fare tickets are valid for one year and allow unlimited stopovers between paid destinations.

From Calgary: Greyhound runs five times daily from its depot (877 Greyhound Way SW, 403/260-0877) to Canmore and Banff, with most services continuing through Lake Louise to Golden and beyond.

From Edmonton: Buses run year-round between Edmonton's depot (10324 103rd St., 780/420-2424) and Jasper along a route through western Canada that extends as far west as Prince Rupert and Vancouver.

From Vancouver: The main Greyhound routes from Vancouver include the TransCanada Highway to Golden, Field, and Banff; a northern route along Highway 5 through Jasper to Edmonton and beyond; and a southern route on Highway 3, through Cranbrook to Radium Hot Springs and on to Banff. The fare between Vancouver and Banff is around $175 one-way. The bus depot in Vancouver is at 1150 Station Street (604/683-8133).

From the United States: If you're traveling from the United States, get yourself to Great Falls, Montana, from where regular services continue north to the Coutts/Sweetgrass port of entry. There you change to a Canadian Greyhound bus for Calgary, where you can make connections to Banff.

When calling for ticket information, ask about any special deals. Other discounts apply to regular-fare tickets bought 7, 14, and 21 days in advance; to travelers 65 and over; and to two people traveling together. Greyhound's **Discovery Pass,** valid for unlimited travel throughout North America, is sold in periods of 7 days ($209), 15 days ($319), 30 days ($429), and 60 days ($539). Passes can be bought 14 or more days in advance online, 7 or more days in advance from any Canadian bus depot, or up to the day of departure from U.S. depots.

From Calgary
International Airport

This airport, 128 kilometers (80 miles) east of Banff, is the main gateway to the Canadian Rockies. In addition to car rental desks, shuttle bus companies are represented opposite the baggage carousels. Companies that offer service out to the Canadian Rockies are **Brewster** (403/762-6767 or 800/661-1152, www.brewster.ca) and **Banff Airporter** (403/762-3396 or 888/449-2901, www.banffairporter.com). Brewster is the only one of these services that continues beyond Lake Louise to Jasper. Reserve a seat by booking over the phone or online in advance. Expect to pay $55 each way to Canmore or Banff and around $65 to Lake Louise. Brewster charges $105 for the Calgary-Jasper run. **Sundog Tours** (780/852-4056 or 888/786-3641, www.sundogtours.com) operates the Mountain Connector, a winter-only service linking Calgary to Jasper via Banff.

Backpacker Bus

For young travelers on a budget, the **Moose Travel Network** (604/297-0255 or 888/244-6673, www.moosenetwork.com) is an excellent way to travel to and around the Canadian

Rockies and beyond. It runs along a number of different routes, including a seven-day loop originating in Vancouver and traveling to Jasper and Banff via Whistler ($589 per person), a four-day Banff-Jasper-Banff trip ($338), and a two-day Banff-Vancouver shuttle ($224). On any of these trips, you can get on and off wherever you please (and jump aboard the next bus as it passes through) or bond with the crowd and stay on the fixed itinerary. Nights are spent at hostels en route. This cost isn't included in the tour, but your reservation is (so you don't need to worry about trying to find an empty bed at each stop). Food is also extra, but often all travelers pitch in a token amount to purchase dinner at a grocery store along the way. Buses run 3-7 times a week through a March-October season.

CAR

Driving to the Canadian Rockies is possible from anywhere in North America but is most convenient if you live in western Canada or the Pacific Northwest. Driving saves money on transportation costs and allows you to bring along camping equipment and sporting gear such as mountain bikes and canoes.

Driver's licenses from all countries are valid in Canada for up to three months. You should also obtain a one-year **International Driving Permit** before leaving home (U.S.-licensed drivers do not require an IDP to drive in Canada) if your license is in a language other than English. Inexpensive and available from most motoring organizations, an IDP allows you to drive in Canada (in conjunction with your regular license), without taking a test, for up to three months. You should also carry vehicle registration papers or rental contracts. Proof of insurance must also be carried, and you must wear seat belts. All highway signs in Canada give distances in **kilometers** and speeds in **kilometers per hour** (kph). The speed limit on most major highways is 100 kph (62 mph).

Insurance

If entering Canada from the United States in your own vehicle, check that your insurance covers travel in Canada. U.S. motorists are advised to obtain a Canadian Non-resident Interprovincial Motor Vehicle Liability Insurance Card, available through U.S. insurance companies, which is accepted as evidence of financial responsibility in Canada.

When renting a vehicle in Canada, you have the option of purchasing a Loss Damage Waiver, along with other types of insurance, such as for your personal effects. Before leaving home, find out if you're already covered. Many people are—through gold credit cards, higher levels of motoring association membership, or home insurance (in the case of personal effects)—and additional coverage may be unnecessary.

Routes in Canada

The TransCanada Highway (Highway 1) stretches from one end of Canada to the other and is the world's longest national highway (7,821 km/4,860 mi from end to end). It passes through the Canadian Rockies towns of Canmore, Banff, and Golden. The first major city east of the mountains is Calgary, 128 kilometers (80 miles) from Banff along the TransCanada. The northern route across western Canada is the Yellowhead Highway, which passes through the town of Jasper, in Jasper National Park, 364 kilometers (226 miles) east of Edmonton. From Vancouver, on the west coast of British Columbia and the major air gateway from Asia, it's 836 kilometers (519 miles) west to Banff along the TransCanada Highway and 781 kilometers (486 miles) northwest to Jasper along Highway 5. The TransCanada and Yellowhead Highways are linked within the Canadian Rockies by the Icefields Parkway, which runs parallel to the Continental Divide between Lake Louise and Jasper, a distance of 230 kilometers (143 miles).

© ANDREW HEMPSTEAD

highway in Kananaskis Country

Routes from the United States

Reaching the Canadian Rockies from the United States is possible via a number of routes. From Seattle, the shortest approach is to follow I-5 north to Vancouver and jump on the TransCanada Highway. If you're traveling north from the Rocky Mountain states, U.S. Highway 93 will provide a warm-up for the mountain scenery north of the border. This route crosses into Canada north of Kalispell, Montana, merging with U.S. Highway 95 from Coeur d'Alene, Idaho, at Cranbrook, then continuing up the west side of the Canadian Rockies to Radium Hot Springs, where you can cut through Kootenay National Park to Banff. Much quicker is I-15, which begins in Los Angeles, looping through Las Vegas and Salt Lake City on its way north to Montana. I-15 enters Canada at the 24-hour Coutts/Sweetgrass border crossing south of Lethbridge, Alberta. From Lethbridge, it's a three-hour drive to Banff, or you can choose to head west to Waterton Lakes National Park. Total distance from Los Angeles to Banff via I-15 is 2,600 kilometers (1,617 miles). From the Midwest and eastern states, there are innumerable options, including I-94 through Minneapolis or crossing into Canada east of the Great Lakes and driving the entire way within Canada.

Getting Around

BUS

Getting around the Canadian Rockies is easiest with your own vehicle because public transportation is limited. **Brewster** (403/762-6767 or 800/661-1152, www.brewster.ca) is primarily a tour company but also runs a scheduled bus service linking Calgary International Airport, Canmore, Banff, and Lake Louise with a summer-only service between Lake Louise and Jasper. **Greyhound** (403/762-1092, www.greyhound.ca) serves the TransCanada Highway, providing a link between Canmore, Banff, Lake Louise, and Golden three times daily. Once daily, buses run through Kootenay National Park, between Banff and Radium Hot Springs. You can also take **Moose Travel Network** buses (604/297-0255 or 888/244-6673, www.moosenetwork.com) between Banff and Jasper.

CAR
Driving in Canada

U.S. and international driver's licenses are valid in Canada. All highway signs give distances in kilometers and speeds in kilometers per hour. Unless otherwise posted, the maximum speed limit on the highways is 100 kph (62 mph).

Use of safety belts is mandatory, and motorcyclists must wear helmets. Infants and toddlers weighing up to nine kilograms (20 pounds) must be strapped into an appropriate children's car seat. Use of a child car seat for larger children weighing 9-18 kilograms (20-40 pounds) is required of British Columbia residents and recommended to nonresidents. Before venturing north of the 49th parallel, U.S. residents should ask their vehicle insurance company for a Canadian Non-resident Inter-provincial Motor Vehicle Liability Insurance Card. You may also be asked to prove vehicle ownership, so carry your vehicle registration form.

If you're a member in good standing of an automobile association, take your membership card—the Canadian AA provides members of related associations full services, including free maps, itineraries, excellent tour books, road- and weather-condition information, accommodations reservations, travel agency services, and emergency road services. For more information, contact the **Alberta Motor Association** (780/430-6800, www.ama.ab.ca) or the **British Columbia Automobile Association** (604/268-5600, www.bcaa.com).

Note: Drinking and driving (with a blood-alcohol level of 0.05 percent or higher) in Canada can get you imprisoned on a first offense and will cost you your license for up to 12 months.

Car Rental

All major car rental agencies have outlets at Calgary and Vancouver International Airports. Car rentals are also available in Banff, Canmore, and Jasper, but it is strongly recommended to rent a vehicle *before* arriving in the Canadian Rockies for two reasons: cost and mileage charges (the now-standard unlimited mileage with major car rentals doesn't apply in Banff, Canmore, or Jasper). Generally, vehicles can be booked through parent companies in the United States. Rates start at $65 per day for a small economy car, $85 for a midsize car, and $95 for a full-size car.

Major rental companies with outlets in Calgary, Edmonton, and Vancouver are **Avis** (800/974-0808, www.avis.ca), **Budget** (800/268-8900, www.budget.com), **Discount** (800/263-2355, www.discountcar.com), **Dollar** (800/800-4000, www.dollar.com), **Enterprise** (800/325-8007, www.enterprise.com), **Hertz** (800/263-0600, www.hertz.ca), **National** (800/227-7368, www.nationalcar.com), and

Rent-A-Wreck (800/327-0116, www.rentaw-reck.ca).

RV Rental

Camper vans, recreational vehicles, and travel trailers are a great way to get around the Canadian Rockies without having to worry about accommodations each night. The downside is cost. The smallest vans, capable of sleeping two people, start at $165 per day with 100 free kilometers (62 miles) per day. Standard extra charges include insurance, a preparation fee (usually around $50 per rental), a linen/cutlery charge (around $60 per person per trip), and taxes. Major agencies, with rental outlets in both Calgary and Vancouver, include **Cruise Canada** (403/291-4963, 800/671-8042 or 800/327-7778, www.cruisecanada.com), **Canadream** (403/291-1000 or 800/461-7368, www.canadream.com), and **Go West** (604/528-3900 or 800/661-8813, www.go-west.com). In most cases, a drop-off fee of $500 applies to drop-offs made in Vancouver from rentals originating in Calgary, or vice versa. At the end of the summer season (early September), look for some great online bargains.

TOURS

For those with limited time, an organized tour is the best way to see the Canadian Rockies. **Brewster Travel Canada** (403/762-6767 or 800/760-6934, www.explorerockies.com) offers day tours and overnight tours throughout the mountains, as well as car rental and accommodation packages. **Rocky Mountaineer** (604/606-7245 or 877/460-3200, www.rockymountaineer.com) offers a wide variety of longer tours in conjunction with rail travel between Vancouver and Banff or Jasper. At the opposite end of the price spectrum, by joining a **Moose Travel Network** (604/777-9905 or 888/244-6673, www.moosenetwork.com) tour you get to see the Canadian Rockies with like-minded budget travelers.

Visas and Officialdom

ENTRY FOR U.S. CITIZENS

Citizens and permanent residents of the United States are required to carry a passport for both entry to Canada and for reentry to the United States. At press time, the U.S. government was developing alternatives to the traditional passport. For further information, see the website http://travel.state.gov. For current entry requirements to Canada, check the Citizenship and Immigration Canada website (www.cic.gc.ca).

ENTRY FOR OTHER FOREIGN VISITORS

All other foreign visitors entering Canada must have a valid passport and may need a visitor permit or Temporary Resident Visa depending on their country of residence and the vagaries of international politics. At present, visas are not required for citizens of the United States, British Commonwealth, or Western Europe. The standard entry permit is for six months, and you may be asked to show onward tickets or proof of sufficient funds to last you through your intended stay. Extensions are available from Citizenship and Immigration Canada offices in Vancouver and Calgary. This department's website (www.cic.gc.ca) is the best source of the latest entry requirements.

CLEARING CUSTOMS

Visitors are allowed to bring in personal items that will be used during a visit, such as cameras, fishing tackle, and equipment for camping, golf, tennis, photography, and so on. You can also bring the following into Canada duty free: reasonable quantities of clothes and personal effects, 50 cigars and 200 cigarettes, 200 grams (seven ounces) of tobacco, 1.14 liters (1.2 quarts) of spirits or wine, food for personal use, and gas (normal tank capacity). Pets from the United States can generally be brought into Canada, with certain caveats. Dogs and cats must be more than three months old and have a rabies certificate showing date of vaccination. Birds can be brought in only if they have not been mixing with other birds, and parrots need an export permit because they're on the endangered species list.

Handguns, automatic and semiautomatic weapons, and sawn-off rifles and shotguns are not allowed into Canada. Visitors with firearms must declare them at the border; restricted weapons will be held by customs and can be picked up on exit from the country. Those not declared will be seized, and charges may be brought. It is illegal to possess any firearm in a national park unless it is dismantled or carried in an enclosed case. Up to 5,000 rounds of ammunition may be imported but should be declared on entry.

On reentering the United States, if you've been in Canada more than 48 hours, you can bring back up to US$400 worth of household and personal items, excluding alcohol and tobacco, duty free. If you've been in Canada fewer than 48 hours, you may bring in only up to US$200 worth of such items duty free.

For further information on all customs regulations, contact **Canada Border Services Agency** (204/983-3500 or 800/461-9799, www.cbsa.gc.ca).

Recreation

The Canadian Rockies are a four-season playground, their great outdoors offering something for everyone. Hiking grabs first place in the popularity stakes; many thousands of kilometers of trails crisscross the entire region. But you can also enjoy canoeing and kayaking, mountain climbing, golfing, horseback riding, photography, skiing and snowboarding, scuba diving, and everything in between. An overview of available outdoor-recreation opportunities is provided in the following sections, and you'll find more detail in the individual travel chapters.

National Park Passes

Unless you're passing directly through, passes are required for entry into all five national parks covered in this book. Monies collected from these passes go directly to Parks Canada for park maintenance and improvements.

A **National Parks Day Pass** is adult $9.80, senior $8.30, child $4.90, to a maximum of $20 per vehicle. It is interchangeable among parks and is valid until 4pm the day following its purchase. An annual **Discovery Pass,** good for entry into all of Canada's national parks and national historic sites for one year from the date of purchase, is adult $67.70, senior $57.90, child $33.30, to a maximum of $136.40 per vehicle. Both types of pass can be purchased at park gates (at the entrance to Banff, Kootenay, Jasper, and Waterton Lakes National Parks), at the tollbooths at either end of the Icefields Parkway, at all park information centers, and at campground fee stations. For more information, check the Parks Canada website (www. pc.gc.ca).

HIKING

The Canadian Rockies are a hiker's paradise. Hiking is free, and the mountains offer some of the world's most spectacular scenery. With exceptions made for the most popular overnight hikes, all trails detailed in this book are day hikes. Anyone of moderate fitness could complete them in the time allotted. Strong hikers will need less time, and if you stop for lunch, it will take you a little longer. Remember, all distances and times are one-way, so allow yourself time at the destination and time to return to the trailhead. Basic trail descriptions are available through local information centers, but anyone planning on focusing their trip around hiking should pick up a copy of the *Canadian Rockies Trail Guide,* authored by Brian Patton and Bart Robinson; the publisher is Summerthought (www.summerthought.com).

Banff National Park holds the greatest variety of trails. Here you can find anything from short interpretive trails with little elevation gain to strenuous slogs up high alpine passes. Trailheads for some of the best hikes are accessible on foot from the town of Banff. Those farther north begin at higher elevations, from which access to the tree line is less arduous. The trails in **Jasper National Park** are oriented more toward the experienced backpacker, offering plentiful routes for long backcountry trips.

Waterton Lakes National Park is small but has a complex trail system geared especially for the day hiker. Many of the hikes in **Yoho National Park** entail significant elevation gain, but they reward your extra effort with spectacular mountain panoramas rivaling those of the more famous parks across the divide. Many less-visited parts of the mountains hold unexpected gems. Examples include Grassi Lakes, near Canmore; Rawson Lake, Kananaskis Country; Fish Lake, Top of the World Provincial Park; and Grande Mountain, near Grande Cache.

Scrambling

The Canadian Rockies hold many peaks that can be reached without ropes or climbing skills, provided you have a good level of fitness and, more important, common sense. Obviously, this type of activity has more inherent dangers

© ANDREW HEMPSTEAD

Pack a picnic lunch to make hiking more enjoyable.

than hiking, but these can be minimized by planning ahead. Check weather forecasts; take food, water, and warm clothing; and be aware of the terrain. Routes to the top of the most popular peaks are flagged with tape or marked with rock cairns showing the way, but you should always check with information centers or locals before attempting any ascent. The Bow Valley offers a good selection of well-traveled scrambles. These include Mount Rundle, Cascade Mountain, and Ha Ling (Chinaman's) Peak.

Backpacking

Most hikers are just out for the day or a few hours, but staying overnight in the backcountry offers many rewards. Some effort is involved in a backcountry trip—you'll need a backpack, lightweight stove, and tent, among other things—but you'll be traveling through country inaccessible to the casual day hiker,

SAFE HIKING

When venturing out on the trails of the Canadian Rockies, using a little common sense will help keep you from getting into trouble. First, don't underestimate the forces of nature; weather can change dramatically anywhere in the mountains at any time. That clear, sunny sky that looked so inviting during breakfast can turn into a driving snowstorm within hours. Go prepared for all climatic conditions (always carry food, a sweater, a waterproof jacket, and matches) and take plenty of water–open slopes can get very hot on sunny days.

All national park visitors centers, as well as those in Kananaskis Country, post daily trail reports and weather forecasts. Check trail conditions before heading out; lingering snow, wildlife closures, or a washed-out trail could ruin your best-laid plans. Also, hikers must register at park information centers for all overnight hikes in national parks.

Topographic maps aren't required for the hikes detailed in this book, but they provide an interesting way to identify natural features. For extended hiking in the backcountry, topo maps are vital. For most hikes, the maps produced by **Gem Trek Publishing** (www.gemtrek.com) are sufficient. You can purchase them from park information centers, bookstores, gas stations, and other outlets throughout the region.

---

well away from the crowds and far from any road. **Lake O'Hara**, in Yoho National Park, is the trailhead for what is generally considered to be Canada's finest backcountry hiking area. The lake is easily accessible; a shuttle bus runs from the highway up an old fire road to this alpine gem. Unlike at other backcountry destinations, visitors to Lake O'Hara not equipped for camping have the option of visiting for just a day. **Mount Assiniboine Provincial Park** is another popular spot far from civilization. Like Lake O'Hara, there's a lodge for hikers not equipped to camp out. Banff and Jasper National Parks also have backcountry lodges. Another option for backcountry accommodations is offered by the **Alpine Club of Canada** (403/678-3200, www.alpineclubofcanada.ca). The club maintains a series of huts, each generally a full-day hike from the nearest road, throughout the Canadian Rockies.

Heli-Hiking

Heli-hiking is an easy way to appreciate high alpine areas without having to gain the elevation on foot. The day starts with a helicopter ride into the alpine, where short, guided hikes are offered and a picnic lunch is served. For details, contact **Alpine Helicopters** (Canmore, 403/678-4802, www.alpinehelicopter.com) or **Robson Helimagic** (250/566-4700 or 877/454-4700, www.robsonhelimagic.com), near Mount Robson Provincial Park. Expect to pay from $429 for 30 minutes of flight time, a guided hike, and a mountaintop lunch. Primarily known for its heli-skiing operations, **Canadian Mountain Holidays** (403/762-7100 or 800/661-0252, www.cmhhike.com) has a summer program of heli-hiking trips, with overnights spent in luxurious backcountry lodges; expect to pay about $750 per person per night, all-inclusive.

CLIMBING AND MOUNTAINEERING

The Canadian Rockies are a mecca for those experienced in climbing and mountaineering, but for those who aren't, instruction is available. **Canmore**, in the Bow Valley, is the self-proclaimed capital of mountain sports. Surrounded by towering peaks of limestone, routes to challenge all levels of ability can be found on the immediate outskirts of town and along narrow canyons that open to the valley.

The distinctive south face of Yamnuska, easily recognized to the north of the TransCanada Highway as you enter the Bow Valley from the east, is the most popular climbing spot in the mountains, with dozens of routes up its sheer 350-meter-high (1,150-foot-high) walls. *Bow Valley Rock* (Rocky Mountain Books, www.rmbooks.com) is an indispensable book for Yamnuska-bound climbers. Experienced climbers should also gather as much information as possible before attempting any unfamiliar routes; quiz locals, hang out at climbing stores, and contact park information centers.

Learning the Ropes

For the inexperienced, the Canadian Rockies are the perfect place to learn to climb. Climbers and mountaineers can't live on past accomplishments alone, so to finance their lifestyle, some turn to teaching others the skills of their sport. Canmore is home to many qualified mountain guides who operate both in and out of Banff National Park. One of these—and one of North America's most respected climbing schools—is **Yamnuska** (403/678-4164, www.yamnuska.com). Learn basic climbing skills over an Outdoor Rock Intro weekend ($345 per person), with the option to make a full climb (an extra $245). The school also offers guided climbs of peaks throughout the Canadian Rockies, wilderness first-aid classes, and ice-climbing instruction.

ROAD CYCLING AND MOUNTAIN BIKING

The Canadian Rockies are perfect for both road biking and mountain biking. On-road cyclists will appreciate the wide shoulders on all main highways, while those on mountain bikes will enjoy the many designated trails. One of the most popular paved routes is the **Legacy Trail** between Banff and Canmore, which links up with the Bow Valley Parkway to Lake Louise. The most challenging and scenic on-road route is the 290-kilometer (180-mile) **Icefields Parkway** between Lake Louise and Jasper (*Outside* magazine rates it as one of North America's 10 best). Most cyclists allow 4-5 days, but it's easy to spend a lot longer on the parkway. With 11 campgrounds, four hostels, and four lodges along the way, you'll have plenty of accommodation options. An extension of the Icefields Parkway is the **Bow Valley Parkway,** the original route between Banff and Lake Louise, which can easily be cycled in one day.

Backroads (510/527-1555 or 800/462-2848, www.backroads.com) offers biking trips through the Canadian Rockies, as well as trips that include hiking and touring. These trips are designed to suit all levels of fitness and all budgets. On the biking trips, around six hours are spent cycling each day. The cost, inclusive of luxury accommodations, is US$3,298, which includes all meals.

Mountain biking is allowed on designated trails throughout the national parks. Park information centers hand out brochures detailing these trails and giving them ratings. The **Canmore Nordic Centre** is home to 70 kilometers (43.5 miles) of biking trails, some steep enough to hold international downhill competitions each summer. Peter Oprsal's *Bow Valley Mountain Bike Trail Guide* covers all the major trails in the Bow Valley; pick up a copy from local bookstores. Bikes can be rented throughout the national parks and Kananaskis Country. Road and town bikes rent for $6-9 per hour and $25-35 per day. All shops rent front- and full-suspension bikes; expect to pay up to $20 per hour and $70 per day for these.

HORSEBACK RIDING

Horses were used for transportation in the mountains by the earliest explorers. Even after the completion of the railway, horses remained as the most practical way to get deep into the backcountry because crossing unbridged rivers and carrying large amounts of supplies were impossible on foot. The names of early outfitters—Tom Wilson, Jim and Bill Brewster, Bill Peyto, Jimmy Simpson, and Curly Phillips were the best known—crop up again and again through the mountains. Another legacy of their trade is that many of the main hiking trails began as horse trails.

The tradition of travel by horseback continues today in the Canadian Rockies; some companies have been operating since before the parks were established. Trail riding is available in Banff, Jasper, Waterton Lakes, and Yoho National Parks, as well as in Canmore, Kananaskis Country, Radium Hot Springs, and Grande Cache. Expect to pay around $35 for a one hour ride (usually covering around 3 km/1.9 mi), $60 for a two-hour ride, and $75-105 for a ride that includes a meal. If you're an experienced rider, consider heading out of the mountains 40 minutes east of Canmore to **Griffin Valley Ranch** (north of Hwy. 1A, 403/932-7433, www.griffinvalleyranch.ca). This sprawling property is one of the few places in western Canada that allows unguided riding. Horse rentals are similarly priced to trail riding; the only additional cost is an annual membership (simply sign a waiver and pay an $80 fee). Trails lead through the valley and to high viewpoints where the panorama extends back to the Canadian Rockies.

Pack Trips and Guest Ranches

Overnight pack trips consist of up to six hours of riding per day, with nights spent at a remote mountain lodge or a tent camp, usually in a scenic location where you can hike, fish, or ride farther. Rates range $175-245 per person per day, which includes the riding, accommodations, and food. These trips are offered by **Brewster Adventures** (403/762-5454 or 800/691-5085, www.brewsteradventures.com), east of Canmore; **Boundary Ranch**

(403/591-7171 or 877/591-7177, www.boundaryranch.com), in Kananaskis Valley; through the south end of Banff National Park by **Warner Guiding & Outfitting** (403/762-4551 or 800/661-8352, www.horseback.com); and in Jasper National Park by **Skyline Trail Rides** (780/852-4215 or 888/852-7787, www.skylinetrail.com) and **Tonquin Valley Adventures** (780/852-1188, www.tonquinadventures.com).

GOLFING

The Canadian Rockies hold special appeal for golfers because some of the world's most scenic courses lie in their midst. All of the best courses are public, lying in national parks or on provincial land, so anyone can play at any time. The scenery alone stands the courses of the Canadian Rockies apart from others, but there are many other reasons that the region is a golf destination in itself. Stanley Thompson, generally regarded as one of the preeminent golf course architects of the early 1900s, designed three courses in the Canadian Rockies, typified by holes aligned with distant mountains, elevated tee boxes, and fairways following natural contours of the land. (As most of Thompson's work was in Canada, he is still little known in the United States.)

The golfing season is fairly short, May-early October, depending on snow cover. (The golf courses at Radium Hot Springs and Golden are the first to open each spring.) But with the long days of summer, there's plenty of time for golfing. Greens fees range from $15 at the historic nine-hole Nordegg Golf Course to $225 for 18 holes at the Banff course. The greens fee at Kananaskis Country Golf Course ($100) is also worth noting: It is regularly featured in *Golf Digest* as North America's best-value course. At the resort courses, greens fees usually include the use of practice facilities and a cart (complete with global positioning system at Silvertip). The sport's popularity in the mountains is such that tee times need to booked well in advance—up to a month for preferred times at some courses.

The Courses

The jewel in the golfing crown is the **Banff Springs Golf Course,** a 27-hole layout that graces the grounds of the Fairmont Banff Springs and is rated one of the world's most scenic courses. The **Jasper Park Lodge Golf Course,** a challenging par-73 course surrounded by spectacular mountain scenery, is of the same high standard. The **Kananaskis Country Golf Course,** a 36-hole, Robert Trent Jones Sr.-designed course built in the 1980s at a cost of $1 million per hole, was the first of the resort-style courses built in the Canadian Rockies. At Canmore, **Silvertip** set a new standard in golf course difficulty in Canada when it opened in 1998. It promotes itself as an extreme experience, and it is: 7,300 yards long, with elevation changes up to 40 meters (130 feet) on any one hole, and a slope rating of 153—the highest of any Canadian course. Across the valley from Silvertip, **Stewart Creek** opened in the summer of 2000, bringing the total number of courses in Canmore to three. Other resort courses are **Radium Resort** (36 holes), at Radium Hot Springs; **Greywolf,** at Panorama Mountain Village; and **Wintergreen,** at Bragg Creek; while the towns of Canmore and Golden offer excellent 18-hole public layouts, as does Waterton Lakes National Park.

ON THE WATER
Canoeing

This traditional form of Canadian transportation is a great way to explore the waterways of the mountains that are otherwise inaccessible—places such as **Vermilion Lakes** in Banff National Park, where beavers, elk, and a great variety of birds can be appreciated from water level. Canoes can be rented on the **Bow River** (in the town of Banff), **Lake Louise,** and **Moraine Lake** in Banff National Park; **Pyramid** and **Maligne Lakes** in Jasper National Park; **Cameron Lake** in Waterton Lakes National Park; and **Emerald Lake** in Yoho National Park. Expect to pay around $20-45 per hour. The more adventurous visitor can rent a canoe and paddle down the Bow River from Lake Louise to downtown Banff.

White-Water Rafting

The rafting season is relatively short, but the thrill of careening down a river laced with rapids is not easily forgotten. Qualified guides operate on many rivers flowing out of the mountains. The **Kicking Horse River,** which flows through Yoho National Park to Golden, is run by companies based in Golden, Lake Louise, and Banff. This is the most popular river for rafting trips. The **Sunwapta River** in Jasper National Park and the upper reaches of the **Fraser River** through Mount Robson Provincial Park are others offering big thrills. For a more sedate river trip, try the **Bow River** in Banff National Park or the **Athabasca River** in Jasper National Park. Both are run commercially. All companies offer half- and full-day trips, including transportation, wet suits, and often light snacks.

Scuba Diving

Being landlocked, the Canadian Rockies are not renowned for scuba diving. A few interesting opportunities do exist, however, and rentals are available in Lethbridge, Calgary, and Edmonton. The old town site of **Minnewanka Landing,** in Banff National Park, has been flooded, and although an easy dive, the site is interesting. **Patricia Lake,** in Jasper National Park, conceals the remains of a secret experiment to build an ice-covered barge that was to be used in the mid-Atlantic as a refueling dock for Allied aircraft. A sunken boat lies at the bottom of **Emerald Bay** in Waterton Lakes National Park, not far from some wagons that fell through the ice many winters ago.

For a list of dive shops and sites, contact the **Alberta Underwater Council** (780/427-9125 or 888/307-8566, www.albertaunderwatercouncil.com).

FISHING

The Canadian Rockies are an angler's delight. Fish are abundant in many lakes and rivers (the exceptions to good fishing are the lakes and rivers fed by glacial runoff, such as Lake Louise), and outfitters provide guiding services throughout the mountains. Many lakes are stocked annually with a variety of trout—most often rainbows—and although stocking was discontinued in the national parks in 1988, populations have been maintained. In Banff National Park, **Lake Minnewanka** is home to the mountains' largest fish—lake trout—as well a variety of other trout and whitefish. This lake, along with **Maligne Lake** in Jasper National Park, are major fishing centers, with boats and tackle for rent and guides offering their services.

Fish Species

Rainbow trout are the fighting fish of the Canadian Rockies; they are to western Canada what bass are to the United States. Although not native, through stocking they are found in lakes and streams throughout the mountains. The Bow River is considered one of the world's great trout rivers, but most of the action happens downstream of Calgary. Wet flies and small spinners are preferred methods of catching these fish. The largest fish found in the region is the **lake trout,** which grows to 18 kilograms (40 pounds). It feeds near the surface after winter breakup and then moves to deeper, colder water in summer. Long lines and heavy lures are needed to hook these giants. **Brown trout,** introduced from Europe, are found in the Upper Bow River (downstream from Banff) and slow-flowing streams in the foothills of Kananaskis Country. They

are most often caught on dry flies, but they are finicky feeders and therefore difficult to hook. **Brook trout** are widespread throughout lower-elevation lakes and streams. **Cutthroat trout** inhabit the cold and clear waters of the highest lakes, which generally require a hike to access. Fishing for cutthroat requires using the lightest of tackle because the water is generally very clear; fly casting is most productive on the still water of lakes, while spinning is the preferred river-fishing method.

Arctic grayling, easily identified by their large dorsal fins, are common in cool, clear streams throughout the far north, but they are not native to the Canadian Rockies; Wedge Pond (Kananaskis Country) is stocked with these delicious fish. **Dolly Varden** can be caught in many high-elevation lakes on the British Columbia side of the mountains; Whiteswan Lake is a local favorite. **Whitefish** are a commonly caught fish in lower-elevation lakes and rivers (many anglers in Alberta call whitefish "arctic grayling," but they are in fact two distinct species-and grayling aren't native to the mountains). Hydroelectric dams, such as those east of Canmore and in the Spray Valley Provincial Park, are popular with anglers chasing whitefish.

Note: The **bull trout** is an endangered species and is a catch-and-release fish. Possession of bull trout—a dark-colored fish with light spots—is illegal. The defining difference between the bull trout and the brook trout, with which it is often confused, is that the bull trout has *no black spots on its dorsal fin;* due to its status, correct identification of this species is especially important.

Regulations and Licenses

Three different licenses are in effect in the Canadian Rockies—one license covers all the national parks, another Albertan waters, and a third the freshwater of British Columbia.

National parks: Licenses are available from

park offices and some sport shops; $10 for a one-day license, $35 for an annual license. The brochure *Fishing Regulations Summary,* available from all park information centers, details limits and closures.

Alberta: Alberta has an automated licensing system, with licenses sold from sporting stores, hardware stores, and gas stations. To use the machines, the vendor needs you to supply a Wildlife Identification Number (WIN) card. These numbers are sold by all license vendors and cost $8 (valid for five years). Once you have your card, it is swiped through a vending machine to purchase a license. An annual license for Canadian residents older than age 16 is $28 (no license required for those 16 years or younger or Albertans older than 64); for nonresidents older than age 16, it is $78, or pay $31 for a one-day license or $55 for five days. The *Alberta Guide to Sportfishing Regulations,* which outlines all the open seasons and bag limits, is available from outlets selling licenses and online at www.mywildalberta.com. In addition to having the entire regulations online, this site also holds statistics for the provincial stocking program (which lakes, when, and how many fish) and details of Alberta's barbless hook rules.

British Columbia: In British Columbia, the cost of a license varies according to your age and place of residence. British Columbia residents pay $38 for a freshwater adult license, good for one year. All other Canadians pay $22 for a one-day license, $38 for an eight-day license, or $65 for a one-year license. Nonresidents of Canada pay $28, $58, and $92, respectively. For more information, visit www.fishing.gov. bc.ca, which offers the same online purchase process as neighboring Alberta.

WINTER RECREATION
Downhill Skiing and Snowboarding

Five world-class winter resorts are perched among the high peaks of the Canadian Rockies. The largest, and Canada's second largest (only Whistler/Blackcomb is larger), is **Lake Louise,** overlooking the lake of the same name in Banff National Park. The resort boasts 1,700 hectares (4,200 acres) of skiing and boarding on four distinct faces, with wide-open bowls and runs for all abilities. Banff's other two resorts are **Sunshine Village,** sitting on the Continental Divide and accessible only by gondola, and **Ski Norquay,** a resort with heart-pounding runs overlooking the town of Banff.

Kananaskis Country is home to **Nakiska,** a resort developed especially for the downhill events of the 1988 Winter Olympic Games in Calgary. **Marmot Basin,** in Jasper National Park, has minimal crowds and a maximum variety of terrain. Across the border in British Columbia, near Golden, **Kicking Horse Mountain Resort** is a big hill with an even bigger reputation for its challenging terrain, while **Panorama** appeals to all levels of ability.

Winter is low season in the mountains, so many accommodations reduce their rates drastically. Lift and lodging package deals at many resorts start around $100 per person per night. Sunshine Village, Kicking Horse, and Panorama have on-slope lodging, while the other resorts are served by shuttle buses from the nearest towns. Most resorts open in early December and close in May.

Heli-Skiing

Helicopters are banned in the national parks of the Canadian Rockies, but two surrounding heli-ski operators provide transfers from Banff and Jasper. One such company is **R.K. Heli-Ski** (250/342-3889 or 800/661-6060, www. rkheliski.com), which is based on the west side of the mountains at Panorama but provides daily transfers from Banff and Lake Louise for a day's heli-skiing or boarding high in the Purcell Mountains. The cost is $740-880 per person. The only other company that offers day trips is **Robson Helimagic,** based west of Jasper at Valemont (250/566-4700 or 877/454-4700, www.robsonhelimagic.com), which charges $745 for a day's skiing on the northern boundary of Mount Robson Provincial Park.

The town of Banff is headquarters for the world's largest heli-skiing operation, **Canadian Mountain Holidays** (403/762-7100 or 800/661-0252, www.cmhski.com), although the skiing and boarding terrain is accessed from 12 upscale lodges scattered throughout eastern British Columbia. Seven-day packages begin at around $6,800 per person, rising to more than $9,000 in the high season.

Other Winter Activities

Many hiking trails provide ideal routes for **cross-country skiing,** and many are groomed for that purpose. The largest concentration of groomed trails is in Kananaskis Country. Other areas are Banff, Jasper, Kootenay, Waterton, and Yoho National Parks. The Canmore Nordic Centre was developed for the 1988 Winter Olympic Games and is now a public facility. The town site in Waterton Lakes National Park all but closes down for winter, but this park is one of the most enjoyable spots for a skiing sojourn. Anywhere you can cross-country ski you can **snowshoe,** a traditional form of winter transportation that is making a comeback. **Sleigh rides** are offered in Banff, Lake Louise, and Jasper.

Winter travel brings its own set of potential hazards, such as hypothermia, avalanches, frostbite, and sunburn. Necessary precautions should be taken. All park information centers can provide information on hazards and advise on current weather conditions.

Accommodations and Camping

Following is a summary of the types of accommodations you can expect to find throughout the Canadian Rockies. Individual properties are detailed in each travel chapter, along with prices and contact information. Nearly all accommodations now have toll-free numbers and websites, through which you can find out more information about each property and make bookings.

Accommodation Taxes

Except for campgrounds and bed-and-breakfasts with fewer than four guest rooms, accommodations collect tax on behalf of various levels of government. In British Columbia, an 8 percent provincial hotel room tax is administered, while in Alberta, a 4 percent Tourism Levy is added. Banff also has a 2 percent Tourism Improvement Fee. These taxes are in addition to the Canada-wide 5 percent goods and services tax. As a general rule, quoted rates don't include any of these taxes.

HOTELS AND MOTELS

Hotels and motels throughout the Canadian Rockies range from substandard road motels to sublime resorts such as the famous Fairmont Banff Springs. Bookings throughout the mountains, but especially in Banff, Lake Louise, and Jasper, should be made as far in advance as possible. Finding inexpensive lodging in the mountain national parks is difficult in summer. By late afternoon, the only rooms left will be in the more expensive categories, and by nightfall all of these will go.

Hotel rooms in Banff begin around $160; those in Jasper and Waterton Lakes are a little less. Accommodation prices are slashed by as much as 50 percent outside summer. Always ask for the best rate available and check local tourist literature for discount coupons. All rates quoted in this handbook are for the cheapest category of rooms during the most expensive time period (summer).

Park-at-your-door, single-story road motels are mostly a thing of the past in the mountains, although Radium Hot Springs, just outside Kootenay National Park, still has many of these motels (one of which proudly boasts "Electric Heat"). In most cases rooms are fine, but check before paying, just to make sure. Most have a few rooms with kitchenettes, but these fill fast. Expect to pay around $80-100 for a double room. You will also find this style of accommodation in Canmore, Waterton town site, and Golden.

Information and Reservations

For a list of all hotels, motels, lodges, and bed-and-breakfasts in Alberta, pick up a copy of *Alberta Accommodation Guide,* available on-line, or order a free copy through **Travel Alberta** (780/427-4321 or 800/252-3782, www.travelalberta.com). The same association produces the *Alberta Campground Guide* (also online). **Tourism British Columbia** (250/387-1642 or 800/435-5622, www.hellobc.com) produces the free *British Columbia Approved Accommodation* brochure, which lists all accommodations and campgrounds in the province.

BED-AND-BREAKFASTS

The bed-and-breakfast phenomenon is well entrenched in Canada. This type of accommodation is a good option if you don't mind sacrificing some privacy to meet locals and to mingle with like-minded travelers. Bed-and-breakfasts are usually private residences, with up to four guest rooms, although bylaws are different throughout the region. Amenities can vary greatly—the "bed-and-breakfast" may be a single spare room in an otherwise regular family home or a full-time business in a beautifully restored heritage home. This uncertainty as to what to expect upon arrival can be off-putting for many people, especially with the possibility of sharing a bathroom with other guests—which is both a common and accepted practice in European bed-and-breakfasts. If having a bathroom to yourself is important to you, clarify with the bed-and-breakfast operator when reserving. Also, as bed-and-breakfasts also function as private residences, book in advance—don't just turn up. Finally, check payment methods when booking; not all establishments take credit or debit cards.

Rates fluctuate greatly, with the least expensive rooms costing $60 s, $70 d and the most expensive almost $300. Bed-and-breakfasts are located in Banff, Canmore, Bragg Creek, and Jasper. In Jasper National Park, a park bylaw that prevented such establishments from serving breakfast was recently lifted; some have started serving meals, but those that don't are still known as private-home accommodations. The best way to find out about individual lodging is from local tourist information centers or from listings in the *Alberta Accommodation Guide* or *British Columbia Approved Accommodation* brochure.

Bed-and-Breakfast Associations and Agencies

The **Western Canada Bed and Breakfast Innkeepers Guild** (www.bcsbestbnbs.com) represents bed-and-breakfasts across the region. The association produces an informative brochure with simple descriptions and a color photo of each property, but it doesn't take bookings. Without the color photos, **Jasper Home Accommodation Association** (www.stayinjasper.com) offers the same kind of literature and an online availability calendar.

Canada-West Accommodations (604/990-6730 or 800/561-3223, www.b-b.com) does take bookings, along with providing recommendations based on your likes and dislikes.

OTHER LODGING OPTIONS
Seasonal Accommodations

As roads through the mountains were improved in the 1920s, the number of tourists arriving

GETTING THE BEST LODGING DEAL

It can't be stressed enough: The Internet is an invaluable tool for searching out the best accommodation deals.

Rates quoted in this book are for a standard double room throughout the high season, which generally extends late June-mid-September. Almost all accommodations are less expensive outside of these busy months. As a general rule of thumb, the more expensive the property, the steeper the discount. For example (and at different ends of the spectrum), the cost of a dorm bed at the Banff Alpine Centre drops $5 per night on September 15, while in downtown Banff, already reasonably priced Brewster's Mountain Lodge halves its rates to $135 in winter, with graduated discounts in spring and fall. Plan on traveling a few weeks on either side of the peak season, then use hotel websites to check when individual properties are offering discounts. Most accommodations post seasonal specials on their websites well in advance.

While you have no influence over seasonal pricing fluctuations, *how* you reserve a room *can* make a difference in how much you pay. Book through a central reservations agency or travel agent, or pay for accommodations as part of a tour package, and you'll pay the full published price.

In some years, getting a room in July and August without advance reservations is almost impossible. In others, hotels will be selling rooms well into the night for a fraction of the published rate. Leaving reservations until the last minute is a risky proposition if you're not prepared to be flexible, but it's a good way to save a lot of money.

Don't be afraid to negotiate during slower times. Even if the desk clerk has no control over rates, there's no harm in asking for a bigger room or one with a better view. Just look for a Vacancy sign hanging out front.

Most hotels offer auto association members an automatic 10 percent discount, and whereas senior discounts apply only to those 60 or 65 and older on public transportation and at attractions, most hotels offer discounts to those over 50. Some chains, such as Best Western, also allow senior travelers a late checkout. Corporate rates are a lot more flexible than in years past; some hotels require nothing more than the flash of a business card for a 10-20 percent discount. Finally, when it comes to frequent flyer programs, you really do need to be a frequent flyer to achieve free flights, but the various loyalty programs offered by hotel chains often provide benefits simply for signing up.

---

by automobile increased greatly. To cater to this new breed of traveler, many bungalow camps were constructed along the highways. Some remain today (mostly in Jasper National Park), offering a high standard of accommodation away from the hustle and bustle of the towns. Generally, they consist of freestanding, self-contained units and are open for the summer only.

Backcountry Huts and Lodges

Throughout the backcountry of the Canadian Rockies is an extensive system of 18 rustic huts managed by the **Alpine Club of Canada** (403/678-3200, www.alpineclubofcanada.ca). Due to their locations around favorite climbing areas, they are most often used by mountaineers as an overnight stop before assaulting some of the park's highest peaks, but they are available to anyone who wishes to take advantage of their remote location. Their accessibility ranges from the Elizabeth Parker Hut (Yoho National Park), which can be reached by bus, to the Neil Colgan Hut, Canada's highest habitable structure, 2,960 meters (9,700 feet) from sea level on a windswept ledge above Moraine Lake. Often of historical significance, each of the huts has a stove, lantern, kitchen utensils, and foam mattresses. Rates range $18-32 per person per night.

Privately operated backcountry lodges are found in Banff, Jasper, and Yoho National

QUINTESSENTIAL MOUNTAIN LODGINGS

You could stay in a basic, boring motel room, but don't. Instead, make reservations at one of the following lodgings, each offering a distinctive mountain experience.

- **Baker Creek Mountain Resort,** Banff National Park
- **Paradise Lodge and Bungalows,** Banff National Park
- **Simpson's Num-ti-jah Lodge,** Banff National Park
- **Mount Assiniboine Lodge,** Mount Assiniboine Provincial Park
- **Paintbox Lodge,** Canmore
- **Mount Engadine Lodge,** Kananaskis Country
- **Cross River Wilderness Centre,** Kootenay National Park
- **Cathedral Mountain Lodge,** Yoho National Park
- **Emerald Lake Lodge,** Yoho National Park
- **Lake O'Hara Lodge,** Yoho National Park
- **Alpine Village,** Jasper National Park
- **Sheep Creek Back Country Lodge & Cabins,** Grande Cache

Parks, as well as Mount Assiniboine Provincial Park. The most luxurious is **Lake O'Hara Lodge** in Yoho National Park. It lies 11 kilometers (6.8 miles) from the nearest public road—access is by shuttle bus—and is surrounded by some of the finest hiking in all the Canadian Rockies. Banff National Park has two backcountry lodges: **Shadow Lake Lodge,** northwest of Banff, and **Skoki Lodge,** east of Lake Louise. Jasper National Park is home to **Tonquin Amethyst Lake Lodge** and **Tonquin Valley Backcountry Lodge.** All require some degree of effort to reach—either on foot or on horseback in summer, or on cross-country skis or snowshoes in winter. **Mount Assiniboine Lodge** is farthest from the road system but can be reached by helicopter. Rates at these lodges begin at $180 per person, including three meals. None have television, but all have running water and a congenial atmosphere.

BACKPACKER ACCOMMODATIONS

Throughout the Canadian Rockies, traditional hostels operated by Hostelling International are still the most common form of accommodation for budget travelers, but other options do exist. Banff and Radium Hot Springs have privately run backpacker lodges, and Banff has a YWCA with dormitory accommodations for men and women. Generally, you need to supply your own sleeping bag or linens, but most places supply extra bedding at a minimal cost.

Hostelling International

Hostelling International operates 12 hostels in the Canadian Rockies. Five of these are in Banff National Park, five in Jasper National Park, and one each in Canmore and Yoho National Parks. Whenever you can, make reservations in advance, especially in summer. Make bookings online at www.hihostels.ca.

All of the hostels are equipped with a kitchen and lounge room, and some have laundries and private rooms. Those in Banff and Lake Louise are world-class, with hundreds of beds as well as libraries and cafés. The five rustic hostels along the Icefields Parkway are evenly spaced, perfect for a bike trip along one of the world's great mountain highways. A sheet or sleeping bag is required at more remote locations, although these can usually be rented. Rates for members are $20-40 per night, nonmembers $24-44. Staying in hostels is an especially good bargain for skiers and snowboarders; packages including accommodation and a day pass at a local resort start at $95.

You don't *have* to be a member to stay in an affiliated hostel of Hostelling International, but membership pays for itself after only a few nights of discounted lodging. Aside from lower rates, benefits of membership vary from country to country but often include discounted air, rail, and bus travel; discounts on car rental; and discounts on some attractions and commercial activities. For Canadians, the membership charge is $35 annually, or $175 for a lifetime membership. For more information, contact **HI-Canada** (613/237-7884, www.hihostels.ca). Joining the Hostelling International affiliate of your home country entitles you to reciprocal rights in Canada, as well as around the world. In the United States, the contact information is **Hostelling International USA** (301/495-1240, www.hiusa.org); annual membership is

adult US$28 and senior 55 and over US$18, or become a lifetime member for US$250. International chapters include **YHA England and Wales** (0870/770-8868, www.yha.org.uk); **YHA Australia** (422 Kent St., Sydney, 02/9261-1111, www.yha.com.au), also based in all capital cities; and **YHA New Zealand** (03/379-9970, www.yha.org.nz). Otherwise, click through the links on the Hostelling International website (www.hihostels.com) to your country of choice.

CAMPING

Camping is the way to stay cheaply in the Canadian Rockies. Each of the five national parks has excellent campgrounds, which have a combined total of 6,000 sites plus large areas set aside for overflow camping. Many of the campgrounds consist of nothing more than picnic tables, drinking water, pit toilets, and firewood ($8 per site per night), but at least one campground in each park has hot showers and full hookups. Each park also has an area set aside for winter camping.

A percentage of sites in the most popular campgrounds can be reserved through the **Parks Canada Campground Reservation Service** (877/737-3783, www.pccamping.ca) for a nonrefundable $11 reservation fee. If you're traveling in the height of summer and require electrical hookups, this booking system is highly recommended. The remaining campsites in the national parks operate on a first-come, first-served basis and often fill by midday in July and August.

Each of the road-accessible provincial parks covered in this book provides camping facilities, usually only with drinking water, picnic tables, and pit toilets. The exceptions are Peter Lougheed and Bow Valley Provincial Parks in Kananaskis Country, where hookups and showers are provided. Campground operations in Kananaskis Country are contracted to private operators but ultimately come under

Hostels in the Canadian Rockies are excellent.

the auspices of the Alberta government (www. albertaparks.ca). This department is also in charge of other campgrounds on public lands, including those in provincial recreation areas along the eastern slopes of the Canadian Rockies. **BC Parks** (www.bcparks.ca) manages similar facilities along the other side of the divide; camp fees range $14-28 per night.

Commercial campgrounds operate in Canmore and Radium Hot Springs, at the entrance to Waterton Lakes National Park, and in Golden, Mount Robson Provincial Park, and Grande Cache. They provide full hookups and have showers but generally lack the natural surroundings found in national and provincial parks. In Kananaskis Country, the privately operated Mount Kidd RV Park boasts a tennis court, recreation room, spa, and sauna.

Backcountry Camping

Backcountry camping in all national parks is $10 per person per night, or purchase an annual pass ($70), valid for unlimited backcountry travel and camping for 12 months from its purchase date. Before heading out, you must register at the respective park information center (regardless of whether you have an annual pass) and pick up a Backcountry Permit (for those without an annual pass, the cost is the nightly camping fee multiplied by the number of nights you'll be in the backcountry). Many popular backcountry campgrounds have quotas, with reservations taken up to three months in advance. The reservation fee is $12 per party per trip. Most campgrounds in the backcountry have pit toilets, and some have bear bins for secure food storage. Fires are discouraged, so bring a stove.

Tips for Travelers

EMPLOYMENT AND STUDY

Banff is especially popular with young workers from across Canada and beyond. Aside from Help Wanted ads in local papers, a good place to start looking for work is the **Job Resource Centre** (314 Marten St., Banff, 403/760-3311, www.jobresourcecentre.com).

International visitors wishing to work or study in Canada must obtain authorization *before* entering the country. Authorization to work will only be granted if no qualified Canadians are available for the work in question. Applications for work and study are available from all Canadian embassies and must be submitted with a nonrefundable processing fee. The Canadian government has a reciprocal agreement with Australia for a limited number of **holiday work visas** to be issued each year. Australian citizens ages 30 and under are eligible; contact your nearest Canadian embassy or consulate. For general information on immigrating to Canada,

contact **Citizenship and Immigration Canada** (604/666-2171, www.cic.gc.ca).

VISITORS WITH DISABILITIES

A lack of mobility should not deter you from traveling to the Canadian Rockies, but you should definitely do some research before leaving home.

If you haven't traveled extensively, start by doing some research at the website of the **Access-Able Travel Source** (www.access-able.com), where you will find databases of specialist travel agencies and lodgings in western Canada that cater to travelers with disabilities. **Flying Wheels Travel** (507/451-5005, www.flyingwheelstravel.com) caters solely to the needs of travelers with disabilities. The **Society for Accessible Travel and Hospitality** (212/447-7284, www.sath.org) supplies information on tour operators, vehicle rentals, specific destinations, and companion services. For frequent

WHAT TO TAKE

You'll find little use for a suit and tie in the Canadian Rockies. Instead, pack for the outdoors. At the top of your must-bring list should be walking or **hiking boots.** Even in summer, you should be geared up for a variety of weather conditions, especially at the change of seasons. Do this by preparing to **dress in layers,** including at least one pair of fleece pants and a heavy long-sleeved top. For dining out, **casual dress** is accepted at all but the most upscale restaurants.

Electrical appliances from the United States work in Canada, but those from other parts of the world will require a current **converter** (transformer) to bring the voltage down. Many travel-size shavers, hair dryers, and irons have built-in converters.

travelers, the annual membership fee (adult US$49, senior US$29) is well worthwhile. *Emerging Horizons* (www.emerginghorizons. com) is a U.S. online quarterly magazine dedicated to travelers with special needs.

Access to Travel (800/465-7735, www. accesstotravel.gc.ca) is an initiative of the Canadian government that includes information on travel within and between Canadian cities. The website also has a lot of general travel information for those with disabilities. The **Canadian National Institute for the Blind** (800/563-2642, www.cnib.ca) offers a wide range of services from offices in Edmonton (780/488-4871) and Vancouver (604/431-2020). Finally, the **Canadian Paraplegic Association** (613/723-1033, www.canparaplegic.org), with chapter offices in Calgary (403/228-3001) and Vancouver (604/324-3611), is another good source of information.

TRAVELING WITH CHILDREN

The natural wonders of the Canadian Rockies are a marvelous place to bring children on a vacation, and luckily for you, many of the best things to do—walking, watching wildlife, and more—don't cost a cent.

Admission and tour prices for children are included throughout the travel chapters of this book. As a general rule, these reduced prices are for children ages 6-16 years. For two adults and two or more children, always ask about family tickets. Children under six nearly always get in free. Most hotels and motels will happily accommodate children, but always try to reserve your room in advance and let the reservations desk know the ages of your kids. Often, children stay free in major hotels, and in the case of some major chains, such as Holiday Inn, eat free also. Generally, bed-and-breakfasts aren't suitable for children and in some cases don't accept kids at all. Ask ahead.

As a general rule when it comes to traveling with children, let them help you plan the trip, looking at websites and reading up on the Canadian Rockies together. To make your vacation more enjoyable if you'll be spending a lot of time on the road, rent a minivan (all major rental agencies have a supply). Don't forget to bring along favorite toys and games from home—whatever you think will keep your kids entertained when the joys of sightseeing wear off.

The websites of **Travel Alberta** (www. travelalberta.com) and **Tourism British Columbia** (www.hellobc.com) have sections devoted to children's activities within the two provinces. Another useful online tool is the website **Travel with Your Kids** (www.travelwithyourkids.com).

Health and Safety

Compared to other parts of the world, Canada is a relatively safe place to visit. That said, wherever you are traveling, carry a medical kit that includes bandages, insect repellent, sunscreen, antiseptic, antibiotics, and water-purification tablets. Good first-aid kits are available through most outdoor shops.

It's a good idea to get health insurance or some form of coverage before heading to Canada if you're going to be there for a while, but check that your plan covers foreign services. Hospital charges vary from place to place but can start at around $1,000 a day, and some facilities impose a surcharge for nonresidents. Some Canadian companies offer coverage specifically aimed at visitors.

If you're on medication, take adequate supplies with you, and get a prescription from your doctor to cover the time you will be away. You may not be able to get a prescription filled at Canadian pharmacies without visiting a Canadian doctor, so don't wait till you've almost run out. If you wear glasses or contact lenses, ask your optometrist for a spare prescription in case you break or lose your lenses, and stock up on your usual cleaning supplies.

Believe it or not, AIDS and other venereal and needle-communicated diseases are as much of a concern in the Canadian Rockies as anywhere in the world today. Take exactly the same precautions you would at home—use condoms, and don't share needles.

Giardia

Giardiasis, also known as beaver fever, is a real concern for those who drink water from backcountry water sources. It's caused by an intestinal parasite, *Giardia lamblia,* that lives in lakes, rivers, and streams. Once ingested, its effects, although not instantaneous, can be dramatic; severe diarrhea, cramps, and nausea are the most common. Preventive measures should always be taken. **Pristine** (www.advancechemicals.ca) is a Canadian company that has developed water bottles with built-in filters; the alternative is boiling water for at least 10 minutes or treating with iodine.

Winter Travel

Travel through the Canadian Rockies during winter months should not be undertaken lightly. Before setting out in a vehicle, check antifreeze levels, and always carry a spare tire and blankets or sleeping bags. **Frostbite** is a potential hazard, especially when cold temperatures are combined with high winds (a combination known as **windchill**). Most often it leaves a numbing, bruised sensation, and the skin turns white. Exposed areas of skin, especially the nose and ears, are most susceptible.

Hypothermia occurs when the body fails to produce heat as fast as it loses it. It can strike at any time of year but is more common during cooler months. Cold weather, combined with hunger, fatigue, and dampness, creates a recipe for disaster. Symptoms are not always apparent to the victim. The early signs are numbness, shivering, slurring of words, dizziness, and, in extreme cases, violent behavior, unconsciousness, and even death. The best way to dress for the cold is in layers, including a waterproof outer layer. Most important, wear headgear. The best treatment for hypothermia is to get the patient out of the cold, replace wet clothing with dry, slowly give hot liquids and sugary foods, and place the victim in a sleeping bag. Warming too quickly can lead to heart attacks.

Information and Services

All prices quoted in this guidebook are in Canadian dollars and cents unless otherwise noted.

Canadian currency is based on dollars and cents, with 100 cents equal to one dollar. Coins come in denominations of 1, 5, 10, and 25 cents, and one and two dollars. The 11-sided, gold-colored, one-dollar coin is known as a "loonie" for the bird featured on it. The unique two-dollar coin is silver with a gold-colored insert. The most common notes are $5, $10, $20, and $50. A $100 bill does exist but is uncommon.

Visa and MasterCard credit and debit cards are also readily accepted in the Canadian Rockies; American Express charge cards are less widely accepted. By using these cards you eliminate the necessity of thinking about the exchange rate—the transaction and rate of exchange on the day of the transaction will automatically be reflected in the bill from your credit-card company. On the downside, you'll always get a better exchange rate when dealing directly with a bank.

It's also handy to carry small amounts of Canadian cash. Banks offer the best exchange rates, but other foreign-currency exchange outlets are available.

Costs

The cost of living in the Canadian Rockies is generally higher than in other parts of Canada, especially when it comes to accommodations. Provincially, the cost of living is lower in Alberta than in British Columbia but higher than in the United States. By planning ahead, having a tent or joining Hostelling International, and being prepared to cook your own meals, it is possible to get by on $80 per person per day. Gasoline is sold in liters (3.78 liters equals one U.S. gallon) and is generally $1.20-1.40 cents per liter for regular unleaded, rising to $1.60 along the Icefields Parkway.

Tipping charges are not usually added to your bill. You are expected to add a tip of 15 percent to the total amount for waiters and waitresses, barbers and hairdressers, taxi drivers, and other such service providers. Bellhops, doormen, and porters generally receive $1 per item of baggage.

Taxes

Canada imposes a 5 percent **goods and services tax (GST)** on most consumer purchases. The British Columbia government imposes its own 7 percent tax (PST) onto everything except groceries and books. Alberta has no provincial tax. So when you are looking at the price of anything, remember that the final cost you pay will include an additional 5-12 percent in taxes.

MAPS AND TOURIST INFORMATION
Maps

The best maps of the Canadian Rockies are produced by **Gem Trek Publishing.** They cover all of the Canadian Rockies, using computer-generated 3-D imagery to clearly define changes in elevation and GPS to plot hiking trails. The backs of maps are filled with trail information as well as tidbits of history.

Maps are available at bookstores, gas stations, and gift shops throughout the Canadian Rockies. In Banff, head to **Mooseprint Books and Gifts** (208 Buffalo St., 403/762-3355) for the full range of Gem Trek maps. In Calgary, **Map Town** (400 5th Ave. SW, 403/266-2241) is a specialist map shop worth stopping at as you pass through. In Vancouver, pick up maps at these specialty bookstores: **International Travel Maps & Books** (530 W. Broadway,

CURRENCY EXCHANGE

At press time, the Canadian dollar had been steady against the greenback since dipping to record lows in 2002, when it was trading at US$1 per CDN$1.65.

At press time, exchange rates (into CDN$) for major currencies are:

- US$1 = $1
- AUS$1 = $0.95
- €1 = $1.55
- HK$10 = $1.60

- NZ$1 = $0.82
- UK£1 = $1.90
- ¥100 = $1.20

On the Internet, check current exchange rates at www.xe.com/ucc.

All major currency can be exchanged at banks in Canmore, Banff, and Jasper, or at airports in the gateway cities of Calgary, Edmonton, and Vancouver. Many Canadian businesses will accept U.S. currency, but you will get a better exchange rate from the banks.

604/879-3621), **The Travel Bug** (3065 W. Broadway, 604/737-1122), or **Wanderlust** (1929 W. 4th Ave., Kitsilano, 604/739-2182).

Park Information

Each of the five national parks has at least one **park information center.** These are the places to head for interpretive displays, all park-related information, trail reports, weather forecasts, and wilderness passes. Individual addresses and websites are listed in the relevant travel chapters. The national parks are managed by **Parks Canada** (www.pc.gc.ca). On the Alberta side of the Canadian Rockies, all other parks are managed by **Tourism, Parks, and Recreation** (www.albertaparks.ca). British Columbia's provincial parks are managed by **BC Parks** (www.bcparks.ca).

Tourism Information

Begin planning your trip by contacting the government tourist offices of Alberta and British Columbia: **Travel Alberta** (780/427-4321 or 800/252-3782, www.travelalberta.com) and **Tourism British Columbia** (250/387-1642 or 800/435-5622, www.hellobc.com). Both will fill your mailbox with useful literature and maps, which can be ordered by phone or through their respective websites.

In Calgary, you'll find an information booth on the arrivals level of the airport. The **Vancouver Visitor Centre** (604/683-2000) is at 200 Burrard Street, although information on the Canadian Rockies is limited. For general tourism information, the towns of Banff, Canmore, Jasper, Radium Hot Springs, and Golden have information centers that provide advice on local attractions, accommodations, and restaurants.

COMMUNICATIONS
Postal Services

Canada Post (www.canadapost.ca) issues postage stamps that must be used on all mail posted in Canada. First-class letters and postcards sent within Canada are $0.61, to the United States $1.05, to foreign destinations $1.81. Prices increase along with the weight of the mailing. You can buy stamps at post offices, automatic vending machines, most hotel lobbies, the airports, many retail outlets, and some newsstands.

Telephones

Alberta and British Columbia have three and four area codes respectively. The **area code** for southern Alberta, including Banff and Canmore, is **403.** The area code for

HEADING FARTHER AFIELD

If your travels take you beyond the Canadian Rockies, you may find the following resources helpful for pretrip planning:

- **Travel Alberta:** 780/427-4321 or 800/252-3782, www.travelalberta.com
- **Tourism British Columbia:** 250/387-1642 or 800/435-5622, www.hellobc.com
- **Yukon Department of Tourism and Culture:** 867/667-5036 or 800/661-0494, www.travelyukon.com
- **Alaska Travel Industry Association:** www.travelalaska.com
- **NWT Tourism:** 867/873-7200 or 800/661-0788, www.spectacularnwt.com
- **Tourism Saskatchewan:** 306/787-9600 or 877/237-2273, www.sasktourism.com
- **Travel Manitoba:** 204/945-3777 or 800/665-0040, www.travelmanitoba.com

northern Alberta, including Jasper National Park, is **780.** The area code **587** covers all of the province. The area code for all of British Columbia except Vancouver and environs is **250.** The area code for Vancouver is **604.** The area codes **778** and **236** overlay the entire province. Unless otherwise noted, all numbers must be dialed with this prefix, including local calls made from within Alberta. The country code for Canada is 1, the same as the United States.

Public phones accept 5-, 10-, and 25-cent coins. Local calls cost $0.35, and most long-distance calls from public phones cost at least $2 for the first minute. Phone cards, available from drug and grocery stores, provide considerable savings for those using public phones.

Internet Access

Most Internet providers allow you to access your email away from your home computer, or open an email account with Hotmail (www.hotmail.com) or Yahoo (www.yahoo.com). Although there are restrictions to the size and number of emails you can store, these services are handy and, best of all, free.

Public Internet access is available throughout the Canadian Rockies. Most lodgings have Wi-Fi or high-speed access from guest rooms (the exception are lodges in remote locations). Except for wilderness hostels, backpacker lodges provide inexpensive Internet access. You'll also find Internet cafés in Banff, Canmore, and Jasper, as well as booths in some regular cafés, and in public areas, such as Cascade Plaza (Banff), where a credit card will allow you to spend as much time as you need online. Aside from a lack of privacy, the downside to these public access points is the lack of a mouse at most terminals—instead you must move around the screen using a touch pad.

WEIGHTS AND MEASURES
The Metric System

Canada officially adopted the metric system back in 1975, though you still hear grocers talking in ounces and pounds, golfers talking in yards, and sailors talking in nautical miles. Metric is the primary unit used in this book, but we've added imperial conversions for readers from the United States, Liberia, and Myanmar, the only three countries that have not adopted the metric system. You can also refer to the metric conversion chart in the back of this book.

Time Zones

Alberta is in the **mountain time zone,** one hour later than Pacific standard time, two hours earlier than eastern standard time. The mountain time zone extends west into southern British

Columbia, which includes Yoho and Kootenay National Parks as well as the towns of Golden and Radium Hot Springs. The rest of British Columbia, including Mount Robson Provincial Park, is in the **Pacific time zone.**

Daylight saving time is in effect from the second Sunday of March to the first Sunday in November. This corresponds with the United States (except Arizona) and all other Canadian provinces (except Saskatchewan).

RESOURCES

Suggested Reading

NATURAL HISTORY

The Atlas of Breeding Birds of Alberta. Edmonton: Federation of Alberta Naturalists, 1992. Comprehensive study of all birds that breed in Alberta with easy-to-read distribution maps, details on nesting and other behavioral patterns, and color plates.

Dettling, Peter. *The Will of the Land.* Victoria: Rocky Mountain Books, 2010. Filled with stunning images, this book includes thoughtful dialogue on the often-controversial relationship between man and wolf.

Dolson, Sylvia. *Bearology.* Whistler: Get Bear Smart Society, 2009. An easy-to-read book filled with bear facts and trivia.

Gadd, Ben. *Canadian Rockies Geology Road Tours.* Canmore: Corax Press, 2009. The best reference for those interested in the geology of the Canadian Rockies. Includes information on almost 300 roadside stops.

Gadd, Ben. *Handbook of the Canadian Rockies.* Canmore: Corax Press, 2009. At over 800 pages and one kilogram (2.2 pounds), this is the classic field guide to the Canadian Rockies. It is in full color, and although bulky for backpackers, it's a must-read for anyone interested in the natural history of the region.

Gray, D. M., and D. H. Male. *Handbook of Snow.* Toronto: Pergamon Press, 1991. Comprehensive guide on everything you ever wanted to know about snow but didn't ask because no one else would have known either.

Hallworth, Beryl, and C. C. Chinnappa. *Plants of Kananaskis Country.* Calgary: University of Calgary Press, 1997. An incredibly detailed book, encompassing more than 400 species of flora, complete with detailed black-and-white illustrations. It could be used in the field anywhere in the Canadian Rockies.

Hare, F. K., and M. K. Thomas. *Climate Canada.* Toronto: John Wiley & Sons, 1974. One of the most extensive works on Canada's climate ever written. Includes a chapter on how the climate is changing.

Herrero, Stephen. *Bear Attacks: Their Causes and Avoidances.* New York: The Lyons Press, 2003. Through a series of gruesome stories, this book catalogs the stormy relationship between people and bruins, provides hints on avoiding attacks, and tells what to do in case you're attacked.

Kerr, Michael. *The Canadian Rockies Guide to Wildlife Watching.* Calgary: Fifth House, 2000. A handy reference for wildlife enthusiasts. Complete with color illustrations and tips to find the best viewing spots.

Lauriault, Jean. *Identification Guide to the Trees of Canada*. Markham, ON: Fitzhenry & Whiteside, 1989. Makes tree identification easy through drawings of leaves. Maps detail distribution of species.

Marty, Sid. *The Black Grizzly of Whiskey Creek*. Toronto: McClelland & Stewart, 2008. True story of a grizzly bear that went on a terrifying rampage near the town of Banff.

Musiani, Marco. *A New Era for Wolves and People*. Calgary: University of Calgary Press, 2009. A detailed analysis of the relationship between wolves and people in both North America and Europe. All contributors are wolf experts; includes stunning images.

Patterson, W. S. *The Physics of Glaciers*. London: Butterworth-Heinemann, 1999. A highly technical look at all aspects of glaciation, why glaciers form, how they flow, and their effect on the environment. The first edition was published in 1969 by Pergamon Press (Toronto).

Rezendes, Paul. *Tracking and the Art of Seeing*. Charlottesville, VA: Camden House Publishing, 1992. This is one of the best of many books dedicated to tracking North American mammals. It begins with a short essay on the relationship of humans with nature.

Scotter, George. *Wildflowers of the Rocky Mountains*. Vancouver: Whitecap Books, 2007. Simplified descriptions, color-coded chapters, and the delicate photography of Halle Flygare combine to create the region's best wildflower field guide.

Sharp, Robert P. *Living Ice: Understanding Glaciers and Glaciation*. Cambridge, England: Cambridge University Press, 1988. A detailed but highly readable book on the formation, types, and results of glaciers.

Sheldon, Ian. *Animal Tracks of the Rockies*. Edmonton: Lone Pine Publishing, 1997. A pocket-sized book that illustrates the tracks of almost all animal species present in the Canadian Rockies.

Slinger, Joey. *Down & Dirty Birding*. Toronto: Key Porter Books, 1996. A hilarious but practical look at the art of bird-watching, with sections of text such as "How to steer clear of people who think bird-watching is better than sex."

Whitaker, John. *National Audubon Society Field Guide to Mammals*. New York: Alfred A. Knopf, 1996. One of a series of field guides produced by the National Audubon Society, this one details mammals through color plates and detailed descriptions of characteristics, habitat, and range.

Wilkinson, Kathleen. *Wildflowers of Alberta*. Edmonton: University of Alberta Press, 1999. Color plates of all flowers found in the mountain national parks and beyond. The detailed color plates and line drawings are indispensable for identification.

HUMAN HISTORY

Barnes, Christine. *Great Lodges of the Canadian Rockies*. Seattle: Sasquatch Books, 1999. This book delves into the history of the many famous mountain lodges—such as the Fairmont properties and Emerald Lake Lodge—and lesser known but equally interesting historic accommodations like Num-Ti-Jah and Skoki. Includes many historical photos.

Engler, Bruno. *Bruno Engler Photography.* Victoria: Rocky Mountain Books, 2002. Swiss-born Engler spent 60 years exploring and photographing the Canadian Rockies. This impressive hardcover book showcases more than 150 of his most timeless black-and-white images.

Hart, E. J. (Ted). *Ain't it Hell.* Banff: Summerthought Publishing, 2008. "Wild" Bill Peyto was one of the most interesting and colorful characters in the history of the Canadian Rockies. This book tells his story through fictional diary entries.

Hart, E. J. (Ted). *Jimmy Simpson: Legend of the Rockies.* Victoria: Rocky Mountain Books, 2009. Details the life of one of the most colorful of the pioneer outfitters in the Canadian Rockies.

Hempstead, Andrew. *Exploring the History of Banff.* Banff: Summerthought Publishing, 2012. A guidebook to 88 historic sites and heritage properties in and around the town of Banff.

Lavallee, Omer. *Van Horne's Road.* Montreal: Railfare Enterprises, 1974. William Van Horne was instrumental in the construction of Canada's first transcontinental railway. This is the story of his dream and the boomtowns that sprang up along the route. Lavallee devotes an entire chapter to telling the story of the railway's push over the Canadian Rockies.

Marty, Sid. *Switchbacks: True Stories from the Canadian Rockies.* Toronto: McClelland & Stewart, 1999. This book tells of Marty's experiences in the mountains and of the people he came in contact with in his role as a park warden. Along the way he describes how his experiences with both nature and fellow humans have shaped his views on conservation today.

McMillan, Alan D. *Native Peoples and Cultures of Canada.* Vancouver: Douglas & McIntyre, 1995. A comprehensive look at the archaeology, anthropology, and ethnography of the native peoples of Canada. The last chapters delve into the problems facing these people today.

Robinson, Bart. *Banff Springs: The Story of a Hotel.* Banff: Summerthought Publishing, 2007. This detailed history of one of the world's best-known hotels includes up-to-date changes, rare black-and-white photographs, and interviews with longtime employees.

Schaffer, Mary T. S. *A Hunter of Peace.* Banff: Whyte Museum of the Canadian Rockies, 2001. This book was first published in 1911 by G. P. Putnam & Sons, New York, under the name *Old Indian Trails of the Canadian Rockies.* Tales of Schaffer's adventures recount the exploration of the Rockies during the turn of the 20th century. Many of the author's photographs appear throughout.

Scott, Chic. *Deep Powder and Steep Rock.* Banff: Assiniboine Publishing, 2009. The biography of Hans Gmoser, the father of heli-skiing. Includes a DVD with three films.

Scott, Chic. *Pushing the Limits.* Victoria: Rocky Mountain Books, 2000. A chronological history of mountaineering in Canada, with special emphasis on many largely unknown climbers and their feats, as well as the story of Swiss guides in Canada and a short section on ice climbing.

Snow, Chief John. *These Mountains are our Sacred Places.* Calgary: Fifth House, 2005. The history of the Stoney people as told by Chief John Snow.

Twigger, Robert. *Voyageur: Across the Rocky Mountains in a Birchbark Canoe.* London: Weidenfeld, 2006. This is the rollicking tale of author Twigger's adventures building a canoe and crossing the Canadian Rockies on a diet of porridge, fish, and whiskey—exactly as Alexander Mackenzie had 200 years previously.

RECREATION

Corbett, Bill. *The 11,000ers.* Calgary: Rocky Mountain Books, 2004. A reference to all 54 mountain peaks in the Canadian Rockies that are higher than 11,000 feet. The author discusses the human history of each, as well as access and popular routes.

Daffern, Gillean. *Kananaskis Country Trail Guide.* Calgary: Rocky Mountain Books, 2012. Five volumes cover all the official and unofficial trails in Kananaskis Country.

Gadd, Ben. *The Canadian Hiker's and Backpacker's Handbook.* Vancouver: Whitecap Books, 2008. Whether you're interested in learning the basics or a seasoned traveler, this is the best book for reading up on your backcountry and hiking skills.

Kane, Alan. *Scrambles in the Canadian Rockies.* Calgary: Rocky Mountain Books, 2002. Routes detailed in this guide lead to summits without the use of ropes or mountaineering equipment.

Martin, John, and Jon Jones. *Sport Climbs in the Canadian Rockies.* Calgary: Rocky Mountain Books, 2011. Details 2,000 routes through the Bow Valley and Banff National Park. Includes maps and photographs.

Mitchell, Barry. *Alberta's Trout Highway.* Red Deer: Nomad Creek Books, 2001. "Alberta's Trout Highway" is the Forestry Trunk Road (Highway 40), which runs the length of the Canadian Rockies, including through the heart of Kananaskis Country. Entertaining and useful descriptions of Mitchell's favorite fishing holes are accompanied by maps and plenty of background information.

Oprsal, Peter. *Bow Valley Mountain Bike Trail Guide.* Canmore: self-published, 2012. Details mountain bike trails in the Canmore, Banff, and Lake Louise areas using simple maps and elevation graphs.

Patton, Brian, and Bart Robinson. *Canadian Rockies Trail Guide.* Banff: Summerthought Publishing, 2011. First published in 1971 and now in its ninth edition, this book covers 230 hiking trails and 3,400 kilometers (2,100 miles) in the mountain national parks as well as in surrounding provincial parks. At least one full page is devoted to each trail, making it the most comprehensive hiking book available.

Patton, Brian, and Bart Robinson. *50 Walks and Hikes in Banff National Park.* Banff: Summerthought Publishing, 2008. The authors of the *Canadian Rockies Trail Guide* detail their favorite short walks and day trips in this full-color guidebook.

Potter, Mike. *Backcountry Banff.* Calgary: Luminous Compositions, 2001. This book's title is a little misleading, for included are many shorter trails that can be enjoyed by everyone. Includes logged distances and readable trail descriptions of over 100 hikes in Banff National Park.

Potter, Mike. *Fire Lookouts in the Canadian Rockies.* Calgary: Luminous Compositions,

1998. This book specializes in hikes to fire lookouts. Trail descriptions are detailed, and each is accompanied by the history of the lookout.

Scott, Chic. *Ski Trails of the Canadian Rockies.* Calgary: Rocky Mountain Books, 2005. After reading this book, it quickly becomes apparent that there is a lot more to wintertime than the downhill alpine resorts. Covering both groomed and backcountry trails, you'll find yourself spoiled for options with this book as a reference.

Spring, Vicky, and Tom Kirkendall. *Glacier-Waterton International Peace Park.* Seattle: Mountaineer Books, 2003. This book concentrates on hiking in the adjacent national parks of Waterton Lakes and Glacier.

GUIDEBOOKS AND MAPS

Gem Trek Publishing. Victoria, BC. This company produces maps for all regions of the Canadian Rockies. Relief shading clearly and concisely shows elevation, and all hiking trails have been plotted using a global positioning system. On the back of most maps are descriptions of attractions and hikes, along with general, practical, and educational information. Highly recommended. Website: www.gemtrek.com.

Hempstead, Andrew. *Moon Alberta* and *Moon British Columbia.* Berkeley, CA: Avalon Travel. Regularly updated guides that comprehensively cover Canada's westernmost provinces.

MapArt. Driving maps for all of Canada, including provinces and cities. Maps are published as old-fashioned foldout versions, as well as laminated and in atlas form. Website: www.mapart.com.

The Milepost. Bellevue, WA: Vernon Publications. This annual publication is a must-have for those traveling through western Canada and Alaska. The maps and logged highway descriptions are incredibly detailed. Most northern bookstores stock *The Milepost,* or call 800/726-4707 or go to www.milepost.com.

Patton, Brian. *Parkways of the Canadian Rockies* Banff: Summerthought Publishing, 2008. A comprehensive map and driving guide to all major highways. Includes color photography and details of many short hikes.

PERIODICALS

The Canadian Alpine Journal. Canmore, AB. The annual magazine of the Alpine Club of Canada, with mountaineering articles from its members and climbers from around the world. Website: www.alpineclubofcanada.ca.

Canadian Geographic. Ottawa: Royal Canadian Geographical Society. Bimonthly publication pertaining to Canada's natural and human histories and resources. Website: www.canadiangeographic.ca.

Explore. Toronto. Bimonthly publication of adventure travel throughout Canada. Website: www.explore-mag.com.

Nature Canada. Ottawa, ON. Quarterly magazine of the Canadian Nature Federation. Website: www.cnf.ca.

Western Living. Vancouver, BC. Lifestyle magazine for western Canada. Includes travel, history, homes, and cooking. Website: www.westernliving.ca.

FREE CATALOGS

Alberta Accommodation Guide. Alberta Hotel & Lodging Association. Lists all hotels, motels, and other lodging in the province. Available at all Tourist Information Centres or by calling 780/427-7321 or 800/252-3782, www.travelalberta.com.

Alberta Campground Guide. Alberta Hotel Association. Lists all campgrounds in the province. Available at all Tourist Information Centres or by calling 780/427-7321 or 800/252-3782, www.travelalberta.com.

British Columbia Approved Accommodation Guide. Tourism British Columbia. Lists all accommodations, including commercial and provincial campgrounds, in the province. Available at all Visitor Information Centres or by calling 250/387-1642 or 800/435-5622, www.hellobc.com.

REFERENCE

Daffern, Tony. *Avalanche Safety for Skiers & Climbers.* Calgary: Rocky Mountain Books, 1992. Covers all aspects of avalanches, including their causes, practical information on how to avoid them, and a section on rescue techniques and first aid.

Guide to Manuscripts: The Fonds and Collections of the Archives, Whyte Museum of the Canadian Rockies. Banff: Whyte Museum of the Canadian Rockies, 1988. This book makes finding items in the museum easy by providing alphabetical lists of all parts of the collection.

Karamitsanis, Aphrodite. *Place Names of Alberta.* Calgary: University of Alberta Press, 1991. Volume 1 alphabetically lists all geographic features of the mountains and foothills, with explanations of each name's origin. Volume 2 does the same for southern Alberta.

Internet Resources

TRAVEL PLANNING

Canadian Tourism Commission
www.canada.travel
Official tourism website for all of Canada.

Tourism British Columbia
www.hellobc.com
Learn more about the province, plan your travels, and order tourism literature.

Travel Alberta
www.travelalberta.com
Similar to the British Columbia tourism website, but includes information on Banff and Jasper National Parks.

PARKS

BC Parks
www.env.gov.bc.ca
This department oversees management of provincial parks in British Columbia. The website details facilities, fees, and seasonal openings of each park.

Parks Canada
www.pc.gc.ca
Official website of the agency that manages Canada's national parks and national historic sites. Website has information on each park and historic site, including fees, camping, and wildlife.

**Parks Canada Campground
Reservation Service**
www.pccamping.ca
Online reservation service for national park campgrounds.

GOVERNMENT

Citizenship and Immigration Canada
www.cic.gc.ca
Check this government website for anything related to entry into Canada.

Environment Canada
www.weatheroffice.gc.ca
Seven-day forecasts from across Canada, including dozens of locations throughout the Canadian Rockies. Includes weather archives such as seasonal trends and snowfall history.

Government of Canada
www.gc.ca
The official website of the Canadian government.

ACCOMMODATIONS

Banff Lodging Co.
www.bestofbanff.com
Operates eight hotels within the town of Banff.

Canadian Rocky Mountain Resorts
www.crmr.com
Small chain of four upscale Canadian Rockies resorts.

Fairmont Hotels and Resorts
www.fairmont.com
Lodging chain that owns famous mountain resorts such as the Banff Springs, Chateau Lake Louise, and Jasper Park Lodge.

Hostelling International-Canada
www.hihostels.ca
Canadian arm of the worldwide organization.

CONSERVATION

Biosphere Institute of the Bow Valley
www.biosphereinstitute.org
Canmore-based organization mandated to gather and circulate information on management of the Bow River watershed. Online references include studies, publications, and human-use guidelines for the region.

Bow Valley Wildsmart
www.wildsmart.ca
This nonprofit organization has put together a wealth of information on how to stay safe in the Bow Valley watershed, including reported wildlife sightings.

Canadian Parks and Wilderness Society
www.cpaws.org
Nonprofit organization that is instrumental in highlighting conservation issues throughout Canada. The link to the Calgary chapter provides local information and a schedule of guided walks.

Yellowstone to Yukon Conservation Initiative
www.y2y.net
Network of 800 groups working on conservation issues in the Canadian Rockies and beyond.

TRANSPORTATION AND TOURS

Air Canada
www.aircanada.ca
Canada's national airline.

Brewster
www.brewster.ca
Banff-based operator offering day trips, airport shuttles, and package tours.

Rocky Mountaineer
www.rockymountaineer.com
Luxurious rail service from Vancouver to Banff and Jasper.

VIA Rail
www.viarail.ca
Passenger rail service across Canada.

PUBLISHERS

Gem Trek
www.gemtrek.com
You can pick up basic park maps free from local information centers, but this company produces much more detailed maps covering all the most popular regions of the Canadian Rockies.

Lone Pine
www.lonepinepublishing.com
Respected for its field guides, this company has books on almost every natural-history subject pertinent to the Canadian Rockies.

Rocky Mountain Books
www.rmbooks.com
Check out this publisher's catalog, and you'll surely be impressed by the list of local history and outdoor recreation guides.

Summerthought Publishing
www.summerthought.com
The world's only publisher devoted solely to publishing books about the Canadian Rockies. If you plan on doing lots of hiking, you'll want a copy of their authoritative *Canadian Rockies Trail Guide.*

Index

List of Maps

MAP SYMBOLS

▦	Expressway	█	Highlight	✗	Airfield	⚲	Golf Course
	Primary Road	○	City/Town	✈	Airport	₽	Parking Area
	Secondary Road	◉	State Capital	▲	Mountain	≜	Archaeological Site
= = = = =	Unpaved Road	⊛	National Capital	✛	Unique Natural Feature	▲	Church
- - - - -	Trail	★	Point of Interest				
·············	Ferry	●	Accommodation	🕈	Waterfall	⛽	Gas Station
━•━•━	Railroad	▼	Restaurant/Bar	♠	Park	⬭	Glacier
	Pedestrian Walkway	■	Other Location	⬚	Trailhead	▨	Mangrove
▥▥▥▥	Stairs	⋀	Campground	⛷	Skiing Area	▨	Reef
						▨	Swamp

CONVERSION TABLES

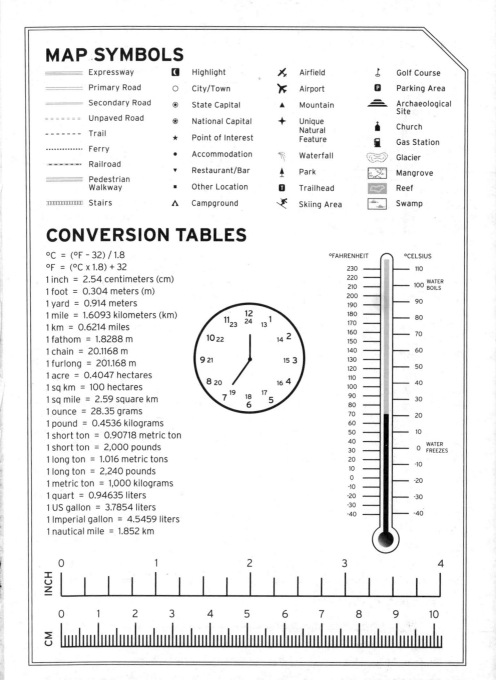

°C = (°F - 32) / 1.8
°F = (°C x 1.8) + 32
1 inch = 2.54 centimeters (cm)
1 foot = 0.304 meters (m)
1 yard = 0.914 meters
1 mile = 1.6093 kilometers (km)
1 km = 0.6214 miles
1 fathom = 1.8288 m
1 chain = 20.1168 m
1 furlong = 201.168 m
1 acre = 0.4047 hectares
1 sq km = 100 hectares
1 sq mile = 2.59 square km
1 ounce = 28.35 grams
1 pound = 0.4536 kilograms
1 short ton = 0.90718 metric ton
1 short ton = 2,000 pounds
1 long ton = 1.016 metric tons
1 long ton = 2,240 pounds
1 metric ton = 1,000 kilograms
1 quart = 0.94635 liters
1 US gallon = 3.7854 liters
1 Imperial gallon = 4.5459 liters
1 nautical mile = 1.852 km

°FAHRENHEIT °CELSIUS

230	110
220	100 WATER BOILS
210	
200	90
190	
180	80
170	
160	70
150	
140	60
130	50
120	
110	40
100	
90	30
80	
70	20
60	
50	10
40	
30	0 WATER FREEZES
20	
10	-10
0	
-10	-20
-20	-30
-30	
-40	-40

MOON CANADIAN ROCKIES

Avalon Travel
a member of the Perseus Books Group
1700 Fourth Street
Berkeley, CA 94710, USA
www.moon.com

Editor: Elizabeth Hollis Hansen
Series Manager: Kathryn Ettinger
Copy Editor: Ann Seifert
Graphics Coordinator: Darren Alessi
Production Coordinator: Darren Alessi
Cover Designer: Darren Alessi
Map Editor: Albert Angulo
Cartographer: Chris Henrick, Kaitlin Jaffe,
  Heather Sparks
Indexer: Greg Jewett

ISBN-13: 978-1-61238-528-0
ISSN: 1546-2129

Printing History
1st Edition – 1999
7th Edition – May 2013
5 4 3 2 1

Front cover photo: Athabasca Falls at dusk, Jasper
  National Park © Yves Marcoux/First Light/Corbis
Title page photo: © Andrew Hempstead
Interior color photos: All © Andrew Hempstead,
  except page 9 and 10 (inset) © 123rf.com

Printed in Canada by Friesens

KEEPING CURRENT

If you have a favorite gem you'd like to see included in the next edition, or see anything
that needs updating, clarification, or correction, please drop us a line. Send your com-
ments via email to feedback@moon.com, or use the address above.